Cattaraugus County New York

SURROGATE COURT ABSTRACTS

Guardianship Edition

Susan E. Stahley

HERITAGE BOOKS
2008

HERITAGE BOOKS
AN IMPRINT OF HERITAGE BOOKS, INC.

Books, CDs, and more—Worldwide

For our listing of thousands of titles see our website
at
www.HeritageBooks.com

Published 2008 by
HERITAGE BOOKS, INC.
Publishing Division
100 Railroad Ave. #104
Westminster, Maryland 21157

Copyright © 2008 Susan E. Stahley

All rights reserved. No part of this book may be reproduced or transmitted in any form or by any means, electronic or mechanical, including photocopying, recording or by any information storage and retrieval system without written permission from the author, except for the inclusion of brief quotations in a review.

International Standard Book Numbers
Paperbound: 978-0-7884-4676-4
Clothbound: 978-0-7884-7263-3

Dedication

To my Hardy family-Dad, Mom, John, Angie, Brenda, Jim and Bob-you all helped mold me into the person I am today.

To my Stahley men, Roland and Matthew, thank you for putting up with the long hours at courthouses and on the computer getting this book ready. I love you both!

And Brenda Hare, who has always believed in me since day one- this book started trying to find any mention of your Worden, Whiting, Clark and Nuzum families.

Table of Contents

Introduction	vii
Abbreviations	ix
A Surnames	1-7
B Surnames	9-40
C Surnames	41-73
D Surnames	75-88
E Surnames	89-95
F Surnames	97-111
G Surnames	113-123
H Surnames	125-148
I Surnames	149-150
J Surnames	151-157
K Surnames	159-170
L Surnames	171-183
M Surnames	185-213
N Surnames	215-223
O Surnames	225-231
P Surnames	233-248
Q Surnames	249-250
R Surnames	251-267
S Surnames	269-307
T Surnames	309-318
U Surnames	319
V Surnames	321-324
W Surnames	325-352
Y Surnames	353
Z Surnames	355
Index	357-405

Introduction

Susan Stahley is a Professional Family History Researcher who researches in Western New York and Northwestern Pennsylvania. For more information on her services and how to order a record if you want a copy of the original papers, please visit http://www.brickwallbuster.com

The Cattaraugus County Courthouse is located in Little, Valley, New York. The information for this book was found in the Surrogate Court in the Cattaraugus County Courthouse. The information was abstracted from the original records which are kept in boxes. The boxes each have multiple files. Each file was searched for family history information and abstracted. In some files there is information such as property owned, money transactions, and other information that wasn't abstracted. This book covers the first seventy-seven boxes and one guardianship file from box 79.

The records in this book are all guardianship records. A child needed a guardian if they were less than 21 years old and had money, land, stocks, etc. that needed to be watched for them. The guardian didn't necessarily adopt or board the child.

Abbreviations List

A-	Aunt
AC	Adopted Cousin
AF	Adopted Father
AKA	Also Known As
AM	Adopted Mother
BL	Brother-in-law
C-	Cousin
FL	Father-in-law
G-	Guardian
GA	Great Aunt
GF	Grandfather (not known if Maternal or Paternal)
GGF	Great-Grandfather
GGM	Great-Grandmother
GM	Grandmother (not known if Maternal or Paternal)
GU	Great-Uncle
HB	Half-brother
HS	Half-Sister
HU	Husband
MA	Maternal Aunt
MG	Maternal Grandparents
MGA	Maternal Great-aunt
MGF	Maternal Grandfather
MGM	Maternal Grandmother
MGU	Maternal Great-Uncle
PA	Paternal Aunt
PG	Paternal Grandparents
PGA	Paternal Great Aunt
PGF	Paternal Grandfather
PGM	Paternal Grandmother
PGU	Paternal Great Uncle
PU	Paternal Uncle
RE	Residence or Resided
U-	Uncle
W-	Wife

Name; Date of Birth; Father; Mother; Siblings; Other Relatives; Notes; Box Number

A Surnames

Helen M. Abbott; 19 November 1895; - ; AM Mary E., died 17 August 1914; - ; AC Ada R. Thurber; - ; 34

Mary Cooper Abbott; December 1878; Joseph Abbott; - ; Evan C. Abbott; - ; Benjamin Cooper left legacy; 34

Frederick C. Achenbach; 28 May 1877; Frederick Achenbach, died August 1878, in Salamanca; Lena, married Mr. Smith; - ; PGF Martin Achenbach; - ; 1

Lena Achenbach; 24 November 1857; - ; - ; - ; child was Frederick C. Achenbach and HU Frederick Achenbach; - ; 1

Elma O. Ackler; 5 Oct 1872; Mr. Ridout ; Maria; - ; HU Lemuel Ackler, FL Peter M. Ackler; - ; 1

Mabel E. Ackley; 27 April 1882; John S. Ackley, died 20 April 1902; Elzina, died 20 August 1938; Mildred Ackley; - ; - ; 71

Mildred Hastings Ackley; 21 January 1888, in Gowanda; John S. Ackley, died 20 April 1902; Elzina, died 20 August 1938; Mabel Ackley; HU Mr. Parker; RE , 1942 in Newark, New York; 71

Carrie Louisa Adams; 27 December 1886; AF Gottlieb Michler; - ; James and Minnie Adams; - ; money from estate of G. Adams, Carrie's biological father was alive, but renounced his rights, AKA Louisa C. Adams; 36

Cornelius Ray Adams; 2 December 1886; James D. Abbey, died June 1888; Sarah E., died July 1891, married Joel R. Adams; - ; AF Joel R. Adams; AKA Cornelius Abbey ; 23

Eugene E. Adams; 21 Feb 1858; - ; - ; - ; - ; G- Roquel N. Rogers; 1

Frances Adams; 21 September 1894; Douglas C. Adams, of Randolph; Mittie; - ; - ; - ; 77

George Lester Adams; 29 May 1896; - ; Addie H.; Phillip Adams; - ; - 23

James Ansel Adams; 28 April 1885; AF Gottlieb Michler; - ; Carrie and Minnie Adams; - ; money from estate of G. Adams and biological father was alive, but renounced his

Name; Date of Birth; Father; Mother; Siblings; Other Relatives; Notes; Box Number

rights; 36

Minnie Ruth Adams; 7 March 1883; - ; - ; James and Carrie Adams; HU Mr. Koop; received money from estate of G. Adams; biological father was alive, but renounced his rights, Minnie RE 1908, Jersey City, Hudson, NJ; 36

Phillip Andrew Adams; 29 May 1896; - ; Addie H.; George Adams; - ; - 23

Thomas Edwin Adams; 26 December 1910; Percy Adams, architect in D.C. December 1917; - ; - ; - ; - ; 34

Eva Adsit; - ; Seldon Adsit; Anna, died before 2 August 1917; - ; - ; - ; 34

Pearl D. Adye; 25 January 1908; Frederick A. Adye; - ; - ; - ; - ; 34

Ines Akers; 8 March 1879; - ; Candis, married Mr. Frank; - ; - ; received pension money, name also seen as Inez; 36

Deborah Ann Akins; 5 Sept 1858; - ; - ; - ; - ; - ; 1

Minnie M. Akins; 11 April 1883; - ; - ; - ; PGF Edward Akins of Poland, Chautauqua, NY; RE 1904, in Jamestown, Chautauqua, NY; G- John Cowen, no relation; 1

Augustus Albro; about 25 September 1856; - ; - ; - ; - ; G Alexander Milks; 1

Stephen Albro; about 1856; - ; - ; - ; - ; G- Alexander Milks; 1

Elizabeth Belle Alden; 31 March 1900; David S. Alden, died before July 1904; M. Belle, died January 1903; Mary Alden, HS Blanche Hubbard, HB Glenn A. Alden; GM Amana P. Whiting, of Eden, Erie, NY; - ; 34

Mary Ann Alden; 18 February 1898; David S. Alden, died before July 1904; M. Belle, died January 1903; Elizabeth Alden, HS Blanche Hubbard, HB Glenn A. Alden; GM Amana P. Whiting, of Eden, Erie, NY; - ; 34

Carrie B. Alexander; about 1867; Franklin Alexander, died September 1870, of Great Valley; Mary; Franklin and Stephen Alexander; - ; money from John Alexander's estate; 36

Franklin Alexander; about 1869; Franklin Alexander, died

Name; Date of Birth; Father; Mother; Siblings; Other Relatives; Notes; Box Number

September 1870, of Great Valley; Mary; Carrie and Stephen Alexander; - ; money from John Alexander's estate; 36

Stephen H. Alexander; about 1870; Franklin Alexander, died September 1870, of Great Valley; Mary; Franklin and Carrie Alexander; - ; money from John Alexander's estate; 36

Elmira B. Alger; about 1876; Webster J. Alger; Olive R., died August 1876, of Allegany; - ; - ; Wm. Hopping, of California, left legacy; 36

Annette Allen; 25 April 1848; Acel Allen; - ; Peter, Jonathan, Eliza, Newton, and Julia Allen and Laura J. Ingersoll (W- of Francis Ingersoll); U- James S. Shaw, - ; 1

Charlotte Louise Allen; 25 May 1916; N. Boyd Allen; Ethel S. died 11 December 1918; - ; - ; Charlotte died 28 March 1930 at Collins, Erie, New York; 1

Dascom Allen; 18 June 1855, Loyal Allen, died June 1865 in Carroll, Chautauqua, NY; Mary Ann, married Mr. Stevens; Frances Allen; - ; - ; 1

Frances Helen Allen; 22 January 1859, Loyal Allen, died June 1865 in Carroll, Chautauqua, NY; Mary Ann, married Mr. Stevens; Dascum Allen; - ; - 1

George Allen; 24 May 1844; - ; - ; - ; - ; G -Peter R. Allen; 1

Harmony R. Allen; 29 July 1856; Norman H. Allen; Rowanna, died March 1863; Norman Allen; - ; - ;1

Herbert Eugene Allen; before June 1857; - ; - ; - ; - ; G- Samuel Allen, Herbert AKA Eugene Allen; 1

Herbert Eugene Allen;18 Jan 1873, - ; Grace M, married Mr. Barber; - ; - ; AKA Eugene Allen; 1

James Allen; 22 Dec 1840; - ; - ; - ; - ; G Peter R. Allen; 1

Julia A. Allen; December 1851; Acel Allen; - ; Peter, Jonathan, Eliza, Newton, and Annette Allen, Laura J. Ingersoll (W- of Francis Ingersoll); U- James S. Shaw, - ; 1

Luther Allen; 20 July 1846; Luther Allen; Lois; HB Norman Allen, HS Louise Judd, HS Augusta Richmond; - ; - ; 1

Mary Lenora Allen; - ; - ; - ; - ; - ; - ; 1

Newton Allen; 24 November 1850; Acel Allen; - ; Peter,

Name; Date of Birth; Father; Mother; Siblings; Other Relatives; Notes; Box Number

Jonathan, Eliza, Julia, and Annette Allen, Laura J. Ingersoll (W- of Francis Ingersoll); U- James S. Shaw, - ; 1

Norman B. Allen; 29 June 1851; Norman H. Allen; Rowanna, died March 1863; Harmony Allen; - ; - ; 1

Winona M. Allen; 18 September 1905; Edward H. Allen, RE 501½ Cumberland, Lebanon, Pennsylvania; - ; - ; - ; RE 1929, King County, Washington; 34

Edwin A. Ames; 28 April 1878; - ; - ; - ; - ; RE Perry, Wyoming, NY, G- Rebecca Brasted; 1

Howard H. Ames; - ; Henry H. Ames, died November 1879, of Salamanca; - ; Mary Jane Scott, Carry Adell Kidder, and William, Lois, Levi and Angie Ames; - ; received pension money; 36

Levi H. Ames; - ; Henry H. Ames, died November 1879, of Salamanca; - ; Mary Jane Scott, Carry Adell Kidder, and William, Lois, Howard and Angie Ames; - ; received pension money; 36

Lois Isabell Ames; about 1872; Henry H. Ames, died November 1879, of Salamanca; - ; Mary Jane Scott, Carry Adell Kidder, and William, Levi, Howard and Angie Ames; - ; received pension money; 36

Franklin C. Amidon; 15 August 1860; Calvin A. Amidon; died September 1862, of Dakota, Minnesota; Clarissa E. Hall, married Mr. Peabody, he resided Boulder, Colorado; - ; MGF William Hall; - ; 1

Bertie D. Amsdell; 12 February 1874; Harmon L. Amsdell; Matilda; Charles and Nettie Amsdell; - ; Major Macapes left legacy; 23

Charles W. Amsdell; 6 August 1871; Harmon L. Amsdell; Matilda; Bertie and Nettie Amsdell; - ; Major Macapes left legacy; 23

Nettie P. Amsdell; 3 November 1876; Harmon L. Amsdell; Matilda; Bertie and Charles Amsdell; - left money in will of Major Macapes; 23

Dorothy Anderson; 15 December 1902; Clarence A. Anderson,

Name; Date of Birth; Father; Mother; Siblings; Other Relatives; Notes; Box Number

died 15 March 1920; Grace V.; - ; HU Mr. McLarney, married 18 Dec 1920; pregnant 6 October 1921; 53

Tacie "Tastacie" Irene Anderson; 9 July 1886; Otto Anderson; - ; - ; PA Hilda Anderson, A- Hilda Brenner (may be the same person as Hilda Anderson); two separate jackets for Tacie Anderson; 3

Frank H. Andrews; about 1895; - ; Jennie; Ruth Andrews; - ; - ; 34

Helen M. Andrews; 18 August 1905; Edwin H. Andrews, died 14 July 1920; May; - ; U- Claude Andrews, U- Frank H. Andrews; A- Ruth Piatt, GA Lizzie Brown; RE 1924, Geneseo Normal School, Geneseo, NY; 34

Ruth Andrews; about 1894; - ; Jennie; Frank Andrews; - ; - ; 34

Ethel May Anthony; about 1891; - ; Lena R., of Olean; - ; - ; father died before December 1898; 77

Bertha M. Archer; 12 Feb 1867; John Archer, died May 1881; Mary J.; Roy and Carrie Archer; HU H. H. Shipperd, married before 31 December 1887; - 3

Carrie B. Archer; 10 July 1877; John Archer, died May 1881; Mary J.; Roy and Bertha Archer; - ; - ; 3

Roy R. Archer: 23 December 1872; John Archer, died May 1881; Mary J.; Carrie and Bertha Archer; - ; - ; 3

Caroline R. Arnold; before December 1868; Ephraim S. Arnold; Emeline, died March 1864 in Conquest, Cayuga, NY; William, Wesley, Susan, Francis, and Fanny Arnold; - ; - ; 1

Dennis E. Arnold; about 1859; Ambrose E. Arnold; Calista H.; Orrin Arnold; - ; - 1

Fanny A. Arnold; before December 1868; Ephraim S. Arnold; Emeline, died March 1864 in Conquest, Cayuga, NY; William, Wesley, Susan, Francis, and Caroline Arnold; - ; - ; 1

Francis D. Arnold; before January 1854; Ephraim S. Arnold; Emeline, died March 1864 in Conquest, Cayuga, NY; William, Wesley, Susan, Fanny, and Caroline Arnold; - ; - ;1

Georgia Ella Arnold; before July 1871; George Arnold, died

Name; Date of Birth; Father; Mother; Siblings; Other Relatives; Notes; Box Number

January 1858, of Buffalo, Erie, NY; Julia P., married Mr. Somers and RE in Turney, Clinton, Missouri; - ; PGF Samuel P. Arnold, left legacy to Georgia, died before July 1871; - ; 1

Lynn D. Arnold; January 1858; Delevan Arnold, died September 1867 in Crawford County, Pennsylvania; Jane; - ; GM Lucy Arnold, A- Armenia Arnold, A- Lucy Arnold, U- Lewis C. Arnold; - ; 1

Orrin N. Arnold; about 1853; Ambrose E. Arnold; Calista H.; Dennis Arnold; - ; - ; 1

Susan C. Arnold; before December 1868; Ephraim S. Arnold; Emeline, died March 1864 in Conquest, Cayuga, NY; William, Wesley, Francis, Fanny, and Caroline Arnold; - ; - ; 1

Wesley J. Arnold; before December 1868; Ephraim S. Arnold; Emeline, died March 1864 in Conquest, Cayuga, NY; William, Susan, Francis, Fanny, and Caroline Arnold; - ; - ; 1

William Arnold; 16 Jan 1854; Horace Arnold; - ; - ; - ; G- Chauncey J. Fox Jr.; 1

William R. Arnold; before January 1854; Ephraim S. Arnold; Emeline, died March 1864 in Conquest, Cayuga, NY; Wesley, Susan, Francis, Fanny, and Caroline Arnold; - ; - ; 1

James R. Arrants; 15 October 1834; William Arrants, died before June 1850; - ; William, Sarah and Thomas Arrants, and Expenance Curtis; PU James Arrants; - ; 55

Sarah Ann Arrants; 27 July 1839; William Arrants, died before June 1850; - ; William, James and Thomas Arrants, and Expenance Curtis; PU James Arrants; - ; 55

Thomas B. Arrants; July 1833; William Arrants, died before June 1850; - ; William, James and Sarah Arrants, and Expenance Curtis; PU James Arrants; - ; 55

Dana D. Ashley; - ; - ; Luella; - ; - ; money from estate of Harmon J. Ashley; 34

Harry Atwell; 14 December 1877; - ; Julia M.; - ; - ; - ; 36

Henry H. Atwood; 18 November 1892; - ; - ; - ; - ; Theresa

Name; Date of Birth; Father; Mother; Siblings; Other Relatives; Notes; Box Number

Atwood left stocks to Henry Atwood, Henry RE November 1913, Pittsburgh, Allegheny, Pennsylvania; 23

Clara Austin; 25 November 1844; E. Austin; - ; - ; - ; G- Lucretia Austin; 1

Edna Austin; 9 January 1880; - ; Rhoda; Elizabeth and Georgiana Austin; - ; - ; 34

Georgiana Austin; 3 November 1876; - ; Rhoda; Elizabeth and Edna Austin; - ; - ; 34

Monroe Austin; about 1847; Henry Austin; - ; - ; - ; G- Philip B. Rich. Monroe went into the army about 1865 and wasn't heard from again; 1

Louisa Axtell; 20 Aug 1848; - ; Louisa, married Mr. Haskins; Theodore Axtell; - ; - ; 1

Theodore F. Axtell; 15 March 1845; - ; Louisa, married Mr. Haskins; Louisa Axtell; - ; - ; 1

Cora Aylesworth; about 1855; Marcus Aylesworth, died June 1870; Maria; Frank, Emmet, Dora, and Victor Aylesworth; C- Lydia Vincent; right to dower given to Electa Aylesworth, for land in Milford, Otsego, NY; 1

Dora Aylesworth; about 1853; Marcus Aylesworth, died June 1870; Maria; Frank, Emmet, Cora, and Victor Aylesworth; C- Lydia Vincent; right to dower given to Electa Aylesworth, for land in Milford, Otsego, NY; 1

Emmet Aylesworth; about 1847; Marcus Aylesworth, died June 1870; Maria; Frank, Dora, Cora, and Victor Aylesworth; C- Lydia Vincent; right to dower given to Electa Aylesworth, for land in Milford, Otsego, NY; 1

Frank Aylesworth; about 1844; Marcus Aylesworth, died June 1870; Maria; Emmet, Dora, Cora, and Victor Aylesworth; C- Lydia Vincent; right to dower given to Electa Aylesworth, for land in Milford, Otsego, NY; 1

Name; Date of Birth; Father; Mother; Siblings; Other Relatives; Notes; Box Number

B Surnames

Katharine L. Babcock; 18 September 1864; Horace Babcock; Mary; Louis Babcock; BL Wm. R. Smallwood; - ; 37

Louis L. Babcock; about 1869; Horace Babcock; Mary; Katharine Babcock; BL Wm. R. Smallwood; - ; 37

Cameron Babinger; 6 September 1905; Leo Babinger, died before December 1919; Minnie C., died before December 1919; - ; MGM Elizabeth Sackinger (born about 1849, of Allegany), PGM Louise Babinger; Cameron was a teacher; 68

Ada Pearl Bacheldor; about 1907; AF Cuyler W. Bacheldor; - ; - ; - ; biological parents had died; 37

Almon Bacon; 10 May 1820; William Bacon, died before July 1833; - ; Chloe and Lodema Bacon; - ; G- Penuel Bacon; 2

Chloe Bacon; - ; William Bacon, died before July 1833; - ; Almon and Lodema Bacon; - ; G- Penuel Bacon; 2

Dana D. Bacon; 29 June 1893; - ; Alice L; - ; - ; - ; 23

Harry M. Bacon; 7 September 1885; - ; May, died January 1905; Edna Steven, and Fred, William, Myrtle and Rolland Bacon; - ; G- William McGeorge; 37

Lodema Bacon; 20 May 1817; William Bacon, died before July 1833; - ; Almon and Chloe Bacon; - ; G- Penuel Bacon; 2

Myrtle M. Bacon; about 1894; - ; May, died January 1905; Edna Steven, and Fred, William, Harry and Rolland Bacon; - ; G- William McGeorge; 37

Rolland Bacon; about 1897; - ; May, died January 1905; Edna Steven, and Fred, William, Harry and Myrtle Bacon; - ; G- William McGeorge; 37

William H. Bacon; about 1892; - ; May, died January 1905; Edna Steven, and Fred, Rolland, Harry and Myrtle Bacon; - ; G- William McGeorge; 37

Libbie Bailey; about 1869; Mr. Shears; Sarah, died 29 June 1886 in Chautauqua County, NY; Emma Shears; HU Grant Bailey;

Name; Date of Birth; Father; Mother; Siblings; Other Relatives; Notes; Box Number

- ; 37

John Paul Baird; 9 July 1881; Charles W. Baird; Pauline Siggins, died 18 August 1887, from Chautuaqua County; - ; PGM Sarah M. Baird, PU George W. Baird, PU John E. Baird, PA Mary R. Gephart, PA Lucretia L. Gardner, MA Mary Siggins, MA Hellen Siggins, MA Jane S. Ferry, MA Sabina E. Parker, MU Walter Siggins, PU Isaac Siggins, C- Rose Baird (daughter of George Baird); money from estate of Helen Siggins; 2

Adorah Baker; about 1858; Augustus Baker; Marietta; Arunah, Henrietta, Nellie and Rensselaer Baker; other relatives were Francis and Rosalinda Baker and Matilda Mann; G- Heman Button; 1

Arunah Baker; about 1855; Augustus Baker; Marietta; Adora, Henrietta, Nellie and Rensselaer Baker; other relatives were Francis and Rosalinda Baker and Matilda Mann; G- Heman Button; 1

Clarissa A. Baker; 17 June 1909; J. A. Baker; Iva, went by Iva Lawton Baker; James Baker; - ; money from estate of Clara E. Baker (estate in Allegany County, NY); 25

Dorothy H. Baker; - ; - ; Mary E., of Allen, Ottawa, Ohio; Florence Baker; - ; 23

Florence M. Baker; - ; - ; Mary E., of Allen, Ottawa, Ohio; Dorothy Baker; - ; 23

Frances Baker; before 1859; - ; Elizabeth; W. Scott and Julian Baker, - ; - ; 2

Henrietta Baker; about 1861; Augustus Baker; Marietta; Arunah, Adora, Nellie and Rensselaer Baker; HU Mr. Crow, other relatives were Francis and Rosalinda Baker and Matilda Mann; AKA Netta Baker; G- Heman Button; 1

James Baker; 20 January 1911; J. A. Baker; Iva, went by Iva Lawton Baker; Clarissa Baker; - ; money from estate of Clara E. Baker (estate in Allegany County, NY); 25

Julian B. Baker; before 1859; - ; Elizabeth; W. Scott and Frances Baker, - ; - ; 2

Name; Date of Birth; Father; Mother; Siblings; Other Relatives; Notes; Box Number

M. Antoinette Baker; before 1859; - ; Marsena; - ; - ; - ; 2

Nellie Baker; about 1865; Augustus Baker; Marietta; Arunah, Adora, Henrietta and Rensselaer Baker; HU Mr. Barber, other relatives were Francis and Rosalinda Baker and Matilda Mann; Nellie died before January 1886, G- Heman Button; 1

Nina Baker; about 1892; Loren Baker; - ; - ; - ; G- Lynn Bean, no relation; 37

Rensselaer Baker; 20 February 1865; Augustus Baker; Marietta; Arunah, Adora, Henrietta and Nellie Baker; other relatives were Francis and Rosalinda Baker and Matilda Mann; G- Heman Button; 1

W. Scott Baker; before 1859; - ; Elizabeth; Frances and Julian Baker, - ; - ; 2

Julia L. Ball; about 1893; - ; Ella M.; - ; - ; - ; 23

Clyde E. Ballard; 11 September 1872; - ; Helen; Henry Ballard; - ; - ; 37

Delta Ballard; 10 January 1866; Charles Ballard, died August 1873 in Otto; Sarahette; - ; GM Susan Colvin, A- Laura Colvin, U- George Colvin; G- George A. Ballard; 1

Gordon C. Barber; 6 February 1909; - ; - ; - ; U- Ben Barber, U- Glenn Barber, A- Linnie M. Harvey, A- Florence I. Masterson, A- Anna Gibbs, all of Buffalo; - ; 25

Josephine Barber; 24 October 1891; - ; - ; Mary and Dominick Barber, - ; Dominick RE 610 N. Union St., Olean; 37

Mary Barber; 13 October 1888; - ; - ; Josephine and Dominick Barber, - ; Dominick RE 610 N. Union St., Olean; 37

Mary Bargy; 14 February 1871; J. M. Bargy; - ; Emma Taylor, Sylvanus, Minnie and Devillo Bargy; A- Emily Millhollen, U- Devillo Bargy; - ; 37

Minnie Bargy; 30 March 1879; J. M. Bargy; - ; Emma Taylor, Sylvanus, Mary and Devillo Bargy; A- Emily Millhollen, U- Devillo Bargy; - ; 37

Sylvanus B. Bargy; January 1864; J. M. Bargy; - ; Emma Taylor, Minnie, Mary and Devillo Bargy; A- Emily Millhollen, U- Devillo Bargy; - ; 37

Name; Date of Birth; Father; Mother; Siblings; Other Relatives; Notes; Box Number

Elva Minnette Barhite; 16 October 1902; Charles Barhite; Helen; Janice and Welcome Barhite; HU Mr. Rhoades, U- Fay Barhite; - ; 25

Janice Barhite; 21 July 1905; Charles Barhite; Helen; Elva and Welcome Barhite; U- Fay Barhite; RE 1926, Ellington, Chautauqua, NY; 25

Welcome Julian Barhite; 16 June 1900; Charles Barhite; Helen; Elva and Janie Barhite; U- Fay Barhite; RE 1921, Ellicott, Chautauqua, NY; 25

Frank W. Barker; 19 Jan 1865; Marshall Barker; Ellen; - ; - ; Phebe P. Morris left legacy; 2

Mary Barker; 8 May 1897; - ; Josephine; Theodore Barker; U- Peter Miller; Isabell Barker left legacy, Mary RE 1918, Toledo, Lucas, Ohio; 36

Theodore Barker; 15 May 1900; - ; Josephine; Mary Barker; U- Peter Miller; Isabell Barker left legacy, Theodore RE 1918, Toledo, Lucas, Ohio; 36

Cortez Barlow; August 1881; - ; - ; Alice Greeley; - ; - ; 37

Carl J. Barnes; 27 June 1877; Clark Barnes; - ; Maud Barnes; - ; - ; 23

Kittie A. Barnes; - ; - ; - ; - ; A- Mrs. Norman E. C. Cowen; money from estates of Armena C. Metcalf and Eva M. Barnes; 37

Mary L. Barnes; - ; - ; - ; - ; - ; file only contains guardian accounts; 37

Maud Barnes; - ; Clark Barnes; - ; Carl Barnes; - ; - ; 23

Rosemond Barnes; 8 February 1898; John W. Barnes; Rose; - ; - ; RE 1918, in Buffalo; 23

Frank Barrett; about 1889; - ; Ida; Thomas, Mark, Leo and Mary; U- James W. Barrett, of LeRoy, Genesee, NY; money from Martin Barrett estate, Father Vaderfoot did Mass for Martin, paid money to St. John's Protectory, "Victoria", West Seneca, NY and Frank's father died 5 April 1894; 36

Helen J. Barrett; 22 April 1852; Asher J. Barrett; - ; - ; - ; - ; 2

Leo Barrett; about 1892; - ; Ida; Thomas, Mark, Frank and Mary;

Name; Date of Birth; Father; Mother; Siblings; Other Relatives; Notes; Box Number

U- James W. Barrett, of LeRoy, Genesee, NY; money from Martin Barrett estate, Father Vaderfoot did Mass for Martin, paid money to St. John's Protectory, "Victoria", West Seneca, NY and Leo's father died 5 April 1894; 36

Mark Barrett; about 1887; ; Ida; Thomas, Leo, Frank and Mary; U- James W. Barrett, of LeRoy, Genesee, NY; money from Martin Barrett estate, Father Vaderfoot did Mass for Martin, paid money to St. John's Protectory, "Victoria", West Seneca, NY and Mark's father died 5 April 1894; 36

Mary Barrett; about 1890; - ; Ida; Thomas, Mark, Frank and Leo; U- James W. Barrett, of LeRoy, Genesee, NY; money from Martin Barrett estate, Father Vaderfoot did Mass for Martin, paid money to St. John's Protectory, "Victoria", West Seneca, NY and Mary's father died 5 April 1894; 36

Thomas "Tommy" Barrett; about 1889;- ; Ida; Mark, Leo, Frank and Mary; U- James W. Barrett, of LeRoy, Genesee, NY; money from Martin Barrett estate, Father Vaderfoot did Mass for Martin, paidmoney to St. John's Protectory, "Victoria", West Seneca, NY and Thomas's father died 5 April 1894; 36

Estella Barse; 31 May 1857; Archibald Barse, died 1865; Sabina, married Mr. Shippy; Rosa and Flora Barse, U- Perry Brown; - ; 2

Flora Barse; before February 1869; Archibald Barse, died 1865; Sabina, married Mr. Shippy; Rosa and Estella Barse, U- Perry Brown; - ; 2

Rosa Barse; before February 1869; Archibald Barse, died 1865; Sabina, married Mr. Shippy; Flora and Estella Barse, U- Perry Brown; - ; 2

Alvina C. Bartlett; 4 May 1908 in Gowanda; Frank Bartelt; Phoebe C.; Arthur W. Bartelt; - ; AKA Alvina C. Bartelt; 25

Blanche Bartlett; 30 June 1874; Martin A. Salisbury; - ; - ; FL Edward L. Bartlett; - ; 37

Gracie Bartlett; March 1879; - ; Emma Razey; - ; PG Daniel E. and Harriet A. Bartlett, MG Almadorus and Sarah Razey, A- Grace Arnold, A- Nellie Lee, A- Franc Bartlett; - ; 37

Name; Date of Birth; Father; Mother; Siblings; Other Relatives; Notes; Box Number

Robert Emerson Bartlett; 28 November 1909; Willis G. Bartlett; Belle M, died December 1916, after cancer operation; - ; MGA Emma Gerber; RE 1931, Kenmore, NY; 23

Arthur Barton; 16 September 1875; - ; - ; - ; - ; - ; 23

Anthony F. Bassinger; 28 May 1876; - ; - ; Fred, Rosa, Mary, Peter, Paul and William Bassinger; U- Peter Bassinger, U- Fred Gilbert; G- Giles Johnson (no relation). Anthony's father died March 1885 and mother died 24 January 1890; 76

Fred M. Bassinger; 26 November 1874; - ; - ; Anthony, Rosa, Mary, Peter, Paul and William Bassinger; U- Peter Bassinger, U- Fred Gilbert; G- Giles Johnson (no relation). Fred's father died March 1885 and mother died 24 January 1890; 76

Mary E. Bassinger; 18 February 1878; - ; - ; Anthony, Rosa, Fred, Peter, Paul and William Bassinger; U- Peter Bassinger, U- Fred Gilbert; RE 1899, in Thomaston, Litchfield, Connecticut, G- Giles Johnson (no relation). Mary's father died March 1885 and mother died 24 January 1890; 76

Paul A. Bassinger; 27 June 1881; - ; - ; Anthony, Rosa, Fred, Peter, Mary and William Bassinger; U- Peter Bassinger, U- Fred Gilbert; G- Giles Johnson (no relation). Paul's father died March 1885 and mother died 24 January 1890; 76

Peter H. Bassinger; 28 January 1880; - ; - ; Anthony, Rosa, Fred, Mary, Paul and William Bassinger; U- Peter Bassinger, U- Fred Gilbert; G- Giles Johnson (no relation). Peter's father died March 1885 and mother died 24 January 1890; 76

Rosa F. Bassinger; 3 August 1883; - ; - ; Anthony, Peter, Fred, Mary, Paul and William Bassinger; HU Mr. Merrill, U- Peter Bassinger, U- Fred Gilbert; G- Giles Johnson (no relation). Rosa's father died March 1885 and mother died 24 January 1890; 76

William "Willie" W. Bassinger; 2 December 1885; - ; - ; Anthony, Peter, Fred, Mary, Paul and Rosa Bassinger; U- Peter Bassinger, U- Fred Gilbert; G- Giles Johnson (no

Name; Date of Birth; Father; Mother; Siblings; Other Relatives; Notes; Box Number

relation). Williams's father died March 1885 and mother died 24 January 1890; 76

Alice Bates; about 1906; Samuel Bates of Buffalo; - ; - ; GM Caroline Moench; - ; 2 and 37

Chloe R. Bates; about 1857; - ; - ; - ; - ; lawyer was Eugene Abuile; 2

Mildred Battles; 19 Dec 1893; - ; Lizzie; Reva Battles; - ; - ; 2 and 37

Reva Battles; 16 June 1896; - ; Lizzie; Mildred Battles; - ; Reva died 23 September 1901; 2 and 37

Edward S. Baxter; 31 October 1910; - ; - ; Richard and Norman Baxter; - ; RE 1931, in Buffalo, NY; 25

Richard S. Baxter; 6 March 1908; - ; - ; Edward and Norman Baxter; - ; - ; 25

Arlene R. Beach; 15 April 1909; Robert T. Beach; Ora M.; Roberta Beach; HU Mr. Stelley; - ; 25

Ellen Beach; about 1861; - ; Esther, died 1869, in Wisconsin; - ; MA Emeline Snyder (W- of Norman Snyder); father lived with her in Silver Creek, Chautauqua, NY, G- John A. Lynde; 1

Flossie Beach; about 1883; - ; Edith; - ; - ; - ; 37

Nellie R. Beach; 2 Nov 1861; Ethan Orlando Beach, AKA Orlando Beach; - ; William J. Beach; HU Mr. Gavin, married by November 1883; G- Edwin F. Beach, Nellie RE April 1883, Madison, NY; 2

Roberta C. Beach; 21 August 1911; Robert T. Beach; Ora M.; Arlene Beach; HU Mr. Demmon; July 1931, had 2 year old daughter and another child on way; 25

William J. Beach; 20 April 1859; Ethan Orlando Beach, AKA Orlando Beach, - ; Nellie R. Beach; - ; G- Millard Beach; 1

Elmina E. Beals; - ; - ; - ; - ; - ; G- Zina Holdridge, file mentions that Elliott Curtiss died, money left to care for Waldo H. Curtis; 2

Leon L. Bean; 22 October 1894; - ; Cora E.; - ; - ; - ; 36

Myron F. Beardsley; 1 March 1892; Fred G. Beardsley; - ; - ; - ;

Name; Date of Birth; Father; Mother; Siblings; Other Relatives; Notes; Box Number

- ; 37

Tillie Beardsley; 10 July 1884; - ; - ; - ; U- Charles Beardsley, of Carrollton; - ; 71

Harriet E. Becker; 1 September 1906; William Becker, died 28 February 1909; Louise A.; M. Alley and Howard T. Becker; - ; - ; 23

Helen Becker; 17 November 1904; Herbert Becker; - ; Madeline Becker; - ; - ; 23

Howard T. Becker; 10 December 1904; William Becker, died 28 February 1909; Louise A.; M. Alley and Harriet Becker; - ; - ; 23

Madeline Becker; 18 July 1906; Herbert Becker; - ; Helen Becker; - ; - ; 23

Louisa Beckman; 19 June 1875; Charles Beckman, died 16 February 1883, of Salamanca; - ; Robert Beckman, HB Charles Beckman; HU Mr. Becker, married 1896 in Bradford, McKean, Pennsylvania; John Schaeder had custody and died 17 September 1887; 38

Robert Beckman; 17 May 1874; Charles Beckman, died 16 February 1883, of Salamanca; - ; Louisa Beckman, HB Charles Beckman; - ; John Schaeder had custody and died 17 September 1887; 38

Blanche M. Beckwith; 5 April 1886; - ; - ; George, Harlow, Rachel, and Stella Beckwith; MGF Charles Charlesworth, U- Orrin O. Beckwith; RE November 1908, in Perry, Wyoming, NY; 2

Douglas Beckwith; 26 June 1861; Luther Beckwith; - ; - ; - ; G- Marvin Austin; 1

George Beckwith; 4 June 1891; - ; - ; Blanche, Harlow, Rachel, and Stella Beckwith; MGF Charles Charlesworth, U- Orrin O. Beckwith; - ; 2

Harlow Beckwith; 22 Jan 1894; - ; - ; George, Blanche, Rachel, and Stella Beckwith; MGF Charles Charlesworth, U- Orrin O. Beckwith; RE Buffalo, Erie, NY; 2

Rachel Beckwith; 10 April 1896; - ; - ; Blanche, Harlow, George,

Name; Date of Birth; Father; Mother; Siblings; Other Relatives; Notes; Box Number

and Stella Beckwith; MGF Charles Charlesworth, U- Orrin O. Beckwith; - ; 2

Stella Beckwith; 24 Oct 1887; - ; - ; George, Harlow, Rachel, and Blanche Beckwith; MGF Charles Charlesworth, U- Orrin O. Beckwith; RE November 1908, Perry, Wyoming, NY; 2

Ellen Beebe; about 1853; Henry Beebe Jr.; - ; Orson and Orvis Beebe; MGF John Valance, PGF Henry Beebe, MU William Valence, PU Daniel Beebe, PU Roland Beebe, PA Permelia Parker, (W- of Corwin D. Parker); - ; 24

Orson Beebe; about 1851; ; Henry Beebe Jr.; - ; Ellen and Orvis Beebe; MGF John Valance, PGF Henry Beebe, MU William Valence, PU Daniel Beebe, PU Roland Beebe, PA Permelia Parker (W- of Corwin D. Parker); indexed under Oren Beebe; 24

Orvis Beebe; about 1851; Henry Beebe Jr.; - ; Orson and Ellen Beebe; MGF John Valance, PGF Henry Beebe, MU William Valence, PU Daniel Beebe, PU Roland Beebe, PA Permelia Parker (W-of Corwin D. Parker); - ; 24

Alice M. Beeman; August 1896; - ; - ; - ; PGM Esther M. Beeman, PU Fred Beeman; - ; 76

Edna I. Bell; 3 September 1879; - ; Eva M.; Ralph Bell; - ; father died 14 December 1890; 37

Ralph E. Bell; 14 September 1881; - ; Eva M.; Edna Bell; - ; father died 14 December 1890; 37

Effie B. Bennehoff; before April 1860; - ; - ; - ; - ; G- W. G. Hornblower, R. Lyle Bennehoff may be Effie's sibling, although no link found in file; 2

R. Lyle Bennehoff: before April 1854; - ; - ; - ; - ; G- W. G. Hornblower, Effie Bennehoff may be R. Lyle's sibling, although no link found in file; 2

Clara P. Bennett; - ; - ; - ; Oliver Bennett; - ; G- Mary E. Bennett (of Franklinville); 75

Elizabeth Bennett; about 1862; Thomas W. Bennett, died 5 March 1861, of Plover, Portage, Wisconsin; Maria, married Mr. Brown; - ; PU Wallace M. Bennett; - ; 23

Name; Date of Birth; Father; Mother; Siblings; Other Relatives; Notes; Box Number

Fanny D. Bennett; about 1857; David Bennett died 1 November 1857; - ; Polly Bennett; GM Jemina Bennett; PU James Willcox, PU Hosea Willcox, PU Jonathan Willcox, PU Ellihu Willcox, PA Fanny Wilcox (W- of Jonathan Willcox); money from estates of James Willcox and Arthur Hinds (GU) and Fanny married son of Jonathan and Fanny Willcox. Fanny's mother died 15 August 1857; 2

Oliver P. Bennett; - ; - ; - ; Clara Bennett; - ; G- Mary E. Bennett (of Franklinville); 75

Polly D. Bennett; about 1855; David Bennett died 1 November 1857; - ; Fanny. Bennett; GM Jemina Bennett; PU James Willcox, PU Hosea Willcox, PU Jonathan Willcox, PU Ellihu Willcox, PA Fanny Wilcox (W- of Jonathan Willcox); money from estates of James Willcox and Arthur Hinds (GU) and Fanny's mother died 15 August 1857; 2

Lucy Maria Benson; about 1848; - ; - ; - ; HU William L. White; G- Joseph Harrington, Lucy died before 24 September 1869, in same envelope with Jane Robinson; 2 and 76

William Hodges Benson; 17 February 1893; John G. Benson; - ; - ; - ; - ; 2

Betsey Bent; about 1833; Hartwell Bent, died before June 1844, of Randolph; - ; Melvina, Horace and Diana Bent; - ; first G- Joseph Stanley (born about 1774), second G- Melzer Pingrey; 76

Diana Bent; about 1840; Hartwell Bent, died before June 1844, of Randolph; - ; Melvina, Horace and Betsey Bent; - ; first G- Joseph Stanley (born about 1774), second G- Melzer Pingrey; 76

Hartwell "Heady" Bent; 29 April 1858; Horace Bent; Helen M.; Henrietta Bent; PA Betsey Topliff, PA Diana Jones, PGA Axy Damon, PGU Harris Aldrich; G- Adams D. Marsh, Hartwell RE 1872, in Meadville, Pennsylvania; 2

Henrietta "Nettie" M. Bent; 17 April 1855; Horace Bent; Helen M.; Hartwell Bent; PA Betsey Topliff, PA Diana Jones, PGA Axy Damon, PGU Harris Aldrich; G- Adams D. Marsh,

Name; Date of Birth; Father; Mother; Siblings; Other Relatives; Notes; Box Number

Henrietta RE 1872, in Meadville, Pennsylvania; 2

Horace Bent; about 1835; Hartwell Bent, died before June 1844, of Randolph; - ; Melvina, Diana and Betsey Bent; - ; first G- Joseph Stanley (born about 1774), second G- Melzer Pingrey; 76

Melvina Bent; about 1831; Hartwell Bent, died before June 1844, of Randolph; - ; Horace, Diana and Betsey Bent; - ; first G- Joseph Stanley (born about 1774), second G- Melzer Pingrey; 76

Julia Spees Bentley; about 1846; Stephen Bentley; - ; - ; - ; G- Burr S. Bentley; 2

Louella Benton; - ; - ; Adeline Leighton; - ; MGF Henry Leighton, another relative was Harriet Simpson (W- of Joseph Simpson); grandfather left her property in Portville; 2

Caroline "Carrie" A. Berry; 23 October 1849; Henry C. Berry; Caroline; Imogene, Leona, Herbert, and William Berry; - ; HU Franklin Brown; Louisa Berry was a deceased sister; 2

Frank W. Berry; 8 August 1871; - ; - ; - ; relatives were: Frank Feehan (Brockville, Ontario, Canada), Mrs. Lilly Hall (Philadelphia, Pennsylvania), Miss Florence Feehan (Philadelphia, Pennsylvania), Mrs. Christiana Berry (Great Valley, NY), Mrs. Anna Loomis (Great Valley), L. P. Berry (Bliss, Wyoming, NY), Horatio N. Berry (Perry, Wyoming, NY); - ; 37

Herbert W. Berry; 23 October 1857; Henry C. Berry; Caroline; Leona, Caroline, Imogene, and William Berry; - ; Louisa Berry was a deceased sister; 2

Imogene "Emma" Berry; 20 January 1853; Henry C. Berry; Caroline; Leona, Caroline, Herbert, and William Berry; - ; Louisa Berry was a deceased sister; 2

Leona Berry; 30 August 1860; Henry C. Berry; Caroline; Herbert, Caroline, Imogene, and William Berry; - ; Louisa Berry was a deceased sister; 2

Leonora J. Berry; 10 July 1896; Alexander Berry; Henrietta S.; - ; - ; - ; 37

Name; Date of Birth; Father; Mother; Siblings; Other Relatives; Notes; Box Number

William Henry Berry; - ; Henry C. Berry; Caroline; Herbert, Caroline, Imogene, and Leona Berry; - ; Louisa Berry was a deceased sister; 2

Gertrude Besecker; 11 August 1901; - ; - ; Lena and Myrtle Dollard and Mrs. Fred Davis; - ; - ; 25

Frank Bettinger; about 1878; Nicholas Bettinger, died 20 August 1881; Hulda Newcomb, married Mr. Zaumetzer; Sarah Bettinger; MGF Thomas Newcomb; - ; 37

Sarah Bettinger; 12 March 1882; Nicholas Bettinger, died 20 August 1881; Hulda Newcomb, married Mr. Zaumetzer; Frank Bettinger; MGF Thomas Newcomb; - ; 37

Lewis Beverly; - ; - ; - ; - ; - ; G- Margaret Beverly; 2

Fred R. Billington; 30 September 1887; - ; - ; - ; GGF Rollin Wright; G- J. Wilson Radley, no relation; 71

Alice M. Bishop; 22 January 1907; - ; Ellen, of Ashford, married Mr. Hollister; - ; - ; money from pension and estate of Harriston P. Bishop; 68

George Bishop; 28 June 1854; George Bishop; Louisa; Sarah and Henry Bishop; - ; received pension money; 2

Henry Bishop; 12 February 1861; George Bishop; Louisa; Sarah and George Bishop; - ; received pension money; 2

Sarah Bishop;15 May 1858; George Bishop; Louisa; Henry and George Bishop; - ; received pension money; 2

Hannah J. Bixby; about 1860; - ; - ; - ; - ; G- Silas F. Mann, Barnes Bixby left legacy; 2

Elizabeth F. Blackmer; - ; Henry Blackmer, died about 1855, of Livonia, Livingston, NY; - ; Sarah Blackmer; PGF Levi Blackmer, died about 1855, of Richmond, Ontario, NY; - ; 25

Sarah L. Blackmer; - ; Henry Blackmer, died about 1855, of Livonia, Livingston, NY; - ; Elizabeth Blackmer; PGF Levi Blackmer, died about 1855, of Richmond, Ontario, NY; - ; 25

Bertha G. Blackwell; about 1891; - ; - ; Florence, Harry, Howard, Joseph, Robert and Morris Blackwell; - ; - ; 24

Florence E. Blackwell; about 1893; - ; - ; Bertha, Harry, Howard, Joseph, Robert and Morris Blackwell; - ; - ; 24

Name; Date of Birth; Father; Mother; Siblings; Other Relatives; Notes; Box Number

Harry A. J. Blackwell; about 1895; - ; - ; Bertha, Florence, Howard, Joseph, Robert and Morris Blackwell; - ; - ; 24

Howard E. Blackwell; about 1898; - ; - ; Bertha, Florence, Harry, Joseph, Robert and Morris Blackwell; - ; - ; 24

Joseph D. Blackwell; about 1901; - ; - ; Bertha, Florence, Harry, Howard, Robert and Morris Blackwell; - ; - ; 24

Robert M. Blackwell; about 1903; - ; - ; Bertha, Florence, Harry, Howard, Joseph and Morris Blackwell; - ; - ; 24

Alice J. Blake; 14 April 1883; Elmer J. Blake, of New Albion; - ; Maude Blake; HU Mr. Dake, C- Walter F. Andrews; - ; 71

Maude Blake; 6 April 1885; Elmer J. Blake, of New Albion; - ; Alice Blake; C- Walter F. Andrews; - ; 71

Harriet Blakely; about 1832; Harry Blakely, died before November 1839, of Perrysburg; - ; Justus, Hiram, Weltha and Otsey Blakely; other relatives were Lurilla Easton, Lodema Easterly, Cloe Aldrich, Laura How and Mrs. Fanny Blakely; G- William Crandall; 76

Hiram Blakely; 1 April 1826; Harry Blakely, died before November 1839, of Perrysburg; - ; Justus, Harriet, Weltha and Otsey Blakely; other relatives were Lurilla Easton, Lodema Easterly, Cloe Aldrich, Laura How and Mrs. Fanny Blakely; G- Fanny Blakely, G- Asher Brown; 77

Justus Blakely; 26 September 1821 Harry Blakely, died before November 1839, of Perrysburg; - ; Harriet, Hiram, Weltha and Otsey Blakely; other relatives were Lurilla Easton, Lodema Easterly, Cloe Aldrich, Laura How and Mrs. Fanny Blakely; G- Fanny Blakely, G- Asher Brown; 77

Otsey Blakely; about 1837; Harry Blakely, died before November 1839, of Perrysburg; - ; Justus, Hiram, Weltha and Harriet Blakely; other relatives were Lurilla Easton, Lodema Easterly, Cloe Aldrich, Laura How and Mrs. Fanny Blakely; G- William Crandall, Otsey lived with Silas Burdick; 76

Weltha Blakely; about 1828; Harry Blakely, died before November 1839, of Perrysburg; - ; Justus, Hiram, Weltha and Harriet Blakely; other relatives were Lurilla Easton, Lodema

Name; Date of Birth; Father; Mother; Siblings; Other Relatives; Notes; Box Number

Easterly, Cloe Aldrich, Laura How and Mrs. Fanny Blakely; G- William Crandall, Weltha lived with Silas Burdick; 76

Emma R. Blanchard; 7 May 1864; Solotus M. Blanchard, died March 1875; Tamerson; Nellie, Washington, Cornelius and Marsevan Blanchard; HU Mr. Hopkins; - ; 37

Erma S. Blanchard; 10 January 1878; - ; Florence D.; Lynn, Harrie and Hattie Blanchard; - ; A. D. Blanchard's funeral was paid out of guardian's account; 37

Harrie B. Blanchard; 26 January 1876; - ; Florence D.; Lynn, Erma and Hattie Blanchard; - ; A. D. Blanchard's funeral was paid out of guardian's account. Indexed as Harry Blanchard; 37

Hattie Blanchard; 6 February 1874; - ; Florence D.; Lynn, Erma and Harrie Blanchard; HU Mr. Kelly ; A. D. Blanchard's funeral was paid out of guardian's account; 37

Lynn Blanchard; 3 May 1872; - ; Florence D.; Harrie, Erma and Hattie Blanchard; - ; A. D. Blanchard's funeral was paid out of guardian's account; 37

Lucius Bliss; 17 Oct 1846; - ; Mary, married Mr. Gleason; Lydia; - ; G- Ele Gleason; 2

Lydia Bliss; 10 Sept 1839; - ; Mary, married Mr. Gleason; Lucius; - ; G- Ele Gleason; 2

Lloyd Nelson Bliton; 11 February 1906; Rupert Bliton, died 2 August 1909; Margaret, of Freedom; Nellie Bliton; - ; - ; 69 and 75

Nellie Elizabeth Bliton; 29 March 1903; Rupert Bliton, died 2 August 1909; Margaret, of Freedom; Lloyd Bliton; HU Mr. Hardy ; - ; 69 and 75

Lena Sophia Block; about 1869; - ; Mary; - ; HU Martin Blemuster, of Springville, Erie, NY; father served in the US Government at time of death; ; 37

Blanch Blood; - ; - ; - ; - ; - ; there is nothing in the file for Blanch, but her name is on envelope with Lucia Blood; 37

Lucia E. Blood; 14 November 1868; Irwin Blood; - ; - ; - ; G- Ephraim Fitts (no relation), in same envelope with Blanch

Name; Date of Birth; Father; Mother; Siblings; Other Relatives; Notes; Box Number

Blood and Lucia's mother died 13 September 1882; 37

Earl Llewellyn Blossom; - ; - ; Leota; Elmer, Ernest, and Eugene Blossom; - ; - ; 37

Elmer Seth Blossom; - ; - ; Leota; Earl, Ernest, and Eugene Blossom; - ; - ; 37

Ernest Ellsworth Blossom; - ; - ; Leota; Earl, Elmer, and Eugene Blossom; - ; - ; 37

Eugene Arthur Blossom; - ; - ; Leota; Earl, Elmer, and Ernest Blossom; - ; - ; 37

Addie Blowers; about 1860; Andrew Blowers; Almira Frank, married Daniel Tracy; Omer and Hassan Blowers ; MGF Jacob Frank, PU Clark Blowers, MU Hiram Frank, MU Reuben Frank, MU Henry Frank, MU Ezra Frank; - ; 2

Amba Blowers; about 1846; - ; Charlotte, who married Nathan L. Coon, of East Otto; Matilda and Annis Blowers; PGF Andrew Blowers, PU Silas Blowers, PU William Blowers, PU Andrew Blowers, PU Clark Blowers; - ; 75

Annis Blowers; about 1848; - ; Charlotte, who married Nathan L. Coon, of East Otto; Matilda and Amba Blowers; PGF Andrew Blowers, PU Silas Blowers, PU William Blowers, PU Andrew Blowers, PU Clark Blowers; - ; 75

Hassan Blowers; about 1862; Andrew Blowers; Almira Frank, married Daniel Tracy; Omer and Addie Blowers ; MGF Jacob Frank, PU Clark Blowers, MU Hiram Frank, MU Reuben Frank, MU Henry Frank, MU Ezra Frank; - ; 2

Matilda Blowers; about 1850; - ; Charlotte, who married Nathan L. Coon, of East Otto; Annis and Amba Blowers; PGF Andrew Blowers, PU Silas Blowers, PU William Blowers, PU Andrew Blowers, PU Clark Blowers; - ; 75

Omer Blowers; about 1857; Andrew Blowers; Almira Frank, married Daniel Tracy; Hassan and Addie Blowers ; MGF Jacob Frank, PU Clark Blowers, MU Hiram Frank, MU Reuben Frank, MU Henry Frank, MU Ezra Frank; - ; 2

Phebe Matilda Blowers; 10 Dec 1848; - ; Mary E. Blowers; - ; MG Smith and Phebe Blowers, PGM Huldah Blowers; - ;

Name; Date of Birth; Father; Mother; Siblings; Other Relatives; Notes; Box Number

2

Amanda M. Boardman; 10 November 1834; - ; - ; - ; HU Edwin A. Boardman; - ; 37

Gardner Boardman; 15 Aug 1873; Thomas Boardman; Ellen, married Mr. Pittman; - ; PGM Arminta Boardman; RE Coin, Page, Iowa; 1

Genevieve Ursula Boardman; 24 September 1906; Lee C. Boardman, of Little Valley; - ; - ; - ; - ; 68

Jerome Stanton Boardman; - ; - ; - ; Nellie and Solomon Boardman; heir of Alfred Ayer; Jerome RE Williamsport, Indiana; 37

Nellie L. Boardman; - ; - ; - ; Jerome and Solomon Boardman; heir of Alfred Ayer; Nellie RE Williamsport, Indiana; 37

Solomon Boardman; - ; - ; - ; Jerome and Nellie Boardman; heir of Alfred Ayer; Solomon RE Williamsport, Indiana; 37

Edna Boberg; 21 January 1897; William J. Boberg; - ; - ; - ; - ; 37

Avena Bockmier; about 1897; - ; - ; Clare, Rheinhart and William Bockmier; U- John B. Bockmier; G- Clare Miller, no relation; 44

Caroline "Carrie" Bockmier; about 1881; Conrad Bockmier, of Allegany; - ; Rosa Bockmier; - ; G- John H. Carls and received money from estate of Andrew Hirt (died 30 November 1898); 71

Clare Bockmier; about 1895; - ; - ; Avena, Rheinhart and William Bockmier; U- John B. Bockmier; G- Clare Miller, no relation; 44

Mary Bockmier; 21 April 1879; Conrad Bockmier; - ; - ; - ; RE April 1900, Oshkosh, Winnebago County, Wisconsin; 1

Rheinhart Bockmier; about 1893; - ; - ; Avena, Clare and William Bockmier; U- John B. Bockmier; G- Clare Miller, no relation; 44

Rosa Bockmier; about 1883; Conrad Bockmier, of Allegany; - ; Caroline Bockmier; HU Mr. Geise; G- John H. Carls and received money from estate of Andrew Hirt (died 30 November 1898); 71

Name; Date of Birth; Father; Mother; Siblings; Other Relatives; Notes; Box Number

William Bockmier; about 1891; - ; - ; Avena, Clare and Rheinhart Bockmier; U- John B. Bockmier; G- Clare Miller, no relation; 44

Charles "Carl" Bolander; 14 July 1888; William Bolander, RE Erie County, NY; - ; Mary; A- Lena Fleckenstein; G- Frank Fleckenstein, money from estate of John J. Reuter, other heirs of John J. Reuter were Lana and Mary Bolander; 2

Mary M. Bolander; 15 June 1885; William Bolander, RE Erie County, NY; - ; Mary; A- Lena Fleckenstein; G- Frank Fleckenstein, money from estate of John J. Reuter, other heirs of John J. Reuter were Lana and Charles Bolander. Mary committed to Buffalo State Hospital as an insane person on 29 March 1906; 2

Alfred Bond; 3 June 1871; Perry Bond, died February 1872; Ava Starks; Angie Bond; U- Warren Bond, U- G. W. Starks, U- Warren Starks; - ; 1

Angie Bond; 14 July 1872; ; Perry Bond, died February 1872; Ava Starks; Alfred Bond; U- Warren Bond, U- G. W. Starks, U- Warren Starks; - ; 1

Ellen Bonesteel; - ; - ; - ; - ; - ; in index, states formerly Edmuns (probably Ellen Edmunds). G- Reuben C. Bonesteel; 1

Beatrice Booth; 11 August 1911;Vance Booth, died by January 1926; Mildred, married Laurence Lockwood; Charlotte, Lucy and Virgil Booth; - ; - ; 25

Charlotte Booth; 3 July 1908; Vance Booth, died by January 1926; Mildred, married Laurence Lockwood; Beatrice, Lucy and Virgil Booth; HU Mr. Carrier; - ; 25

Lucy Booth; - ;Vance Booth, died by January 1926; Mildred, married Laurence Lockwood; Charlotte, Beatrice and Virgil Booth; - ; - ; 25

Virgil Booth; 4 August 1905; Vance Booth, died by January 1926; Mildred, married Laurence Lockwood; Charlotte, Beatrice and Lucy Booth; - ; - ; 25

Jennie Richmond Borden; 24 September 1885; - ; Elizabeth, lived 123 S. 2nd St, Olean; - ; - ; G- J. E. Worden and

Name; Date of Birth; Father; Mother; Siblings; Other Relatives; Notes; Box Number

received money from estate of Geo. A. Borden; 71

Gordon Boser; 12 December 1897; - ; Lena; - ; - ; received money from insurance on Henry Boser; 37

Clark Boutell; 21 October 1847; Charles Boutell, died before September 1863; Cynthia, of Salamanca, married Mr. Waite; Jannette Boutell; - ; - ; 76

Jannette H. Boutell; 16 February 1845;Charles Boutell, died before September 1863; Cynthia, of Salamanca, married Mr. Waite; Clark Boutell; - ; - ; 76

Clark Roff Boutelle; 18 August 1903; Calvin Boutelle; Florence Roff; - ; MGM Ida Roff; Calvin was in the WNY Society for the Protection of Homeless and Dependent Children; 25

Lewis L. Bouton; 1833; Lewis Bouton; Clarissa, died before January 1835; - ; heir of Ezra Kent; - ; 77

Daisy Bowen; 26 September 1881; Judson Bowen; Esther; - ; HU Mr. Carthell; - ; 24

Ernest Bowen; about 1885; - ; Hattie, married Mr. Rainey; William and Leonard Bowen; - ; money from estate of Charles Bowen; 38

Ethel R. Bowen; about 1905; Charles L. Bowen, died before 27 September 1913; - ; Lou and Lawrence Bowen; PGM Effie F. Bowen; - ; 24

George Bowen; about 1856; - ; Susan P., married Mr. Johnson; Luzerne; - ; - ; 2

Hettie S. Bowen; 23 December 1873; Hector S. Bowen; Juliette Woodworth, married Mr. Benson; - ; MG Charles and Olive Woodworth, MA Delia A. Woodworth, MU Zebbie A. Woodworth, MU Victor C. Woodworth; - ; 37

Lawrence N. Bowen; about 1911; Charles L. Bowen, died before 27 September 1913; - ; Lou and Ethel Bowen; PGM Effie F. Bowen; - ; 24

Leonard Bowen; about 1883; - ; Hattie, married Mr. Rainey; William and Ernest Bowen; - ; money from estate of Charles Bowen; 38

Lou E. Bowen; about 1903; Charles L. Bowen, died before 27

Name; Date of Birth; Father; Mother; Siblings; Other Relatives; Notes; Box Number

September 1913; - ; Lawrence and Ethel Bowen; PGM Effie F. Bowen; - ; 24

Luzerne Bowen; about 1854; - ; Susan P., married Mr. Johnson; George; - ; - ; 2

Lucy Ann Bowen; - ; - ; - ; - ; HU Jesse Bowen; G- John Dow; 2

Susie Bowen; about 1897; - ; - ; Victor Bowen; second C- Frank Bowen; father left children and he lived outside of Cattaraugus County; 37

Victor Bowen; about 1899; - ; - ; Susie Bowen; second C- Frank Bowen; father left children and he lived outside of Cattaraugus County; 37

William Bowen; about 1881; - ; Hattie, married Mr. Rainey; Leonard and Ernest Bowen; - ; money from estate of Charles Bowen; 38

Fred E. Boyce; about 1855; - ; - ; - ; - ; G- Morris W. Butterfield; 2

George W. Boyce; about 1854; - ; - ; - ; - ; G- Morris W. Butterfield; 2

Edward D. Boyle; 5 February 1866; Peter Boyle, died 22 December 1882, in Carrollton; Margaret; William, Mary and Nellie Boyle; W- Hattie; - ; 36

Mary Maud Boyle; 9 August 1875; Peter Boyle, died 22 December 1882, in Carrollton; Margaret; Edward, Mary and Nellie Boyle; HU Mr. McIntyre; Edward Boyle, and W- Hattie, took care of her; 36

Nellie Boyle; September 1867; Peter Boyle, died 22 December 1882, in Carrollton; Margaret; William, Edward and Mary Boyle; - ; - ; 36

William Peter Boyle; 6 September 1877; Peter Boyle, died 22 December 1882, in Carrollton; Margaret; Edward, Mary and Nellie Boyle; - ; Edward Boyle, and wife Hattie, took care of him; 36

Beatrice Bozard; 11 July 1903; - ; Eva L, 1926, RE 82 N. Bennett St., Bradford, PA; Clifford Bozard; - ; RE 51 Adams St., Salamanca, NY and money from estate of Truman C.

Name; Date of Birth; Father; Mother; Siblings; Other Relatives; Notes; Box Number

Bozard; 24

Clifford Bozard; 11 April 1906; - ; Eva L, 1926, RE 82 N. Bennett St., Bradford, PA; Beatrice Bozard; - ; RE 51 Adams St., Salamanca, NY, RE 1927, in Bradford, PA and money from estate of Truman C. Bozard; 24

Hanford Bozard; 1 December 1900; Alphonzo A. Bozard; Luella, of Allegany; - ; - ; money from estate of Orrin S. Bennett; 68

Ella A. Bradley; 17 February 1852; - ; - ; - ; - ; G- Milton Waldo; 2

Georgia L. Bradley; about April 1860; Samuel Bradley, died November 1867; Aditha; Samuel H. Bradley; - ; - ; 2

Lydia E. Bradley; 29 September 1855; - ; Eliza; Watia A.Bradley PGF Levi Bradley, U- Alvin L. Bradley; - ; 2

Mary E. Bradley; 1 July 1874; John Bradley, Florence Wright, died 18 June 1876, of Machias; - ; MGF Eleakim Wright (died 28 April 1876), PU Arthur Wright, A- Cornelia Lingenfelder, A- Miriam Little; RE Allegan County, Michigan, G- Oristus A. Conrad; 1

Watia A. Bradley; 1 Jan 1861; - ; Eliza; Lydia A.Bradley; PGF Levi Bradley, U- Alvin L. Bradley; - ; 2

Edna M. Bradt; 31 March 1886; J. N. Bradt; - ; Hazel Bradt; - ; money from estate of Amanda Cone; 37

Hazel A. Bradt; 18 December 1889; J. N. Bradt; - ; Edna Bradt; - ; money from estate of Amanda Cone; 37

Ella Brainard; 22 October 1855; - ; - ; - ; - ; G- Zina Holdridge; 2

Anna May Brand; 4 May 1894; - ; Anna, married Mr. Palmer; Richard, Lois, and Gladys Brand; U- David Brand; G- Charles Merrill. Children were wards of WNY Society for the Protection of Homeless and Dependent Children; 2 and 36

Gladys Brand; July 1898; - ; Anna, married Mr. Palmer; Richard, Lois, and Anna Brand; U- David Brand; G- Charles Merrill. Children were wards of WNY Society for the Protection of Homeless and Dependent Children; 2 and 36

Name; Date of Birth; Father; Mother; Siblings; Other Relatives; Notes; Box Number

Lois Brand; 31 July 1898; - ; Anna, married Mr. Palmer; Richard, Gladys, and Anna Brand; U- David Brand; G- Charles Merrill. Children were wards of WNY Society for the Protection of Homeless and Dependent Children; 2 and 36

Nellie Blanchard Brand; - ; Solotus M. Blanchard, died March 1875; Tamerson; Emma, Washington, Cornelius and Marsevan Blanchard; HU Mr. Brand; - ; 37

Richard Brand; 23 July 1892; - ; Anna, married Mr. Palmer; Richard, Gladys, and Anna Brand; U- David Brand; G- Lois Merrill. Children were wards of WNY Society for the Protection of Homeless and Dependent Children; 2 and 36

Frederick Brandel; 2 June 1889; - ; Paulena; John Brandel; - ; - ; 37

John Brandel; 15 May 1881; - ; Paulena; Frederick Brandel; - ; - ; 37

Robert G. Brandel, Jr.; 12 December 1906; Robert G. Brandel, Sr.; - ; Lena Karl; - ; - ; 26

Floris A. Bridenbaker; about 1894; William E. Bridenbaker, lived 253 Swan St., Buffalo, NY; - ; Pearl Bridenbaker; A- Ida M. Greene; money from estate of Lafayette Rogers, Oma Rogers was mentioned as receiving part of Lafayette Rogers's estate; 37

Pearl A. Bridenbaker; about 1891; William E. Bridenbaker, lived 253 Swan St., Buffalo, NY; - ; Floris Bridenbaker; A- Ida M. Greene; money from estate of Lafayette Rogers, Oma Rogers was mentioned as receiving part of Lafayette Rogers's estate; 37

Adda "Addie" Brissee; 20 June 1872; - ; - ; Frank Brissee; - ; G- Welcome Camp; 2

Catharine Broderick; about 1883; Michael Broderick, died 4 October 1893; Mary; Thomas, Mary, Maggie, Ellen, Rose and Elizabeth Broderick; - ; - ; 37

Elizabeth Broderick; about 1887; Michael Broderick, died 4 October 1893; Mary; Thomas, Mary, Maggie, Ellen, Rose and Catharine Broderick; - ; - ; 37

Name; Date of Birth; Father; Mother; Siblings; Other Relatives; Notes; Box Number

Ellen Broderick; about 1881; Michael Broderick, died 4 October 1893; Mary; Thomas, Mary, Maggie, Elizabeth, Rose and Catharine Broderick; - ; - ; 37

Joseph Broderick; - ; - ; - ; - ; - ; G- Armenia Broderick, of Salamanca; 71

Maggie Broderick; about 1880; Michael Broderick, died 4 October 1893; Mary; Thomas, Mary, Ellen, Elizabeth, Rose and Catharine Broderick; - ; - ; 37

Mary Broderick; 27 September 1878; Michael Broderick, died 4 October 1893; Mary; Thomas, Maggie, Ellen, Elizabeth, Rose and Catharine Broderick; - ; - ; 37

Rose Broderick; about 1885; Michael Broderick, died 4 October 1893; Mary; Thomas, Mary, Ellen, Elizabeth, Maggie and Catharine Broderick; - ; - ; 37

Thomas M. Broderick; 24 March 1876; Michael Broderick, died 4 October 1893; Mary; Rose, Mary, Ellen, Elizabeth, Maggie and Catharine Broderick; - ; - ; 37

John W. Brooker; 19 April 1894; - ; - ; - ; - ; - ; 24

Leola Evelyn Brooks; 9 June 1906; Carl E. Brooks; - ; - ; HU Mr. Pierson; attended State Normal School in Fredonia; 26

Martha Brooks; 2 February 1848; Orator Warren Meacham; - ; - ; - ; G- Edwin S. King; 2

Maud D. Brooks; 10 Jan 1879; - ; - ; - ; BL Asa Couse; - ; 1

Thomas Brothers; 4 Jan 1880; - ; Mary; - ; - ; G- William V. Smith, not related; 3

Achsah Brown; about 1884; Henry C. Brown; - ; Lyman, Charles and Lillian Brown; - ; - ; 38

Archibald Brown; 9 May 1878; N. S. Brown; - ; Harriet Stevenson, Sarah Graham, Albert, Arthur, Grace, James, Ellen and Olive Brown; - ; G- George H. Whiting, no relation; 38

Bessie E. Brown: about 1886; - ; - ; - ; BL Truman D. Keyes; father resided in Colorado for health; 1

Clara H. Brown; about 1876; - ; - ; - ; - ; G- William E. Wheeler, not related; 24

Name; Date of Birth; Father; Mother; Siblings; Other Relatives; Notes; Box Number

Charles E. Brown; about 1875; Henry C. Brown; - ; Lyman, Achsah and Lillian Brown; - ; - ; 38

Cressie L. Brown; 17 August 1887; Charles Brown, died before December 1898; Mary "Mettie" E., of Napoli; - ; - ; received pension money, RE 1900, in Forestville, Chautauqua, NY; 71

Dean Brown; 5 Aug 1891; - ; Nancy; Ellis Brown; - ; - ; 2

Delila Brown; about 1863; James Brown; Sarah Hedden, died April 1899; Nettie Brown; MU John Hedden, MU William Hedden, PU George Brown, PU John Brown and PU Harvey Brown; 37

Effa S. Brown; 7 February 1891; - ; Nettie B., married Mr. Phillips by 1904; Eva Brown; - ; - ; 2

Eliza Brown; 26 January 1849; Eli S. Felch; - ; - ; HU David Edwin Brown; - ; 2

Eliza Jane Brown; July 1835; Ezra Brown; - ; Daniel Brown; - ; - ; 2

Ellen Brown; 21 December 1875; N. S. Brown; - ; Harriet Stevenson, Sarah Graham, Albert, Arthur, Grace, James, Archibald and Olive Brown; - ; G- George H. Whiting, no relation; 38

Ellis E. Brown; 18 May 1877; - ; Nancy; Dean Brown; - ; - ; 2

Emma Brown; 1860; Charles Brown; - ; - ; PU Nathaniel S. Brown, MU Philander Locke; - ; 2

Eva L. Brown; 16 September 1886; - ; Nettie B., married Mr. Phillips by 1904; Effa S. Brown; HU Mr. German, married between 1906 and 1907; - ; 2

Floyd Brown; 14 February 1876; - ; - ; - ; - ; G- Fred Truby, no relation; 38

Gracie Brown; about 1881; N. S. Brown; - ; Harriet Stevenson, Sarah Graham, Albert, Arthur, Ellen, James, Archibald and Olive Brown; - ; G- George H. Whiting, no relation; 38

Gust Brown; 23 February 1899; Alfred Brown, supported in County Home; - ; Peter Brown; - ; G- John W. Sharpe, brother Carl A. Brown died; 25

Harry B. Brown; 18 December 1888; - ; Carrie E.; Lynn, Merrill,

Name; Date of Birth; Father; Mother; Siblings; Other Relatives; Notes; Box Number

Robert, and Leslie Brown; - ; - ; 26

Harry L. Brown; 4 July 1880; - ; - ; - ; BL William H . Hazard; - ; 1

James Brown; 4 April 1873; N. S. Brown; - ; Harriet Stevenson, Sarah Graham, Albert, Arthur, Ellen, Gracie, Archibald and Olive Brown; - ; G- George H. Whiting, no relation; 38

Laura L. Brown; 15 August 1823; Silas Brown, died before March 1837; - ; - ; - ; G- Thomas White; 77

Leroy W. Brown;19 July 1829; David Brown, died before May 1846; - ; - ; - ; AKA Warren Leroy Brown, G- William V. Smith and money from Ichabod Smith estate; 77

Leslie L. Brown; 26 August 1886; - ; Carrie E.; Harry, Merrill, Robert, and Lynn Brown; - ; - ; 26

Lillian Brown; about 1882; Henry C. Brown; - ; Lyman, Achsah and Charles Brown; - ; - ; 38

Louisa A. Brown; 19 June 1902; D. Alton Brown, of Randolph; Grace E.; Victor Brown; - ; - ; 69

Lyman Brown; about 1873; Henry C. Brown; - ; Lillian, Achsah and Charles Brown; - ; - ; 38

Lynn Brown; - ; - ; Carrie E.; Harry, Merrill, Robert, and Leslie Brown; - ; - ; 26

Malcolm A. Brown; 25 January 1902; - ; Ruby; - ; relatives were Edith M. Brown Cromie (Palm Beach, Florida), Allan R. Brown (Ilion, NY); Marilda Brown left legacy, Malcolm's RE Saranac Lake, Franklin, NY; 26

Merrill Brown; - ; - ; Carrie E.; Harry, Leslie, Robert, and Lynn Brown; - ; - ; 26

Mildred Stout Brown; 15 August 1907; Herbert Stout, died 16 May 1917; Etta, died 20 August 1911; - ; AF Florian Brown, (adopted 7 June 1917), AM and A- Elizabeth (W- of Florian), PGM Minnie Stout, MGM Catherine Osgood, Millard Wilkinson convicted of manslaughter April 1918 and ordered to pay $750 to Mildred Stout; 61

Nettie O. Brown; 28 November 1867; James Brown; Sarah Hedden, died April 1899; Delila Brown; MU John Hedden,

Name; Date of Birth; Father; Mother; Siblings; Other Relatives; Notes; Box Number

MU William Hedden, PU George Brown, PU John Brown and PU Harvey Brown; - ; 37

Olive Brown; about 1880; N. S. Brown; - ; Harriet Stevenson, Sarah Graham, Albert, Arthur, Ellen, Gracie, Archibald and James Brown; - ; G- George H. Whiting, no relation; 38

Richard Danforth Brown; 21 September 1908; Wallace R. Brown, died by September 1925; Mary L.; - ; - ; RE 1926, in Valley Ranch School for Boys, Valley, Wyoming; 25

Robert Brown; 9 June 1901; - ; Carrie E.; Harry, Leslie, Merrill, and Lynn Brown; - ; - ; 26

Sarah Brown; 26 July 1859; Mr. Williams ; - ; - ; HU Ellis Brown; G- Mr. Ingersoll; 2

Simon Edward Brown; January 1903; Thos. E. Brown; - ; - ; GU J. T. Hanratty; G- Irving E. Worden; 25

Victor A. Brown; 16 May 1899; D. Alton Brown, of Randolph; Grace E.; Louisa Brown; - ; - ; 69

John A. Bruce; about 1859; Charles Bruce; - ; - ; U- Reuben Archer; John died 28 December 1871, he received money from estate of Benson Archer; 2

Hazel Brushingham; about 1891; Timothy J. Brushingham; - ; - ; - ; - ; 37

Margaret Brushingham; 9 May 1860; - ; - ; - ; - ; also indexed under Margret Bushingham, G- Peter O'Laughlin; 1

Charlotte F. Bryant; - ; Isaac Bryant; Cordelia, married Mr. Loop; - ; - ; received pension money; 1

Clara E. Bucher; 24 March 1888; - ; - ; Jacob W. Bucher, of Allegany; - ; received money from estate of William Bucher; 71

Alfred C. Buck; 18 May 1860; - ; Abigail; - ; - ; - ; 2

Henry Buck; about 1880; - ; Louisa; - ; - ; - ; 37

William Buffin; 7 May 1881; - ; Nina, went by Nina Enders; Mildred, Celia, Charles, William, Alfred, Louis, and Isabella Enders; - ; AKA Walter Enders Buffin; 41

Frances V. Buffington; 25 December 1880; - ; Florence A.; Helen, William and S. Arline Buffington; - ; - ; 37

Name; Date of Birth; Father; Mother; Siblings; Other Relatives; Notes; Box Number

Helen C. Buffington; 17 May 1876, in Salamanca; - ; Florence A.; Frances, William and S. Arline Buffington; - ; - ; 38

S. Arline Buffington; 18 October 1874; - ; Florence A.; Frances, William and Helen Buffington; - ; - ; 38

Willie J. Buffington; 22 January 1878; - ; Florence A.; Frances, Helen and S. Arline Buffington; - ; - ; 38

Jane Bugsbey; about 1820; - ; - ; - ; - ; G- Spencer Pitcher, file states Charles Chamberlain died 29 August 1828 at Great Valley, in same envelope as Sarah Bugsbey; 77

Sarah Bugsbey; about 1822; - ; - ; - ; - ; G- Spencer Pitcher, file states Charles Chamberlain died 29 August 1828 at Great Valley, in same envelope as Jane Bugsbey; 77

Beremis Bull; June 1869; - ; - ; - ; PGF William Bull, PU Henry Bull, PU Perus Bull; AKA Bernice Bull, received money from Fayette Bull's estate and Elizabeth Gifford's legacy; 1

Leah H. Bull; 5 March 1882; Wallace Bull; - ; - ; HU Mr. Ribble; - ; 26

Cady R. Bullock; 6 January 1910; Milton P. Bullock, married Luella, died 12 May 1920; Marcia L.; Orrin and Phillip Bullock; PGM Anna A. Bullock; G- Guy C. Ames; 24

Orrin J. Bullock; 19 May 1902; Milton P. Bullock, married Luella, died 12 May 1920; Marcia L.; Cady and Phillip Bullock; PGM Anna A. Bullock; G- Guy C. Ames; 24

Phillip M. Bullock; 4 August 1901; Milton P. Bullock, married Luella, died 12 May 1920; Marcia L.; Cady and Orrin Bullock; PGM Anna A. Bullock; G- Guy C. Ames; 24

Warner J. Bullock; about 1901; Charles G. Bullock; - ; - ; - ; - ; 37

Glenn J. Bunce; 31 March 1877; Sanford C. Bunce, of Troy, Crawford, Pennsylvania; - ; - ; - ; - ; 37

Grace Lewis Burch; 5 June 1895; William Lewis; - ; - ; HU Mr. Burch, PGF Stephen Burr; AKA Grace Burr, G- James H. Burr; 24

Byron Burdett; - ; - ; - ; - ; - ; lived with W. H. Beecher from September 1864; 2

Name; Date of Birth; Father; Mother; Siblings; Other Relatives; Notes; Box Number

Helen L. Burdick; 27 July 1890; - ; Nellie, married Mr. Babbitt; - ; HU Mr. Sanders; - ; 26

Samuel Byron Burdick; 7 Sept 1861; Samuel Burdick, lived in Huntington, Fairfield, Connecticut and died November 1862 in the U. S. Services; - ; - ; MG William and Ann Beecher; - ; 1

Samuel B. Burditt; - ; - ; - ; - ; - ; G- William H. Beecher; 2

Ida May Burger; 12 October 1866; Charles A. O'Brien; - ; - ; HU Alexander Burger; G- Ernest Truby; 1

Christine N. Burkhalder; 2 December 1891; Nicholas Burkhalder; - ; Lucile Burkhalder; - ; - ; 24

Lucile B. Burkhalder; 10 October 1894; Nicholas Burkhalder; - ; Christine Burkhalder; - ; - ; 24

Emma Burkhalter; 15 Dec 1857; Nicholas Burkhalter, died April 1871; - ; Nicholas, George, Louisa, Caroline, Henry Burkhalter; U- Philip Griner; - ; 2

George Burkhalter; 1 July 1854; Nicholas Burkhalter, died April 1871; - ; Nicholas, Emma, Louisa, Caroline, Henry Burkhalter; U- Philip Griner; - ; 2

Henry Burkhalter; 1856; Nicholas Burkhalter, died April 1871; - ; Nicholas, Emma, Louisa, Caroline, George Burkhalter; U- Philip Griner; - ; 2

Louisa Burkhalter; 24 January 1853; Nicholas Burkhalter, died April 1871; - ; Nicholas, Emma, Henry, Caroline, George Burkhalter; U- Philip Griner; - ; 2

Nicholas Burkhalter; 28 December 1850; Nicholas Burkhalter, died April 1871; - ; Louisa, Emma, Henry, Caroline, George Burkhalter; U- Philip Griner; - ; 2

Adel Burlingame; - ; - ; Hannah; Isabelle and Ira Burlingame; - ; G- Philo Burlingame; 2

Fred Burlingame; 1890 or 1891; George Burlingame, died before September 1896 at work at Pierce and Company Tannery; - ; George, May, John, and Walter Burlingame; PGM Emeline Burlingame (of Olean, died before June 1907), MG Conrad and Rosina Bender; first G- Alfred Austin, second G- Samuel

Name; Date of Birth; Father; Mother; Siblings; Other Relatives; Notes; Box Number

Passmore (no relation), lived with W. Wright; 71

George D. Burlingame; about 1885; George Burlingame, died before September 1896 at work at Pierce and Company Tannery; - ; Fred, May, John, and Walter Burlingame; PGM Emeline Burlingame (of Olean, died before June 1907), MG Conrad and Rosina Bender; first G- Alfred Austin, second G- Samuel Passmore (no relation), sent to Randolph Home; 71

Ira Burlingame; - ; - ; Hannah; Isabelle and Adel Burlingame; - ; G- Philo Burlingame; 2

Isabelle Burlingame; - ; - ; Hannah; Adel and Ira Burlingame; - ; G- Philo Burlingame; 2

John Burlingame; 1888 or 1889; George Burlingame, died before September 1896 at work at Pierce and Company Tannery; - ; Fred, May, George, and Walter Burlingame; PGM Emeline Burlingame (of Olean, died before June 1907), MG Conrad and Rosina Bender; first G- Alfred Austin, second G- Samuel Passmore (no relation), lived with L. H. Garr; 71

May Burlingame; 1886 or 1887; George Burlingame, died before September 1896 at work at Pierce and Compnay Tannery; - ; Fred, John, George, and Walter Burlingame; HU Mr. Edel PGM Emeline Burlingame, of Olean (died before June 1907), MG Conrad and Rosina Bender; first G- Alfred Austin, second G- Samuel Passmore (no relation); 71

Walter W. Burlingame; 12 March 1893; George Burlingame, died before September 1896 at work at Pierce and Company Tannery; - ; Fred, May, George, and John Burlingame; PGM Emeline Burlingame (of Olean, died before June 1907), MG Conrad and Rosina Bender; first G- Alfred Austin, second G- Samuel Passmore (no relation); 71

Beatrix Burlingham; 7 December 1879; Amos C. Burlingham, died before October 1896; Emma E., of Olean; Charles, Margaret, Elnathan, and William Burlingham; - ; - ; 71

Charles D. Burlingham; born 28 January 1887 or 28 September 1884; Amos C. Burlingham, died before October 1896;

Name; Date of Birth; Father; Mother; Siblings; Other Relatives; Notes; Box Number

Emma E., of Olean; Beatrix, Margaret, Elnathan, and William Burlingham; - ; - ; 71

Elnathan "Nate" Burlingham; 2 October 1881; Amos C. Burlingham, died before October 1896; Emma E., of Olean; Beatrix, Margaret, Charles, and William Burlingham; - ; - ; 71

Margaret Burlingham; 25 September 1884; Amos C. Burlingham, died before October 1896; Emma E., of Olean; Beatrix, Elnathan, Charles, and William Burlingham; - ; - ; 71

William D. Burlingham; 28 September 1878; Amos C. Burlingham, died before October 1896; Emma E., of Olean; Beatrix, Elnathan, Charles, and Margaret Burlingham; - ; - ; 71

Mark D. Burrell; 23 June 1876; William M. Burrell; Laurie J.; - ; - ; - ; 37

William M. Burrill; 2 January 1850; David Burrill; - ; - ; MGM Matilda Champlain; - ; 2

Jerry M. Burroughs; Arctus P. Burroughs, died December 1864; Susan; - ; - ; found in index as Jerry M. Burrell; 2

Frank C. Burt;1 November 1865; Hezekiah O. Burt; - ; - ; - ; - ; 2

Beatrice Burton; about 1901; Charles Burton; - ; Lillian Burton; U- Charles Phelps, U- William Phelps; 18 April 1910, committed to WNY Soc. for the Protection of Homeless and Dependent Children, they were homeless, Beatrice RE with William Phelps in Carthage, Jasper, Missouri; 24

Lillian Burton; about 1898; Charles Burton; - ; Lillian Burton; U- Charles Phelps, U- William Phelps; 18 April 1910, committed to WNY Soc. for the Protection of Homeless and Dependent Children, they were homeless, Lilliam RE with Charles Phelps in Carthage, Jasper, Missouri; 24

William M. Bury;15 July 1901; William G. Bury, died by 18 May 1918; - ; - ; - ; G- Iona H. Bury; 26

Walter Busekist; 23 November 1900; John W. Busekist; - ; - ; - ; money from estate of Henry Gold; 37

Name; Date of Birth; Father; Mother; Siblings; Other Relatives; Notes; Box Number

Clark Bush; 19 August 1881; - ; - ; - ; A- Julia A. Davis, of Kennedy, Chautauqua, NY; RE Oberlin, Decatur, Kansas; 24

Harry Bush; about 1899; - ; foster mother, Julia Bush (not her maiden name); - ; - ; - ; 37

Arthur M. Butler; 25 September 1851; Horace D. Butler; Alzina; Lydia, Jasper, Horace, and Olivia Butler; and Loretta L. Oyer; - ; - ; 1

Donald M. Butler; January 1900; - ; - ; Lillian Butler; - ; - ; 36

F. Louise Butler; 21 July 1863/4; - ; Elizabeth A.; - ; - ; - ; 1

Lillian E. Butler; 25 March 1897; - ; - ; Donald Butler; - ; she was an inmate at The Craig Colony for Epileptics at Sonyea, NY ; 36

Louisa M. Butler; 11 May 1847; Patrick Butler; - ; Seneca H. Butler; - ; G- William Hopkins; 2

Lydia A. Butler; 5 May 1848; Horace D. Butler; Alzina; Arthur, Jasper, Horace, and Olivia Butler; and Loretta L. Oyer; - ; - ; 1

Mary Ellen Butler; 18 November 1861; Alvin Butler, married 1 January 1861, died February 1865, cause of death listed as disease from account of war; Henrietta, married Cyrus Slocomb (had one child by Cyrus, she and Cyrus Slocum separated); - ; PGF Joseph Butler, PU Wilder Butler; G- Caleb B. Brown, G- Rowland C. Harmon, Mary RE June 1880, Cheshire, Allegan, Michigan; 2

Olivia D. Butler; 19 April 1845; - ; Alzina; Arthur, Jasper, Horace, and Lydia Butler; and Loretta L. Oyer; - ; - ; 1

Seneca H. Butler; 20 October 1848; Patrick Butler; Maria M., married Mr. Bacon; Louisa M. Butler; A- Alzina Butler; G- William Hopkins; 2

Caroline A. Button; - ; - ; Polly; David, Reuben, Jonas, and Harvey Button; - ; - ; 2

Charles F. Button; 6 July 1818; Charles Button, died 28 October 1832; Naomi; Hannah Beckwith, (W- of Simon Beckwith), Lyman, Lucetta, Sophia, Heman, Jonas, and Jesse Button; - ; - ; 2

Name; Date of Birth; Father; Mother; Siblings; Other Relatives; Notes; Box Number

David M. Button; - ; - ; Polly; Reuben, Caroline, Jonas, and Harvey Button; - ; - ; 2

Heman G. Button; 1 May 1814; Charles Button, died 28 October 1832; Naomi; Hannah Beckwith (W- of Simon Beckwith), Lyman, Lucetta, Sophia, Charles, Jonas, and Jesse Button; - ; - ; 2

Horace Stillwell Button; 25 January 1891; - ; Mary Belle Melrose; Margaret Button; MU Clifton S. Melrose; - ; 38

Jonas K. Button; 3 May 1821; Charles Button, died 28 October 1832; Naomi; Hannah Beckwith (W- Simon Beckwith), Lyman, Lucetta, Sophia, Charles, Heman, and Jesse Button; - ; - ; 2

Jonas K. Button; - ; - ; Polly; Reuben, Caroline, David, and Harvey Button; - ; - ; 2

Jonas K. Button; 21 April 1870; Jonas K. Button; - ; Peter Button; - ; - ; 2

Jonas K. Button; 4 December 1889; - ; Harriett M.; Jane, Louise, Peter, and Leon A. Button; - ; father died 1 September 1907; 2

Leon A. Button; February 1892; - ; Harriett M.; Jane, Louise, Peter, and Jonas A. Button; - ; father died 1 September 1907; 2

Louise C. Button; 15 November 1887; - ; Harriett M.; Jane, Leon, Peter, and Jonas A. Button; - ; father died 1 September 1907; 2

Lyman Button; - ; Charles Button, died 28 October 1832; Naomi; Hannah Beckwith (W- of Simon Beckwith), Heman, Lucetta, Sophia, Charles, Jonas, and Jesse Button; - ; - ; 2

Margaret Button; 15 May 1896; - ; Mary Belle Melrose; Horace Button; MU Clifton S. Melrose; - ; 38

Peter Button; July 1895; - ; Harriett M.; Jane, Leon, Louise, and Jonas A. Button; - ; father died 1 September 1907; 2

Reuben C. Button; 25 November 1840; - ; Polly; Jonas, Caroline, David, and Harvey Button; - ; - ; 2

Frances M. Buxton; 2 November 1908; Charles E. Buxton, died

Name; Date of Birth; Father; Mother; Siblings; Other Relatives; Notes; Box Number

1 June 1915, at Randolph; - ; - ; PGF John Buxton, born about 1826; mother died about 1913 at Randolph, G- Clarence B. Buxton (of Richmond, Virginia); 69

Lizzie Buxton; - ; - ; - ; - ; - ; G- Charles Buxton; 75

Paul Sheldon Byrne; about 1894; Peter E. Byrne; Jeannette, married Mr. Boswer; Robert Byrne; - ; RE Butler, Butler, Pennsylvania, money from estate of Adaline G. Colwell, G- Miles Shakely; 38

Robert E. Byrne; about 1896; Peter E. Byrne; Jeannette, married Mr. Boswer; Paul Byrne; - ; RE Butler, Butler, Pennsylvania, money from estate of Adaline G. Colwell, G- Miles Shakely; 38

Augusta E. Byron; about 1892; - ; Emma, died before January 1902; John and Nellie Byron; - ; G- Augustus Byron; 24

John Edward Byron; about 1893; - ; Emma, died before January 1902; Augusta and Nellie Byron; - ; G- Augustus Byron; 24

Nellie D. Byron; about 1895; - ; Emma, died before January 1902; Augusta and John Byron; - ; G- Augustus Byron; 24

Name; Date of Birth; Father; Mother; Siblings; Other Relatives; Notes; Box Number

C Surnames

Alice L. Cady; 8 March 1862; John Cady, died in Civil War; Melissa, married Mr. Treadaway; Josiah, Carlina, and Betsey Cady; MA Polly Cox; received pension money; 4

Betsey C. Cady; 22 June 1854; John Cady, died in Civil War; Melissa, married Mr. Treadaway; Josiah, Carlina, and Alice Cady; MA Polly Cox; received pension money; 4

Carlina A. Cady; 30 September 1859; John Cady, died in Civil War; Melissa, married Mr. Treadaway; Josiah, Betsey, and Alice Cady; MA Polly Cox; received pension money; 4

Josiah W. Cady; 8 September 1855; John Cady, died in Civil War; Melissa, married Mr. Treadaway; Carlina, Betsey, and Alice Cady; MA Polly Cox; received pension money; 4

Charles H. Cagwin; 9 April 1868; Isaac A. Cagwin, died June 1877, of Machias; Jane B., married Mr. Hall; Jessie Cagwin; PU Alexander Cagwin, of Verona, Oneida, NY; there are two separate Charles Cagwins in the same envelope; 39

Charles J. Cagwin; about 1858; Charles H. Cagwin, died May 1864, of Yorkshire; C. Hellen; Florence Cagwin; - ; there are two separate Charles Cagwins in the same envelope; 39

Florence N. Cagwin; about 1863; Charles H. Cagwin, died May 1864, of Yorkshire; C. Hellen; Charles J. Cagwin; - ; - ; 39

Jessie M. Cagwin; about 1865; Isaac A. Cagwin, died June 1877, of Machias; Jane B., married Mr. Hall; Charles H. Cagwin; HU Mr. Coe, PU Alexander Cagwin, of Verona, Oneida, NY; - ; 39

Larry L. Cain; 4 October 1845; Seth Cain; - ; - ; - ; - ; 4

George C. Calkins; 8 or 15 June 1883; George M. Calkins, died February 1900, of Ellicottville; - ; - ; PG George and Sally Calkins, MU Wm. E. Collins (AKA William E. Batt), MU Volney Batt, PU Thomas Calkins (of Bird, NY), MA Nancy L. Drown; mother died July 1883; 39

Clifford Camp; 8 May 1885; - ; Jennie, married Mr. Button; - ; - ; received money from estate of Austin Camp; 38

Name; Date of Birth; Father; Mother; Siblings; Other Relatives; Notes; Box Number

Flora A. Camp; 8 September 1884; - ; Emma V., of Franklinville, married Mr. Sayles; - ; - ; received money from estate of Mary Mitchell (of Machias), Flora Camp Stein also mentioned in papers, Flora's father died 1 February 1897; 71

Robert Camp; 30 December 1872; - ; - ; - ; - ; G- Aleanzor M. Farrar; 4

Bertha M. Campbell; about 1879; - ; Adeline M.; Edna S. Campbell; - ; - ; 4

Bertrand "Bertie" L. Campbell; 27 September 1876; - ; Minnie E. Stone, married Henry S. Weed; Lizzie Campbell; MG R. L. and E. L. Stone; U- A. O. Stone, U- A. W. Stone, U- M. D. Colby, U- S. M.. Bliss, U- Fred D. Schulz; A- Flora J. Bliss, A- Eda B. Colby, A- Mary A. Shulz A- Anne G./Gertie A. Stone; RE 1897, in Pomfret, Chautauqua, NY, inherited property in Grand Valley, Warren, Pennsylvania, Bertrand's father died 26 August 1886; 38

Charles S. Campbell; 4 September 1885; Dewitt Campbell; - ; Harry and William Campbell; - ; - ; 39

Edna S. Campbell; about 1881; - ; Adeline M.; Bertha S. Campbell; - ; - ; 4

Harry Dean Campbell; 22 May 1882; Dewitt Campbell; - ; Charles and William Campbell; - ; - ; 39

Howe A. Campbell; 23 April 1896; - ; Martha L.; Ruth Campbell and Maude C. Wiltse; A- Mrs. Manley D. Holt; father died 5 December 1901; 38

Lizzie L. Campbell; 26 November 1883; - ; Minnie E. Stone, married Henry S. Weed; Bertrand Campbell; HU Mr. Rowan, MG R. L. and E. L. Stone; U- A. O. Stone, U- A. W. Stone, U- M. D. Colby, U- S. M.. Bliss, U- Fred D. Schulz; A- Flora J. Bliss, A- Eda B. Colby, A- Mary A. Shulz A- Anne G./Gertie A. Stone; RE 1897, in Pomfret, Chautauqua County, NY, inherited property in Grand Valley, Warren, Pennsylvania, Lizzie's father died 26 August 1886; 38

Ruth E. Campbell; - ; - ; Martha L.; Howe Campbell and Maude C. Wiltse; A- Mrs. Manley D. Holt; Ruth's father died 5

Name; Date of Birth; Father; Mother; Siblings; Other Relatives; Notes; Box Number

December 1901; 40

William Campbell; 18 July 1880; Dewitt Campbell; - ; Harry and Charles Campbell; - ; - ; 39

C. Porter Canfield; about 1857; Samuel Canfield, died October 1874, in Ashford; Fanny; Lucy, Minnie, Fanny and Cornelius Canfield; MU Walter Fairbanks; - ; 39

Cornelius S. Canfield; about 1859; Samuel Canfield, died October 1874, in Ashford; Fanny; Lucy, Minnie, Fanny and C. Porter Canfield; MU Walter Fairbanks; - ; 39

Cory S. Canfield; 24 February 1852; Sylvester Canfield, died September 1852; - ; - ; PU George W. Canfield, PU Henry W. Canfield, PU Porter W. Canfield, MU Charles B. Cole, MA Caroline B. Cole, A- Clarissa W. Gray; mother died November 1863; 4

Fanny Canfield; about 1873; Samuel Canfield, died October 1874, in Ashford; Fanny; Lucy, Minnie, Cornelius and C. Porter Canfield; MU Walter Fairbanks; - ; 39

Lucy A. Canfield; about 1863; Samuel Canfield, died October 1874, in Ashford; Fanny; Minnie, Fanny Cornelius and C. Porter Canfield; MU Walter Fairbanks; - ; 39

Minnie A. Canfield; about 1865; Samuel Canfield, died October 1874, in Ashford; Fanny; Lucy, Fanny Cornelius and C. Porter Canfield; MU Walter Fairbanks; - ; 39

Benjamin Capron; 23 November 1822; Ephraim Capron, died before February 1839; - ; Joseph Capron; - ; G- Abel Demmon; 77

Joseph Capron; 3 August 1830; Ephraim Capron, died before February 1839; - ; Benjamin Capron; - ; G- Asa Sanders; 77

Eleanore Grace Carbach; 6 November 1902; - ; Gertrude; - ; - ; Eleanore died about July 1909; 52

Lola Ruth Card; 5 April 1901; - ; Flora A., died by May 1916; Jay and William H. Card; GM Sylvia A. Griswold; received money from estates of John M. Card and mother; 27

George Robert Carlberg; 12 November 1908; - ; Lulu M., married Mr. Phillips between 1923 and 1924; Grace and

Name; Date of Birth; Father; Mother; Siblings; Other Relatives; Notes; Box Number

Mildred Carlberg; - ; received money from estate of Christina Maria Carlberg; 53

Grace Evelyne Carlberg; 5 February 1906; - ; Lulu M., married Mr. Phillips between 1923 and 1924; George and Mildred Carlberg; - ; received money from estate of Christina Maria Carlberg; 53

Mildred Irene Carlberg; 21 February 1904; - ; Lulu M., married Mr. Phillips between 1923 and 1924; George and Grace Carlberg; HU Mr. Bewley; received money from estate of Christina Maria Carlberg; 53

Alonzo Leroy Carling; 12 December 1850; Samuel Carling; Lovina, married Mr. Curtis; Emeline and Samuel Carling; W-Alvinah (married Mr. Studley), Samuel Carling (born 14 January 1875) was Alonzo's son; Alonzo died before January 1881; 4

Dorothy Adah Carling; 23 October 1899; - ; Ada E.; Mildred Carling; - ; father died before 26 February 1914; 53

Emeline Louisa Carling; 14 May 1858; Samuel Carling; Lovina, married Mr. Curtis; Alonzo and Samuel Carling; HU Mr. Grey; - ; 4

Mildred Louise Carling; 25 June 1909; - ; Ada E.; Dorothy Carling; - ; father died before 26 February 1914; 53

Samuel E. Carling; 11 April 1854; Samuel Carling; Lovina, married Mr. Curtis; Alonzo and Emeline Carling; - ; - ; 4

Cleatus Carls; 28 July 1902; J. J. F. Carls, of Allegany; - ; John, Lewis, Kenneth, and Florence Carls; - ; received money from estate of Mary Carls; 53

Florence Carls; 1 September 1910; J. J. F. Carls, of Allegany; - ; John, Lewis, Kenneth, and Cleatus Carls; - ; received money from estate of Mary Carls; 53

John J. F. Carls; 2 March 1901; J. J. F. Carls, of Allegany; - ; Florence, Lewis, Kenneth, and Cleatus Carls; - ; received money from estate of Mary Carls; 53

Kenneth Carls; 12 July 1908; J. J. F. Carls, of Allegany; - ; Florence, Lewis, John, and Cleatus Carls; - ; received

Name; Date of Birth; Father; Mother; Siblings; Other Relatives; Notes; Box Number

money from estate of Mary Carls; 53

Lewis Carls; 3 October 1906; J. J. F. Carls, of Allegany; - ; Florence, Kenneth, John, and Cleatus Carls; - ; received money from estate of Mary Carls; 53

Millie Carlson; 16 January 1885; Benjamin J. Carlson; - ; Tillie Carlson; - ; G- William E. Wheeler; 38

Tillie Carlson; 15 April 1883; Benjamin J. Carlson; - ; Millie Carlson; - ; G- William E. Wheeler; 38

Lewis Carmatz; 30 October 1901; William Carmatz, died before 26 January 1905; Ida; Sylvia Carmatz; - ; - ; 27

Sylvia Carmatz; 22 September 1903; William Carmatz, died before 26 January 1905; Ida; Lewis Carmatz; - ; - ; 27

Emma Carpenter; 29 March 1863; James M. Carpenter, died 21 July 1864, in Nashville, Tennessee, while in military service; Sarah J. Wilcox, married Mr. Butcher; - ; PG John and Sally Carpenter, MG Hosea and Elizabeth Wilcox; - ; 4

Floyd Carpenter; 11 October 1880; Stephen Carpenter; - ; Nelson and Lee Carpenter; MGF George Isaman; in same envelope as George Carpenter; 39

George Carpenter; 31 May 1881; Charles Carpenter; - ; - ; - ; in same envelope as Floyd, Lee and Nelson Carpenter; 39

Harriet Carpenter; 13 October 1879; - ; Jane, married Mr. Older; - ; HU Mr. Law; received pension money; 4

Lee Carpenter; 12 July 1885; Stephen Carpenter; - ; Nelson and Floyd Carpenter; MGF George Isaman; in same envelope as George Carpenter; 39

Nelson Carpenter; 17 May 1883; Stephen Carpenter; - ; Lee and Floyd Carpenter; MGF George Isaman; in same envelope as George Carpenter; 39

Allie J. Carr; about 1877; - ; Mary E., married Mr. Hall; - ; - ; - ; 38

Viola Ruth Carr; 2 August 1909; - ; Hazel M.; - ; other relative was William A. Carr; - ; 28

Adel Carrier; 13 November 1864; Timothy Carrier; Lefa Farnum; Sarrah, Lucy, Grace, Frances, Carrie and Alice

Name; Date of Birth; Father; Mother; Siblings; Other Relatives; Notes; Box Number

Carrier; PGF David Farnum; Joseph Green left part of estate; 4

Alice Carrier; 28 January 1859; Timothy Carrier; Lefa Farnum; Sarrah, Lucy, Grace, Frances, Carrie and Adel Carrier; PGF David Farnum; Joseph Green left part of estate; 4

Carrie Carrier; 12 September 1856; Timothy Carrier; Lefa Farnum; Sarrah, Lucy, Grace, Frances, Alice and Adel Carrier; PGF David Farnum; Joseph Green left part of estate; 4

Frances Carrier; 12 January 1855; Timothy Carrier; Lefa Farnum; Sarrah, Lucy, Grace, Carrie, Alice and Adel Carrier; PGF David Farnum; Joseph Green left part of estate; 4

Grace Carrier; 25 October 1870; Timothy Carrier; Lefa Farnum; Sarrah, Lucy, Frances, Carrie, Alice and Adel Carrier; PGF David Farnum; Joseph Green left part of estate; 4

Lucy Carrier; 31 July 1868; Timothy Carrier; Lefa Farnum; Sarrah, Grace, Frances, Carrie, Alice and Adel Carrier; PGF David Farnum; Joseph Green left part of estate; 4

Sarrah Carrier; 22 May 1861; Timothy Carrier; Lefa Farnum; Grace, Lucy, Frances, Carrie, Alice and Adel Carrier; PGF David Farnum; Joseph Green left part of estate; 4

Wilbert H. Carringer; 28 August 1863; Step-father James M. McLaughlin; - ; HB James McLaughlin, HS Mary McLaughlin; A- Sarah E. Curry, U- David E. Curry; - ; 4

Angela Carroll; 9 October 1902; Lawrence Carroll, died 12 October 1902; Julia A.; - ; PG John and Margaret Carroll, PU Daniel Carroll, PU John Carroll, PA Mary Carroll; G- James Bixby; 38

Joseph Sherman Carroll; 27 December 1899; - ; Myrtle; - ; - ; G- Delbert Hall; 54

William L. Carter; 3 December 1905; - ; - ; Cleveland G. Carter;

Name; Date of Birth; Father; Mother; Siblings; Other Relatives; Notes; Box Number

- ; - ; 27

Charles A. Cartwright; 1897; - ; Mary B., married Mr. Fisher; Levi and Mary Cartwright; - ; received pension money; 53

Levi A. Cartwright; April 1899; - ; Mary B., married Mr. Fisher; Charles and Mary Cartwright; - ; received pension money; 53

Mary B. Cartwright; about 1905; - ; Mary B., married Mr. Fisher; Charles and Levi Cartwright; - ; received pension money; 53

Louisa Cary; 30 July 1842; - ; - ; - ; - ; G- Abigail Gibson; 4

Phebe Ann Cary; 23 January 1844; Josiah Cary, died between November 1857 and November 1865; - ; Susan and William Cary; GM Phebe Butler, A- Eliza Howard (wife of Plara Howard); - ; 4

Susan Eliza Cary; 27 March 1849; Josiah Cary, died between November 1857 and November 1865; - ; Phebe and William Cary; GM Phebe Butler, A- Eliza Howard (wife of Plara Howard); - ; 4

William Howard Cary; 23 January 1846; Josiah Cary, died between November 1857 and November 1865; - ; Phebe and Susan Cary; GM Phebe Butler, A- Eliza Howard (wife of Plara Howard); - ; 4

E. Ralph Case; 1 August 1888; Edward N. Case; - ; - ; - ; - ; 27

Emerson Case; 18 May 1902; Elliott J. Case, died before November 1905; Maude M.; Theresa Case; PU Dean Case; - ; 27

Theresa Maud Case; 14 August 1899; Elliott J. Case, died before November 1905; Maude M.; Emerson Case; PU Dean Case; - ; 27

Carrie Casey; - ; Dennis Casey; Mariah, died December 1878, of Hinsdale; Marion, John and Francis Casey; U- Edmond Casey, U- John Casey, A- Ellen O'Hern, A- Mary O'Hern; - ; 39

Francis C. Casey; - ; Dennis Casey; Mariah, died December 1878, of Hinsdale; Marion, John and Carrie Casey; U- Edmond Casey, U- John Casey, A- Ellen O'Hern, A- Mary

Name; Date of Birth; Father; Mother; Siblings; Other Relatives; Notes; Box Number

O'Hern; - ; 39

John A. Casey; - ; Dennis Casey; Mariah, died December 1878, of Hinsdale; Marion, Francis and Carrie Casey; U- Edmond Casey, U- John Casey, A- Ellen O'Hern, A- Mary O'Hern; - ; 39

Marion Casey; - ; Dennis Casey; Mariah, died December 1878, of Hinsdale; John, Francis and Carrie Casey; U- Edmond Casey, U- John Casey, A- Ellen O'Hern, A- Mary O'Hern; - ; 39

William Herman Castor; 9 November 1901; - ; - ; - ; - ; G- Fred Butcher, needed guardian to enlist in Navy, but couldn't after physical exam, was in NYS Society for Protection of Homeless and Dependent Children; 53

Darwin Caswell; 21 April 1889; - ; Orlinda; Merl, Lora and Media Caswell; - ; - ; 4

Grace G. Caswell; 28 March 1863; Calvin Caswell; - ; - ; HU Mr. Wheeler; G- Charles Caswell; 4

Lora Caswell; 4 June 1891; - ; Orlinda; Media, Merl and Darwin Caswell; - ; - ; 4

Media Mary Caswell; 1 July 1876; - ; Orlinda; Merl, Lora and Darwin Caswell; - ; - ; 4

Merl Caswell; 8 November 1883; - ; Orlinda; Media, Lora and Darwin Caswell; - ; - ; 4

Thomas Caswell; 7 February 1867; - ; - ; Warren Caswell; - ; G- Reuben Archer, died 21 September 1876; money from estate of Sylvester Caswell; RE 1884, in Marathon County, Wisconsin; 38

Warren Caswell; 7 November 1863; - ; - ; Thomas Caswell; - ; G- Reuben Archer, died 21 September 1876; money from estate of Sylvester Caswell; RE 1884, in Marathon County, Wisconsin; 38

Josephine "Jossie" Caughlin; 8 February 1867; Patrick Caughlin, died 1874; - ; - ; - ; RE with G- John Hughs; 38

Maynard J. Cettel; 14 November 1890; - ; - ; - ; U- Harlan Quackenbush; G- Louis J. Thrasher; 39

Name; Date of Birth; Father; Mother; Siblings; Other Relatives; Notes; Box Number

Clifford D. Chaffee; 4 January 1888; - ; Ida M., of Olean; - ; PGF William D. Chaffee, of Le Raysville, Pennsylvania; father died before May 1902; 71

Adelaide Chamberlain; about 1914; Fred B. Chamberlain; - ; - ; - ; G- George H. Ansley, Adelaide lived with Mrs. Margaret Murphy at 3304 E. 3rd St., Tulsa, Oklahoma; 53

Emma E. Chamberlain; October 1855; - ; Harriet, died June 1875; Willis Chamberlain; PU Charles Chamberlain, PU George Chamberlain; - ; 4

Floyd B. Chamberlain; 21 September 1897; Henry Chamberlain, died before April 1918, of Salamanca; Anna, of Salamanca; - ; W- Verna, married by 1917. Other relatives were Mabel Brow (of Salamanca), Carrie Mason (of Canandaigua), Roy Chamberlain (of Salamanca); - ; 53

Mancer Chamberlain; about 1851; - ; - ; - ; - ; G- Almira Chamberlain, of Great Valley; 75

Ralph Roscoe Chamberlain; 2 August 1873; - ; Emma; - ; - ; - ; 4

Willis A. Chamberlain; 3 March 1863; - ; Harriet, died June 1875; Emma Chamberlain; PU Charles Chamberlain, PU George Chamberlain; - ; 4

C. Huested Chamberlin; 9 February 1885; - ; Patience; George Chamberlin; - ; G- Frank Bartlett, no relationship; 40

Clara N. Chamberlin; 19 February 1871; Henry Chamberlin, died before December 1889; Emma; - ; - ; - ; 38

George L. Chamberlin; 26 February 1878; - ; Patience; C. Huested Chamberlin; - ; G- Frank Bartlett, no relationship; 40

Bula Chambers; 4 October; - ; - ; - ; HU Mr. Chambers, GM Jane Sawers; - ; 39

William Perry Chambers; 9 November 1873; Oliver P. Chambers, died March 1875, of Great Valley; Lucy E. Chamberlain, married Mr. Mason; - ; MGP William A., born about 1819, and Emily, born about 1825, Chamberlain, A- Mary Church (born about 1853), A- Sophronia Markham, (born about 1847), A- Mrs. Emily Washburn (born about

Name; Date of Birth; Father; Mother; Siblings; Other Relatives; Notes; Box Number

1859), C- Mrs. Elta Martin (born about 1853), C-Miss Emma Washburn (born about 1874); G- Norman Rust (died February 1884), G- Mark Church, William received pension money; 39

Hannah I. Champlin;19 March 1898; - ; - - ; - ; - ; money from estate of John B. F. Champlin, in same envelope with Pauline M. Champlin; 36

Malia Helen Champlin; - ; - ; - ; - ; - ; there is only half a sheet of paper in her file; 76

Pauline M. Champlin; 22 February 1896; - ; - ; - ; - ; received money from estate of John B. F. Champlin and in same envelope with Hannah I. Champlin; 36

William Pettis Champlin; 13 October 1826; - ; Lydia, surname was Pettis at time of death, died before April 1845, of Newport, Rhode Island; - ; - ; G- Elizabeth Champlin; 76

Clarence L. Chandler; 3 May 1872; Charles Chandler; - ; Roy Chandler; - ; RE Jamesville, Waseca, Minnesota; 38

Ella F. Chandler; about 1856; - ; - ; - ; - ; G- Horace B. Harrington; 4

Roy P. Chandler; 9 September 1879; Charles Chandler; - ; Clarence Chandler; - ; RE Jamesville, Waseca, Minnesota; 38

Albert Chapin; about 1889; - ; Nancy E.; Lois, Frank, Welcome and Hattie Chapin; - ; money from estate of Fearette Chapin; 39

Frank Chapin; about 1892; - ; Nancy E.; Lois, Albert, Welcome and Hattie Chapin; - ; money from estate of Fearette Chapin; 39

Hattie Chapin; about 1882; - ; Nancy E.; Lois, Albert, Welcome and Frank Chapin; - ; money from estate of Fearette Chapin; 39

Lois Chapin; about 1887; - ; Nancy E.; Hattie, Albert, Welcome and Frank Chapin; - ; money from estate of Fearette Chapin; 39

Welcome Chapin; about 1894; - ; Nancy E.; Hattie, Albert, Lois and Frank Chapin; - ; money from estate of Fearette Chapin;

Name; Date of Birth; Father; Mother; Siblings; Other Relatives; Notes; Box Number

39

Ara Chapman; 11 May 1861; Daniel Chapman, died 1881-1882; - ; Myron, Hattie, Frank, and Emory Chapman and Mabel A. Card; - ; - ; 4

Benjamin F. Chapman; about 1860; - ; - ; - ; - ; G- Rathbun Chapman; 6

Elmer E. Chapman; 10 March 1872; - ; - ; - ; - ; received money from estate of Welcome Chapman; 4

Frank A. Chapman; about 1827, Townsend Chapman, died June 1864 in Alexandria, Virginia, while serving in Civil War; Matilda A., married Mr. Metcalf; - ; PGM Rhoda Chapman; - ; 4

Frank E. Chapman; 4 October 1863; Daniel Chapman, died 1881-1882; - ; Myron, Hattie, Ara, and Emory Chapman and Mabel A. Card; - ; - ; 4

Hattie T. Chapman; 28 September 1861; Daniel Chapman, died 1881-1882; - ; Myron, Frank, Ara, and Emory Chapman and Mabel A. Card; HU Mr. Card; - ; 4

Hiram W. Chapman; about 1857; - ; - ; - ; - ; G- Rathbun Chapman; 6

Caroline M. Chase; 28 March 1862; James F. Chase, died July 1863, was a private in Company D, 154th Regiment, NY State Volunteers; Maria, married a Mr. Kellogg; - ; - ; received pension money; 14

Rose Chase; 28 February 1881; - ; - ; - ; first HU Horace Chase (died 12 September 1896), second HU Mr. Lyne; - ; 4

Carrie C. Cheeseman; 9 August 1858; - ; Mary E.; Charlie, Louis, Nellie, and Rollin Cheeseman; - ; RE Richfield, Hennepin, Minnesota; 39

Charlie H. Cheeseman; 23 March 1861; - ; Mary E.; Carrie, Louis, Nellie, and Rollin Cheeseman; - ; RE Richfield, Hennepin, Minnesota; 39

Louis H. Cheeseman; - ; - ; Mary E.; Carrie, Charlie, Nellie, and Rollin Cheeseman; - ; RE Richfield, Hennepin, Minnesota; 39

Name; Date of Birth; Father; Mother; Siblings; Other Relatives; Notes; Box Number

Nellie E. Cheeseman; - ; - ; Mary E.; Carrie, Charlie, Louis, and Rollin Cheeseman; - ; RE Richfield, Hennepin, Minnesota; 39

Rollin D. Cheeseman; 27 September 1856; - ; Mary E.; Carrie, Charlie, Louis, and Nellie Cheeseman; - ; RE Richfield, Hennepin, Minnesota; 39

Florence N. Cheney; about 1863; - ; - ; - ; HU Lyman Cheney; C. J. Cagwin is listed as the only other heir-at-law of estate she was an heir to; 38

Jonas K. Cheney; 29 September 1876; Monroe G. Cheney; - ; - ; MGF Jonas K. Button left legacy to Jonas K. Cheney; - ; 4

Edith Childs; 14 March 1896; - ; - ; - ; BL John C. Childs; - ; 39

Maud Childs; 11 May 1868; - ; Sarah W.; - ; - ; - ; 4

Hazel Chittenden; 18 October 1905; - ; - ; Marion and Robert Chittenden; HU Mr. Wedlock, GM Martha F. Lyons (died 12 May 1911, in Olean), PU- Jared Chittenden, PU- Louis Chittenden, U-Thomas Scott; - ; 53

Marion Chittenden; September 1901; - ; - ; Hazel and Robert Chittenden; GM Martha F. Lyons (died 12 May 1911, in Olean), PU- Jared Chittenden, PU- Louis Chittenden, U-Thomas Scott; - ; 53

Robert Chittenden; 10 March 1903; - ; - ; Hazel and Marion Chittenden; GM Martha F. Lyons (died 12 May 1911, in Olean), PU- Jared Chittenden, PU- Louis Chittenden, U-Thomas Scott; - ; 53

Howard N. Church; 23 April 1873; Nelson Church, died January 1874, of Allegany; Kittie Kenyon, married Edward Torrey; - ; MGM Mary A. Kenyon, A- Aletha O. Kenyon, U- Charles Kenyon; - ; 38

Florence Churchill; about 1882; Frank Churchill, of Salamanca; - ; - ; - ; G- Carl A. Kammire. Florence needed a guardian for a claim for personal injury against Jamestown Electric Street Railway County, because on 4 September 1899 she had to jump from a car on Main between 5th and 6th St. in Olean because someone lost control of the car; 71

Name; Date of Birth; Father; Mother; Siblings; Other Relatives; Notes; Box Number

Clarissa Clark; 17 February 1833; Asahel Clark, died before December 1847, of Massachusetts; - ; Jane and Lucius Clark; step-father was Lawrence Weber; - ; 27

Eugene Clark; about 1894; - ; - ; - ; C- Robert E. Witherel; - ; 40

Francis B. Clark; 20 August 1895; John H. Clark; - ; Lorena Clark; - ; RE 1916, in Jamestown, Chautauqua, NY, G- Arthur Bedell, and money from estate of Ellen Clark; 38

Georgie E. Clark; 13 May 1876; - ; - ; M. Lena Clark; MGF Andrew C. Adams, MU A. Clark Adams, A- Frances Smith; AKA Georgia Clark; 38

Jane Clark; 16 February 1831; Asahel Clark, died before December 1847, of Massachusetts; - ; Clarissa and Lucius Clark; step-father was Lawrence Weber; - ; 27

Lorena Clark; - ; John H. Clark; - ; Francis Clark; - ; RE 1916, in Jamestown, Chautauqua, NY, G- Arthur Bedell, and Lorena received money from estate of Ellen Clark; 38

Lucius Clark; 27 September 1834; Asahel Clark, died before December 1847, of Massachusetts; - ; Clarissa and Jane Clark; step-father was Lawrence Weber; - ; 27

Lydia May Clark; about 1900; Andy J. Clark; - ; - ; - ; mother died 26 June 1905; 39

M. Helene Clark; 18 September 1902; Morris Clark, died 25 January 1919; - ; Lila Clark; - ; RE with Mrs. George Henry, 49 Copeland Place, Buffalo, NY. M. Helene attended University of Michigan at Ann Arbor, Michigan, and Otterbein College in Westerville, Ohio. She also received money from estate of Mary J. Davis; 27

M. Lena Clark; 3 January 1875; - ; - ; Georgie Clark; MGF Andrew C. Adams, MU A. Clark Adams, A- Frances Smith; - ; 38

Maynard Clark; 31 July 1904; - ; Bertha May, died before 22 September 1908; - ; foster father was George Bullock, of Franklinville; G- Della Bullock, G- Stephen Horton. Maynard lived with Stephen, possibly GU; 40 and 53

William E. Clark; - ; William Clark; Hannah Archer; Frank and

Name; Date of Birth; Father; Mother; Siblings; Other Relatives; Notes; Box Number

Orin Clark; MU John Archer, C- Allen Archer; parents separated; 4

Olin J. Clausen; 20 October 1849; - ; Minerva A.; - ; PA Emily Barrett, wife of Simeon Barrett, A- Julie Clawson; - ; 4

Isabelle E. Clements; 16 September 1904; - ; Cora; - ; - ; father died before 13 August 1913; 53

George M. Cleveland; 1 July 1877; - ; Juliette, married Mr. Spencer; - ; - ; needed guardian to receive pension money; 39

Adella J. Clough; about 1859; - ; Amyra W. C., married Mr. Lyman; Lester A. Clough; - ; received pension money ; 4

Lester A. Clough; about 1861; - ; Amyra W. C., married Mr. Lyman; Adella Clough; - ; received pension money ; 4

Bessie Coast; 19 July 1884; Fleming Coast; Mary; Emilie and Mary Gladys Coast; PGF John Coast (died 8 October 1903), A- Emma Conklin; G- Emilie Coast Murphy (perhaps her sister); 4

Edith Coast; 4 May 1885; - ; - ; - ; HU J. Weston Coast; - ; 71

Emilie Coast; June 1882; Fleming Coast; Mary; Bessie and Mary Gladys Coast; PGF John Coast (died 8 October 1903), A- Emma Conklin; - ; 4

J. Weston Coast, Jr.; 7 March 1885; John Weston Coast, lived in Olean; - ; - ; W- Edith; - ; 71

Mary Gladys Coast; 25 November 1889; Fleming Coast; Mary; Bessie and Emilie Gladys Coast; PGF John Coast (died 8 October 1903), A- Emma Conklin; G- Emilie Coast Murphy, (perhaps her sister); 4 and 71

Rhea Cobb; 23 April 1896; - ; Ida V.; - ; - ; RE Ridgeway, Orleans, NY, G- J. D. Laing, no relation; 39

Joseph P. Coffey; 27 August 1904; - ; Winifred G.; - ; - ; - ; 55

John L. Cogswell; 23 August 1859; Mason W. Cogswell; - ; Perry M. Cogswell; - ; money from estate of P. M. Brooks; 4

Perry M. Cogswell; 10 February 1862; Mason W. Cogswell; - ; John M. Cogswell; - ; money from estate of P. M. Brooks; 4

Fannie Cohen; about 1893; Louis Cohen; Betsey; Mollie, Michael, Samuel and Israel Cohen; - ; G- William M.

Name; Date of Birth; Father; Mother; Siblings; Other Relatives; Notes; Box Number

Abrams Jr.; 27

Israel Cohen; about 1896; Louis Cohen; Betsey; Mollie, Michael, Samuel and Fannie Cohen; - ; G- William M. Abrams Jr.; 27

Michael Cohen; about 1889; Louis Cohen; Betsey; Mollie, Israel, Samuel and Fannie Cohen; - ; G- William M. Abrams Jr.; 27

Mollie Cohen; about 1887; Louis Cohen; Betsey; Michael, Israel, Samuel and Fannie Cohen; - ; G- William M. Abrams Jr.; 27

Samuel Cohen; about 1891; Louis Cohen; Betsey; Michael, Israel, Mollie and Fannie Cohen; - ; G- William M. Abrams Jr.; 27

Alice E. Colburn; 6 April 1865; Josiah D. Colburn; Helen A., died March 1872; - ; - ; RE Chittenango, Madison, NY; 4

Ada M. Cole; about 1872; Americus V. Cole; Anna Maria; Hannah, Truman, Lelie, George and Myrtal Cole; A- Sophia Hermance, A- Mary J. Kinne, A- Libbie Curtindall; G- Edwin F. Davis; 38

Alzera F. Cole; 22 March 1847; Richard B. Cole, died before August 1861; Sally; Elizabeth, Theodore and Ellen Cole; PA Eunice (W- of John Watenpaugh), PA Maria (W- of Ralph Johnson); - ; 76

Asahel Cole; about 1823; Daniel Cole, died March 1826, in Freedom; - ; Nancy, William, Daniel and Maryan Cole; - ; G- Joseph Cole (of Lima, Livingston, NY); 77

Clifton T. Cole; 9 February 1855; Theodore R. Cole, died in October 1872; Eliza M. Searl; - ; MGF Matthew Searl; - ; 4

Daniel Harrison Cole; about 1824; Daniel Cole, died March 1826, in Freedom; - ; Nancy, William, Asahel and Maryan Cole; - ; G- Joseph Cole (of Lima, Livingston, NY); 77

Elizabeth A. Cole; 23 June 1852; Richard B. Cole, died before August 1861; Sally; Alzera, Theodore and Ellen Cole; PA Eunice (W- of John Watenpaugh), PA Maria (W- of Ralph Johnson); - ; 76

Ellen Cole; 27 May 1840; Richard B. Cole, died before August 1861; Sally; Alzera, Theodore and Elizabeth Cole; PA

Name; Date of Birth; Father; Mother; Siblings; Other Relatives; Notes; Box Number

Eunice (W- of John Watenpaugh), PA Maria (W- of Ralph Johnson); - ; 76

George E. Cole; about 1868; Americus V. Cole; Anna Maria; Hannah, Truman, Lelie, Ada and Myrtal Cole; A- Sophia Hermance, A- Mary J. Kinne, A- Libbie Curtindall; G- Edwin F. Davis; 38

Gerald Cole; 11 October 1909; Arthur Cole; - ; Maurice Cole; PU Thomas Cole; - ; 52

Hannah J. Cole; about 1859; Americus V. Cole; Anna Maria; George, Truman, Lelie, Ada and Myrtal Cole; A- Sophia Hermance, A- Mary J. Kinne, A- Libbie Curtindall; G- Edwin F. Davis; 38

Lelie E. Cole; about 1863; Americus V. Cole; Anna Maria; George, Truman, Hannah, Ada and Myrtal Cole; A- Sophia Hermance, A- Mary J. Kinne, A- Libbie Curtindall; AKA Lillian Cole, G- Edwin F. Davis; 38

Maryan Charlotte Cordelia Cole; about 1825; Daniel Cole, died March 1826, in Freedom; - ; Nancy, William, Asahel and Daniel Cole; - ; G- Joseph Cole (of Lima, Livingston, NY); 77

Maurice Cole; 2 July 1901; Arthur Cole; - ; Gerald Cole; PU Thomas Cole; - ; 52

Nancy Cole; about 1821; Daniel Cole, died March 1826, in Freedom; - ; Maryan, William, Asahel and Daniel Cole; - ; G- Joseph Cole (of Lima, Livingston, NY); 77

Theodore R. Cole; 31 August 1843; Richard B. Cole, died before August 1861; Sally; Alzera, Ellen and Elizabeth Cole; PA Eunice (W- of John Watenpaugh), PA Maria (W- of Ralph Johnson); - ; 76

Truman D. Cole; about 1861; Americus V. Cole; Anna Maria; George, Lelie, Hannah, Ada and Myrtal Cole; A- Sophia Hermance, A- Mary J. Kinne, A- Libbie Curtindall; AKA Delos Cole, G- Edwin F. Davis; 38

William Cole; about 1819; Daniel Cole, died March 1826, in Freedom; - ; Maryan, Nancy, Asahel and Daniel Cole; - ; G-

Name; Date of Birth; Father; Mother; Siblings; Other Relatives; Notes; Box Number

Joseph Cole (of Lima, Livingston, NY); 77

Edward M. Coleman; 4 June 1893; - ; - ; - ; MA Elizabeth Marth; received money from estate of E. G. Coleman; 63

Elizabeth Blair Coleman; 30 March 1895; - ; - ; Marjorie Coleman; A- Lydia C. Blair; parents estates in Tioga County, NY; 28

Marjorie Blair Coleman; 31 August 1893; - ; - ; Elizabeth Coleman; A- Lydia C. Blair; parents estates in Tioga County, NY; 28

Albert J. Colf; about December 1860; John D. Colf, died April 1874, of Machias; Mary Clark; Altie and Herbert Colf; PGM Edie Colf, PU Erastus Colf, PU Jehiel Colf, PU Delevan Colf, MU Warner F. Clark, MU John B. Clark, MU Ephraim V. Clark; file in same envelope with Cora Smith, and Nora, Matie, Emory, Viola and Grover Colf; 38

Altie Jane Colf; 2 May 1869; John D. Colf, died April 1874, of Machias; Mary Clark; Albert and Herbert Colf; PGM Edie Colf, PU Erastus Colf, PU Jehiel Colf, PU Delevan Colf, MU Warner F. Clark, MU John B. Clark, MU Ephraim V. Clark; file in same envelope with Cora Smith, and Nora, Matie, Emory, Viola and Grover Colf; 38

Emory Colf; about 1880; - ; - ; Cora Smith, and Matie, Nora, Viola and Grover Colf; - ; received money from estate of Delevan Colf, G- Andrew B. Neff, in same envelope as Cora Smith, and Herbert, Altie and Albert Colf; 38

Grover Colf; about 1886; - ; - ; Cora Smith, and Matie, Nora, Viola and Emory Colf; - ; received money from estate of Delevan Colf, G- Andrew B. Neff, in same envelope as Cora Smith, and Herbert, Altie and Albert Colf; 38

Herbert R. Colf; 26 November 1864; John D. Colf, died April 1874, of Machias; Mary Clark; Albert and Altie Colf; PGM Edie Colf, PU Erastus Colf, PU Jehiel Colf, PU Delevan Colf, MU Warner F. Clark, MU John B. Clark, MU Ephraim V. Clark; file in same envelope with Cora Smith, and Nora, Matie, Emory, Viola and Grover Colf; 38

Name; Date of Birth; Father; Mother; Siblings; Other Relatives; Notes; Box Number

Matie Colf; about 1878; - ; - ; Cora Smith, and Grover, Nora, Viola and Emory Colf; - ; received money from estate of Delevan Colf, G- Andrew B. Neff, in same envelope as Cora Smith, and Herbert, Altie and Albert Colf; 38

Nora Colf; about 1875; - ; - ; Cora Smith, and Grover, Matie, Viola and Emory Colf; - ; received money from estate of Delevan Colf, G- Andrew B. Neff, in same envelope as Cora Smith, and Herbert, Altie and Albert Colf; 38

Robert L. Colf; 24 August 1882; Clinton Matthewson, in Buffalo Hospital for Insane; - ; - ; GM Emma Colf; - ; 40

Viola Colf; about 1883; - ; - ; Cora Smith, and Grover, Matie, Nora and Emory Colf; - ; received money from estate of Delevan Colf, G- Andrew B. Neff, in same envelope as Cora Smith, and Herbert, Altie and Albert Colf; 38

James A. Collins; 24 June 1908; Daniel Collins; - ; - ; - ; G- Lola B. Collins, he worked on a boat in Great Lakes during Summer of 1927; 28

Jeanne E. Collins; 2 September 1911; Timothy Collins, died before 30 January 1922; Mary; Josephine and John Collins; - ; - ; 54

John J. Collins; about 1900; - ; - ; Robert and Daniel Collins, and Marie Runge; - ; RE 1111 W. State St., Olean; 54

John W. Collins; 8 June 1909; Timothy Collins, died before 30 January 1922; Mary; Josephine and Jeanne Collins; - ; - ; 54

Josephine M. Collins; 14 October 1907; Timothy Collins, died before 30 January 1922; Mary; John and Jeanne Collins; - ; - ; 54

Mary Ann Collins; 14 November 1842; - ; - ; - ; - ; G- William Baxter; 4

Robert E. Collins; April 1911; - ; - ; John and Daniel Collins, and Marie Runge; - ; RE 1111 W. State St., Olean; 54

George M. Colvin; May 1902; - ; - ; Marie Cramer; - ; two brothers served in Army in France; 54

Iona I. Colvin; 4 October 1871; Barton Colvin, resided in Wexford County, Michigan; Alma, died August 1875;

Name; Date of Birth; Father; Mother; Siblings; Other Relatives; Notes; Box Number

Marvin Colvin; HU Mr. Kellogg; - ; 38

Marvin D. Colvin; 13 February 1874; Barton Colvin, resided in Wexford County, Michigan; Alma, died August 1875; Iona Colvin; - ; - ; 38

Phebe M. Colvin; 11 June 1859; - ; - ; - ; HU Morris Colvin; G- Theodore M. Dewey; 4

Andrew Competiro; about 1895; Joseph Competiro; - ; - ; - ; - ; 40

John J. Condon; 25 October 1876; John Condon, of Olean; - ; William, Johnanna, Mary, Margaret and Nellie Condon; - ; money from judgment against John and Jane Allen, first G- William Pierce, (no relation), second G- John L. Baxter; 76

Johnanna Condon; about 1881; John Condon, of Olean; - ; William, John, Mary, Margaret and Nellie Condon; HU Mr. Donovan ; received money from judgment against John and Jane Allen, first G- William Pierce, (no relation), second G- John L. Baxter; 76

Margaret Condon; 1884 or 1885; John Condon, of Olean; - ; William, Johnanna, Mary, John and Nellie Condon; - ; received money from judgment against John and Jane Allen, first G- William Pierce, (no relation), second G- John L. Baxter; 76

Mary Condon; 19 January 1882; John Condon, of Olean; - ; William, Johnanna, Margaret, John and Nellie Condon; - ; received money from judgment against John and Jane Allen, first G- William Pierce, (no relation), second G- John L. Baxter; 76

Nellie Condon; 1885 or 1886; John Condon, of Olean; - ; William, Johnanna, Margaret, John and Mary Condon; - ; received money from judgment against John and Jane Allen, first G- William Pierce, (no relation), second G- John L. Baxter; 76

William Condon; about 1874 John Condon, of Olean; - ; Nellie, Johnanna, Margaret, John and Mary Condon; - ; received money from judgment against John and Jane Allen, first G-

Name; Date of Birth; Father; Mother; Siblings; Other Relatives; Notes; Box Number

William Pierce, (no relation), second G- John L. Baxter; 76

Hazel Conhiser; 8 November 1895; - ; Caroline; Frank H. Conhiser; - ; - ; 38

Mary A. Conklin; 13 January 1852; - ; - ; Alice and Millard Conklin; - ; G- Emory Conklin, money from Zachary Conklin's estate; 4

Millard Conklin; 23 January 1850; - ; - ; Alice and Mary Conklin; - ; G- Emory Conklin, received money from Zachary Conklin's estate; 4

Millard F. Conkling; 23 January 1850; Samuel Conkling; - ; - ; - ; G- Edgar Fuller, see Millard Conklin above; 4

Bertha Connell; about 1888; - ; Margaret F.; Blanche, Frances and Eunice Connell; - ; RE 53 Garden Ave., Rochester, NY, money from estates of Owen Connell from Plainsville, Pennsylvania, and Peter Connell from McKean County, Pennsylvania; 27

Blanche Connell; about 1886; - ; Margaret F.; Bertha, Frances and Eunice Connell; - ; RE 53 Garden Ave., Rochester, NY, received money from estates of Owen Connell from Plainsville, Pennsylvania, and Peter Connell from McKean County, Pennsylvania; 27

Eunice Connell; about 1899; - ; Margaret F.; Bertha, Frances and Blanche Connell; - ; RE 53 Garden Ave., Rochester, NY, received money from estates of Owen Connell from Plainsville, Pennsylvania, and Peter Connell from McKean County, Pennsylvania; 27

Frances Connell; about 1895; - ; Margaret F.; Bertha, Eunice and Blanche Connell; - ; RE 53 Garden Ave., Rochester, NY, received money from estates of Owen Connell from Plainsville, Pennsylvania, and Peter Connell from McKean County, Pennsylvania; 27

Gertrude M. Connell; about 1887; John Connell, died before December 1906; Mary; Martin, James and John Connell; and Mayme H. Connell Dawson; - ; received money from estate of Lawrence Connell, child was part owner of real estate on

Name; Date of Birth; Father; Mother; Siblings; Other Relatives; Notes; Box Number

corners of Oak and Maple Streets in Olean; 40

James Connell; about 1892; John Connell, died before December 1906; Mary; Martin, Gertrude and John Connell; and Mayme H. Connell Dawson; - ; received money from estate of Lawrence Connell, child was part owner of real estate on corners of Oak and Maple Streets in Olean; 40

John Connell; 14 February 1898; John Connell, died before December 1906; Mary; Martin, Gertrude and James Connell; and Mayme H. Connell Dawson; - ; received money from estate of Lawrence Connell, child was part owner of real estate on corners of Oak and Maple Streets in Olean; 40

Martin Connell; about 1889; John Connell, died before December 1906; Mary; John, Gertrude and James Connell; and Mayme H. Connell Dawson; - ; received money from estate of Lawrence Connell, child was part owner of real estate on corners of Oak and Maple Streets in Olean; 40

Benjamin Connors; 3 September 1880; - ; Maria; Edward, Charles, James, Susan, Jessie, Gertrude and Emma Connors; - ; G- John Costigan, G-Silas Seymour; 38

Benjamin P. Connors; 15 December 1879; - ; - ; - ; G- John J. Costigan; 4

Bessie Connors; - ; - ; - ; - ; G- Margaret Connors, in same envelope with Lawrence and Rose Connors; 76

Charles Connors; 17 March 1878; - ; Maria; Edward, Benjamin, James, Susan, Jessie, Gertrude and Emma Connors; - ; G- John Costigan, G-Silas Seymour; 38

Edward Connors; 13 March 1876; - ; Maria; Charles, Benjamin, James, Susan, Jessie, Gertrude and Emma Connors; - ; G- John Costigan, G-Silas Seymour; 38

Emma Connors; 27 November 1889; - ; Maria; Charles, Benjamin, James, Susan, Jessie, Gertrude and Edward Connors; - ; G- John Costigan, G-Silas Seymour; 38

Gertrude Connors; 30 November 1885; - ; Maria; Charles, Benjamin, James, Susan, Jessie, Emma and Edward Connors; - ; G- John Costigan, G-Silas Seymour; 38

Name; Date of Birth; Father; Mother; Siblings; Other Relatives; Notes; Box Number

James Connors; 4 March 1874; - ; Maria; Charles, Benjamin, Gertrude, Susan, Jessie, Emma and Edward Connors; - ; G-John Costigan, G-Silas Seymour; 38

Jessie Connors; 25 May 1883; - ; Maria; Charles, Benjamin, Gertrude, Susan, James, Emma and Edward Connors; - ; G-John Costigan, G-Silas Seymour; 38

Josephine C. Connors; 22 May 1892 ; Michael J. Connors; - ; - ; - ; G- William J. Weller; 40

Lawrence Connors; - ; - ; - ; - ; G- Margaret Connors, in same envelope with Bessie and Rose Connors; 76

Rose Connors; - ; - ; - ; - ; G- Margaret Connors, in same envelope with Bessie and Lawrence Connors; 76

Susan M. Connors; 25 September 1881; - ; Maria; Charles, Benjamin, Gertrude, James, Emma and Edward Connors; - ; G- John Costigan, G-Silas Seymour; 38

Charles Conrad; 22 December 1874; H. J. Conrad; - ; Wallace Conrad, Lena Swarts, Elta Pettit, and Elva Conrad; GM Huldah Chamberlin, U-Wales Chamberlin; received money from estate of C. J. Chamberlin; 38

Wallace Conrad; 20 September 1876; H. J. Conrad; - ; Charles Conrad, Lena Swarts, Elta Pettit, and Elva Conrad; GM Huldah Chamberlin, U-Wales Chamberlin; received money from estate of C. J. Chamberlin; 38

John Constantino; 15 August 1907; - ; - ; - ; - ; G- Michael C. Wuersett; 40

Bertha Cookingham; 25 February 1903; Walter J. Cookingham; Cora; - ; HU Leon S. Dort, GM Catherine L. Mauer, died 21 July 1921; Bertha gave birth on 29 October 1921; 5

Henry A. Cooley; 28 November 1900; William H. Cooley; - ; - ; - ; 52

Helen M. Cooney; 22 August 1910; Michael J. Cooney, of 176 River St., Salamanca; Mary C.; - ; - ; - ; 63

Thomas Cooney; 8 September 1883; Michael Cooney; Mary, of Randolph; - ; - ; - ; 71

Abigail A. Cooper; 23 December 1844; Silas W. Cooper; - ;

Name; Date of Birth; Father; Mother; Siblings; Other Relatives; Notes; Box Number

Emma Jane and Christiana Cooper; MGM Rebecca Cooper; G- Thomas Caneen; 4

Christiana D. Cooper; 4 December 1849; Silas W. Cooper; - ; Emma Jane and Abigail Cooper; PGM Rebecca Cooper; G- Thomas Caneen; 4

Cora D. Cooper; about 1871; Harvey A. Cooper, died September 1872 in DuPage County, Illinois, but was of Hinsdale; - ; - ; PGM Polly Cooper; needed guardian to receive pension; 38

Doris Iola Cooper;14 August 1903; Merrill Mills; - ; - ; HU Mr. Hare; received money from U. S. Government; 27

Emma Jane Cooper; 29 December 1846; Silas W. Cooper; - ; Christiana and Abigail Cooper; MGM Rebecca Cooper; G- Thomas Caneen; 4

Erbika Cooper; 20 November 1859; Sylus Cooper, died 6 March 1860; Margaret; - ; PGF Elish Cooper; - ; 4

Florence A. Cooper; about 1849; George W. Cooper; - ; - ; HU Mr. Kent; RE 1870, Fond Du Lac County, Wisconsin, Florence's lawyer was William F. Kent; 27

Ellen Coot; 15 December 1879; - ; Nettie; Jennie Coot; - ; Mary Coot left legacy; 38

Jennie Coot; 25 May 1876; - ; Nettie; Ellen Coot; - ; Mary Coot left legacy; 38

Paul H. Corbett; about 1910; - ; Emma, RE 201 Broad St., Salamanca; Shirley Corbett; - ; - ; 54

Shirley E. Corbett; about 1908; - ; Emma, RE 201 Broad St., Salamanca; Paul Corbett; - ; - ; 54

John Elsworth Corkins; 6 April 1881; Patrick Corkins; - ; - ; - ; money from estate of Florilla Bishop and Julia Corkins; 38

Ida Cormya; about 1857; - ; - ; - ; HU Frank Cormya; RE Emporium, Cameron, Pennsylvania, left property in Cattaraugus County; 4

William Edgar Cornwell; 12 March 1910; Charles R. Cornwell, died 28 April 1920; Elizabeth; - ; - ; received relief check from Pennsylvania Railroad Co.; 55

Reuben R. Corsaw; 11 July 1889; Devillo Corsaw; Sarah E., died

Name; Date of Birth; Father; Mother; Siblings; Other Relatives; Notes; Box Number

before May 1893; - ; - ; Reuben died 21 June 1893; 39

Ellen A. Corsett; 22 September 1898; Lincoln A. Corsett; Carrie A.; - ; - ; RE 121 N. 3rd St., Olean; 39

Harold L. Corsett; 3 January 1894; Lincoln A. Corsett; Carrie A.; - ; - ; received money from estate of Ellen Corsett; 27

Marion I. Corwin; 4 May 1899; - ; - ; - ; U- Bartholomew F. McCloskey; - ; 40

Wells Brooks Coss; about 1868; Charles Coss; Helen; - ; MGM Helen Brooks left Wells a legacy; Wells died 1874; 38

Claude Costello; 15 June 1891; - ; Ida; George Costello; - ; John Costello left legacy, file mentioned Smith Parish; 63

George Costello; 2 October 1893; - ; Ida; Claude Costello; - ; John Costello left legacy, file mentioned Smith Parish; 63

Marion Costello; 30 October 1904; - ; Esther, married Mr. Inman, of Conewango; Mildred Costello;- ; father died 22 July 1917; 54

Mildred Costello; 29 January 1907; - ; Esther, married Mr. Inman, of Conewango; Marion Costello;- ; father died 22 July 1917; 54

Ellen Elizabeth Cotrael; 26 June 1875; Hiram S. Cotrael; - ; Mary Cotrael; - ; Jonathon P. Cotrael left legacy; 38

Karl Cotrael; about 1876; Carlton Cotrael; - ; - ; - Jonathon P. Cotrael left legacy; 36

Mary Isabel Cotrael; 19 July 1880; Hiram S. Cotrael; - ; Ellen Cotrael; - ; received legacy from Jonathon P. Cotrael; 38

Louis B. Cotton; 21 August 1871; Charles Cotton; Mariah M.; - ; - ; - ; 4

George F. Councilman; 23 July 1874; - ; - ; Ira W. Councilman (born about 1853), Andrew J. Councilman (born about 1855), John J. Councilman (born about 1866), Rose E. Spencer (born about 1851), Lelia Culver (born about 1860), and Julia M. Culver (born about 1862); - ; - ; 36

Edna Courter; 2 September 1889; - ; - ; - ; HU Mr. Simpson, C- G. W. Brown; - ; 4

Benjamin Frank Courtright; 16 April 1907; William Courtright,

Name; Date of Birth; Father; Mother; Siblings; Other Relatives; Notes; Box Number

of East Randolph; Reba, died 27 January 1927; - ; - ; money from estate of Mary H. Amsbry, of Montrose, Pennsylvania. Benjamin attended St. John's Military Academy, at Manlius, NY; 55

Albert L. Cousins; August 1903; - ; - ; - ; relative was Paul Cousins; married and had two children by December 1923, worked for Pennsylvania RR company. Albert's mother lived in Buffalo, NY, and he received money from estate of Ella C. Carlisle; 27

James Cousins; 28 September 1908; - ; - ; - ; relatives were Paul and Albert Cousins; mother in Gowanda State Hospital, as insane person. James resided with Alva Smith, G- George Eaton, no relation, and was in army 1922 to 1925; 63

Anthony Covert; 4 August 1896; John Covert; - ; Glenn and Leo Covert; - ; two files and received money from estate of Almira Covert; 39

Glenn A. Covert; 2 October 1880; John Covert; - ; Anthony and Leo Covert; - ; RE Minneapolis, Hennepin, Minnesota , two files and received money from estate of Almira Covert; 39

Leo E. Covert; 23 February 1893; John Covert; - ; Anthony and Leo Covert; - ; two files and received money from estate of Almira Covert; 39

Earl Cowen; 2 November 1895; - ; Anna K., married Levi Slater; - ; - ; - ; 40

Edgar Cowley; - ; Horace Cowley, of Ionia County, Michigan; - ; - ; - ; G- Orlo Cowley, of Mecosta County, Michigan; 4

Ethel M. Cox; about 1881; Howard S. Cox; - ; Lloyd and Fred Cox; HU Mr. Dodge; G- Augusta M. Cox; 39

Fred E. Cox; about 1883; Howard S. Cox; - ; Lloyd and Ethel Cox; - ; G- Augusta M. Cox; 39

Lloyd D. Cox; about 1886; Howard S. Cox; - ; Fred and Ethel Cox; - ; G- Augusta M. Cox; 39

Mary E. Cox; 19 January 1862; William Hawkins; - ; - ; HU Howard Cox, married 18 February 1880; PGF John Hawkins, MGF James Mersch; RE 1883, Springville, NY, and Mary's

Name; Date of Birth; Father; Mother; Siblings; Other Relatives; Notes; Box Number

mother died 1862; 4

Morris Cradduck; 17 May 1896 ; - ; Alice, died by March 1898; Fred Cradduck; - ; - ; 40

Burt F. G. Cram; about 1878; Henry D. Cram, died 3 October 1887, in State Line, Pennsylvania; Eva; Harry Cram; - ; - ; 38

Harry D. Cram; about 1873; Henry D. Cram, died 3 October 1887, in State Line, Pennsylvania; Eva; Burt Cram; - ; - ; 38

Addie R. Crandall; 7 Dec 1864; - ; - ; - ; HU Guy B. Crandall; - ; 5

Clea H. Crandall; 31 October 1907; - ; Jessie; Orville and Harvey Crandall and Edith Myers; - ; - ; 28

Earl B. Crandall; 29 January 1887; Frank E. Crandall; - ; - ; - ; - ; 38

Frank Crandall; about 1865; Lemuel Crandall; Loretta E., died January 1877, of Persia; - ; GM Marietta Strickland, U- James Borden, A- Henrietta Borden, U- William E. Hunt; - ; 75

Gladys Leah Crandall; 28 December 1903; Curtis J. Crandall; - ; - ; - ; - ; 40

Orville B. Crandall; 19 July 1905; - ; Jessie; Clea and Harvey Crandall and Edith Myers; - ; - ; 28

Elsie Crane; 2 December 1891; Ulysses Crane, residence unknown; - ; Stanley Crane and Rena B. (W- of Gilbert Laidlaw); - ; money from estate of Elijah Chaffee; 40

Emma E. Crane; 5 December 1864; - ; Julia E.; - ; - ; - ; 38

Jennie Crane; 11 May 1863; - ; - ; - ; HU Mr. Adams, MG Franklin and Abigail Hinman, PGM Lucy Tripp, MU Byron Hinman, MU Richard Hinman, MU Truman Hinman, MU Francis Hinman, MA Mary Wait, MA Emily Brown, MA Lovinda Grimells, MA Matilda Hinman, MA Alice Hinman, PU Lorenzo Crane, PU Alex. Crane, PA Theodora Sherman; father wasn't a resident of Cattaraugus County, G- Imogene Stone (was Ms. Hinman in 1874, possibly mother); 6

Stanley Crane; 14 August 1890; Ulysses Crane, residence unknown; - ; Elsie Crane and Rena B. (W- of Gilbert

Name; Date of Birth; Father; Mother; Siblings; Other Relatives; Notes; Box Number

Laidlaw); - ; money from estate of Elijah Chaffee; 40

Ruth Alberta Crannell; 12 August 1902; - ; went by Bertha Luther Crannell in September 1919; - ; - ; RE 310 N. Clinton St., Olean and received U.S. Government Insurance money on life of Luther Crannell, deceased; 28

Herbert Crawford; 25 March 1909; John Crawford; Ellen; - ; - ; - ; 28

Isabelle F. Crawford; 5 June 1884; James Crawford, died September 1893; Bridget; Mary A., Margaret E., and Loretta B. Crawford; - ; - ; 4

Loretta B. Crawford; 6 November 1889; James Crawford, died September 1893; Bridget; Mary A., Margaret and Isabelle Crawford; - ; - ; 4

Margaret E. Crawford; 5 February 1879; James Crawford, died September 1893; Bridget; Mary A., Loretta and Isabelle Crawford; - ; - ; 4

Mary A. Crawford; about 1882; James Crawford, died September 1893; Bridget; Margaret., Loretta and Isabelle Crawford; - ; - ; 4

Vernon W. Croker; 16 October 1911; Daniel Croker, of Perrysburg; Annie M., died before January 1928; - ; - ; - ; 63

Frank Crook; 25 September 1906; Fred Crook, died 1917; Isabella Sutherland, died 2 December 1919; George Crook and Ralph Sutherland; step-father was Herman Gilbert (married Isabella 27 December 1918, in Allegany), MG Edward and Mary Elizabeth Sutherland (Isabella indentured to them 1878, they legally adopted Isabella). Mary E. Sutherland (died 27 April 1920, in Limestone), PG Charles and Mina Crook, Mary E. Sutherland's sister is Harriet Adsit and Mary E. Sutherland's brothers are Alfred and Volorous Swift; - ; 53

George Crook; 30 July 1904; Fred Crook, died 1917; Isabella Sutherland, died 2 December 1919; Frank Crook and Ralph Sutherland; step-father was Herman Gilbert (married Isabella 27 December 1918, in Allegany), MG Edward and Mary

Name; Date of Birth; Father; Mother; Siblings; Other Relatives; Notes; Box Number

Elizabeth Sutherland (Isabella indentured to them 1878, they legally adopted Isabella). Mary E. Sutherland (died 27 April 1920, in Limestone), PG Charles and Mina Crook, Mary E. Sutherland's sister is Harriet Adsit and Mary E. Sutherland's brothers are Alfred and Volorous Swift; - ; 53

Henry Maurice Crook; 30 August 1853; - ; - ; - ; - ; G- Mason Smith, Cyrenia Crook signed paper that she knew Henry well; 5

Emmet H. Crosby; 24 May 1867; - ; Miranda, married Mr. Webster; - ; - ; received legacy from Horatio Crosby; 5

Almira Ann Cross; about 1853; - ; Betsey Carr, of Randolph; Derdick and Stephen Cross; MGF Daniel Carr, PU Isaiah Cross; 75

Caroline Cross; 5 November 1846; Luther Cross, died 1 December 1849; Eliza Ann Bond, married Mr. Mallory, lived near Yankee Station, Iowa, by 1860; - ; PG Reuben and Amanda Cross, MU Marshall Bond, MA Maria McClure (wife of Henry); Caroline had a child that died, the supposed father of her child was U-, Henry McClure; 4

Cora E. Cross; 25 April 1877; William H. Cross, of York County, Nebraska; - ; Isaiah, Ella and Garwood Cross; MG Garwood M. Torrance (died 16 June 1885, in Randolph) and Persis Torrance, MA Emeline M. Boyington, MA Mary M. Babcock, MU Mitchell Torrance, MU Joel B. Torrance, PA Alice Frary, PA Sarah J. Torrance, PA Eva Cross, PU Francis J. Cross, PU Asa B. Cross, PU George W. Cross; - ; 39

Derdick L. Cross; about 1852; - ; Betsey Carr, of Randolph; Almira and Stephen Cross; MGF Daniel Carr, PU Isaiah Cross; - ; 75

Ella Cross; 27 July 1875; William H. Cross, of York County, Nebraska; - ; Isaiah, Cora and Garwood Cross; MG Garwood M. Torrance (died 16 June 1885, in Randolph) and Persis Torrance, MA Emeline M. Boyington, MA Mary M. Babcock, MU Mitchell Torrance, MU Joel B. Torrance, PA Alice Frary, PA Sarah J. Torrance, PA Eva Cross, PU Francis

Name; Date of Birth; Father; Mother; Siblings; Other Relatives; Notes; Box Number

J. Cross, PU Asa B. Cross, PU George W. Cross; - ; 39

Garwood William Cross; 9 December 1869; William H. Cross, of York County, Nebraska; - ; Isaiah, Cora and Ella Cross; MG Garwood M. Torrance (died 16 June 1885, in Randolph) and Persis Torrance, MA Emeline M. Boyington, MA Mary M. Babcock, MU Mitchell Torrance, MU Joel B. Torrance, PA Alice Frary, PA Sarah J. Torrance, PA Eva Cross, PU Francis J. Cross, PU Asa B. Cross, PU George W. Cross; - ; 39

Gertrude R. Cross; 19 October 1894; - ; Lizzie A., married Mr. Miller after January 1917; Hilda Cross; needed guardian to receive pension money and money from lawsuit: Cross versus Cross 1910-1911; 52

Hawley R. Cross; 15 May 1848; Hawley Cross; - ; - ; - ; G- John Hillenbrand (from Canisteo, Steuben, NY); 5

Hilda M. Cross; 28 September 1902 - ; Lizzie A., married Mr. Miller after January 1917; Gertrude Cross; needed guardian to receive pension money and money from lawsuit: Cross versus Cross 1910-1911; 52

Isaiah Cross; 9 October 1872; William H. Cross, of York County, Nebraska; - ; Garwood, Cora and Ella Cross; MG Garwood M. Torrance (died 16 June 1885, in Randolph) and Persis Torrance, MA Emeline M. Boyington, MA Mary M. Babcock, MU Mitchell Torrance, MU Joel B. Torrance, PA Alice Frary, PA Sarah J. Torrance, PA Eva Cross, PU Francis J. Cross, PU Asa B. Cross, PU George W. Cross; - ; 39

Stephen A. Cross; about 1850; - ; Betsey Carr, of Randolph; Almira and Derdick Cross; MGF Daniel Carr, PU Isaiah Cross; - ; 75

Jennie Crowe; - ; - ; - ; - ; - ; G- Imogene Stone; 76

Mary G. Crowley; 6 March 1873; Rodney Crowley; Jane M.; - ; - ; - ; 38

Edwin L. Crumb; 25 December 1830 ; Culver Crumb; Mary; - ; - ; - ; 5

Name; Date of Birth; Father; Mother; Siblings; Other Relatives; Notes; Box Number

Emeline Crumb; 10 September 1849; Chauncey Crumb; - ; - ; PA Deborah Bailey; - ; 4

Olive Marie Crumb; 3 May 1905; Chiles M. Crumb; Mary E., married Mr. Little, she was blind; Sylvia Crumb; PU- Kingsley D. Crumb; RE 1708 Holland St., Erie, Erie, Pennsylvania; 28

Sylvia Joyce Crumb; 4 February 1902; Chiles M. Crumb; Mary E., married Mr. Little, she was blind; Olive Crumb; PU- Kingsley D. Crumb; RE 1708 Holland St., Erie, Erie, Pennsylvania; 28

Gordon C. Cuit; 31 October 1826; Roger Cuit, died before March 1846, of Ellicottville; - ; - ; - ; G- Gordon Coit, of Buffalo; 77

Hattie A. Cullen; 31 January 1871; Samuel Cullen; - ; Lucy and Montreville Cullen; HU Mr. Whitford, MGF Joseph M. Riddle, MU James Riddle, PU Joseph Cullen, another relative was Ann Busley; G- C. A. Benson, no relation; 42

Lucy H. Cullen; 15 June 1867; Samuel Cullen; - ; Hattie and Montreville Cullen; HU Mr. Ellis, MGF Joseph M. Riddle, MU James Riddle, PU Joseph Cullen, another relative was Ann Busley; G- C. A. Benson, no relation; 42

Montreville J. Cullen; 27 October 1876; Samuel Cullen; - ; Hattie and Lucy Cullen; MGF Joseph M. Riddle, MU James Riddle, PU Joseph Cullen, another relative was Ann Busley; G- C. A. Benson, no relation; 42

Margaret Cullinan; 21 March 1872; - ; Sarah; Theresa and Mary Cullinan; - ; G- T. H. Dowd; 39

Mary C. Cullinan; 9 June 1879; - ; Sarah; Theresa and Margaret Cullinan; - ; G- T. H. Dowd; 39

Theresa Cullinan; 26 March 1873; - ; Sarah; Mary and Margaret Cullinan; - ; G- T. H. Dowd; 39

Cary Culver; 24 February 1841; Lyman Culver, died before August 1852, of Colsdpring; Sarah; Mary Culver; - ; - ; 77

Mary Culver; 12 September 1844; Lyman Culver, died before August 1852, of Colsdpring; Sarah; Cary Culver; - ; - ; 77

Name; Date of Birth; Father; Mother; Siblings; Other Relatives; Notes; Box Number

Leonard A. Cummings; - ; Joseph Cummings; Eliza; Philander and Sarah Cummings; - ; - ; 5

Philander Cummings; - ; Joseph Cummings; Eliza; Leonard and Sarah Cummings; - ; - ; 5

Sarah Ann Cumming; - ; Joseph Cummings; Eliza; Leonard and Philander Cummings; - ; - ; 5

Mildred M. Cunningham; 7 May 1904; - ; - ; - ; HU Mr. Shaw, MU Harry B. Smith; RE 1925, Erie, Pennsylvania, mother died about 1907 and father abandoned family; 52

Agnes M. Currie; 9 February 1898; - ; Olive, married Mr. Davidson; Ella, Andrew, and Roy Currie; HU Mr. Morgan, PU Alexander Currie, PU James Currie; received money from estate of Andrew Currie; 54

Andrew Bruce Currie; 5 May 1900; - ; Olive, married Mr. Davidson; Ella, Agnes, and Roy Currie; PU Alexander Currie, PU James Currie; received money from estate of Andrew Currie; 54

Ella May Currie; 25 June 1896; - ; Olive, married Mr. Davidson; Andrew, Agnes, and Roy Currie; PU Alexander Currie, PU James Currie; received money from estate of Andrew Currie; 54

Max F. Currie; 21 January 1911; - ; Hazel M.; - ; - ; father died before September 1912, G- Alexander McCall, received money from estate in Toronto, Canada; 53

Roy Currie; 6 January 1907 ; - ; Olive, married Mr. Davidson; Andrew, Agnes, and Roy Currie; PU Alexander Currie, PU James Currie; received money from estate of Andrew Currie and he has two files; 54

John F. Curry; about 1868; Richard Curry, died March 1872; Mary A., married Mr. Crandall between 1876 and 1889; - ; - ; - ; 5

Abiah "Burr" Curtis; 5 August 1843; Smith Curtis; Ann Ross; Susan and Amelia Curtis; GM Sally Baker, PU William Curtis, PU Joseph Curtis, U- Zenos Ross, U- Edwin Ross, U- Joseph Ross, U- Wilber Ross, A- Amelia Ann Ross, A- Sally

Name; Date of Birth; Father; Mother; Siblings; Other Relatives; Notes; Box Number

Mixer, C- James M. Lyon; - ; 5

Amelia Curtis; 3 April 1846; Smith Curtis; Ann Ross; Susan and Abiah Curtis; GM Sally Baker, PU William Curtis, PU Joseph Curtis, U- Zenos Ross, U- Edwin Ross, U- Joseph Ross, U- Wilber Ross, A- Amelia Ann Ross, A- Sally Mixer, C- James M. Lyon; - ; 5

Byron E. Curtis; June 1861; William Curtis; - ; Willie Curtis; MG Isaac W. and Rebecca Fisher; GU Silas W. Fisher, GU Everett Fisher, GA Betsey Marble, Half-U- Andrew Bailey, Half-U- James Bailey, Alice Fisher (niece); - ; 5

Charles Curtis; 17 September 1857; Elliott Curtis; Elmina, married Mr. Barker; Waldo Curtis; MGU Zina Holdridge, MGU Price Holdridge, MGA Mary Hatch (wife of Stephen Hatch); - ; 5

Helen A. Curtis; 21 August 1910; Rensselaer Leigh Curtis, died 18 September 1924; Mary P.; Ruth Curtis; - ; RE 28 Second Ave., Franklinville; 28

Howard Curtis; 22 March 1893; - ; - ; - ; - ; G- David Stark, no relation; 40

Julia "Ettie" Curtis; 17 July 1856; Joseph Curtis, died before November 1871; Catharine, died before November 1871; - ; - ; G- G. W. Drake; 75

Leslie L. Curtis; about 1898; Thomas Curtis, died 26 December 1905, of Knapp Creek,; Margaret H., born about 1858; Logan and Mary Curtis; - ; attended Syracuse University, money from Henry Curtis's estate (of Belvedere, Boone, Illinois); 40

Logan H. Curtis; 21 February 1891; Thomas Curtis, died 26 December 1905, of Knapp Creek; Margaret H., born about 1858; Leslie and Mary Curtis; - ; money from estate of Henry Curtis (from Belvedere, Boone, Illinois); 40

Mary Curtis; 2 March 1889; Thomas Curtis, died 26 December 1905, of Knapp Creek; Margaret H., born about 1858; Leslie and Logan Curtis; - ; attended Syracuse University, money from estate of Henry Curtis (from Belvedere, Boone, Illinois); 40.

Name; Date of Birth; Father; Mother; Siblings; Other Relatives; Notes; Box Number

Ruth M. Curtis; 11 November 1908; Rensselaer Leigh Curtis, died 18 September 1924; Mary P.; Helen Curtis; - ; RE 28 Second Ave., Franklinville; 28

Susan Curtis; 1 October 1850; Smith Curtis; Ann Ross; Amelia and Abiah Curtis; GM Sally Baker, PU William Curtis, PU Joseph Curtis, U- Zenos Ross, U- Edwin Ross, U- Joseph Ross, U- Wilber Ross, A- Amelia Ann Ross, A- Sally Mixer, C- James M. Lyon; - ; 5

Waldo H. Curtis; 1 May 1856; Elliott Curtis; Elmina, married Mr. Barker; Charles Curtis; MGU Zina Holdridge, MGU Price Holdridge, MGA Mary Hatch (W- of Stephen Hatch); - ; 5

Willie Curtis; January 1863; William Curtis; - ; Byron Curtis; MG Isaac W. and Rebecca Fisher; GU Silas W. Fisher, GU Everett Fisher, GA Betsey Marble, Half-U- Andrew Bailey, Half-U- James Bailey, Alice Fisher (niece); - ; 5

Madelyn A. Cyener; about 1906; - ; Alice; - ; - ; 39

Name; Date of Birth; Father; Mother; Siblings; Other Relatives; Notes; Box Number

D Surnames

Joseph G. Dahar; 13 February 1900;- ; - ; - ; C- Simon J. Simon; - ; 6

Ada "Addie" Damon; about 1861; Daniel Damon; Emeline, married Mr. Jackson; Emma and Ralph Damon; PGF Martin Damon, A- Sally Hopkins, A- Eurnice Burns, PU- Lyman Damon, PU Henry Damon; - ; 40

Emma Damon; about 1867; Daniel Damon; Emeline, married Mr. Jackson; Ada and Ralph Damon; PGF Martin Damon, A- Sally Hopkins, A- Eurnice Burns, PU- Lyman Damon, PU Henry Damon; - ; 40

Minnie Damon; about 1877; - ; Melvina; Myra Damon; - ; G- Cary Damon, received money from estate of Lyman Damon, file also mentions Edward Adams; 40

Myra Damon; about 1875; - ; Melvina; Minnie Damon; - ; G- Cary Damon, received money from estate of Lyman Damon, file also mentions Edward Adams; 40

Ralph Damon; 10 July 1858; Daniel Damon; Emeline, married Mr. Jackson; Ada and Emma Damon; PGF Martin Damon, A- Sally Hopkins, A- Eurnice Burns, PU- Lyman Damon, PU Henry Damon; - ; 40

William M. Damon; 27 October 1874; - ; - ; - ; PGF Edmund Damon, GM Margaret Fitch, GU Harrison Blodget, PU Hiram Damon; mother died 18 September 1886, received money from estate of Mary Ashdown; 41

Frank G. Dana; 4 April 1881; Frank Dana; Kate, died 1 March 1892; Ivy, Minnie, Susie, and Warner Dana; PGF George H. Dana, U- N. Stewart Dana, U- Lawrence Dana; lived with N. Stewart Dana, in Bradford, Pennsylvania. RE 1903, in Hancock County, Ohio; 5

Ivy M. Dana; about 1884; Frank Dana; Kate, died 1 March 1892; Frank, Minnie, Susie, and Warner Dana; PGF George H. Dana, U- N. Stewart Dana, U- Lawrence Dana; lived with

Name; Date of Birth; Father; Mother; Siblings; Other Relatives; Notes; Box Number

George H. Dana in Duke Center, Pennsylvania; 5

Minnie A. Dana;16 March 1874; Frank Dana; Kate, died 1 March 1892; Frank, Ivy Susie, and Warner Dana; PGF George H. Dana, U- N. Stewart Dana, U- Lawrence Dana; - ; 5

Susie Dana; - ; Frank Dana; Kate, died 1 March 1892; Frank, Ivy Minnie, and Warner Dana; PGF George H. Dana, U- N. Stewart Dana, U- Lawrence Dana; Susie died 26 October 1891; 5

Warner J. Dana; 6 June 1889; Frank Dana; Kate, died 1 March 1892; Frank, Ivy Minnie, and Warner Dana; PGF George H. Dana, U- N. Stewart Dana, U- Lawrence Dana; RE Knapp Creek with Lawrence Dana; 5

Edwin Daniels; 1 November 1824; Ethern Daniels, died before January 1836, of Ashford; - ; - ; - ; G- Emerson Fay; 77

George L. Darbee; February 1859; - ; Mary M. Flowers, of Dayton; Willie Darbee; PGF Azariah Darbee, MGF George Flowers, other relatives were two PU, four PA, one MU, four HB and one HS; - ; 75

Gladys I. Darbee; 27 June 1898; - ; Anna L., married Mr. Matthewson; Hoyt Darbee; - ; - ; 40

Hoyt R. Darbee; 29 May 1897; - ; Anna L., married Mr. Matthewson; Gladys Darbee; - ; - ; 40

Willie M. Darbee; 23 November 1856; - ; Mary M. Flowers, of Dayton; George Darbee; PGF Azariah Darbee, MGF George Flowers, other relatives were two PU, four PA, one MU, four HB and one HS; - ; 75

Fry B. Darling; about 1885; - ; Clara, married Mr. Wood; - ; - ; - ; 41

John P. Darling; - ; John L. Darling; Lovina E.; - ; - ; G- Judson Darling; 5

Rena Darling; 9 February 1903; Urban Prescott; Lillian; Mildred, Jennings and Norton Prescott, HB John Prescott; second C- Lincoln R. Vibbard, HU Robert Darling; RE 1924, in Arcade, NY; 28

Ruby V. Darling; October 1878; George Darling; Loraine; - ; - ;

Name; Date of Birth; Father; Mother; Siblings; Other Relatives; Notes; Box Number

her parents did not live together; 40

Alfred Davies; about 1912; - ; - ; Maurice, Carl, Rena, Gladys, and Norman Davies; PGF John J. Davies; received money from estate of David J. Davies; 40

Carl Davies; about 1909; - ; - ; Maurice, Alfred, Rena, Gladys, and Norman Davies; PGF John J. Davies; received money from estate of David J. Davies; 40

Gladys L. Davies; about 1898; - ; - ; Maurice, Alfred, Rena, Carl, and Norman Davies; PGF John J. Davies; received money from estate of David J. Davies; 40

Maurice Davies; about 1907; - ; - ; Gladys, Alfred, Rena, Carl, and Norman Davies; PGF John J. Davies; AKA Morris Davies, RE Marion, Ohio, money from David J. Davies's estate; 40

Norman L. Davies; about 1897; - ; - ; Maurice, Alfred, Rena, Carl, and Gladys Davies; PGF John J. Davies; received money from estate of David J. Davies; 40

Rena Davies; September 1900; - ; - ; Maurice, Alfred, Norman, Carl, and Gladys Davies; PGF John J. Davies; received money from estate of David J. Davies; 40

Adelbert Davis; about 1858; - ; - ; Emory Davis; - ; G- Sarah Davis; 6

Alberta A. Davis; 1 July 1859; Mr. Elwell; - ; - ; HU Harry Davis; first G Maria Welch, second G Joseph Peaslee; 6

Clarence Davis; 23 April 1902, in Ellicottville; Thomas Davis, died before November 1918; Mary E., died before November 1918, she had nine children; Fred and Benjamin F. Davis, Nettie M. Miner, Jessie V. Hadley (W- of Frederick Hadley), and Dora Hopkins; - ; RE 1923, in St. Paul, Ramsey, Minnesota, lived in Hotel Elgin; 28

Daniel A. Davis; 21 July 1831; Lyman Davis, of Yorkshire; - ; Joshua Davis; - ; - ; 77

Emory W. Davis; about 1855; - ; - ; Adelbert Davis; - ; G- Sarah Davis; 6

Fred Davis; 10 July 1898; Thomas Davis, died before November

Name; Date of Birth; Father; Mother; Siblings; Other Relatives; Notes; Box Number

1918; Mary E., died before November 1918, she had nine children; Clarence and Benjamin F. Davis, Nettie M. Miner, Jessie V. Hadley (W- of Frederick Hadley), and Dora Hopkins; - ; Fred was married by November 1918; 28

Joshua Davis; August 1841; Lyman Davis, of Yorkshire; - ; Daniel Davis; - ; - ; 77

Mary T. Davis; 12 October 1909; William A. Davis; - ; - ; - ; RE 209 South Fourth St., Olean, NY; 28

Archie Dawley; 23 May 1892; - ; Rose L., married Mr. Valentine; Beulah Dawley; - ; G- Victor Ames (no relation), money from pension and John M. Dawley's estate; 40

Beulah Dawley; 3 February 1898; - ; Rose L., married Mr. Valentine; Archie Dawley; - ; G- Victor Ames (no relation), money from pension and John M. Dawley's estate; 40

James Dawson; 6 March 1869; - ; Ellen Hill, died January 1875, of Persia; - ; PGM Mrs. James Dawson, MGF Millen T. Hill, A- Mary Dawson. A- Jennie Walker, PU- Henry K. Dawson PU- Alexander Dawson; - ; 40

Catherine Day; 9 February 1900; William A. Day, Sr., died before March 1911; Anna B., RE Niagara Falls, NY in 1925; Morgan and William Day; - ; received pension money; 28

Charles H. Day: about 1885; Charles O. Day; Lucy S.; Ida L. and Harriet A. Day; - ; - ; 7

Edna Day; 6 March 1901; William T. Day; Mary J.; Reuben and Myrtle Day and Irene Goodman; HU Mr. Odell; left estate by Susana Hofer; 5

Flora Day; 23 April 1860; Salmon Day; - ; Georgia and Leroy Day; HU Peter Drown, PU Hartson Day; - ; 5

George W. Day; 1 February 1860; Asahel Day; - ; - ; - ; G- George W. Cable; 6

Georgia Day; - ; Salmon Day; - ; Flora and Leroy Day; PU Hartson Day; - ; 5

Harriet A. Day; 7 December 1844; - ; - ; - ; - ; G- Hiram Davis; 75

Harriet A. Day; about 1879; Charles O. Day; Lucy S.; Ida L. and

Name; Date of Birth; Father; Mother; Siblings; Other Relatives; Notes; Box Number

Charles Day; - ; - ; 7
Ida L. Day; 12 September 1875; Charles O. Day; Lucy S.; Harriet and Charles Day; - ; - ; 7
Leroy Day; October 1857; Salmon Day; - ; Flora and Georgia Day; PU Hartson Day; - ; 5
Morgan R. Day; 7 October 1902; William A. Day, Sr., died before March 1911; Anna B., RE Niagara Falls, NY in 1925; Catherine and William Day; - ; received pension money; 28
William A. Day Jr.; 17 February 1898; William A. Day, Sr., died before March 1911; Anna B., RE Niagara Falls, NY in 1925; Catherine and Morgan Day; - ; received pension money; 28
Ernest P. Dean; - ; - ; - ; - ; G- Joseph Hazard, no relation; 40
Virginia B. Dean; 6 December 1864; Merwin Dean, died 6 August 1876; Euretta, died 19 September 1879; Edith A. Dean, born 7 January 1862; HU Mr. Fullam, married by December 1882; received pension money; 5 and 8
Worthy Dean; - ; - ; - ; - ; - ; G- Bethuel McCoy; 77
Alvin F. Dechow; 11 September 1892; - ; - ; - ; PGF Frederick D. Dechow; filed mentioned that William W. Dechow died between June 1893 and July 1894; 40
Frederick "Fred" Deibler; 2 September 1863; Sylvester Dibler, died before March 1865; - ; - ; MGF Edward C. Squires, PU William Dibler, PU Joseph Dibler, PU Nathan Dibler, PA Esther Dibler; last name also seen as Dibbler and Dibler; 75
Louis J. Delaney; 7 February 1886; Michael Delaney; - ; - ; A- Marguerite Delaney; - ; 6
Floyd Delmage; 18 May 1889; Sheldon L. Delmage, died 6 January 1897, of Olean; Cora; John Delmage; - ; G- Levi C. Kenner; 55
John Delmage; 20 January 1887; Sheldon L. Delmage, died 6 January 1897, of Olean; Cora; Floyd Delmage; - ; G- Levi C. Kenner; 55
Jessie Demmon; 10 October 1888; - ; Mertie; Enos Demmon; - ; - ; 5
Raymond Good Dempsey; 1902; Raymond M. Dempsey; - ; - ;

Name; Date of Birth; Father; Mother; Siblings; Other Relatives; Notes; Box Number

- ; he died about 1913; 6

Myrtle May Derby; 21 January 1886; Mr. Frank; Eveline; - ; - ; - ; 40

Ralph W. Dermont; about 1892; - ; Emegene P, married Mr. Milks by 1903; Ray Dermont; - ; money from William Dermont's estate; 40

Ray M. Dermont; about 1896; - ; Emegene P, married Mr. Milks by 1903; Ralph Dermont; - ; received money from estate of William Dermont; 40

Ellen Victoria Devereux; 12 April 1898; - ; Mary, married Mr. McElfresh; Mary Devereux; - ; - ; 28

Mary Elizabeth Devereux; 2 July 1901; - ; Mary, married Mr. McElfresh; Ellen Devereux; - ; - ; 28

James Horace Dewey; 12 May 1864; - ; Hannah U.; John Dewey; - ; money from Alanson Dewey's estate and her father died 14 May 1879; 5

John A. Dewey; 28 January 1862; - ; Hannah U.; James Dewey; - ; received money from estate of Alanson Dewey and her father died 14 May 1879; 5

Clarence E. Dewitt; 16 June 1872; - ; Chloe L.; Florette and Mary Dewitt; - ; stated that Clinton E. Dewitt died 11 April 1882; 41

Florette Dewitt; 13 November 1877; - ; Chloe L.; Clarence and Mary Dewitt; - ; stated that Clinton E. Dewitt died 11 April 1882; 41

Mary E. Dewitt; 29 December 1873; - ; Chloe L.; Florette and Clarence Dewitt; HU Mr. Tullie, married by September 1894; stated that Clinton E. Dewitt died 11 April 1882; 41

Lizzie Dexter; 12 May 1893; - ; step-mom was Jennie R. Dexter (not her maiden name), of Bear Lake, Warren, Pennsylvania; Norman H. Dexter; C- Charles Buxton; received settlement on insurance of Henry P. Dexter; 6

Edna Deyoe; 16 February 1901; - ; Flora; Leona and Velma Deyoe; - ; - ; 40

Leona Deyoe; 1 April 1897; - ; Flora; Edna and Velma Deyoe; - ;

Name; Date of Birth; Father; Mother; Siblings; Other Relatives; Notes; Box Number

- ; 40

Velma Deyoe; 14 June 1904; - ; Flora; Edna and Leona Deyoe; - ; - ; 40

Mary Adell Dibble; - ; Daniel J. Dibble, died 29 March 1865; Mary Green; - ; HU Mr. Whitney, PGF Benedict Dibble, MG Hiram and Eliza Green, PU Mason Dibble, MU James H. Green, MA Adelia Knight (W- of Oliver A. Knight), MA Mrs. Evan Peet, MA Charlotte Cheeseman (W- of Morris Cheeseman), MA Louisa Cagwin (W- of James Cagwin), MA Mrs. George Beardsley, MA Flora London, MA Helen Cagwin; - ; 5

Charles A. Dickson; May 1895; Weldon Dickson; Anna; - ; - ; - ; 40

John F. Didas; 6 May 1906; John F. Didas, died by 17 November 1926; Bessie C.; Mary and Kathleen Didas; - ; RE 1927, 86 Myrtle Ave., Hornell; 28

Kathleen E. Didas; 25 May 1915; John F. Didas, died by 17 November 1926; Bessie C.; Mary and Kathleen Didas; - ; Kathleen died 11 June 1929; 28

Frank George Dieter; 7 October 1888; George Dieter; - ; George Dieter; - ; - ; 40

George Frederick Dieter; 22 October 1890; George Dieter; - ; Frank Dieter; - ; - ; 40

Lillian M. Dilts; 16 May 1860; Gilbert Dilts, died before November 1866; Lydia, of Franklinville, married Mr. Sprague; William Dilts; MGM Athalia Fitch; received pension money; 75

William Henry Dilts; 12 February 1852; Gilbert Dilts, died before November 1866; Lydia, of Franklinville, married Mr. Sprague; Lillian Dilts; MGM Athalia Fitch; received pension money; 75

John Dinan; - ; John Dinan, died September 1865, of Ellicottville; - ; - ; U- Michael Dinan, of Rochester, Monroe, NY; - ; 75

Dora Dinder; 14 February 1870; Ernest Dinder; Lena Warters,

Name; Date of Birth; Father; Mother; Siblings; Other Relatives; Notes; Box Number

married Mr. Boswick; - ; HU Mr. Hyde (married before 1891), MGF Joseph Warters; received pension money; 5

James Dirksen; 15 January 1903; - ; - ; - ; MGF Marshall Strain; RE Elkins, West Virginia, with Jennie Kehoe; 5

Bernice E. Ditcher; 28 July 1908; Glenn M. Ditcher, died 27 October 1917; Edna F.; Ralph and LaVern Ditcher; - ; Mrs. F. M. Green, of Mountain Home, Arkansas, wrote letter in 1932 about children.; 6

John D. Ditcher; 22 January 1894; Christopher Ditcher; - ; Glenn Ditcher; - ; - ; 40

LaVern J. Ditcher; 30 March 1911; Glenn M. Ditcher, died 27 October 1917; Edna F.; Ralph and Bernice Ditcher; - ; Mrs. F. M. Green, of Mountain Home, Arkansas, wrote letter in 1932 about children.; 6

Ralph T. Ditcher; 25 March 1907; Glenn M. Ditcher, died 27 October 1917; Edna F.; LaVern and Bernice Ditcher; - ; Mrs. F. M. Green, of Mountain Home, Arkansas, wrote letter in 1932 about children.; 6

Anna Diver; between 1887 and 1889; - ; Jane; John and William Diver; - ; G- John T. Baxter; 41

John Diver; 1884 or 1885; - ; Jane; Anna and William Diver; - ; G- John T. Baxter; 41

William Diver; 1889 or 1890; - ; Jane; Anna and John Diver; - ; G- John T. Baxter; 41

Arnold Dixon; 8 July 1908; Andrew Dixon; - ; William and Thomas Dixon; - ; worked on farm of George F. Cheek; 28

Julia Dobkowski; 3 February 1904; Alexander Cyzmanowski; Victoria; - ; HU John Dobkowski, died before March 1924; there was a cause of action against Buffalo, Rochester and Pittsburgh Railraod for death of husband, had child by March 1924; 28

Almon Carleton Dodge; 27 June 1871; Myron Dodge, died about 1883, of Olean; Myra A.; Lottie and Ruth Dodge; - ; - ; 40

Ethel M. Dodge; 10 May 1881; - ; - ; - ; HU C. I. Dodge; RE Rushford, NY, temporary G- Augusta Coxes; 5

Name; Date of Birth; Father; Mother; Siblings; Other Relatives; Notes; Box Number

George H. Dodge; 17 April 1848; Horace G. Dodge, died before December 1865; - ; - ; - ; G- Eliza Ann Dodge, of Farmersville; 75

Lottie Emma Dodge; 4 July 1877; Myron Dodge, died about 1883, of Olean; Myra A.; Almon and Ruth Dodge; - ; - ; 40

Ruth Ellen Dodge; 5 January 1880; Myron Dodge, died about 1883, of Olean; Myra A.; Almon and Lottie Dodge; - ; - ; 40

Anastatia Dollard; about 1888; Matthew P. Dollard; - ; Jane A. Dollard; - ; - ; 40

Jane A. Dollard; about 1889; Matthew P. Dollard; - ; Anastatia. Dollard; - ; - ; 40

Jennie A. Donaldson; 30 November 1897; Daniel Donaldson, died 7 April 1908; Lydia, married Edward Gerwitz; Viola Donaldson; - ; - ; 5

Nellie M. Donaldson; 17 June 1871; John Donaldson, died 11 January 1886; Laura; - ; HU Mr. Cool, PGM Mrs. Phillips (RE Wyoming County, NY), MU Andrew J. Galigar, MA Mary Galigar; G- Oscar F. Beach. There were half-aunts and half uncles on the paternal side named Phillips in Wyoming County, NY. RE 1892, in Hulberton, (Town of Murray), Orleans, NY; 40

Viola M. Donaldson; 7 September 1901; Daniel Donaldson, died 7 April 1908; Lydia, married Edward Gerwitz; Jennie Donaldson; - ; - ; 5

Gelson Donan; 3 September 1865; - ; - ; - ; - ; G- Earl Patton, Gelson's parents died before December 1913, needed guardian to enlist in Army; 75

James Donegan; - ; James Donegan, died before September 1866, of Olean, served in Co I. 154th Reg, NY Vol.; Mary, married Patrick O'Keefe; John, Mary, Thomas and Jerry Donegan and Catharine Handrahan; - ; received pension money; 75

Jerry Donegan; - ; James Donegan, died before September 1866, of Olean, served in Co I. 154th Reg, NY Vol.; Mary, married Patrick O'Keefe; John, Mary, Thomas and James Donegan and Catharine Handrahan; - ; received pension money; 75

Name; Date of Birth; Father; Mother; Siblings; Other Relatives; Notes; Box Number

John Donegan; about 1851; James Donegan, died before September 1866, of Olean, served in Co I. 154th Reg, NY Vol.; Mary, married Patrick O'Keefe; Jerry, Mary, Thomas and James Donegan and Catharine Handrahan; - ; received pension money; 75

Mary Donegan; - ; James Donegan, died before September 1866, of Olean, served in Co I. 154th Reg, NY Vol.; Mary, married Patrick O'Keefe; John, Jerry, Thomas and James Donegan and Catharine Handrahan; - ; received pension money; 75

Thomas Donegan; - ; James Donegan, died before September 1866, of Olean, served in Co I. 154th Reg, NY Vol.; Mary, married Patrick O'Keefe; John, Jerry, Mary and James Donegan and Catharine Handrahan; - ; received pension money; 75

Francis J. Donnellan; about 1903; Michael J. Donnellan; - ; Margaret Donnellan; - ; - ; 5

Margaret Donnellan; 19 February 1899; Michael J. Donnellan; - ; Francis Donnellan; - ; - ; 5

Margaret Donnelly; about 1902; John Donnelly; Mary; - ; - ; - ; 5

Aileen Donovan; about 1897; - ; - ; William, Daniel, James and Catherine Donovan; MU James M. White; father abandoned the family; 28

Catherine Donovan; about 1904; - ; - ; William, Daniel, James and Aileen Donovan; MU James M. White; father abandoned the family; 28

Daniel Donovan; about 1894; - ; - ; William, Catherine, James and Aileen Donovan; MU James M. White; father abandoned the family; 28

James Donovan; about 1900; - ; - ; William, Catherine, Daniel and Aileen Donovan; MU James M. White; father abandoned the family; 28

William Donovan; about 1892; - ; - ; William, Catherine, James and Aileen Donovan; MU James M. White; father abandoned the family; 28

Name; Date of Birth; Father; Mother; Siblings; Other Relatives; Notes; Box Number

Eliza Dooley; - ; Jeremiah Dooley, died March 1863; - ; Mary and Richard Dooley; PU William Dooley; G- John Slattery; 6

Mary Dooley;14 October 1857; Jeremiah Dooley, died March 1863; - ; Eliza and Richard Dooley; PU William Dooley; G- John Slattery; 6

Richard Dooley; 10 Feburary 1856; Jeremiah Dooley, died March 1863; - ; Eliza and Mary Dooley; PU William Dooley; G- John Slattery; 6

Frederick Dorr; 2 October 1887; - ; - ; Alva Wilson, and Lottie and Mary Dorr; PU Frank Dorr (of Bowling Green, Ohio), PU Henry Dorr; G- Fred W. Dorr; money from John Dorr Jr.'s estate; 40

Lottie Dorr; October 1882; - ; - ; Alva Wilson, and Frederick and Mary Dorr; PU Frank Dorr, of Bowling Green, Ohio, PU Henry Dorr; G- Fred W. Dorr; received money from estate of John Dorr Jr.; 40

Margaret "Maggie" Dorr; 22 November 1861; Christopher Ritzaur; Annie; - ; HU Frederick Dorr; - ; 6

Mary G. Dorr; about 1891; - ; - ; Alva Wilson, and Frederick and Lottie Dorr; PU Frank Dorr (of Bowling Green, Ohio), PU Henry Dorr; G- Fred W. Dorr; received money from estate of John Dorr Jr.; 40

Alfred J. Dougherty; 10 September 1903; Alfred J. Dougherty; Alice P.; - ; - ; - ; 5

Mildred Dow; - ; - ; - ; - ; - ; G- S. H. Seymour; 76

Leon Doyle; 13 December 1899; Thomas Doyle; Junie F.; - ; - ; - ; 40

Florence E. Draper; 29 June 1891; - ; - ; Lois Draper; HU Mr. Fielden; G- Flora E. Harmon; 28

Lois C. Draper; 19 July 1889; - ; - ; Florence Draper; HU Mr. Jewett; G- Flora E. Harmon; 28

Lottie Luella Drayer; - ; Frederick Drayer, AKA Henry F. B. Drayer; - ; Mary B. Mould, William Drayer (born about 1888), Emerson Drayer (born about 1880), Minnie Drayer (born about 1892), Mrs. Charles Waldron (born about 1882);

Name; Date of Birth; Father; Mother; Siblings; Other Relatives; Notes; Box Number

    A- Mrs. John Kelly (Lottie lived with), U- John Drayer (born about 1874), A- Mrs. George Stowell (born about 1871), U- Theodore Drayer (born about 1859), A- Mrs. John Yorch (born about 1854), U- Hubert Drayer (born about 1873); - ; 75

Ethel J. Dreaver; about 1896; - ; - ; Clark Dreaver; - ; money from pension and estates of William and Sarah Dreaver; 40

Clara Dreppensted; about 1897; - ; - ; - ; PGF Henry Dreppensted; G- Charles Nies; 40

Cephas B. Dresser; 5 July 1839; - ; - ; - ; - ; G- Heman G. Button; 75

Arthur S. Driscoll; 25 December 1883; - ; - ; Winifred Keating and Sarah, John, James and William Driscoll; GM Bridget Preston, U- James Preston; - ; 41

James B. Driscoll; 12 January 1892; - ; - ; Winifred Keating and Sarah, John, Arthur and William Driscoll; GM Bridget Preston, U- James Preston; - ; 41

John F. Driscoll; 28 August 1880; - ; - ; Winifred Keating and Sarah, Arthur, James and William Driscoll; GM Bridget Preston, U- James Preston; - ; 41

Robert E. Driscoll; 2 December 1895; - ; - ; - ; - ; G- Charles Smith, had a claim against O. W. Pierce for personal injury; 41

Sarah W. Driscoll; 31 Decmeber 1891; - ; - ; Winifred Keating and John, Arthur, James and William Driscoll; GM Bridget Preston, U- James Preston; - ; 41

William J. Driscoll;13 March 1884; - ; - ; Winifred Keating and John, Arthur, James and Sarah Driscoll; GM Bridget Preston, U- James Preston; - ; 41

Lillian Belle Drown; 27 February 1858; Oliver T. Drown, died October 1870, of Ellicottville; Harriet L; May Drown; - ; - ; 75

May Drown; about 1864; Oliver T. Drown, died October 1870, of Ellicottville; Harriet L; Lillian Drown; - ; - ; 75

John Duffy; 18 July 1910; - ; - ; Marguerite Duffy; GM Margaret

Name; Date of Birth; Father; Mother; Siblings; Other Relatives; Notes; Box Number

Kehoe; - ; 28

J. Hanford Duke; - ; Joseph Duke, died December 1884; Emily; Myron Duke; - ; G- Eugene P. Whitcomb, G- Andrew J. Applebee; 6

Myron Duke; 3 December 1875; Joseph Duke, died December 1884; Emily; J. Hanford Duke; - ; G- Eugene P. Whitcomb, G- Andrew J. Applebee; 6

Anna Dulian; 29 August 1905; Joseph Dulian, died 1929; - ; Rose Dulian; RE Rocky Crest Sanitarium (Rock City Hill) for tuberculosis, received money from Louis Dullian's life insurance; 5

Rose Dulian; 3 June 1911; Joseph Dulian, died 1929; - ; Anna Dulian; RE Buffalo, at St. Agnes Training School, received money from Louis Dullian's life insurance; 5

Alice M. Dunbar; 14 July 1864; - ; - ; Arthur W. Dunbar; PA Mrs.Henry White; father RE Military Post, Boreman, Territory of Dakota; 6

Arthur W. Dunbar; 7 September 1869; - ; - ; Alice Dunbar; PA Mrs. Henry White; father RE Fort Yates. Arthur RE November 1890, in San Francisco, California; 6

Eloise Duncan; 1 November 1904; - ; Addie; - ; - ; GF left legacy; 5

Donald Dunlavey; - ; - ; - ; - ; - ; money from John Dunlavey's estate; 75

Francis Bernard Dunlavey; 23 May 1879; - ; Mary; - ; GM Mary Harvey; - ; 40

Mabel Dunlavey; 5 September 1876; - ; Margaret; - ; - ; - ; 40

Clair J. Dunn; 9 February 1911; Patrick Dunn; Alice C.; - ; - ; RE 202 Irving St., Olean, NY; 28

Leland E. Durfee; 21 August 1900; - ; Mary G.; - ; - ; father died 29 November 1902, money from Elmer E. Durfee's estate; 28

Duncan C. Dusenberry; 21 April 1890; - ; Helen T., of Portville; Edgar and William Dusenberry; U- Edgar G. Dusenberry; father died before December 1899 ; 71

Edgar T. Dusenberry; 8 May 1885; - ; Helen T., of Portville;

Name; Date of Birth; Father; Mother; Siblings; Other Relatives; Notes; Box Number

Duncan and William Dusenberry; U- Edgar G. Dusenberry; father died before December 1899 ; 71

William A. Dusenberry; 24 September 1879; - ; Helen T., of Portville; Duncan and Edgar Dusenberry; U- Edgar G. Dusenberry; father died before December 1899 ; 71

Berlin F. Dutton; 4 July 1858; Franklin Dutton; Catherine Wait, married Mr. Sibling; Franklin B. Dutton; MGM Irene Hubbard, MU John Wait, MA Abbey Wyman, MA Almina Green; - ; 6

Franklin B. Dutton; 25 January 1860; Franklin Dutton; Catherine Wait, married Mr. Sibling: Berlin Dutton; MGM Irene Hubbard, MU John Wait, MA Abbey Wyman, MA Almina Green; - ; 6

Gertrude Dutton; 17 November 1886 ; Thomas Dutton; - ; James, Joseph, Margaret, Mary, Peter and Thomas Dutton; - ; - ; 5

James Dutton; 5 July 1881; Thomas Dutton; - ; Gertrude, Joseph, Margaret, Mary, Peter and Thomas Dutton; - ;   - ; 5

Joseph Dutton; 13 November 1893; Thomas Dutton; - ; Gertrude, James, Margaret, Mary, Peter and Thomas Dutton; - ; - ; 5

Margaret Dutton; 29 January 1892; Thomas Dutton; - ; Gertrude, James, Joseph, Mary, Peter and Thomas Dutton; - ; - ; 5

Mary Dutton; 13 April 1883; Thomas Dutton; - ; Gertrude, James, Joseph, Margaret, Peter and Thomas Dutton; - ; - ; 5

Peter Dutton; 11 July 1890; Thomas Dutton; - ; Gertrude, James, Joseph, Margaret, Mary and Thomas Dutton; - ; - ; 5

Sally Ann Dutton; July 1845; Ransom Dutton, died before November 1854; Harriet S., of Freedom; - ; - ; - ; 75

Thomas Dutton; 22 July 1884; Thomas Dutton; - ; Gertrude, James, Joseph, Margaret, Mary and Peter Dutton; - ; - ; 5

Nellie B. Dye; 3 September 1868; Nathan A. Dye; - ; Mason M. Dye; - ; - ; 6

Belle Dyer; 22 May 1870; - ; - ; - ; HU Mr. Witter, MU Nelson I. and Mary E. Norton; - ; 6

Name; Date of Birth; Father; Mother; Siblings; Other Relatives; Notes; Box Number

E Surnames

Adaline Earl; about 1865; William Earl, died April 1869, of Salamanca, served in the 37th NY Reg.; - ; Frederick Earl; HU Wilbur J. Stebbins (married 9 October 1881 and later separated), MGF Chester B. Starks, PG Lewis and Ann Earl, U- Isaac Winship, U- Charles Winship, U- Fred Starks, U-Wesley Starks, U- J. W. Starks, U- Alfred Earl, U- Thomas Earl, A- Adaline Winship, A- Evaline Winship, A- Malissa Starks, A- Alyeretta Starks; G- Horace Woodsworth; 60

Frederick " Fred" Earl; 23 August 1859; William Earl, died April 1869, of Salamanca, served in the 37th NY Reg.; - ; Adaline Earl; MGF Chester B. Starks, PG Lewis and Ann Earl, U- Isaac Winship, U- Charles Winship, U- Fred Starks, U- Wesley Starks, U- J. W. Starks, U- Alfred Earl, U- Thomas Earl, A- Adaline Winship, A- Evaline Winship, A- Malissa Starks, A- Alyeretta Starks; G- Horace Woodsworth; 60

Lillian Easterly; 22 March 1892; Henry Easterly, died 11 November 1894, in Cumberland County, Tenn.; Bertha, married Mr. Snyder and lived in Yorkshire; - ; HU Mr. Tollett, GM Huldah Easterly, U-Price Easterly (of Hamlet, Chautauqua, NY). Eugene Patterson was related to Huldah, and lived in Devereaux, NY; Lillian RE Crab Orchard, Cumberland, Tenn., Henry and Bertha Easterly divorced; 41

Norman F. Eastman; 7 March 1818; John Eastman, died before April 1836, of Bennington County, Vermont; - ; William Eastman; - ; G- John Perkins; 77

William Eastman; 20 February 1820; John Eastman, died before April 1836, of Bennington County, Vermont; - ; Norman Eastman; - ; G- John Perkins; 77

Hazel L. Easton; 1 June 1900; - ; Ellen J.; Ruby and Nina Easton; - ; - ; 41

Nina B. Easton; 22 February 1891; - ; Ellen J.; Ruby and Hazel Easton; - ; - ; 41

Name; Date of Birth; Father; Mother; Siblings; Other Relatives; Notes; Box Number

Ruby P. Easton; 4 January 1897; - ; Ellen J.; Nina and Hazel Easton; - ; - ; 41

Tappan S. Eaton; 5 January 1863; Tappan E. Eaton, died in U.S. Service; Emma M, married Almon Bonesteel on 12 December 1865; - ; - ; RE 1884, Corry, Erie, Pennsylvania, Tappan received pension money; 7

John Eberhardt; 17 March 1887; - ; - ; - ; - ; G- Sylvester E. Ford, Lizzie Eberhardt left John a legacy; 7

Esther L. Eberhart; about 1910; - ; Susie M. Casey; - ; MG Charles W. and Martha Casey; - ; 30

Ethel E. Eddy; - ; - ; - ; - ; - ; G- Enos Eddy; 75

Virginia Freeman Eddy; 25 September 1898; Lorin L. Eddy, left a widow who went by name of Rosalie B. Cronin; - ; - ; - ; RE Arlington, Middlesex, Massachusetts, received legacy from Elvira L. Eddy, Virginia's guardianship papers were filed in Middlesex County, Mass, and copies are in Cattaraugus County Surrogate Office; 42

Dorothy Edel; 10 April 1904; - ; Catherine, married Mr. Yeager; Lillian Edel; HU Mr. Sellinger; - ; 7

Lillian Edel; 2 October 1905; - ; Catherine, married Mr. Yeager; Dorothy Edel; - ; - ; 7

Clarence L. Edick; 11 March 1877; Andrew J. Edick; - ; - ; U- Cyrus W. Ingersoll; RE 1898, in Villanova, Chautauqua, NY, mother died 4 July 1885, money from Mary Ann Markham's estate; 41

Arthur E. Edmonds; 15 March 1881; Fred Edmonds; - ; - ; PGM Lavaca (wife of Eleazer Fairbanks, of Fawn River, Michigan), GU- William H. Barrett who is Lavancha's brother; - ; 41

Burrett Edmunds; about 1859; Austin Edmunds, died before June 1865; Jane; Ellen, Chester and Emily Edmunds; PG Salem and Ruth Edmunds, MGM Sally Deming, A- Esther Deming, A- Betsey Noldes, U- Thomas Demming, U- Joseph Demming; - ; 75

Chester Edmunds; about 1856; Austin Edmunds, died before

Name; Date of Birth; Father; Mother; Siblings; Other Relatives; Notes; Box Number

June 1865; Jane; Ellen, Burrett and Emily Edmunds; PG Salem and Ruth Edmunds, MGM Sally Deming, A- Esther Deming, A- Betsey Noldes, U- Thomas Demming, U- Joseph Demming; - ; 75

Ellen Edmunds; about 1852; Austin Edmunds, died before June 1865; Jane; Chester, Burrett and Emily Edmunds; PG Salem and Ruth Edmunds, MGM Sally Deming, A- Esther Deming, A- Betsey Noldes, U- Thomas Demming, U- Joseph Demming; - ; 75

Emily Edmunds; about 1854; Austin Edmunds, died before June 1865; Jane; Chester, Burrett and Ellen Edmunds; PG Salem and Ruth Edmunds, MGM Sally Deming, A- Esther Deming, A- Betsey Noldes, U- Thomas Demming, U- Joseph Demming; - ; 75

Florence Edwards; 21 January 1903; - ; Alice; - ; HU Mr. Pringle; G- Irving E. Worden, received money from grandfather estate and father's life insurance policy; 30

Leister Eells; 27 June 1848; - ; - ; - ; - ; G- William H. Eells, of Perrysburg; 75

Florence Eglington; 7 September 1904; - ; Eliza, married Mr. Yarnell; John Eglington; - ; father resided in Toronto, Canada; 49

John Amos Eglington; 3 January 1906; - ; Eliza, married Mr. Yarnell; Florence Eglington; - ; father resided in Toronto, Canada; 49

Iva Ehman; 13 March 1902; Frank Ehman; - ; Laurena Ehman; - ; - ; 30

Laurena Ehman; 9 August 1900; Frank Ehman; - ; Iva Ehman; - ; also seen as Lorena Ehman; 30

Coletta Eisert; about 1896; George Eisert; Anna; George and Rose Eisert; - ; - ; 41

George Eisert; - ; George Eisert; Anna; Coletta and Rose Eisert; - ; - ; 41

Rose Eisert; - ; George Eisert; Anna; Coletta and George Eisert; - ; - ; 41

Name; Date of Birth; Father; Mother; Siblings; Other Relatives; Notes; Box Number

Charles Edward Eldridge; 20 February 1898; - ; - ; - ; - ; mother died 18 February 1905, father died 10 August 1903, RE 203 Knight St., Olean, G- Herbert C. Perkins, and Charles joined National Guard; 30

Clara E. Eldridge; 5 July 1853; Daniel J. Eldridge, died before May 1864; Martha Crook; Francis, Ophelia and Lemuel Eldridge; MGF Charles Crook, of Salamanca; - ; 75

Francis D. Eldridge; 5 January 1857; Daniel J. Eldridge, died before May 1864; Martha Crook; Clara, Ophelia and Lemuel Eldridge; MGF Charles Crook, of Salamanca; - ; 75

Ophelia Eldridge; 17 January 1846; Daniel J. Eldridge, died before May 1864; Martha Crook; Clara, Francis and Lemuel Eldridge; MGF Charles Crook, of Salamanca; - ; 75

Lemuel S. Eldridge; 3 May 1847; Daniel J. Eldridge, died before May 1864; Martha Crook; Clara, Francis and Ophelia Eldridge; MGF Charles Crook, of Salamanca; - ; 75

Howard Ransom Elliott; 20 August 1901; - ; Margaret; - ; - ; RE 1923, Sturgeon Bay, Door, Wisconsin; 30

Cecile Elliott; about 1897; Robert M. Elliott; - ; Gladys Elliott Whiting; - ; - ; 36

Claude M. Elliott; about 1901; Robert M. Elliott; - ; - ; - ; - ; 41

Lucy P. Elliott; about 1832; David P. Elliott; - ; - ; - ; G- James Borden; 7

Burt E. Ellis; about 1859; John D. Ellis, died July 1868; Elizabeth A.; - ; only other relatives were Henry, Giles and John Ellis; G- William H. Ellis; 7

Minnie Ellis; 15 June 1867; - ; Sophia, her last name at time of petition was Louis; - ; HU Will A. Ellis; - ; 7

Pearle Ellis; - ; - ; - ; - ; - ; - ; Box 75

Shelon W Ellis; - ; Reuben H. Ellis, of Beaverdam, Dodge, Wisconsin; - ; - ; - ; - ; 77

Anna Marie Ellithorpe; 12 September 1890; Millard J. Ellithorpe; - ; - ; - ; - ; 41

Alberta A. Elwell; 1 July 1859; Michael E. Elwell, died before December 1865; - ; Maria E. Boorn; U- Joseph Peaslee, U-

Name; Date of Birth; Father; Mother; Siblings; Other Relatives; Notes; Box Number

Daniel Peaslee, A- Elizabeth Peaslee, A- Syntha Peaslee; - ; 75

Vangie Elwell; 30 November 1882; - ; Ettie, married Henry Ackler between 1892 and 1894, and married Mr. Brown by 1903; - ; HU Mr. Peters; money from Josiah Elwell's estate; 41

Carrie G. Ely; 24 July 1887; Charles Gage, lived in New Jersey; AM Caroline; - ; AF William Ely, of Franklinville; received money from estate of Harrison Vaughn; 71

Clara M. Emerson; 13 July 1875; - ; Sarah C.; Lowell and Lovinia Emerson; - ; received money from estate of William F. Emerson, who died 10 July 1893; 41

Lovinia E. Emerson; 15 March 1886; - ; Sarah C.; Lowell and Clara Emerson; - ; received money from estate of William F. Emerson, who died 10 July 1893; 41

Lowell C. Emerson; 6 November 1879; - ; Sarah C.; Lovinia and Clara Emerson; - ; received money from estate of William F. Emerson, who died 10 July 1893; 41

Alfred M. Enders; 20 June 1911; - ; Nina; William W. Buffin, Celia, Charles, William, Mildred, Louis, and Isabella Enders; - ; - ; 41

Celia Enders; 14 May 1902; - ; Nina; William W. Buffin, Charles, William, Mildred, Louis, and Isabella Enders; - ; - ; 41

Charles Enders; 14 February 1900; - ; Nina; William W. Buffin, Celia, William, Mildred, Louis, and Isabella Enders; - ; - ; 41

Isabella Enders; 19 June 1895; - ; Nina; William W. Buffin, Celia, William, Mildred, Louis, and Charles Enders; - ; - ; 41

Louis Enders; 18 April 1897; - ; Nina; William W. Buffin, Celia, William, Mildred, Isabella, and Charles Enders; - ; - ; 41

Mildred Enders; 20 September 1904; - ; Nina; William W. Buffin, Celia, William, Louis, Isabella, and Charles Enders; - ; - ; 41

Name; Date of Birth; Father; Mother; Siblings; Other Relatives; Notes; Box Number

William J. Enders; 29 September 1908; - ; Nina; William W. Buffin, Celia, Mildred, Louis, Isabella, and Charles Enders; - ; - ; 41

Berger Engblom; 6 January 1893; - ; - ; Frank Engblom; C- Clara C. Nordine; - ; 42

Frank Engblom; 20 March 1894; - ; - ; Berger Engblom; C- Clara C. Nordine; - ; 42

George Leonard Enos; - ; Silas F. Enos; - ; - ; - ; G- David Flagg; 30

Emma Erhart; about 1882; - ; Mary; Grace Erhart; U- Lewis Erhart; - ; 30

Grace Erhart; about 1886; - ; Mary; Emma Erhart; U- Lewis Erhart; - ; 30

Julia Erhart; about 1860; - ; - ; Lewis and Leo Erhart; - ; G- George Strahuber; 7

Leo Erhart; about 1858; - ; - ; Lewis and Julia Erhart; - ; G- George Strahuber; 7

Lewis Erhart; about 1856; - ; - ; Leo and Julia Erhart; - ; G- George Strahuber; 7

Leslie J. Ernest; 31 July 1900; - ; Christina; William Ernest; - ; - ; 41

William J. Ernest; 29 April 1896; - ; Christina; Leslie Ernest; - ; - ; 41

Tina M. Essensa; 24 October 1896; Frank Miller, RE Coryville, Pennslyvania; - ; - ; HU Hedley A. Essensa, died 14 March 1918, result of a wreck in Portageville, NY; RE 302 S. 8th St., Olean; 41

Earl J. Essex; 15 November 1869; Cyrenius B. Essex, died between 1886 and 1887; - ; Mary Darbee; GM Martha M. Sweeten, U- Wallace B. Sweeten (of Altoona, Dakota), U- John Sweeten (of Portville), U- Marshall Sweeten (of Gerry, NY), A- Deliah Charlesworth (of Adrian, MO), A- Calphernia Morris (of Allegany), A- Elnora Miller (of Fredonia), A- Lavantia Essex (of Franklinville), C- Lillie Moscriss; - ; 7

Name; Date of Birth; Father; Mother; Siblings; Other Relatives; Notes; Box Number

William Essner; 18 December 1880; - ; - ; - ; - ; G- John E. Wheeler; 41

Frank Evans; 25 October 1878; Wm. H. Evans; - ; Fred Evans; MG Evan and Margarett Owens, of Centerville, Allegany, NY, file mentions Elizabeth Evans, who died 15 April 1886 in Farmersville; 41

Fred Evans; 18 July 1880; Wm. H. Evans; - ; Frank Evans; MG Evan and Margarett Owens, of Centerville, Allegany, NY, file mentions Elizabeth Evans, who died 15 April 1886 in Farmersville; 41

Irene D. Evans; 20 April 1912; Harry E. Evans; - ; Ruth Evans; MGF Fred O. Langworthy; - ; 41

Jessie Mary Evans; 10 December 1893; - ; - ; - ; A- Elizabeth Austin; file mentions Morris F. Evans; 41

John B. Evans; 9 May 1862; - ; Sarah, married Mr. Reese; - ; - ; - ; 7

Mamie B. Evans; about 1888; David H. Evans; Mary J.; Sadie, William and John Evans, and Anna Bessey; - ; - ; 41

Ruth E. Evans; 1 August 1910; Harry E. Evans; - ; Irene Evans; MGF Fred O. Langworthy; - ; 41

Sadie J. Evans; about 1886; David H. Evans; Mary J.; Mamie, William and John Evans, and Anna Bessey; - ; - ; 41

Eleanor C. Evens; 28 March 1861; Evander Evens, died before July 1864; Betsey E., died 12 June 1864; Francis and Sylvester Evens; PU Sylvester R. Evens; received pension money; 75

Francis J. Evens; 30 March 1859; Evander Evens, died before July 1864; Betsey E., died 12 June 1864; Eleanor and Sylvester Evens; PU Sylvester R. Evens; received pension money; 75

Sylvester R. Evens; 3 July 1857; Evander Evens, died before July 1864; Betsey E., died 12 June 1864; Francis and Eleanor Evens; PU Sylvester R. Evens; received pension money; 75

Ruth E. Everts; about 1877; AF Orsemus Everts; - ; - ; HU David Davies, GF Ephraim S. Arnold, U- William Arnold; - ; 41

Name; Date of Birth; Father; Mother; Siblings; Other Relatives; Notes; Box Number

F Surnames

Allen Failing; 13 October 1835; Charles Failing, died before March 1850; Emily Daniels; Emily Failing; MGF Samuel Daniels, MU Joseph Daniels, MU Samuel Daniels, A-Betsey, (W- of Frederick Noyes); - ; 74

Emily Failing; 4 March 1839; Charles Failing, died before March 1850; Emily Daniels; Allen Failing; MGF Samuel Daniels, MU Joseph Daniels, MU Samuel Daniels, A-Betsey, (W- of Frederick Noyes); - ; 74

Daisy Fairchild; January 1907; James W. Fairchild, died 21 or 22 January 1909, editor of "Portville Review"; - ; - ; MG Mr. and Mrs. Amos Parsons, PGM R. Rosalia Fairchild (born about 1847, Daisy had lived with her since birth), PU Fred W. Fairchild (born about 1873), PU Bruce Fairchild (born about 1871), PU Lewis L. Fairchild (born about 1875), PU Robert E. Fairchild (born about 1880), PA Mary A. Fairchild (born about 1878), PA Florence Fairchild (born about 1887), PA Nellie S. Fairchild (born about 1890), MA Orville A. Eastman (Clarksville, Allegany, NY); mother died 17 January 1907; 7

Florence M. Fairchild; November 1886; James H. Fairchild, died 5 March 1906, in Portville; Rose; Nellie, Bruce, Fred, Mary, Robert and James Fairchild; niece was Ella Swetland, nephew was Henry E. Denning, A- Mrs. M. D. Fairchild; - ; 42

Mildred H. Fairchild; about 1893; - ; - ; Bertha Fairchild; - ; needed guardian to receive pension money; 42

Nellie S. Fairchild; July 1889; James H. Fairchild, died 5 March 1906, in Portville; Rose; James, Bruce, Fred, Mary, Robert and James Fairchild; niece was Ella Swetland, nephew was Henry E. Denning, A- Mrs. M. D. Fairchild; - ; 42

Muriel Falconer; 23 August 1888; Charles Falconer; Elizabeth J.; - ; - ; received money from estate of Eunice A. Green; 41

Name; Date of Birth; Father; Mother; Siblings; Other Relatives; Notes; Box Number

John E. Fancher; March 1879; Charles Fancher; - ; Lynn Fancher; - ; - ; 7

Lynn C. Fancher; March 1881; Charles Fancher; - ; John Fancher; - ; - ; 7

Frank M. Farley; about 1882; - ; Ann; Georgiana, Harry, Leon, Julia and Kathryn Farley; - ; - ; 41

Georgiana "George" Farley; about 1883; - ; Ann; Frank, Harry, Leon, Julia and Kathryn Farley; - ; RE 1914, in Buffalo, NY ; 41

Harry Farley; about 1888; - ; Ann; Georgiana, Frank, Leon, Julia and Kathryn Farley; - ; - ; 41

Kathryn "Katie" Farley; about 1880; - ; Ann; Frank, Harry, Leon, Julia and Georgiana Farley; HU Mr. English, HU Mr. Hollis; RE 1914, in Brooklyn, NY ; 41

Julia Farley; about 1894; - ; Ann; Georgiana, Frank, Leon, Harry and Kathryn Farley; - ; - ; 41

Leon J. Farley; about 1891; - ; Ann; Georgiana, Frank, Julia, Harry and Kathryn Farley; - ; - ; 41

Edith Farnum; 14 March 1886; A. H. Farnum, died before November 1895; Josephine; Gertrude, Maude, Jennie, Willie and Ellen Farnum; - ; - ; 42

Ellen Farnum; 16 July 1887; A. H. Farnum, died before November 1895; Josephine; Gertrude, Maude, Jennie, Willie and Edith Farnum; - ; - ; 42

Gertrude Farnum; 15 June 1879; A. H. Farnum, died before November 1895; Josephine; Ellen, Maude, Jennie, Willie and Edith Farnum; - ; - ; 42

Jennie Farnum; 14 March 1880; A. H. Farnum, died before November 1895; Josephine; Ellen, Maude, Gertrude, Willie and Edith Farnum; - ; - ; 42

Maude Farnum; 22 May 1875; A. H. Farnum, died before November 1895; Josephine; Ellen, Jennie, Gertrude, Willie and Edith Farnum; - ; - ; 42

Willie Farnum; 14 June 1891; A. H. Farnum, died before November 1895; Josephine; Ellen, Jennie, Gertrude, Maude

Name; Date of Birth; Father; Mother; Siblings; Other Relatives; Notes; Box Number

and Edith Farnum; - ; - ; 42

Willie Farnum; 20 June 1889; - ; - ; Ella F. Shorts and Edith Farnum; - ; G- A. D. Bedell, and in same envelope with Jennie, Gertrude, Maude, Edith, Willie and Ellen Farnum; 42

Luna Farrar; August 1847; Royal C. Farrar, of Machias; - ; - ; - ; - ; 74

Ellen F. Farrington; 13 December 1885; Edward H. Farrington, of Franklinville; Sarah; Irving, F. Vernal, Forrest, Harry and Howard Farrington; - ; - ; 72

F. Vernal Farrington; 22 December 1891; Edward H. Farrington, of Franklinville; Sarah; Irving, Ellen, Forrest, Harry and Howard Farrington; - ; - ; 72

Forrest F. Farrington; 11 February 1894; Edward H. Farrington, of Franklinville; Sarah; Irving, Ellen, F. Vernal, Harry and Howard Farrington; - ; - ; 72

Harry B. Farrington; 4 July 1883; Edward H. Farrington, of Franklinville; Sarah; Irving, Ellen, F. Vernal, Forrest and Howard Farrington; - ; - ; 72

Howard P. Farrington; 22 November 1881; Edward H. Farrington, of Franklinville; Sarah; Irving, Ellen, F. Vernal, Forrest and Harry Farrington; - ; - ; 72

Daniel G. Farwell; 8 October 1885; Abram M. Farwell; - ; Mabel, Eugene and Elizabeth Farwell; - ; - ; 42

Elizabeth D. Farwell; 12 October 1874; Abram M. Farwell; - ; Mabel, Eugene and Daniel Farwell; - ; - ; 42

Eugene B. Farwell; 20 May 1871; Abram M. Farwell; - ; Mabel, Elizabeth and Daniel Farwell; - ; - ; 42

Helen N. Farwell; 24 August 1902; Arthur M. Farwell; Flora A.; - ; - ; - ; 7

Mabel P. Farwell; 13 April 1879; Abram M. Farwell; - ; Eugene, Elizabeth and Daniel Farwell; - ; - ; 42

Margaret Faurquharson; 5 April 1870; - ; - ; - ; A- Sarah C. Howard; G- J. Eugene Van Deusen; 7

Elsie M. Fay; 14 January 1868; Cyrus M. Fay; Ellen; - ; - ; - ; 42

James S. Fay; 28 May 1849; Warren R. Fay, died before

Name; Date of Birth; Father; Mother; Siblings; Other Relatives; Notes; Box Number

December 1865; - ; - ; - ; G- Jonas K. Button; 75

Albert Fee; 2 May 1862; Owen Fee, died June 1862; Catherine, married Mr. Sera; James, Charles, and Eugene Fee; - ; received pension money; 8

Frances G. Fee; 25 June 1887; Eugene Fee; Nellie I.; James Fee and Margaret Banson; - ; - ; 7

James Fee; 11 February 1860; Owen Fee, died June 1862; Catherine, married Mr. Sera; Albert, Charles, and Eugene Fee; - ; received pension money; 8

Clara Lenore Fegley; - ; Jessiah Fegley; Lena M.; Jesse Fegley; - ; - ; 7

Jesse C. Fegley; 2 Dec 1906; Jessiah Fegley; Lena M.; Clara Fegley; - ; RE 1928, in Rochester, NY; 7

George Felch; 9 September 1841; Eli S. Felch, died before September 1859; Mary; Perry, Sullivan and John Felch; - ; G- Daniel Brown; 75

John Felch; 29 December 1843; Eli S. Felch, died before September 1859; Mary; Perry, Sullivan and George Felch; - ; died 17 October 1864 in Savannah, Georgia, G- Daniel Brown; 75

Sullivan Felch; 16 August 1846; Eli S. Felch, died before September 1859; Mary; Perry, John, and John Felch; - ; G- Daniel Brown; 75

Francis Horth Fellows; - ; - ; - ; - ; - ; married name is Fellows, G- Andrew C. Rickars, see box 46 under Frances Horth; 43

Addie A. Felt; about 1860; Mr. Ciples ; Abigail, died 1 May 1860; - ; HU Mr. Felt, GF William Valkenbury or Valkenburg (died 30 January 1878, he left estate in La Porte, Indiana); - ; 8

Clement Felt; 3 August 1893; John Felt; Agnes, died 6 September 1910, she was pregnant at time of her death; Coletta Felt; - ; - ; 8

Coletta M. Felt; 8 February 1891; John Felt; Agnes, died 6 September 1910, she was pregnant at time of her death; Clement Felt; - ; - ; 8

Name; Date of Birth; Father; Mother; Siblings; Other Relatives; Notes; Box Number

Erie E. Fenton; 1 July 1859; - ; - ; - ; - ; first G- Melvin A. Crowley, second G- Reuben Fenton (of Jamestown); 8

George Fenton; April 1872; - ; - ; - ; - ; file in with George, Mary, Seth and Joseph Fenton; 42

George W. Fenton; 2 September 1851; Charles Fenton; step-mom was Annie; Mary, Seth and Joseph Fenton; PGF John A. Fenton, U- Henry Blackmere; G- Matthew Murphy; 42

Joseph Fenton; 6 June 1866; Charles Fenton; step-mom was Annie; Mary, Seth and George Fenton; PGF John A. Fenton, U- Henry Blackmere; G- Matthew Murphy; 42

Leo Fenton; 23 November 1901; Joseph Fenton; Rill, married Mr. Gillmaster and moved to Monroeville, Ohio; - ; PU Seth Fenton, PU George Fenton; Joseph Fenton's estate settled in Erie County, Ohio; 8

Mary Fenton; April 1873; - ; - ; - ; - ; file in with George, Mary, Seth and Joseph Fenton; 42

Mary Fenton; 28 July 1855; Charles Fenton; step-mom was Annie; George, Seth and George Fenton; PGF John A. Fenton, U- Henry Blackmere; G- Matthew Murphy; 42

Mary Myrtle Fenton; 1 February 1891; - ; - ; William Fenton, U- Eugene Lawler; G- George A. Fox, received money from life insurance on Bridget Fenton; 42

Maude L. Fenton; 1 January 1875; George W. Fenton; - ; - ; - ; - ; 8

Seth Fenton; July 1875; Charles Fenton; step-mom was Annie; George, Mary and George Fenton; PGF John A. Fenton, U- Henry Blackmere; G- Matthew Murphy; 42

William Clarence Fenton; 10 May 1886; - ; - ; William Fenton, U- Eugene Lawler; G- George A. Fox, received money from life insurance on Bridget Fenton; 42

Helen Louise Feutcher; 8 May 1905; - ; - ; Fred Feutcher, Emma K. Thompson and Mary Sullivan; - ; file also mentions a Charles Feutcher; 42

Velma E. Fie; 8 February 1909; Albert C. Crotzer; Fannie E., RE 532 N. 8th St., Olean; - ; HU William Fie, had a child by 29

Name; Date of Birth; Father; Mother; Siblings; Other Relatives; Notes; Box Number

December 1927; - ; 42

Bell Findlay; 1 August 1869; John E. Findlay, lived in Denver, Colorado; - ; - ; A- Mrs. Charles Taylor; mother died about 1871; 7

Albert Fingerlos; about 1895; - ; Ina, married Mr. Parker; Clara, Arthur and Clinton Fingerlos; - ; an heir of Wm. Fingerlos, other heirs are George and Fred Fingerlos; 43

Arthur Fingerlos; about 1892; - ; Ina, married Mr. Parker; Clara, Albert and Clinton Fingerlos; - ; an heir of Wm. Fingerlos, other heirs are George and Fred Fingerlos; 43

Clara Fingerlos; about 1898; - ; Ina, married Mr. Parker; Arthur, Albert and Clinton Fingerlos; - ; an heir of Wm. Fingerlos, other heirs are George and Fred Fingerlos; 43

Clinton Fingerlos; about 1900; - ; Ina, married Mr. Parker; Arthur, Albert and Clara Fingerlos; - ; an heir of Wm. Fingerlos, other heirs are George and Fred Fingerlos; 43

M. Nettie Finley; 29 July 1860; - ; Jane M, married a Mr. Paisley; - ; HU Mr. Ames; - ; 8

Catherine Finn; 1 Jan 1903; - ; - ; Richard, Delia and Mary Finn; - ; Edward Finn was a deceased brother, whose Government War Insurance she received, she RE in St. Elizabeth's Convent; 7

Henry H. Firman; 1 October 1838; - ; - ; - ; - ; G- Harrison Firman; 75

Ethel A. Fischer; - ; - ; Alta; - ; - ; RE 1912, in Erie, Erie, Pennsylvania ; 42

George N. Fish; 16 March 1879; Harrison Fish; Rosaltha; William Fish; - ; - ; 42

Herbert E. Fish; 3 September 1875; M. Herrick Fish; Emma F.; Jennie Fish; - ; G- Edwin Baker, no relation; 42

Jennie May Fish; 11 November 1877; M. Herrick Fish; Emma F.; Herbert Fish; - ; G- Edwin Baker, no relation; 42

William S. Fish; 19 August 1881; Harrison Fish; Rosaltha; George Fish; - ; - ; 42

Allen H. Fisher; - ; George Fisher, died in Kill Buck; - ; - ; - ; - ;

Name; Date of Birth; Father; Mother; Siblings; Other Relatives; Notes; Box Number

72

Anna Fisher; about 1867; John Fisher, died April 1877, of Ashford; Eva; Jacob, Catherine, Charles, Caroline and John Fisher; GM Isabel Ziedel, U- Jacob Ulmer; - ; 42

Caroline Fisher; - ; John Fisher, died April 1877, of Ashford; Eva; Jacob, Catherine, Charles, Anna and John Fisher; GM Isabel Ziedel, U- Jacob Ulmer; - ; 42

Catherine Fisher; about 1874; John Fisher, died April 1877, of Ashford; Eva; Jacob, Caroline, Charles, Anna and John Fisher; GM Isabel Ziedel, U- Jacob Ulmer; - ; 42

Charles Fisher; about 1869; John Fisher, died April 1877, of Ashford; Eva; Jacob, Caroline, Catherine, Anna and John Fisher; GM Isabel Ziedel, U- Jacob Ulmer; - ; 42

Edith Fisher; 20 January 1892; Charles Fisher; - ; - ; - ; G- Joseph Burmaster, in her file there is a receipt that a note was paid to the Lutheran Church, in Plato, NY.; 8

Harold Fisher; 7 June 1902; Samuel Fisher; - ; - ; - ; - ; 8

Jacob Fisher; about 1865; John Fisher, died April 1877, of Ashford; Eva; Charles, Caroline, Catherine, Anna and John Fisher; GM Isabel Ziedel, U- Jacob Ulmer; - ; 42

John Fisher; - ; John Fisher, died April 1877, of Ashford; Eva; Charles, Caroline, Catherine, Anna and Jacob Fisher; GM Isabel Ziedel, U- Jacob Ulmer; - ; 42

Montrose H. Fisher; about 1850; Harmon Fisher, died 29 November 1862, of Little Valley; Nancy H., of New Albion, married Mr. Dye; Nancy I. Fisher; other relatives are Dorcas Puddy, Harvey J. Fisher and Eleanor Ellis; AKA Harmon M. Fisher, he has two envelopes, one under Harmon Fisher and one under Montrose Fisher; 75

Nancy I. Fisher; about 1863; Harmon Fisher, died 29 November 1862, of Little Valley; Nancy H., of New Albion, married Mr. Dye; Montrose. Fisher; other relatives are Dorcas Puddy, Harvey J. Fisher and Eleanor Ellis; - ; 75

Nina M. Fisher; 14 October 1898 or 1899; Joel M. Fisher, committed suicide; - ; Otis and Zana Fisher; A- Clara May

Name; Date of Birth; Father; Mother; Siblings; Other Relatives; Notes; Box Number

Fisher, and other relatives are Olive Young, Mabel Mann and Theodore Stoddard; Nina was was "somewhat deaf", lived with Mabel Mann, Nina received money from estate of Leon J. Fisher; 41

Otis K. Fisher; 13 December 1904; Joel M. Fisher, committed suicide; - ; Nina and Zana Fisher; A- Clara May Fisher, and other relatives are Olive Young, Mabel Mann and Theodore Stoddard; lived with Nina Fisher after 4 May 1916, Otis received money from estate of Leon J. Fisher; 41

Zana L. Fisher; 22 July 1907; Joel M. Fisher, committed suicide; - ; Nina and OtisFisher; A- Clara May Fisher, and other relatives are Olive Young, Mabel Mann and Theodore Stoddard; lived with Walter West after 4 May 1916, Zana received money from estate of Leon J. Fisher; 41

Mabel Fisk; 10 June 1899; Merle W. Fisk; - ; - ; MGF Horace Brown, died 2 September 1904, of Cherry Creek; - ; 43

Norman C. Fisk; 1 August 1848; - ; Betsey A., of Lyndon, married Mr. Seely; - ; - ; father died before November 1859, G- Silas S. Seely; 74

Adda Fitch; - ; Asaph Fitch, died June 1865, of Franklinville; Caroline; Emma Fitch; - ; - ; 74

Cynthia M. Fitch; 19 January 1895; - ; Laura; - ; - ; - ; 42

Emma Fitch; about 1853; Asaph Fitch, died June 1865, of Franklinville; Caroline; Adda Fitch; - ; - ; 74

Frank Fitch; - ; - ; - ; - ; - ; G- Daniel Brown, in same envelope as George Fitch; 75

George Fitch; - ; - ; - ; - ; - ; G- Daniel Brown, in same envelope as Frank Fitch; 75

Anna Fitzgerald; 13 March 1902; Michael Fitzgerald; Mary; Helen and Edward Fitzgerald; PA Anna McCabe; baptism in Austin, Pennsylvania by Rev. O'Brien, christening name was Bridget, inherited money from insurance from Ladies Catholic Benevolent Assoc.; 8

Edward Fitzgerald; 8 February 1901; Michael Fitzgerald; Mary; Helen and Anna Fitzgerald; PA Anna McCabe; inherited

Name; Date of Birth; Father; Mother; Siblings; Other Relatives; Notes; Box Number

money from insurance from Ladies Catholic Benevolent Assoc.; 8

Helen Fitzgerald; 8 January 1898; Michael Fitzgerald; Mary; Edward and Anna Fitzgerald; PA Anna McCabe; RE Sisters of Good Sheperd in Buffalo, NY, inherited money from insurance from Ladies Catholic Benevolent Assoc.; 8

Julia Fitzgerald;13 September 1898; Owen Fitzgerald; Bridget; Nicholas Fitzgerald, of Mendora, Mercer, Ohio; 7

Sarah Virginia Fitzpatrick; 22 December 1909; Malachy G. Fitzpatrick; Mary F.; Mildred Davis and Mary Fitzpatrick; - ; attended Syracuse University; 42

Leonarda Marinda Mary Flagg; - ; - ; - ; - ; G- Irma Flagg, only bond is in file; 43

Mattie A. Flagg; 3 May 1859; - ; Ann Cline, died October 1866; - ; MGF John W. Cline, MA Maryette Frants (W- of Edward Frants), MA Lucinda Kerr, PU William Flagg; - ; 8

Katie Flyte; 4 April 1872; - ; - ; - ; HU Mr. Benhan, PU Alfred Flyte, U- Jacob Flyte, U- George Flyte, A- Sarah Job; RE August 1888 in Portville; April 1893 RE Cuba; 8

Edward Fobes; 28 January 1864; George N. Fobes, died before 17 August 1881; Amanda; George, Mary, Frederick, and Walter Fobes; - ; - ; 42

Frederick D. Fobes; 26 January 1873; George N. Fobes, died before 17 August 1881; Amanda; George, Mary, Edward, and Walter Fobes; - ; - ; 42

George Fobes; 2 April 1865 or 1866; George N. Fobes, died before 17 August 1881; Amanda; Frederick, Mary, Edward, and Walter Fobes; - ; - ; 42

Mary Clara Fobes; 29 July 1868; George N. Fobes, died before 17 August 1881; Amanda; George, Frederick, Edward, and Walter Fobes; - ; - ; 42

Walter Fobes; 9 January 1875 or 1876; George N. Fobes, died before 17 August 1881; Amanda; George, Frederick, Edward, and Mary Fobes; - ; - ; 42

Cora Folts; 28 February 1872; Jeremiah Folts - ; - ; - ; - ; 8

Name; Date of Birth; Father; Mother; Siblings; Other Relatives; Notes; Box Number

Timothy Folts/Foltz; about 1890; - ; - ; - ; U- Henry Schutt; father was insane and confined to Gowanda Hospital and Timothy received money from estate of John M. Schutt; 43

Frank Foote; about 1859; - ; Agnes Galloway; Mary Foote; MGF Jacob Galloway, MU George Galloway, PU Henry Foote, PU Larmon Foote; - ; 8

Heli Foote; 18 February 1843; Prosper Foote; - ; William Foote; PU Heli Foote, MA Ann Eliza Wood (W- of John Wood); - ; 8

Henry Foote; 1 August 1846; Lucius Foote; - ; Larmon Foote; PU Ransford Foote, of Concord, Erie, NY; 8

Larmon Foote; 27 November 1844; Lucius Foote; - ; Henry Foote; PU Ransford Foote, of Concord, Erie, NY; 8

Mary Foote; 11 April 1861; - ; Agnes Galloway; Frank Foote; MGF Jacob Galloway, MU George Galloway, PU Henry Foote, PU Larmon Foote; - ; 8

Melvin Foote; - ; Rufus Foote; - ; - ; - ; G- Orrin Lawrence and Melvin received legacy from estate of grandfather; 8

William Foote; 9 November 1842; Prosper Foote; - ; Heli Foote; PU Heli Foote, MA Ann Eliza Wood (W- of John Wood); - ; 8

Elizabeth Ford; about 1882; Patrick Ford; Elizabeth, married Mr. Kennedy; William Ford; - ; received pension money; 43

Freda Belle Ford; 29 August 1901; Duane Ford; Jennie McStay; Millard, Kenneth, and Victor Ford; - ; G- William Currie; 8

Kenneth Antony Ford; 17 October 1899; Duane Ford; Jennie McStay; Millard, Freda, and Victor Ford; - ; G- William Currie; 8

Millard Stanley Ford; 1 October 1897; Duane Ford; Jennie McStay; Kenneth, Freda, and Victor Ford; - ; G- William Currie; 8

Victor Harold Ford; 13 December 1895; Duane Ford; Jennie McStay; Kenneth, Freda, and Millard Ford; - ; G- William Currie; 8

William Ford; about 1884; Patrick Ford; Elizabeth, married Mr.

Name; Date of Birth; Father; Mother; Siblings; Other Relatives; Notes; Box Number

Kennedy; Elizabeth Ford; - ; received pension money; 43

Clara Forester; 16 June 1907; David Forester, was tried in Little Valley for having relations with his daughter; - ; - ; - ; RE Salvation Army in Buffalo, G-Mary E. Lettis; 8

Depuy Fosket; 21 August 1848; - ; Mary R., of South Valley, married Mr. Flagg; - ; - ; - ; 75

Romenzo Foskit; 14 September 1850; - ; - ; - ; - ; G- Mary R. Flagg; 75

Augusta Foster; about 1873; - ; - ; - ; HU Burt A. Foster; - ; 42

Frances Foster; 24 March 1893; Albert W. Foster; - ; - ; - ; received money from estate of Rachel Foster; 43

Frederick B. Foster; 11 July 1873; - ; - ; - ; GM Lucinda Lovewell; G-Walter Walrath, no relationship; 8

Caroline L. Fox; about 1895; - ; Emily A.; Laura, Elizabeth, George, Eleanor and Marion Fox; - ; - ; 7

Charles D. Fox; 15 August 1903; Charles E. Fox, RE 515 N. 7th St., Olean; - ; Paul Fox; - ; - ; 42

Charles E. Fox; 27 January 1864; - ; Eunice, married Mr. Little; - ; - ; G- Richard Little, no relation; 42

Eleanor Fox; about 1904; - ; Emily A.; Laura, Elizabeth, George, Caroline and Marion Fox; - ; - ; 7

Elizabeth Fox; about 1898; - ; Emily A.; Laura, Eleanor, George, Caroline and Marion Fox; - ; - ; 7

George C. D. Fox; about 1899; - ; Emily A.; Laura, Elizabeth, Eleanor, Caroline and Marion Fox; - ; - ; 7

George K. Fox; 31 October 1871; William H. Fox; Parma Dulcenia Knight; - ; PGF George Knight; - ; 42

Laura A. Fox; about 1893; - ; Emily A.; George, Elizabeth, Eleanor, Caroline and Marion Fox; - ; - ; 7

Marion Fox; about 1908; - ; Emily A.; George, Elizabeth, Eleanor, Caroline and Laura Fox; - ; - ; 7

Mary Fox; 19 January 1905; William H. Fox, died before 6 March 1919; Anna M.; William and Richard Fox; - ; G- Ernest Wies. Mary RE 1924, with Mr. Kane, no relation, while attending school in Buffalo and received money from

Name; Date of Birth; Father; Mother; Siblings; Other Relatives; Notes; Box Number

estate of Theresa Fox; 43

Paul Raymond Fox; 19 February 1910; Charles E. Fox, RE 515 N. 7th St., Olean; - ; Charles Fox; - ; - ; 42

Richard Fox; 7 May 1901; William H. Fox, died before 6 March 1919; Anna M.; William and Mary Fox; - ; G- Ernest Wies and received money from estate of Theresa Fox; 43

William H. Fox; 4 September 1903; William H. Fox, died before 6 March 1919; Anna M.; Richard and Mary Fox; - ; G- Ernest Wies, RE 1919, Army 9th Regiment, Great Lakes, Illinois and received money from estate of Theresa Fox; 43

Irene Anna Frame; 1 November 1921; Herman C. Frame; Anna C.; Rena Frame; - ; - ; 42

Rena Adele Frame; 5 July 1923; Herman C. Frame; Anna C.; Irene Frame; - ; - ; 42

Dorothy M. France; 20 January 1903; - ; May Stiles; Howard G. France; HU Mr. Rogers; RE Millersburgh, Elkhart, Indiana; 7

Eleanor France; 3 April 1902; George P. France, resided in Sarnia, Ontario; Charlotte L. Reed, married Mr. White, and resided at 83 Bratte St. Cambridge, Massachusetts; - ; MGF Newton Reed; parents divorced, G-Mark Holmes, RE May 1917, lived in Peublo Viejo, Puerto Rico with grandfather; 8

Howard G. France; 31 October 1901; - ; May Stiles; Dorothy France; - ; RE Millersburgh, Elkhart, Indiana; 7

Annie C. W. Franchot; 17 December 1888; N. V. V. Franchot; Annie C. W.; - ; - ; - ; 8

Abraham Frank; Summer, about 1833; Solomon Frank, died before March 1844, of Ashford; Mary Ann, married Mr. Shafner; - ; U-Jacob Frank and other relatives are Abram Frank and Edward Nye; - ; 77

Ella J. Frank; 20 May 1867; Almon Frank; Sarah A; - ; - ; G- Jacob Moore and Ella is inheriting land from Eliza McMillen (late of Madison County, NY); 8

Ellen A. Frank; 20 September 1910; Bert B. Frank, died 20 September 1924, of West Valley; - ; Mildred Frank; HU Mr. Crosgrove, A- Katherine P. Duncan; mother died about 1916;

Name; Date of Birth; Father; Mother; Siblings; Other Relatives; Notes; Box Number

42
Ethel M. Frank; 21 July 1884; - ; - ; HS Allie Bedell; - ; - ; 72
Fred P. Frank; - ; - ; - ; Goldie Frank; - ; G- Candis M. Frank; 75
Goldie Frank; - ; - ; - ; Fred Frank; HU Mr. Ellwood, married in 1900; G- Candis M. Frank; 75
Jessie Eliza Frank; 13 or 30 July 1875; Ezra Frank; - ; - ; HU Mr. Warner, married by 1892; received legacy from Eliza McMullen (of Madison County, NY); 42
Manley J. Frank; 11 November 1877; Henry Frank; Alice E., married Mr. Lovett; - ; - ; - ; 42
Mildred I. Frank; 26 July 1907; Bert B. Frank, died 20 September 1924, of West Valley; - ; Ellen Frank; HU Mr. Crosgrove, A- Katherine P. Duncan; mother died about 1916; 42
Arden M. Frary; 23 September 1847; - ; Mary Ann E. Higbee, married Mr. Thompson; - ; MGF David Higbee; - ; 8
William E. Freel; about 1895; - ; Anna, married Mr. Driscoll; - ; - ; G- Michael Freel; 42
Alfred Freeman; about 1870; - ; Melissa; - ; - ; - ; 42
Hiram Freeman; 24 August 1838; - ; - ; - ; - ; G- Phineas Freeman, Hiram received a land warrant for 40 acres issued under the Act of Congress passed 28 September 1850, No. 55, 499, from estate of Caleb Freeman; 7
Phebe Freeman; 30 April 1847; Hiram Freeman; - ; - ; - ; - ; 8
Amos L. French; 14 April 1867; Francis French, died September 1867; - ; Linus and Mary French; - ; G- Eliphalet Carpenter; 8
Anna French; 14 December 1862; - ; - ; - ; HU Mr. Vaughn; G- Eliphalet Carpenter; 8
Guy French; about 1893; George French; - ; Leland French; - ; - ; 43
Leland French; about 1899; George French; - ; Guy French; - ; - ; 43
May H. French; 12 December 1909; - ; Jessimyne, RE 413 N. 9th St, Olean; Iris French (born about 1905); - ; - ; 42

Name; Date of Birth; Father; Mother; Siblings; Other Relatives; Notes; Box Number

M. Maurice Friel; 14 May 1888; - ; Margaret ; - ; - ; received money from estate of Patrick Friel; 8

Clarence Scofield Frier; 17 February 1886; - ; Ida M.; Florence Frier; PU A. Burdette Scofield; RE 1906, in Pittsburgh, Pennsylvania; 43

Florence Viola Frier; 29 June 1891; - ; Ida M.; Clarence Frier; PU A. Burdette Scofield; RE 134 S. Clinton St., Olean; 43

Roxania M. Frisby; 12 June 1849; - ; - ; - ; - ; G- Charles M. Danley; 75

Edith L. Fritz; about 1882; Hosea Shipman; - ; - ; HU John Fritz (died 15 September 1901 in Wirt, Allegany, NY), son is Harry D. Fritz; - ; 72

Harry D. Fritz; about 1901; John Fritz, died 15 September 1901 in Wirt, Allegany, NY; Edith Shipman; - ; MGF Hosea Shipman; - ; 72

Alice Fuller; 6 December 1846; - ; - ; - ; - ; received money from Zachary Conklin's estate and in same envelope as Mary A. Conklin and Millard Conklin; 4

Catherine Fuller; 20 February 1901; Taylor C. Fuller; - ; John and Floy Ruth Fuller; HU Mr. Butler; - ; 7

Cora L. Fuller; about 1882; - ; Augusta A.; Wilma Fuller; HU Mr. Pendlebury, PU George W. Weast; G-Daniel A. Bond; 7

Floy Ruth Fuller; 7 December 1903; Taylor C. Fuller; - ; John and Catherine Fuller; HU Mr. Day; - ; 7

Freda Fuller; 29 August 1903; - ; - ; Anna Green; HU Forrest M. Fuller; she had ten siblings; 7

Henry T. Fuller; about 1863; Henry Fuller, of Little Valley, died 2 July 1863; Adelaide, of Coventry, Kent County, Rhode Island, married Daniel P. Baker on 8 January 1871; - ; PG Benjamin and Ann Fuller, PA Clara Fuller (born about 1851); money from Lyman Twomley's estate, of Little Valley (Urania was wife of Lyman, and Minnie was their adopted daughter. The Twomley's attended the First Methodist Church), Henry received pension money; 74.

John Fuller; 19 December 1905; Taylor C. Fuller; - ; Floy

Name; Date of Birth; Father; Mother; Siblings; Other Relatives; Notes; Box Number

and Catherine Fuller; - ; - ; 7

Wilma A. Fuller; about 1880; - ; Augusta A.; Cora Fuller; HU Mr. Ferrin, PU George W. Weast; G-Daniel A. Bond; 7

Leila S. Furlong; - ; - ; Allie, admitted to Gowanda State Hospital; William Furlong; PU Wm. C. Furlong, A- Eliza Warren; - ; 7

William C. Furlong; - ; - ; Allie, admitted to Gowanda State Hospital; Lelia Furlong; PU Wm. C. Furlong, A- Eliza Warren; - ; 7

Name; Date of Birth; Father; Mother; Siblings; Other Relatives; Notes; Box Number

G Surnames

Elizabeth E. Gabel; 21 April 1897; - ; - ; George A. Gabel; - ; - ; 44

Emil Gadzik; 10 December 1903; Andrew Gadzik, of Olean; - ; Helen Griffith, Rudolph, Margaret and Irene Gadzik; - ; - ; 70

Margaret Gadzik; about 1907; Andrew Gadzik, of Olean; - ; Helen Griffith, Rudolph, Emil and Irene Gadzik; - ; - ; 70

Rudolph Gadzik; 10 June 1904; Andrew Gadzik, of Olean; - ; Helen Griffith, Margaret, Emil and Irene Gadzik; - ; - ; 70

Albert A. Gaensslen or Gaenssler; 25 June 1884; Henry Gaenssler; Frances; Harmony Gaenssler; - ; legacy from Albul Gaenssler; 44

Harmony A. Gaensslen or Gaenssler; 9 April 1880; Henry Gaenssler; Frances; Albert Gaenssler; - ; legacy from Albul Gaenssler; 44

Bernard Kinney Gage; about 1890; Bernard Gage; - ; - ; - ; - ; 9

Fern Gage; - ; J. W. Gage; Emma J.; Ora, Floyd and Fred Gage; - ; - ; 9

Floyd A. Gage; 14 Septmeber 1890; J. W. Gage; Emma J.; Ora, Fern and Fred Gage; - ; - ; 9

Fred R. Gage; 3 January 1886; J. W. Gage; Emma J.; Ora, Fern and Floyd Gage; - ; - ; 9

Ora J. Gage; 17 May 1888; J. W. Gage; Emma J.; Fred, Fern and Floyd Gage; - ; - ; 9

Ruth E. Gage; 27 February 1885; - ; - ; Van Norman Gage, the other siblings adopted into various families throughout Franklinville; U- David Vaughn; - ; RE 1906, Elk Grove, Sacramento, California, father lived in New Jersey, received money from Harrison Vaughn's estate; -

Van Norman Gage; 29 December 1882; - ; - ; Ruth Gage, the other siblings adopted into various families throughout Franklinville; U- David Vaughn; RE 1906, Elk Grove, Sacramento, California, father lived in New Jersey, ; received money from Harrison Vaughn's estate; -

Name; Date of Birth; Father; Mother; Siblings; Other Relatives; Notes; Box Number

Francis E. Gallagher; 27 November 1884; Charles E. Gallagher; - ; Charles E. Gallagher, Jr., (of Uhrichsville, Tuscarawas, Ohio), and Ralph Gallagher; - ; - ; -

Ralph W. Gallagher; 27 May 1881; Charles E. Gallagher; - ; Charles E. Gallagher, Jr. (of Uhrichsville, Tuscarawas, Ohio), and Francis Gallagher; - ; - ; -

Jennie (Regina) Gallets; 26 September 1893; Jacob Gallets, of Allegany; - ; - ; - ; - ; 72

Martin Galloway; 28 September 1833; - ; - ; - ; - ; G- Charles Galloway; 75

Augusta M. Gardner; 18 October 1859; Decatur Gardner, died January 1867; Julia, married Mr. Weatherly, died May 1874; Luella and Viola Gardner; HU Mr. Hogan; received money from pension; 9

F. Ross Gardner; 29 May 1890; George D. Gardner, of Conewango; - ; Lorena Gardner; - ; received legacy from Emma Aldrich, of Conewango; 72

Lorena C. Gardner; 25 July 1893; George D. Gardner, of Conewango; - ; F. Ross Gardner; - ; received legacy from Emma Aldrich, of Conewango; 72

Luella M. Gardner; 2 September 1861; Decatur Gardner, died January 1867; Julia, married Mr. Weatherly, died May 1874; Augusta and Viola Gardner; HU Mr. Smith, BIL Charles Kast; received money from pension; 9

Margaret Gardner; 6 May 1899; John T. Gardner, of Randolph; Carrie B.; - ; - ; received money from estate of Margaret D. Brown and file mentions a Veeder D. Gardner; 70

Viola A. Gardner; - ; Decatur Gardner, died January 1867; Julia, married Mr. Weatherly, died May 1874; Augusta and Luella Gardner; HU Mr. Whitehead; received money from pension; 9

Elizabeth M. Garvey; 6 August 1909; - ; Ella B., of Cattaraugus; - ; GA Claribel Pratt; father died before November 1928; 70

Louis Garwood; about 1862; William Garwood; Rebecca; - ; - ; - ; 9

Name; Date of Birth; Father; Mother; Siblings; Other Relatives; Notes; Box Number

Mary G. Gaskill; 24 September 1874; - ; Winnifred; - ; C- Nicholas Hickey; - ; 44

Grace F. Gates; 23 September 1885; - ; - ; - ; MU Joseph E. Lafferty, of New Hudson; parents died before December 1904; 72

Anthony W. Gavin; November 1859; Cornelius Gavin; - ; James and Hattie Gavin; U- James Clary; - ; 9

Hattie F. Gavin; 21 June 1861; Cornelius Gavin; - ; James and Anthony Gavin; U- James Clary; - ; 9

James C. Gavin; 22 March 1863; Cornelius Gavin; - ; Hattie and Anthony Gavin; U- James Clary; - ; 9

Clara Bell or Claribel Gay; - ; Frank Gay, lived in Corry, Pennsylvania; - ; - ; A- Angeline M. Davis, C- Charles W. Davis; - ; 9

John Geary; 14 November 1907; - ; Ellen J., of 212 S. Barry St., Olean; - ; - ; father died before May 1926; 69

Leo F. Geary; 1 June 1899; - ; Laura, of Olean, married Mr. Sage; - ; PGF Thomas F. Geary, of Allegany; - ; 69

Frances M. Geise; about 1887; - ; Cynthia, of Hinsdale; Rosa and Veronica Geise; - ; - ; 72

Rosa L. Geise; 22 September 1881; - ; Cynthia, of Hinsdale; Frances and Veronica Geise; - ; - ; 72

Veronica I. Geise; about 1890; - ; Cynthia, of Hinsdale; Frances and Rosa Geise; - ; - ; 72

Anna Geisser; - ; - ; Mary, Jacob, and Agnes Geisser; - ; parents died before July 1904, G- Francis B. Brown, no relation; 72

Agnes Catherine Geisser; 8 September 1889; - ; Mary, Jacob, and Anna Geisser; - ; RE 1910, lived at 47 N. Main St., Hornell, parents died before July 1904, G- Francis B. Brown, no relation; 72

Jacob Geisser; 26 October 1887; - ; Mary, Agnes, and Anna Geisser; - ; RE 1910, Turtlepoint, Pennsylvania, parents died before July 1904, G- Francis B. Brown, no relation; 72

Mary Rose Geisser; 16 January 1885; - ; Agnes, Jacob, and Anna Geisser; - ; RE 1910, Turtlepoint, Pennsylvania, parents died

Name; Date of Birth; Father; Mother; Siblings; Other Relatives; Notes; Box Number

before July 1904, G- Francis B. Brown, no relation; 72

Minnie Geran; 12 May 1880; Michael Geran, of Carrollton; - ; - ; - ; - ; 72

Ernest Gergley; about 1909; John Gergley, died 21 December 1911; Mary; John and Mary Gergley; PU Thomas Gergel (of Olean. Name changed in this country, and neither Thomas or John has much education); G- Shep L. Vibbard, other heirs mentioned were Anna (born about 1908), and Julia (born about 1910); 69

John Gergley; about 1904; John Gergley, died 21 December 1911; Mary; Ernest and Mary Gergley; PU Thomas Gergel (of Olean. Name changed in this country, and neither Thomas or John has much education); G- Shep L. Vibbard, other heirs mentioned were Anna (born about 1908), and Julia (born about 1910); 69

Mary Gergley; about 1907; John Gergley, died 21 December 1911; Mary; Ernest and John Gergley; PU Thomas Gergel (of Olean. Name changed in this country, and neither Thomas or John has much education); G- Shep L. Vibbard, other heirs mentioned were Anna (born about 1908), and Julia (born about 1910); 69

Amelia O. Gerringer; 28 November 1889; - ; - ; Adam and Mary Gerringer; - ; parents died before August 1906 72

Gladys Gerringer; - ; - ; - ; Marion and Lucille Gerringer; - ; G- Mary E. Gerringer; 43

Lucille Gerringer; - ; - ; - ; Marion and Gladys Gerringer; - ; G- Mary E. Gerringer; 43

Marion Gerringer; - ; - ; - ; Lucille and Gladys Gerringer; - ; G- Mary E. Gerringer; 43

Mary A. Gerringer; 9 August 1887; - ; - ; Adam and Amelia Gerringer; - ; parents died before August 1906 72

Donald Paul Geuder; 26 January 1911; George Geuder, of 812 W. Henley St., Olean; Lena; - ; - ; - ; 69

Edward K. Geuder; 9 September 1904; John H. Geuder, died before January 1922; Anna L., died before January 1922;

Name; Date of Birth; Father; Mother; Siblings; Other Relatives; Notes; Box Number

Emma Wallace, Eda G. Vaughn (W- of Carl Vaughn), and Arthur and Edwin Geuder; - ; RE 128 N. Barry St., Olean 69

Edwin S. Geuder; 9 September 1904; John H. Geuder, died before January 1922; Anna L., died before January 1922; Emma Wallace, Eda G. Vaughn (W- of Carl Vaughn), and Arthur and Edward Geuder; - ; RE 128 N. Barry St., Olean; 69

Mersel Gibbons; 23 April 1893; - ; - ; - ; HU Mr. Taite, U- Lucius Lowell; RE 1914, Wellsville, money from estate of Verna Lowell (of Machias), father abandoned her; 72

Albert Gibby; 27 May 1866; Joseph Gibby, died April 1872, of Freedom; - ; William, Charles and Thomas Gibby; U- William Lewis; - ; 43

Charles Gibby; 20 September 1859; Joseph Gibby, died April 1872, of Freedom; - ; William, Albert and Thomas Gibby; U- William Lewis; - ; 43

Joyce Gibby; about 1889; - ; Cora B., of Portville; - ; - ; father died before January 1909; 72

Thomas Gibby; 16 March 1868; Joseph Gibby, died April 1872, of Freedom; - ; William, Albert and Charles Gibby; U- William Lewis; - ; 43

William Gibby; 4 February 1861; Joseph Gibby, died April 1872, of Freedom; - ; Thomas, Albert and Charles Gibby; U- William Lewis; - ; 43

Daniel Gibson; 8 March 1842; Nehemiah L. Gibson, died before April 1854; - ; William, Nathan and Alonzo Gibson and Rebecca Carver; - ; - ; 75

Elton Gifford; about 1888; - ; - ; - ; - ; - ; 44

Sarah Gifford; about 1884; - ; - ; - ; - ; - ; 44

Ella M. Gilbert; about 1882; Edward Gilbert, died 6 July 1897, Sergeant in Company A, 37th Regiment; - ; Nora Gayton, Clara Brooks, and Charles, Fred, Marin and Will Gilbert; A- Amanda Middleton; - ; 41

Alice Elizabeth Giles; August 1847; John L. Giles, died before May 1855, of Dayton; - ; Jonathan Giles; PGF Cyrus Giles,

Name; Date of Birth; Father; Mother; Siblings; Other Relatives; Notes; Box Number

MGF Jonathan Deremer; - ; 75

Jonathan Melvin Giles; 22 August 1847; John L. Giles, died before May 1855, of Dayton; - ; Alice Giles; PGF Cyrus Giles, MGF Jonathan Deremer; - ; 75

Melvin N. Gillet; 9 December 1846; - ; Catharine, died before November 1862; Sarah Gillet; - ; G- James Freeland; 75

Sarah J. Gillet; 29 March 1844; - ; Catharine, died before November 1862; Melvin Gillet; - ; G- James Freeland; 75

John Henry Gilliat; about 1885; - ; Rachael E., of Ellicottville; Robert and Ruth Gilliat; - ; father died before February 1901, received money from estate of Thomas Gilliat; 72

Robert Fulton Gilliat; about 1887; - ; Rachael E., of Ellicottville; John and Ruth Gilliat; - ; father died before February 1901, received money from estate of Thomas Gilliat; 72

Ruth Gertrude Gilliat; about 1892; - ; Rachael E., of Ellicottville; John and Robert Gilliat; - ; father died before February 1901, received money from estate of Thomas Gilliat; 72

Mary Katherine Gilligan; 30 March 1902; Dennis Gilligan; - ; - ; - ; G-Catherine Gilligan Freel; 44

Ethel A. Ginader; about 1887; John G. Ginader, Clergyman for ME Church; - ; - ; - ; - ; 72

Amanda Gleason; 23 November 1844; - ; - ; Mary Ann Gleason; U- James M. Senter, U- Lambert Whitney, in same envelope as Jane and Ira Gleason; 75

Ira T. Gleason; 1856; - ; Maria C. Farwell; HS Jane Gleason; MG John H. and Catharine Farwell, MU Samuel Farwell, MU John Farwell, MA Mary L. Lockwood; in same envelope with Mary Ann and Amanda Gleason; 75

Jane K. Gleason; 19 June 1851; - ; Step-mom was Maria C; HB Ira T. Gleason; - ; in same envelope with Mary Ann and Amanda Gleason; 75

Mary Ann Gleason; 20 July 1839; - ; - ; Amanda Gleason; U- James M. Senter, U- Lambert Whitney, in same envelope as Jane and Ira Gleason; 75

Name; Date of Birth; Father; Mother; Siblings; Other Relatives; Notes; Box Number

Mary Godding; 29 May 1818; Asa Godding, died 28 July 1826 at Shrewsbury, Vermont; Matilda, died 16 October 1831; Sabra Godding; - ; petitioner was Levi Godding, G- David Colburn (of Shrewsbury, Vermont); 76

Sabra A. Godding; 16 August 1821; Asa Godding, died 28 July 1826 at Shrewsbury, Vermont; Matilda, died 16 October 1831; Mary Godding; - ; petitioner was Levi Godding, G- David Colburn (of Shrewsbury, Vermont); 76

Jennie Velma Godfrey; about 1865; - ; Dolly; Lillian Godfrey; - ; G- Luman A. Bentley; RE Eaton Rapids, Eaton, Michigan, heir of Silas Godfrey, also left legacy by Hanley R. Finch; 43

Kenneth W. Godfrey; 12 January 1905; I. M. Godfrey, of Olean; - ; - ; - ; received money from estate of Fred C. Olds; 69

Lillian Godfrey; about 1862; - ; Dolly; Jennie Godfrey; - ; G- Luman A. Bentley; RE Eaton Rapids, Eaton, Michigan, heir of Silas Godfrey, also left legacy by Hanley R. Finch; 43

Ada L. Goltz; 6 January 1878; Frederick W. Goltz, lived 66 Second St., Olean; - ; - ; - ; - ; 72

Edna Good; 29 June 1908; - ; Martha, of 281 South Ave, Bradford; - ; - ; father died before May 1927; 69

Allen Goodemote; about 1831; David Goodemote, died before October 1838, of Ashford; - ; Charity and Mary Ann Goodemote; U- Philip Goodemote; G- James D. Searl; 77

Charity Goodemote; October 1829; David Goodemote, died before October 1838, of Ashford; - ; Allen and Mary Ann Goodemote; U- Philip Goodemote; G- James D. Searl; 77

James P. Goodemote; - ; - ; - ; - ; - ; - ; 75

Mary Ann Goodemote; about 1833; David Goodemote, died before October 1838, of Ashford; - ; Allen and Charity Goodemote; U- Philip Goodemote; G- James D. Searl; 77

Clara M. Gooden; - ; Charles A. Gooden, lived in Jamestown; - ; Harold C. Gooden; - ; - ; 9

Harold C. Gooden; - ; Charles A. Gooden, lived in Jamestown; - ; Clara Gooden; - ; - ; 9

Adam Goodford; 24 December 1892; - ; - ; Mary Weirchock, of

Name; Date of Birth; Father; Mother; Siblings; Other Relatives; Notes; Box Number

51 Atlantic St., Salamanca; other relatives were Stephen Beres, Josephine Grey, and George Goodford; - ; 69

Helen Goodford; - ; - ; William and George Goodford and Julia Gray; - ; G- Mary Wierchock, received money from US Veteran's Bureau for death of John T. Goodford; 69

William Goodford; - ; - ; Helen and George Goodford and Julia Gray; - ; G- Mary Wierchock, received money from US Veteran's Bureau for death of John T. Goodford; 69

Allman J. Goodrich; about 1858; Orestus H. Goodrich; - ; - ; MGM Sally Kirby; G- Justus J. Scott; 75

Arthur Lee Goodrich; about 1908; George L. Goodrich; - ; Elton Goodrich; - ; - ;69

Ellen P. Goodrich; - ; Zenas Goodrich; - ; Mary and Sarah Goodrich; - ; G- Lewis Bouton; 9

Elton Guy Goodrich; about 1906; George L. Goodrich; - ; Arthur Goodrich; - ; - ;69

Mary A. Goodrich; - ; Zenas Goodrich; - ; Ellen and Sarah Goodrich; - ; G- Lewis Bouton; 9

Sarah E. Goodrich; - ; Zenas Goodrich; - ; Ellen and Mary Goodrich; - ; G- Lewis Bouton; 9

Carroll B. Goodsell; 14 August 1904; - ; Mildred, of 135 Clinton St., Salamanca, married Mr. Schaich; - ; - ; father at Oil City, Pennsylvania; 69

Charles J. Goodsell; 31 August 1907; - ; Loryne, of 37 Maple St., Salamanca; Helen Goodsell; - ; father died before September 1923, received money from estate of Charles Goodsell; 69

Helen A. Goodsell; 30 March 1906; - ; Loryne, of 37 Maple St., Salamanca; Charles Goodsell; HU Mr. Paisley, married about 1925; father died before September 1923, received money from estate of Charles Goodsell; 69

Orville Gordan; 5 April 1855; Isaac Gordan, of Pine Island, Gooden, Minnesota; - ; Willard Gordan; - ; - ; 75

Willard Gordan; 11 July 1857; Isaac Gordan, of Pine Island, Gooden, Minnesota; - ; Orville Gordan; - ; - ; 75

Anne "Annie" M. Gordon; 1885 or 1886; John W. Gordon, lived

Name; Date of Birth; Father; Mother; Siblings; Other Relatives; Notes; Box Number

in West Bay City, Bay, Michigan; Elizabeth J., died 26 August 1897; Nellie Gordon; - ; - ; 72

Emma Gordon; - ; - ; Anne W., of Topeka, Kansas; - ; - ; received money from estate of Walter Gordon; 72

Nellie Gordon; 1886 or 1887; John W. Gordon, lived in West Bay City, Bay, Michigan; Elizabeth J., died 26 August 1897; Anne Gordon; - ; - ; 72

Emily A. Goudie; - ; - ; - ; - ; - ; RE 1881 Buffalo, G- Heman Nickless; 9

Arden "Artie" Gould; 4 May 1870; - ; Amelia; Minerva Gould; - ; - ; 43

Elsie Elizabeth Gould; 29 March 1875; William C. Gould; Margaret A., died May 1877, of Great Valley; Margaret Gould; - ; she was sent to school in Emporia, KS; 43

Margaret Mary Gould; 15 August 1876; William C. Gould; Margaret A., died May 1877, of Great Valley; Elsie Gould; - ; - ; 43

Minerva Gould; 14 August 1876; - ; Amelia; Arden Gould; - ; - ; 43

Vera M. Graves; 30 August 1897; - ; Mabel M., married George Newton; - ; GM Carlia Abbey; father died about 1900; 43

Alice Gray; about 1905; David, died before 30 January 1922; Hannah; - ; - ; - ; 43

Bertha M. Green; 17 September 1881; - ; - ; - ; HU Mr. Clark, married before 1900, U-Freeman Green, U- Frank Green, A- Eva Painter, A- Martha Green; parents died before June 1899, G- William A. Day, no relation; 72

Fred R. Green; 13 October 1895; Niles Green; Nora, died before April 1916; Frank Green; PGM Louisa H. Green (left legacy), A- Bessie Norton,; Fred hadn't lived with his father since he was 6 weeks old; 43

Herman A. Green; 23 April 1887; Albert Green; - ; - ; A- Henrietta Barnhart; - ; 41

Carrie P. Greiner/Griner; 9 December 1898; Philip Griner, died 17 January 1904, of Dayton; Laura, married Mr. Wiegand; - ;

Name; Date of Birth; Father; Mother; Siblings; Other Relatives; Notes; Box Number

- ; - ; 43 and 44

Ray Grierson; 30 August 1878; Ray Grierson, died before December 1894; Helen; - ; - ; G- William Monton, no relation; 44

Genevieve Griffin; 8 April 1900; - ; - ; Ilene and Marie Griffin; - ; G- James Gallup, G- Fred Gallup; 70

Ilene Griffin; 8 September 1898; - ; - ; Genevieve and Marie Griffin; - ; G- James Gallup, G- Fred Gallup; 70

Marie Griffin; 5 August 1895; - ; - ; Genevieve and Ilene Griffin; - ; G- James Gallup, G- Fred Gallup; 70

Catherine Sigman Griffiths; 12 October 1903; Phillip J. Griffith; Alberta; Gertrude Griffiths; GA Catherine Pfleuger, died 7 May 1918 in Cattaraugus; RE 1180 W. Euclid Ave, Detroit, Wayne, Michigan; 70

Gertrude Griffiths; 19 April 1908; Phillip J. Griffith; Alberta; Catherine Griffiths; GA Catherine Pfleuger, died 7 May 1918 in Cattaraugus; RE 1929, 1180 W. Euclid Ave, Detroit, Wayne, Michigan; 70

Caroline A. Grimes; 25 April 1857; James Grimes; Caroline C.; Eugene and Grace Grimes; PG James and Hannah Grimes; - ; 9

Eugene H. Grimes; 23 September 1855; James Grimes; Caroline C.; Caroline and Grace Grimes; PG James and Hannah Grimes; - ; 9

Grace L. Grimes; 1 November 1860; James Grimes; Caroline C.; Caroline and Eugene Grimes; PG James and Hannah Grimes; - ; 9

Abba " Abbie" Eugene Griswold; November 1866; Jerome S. Griswold, died before 19 April 1881; - ; - ; - ; G- Edwin S. Griswold; 43

Maude Griswold; 5 September 1893; - ; Caroline; - ; - ; - ; 43

Myrtle M. Groat; 30 June 1888; Frank Groat, died 27 March 1891; Frankie Scott, died 13 February 1897; - ; PG John Groat, MG Elbert Scott, PU Jasper Groat, PU Charles Groat, PU Earl Groat, MU Bert Scott, A-Mary Olthof (W- of

Name; Date of Birth; Father; Mother; Siblings; Other Relatives; Notes; Box Number

Henry B. Olthof); G- James L. West (born about 1838); 9

Roy Grover; about 1894; - ; - ; - ; PGF Gustavius Grover, Frank A. Grover is another relative; received money from estate of Emerette Stebbins; 70

Mildred Guay; May 1898; - ; - ; Anna E. Krott; - ; - ; 43

Fred Guild; 22 November 1860; Charles Guild; - ; Mary Guild; - ; G- William P. Guild; 9

Mary E. Guild; 17 July 1857; Charles Guild; - ; Fred Guild; HU Mr. Wildrick ; G- William P. Guild; 9

W. Standish Guild; 3 May 1896; - ; Emma, married Mr. Pierce; - ; - ; - ; 44

Donald Adams Gunnison; 9 January 1908 ; - ; Genevieve, last name was Adams at time of petition; - ; - ; attended Dr. Horace Mann School; 43

Callie Jane Guthrie; 29 December 1874; - ; - ; - ; - ; G- Norman Wheeler (in Arkport, Steuben, NY); 44

Cora A. Guthrie; about 1879; - ; Carrie, died 14 June 1904 in Humphrey; Leslie Guthrie; - ; - ; 41

Leslie Guthrie; 12 November 1883; - ; Carrie, died 14 June 1904 in Humphrey; Cora Guthrie; - ; - ; 41

Laura A. Guy; 15 June 1861; Timothy Guy, died March 1869; - ; Lydia Guy; MGM Barbara Heath, A- Catharine Stickney; G- Horace C. Young; 9

Lydia E. Guy; 15 July 1863; Timothy Guy, died March 1869; - ; Laura Guy; MGM Barbara Heath, A- Catharine Stickney; G- Horace C. Young; 9

Name; Date of Birth; Father; Mother; Siblings; Other Relatives; Notes; Box Number

H Surnames

Norman Haase; 5 August 1910; - ; Carrie, lived 324 N. 11th St., Olean; August Haase; - ; G- William G. Wiedman, no relation; 64

Ralph Haberly; 25 December 1908; Fred Haberly; Elnora; - ; - ; - ; 45

Lewis A. Hackett; 14 April 1878; George Hackett; - ; - ; - ; - ; 44

Alfred E. Hadaway; 29 December 1856; James Hadaway, died February 1868, of Montcalm County, Michigan; Charlotte, of Great Valley, married Mr. Wood before 1877; Irena Hadaway; - ; - ; 75

Irena N. Hadaway; 22 January or February 1861; James Hadaway, died February 1868, of Montcalm County, Michigan; Charlotte, of Great Valley, married Mr. Wood before 1877; Alfred Hadaway; - ; - ; 75

Brayton Hadley; 24 February 1885; - ; - ; - ; MGF Truman Stocking, PGF Hartwell Hadley; G- Herbert Hadley and received money from estate of Palmer Hadley; 9

John Hadley; 30 December 1812; Nathan Hadley, died before January 1831; - ; - ; - ; G- Owen Burleson; 76

Dorothy M. Hahn; 17 November 1904; Daniel John Hahn, RE Oakland, Alameda, California at 5665 Keith Ave.; - ; - ; - ; money from estate of Susan Guenther (W- of Henry Guenther); 11

Charles F. Haight; 24 September 1883; Frank E. Haight; - ; - ; - ; RE Winfield, Crowley, Kansas and money from Charles F. Graves' estate ; 12

Sarah Haight; December 1850; Joseph Haight, died before January 1856; - ; - ; AF Jefferson Hasley (biological mother gave Sarah to him when Sarah was 5 years old); biological mother died shortly after December 1855. Sarah Haight's brother died in service; 75

Charles Haire; 23 September 1889; - ; Margaret; - ; - ; RE

Name; Date of Birth; Father; Mother; Siblings; Other Relatives; Notes; Box Number

Shinglehouse, Pennsylvania, married 1 December 1906, but his wife died, G- Ella M. Walsh Haire; 45

Edwin Hale; 15 October 1838; Nathaniel Hale, died before July 1846; Sylvia, of New Albion, married Ira Bartholomew; Martha Hale; - ; - ; 76

Martha Hale; 1 December 1836; Nathaniel Hale, died before July 1846; Sylvia, of New Albion, married Ira Bartholomew; Edwin Hale; - ; - ; 76

S. Lewis Hale; - ; Edson J. Hale; - ; - ; - ; - ; 45

Charles Haley; 11 February 1908; - ; Caroline; - ; - ; G- Thos. R. Haley (28 Chestnut St., Salamanca); 45

Anna Hall; - ; - ; - ; - ; HU Mr. Lingenfelter; in same envelope as William Hall; 75

Artell Hall; 14 September 1876; Charles Hall; Marion; Irving Hall; MA Mrs. Manley Milks; - ; 44

Charles W. Hall; 12 Jan 1903; - ; - ; Clarence and Rachael Hall; MGF Justus Worden; - ; 12

Clarence E. Hall; 21 May 1905; - ; - ; Charles and Rachael Hall; MGF Justus Worden; - ; 12

Elmer O. Hall; 28 June 1884; - ; Allie, married Mr. Klutsenbaker; Nellie Hall; A- Frances M. Hall (moved to Oakland by 1905, also lived in Payne County, Oklahoma); RE Tescott, Ottawa, Kansas; 12

Floyd Hall; - ; - ; - ; - ; - ; in same envelope as Gladys, Lawrence and Mildred Hall; 46

Gladys Hall; - ; - ; - ; - ; - ; in same envelope as Floyd, Lawrence and Mildred Hall; 46

Glenn P. Hall; 13 September 1889; Azariah Hall; - ; - ; - ; G- Ross Phillips, money from estate of Satira Perry (of Kiantone, NY); 9

Irving A. Hall; 15 March 1873; Charles Hall; Marion; Artell Hall; MA Mrs. Manley Milks; - ; 44

Lawrence Hall; - ; - ; - ; - ; - ; in same envelope as Floyd, Gladys and Mildred Hall; 46

Mildred Irene Hall; - ; - ; - ; - ; - ; in same envelope as Floyd,

Name; Date of Birth; Father; Mother; Siblings; Other Relatives; Notes; Box Number

Gladys and Lawrence Hall; 46

Nellie Hall; 16 August 1879; - ; Allie, married Mr. Klutsenbaker; Elmer Hall; A- Frances M. Hall (moved to Oakland by 1905, also lived in Payne County, Oklahoma) ; RE Tescott, Ottawa, Kansas; 12

Phyllis K. Hall; 7 October 1911; Bert H. Hall; - ; - ; HU Mr. Frank; - ; 64

Rachael Hall; 20 May 1908; - ; - ; Charles and Clarence Hall; HU Mr. Canfield, MGF Justus Worden; - ; 12

Wano D. Hall; 31 December 1894; - ; - ; - ; PU Alexander Hall; father was in Kansas ; 45

William Hall; - ; - ; - ; - ; - ; - ; 75

Mary A. Halley; about 1859; - ; - ; - ; - ; G- John L. Eddy; 44

Sarah Frances Halpin; 12 October 1891; William Halpin; Sarah J.; - ; - ; - ; 44

Emil Halsen; about 1892; - ; - ; Edward Halsen; - ; - ; 9

Charles S. Hamilton; - ; - ; Lucinda, married Mr. Pritchard; Ira, Samuel and William Hamilton; - ; - ; 44

Ira E. Hamilton; 20 August 1859; - ; Lucinda, married Mr. Pritchard; Charles, Samuel and William Hamilton; - ; - ; 44

Milford C. Hamilton: about 1897; - ; - ; - ; U- Claude Armstrong; needed guardian to work for Pennsylvania RR County; 45

Samuel Leory Hamilton; 20 May 1855; - ; Lucinda, married Mr. Pritchard; Charles, Ira and William Hamilton; - ; - ; 44

William E. Hamilton; 14 June 1857; - ; Lucinda, married Mr. Pritchard; Charles, Ira and Samuel Hamilton; - ; - ; 44

Catharine Handrahan; 23 March 1850; James Donegan, of 154th Regt.; Mary, wife of Patrick O'Keefe; Thomas, Mary, John, James and Jerry Donegan; - ; - ; 75

Alta Pearl Hanley; 17 August 1884; George W. Hanley died 11 July 1887; - ; Carrie Hanley; HU Mr. Way, MGF Artimus Hall; RE September 1951, 236 ½ W. 5th St, Erie, Pennsylvania; 12

Carrie Georgia Hanley; 14 July 1881; George W. Hanley died 11 July 1887; - ; Alta Hanley; MGF Artimus Hall; RE

Name; Date of Birth; Father; Mother; Siblings; Other Relatives; Notes; Box Number

September 1951, 236 ½ W. 5th St, Erie, Pennsylvania; 12

Clyde James Hannagen; 7 July 1900; - ; Etta L., of Randolph, married Hubert Miller; Mary Hannagen; - ; received money from estate of James Hannagen,. The administrator of James' estate lived in Oregon City, Oregon; 64

Mary Elizabeth Hannagen; 21 September 1902; - ; Etta L., of Randolph, married Hubert Miller; Clyde Hannagen; - ; money from James Hannagen's estate. The administrator of James' estate lived in Oregon City, Oregon; 64

Annie I. Hannegan; 1 January 1889; James Hannegan; - ; Mina, George, Mary Ellen and Martha Hannegan; - ; - ; 10

George Hannegan; 3 August 1884; James Hannegan; - ; Mina, Annie, Mary Ellen and Martha Hannegan; - ; - ; 10

Martha Josephine Hannegan; 24 July 1881; James Hannegan; - ; Mina, Annie, Mary Ellen and George Hannegan; - ; - ; 10

Mary Ellen Hannegan; 24 July 1881; James Hannegan; - ; Mina, Annie, Martha and George Hannegan; 10

Mina Marie Hannegan; 2 April 1897; James Hannegan; - ; Mary Ellen, Annie, Martha and George Hannegan; - ; - ; 10

Raymond Hannifan; 14 September 1903; George M. Hannifan; - ; - ; - ; - ; 45

Eda Bell Hanson; about 1892; - ; Luella; - ; - ; - ; 46

Clara Harbeck; 13 August 1893; Roscoe Harbeck; Eliza; Frederick and Victor Harbeck; - ; - ; 46

Frederick G. Harbeck; 19 March 1890; Roscoe Harbeck; Eliza; Clara and Victor Harbeck; - ; - ; 46

Victor Harbeck; 5 December 1895; Roscoe Harbeck; Eliza; Clara and Frederick Harbeck; - ; - ; 46

Albert Hare; 16 June 1891; - ; Ida, of Kane, McKean, Pennsyvania, married John F. Davis; Benjamin, Ethel and Millard Hare; PG Thomas and Maria Hare, of Randolph; G-Darwin Congdon; 67

Alta Hare; 26 September 1905; - ; - ; - ; HU Stanley Swiderski (married December 1924), MGF Julius Gartske (of Dunkirk); RE 1926, 387 Mass. Ave. and went to the Lima Seminary

Name; Date of Birth; Father; Mother; Siblings; Other Relatives; Notes; Box Number

(also known as the Genesee Weslyan Seminary), in Lima, NY, she was supported by her distant cousin, Martha Goodale. Alta was pregnant 25 March 1926 and baby was due in 2 weeks, G- Rev. William A. Thorton; 10

Benjamin Hare; 10 December 1887; - ; Ida, of Kane, McKean, Pennsyvania, married John F. Davis; Albert, Ethel and Millard Hare; PG Thomas and Maria Hare, of Randolph; G- Darwin Congdon; 67

Ethel Hare; 3 January 1890; - ; Ida, of Kane, McKean, Pennsyvania, married John F. Davis; Albert, Benjamin and Millard Hare; PG Thomas and Maria Hare, of Randolph; G- Darwin Congdon; 67

Millard Hare; 4 April 1896; - ; Ida, of Kane, McKean, Pennsyvania, married John F. Davis; Albert, Benjamin and Ethel Hare; PG Thomas and Maria Hare, of Randolph; G- Darwin Congdon; 67

Florence Harkness; April 1852; Joseph Harkness, died before February 1866; Hema Johnson; Frances and William Harkness; MU Elisha Johnson; - ; 75

Frances Harkness; about 1858; Joseph Harkness, died before February 1866; Hema Johnson; Florence and William Harkness; MU Elisha Johnson; - ; 75

William Harkness; about 1856; Joseph Harkness, died before February 1866; Hema Johnson; Florence and Frances Harkness; MU Elisha Johnson; - ; 75

William Harning; 11 March 1866; - ; Sophia, married Mr. Oldbenburg; - ; - ; G- Erastus Daley, no relation; 11

Iola V. Harns; 12 October 1862; - ; Celina Larabee, married Mr. Rolfe; Libbie J. Harns; HU Mr. Rhoades, MGM Lorinda Larabee, MU Fayette C. Larabee, MU Amos Larabee, MU Nathan Larabee, A- Roby Spaulding; G- John H. Safford, Theodore Harns left the state in December 1869 (possibly her father); 10

Libbie J. Harns; 4 August 1866; - ; Celina Larabee, married Mr. Rolfe; Iola Harns; HU Mr. Vergith, MGM Lorinda Larabee,

Name; Date of Birth; Father; Mother; Siblings; Other Relatives; Notes; Box Number

MU Fayette C. Larabee, MU Amos Larabee, MU Nathan Larabee, A- Roby Spaulding; G- John H. Safford, Theodore Harns left NY in December 1869 (possibly her father); 10

Carrie Jenette Harrington; about 1895; - ; Georgia E.; Josephine, Myrtie, LaMott Harrington, and Mildred Ohmer; - ; father died before January 1910; 71

Josephine Harrington; about 1891; - ; Georgia E.; Carrie, Myrtie, LaMott Harrington, and Mildred Ohmer; - ; father died before January 1910; 71

LaMott Harrington; 9 February 1900; - ; Georgia E.; Carrie, Myrtie, Josephine Harrington, and Mildred Ohmer; - ; father died before January 1910; 71

Myrtie Harrington; about 1891; - ; Georgia E.; Carrie, LaMott, Josephine Harrington, and Mildred Ohmer; - ; father died before January 1910; 71

Elsie M. Harrison; 5 December 1883; - ; - ; - ; C- Mrs. Henry J. Stannard; received money from estate of G. Wilks Harrison (of East Otto); 67

Joseph H. Harrison; September 1879; Charles H. Harrison; - ; Susan Harrison; - ; - ; 9

Susan J. Harrison; 22 April 1877; Charles H. Harrison; - ; Joseph Harrison; - ; - ; 9

Floyd Harson; 24 May 1895; Julius Harson, of Ellicottville; Flora; - ; - ; - ;75

William Hartley; 30 August 1881; - ; Mary, of Ellicottville; - ; - ; G- Michael Duran, no relation; 64

Joseph Hartung; 12 September 1871; Joseph Hartung, died June 1874; Sophia, married Mr. Bockmier; Sophia Hartung; PG John and Catherine Hartung, A- Mary Shrader; - ; 10

Sophia Hartung; 1 July 1870; Joseph Hartung, died June 1874; Joseph, married Mr. Bockmier; Joseph Hartung; PG John and Catherine Hartung, A- Mary Shrader; - ; 10

Anna G. Hartwig; 17 May 1905; Frank Hartwig; Caroline; Harriet (born about 1900 and died 4 February 1919); HU Jos. Rogers, RE 503 N. 4th St., Olean; - ; 45

Name; Date of Birth; Father; Mother; Siblings; Other Relatives; Notes; Box Number

Earl Harvey; 24 August 1908; - ; Mary, married Fred Widrig; - ; GM May Gerwite; - ; 49

Ethel Harvey; 12 August 1882; - ; - ; - ; U- Enos Eddy; - ; 44

Ida Harvey; about 1883; John Harvey; - ; Kate Harvey; - ; - ; 44

John A. Harvey; 3 November 1865; - ; - ; - ; - ; G- Alfred P. Harvey, money from estate of Adam Dockstader; 10

Mary S. Harvey; 30 July 1891; - ; - ; - ; - ; - ; 44

Kate Harvey; about 1884; John Harvey; - ; Ida Harvey; - ; - ; 44

Katerene/ Catherine Hassen; about 1900; foster father was Louie St. Louis; - ; - ; - ; residence of parents unknown, G- James P. Casey; 45

Clyde C. Hatzell; 12 December 1911; Carl C. Hatzell; Emily; William and Robert Hatzell, and Pearl Dake; - ; - ; 46

Effie Hawkins: 31 August 1863; Lorenzo Hawkins, died 18 June 1869 in Lafayette, McKean, Pennsylvania; Betsey, married William Barber; had ten siblings, one of the siblings was Arthur Hawkins, HB Willie Hawkins; A-Roxana Hawkins (W- of Elijah Hawkins); A- Mary Pupple (W- of William T. Pupple); - ; 10

George Hawkins; 16 December 1861; Orson P. Hawkins; - ; - ; - ; G- Mary A. Hawkins; 10

Caroline E. Hawley; 11 November 1840; Alonzo Hawley, of Hinsdale; - ; Lucy, Frances, Frederick and Jonathan Hawley; - ; - ; 75

Fannie Maude Hawley; 3 February 1876; Horace E. Hawley; - ; - ; GM Ellen Tucker; - ; 47

Frances M. Hawley; 12 April; 1842; Alonzo Hawley, of Hinsdale; - ; Lucy, Caroline, Frederick and Jonathan Hawley; - ; - ; 75

Frederick A. Hawley; 25 May 1845; Alonzo Hawley, of Hinsdale; - ; Lucy, Caroline, Frances and Jonathan Hawley; - ; - ; 75

Jonathan F. Hawley; 24 June 1853; Alonzo Hawley, of Hinsdale; - ; Lucy, Caroline, Frances and Frederick Hawley; - ; - ; 75

Name; Date of Birth; Father; Mother; Siblings; Other Relatives; Notes; Box Number

Lucy E. Hawley; 22 September 1849; Alonzo Hawley, of Hinsdale; - ; Jonathan, Caroline, Frances and Frederick Hawley; - ; - ; 75

Lydia Hawley; July 1836; Aretus Hawley, of Napoli; - ; - ; - ; received legacy left by Jesse D. Hawley; 76

Augustine F. Hayden; May 1842; Ebenezer W. Hayden, died in Wisconsin; Lucretia M., died in Wisconsin; Edward Hayden; PGM Asenath Hayden, U-Augustus Hayden, A- Augusta C. Terry; - ; 75

Edward L. Hayden; - ; Ebenezer W. Hayden, died in Wisconsin; Lucretia M., died in Wisconsin; Augustine Hayden; PGM Asenath Hayden, U-Augustus Hayden, A- Augusta C. Terry; - ; 75

Laura Hayes; 5 March 1895; - ; - ; - ; - ; G- Anna A. Moore and received legacy from Eva K. Hayes; 75

Mary A. Oosterhoudt Haynes; 20 February 1881; Mr. Oosterhoudt ; Louisa ; - ; HU Sterling Haynes, U- Henry Allen; - ; 45 and 67

Carrie Hays; 8 July 1904; - ; Lena M.; Frankie and Mary Jane Hays; - ; - ; 45

Frankie Hays; 5 October 1902; - ; Lena M.; Carrie and Mary Jane Hays; - ; - ; 45

Mary Jane Hays; 1 May 1906; - ; Lena M.; Carrie and Frankie Hays; - ; - ; 45

Seward R. Hays; - ; - ; Annette Vosburgh; - ; MGF John Vosburgh, died 1 March 1872; - ; 44

Arthur D. Hazard; about 1859; Joseph Hazard, died May 1875; Susan; Theodore and Willie Hazard; - ; - ; 44

Theodore L. Hazard; about 1861; Joseph Hazard, died May 1875; Susan; Arthur and Willie Hazard; - ; - ; 44

Willie H. Hazard; about 1865; Joseph Hazard, died May 1875; Susan; Arthur and Theodore Hazard; - ; - ; 44

Polly E. Hazzard; 29 September 1866; - ; Helen M., died before 31 August 1885; - ; HU Mr. Weible; father was prospecting out west since her birth, G- Edwin Bell, no relation; 12

Name; Date of Birth; Father; Mother; Siblings; Other Relatives; Notes; Box Number

Charles Heath; 14 February 1856; - ; - ; - ; - ; G- James W. Phelps;11

Walter Heath; 26 or 31 October 1861; Henry Heath; - ; - ; - ; G- H. D. Didcock, friend; 11

Ethel Hehir; 28 October 1908; Edward C. Hehir, of Ischua; - ; William Hehir; PGM Mary Hehir, A- Agnes Hehir; - ; 64

William Hehir; 12 April 1911; Edward C. Hehir, of Ischua; - ; Ethel Hehir; PGM Mary Hehir, A- Agnes Hehir; - ; 64

Sigurd Helland; 13 June 1886; - ; - ; - ; - ; parents in Norway, G- George Peterson; 67

Alberta Helms; about 1907; Mark C. Helms, died 8 June 1906; China B.; Benson Helms; - ; - ; 11

Benson Helms; about 1906; Mark C. Helms, died 8 June 1906; China B.; Alberta Helms; - ; - ; 11

Emma B. Helms; about 1853; - ; Mary A.; Mary Helms; - ; - ; 44

John C. Helms; about 1849; - ; - ; - ; - ; G- M. Van Benson; 75

Lorano O. Helms; 27 January 1908; Verland M. Helms; Daisy; - ; - ; received money from estate of Olive E. Helms; 45

Mary A. Helms; about 1851; - ; Mary A.; Emma Helms; - ; - ; 44

Charles Helser; about 1859; Thomas Helser; Moneyck; Francis and Joseph Helser; - ; G- Noah Little; 75

Francis Helser; 2 August 1851; Thomas Helser; Moneyck; Charles and Joseph Helser; - ; G- Noah Little; 75

Joseph Helser; 15 August 1855; Thomas Helser; Moneyck; Charles and Francis Helser; - ; G- Noah Little, money from uncle and brother's bounty; 10 and 75

Edna K. Helvering; 12 February 1889; - ; Kathryn; - ; HU Mr. Beattie; money from B. R. R. Trainmen insurance; 12

Ethel Henderson; about 1886; - ; Mary A.; - ; - ; - ; 44

Alson W. Henley; 15 November 1911; - ; - ; - ; - ; U- Wesley Hitchcock; father resided in Mt. View, California, mother died about 1911; 46

Julia Hennesey; - ; Timothy Hennesey, died May 1865, of Mansfield; Ann, married Mr. Little; Rebecca and Mary Hennesey; - ; - ; 75

Name; Date of Birth; Father; Mother; Siblings; Other Relatives; Notes; Box Number

Mary Ann Hennesey; - ; Timothy Hennesey, died May 1865, of Mansfield; Ann, married Mr. Little; Rebecca and Julia Hennesey; - ; - ; 75

Rebecca Hennesey; - ; Timothy Hennesey, died May 1865, of Mansfield; Ann, married Mr. Little; Mary and Julia Hennesey; - ; - ; 75

Anna Hennessy; 19 May 1897; - ; - ; Mary (RE with Feltons in Titusville) and two brothers whereabouts unknown; - ; father whereabouts unknown, AKA Anna Hurley, RE with Mrs. Timothy Hurley (of 116 Water Sr., Olean, from 1908-1913), G- Mary Hurley, money from estate Hannah Hurley; 64

James H. Hennessy; 14 October 1896; James Hennessy; Catherine; - ; - ; - ; 46

Carlisle Henry; about 1876; - ; Katherine; Lena, Lewis and Lula Henry; - ; money from estate of Joseph Henry; 12

Elmer Henry; about 1901; - ; - ; Vincent Henry and Irene Henry McCann; - ; - ; 11

Hollice Henry; 13 February 1893; - ; Ann; Joseph, Nellie and Perry Henry; - ; - ; 12

Joseph P. Henry; 6 September 1877; - ; Ann; Hollice, Nellie and Perry Henry; - ; - ; 12

Lena A. Henry; about 1875; - ; Katherine; Carlisle, Lewis and Lula Henry; HU Mr. Chaffee; money from Joseph Henry's estate; 12

Lewis A. Henry; about 1878; - ; Katherine; Lena, Carlisle and Lula Henry; - ; money from estate of Joseph Henry; 12

Lula B. Henry; about 1886; - ; Katherine; Lena, Carlisle and Lewis Henry; - ; money from estate of Joseph Henry; 12

Nellie M. Henry; 6 August 1883; - ; Ann; Hollice, Perry and Joseph Henry; HU Mr. Morton ; - ; 12

Perry W. Henry; 7 July 1880; - ; Ann; Hollice, Nellie and Joseph Henry; - ; - ; 12

Vincent Henry; about 1899; - ; - ; Elmer Henry and Irene Henry McCann; - ; - ; 11

Alberta Babb Herrick; December 1876; - ; Belle; - ; - ; - ; 11

Name; Date of Birth; Father; Mother; Siblings; Other Relatives; Notes; Box Number

Emery F. Herrick; 2 June 1857; Stephen M. Herrick; Marian, died November 1875; Glenn, Willie and Marvin Herrick; PGM Mary Herrick; - ; 10

Eva M. Herrick; 11 May 1885; John Herrick; - ; - ; - ; G- George W. Cary; 9

Glenn W. Herrick; 5 Jan 1870; Stephen M. Herrick; Marian, died November 1875; Emery, Willie and Marvin Herrick; PGM Mary Herrick; - ; 10

John L. Herrick; 26 May 1908; John P. Herrick; - ; Virginia and Paul Herrick; MGF Lafayette Young (died 15 November 1926 in Des Moines, Iowa), MU Lafayette Young, Jr., MU Harold Young; Lafayette's wife died 19 December 1926; 46

Marvin E. Herrick; August 1860; Stephen M. Herrick; Marian, died November 1875; Emery, Willie and Glenn Herrick; PGM Mary Herrick; - ; 10

Paul Y. Herrick; 2 March 1910; John P. Herrick; - ; Virginia and John Herrick; MGF Lafayette Young (died 15 November 1926 in Des Moines, Iowa), MU Lafayette Young, Jr., MU Harold Young; Lafayette's wife died 19 December 1926; 46

Virginia Herrick; 13 November 1906; John P. Herrick; - ; Paul and John Herrick; MGF Lafayette Young (died 15 November 1926 in Des Moines, Iowa), MU Lafayette Young, Jr., MU Harold Young; Lafayette's wife died 19 December 1926; 46

Willie Herrick; February 1863; Stephen M. Herrick; Marian, died November 1875; Emery, Marvin and Glenn Herrick; PGM Mary Herrick; - ; 10

Charles D. Hevenor; 11 April 1877; William Hevenor; - ; Edward Hevenor; - ; - ; - ; 44

Edward A. Hevenor; 13 June 1882; William Hevenor; - ; Charles Hevenor; - ; - ; - ; 44

Iva Charlotte Hevenor; - ; Harvey Hevenor; Charlotte J., died 27 November 1889, in Jamestown, NY; - ; - ; - ; 44

Guy C. Hickey; 4 July 1876; - ; Margaret; - ; - ; - ; 44

Frank Harrison Higgins; 5 July 1886; - ; Kate C.; - ; - ; - ; 67

Charles H. Hildum; 21 December 1904; Charles C. Hildum; - ;

Name; Date of Birth; Father; Mother; Siblings; Other Relatives; Notes; Box Number

- ; - ; mother died 1918; 12

Addie H. Hill; 13 August 1883; - ; Alma M., of Conewango; Ray Hill; - ; received money from estate of L. D. Hill; 67

Alice L. Hill; about 1869; Levi M. Hill, was confined as insane person at Willard Asylum at Romulus, NY, and also at Ovid, Seneca, NY; Mary R. died before July 1885; Delevan S. Hill; U- Delevan W. Scudder, U- Hezekiah B. Scudder, A- Alice Rice, A- Ada Scudder; first G- Ezekiel J. Scudder, second G- Nicholas Angle (moved to Minnesota), third G- Asahel Crowley (not related), money from estate of Mark H. Beecher (of Orleans County); 10

Bertha M. Hill; 10 August 1896; - ; Henrietta; - ; - ; father was in Isle of Princes, he abandoned his family, G- Max E. Hill, received money from estate of Leroy N. Hill; 45

Delevan S. Hill; about 1871; Levi M. Hill, was confined as insane person at Willard Asylum at Romulus, NY, and also at Ovid, Seneca, NY; Mary R. died before July 1885; Alice Hill; U- Delevan W. Scudder, U- Hezekiah B. Scudder, A- Alice Rice, A- Ada Scudder; first G- Ezekiel J. Scudder, second G- Nicholas Angle (moved to Minnesota), third G- Asahel Crowley (not related), received money from estate of Mark H. Beecher, of Orleans County; 10

James Cannon Hill; 28 April 1906; Sidney H. Hill, of Friendship, NY; Elizabeth; - ; W- Clarise; G- James Comstock, James wanted to be professional boxer; 45

Ray C. Hill; 19 October 1879; - ; Alma M., of Conewango; Addie Hill; - ; received money from estate of L. D. Hill; 67

Mary Hillebert; 8 February 1859; Nelson Hillebert; Eleanor; Warren Hillebert; - ; - ; 10

Warren Hillebert; 21 August 1850; Nelson Hillebert; Eleanor; Mary Hillebert; - ; - ; 10

Katherine F. Hillmiller; 21 March 1895; - ; - ; - ; HU Mr. Ferrara; G- Regina Hillmiller; 44

Sofie Hillmiller; 23 September 1897; - ; - ; - ; - ; G- Regina Hillmiller; 44

Name; Date of Birth; Father; Mother; Siblings; Other Relatives; Notes; Box Number

Mary Adeline Hinman; 30 January 1878; Benjamin B. Hinman; - ; - ; - ; mother died April 1890; 44

Bennie B. Hinman; 26 December 1875; Benjamin B. Hinman; - ; - ; - ; - ; 11

DeForest Hinman; 14 August 1882; Alfred Hinman, died before 19 October 1893; Elizabeth; Mabel and Emery Hinman; - ; G- Walter Walrath; 11

Donald F. Hinman; about 1904; - ; Anna B. of Black Creek, NY, married Mr. Bates; - ; - ; Donald lived with S. D. Stone; 11

Emery A. Hinman; 8 December 1875; Alfred Hinman, died before 19 October 1893; Elizabeth; Mabel and DeForest Hinman; - ; G- Walter Walrath; 11

Evelyn Hinman; 6 May 1901; Manley Hinman; - ; - ; - ; money from Margaret Masoner; 11

Mabel Hinman; June 1885; Alfred Hinman, died before 19 October 1893; Elizabeth; Emery and DeForest Hinman; HU Mr. Metts ; G- Walter Walrath; 11

Mayme E. Hinman; 31 December 1888; Anson Hinman, died before 6 May 1897; Mary E.; - ; - ; G- Homer Hollister; 11

Oscar B. Hinman; 20 March 1884; - ; Step-mom was Jennie ; - ; - ; first G- Hoyt Hinman, second G- James W. Mulcay, third G- Walter Hubbard, no relation; 12

Bert Hinze; 22 May 1890; - ; Matilda, died before September 1917; Dorothy and John Hinze; - ; - ; 45

Dorothy Hinze; 22 March 1901; - ; Matilda, died before September 1917; Bert and John Hinze; HU Walter Drepensted; - ; 45

John Hinze; 20 May 1895; - ; Matilda, died before September 1917; Bert and Dorothy Hinze; - ; - ; 4

Allice Hitchcock; 12 February 1855; George Hitchcock, died April 1856, of Humphrey; Jane, married Mr. Williams; - ; - ; G- Hollis Scott; 75

Amelia Hitchcock; 13 October 1857; - ; Ruth; Elsie Hitchcock; HU Mr. Pritchard; heir of Jos. Hitchcock; 11

Charlie Hitchcock; about 1855; - ; - ; Edward Hitchcock; - ; heir

Name; Date of Birth; Father; Mother; Siblings; Other Relatives; Notes; Box Number

of Jos. Hitchcock; 11

Elsie Hitchcock; 8 January 1859; - ; Ruth; Amelia Hitchcock; HU Mr. Schoonhover; heir of Jos. Hitchcock; 11

Emma R. Hitchcock; 7 September 1883; - ; - ; William Hitchcock; HU Mr. Nuda; G- Charles Eugene Hitchcock; 64

Ida Hitchcock; - ; - ; Emma, married Welcome J. Dawton; - ; - ; received money from estate of Henry Hitchcock; 44

William G. Hitchcock; 7 August 1877; - ; - ; Emma Hitchcock; - ; G- Charles Eugene Hitchcock; 64

Merrill A. Hoag; about 1873; Morris J. Hoag; - ; - ; - ; - ; 46

Minnie Hoaker; 27 October 1866; Lawrence Hoaker, died June 1875; Frederica, married Christian Deitt; - ; HU Mr. Block, MA Mary Bierns, MA Christiana Miller, MA Johanna Ocherich; - ; 11

Fred Hodges; 13 April 1876; Jerome Hodges; Laura V., died before June 1893; Halla Hodges; - ; - ; 47

Halla "Hallie" Hodges; 31 August 1872; Jerome Hodges; Laura V., died before June 1893; Fred Hodges; - ; - ; 47

Wilbur Hodson; 13 June 1901; - ; Clara B., lived at Pennsylvania Soldiers and Sailors Home in Erie, Pennsylvania; - ; A- Agnes Hendershot; RE Erie County, Pennsylvania, received money from estate of Mrs. Sarah Welsh; 12

Elizabeth "Bessie" T. Hoffmire; 3 October 1886; - ; Emma; - ; - ; G- Josiah Madara; 9

Clara "Nellie" E. Hogan; 25 May 1889; - ; - ; Martin and William J. Hogan; - ; - ; 44

Martin Phillip Hogan; 28 October 1885; - ; - ; Clara and William J. Hogan; - ; - ; 44

Anna C. Hogg; 13 June 1885; - ; Mina, of Franklinville; Ethel Hogg; - ; father died before April 1896; 75

Ethel Mary Hogg; 1 March 1889; - ; Mina, of Franklinville; Anna Hogg; - ; father died before April 1896; 75

Helen Holbrook; May 1896; - ; - ; Rollin, Mac and Orpha Holbrook; - ; money from Martin F. Holbrook's estate; 46

Mac Holbrook; 2 February 1893; - ; - ; Rollin, Helen and Orpha

Name; Date of Birth; Father; Mother; Siblings; Other Relatives; Notes; Box Number

Holbrook; - ; money from Martin F. Holbrook's estate; 46

Orpha Jeanette Holbrook; - ; - ; - ; Rollin, Helen and Mac Holbrook; - ; money from Martin F. Holbrook's estate; 46

Robert Holbrook; about 1903; - ; Jessie, married Mr. Rich; Rollin W. Holbrook (RE Selon Springs, Maryland, and worked in patent office); - ; - ; 11

Rollin W. Holbrook; 26 April 1891; - ; - ; Orpha, Helen and Mac Holbrook; - ; money from Martin F. Holbrook's estate; 46

Amelia Holland; November 1847; - ; - ; - ; MG Abel and Polly Rice, PG Nathaniel and Amelia Holland, MU Clark Rice, PU Lott Holland, MA Lovina Harmon, MA Louisa Ann Day, MA Sylvia Rice; - ; 75

Harlin Hollister; - ; Robert Hollister, died October 1829, of Machias; - ; Major Hollister; - ; G- John Hollister; 76

Major Hollister; about 1817; Robert Hollister, died October 1829, of Machias; - ; Harlin Hollister; - ; G- Elihu Hollister; 76

Peter Hollod; 2 July 1910; - ; - ; - ; third C- John Bazo; - ; 64

Alma Holmes; 28 December 1852; Delos Holmes, died before April 1867; - ; Hervey Holmes; PA Phebe (W- of Isaac Reed), PA Betsey (W- of James Mercer); G- Sylvester Holmes (of Lee, Oneida, NY); 75

Blanche L. Holmes; 19 October 1879; Burton Holmes; - ; Mayme Holmes; HU Mr. Manning; RE 1900, Sardinia, Erie, NY, received money from estate of James Higgins; 9

Ernest R. Holmes; 8 March 1898; Burnom M. Holmes; - ; Nina E. Holmes; - ; - ; 44

Hervey Holmes; 8 May 1855; Delos Holmes, died before April 1867; - ; Alma Holmes; PA Phebe (W- of Isaac Reed), PA Betsey (W- of James Mercer); G- Sylvester Holmes, of Lee, Oneida, NY; 75

Mayme H. Holmes; 6 August 1876; Burton Holmes; - ; Blanche Holmes; HU Mr. Smith; received money from estate of James Higgins; 9

Nina E. Holmes; 15 September 1901; Burnom M. Holmes; - ;

Name; Date of Birth; Father; Mother; Siblings; Other Relatives; Notes; Box Number

Ernest Holmes; - ; - ; 44

Andrew Jacob Holzwarth; 23 March 1870; Christian Holzwarth, died November 1875; Elizabeth; Laura Holzwarth; GM Hannah Oyer, U- Edwin Greene, A- Ellen Houck, A- Adell Parker, A- Ida Parker, C- John Rohrick, C- Frederick Rohrick; G- John Longhans; 10

Laura E. Holzwarth; 3 November 1867; Christian Holzwarth, died November 1875; Elizabeth; Andrew Holzwarth; HU Mr. Butts, GM Hannah Oyer, U- Edwin Greene, A- Ellen Houck, A- Adell Parker, A- Ida Parker, C- John Rohrick, C- Frederick Rohrick; G- John Longhans; 10

Emma Homer; 2 July 1877; Jacob Homer; - ; Lena Homer; - ; G- Fredrick Smith, not related; 11

Lena Homer; 19 May 1879; Jacob Homer; - ; Emma Homer; - ; G- Fredrick Smith, not related; 11

Otis Hooker; 9 June 1850; Stephen Hooker; - ; HB William Hooker, sisters are Mrs. T. J. Parker and Mrs. Crandall; - ; first G- George Wells, G- Lemuel Hall, no relation; 11

Edgar E. Hooper; 19 September 1891; Cye Hooper; Edith; - ; - ; parents were separated; 9

Frank D. Hooper; 19 July 1888; - ; Jessie C., married E. W. Read; - ; - ; Frank died 2 January 1909, Elizabeth M. Johns left legacy; 9

Emma L. Hopkins; 7 May 1865; - ; - ; - ; - ; G- Jamerson D. Blanchard; 10

Richard P. Horner; about 1894; Philetus L. Holmes, of Philadelphia, Pennsylvania; Marcia B., lived in Olean; - ; - ; received money from estate of William B. Pierce; 44

Ethelene Mosher Horning; 24 January 1897; - ; name at time of her death Millie B. Seelman; - ; HU William Horning, married 1 January 1914; - 46

Ada Horth; 26 December 1874; - ; - ; Frances Horth; BIL Andrew Rickard; - ; 46

Ada Horth; - ; George Horth, died January 1870; - ; De Hart Horth; HU Mr. Waite, adopted MGF Justus Thomas; - ; 10

Name; Date of Birth; Father; Mother; Siblings; Other Relatives; Notes; Box Number

Cassie Horth; - ; Alexander Horth, died April 1860; Sally Pratt; Mark, Ida May and Lydia J. Horth and Rositha McKoon; PU Hiram Horth, MU Delos Pratt; - ; 10

De Hart Horth; - ; George Horth, died January 1870; - ; Ada Horth; adopted MGF Justus Thomas; - ; 10

Eleanor R. Horth; August 1847; - ; - ; Marcus Horth; A- Rachel Herrick, U- Benjamin Horth; - ; 11

Frances Horth; 16 March 1876; - ; - ; Ada Horth; BIL Andrew Rickard; see Box 43 under Francis Horth Fellows ; 46

Ida May Horth; - ; Alexander Horth, died April 1860; Sally Pratt; Mark, Cassie and Lydia J. Horth and Rositha McKoon; PU Hiram Horth, MU Delos Pratt; - ; 10

Marcus A. Horth; November 1842; - ; - ; Eleanor Horth; A- Rachel Herrick, U- Benjamin Horth; - ; 11

Elmer E. Horton; 7 November 1872; Edward Horton, died March 1875; Dulcina, married a Mr. Harvey; - ; other relatives were Nancy Annis, Manley and Delaney Kilburn, John, Albert, William and Angeline Horton, Amelia Swetland and Martha Conklin; Elmer was indicted of felony and needed guardian to receive pension money; 11

Addison Hotchkiss; about 1849; - ; - ; Asahel Hotchkiss; - ; G- Wesley Moore; 11

Asahel Hotchkiss; about 1849; - ; - ; Addison Hotchkiss; - ; G- Wesley Moore;

Bessie L. Hotchkiss; 13 March 1870; - ; Rachel Amanda (Amanda R.), married Mr. Weaver and moved to Albany, NY, by 1890; - ; - ; father died before 5 October 1885.; 10

Lorraine Hotchkiss; about 1855; - ; - ; - ; HU John Hotchkiss; - ; 44

Esther Hotton; 20 June 1894; Nicholas Hotton; Louis B.; Nicholas and Harold Hotton; - ; - ; 9

Harold J. Hotton; 4 March 1886; Nicholas Hotton; Louis B.; Nicholas and Esther Hotton; - ; - ; 9

Nicholas J. Hotton, Jr.; 12 May 1889 ; Nicholas Hotton; Louis B.; Harold and Esther Hotton; - ; - ; 9

Name; Date of Birth; Father; Mother; Siblings; Other Relatives; Notes; Box Number

Burton Houghtailing; 9 February 1879; Budd Houghtailing; Adell Cooley; - ; PGF Alvah Houghtailing, MGF Ebenezer Cooley, PU John Houghtailing, PU Bird Houghtailing; MU Oliver Cooley; - ; 12

Blanche Houghtaling; 9 April 1886; Bird Houghtaling; Rose; Guy Houghtaling; HU Mr. Grose; RE 1912, Niagara Falls, G- George L. Folts, not related; 9

Guy Houghtaling; 13 May 1891; Bird Houghtaling; Rose; Blanche Houghtaling; - ; RE 1912, Niagara Falls, G- George L. Folts, not related; 9

Blanche Howard; about 1874; Roderick Howard; - ; Grace, Ernest, Earl, Cora, William, Claude and Clide Howard; - ; - ; 44

Claude Howard; - ; Roderick Howard; - ; Grace, Ernest, Earl, Cora, William, Blanche and Clide Howard; - ; - ; 44

Clide Howard; 22 May 1871; Roderick Howard; - ; Grace, Ernest, Earl, Cora, William, Blanche and Claude Howard; - ; - ; 44

Cora Howard; about 1885; Roderick Howard; - ; Grace, Ernest, Earl, Clide, William, Blanche and Claude Howard; - ; - ; 44

Earl Howard; about 1883; Roderick Howard; - ; Grace, Ernest, Cora, Clide, William, Blanche and Claude Howard; - ; - ; 44

Ernest Howard; about 1881; Roderick Howard; - ; Grace, Earl, Cora, Clide, William, Blanche and Claude Howard; - ; - ; 44

Grace Howard; about 1877; Roderick Howard; - ; Ernest, Earl, Cora, Clide, William, Blanche and Claude Howard; - ; - ; 44

William Howard; 30 May 1868; Roderick Howard; - ; Ernest, Earl, Cora, Clide, Grace, Blanche and Claude Howard; - ; - ; 44

William Howard; 16 July 1858; - ; - ; - ; - ; G- Wallace Rich; 11

Arlie Howe; 23 August 1890; J. M. Howe; - ; Charlotte Howe; - ; - ; 12

Charlotte E. Howe; 31 December 1886; J. M. Howe; - ; Arlie Howe; HU Mr. Orsburn; received money from estate of John Sewall Sanderson; 12

Name; Date of Birth; Father; Mother; Siblings; Other Relatives; Notes; Box Number

Victor A. Howe; 26 April 1842; - ; Matilda E.; Victoria Howe; - ; - ; 11

Victoria A. Howe; 26 April 1842; - ; Matilda E.; Victor Howe; - ; - ; 11

Floyd Hoxie; about 1887; - ; Etta; - ; - ; G- Charles Brown; 44

Belle L. Hubbard; - ; Mark A. Hubbard, died before July 1870; - ; - ; - ; G- Oliver P. Coon, papers filed in McKean County, Pennsylvania, money from Russell Hubbard's estate; 75

Ella C. Hubbard; 1 March 1858 or 1860; - ; - ; - ; - ; RE Kalamazoo County, Michigan, G- Eugene Nash; 11

Ethel M. Hubbard; 12 October 1885; - ; Grace A.; Ralph Hubbard; - ; money from estate Miner E. Hubbard's estate; 9

Florence Hubbard; 23 June 1902; Walter S. Hubbard, died before 1908; Ethel B., died 1919; Leola Hubbard; A- Mrs. George W. Houck, of Buffalo, NY, A- Florence A. Houck; - ;45

Leola Hubbard; 15 November 1903; Walter S. Hubbard, died before 1908; Ethel B., died 1919; Florence Hubbard; A- Mrs. George W. Houck, of Buffalo, NY, A- Florence A. Houck; RE 1928, in Boston, Massachusetts; 45

Lora Delana Hubbard; - ; Clarence G. Hubbard, lived in Spokane, Washington; Blanche M.; - ; - ; received money from estate of Esther L. Hubbard; 9

Marvin Hubbard; 17 March 1894; - ; Ella, married Mr. Price; Emmett Hubbard; - ; father died before April 1912; 79

Ralph M. Hubbard; 22 May 1881; - ; Grace A.; Ethel M. Hubbard; - ; money from Miner E. Hubbard's estate; 9

William M. Hubbard; about 1855; Manley Hubbard; Jemina, died May 1858; - ; - ; - ; 11

Thomas Ostrom Hubbell; 1905; Wesley C. Hubbell, of Randolph; Bertha M. Ostrom; - ; PG Thomas L. Ostrum (of Randolph, died 4 December 1910) and Helen L. Ostrum; - ; 66

Nora A. Huff; about 1863; - ; Lenora; - ; - ; - ; 44

Michael C. Hufstader; - ; - ; - ; - ; - ; only bond exists in

Name; Date of Birth; Father; Mother; Siblings; Other Relatives; Notes; Box Number

envelope; 76

Floyd W. Huggins; 4 February 1894; - ; - ; - ; C- Charles Huggins; money from estate Emma C. Huggins's estate; 12

Glenn R. Huggins; about 1890; Elmore Huggins, of Salamanca; - ; - ; - ; - ;67

Marshall C. Huggins; 18 December 1884; - ; Elizabeth; - ; - ; - ; 9

Anna Hughes; 27 February 1897; John Hughes, died 4 May 1905 in Pittsburgh, Pennsylvania; Mary, RE 108 N. 6th St., Olean, NY; J. Les, Margaret, James, Katherine, Theresa and Dorothea Hughes; HU Mr. Murphy, GM Margaret Hogan (died 1906); - ; 46

Dorothea Hughes; 21 May 1898; John Hughes, died 4 May 1905 in Pittsburgh, Pennsylvania; Mary, RE 108 N. 6th St., Olean, NY; J. Les, Margaret, James, Katherine, Theresa and Anna Hughes; GM Margaret Hogan (died 1906); - ; 46

Emma L. Hughes; 2 January 1852; George Hughes, died before November 1867; - ; - ; - ; G- Sophronia Phillips (of Allegany); 75

Frank Fakir Hughes; - ; - ; - ; - ; - ; - ; 44

Harry Ara Hughes; - ; - ; - ; - ; - ; - ; 44

Henry Hughes; 7 December 1895; - ; - ; - ; - ; G- William Hughes; 45

J. Les Hughes; 17 August 1893; John Hughes, died 4 May 1905 in Pittsburgh, Pennsylvania; Mary, RE 108 N. 6th St., Olean, NY; Dorothea, Margaret, James, Katherine, Theresa and Anna Hughes; GM Margaret Hogan (died 1906); - ; 46

James Hughes; 18 May 1896; John Hughes, died 4 May 1905 in Pittsburgh, Pennsylvania; Mary, RE 108 N. 6th St., Olean, NY; Dorothea, Margaret, J. Les, Katherine, Theresa and Anna Hughes; GM Margaret Hogan (died 1906); - ; 46

John D. Hughes; 12 December 1888; James S. Hughes, died 25 September 1895 in Bradford, Pennsylvania; Margaret, died 26 October 1898, in Bradford, Pennsylvania; - ; PA Ellen F. Hughes; - ; 46

Name; Date of Birth; Father; Mother; Siblings; Other Relatives; Notes; Box Number

Katherine Hughes; 29 September 1888; John Hughes, died 4 May 1905 in Pittsburgh, Pennsylvania; Mary, Re 108 N. 6th St., Olean, NY; Dorothea, Margaret, J. Les, James, Theresa and Anna Hughes; GM Margaret Hogan (died 1906); - ; 46

Margaret Hughes; 27 November 1894; John Hughes, died 4 May 1905 in Pittsburgh, Pennsylvania; Mary, RE 108 N. 6th St., Olean, NY; Dorothea, Jamest, J. Les, Katherine, Theresa and Anna Hughes; GM Margaret Hogan (died 1906); - ; 46

Theresa Hughes; 26 March 1903; John Hughes, died 4 May 1905 in Pittsburgh, Pennsylvania; Mary, RE 108 N. 6th St., Olean, NY; Dorothea, James, J. Les, Katherine, Margaret and Anna Hughes; GM Margaret Hogan (died 1906); - ; 46

Adaliza Hughey; about 1850; - ; - ; - ; - ; G- George Hughey, of Ashford; 75

Guy M. Hughey; 23 May 1885; - ; - ; Claude and Neil Hughey; - ; - ; 9

Neil J. Hughey; 5 September 1883; - ; - ; Claude and Guy Hughey; - ;   - ; 9

Arthur Hull; 12 April 1860; Samuel Hull, died before January 1865; Emeline Howard; - ; MGF Henry Howard, PU Collins Spencer; - ; 75

Robert Humes; 10 October 1881; Jackson Humes, died 1889; Eleanor, died September 1893; - ; GM Mary R. Placher, lived in Fairfield, Illinois; - ; 12

Seymour Adelbert Humphrey; about 1858; Seymour Humphrey; Eliza A., married Mr. Rose; - ; - ; received pension money; 11

Frances "Franny" L. Hunt; 1 September 1850; Hiram B. Hunt; Mariette B.; Loretta E. Hunt; U- William E. Hunt, U- Andrew Borden; another name mentioned was Constant B. Allen; 10

Loretta E. Hunt; 11 August 1846 Hiram B. Hunt; Mariette B.; Loretta E. Hunt; HU Mr. Crandall, U- William E. Hunt, U- Andrew Borden; another name mentioned was Constant B.

Name; Date of Birth; Father; Mother; Siblings; Other Relatives; Notes; Box Number

Allen; 10

Thomas E. Hunt; 8 June 1910; - ; Anna, of 156 Broad St., Salamanca; Marian Lowe and Dorothy Bradford; - ; father died 11 November 1930; 64

Emily L. Huntington; 9 July 1846; Arnold Huntington, died before February 1855; - ; Monroe, Maria, Lafayette, and George Huntington and Betsey Woodworth; U- David Huntington, U- Trumbull Huntington, U- Horace Huntington, U- Henry Huntington; G- John C. Gardner; 75

Elmer Huntington; - ; - ; Nancy; - ; - ; - ; 44

Fayette G. Huntington; about 1851; Henry Huntington, died 27 March 1863, of Conewango; Rachel; - ; - ; G- Hezekiah Burt; 75

Maria L. Huntington; 7 May 1835; Arnold Huntington, died before February 1855; - ; Monroe, Emily, Lafayette, and George Huntington and Betsey Woodworth; U- David Huntington, U- Trumbull Huntington, U- Horace Huntington, U- Henry Huntington; G- John C. Gardner; 75

Monroe H. Huntington; 4 July 1839; Arnold Huntington, died before February 1855; - ; Maria, Emily, Lafayette, and George Huntington and Betsey Woodworth; U- David Huntington, U- Trumbull Huntington, U- Horace Huntington, U- Henry Huntington; G- John C. Gardner; 75

Ella Huntley; about 1855; - ; - ; - ; HU DeRoy Huntley, of Machias; - ; 75

Alice A. Hunton; about 1864; John M. Hunton, died November 1864; Susan; - ; - ; received pension money; 11

Elbridge G. Hunton; 10 May 1874; Eugene A.; Cora, died November 1881, of New Albion; Nellie Hunton; - ; received money from estate of Arminta Boardman; 47

Nellie A. Hunton; 20 November 1875; Eugene A.; Cora, died November 1881, of New Albion; Elbridge Hunton; - ; received money from estate of Arminta Boardman; 47

Ashahel A. Hurd; about 1844; Ashahel Hurd; Rebecca E.; Ellen Hurd; - ; G- William Knowlton; 11

Name; Date of Birth; Father; Mother; Siblings; Other Relatives; Notes; Box Number

Clarence Hurd; 9 May 1888; - ; - ; Francis Hurd; U- Thomas P. Butler; - ; 9

Edith Hurd; 12 February 1876; Nelson B. Hurd; Madellon, died 27 February 1876; - ; - ; - ; 44

Ellen E. Hurd; about 1840; Ashahel Hurd; Rebecca E.; Ashahel Hurd; - ; G- William Knowlton; 11

Francis Hurd; 19 February 1885; - ; - ; Clarence Hurd; U- Thomas P. Butler; - ; 9

Mary Emily Hurd; 24 July 1873; Philander Hurd; - ; - ; - ; G- I. R. Leonard, received money from estate of GF; 10

Earl B. Hurlbert; about 1909; George C. Hurlbert, residing at 651 Wildwood Ave., Salamanca; Annie, died about Nov. 1922; Mildred and Lee Hurlbert; - ; - ; 10

Henry Hurlbert; about 1876; Edwin G. Hurlbert, died 4 July 1885; - ; John Hurlbert; MGF Benjamin Thomas; Edwin married again after first wife's death and had another daughter, Edwin supposedly committed suicide, Henry's mother died between 1879 and 1881, G- Ransom Terry; 12

John Hurlbert; about 1875; Edwin G. Hurlbert, died 4 July 1885; - ; Henry Hurlbert; MGF Benjamin Thomas; Edwin married again after first wife's death and had another daughter, Edwin supposedly committed suicide, Henry's mother died between 1879 and 1881, G- Ransom Terry; 12

Lee G. Hurlbert; 27 October 1905; George C. Hurlbert,RE 651 Wildwood Ave., Salamanca; Annie, died about Nov. 1922; Mildred and Earl Hurlbert; - ; RE 1926, Chelsea, Suffolk, Massachusetts ; 10

Mildred Hurlbert; about 1911; George C. Hurlbert, RE 651 Wildwood Ave., Salamanca; Annie, died about Nov. 1922; Lee and Earl Hurlbert; - ; - ; 10

Marion L. Hurley; 19 August 1897; Jerry Hurley; Nora, admitted to Gowanda State Hospital as an insane person; - ; - ; RE NY City by 1918, G- Mary Boyce; 14

Mabel Hutchinson; 21 November 1903; Sanford L. Hutchinson; - ; - ; HU Mr. Reeves, married Summer of 1923; RE 1924, in

Name; Date of Birth; Father; Mother; Siblings; Other Relatives; Notes; Box Number

Arcade; 45
Henry W. Huyck; 5 July 1841; Wilbur H. Huyck, of Franklinville; - ; - ; - ; - ;75

Name; Date of Birth; Father; Mother; Siblings; Other Relatives; Notes; Box Number

I Surnames

Harlow F. Ingersoll; 13 December 1856; Francis D. Ingersoll, died before November 1862; - ; Lovica and John Ingersoll; PGF Josephus Ingersoll, PU Cyrus Ingersoll, PU Harmon Ingersoll, MU Jonathan B. Allen, Harlow's mom C- was Norman Allen; - ;75

John Ingersoll; 30 November 1858; Francis D. Ingersoll, died before November 1862; - ; Lovica and Harlow Ingersoll; PGF Josephus Ingersoll, PU Cyrus Ingersoll, PU Harmon Ingersoll, MU Jonathan B. Allen, John's mom C- was Norman Allen; - ;75

Lovica Ingersoll; 4 October 1854; Francis D. Ingersoll, died before November 1862; - ; John and Harlow Ingersoll; PGF Josephus Ingersoll, PU Cyrus Ingersoll, PU Harmon Ingersoll, MU Jonathan B. Allen, Lovica's mom C- was Norman Allen; - ;75

Cora Inman; about 1880; Lowell D. Inman; - ; Lynn Inman; U- John J. Inman; - ; 47

Lynn Inman; about 1879; Lowell D. Inman; - ; Cora Inman; U- John J. Inman; - ; 47

Charles Curtis Irish; 5 May 1904; R. Henry Irish; - ; Simon Irish; - ; G- Stanley A. Neilson; 14

Simon Irish; 24 January 1889; R. Henry Irish; - ; Charles Irish; - ; - ; 14

Bernice Irwin; 13 January 1910; - ; Flora; Marian, Bruce and Thomas Irwin; - ; G- Augustus C. Bussler, received money from estate of Wm. Irwin; 47

Bruce Irwin; 1 April 1908; - ; Flora; Marian, Bernice and Thomas Irwin; - ; also went by Bruce Irwin Starr, RE 1929, in Royal Oak, Oakland, Michigan, G- Augustus C. Bussler, received money from estate of Wm. Irwin; 47

Marian R. Irwin; 8 December 1906; - ; Flora; Bernice, Bruce and Thomas Irwin; - ; G- Augustus C. Bussler, received money

Name; Date of Birth; Father; Mother; Siblings; Other Relatives; Notes; Box Number

from estate of Wm. Irwin; 47

Thomas Irwin; 22 August 1903; - ; Flora; Marian, Bernice and Bruce Irwin; - ; also went by Thomas Irwin Starr, RE 1924, in Royal Oak, Oakland, Michigan, G- Augustus C. Bussler, received money from estate of Wm. Irwin; 47

De Vere Isaman; 11 November 1884; - ; Sarah; Lyman Isaman; - ; father died before June 1895, De Vere received money from estate of George Isaman; 14

Lyman Isaman; 1 March 1878; - ; Sarah; De Vere Isaman; - ; father died before June 1895, Lyman received money from estate of George Isaman; 14

John Ivers; 14 January 1878; - ; - ; Michael Ivers; MU William Gavin, PU John E.Ivers; - ;14

Michael Ivers; March 1879; - ; - ; John Ivers; MU William Gavin, PU John E. Ivers; - ;14

Name; Date of Birth; Father; Mother; Siblings; Other Relatives; Notes; Box Number

J Surnames

Cecil Jackson; - ; - ; - ; Mabel Jackson; other relatives are George Jackson, Florence Brown, and Sadie Cornell; G- David M. Brown; 47

Jay Jackson; 16 October 1889; - ; Angie, married Mr. Fuller; - ; - ; - ; 12

Mabel Jackson; - ; - ; - ; Cecil Jackson; other relatives are George Jackson, Florence Brown, and Sadie Cornell; G- David M. Brown; 47

Amelia Jacobson; 26 November 1893; - ; - ; - ; - ; G- Andrea Franzen; 47

Clyde A. Jacques; 10 February 1909; Delos Jacques; - ; - ; - ; - ; 47

Anna Jahn; about 1885; Anthony Jahn, "lunatic" committed to Buffalo State Asylum on 9 July 1894; Paulina; Rosa, Elizabeth, and Arthur Jahn; - ; - ; 13

Arthur Jahn; about 1891; Anthony Jahn, "lunatic" committed to Buffalo State Asylum on 9 July 1894; Paulina; Rosa, Elizabeth, and Anna Jahn; - ; - ; 13

Elizabeth Jahn; about 1889; Anthony Jahn, "lunatic" committed to Buffalo State Asylum on 9 July 1894; Paulina; Rosa, Arthur, and Anna Jahn; - ; - ; 13

Rosa P. Jahn; about 1887; Anthony Jahn, "lunatic" committed to Buffalo State Asylum on 9 July 1894; Paulina; Elizabeth, Arthur, and Anna Jahn; - ; - ; 13

Frank D. James; about 1883; James James; - ; George James; - ; - ; 13

George I. James; 5 September 1887; James James; - ; Frank James; - ; - ; 13

A. Cortez Jaquay; 12 August 1908; Earl F. Jaquay; - ; Kenneth and Otto Jaquay; - ; money from Mortimer Jaquay's estate; 47

Kenneth M. Jaquay; February 1911; Earl F. Jaquay; - ; A. Cortez

Name; Date of Birth; Father; Mother; Siblings; Other Relatives; Notes; Box Number

and Otto Jaquay; - ; money from Mortimer Jaquay's estate; 47

Otto Theodore Jaquay; 29 May 1905; Earl F. Jaquay; - ; A. Cortez and Kenneth Jaquay; - ; received money from estate of Mortimer Jaquay; 47

Claribel Jefferds; 15 September 1861; F. Jefferds; Luarancy Willard; Willard, Melville, and Samuel Jefferds; MU Owel Willard, MA Julia Shimerski, PU Liberty Jeffords, PA Mrs. Dean P. Howe; - ; 14

Melville O. Jefferds; 20 February 1854; F. Jefferds; Luarancy Willard; Willard, Claribel, and Samuel Jefferds; MU Owel Willard, MA Julia Shimerski, PU Liberty Jeffords, PA Mrs. Dean P. Howe; - ; 14

Samuel C. Jefferds; 20 September 1859; F. Jefferds; Luarancy Willard; Willard, Claribel, and Melville Jefferds; MU Owel Willard, MA Julia Shimerski, PU Liberty Jeffords, PA Mrs. Dean P. Howe; AKA Lamont Jefferds; 14

Willard D. Jefferds; 28 June 1849; F. Jefferds; Luarancy Willard; Samuel, Claribel, and Melville Jefferds; MU Owel Willard, MA Julia Shimerski, PU Liberty Jeffords, PA Mrs. Dean P. Howe; - ; 14

Donald Jenkel; 8 June 1905; Henry Jenkel; - ; Henry C. Jenkel; - ; money from insurance on war risk on Frank Jenkel; 47

Lovett F. Jenks; 25 December 1846; - ; Latisa B.; Orson Jenks; MA Eliza (W-of Hiram Blanchard), MA Tamasin (W- of Solotus Blanchard); G- Bucklin Jenks; 75

Orson A. Jenks; 22 August 1840; - ; Latisa B.; Lovett Jenks; MA Eliza (W-of Hiram Blanchard), MA Tamasin (W- of Solotus Blanchard); G- Bucklin Jenks; 75

Hazel M. Jewell; 7 March 1889; AF Moses Jewell; AM Angie; - ; - ; biological parents RE British Columbia and abandoned Hazel at the Rochester Orphan Asylum; 47

William Ward Jewell; 3 January 1876; - ; - ; - ; U- M. A. Jewell; - ; 14

Eli Jimerson; 1 September 1858; - ; - ; - ; - ; G- Jane Snow, in same envelope with Alice Pierce and Lucinda Seneca; 26

Name; Date of Birth; Father; Mother; Siblings; Other Relatives; Notes; Box Number

Mary Ann Jimerson; 31 January 1849; Robert Jimerson; - ; - ; - ; G- William C. Hoag, Mary needed guardian for bounty claim and pension money; 75

Charlotte E. Johns; 16 August 1882; - ; Susan C. Arnold at time of filing, married Mr. Knight; - ; - ; received money from estate of James B. Jones; 13

Edris Johns; 11 December 1906; John J. Johns; - ; Edward, Harold and Wesley Johns; - ; received money from estate of Thomas Johns; 13

Edward P. Johns; 22 February 1898; John J. Johns; - ; Edris, Harold and Wesley Johns; - ; received money from estate of Thomas Johns; 13

Harold Johns; 24 October 1901; John J. Johns; - ; Edris, Edward and Wesley Johns; - ; received money from estate of Thomas Johns; 13

Wesley Johns; 25 March 1901; John J. Johns; - ; Edris, Edward and Harold Johns; - ; received money from estate of Thomas Johns; 13

Celia M. Johnson; 19 February 1852; Thomas Johnson, died March 1861; Emily Prosser, married Franklin Butcher, she died June 1865; Ellen, Kate and Richard Johnson; MGF Daniel Prosser, PGF Ralph Johnson; - ;13

Charles Johnson; 7 February 1843; - ; Deborah; - ; - ; G- Jane Newkirk; 13

Duane E. Johnson; 20 March 1898; - ; Hattie; - ; - ; father died before 30 March 1908; 13

Edith C. Johnson; 28 March 1891; - ; Elida A., she married a Mr. Livermore; - ; - ; letter in file from probate judge in Morgan County, Alabama, received money from estates of Lucinda A. Johnson and Elton E. Johnson; 13

Edward Webster Johnson; 27 January 1879; John A. Johnson, RE Los Angeles, California, by 1900; Caroline F. Webster, died 31 May 1880; - ; - ; money from insurance for Hugh Webster; 13

Ellen B. Johnson; 20 July 1856; Thomas Johnson, died March

Name; Date of Birth; Father; Mother; Siblings; Other Relatives; Notes; Box Number

    1861; Emily Prosser, married Franklin Butcher, she died June 1865; Celia, Kate and Richard Johnson; MGF Daniel Prosser, PGF Ralph Johnson; - ; 13

Florence A. Johnson; 1 February 1901; - ; Olga, she married Mr. Schrader; Mabel, Raymond and Milton Johnson; HU Mr. Hall; AKA Florence Palm; 13

Henry Johnson Jr.; 25 July 1889; Mr. Doty; - ; - ; GF Henry Johnson, died 19 December 1909; Mr. Doty was divorced from Henry's mother on grounds of adultery, Mr. Doty was convicted of a felony and was in a state prison and Henry's G- Sarah Taggart; 47

Kate A. Johnson; 4 September 1854; Thomas Johnson, died March 1861; Emily Prosser, married Franklin Butcher, she died June 1865; Celia, Ellen and Richard Johnson; MGF Daniel Prosser, PGF Ralph Johnson; - ; 13

Lee A. Johnson; 6 March 1882; - ; - ; - ; - ; AKA Almon Lee Johnson, G- Orton A. Johnson, money from Almira Ingersoll's estate; 13

Mabel V. Johnson; 26 January 1899; - ; Olga, she married Mr. Schrader; Florence, Raymond and Milton Johnson; HU Mr. Good; AKA Mabel Palm; 13

Marcus N. Johnson: born 1 October 1855; Calvin Johnson; Frances; - ; PGF Giles Johnson; PU Corydon Johnson, PU Giles Johnson, PU Bela Johnson; G- Norman Allen; 13

Milton F. Johnson; 13 August 1905; - ; Olga, she married a Mr. Schrader; Florence, Raymond and Mabel Johnson; - ; AKA Milton Palm; 13

Raymond A. Johnson; 28 December 1902; - ; Olga, she married Mr. Schrader; Florence, Milton and Mabel Johnson; - ; AKA Raymond Palm; 13

Richard P. Johnson; 19 March 1850; Thomas Johnson, died March 1861; Emily Prosser, married Franklin Butcher, she died June 1865; Celia, Ellen and Kate Johnson; MGF Daniel Prosser, PGF Ralph Johnson; - ; 13

Alice May Jolls; 30 June 1874; - ; - ; - ; U- Charles Carpenter,

Name; Date of Birth; Father; Mother; Siblings; Other Relatives; Notes; Box Number

Maternal C-Arthur D. Carpenter; Alice's parents died in Titusville, Crawford, Pennsylvania, all four of Alice's siblings lived in Colorado , their guardian is Hamilton Bunce; 47

Angie M. Jolls; 17 September 1879; Warren Jolls; Elizabeth, married Mr. Wood by 1905; Willard, Earl, Elbert, and Ara Jolls; - ; - ; 13

Ara A. Jolls; 13 October 1884; Warren Jolls; Elizabeth, married Mr. Wood by 1905; Willard, Earl, Elbert, and Angie Jolls; - ; - ; 13

Earl A. Jolls; 9 February 1907; John W. Jolls; - ; Merle and Hilda Jolls; - ; - ; 47

Earl W. Jolls; 27 December 1877; Warren Jolls; Elizabeth, married Mr. Wood by 1905; Willard, Ara, Elbert, and Angie Jolls; - ; - ; 13

Elbert Glenn Jolls; 28 September 1874; Warren Jolls; Elizabeth, married Mr. Wood by 1905; Willard, Ara, Earl and Angie Jolls; - ; - ; 13

Hilda B. Jolls; 20 July 1896; John W. Jolls; - ; Merle and Earl Jolls; - ; - ; 47

Merle D. Jolls; 23 November 1894; John W. Jolls; - ; Hilda and Earl Jolls; - ; - ; 47

Willard Burton Jolls; 21 December 1870; Warren Jolls; Elizabeth, married Mr. Wood by 1905; Elbert, Ara, Earl and Angie Jolls; - ; - ; 13

Anne Jones: born 28 May 1886; - ; Catharine; Cathrine, Thomas and Richard Jones; cousins were Elizabeth C., David H., William H. and Catherine E. Jones; RE England; 13

Catharine Jones; about 1855; Morris Jones; - ; Mary, Thomas, and Richard Jones; U- Hugh Jones, U- Thomas Jones; - ; 13

Cathrine Jones; 21 January 1883; - ; Catharine; Anne, Thomas and Richard Jones; cousins were Elizabeth C., David H., William H. and Catherine E. Jones; RE England; 13

Charity J. Jones; 19 October 1863; John W. Jones, died before May 1867; Amelia Damon, married Mr. Nicks; William and

Name; Date of Birth; Father; Mother; Siblings; Other Relatives; Notes; Box Number

Lydia Jones; MGF William H. Damon, PU Oliver Jones; G- Elihu Stewart; 13

Charles Benjamin Jones; - ; Benjamin Jones, died 3 August 1828, of Olean; - ; Ellen and Homer Jones; - ; G- Olive M. Jones and only bond in file in Box 76; 76 and 77

Daniel F Jones; November 1843; Frederick Jones; Permelia, married Mr. Chase; Isaac, Lyman and Silas Jones; - ; G- John Baillet; 13

Dorothy E. Jones; June 1904; Evan L. Jones; - ; Lloyd G. Jones, Vera M. Thompsett and Maud E. Read; - ; - ; 47

Elizabeth C. Jones; - ; - ; - ; - ; - ; - ; 13

Ellen Matilda Jones; - ; Benjamin Jones, died 3 August 1828, of Olean; - ; Charles and Homer Jones; - ; G- Olive M. Jones and only bond in file in Box 76; 76 and 77

Homer Hatch Jones:; - ; Benjamin Jones, died 3 August 1828, of Olean; - ; Charles and Ellen Jones; - ; G- Olive M. Jones and only bond in file in Box 76; 76 and 77

Isaac N. Jones; 14 June 1845; Frederick Jones; Permelia, married Mr. Chase; Daniel, Lyman and Silas Jones; - ; G- John Baillet; 13

Lydia A. Jones; 25 December 1860; John W. Jones, died before May 1867; Amelia Damon, married Mr. Nicks; William and Charity Jones; MGF William H. Damon, PU Oliver Jones; G- Elihu Stewart; 13

Lyman J. Jones; 23 March 1850; Frederick Jones; Permelia, married Mr. Chase; Daniel, Isaac and Silas Jones; - ; G- John Baillet; 13

Mary Jones: born about 1849; Morris Jones; - ; Catharine, Thomas, and Richard Jones; U- Hugh Jones, U- Thomas Jones; - ; 13

Nina M. Jones; 26 March 1889; - ; Hattie ; William, John and David Jones; - ; - ; 13

Ora Jones; 3 August 1869; C. M. Jones, died 4 December 1882; Sophia B.; Verna Jones; - ; - ; 47

Pearl Jones; 10 May 1882; James Jones, served in the Civil War;

Name; Date of Birth; Father; Mother; Siblings; Other Relatives; Notes; Box Number

Emma, married Mr. Fitzpatrick; - ; - ; - ; 47

Richard Jones; about 1858; Morris Jones; - ; Catharine, Thomas, and Mary Jones; U- Hugh Jones, U- Thomas Jones; - ; 13

Richard H. Jones; 9 May 1880; - ; Catharine; Anne, Thomas and Cathrine Jones; cousins were Elizabeth C., David H., William H. and Catherine E. Jones; RE England; 13

Silas Jones; 16 June 1848; Frederick Jones; Permelia, married Mr. Chase; Daniel, Isaac and Lyman Jones; - ; G- John Baillet; 13

Thomas Jones; about 1852; Morris Jones; - ; Catharine, Richard, and Mary Jones; U- Hugh Jones, U- Thomas Jones; - ; 13

Thomas R. Jones; 28 May 1881; - ; Catharine; Anne, Richard, and Cathrine Jones; cousins were Elizabeth C., David H., William H. and Catherine E. Jones; RE England and 1926, Elm Grove, Iowa; 13

Verna S. Jones; 22 June 1873; C. M. Jones, died 4 December 1882; Sophia B.; Ora Jones; - ; - ; 47

Wilbur A. Jones; 24 January 1881; - ; - ; - ; - ; G- Edgar L. Moore (no relation), money from Lyman Jones' estate ; 13

William H. Jones; 19 August 1858; John W. Jones, died before May 1867; Amelia Damon, married Mr. Nicks; Lydia and Charity Jones; MGF William H. Damon, PU Oliver Jones; G- Elihu Stewart; 13

Evelyn Jordan; 4 December 1903; Clare Jordan, RE Illinois; Ruth; - ; A- Belle Smith Herrick; Evelyn resides with Belle Smith Herrick at 307 N. Clinton St., Olean; 47

Edith Joslyn; 30 July 1876; - ; Adelaide; Martin Joslyn; - ; - ; 47

Martin Joslyn; 16 February 1880; - ; Adelaide; Edith Joslyn; - ; - ; 47

Catherine Joy; 3 January 1905; - ; - ; Mary Joy; A- Mary Marron; G- James McMurray, removed by Onondaga County Court; 13

Mary Joy; 19 December 1903; - ; - ; Catherine Joy; A- Mary Marron; G- James McMurray, removed by Onondaga County Court; 13

Name; Date of Birth; Father; Mother; Siblings; Other Relatives; Notes; Box Number

K Surnames

Addie Kafer; about 1867; Jacob Kafer, abandoned family January 1875; - ; - ; other relative was John Laughenthall; Addie died 15 February 1881; 48

Edward Kane; 21 September 1901; John Kane, died 12 June 1921 in Olean; - ; Margaret, John, Daniel, James and Thomas Kane, and Anna Zimbauer; - ; RE 1321 N. Union St., Olean, employed at Vacuum Oil County; 47

Ella Kane; about 1868; Peter Kane, died February 1872, of Great Valley; Eve Eliza, married Mr. Frank; John and Otis Kane; - ; - ;75

Honara (Hannah) Kane; 4 May 1865; Casey Kane; Eliza, married Mr. Robinson; - ; - ; - ; 14

John Kane; about 1853; Peter Kane, died February 1872, of Great Valley; Eve Eliza, married Mr. Frank; Ella and Otis Kane; - ; - ;75

Margaret Kane; 22 January 1906; John Kane, died 12 June 1921 in Olean; - ; John, Edward, Daniel, James and Thomas Kane, and Anna Zimbauer; - ; RE with with William Lawler, 108 N. 10th St., Olean; 47

Otis H. Kane; about 1855; Peter Kane, died February 1872, of Great Valley; Eve Eliza, married Mr. Frank; Ella and John Kane; - ; - ;75

Frank Karczewski;10 June 1909; Stanley Karczewski, resided at 175 Atlantic St., Salamanca; Pauline; - ; - ; Erie RR cut off fingers on right hand; 47

Irene M. Karl; about 1891; - ; - ; Rose M. Reedy, married to T. F. Reedy; - ; received money from estate of Mary Karl; 48

James Emmet Karl; about 1908; John E. Karl, 210 S. Clinton St., Olean; Bessie; Michael Karl; - ; others mentioned in file are Ruth, Claude, Joseph, Winnifred, and John Karl; 48

Michael John Karl; about 1910; John E. Karl, 210 S. Clinton St., Olean; Bessie; James Karl; - ; others mentioned in file are

Name; Date of Birth; Father; Mother; Siblings; Other Relatives; Notes; Box Number

Ruth, Claude, Joseph, Winnifred, and John Karl; 48

Ada O. Kautz; 15 August 1885; - ; - ; Oscar, William and Paul Kautz; 15

Oscar O. Kautz; 29 October 1886; - ; - ; Ada, William and Paul Kautz; 15

William E. Kautz; 4 May 1889; - ; - ; Ada, Oscar and Paul Kautz; 15

Edgar Keating; about 1890; - ; - ; - ; PU Patrick Keating, MU James Griffin, PU John Griffin; Edgar had lived with Mary Hogan since he was two; 14

May E. Keating; 9 May 1884; - ; Minnie A.; - ; - ; - ; 48

Winifred Keating; 27 February 1894; - ; - ; William, Sarah, John, James and Arthur Driscoll; GM Bridget Preston, U- James Preston; - ; 41

Raymond C. Keen; 4 December 1903; - ; Luella, married Mr. Bullock; - ; - ; - ;48

Catharine "Katie" A. Keenan; about 1870; Michael Keenan; - ; - ; - ; received money from estate of Patrick Keenan; 48

Evelyn M. Keim; about 1887; - ; Julia, of Olean; - ; - ; father died before October 1906; 75

George W. Keller; 10 March 1898; - ; - ; - ; other relatives were Eugene W. Keller (born about 1893, in France with American Expeditionary Forces), Arthur Keller (born about 1895, in Hagerstown, MO) and Helen L. Keller (born about 1900, in Hanover, Pennsylvania); RE with Mrs. Agnes Lang (wasn't related, lived at 122 S. 2nd St., Olean), needed G- to obtain marriage license; 48

Cecil B. Kelley; 22 August 1900; - ; Vesta; - ; - ; father died before August 1913, G- Elmer E. Kelley, received money from estate of Ezekiel Kelley; 14

Bernard Kelley; about 1895; Thomas Kelley, died before November 1896; step-mom was Mary; Mary, Thomas, Sarah and Joseph Kelley; - ; - ;14

Joseph Kelley; about 1893; Thomas Kelley, died before November 1896; step-mom was Mary; Mary, Thomas, Sarah

Name; Date of Birth; Father; Mother; Siblings; Other Relatives; Notes; Box Number

and Bernard Kelley; - ; - ;14

Mary Kelley; about 1885; Thomas Kelley, died before November 1896; step-mom was Mary; Joseph, Thomas, Sarah and Bernard Kelley; - ; - ;14

Sarah Kelley; about 1890; Thomas Kelley, died before November 1896; step-mom was Mary; Joseph, Thomas, Mary and Bernard Kelley; - ; - ;14

Thomas Kelley; about 1887; Thomas Kelley, died before November 1896; step-mom was Mary; Joseph, Sarah, Mary and Bernard Kelley; - ; - ;14

John E. Kelly; 16 October 1850; Nelson Kelly, died before August 1862; - ; Mary and Warren Kelly; U- David Whipple, PGF Eddy Kelly; - ; 75

Mary E. Kelly; 11 August 1847; Nelson Kelly, died before August 1862; - ; John and Warren Kelly; U- David Whipple, PGF Eddy Kelly; - ; 75

Warren J. Kelly; 6 October 1845; Nelson Kelly, died before August 1862; - ; John and Mary Kelly; U- David Whipple, PGF Eddy Kelly; - ; 75

Flora W. Kelsey; about 1851; Truman Kelsey, died before June 1861; - ; Wealtha, Maria, Kathalo, Samuel and Stephen Kelsey and Mrs. Hughes; U- Darwin Kelsey; - ; 75

Maria Kelsey; about 1844; Truman Kelsey, died before June 1861; - ; Wealtha, Flora, Kathalo, Samuel and Stephen Kelsey and Mrs. Hughes; U- Darwin Kelsey; - ; 75

Stephen R. Kelsey; about 1848; Truman Kelsey, died before June 1861; - ; Wealtha, Flora, Kathalo, Samuel and Maria Kelsey and Mrs. Hughes; U- Darwin Kelsey; - ; 75

Wealtha A. Kelsey; about 1842; Truman Kelsey, died before June 1861; - ; Stephen, Flora, Kathalo, Samuel and Maria Kelsey and Mrs. Hughes; U- Darwin Kelsey; - ; 75

Lydia Kendall; 10 April 1842; Ezekiel Pierce, of Yorkshire; - ; - ; - ; - ; 75

Nathaniel T. Kendall; 13 or 30 November 1839; - ; - ; - ; - ; G- Henry M. Dean; 75

Name; Date of Birth; Father; Mother; Siblings; Other Relatives; Notes; Box Number

Mary Kennan; 20 January 1858; Lucius J. Kennan, died June 1864, of Randolph; Adeline, married Mr. Smith; - ; - ; needed guardian to receive pension money; 75

Cornelius A. Kennedy; about 1900; Cornelius A. Kennedy, Sr.; Catherine; - ; - ; - ; 48

Elizabeth Kennedy; about 1892; - ; - ; Francis, Henry, Mary, Nora and William Kennedy; U- Michael McDermott; parents died before March 1905, money from Margaret Kennedy's estate; 14

Francis "Frank" Kennedy; 28 December 1888; - ; - ; Elizabeth, Henry, Mary, Nora and William Kennedy; U- Michael McDermott; parents died before March 1905, RE Bradford by 1908, money from Margaret Kennedy's estate; 14

Henry Kennedy; about 1877; - ; - ; Elizabeth, Francis, Mary, Nora and William Kennedy; U- Michael McDermott; parents died before March 1905, he received money from estate of Margaret Kennedy; 14

Mary M. Kennedy; about 1890; - ; - ; Elizabeth, Francis, Henry, Nora and William Kennedy; U- Michael McDermott; parents died before March 1905, she received money from estate of Margaret Kennedy; 14

Nora Kennedy; about 1894; - ; - ; Elizabeth, Francis, Henry, Mary and William Kennedy; U- Michael McDermott; parents died before March 1905, she received money from estate of Margaret Kennedy; 14

William J. Kennedy; 29 January 1886; - ; - ; Elizabeth, Francis, Henry, Mary and Nora Kennedy; U- Michael McDermott; parents died before March 1905, he received money from estate of Margaret Kennedy; 14

Anna "Annie" A. Kennicott; 3 October 1849; Leander W. Kennicott, died before May 1861; Mary Milk, died before May 1861; Ella Kennicott; PG John and Sophronia Kinnicutt, PU John Kinnicutt, MA Deborah Case, MU John Milks, MU Benjamin George Milks, MU Giles Milks, MU Hiram Milks, MU Martin Milks; - ; 75

Name; Date of Birth; Father; Mother; Siblings; Other Relatives; Notes; Box Number

Ella Elvina Kennicott or Kinnicutt; 26 October 1847; Leander W. Kennicott, died before May 1861; Mary Milk, died before May 1861; Anna Kennicutt; PG John and Sophronia Kinnicutt, PU John Kinnicutt, MA Deborah Case, MU John Milks, MU Benjamin George Milks, MU Giles Milks, MU Hiram Milks, MU Martin Milks; - ; 75

Bessie Kent; about 1904; - ; Emma O.; James, Justus, Kenneth, and Mary Kent; - ; father died before February 1916; 14

James Kent; about 1908; - ; Emma O.; Bessie, Justus, Kenneth, and Mary Kent; - ; father died before February 1916; 14

Justus Kent; about 1906; - ; Emma O.; Bessie, James, Kenneth, and Mary Kent; - ; father died before February 1916; 14

Kenneth Kent; about 1910; - ; Emma O.; Bessie, James, Justus, and Mary Kent; - ; father died before February 1916; 14

Mary Louisa Kent; about 1902; - ; Emma O.; Bessie, James, Justus, and Kenneth Kent; - ; father died before February 1916; 14

Charles F. Keppel; 13 May 1881; - ; Lizzie; - ; - ; father died before June 1888, money from John G. Keppel's estate; 14

Frank Kesler; 19 March 1860; Leopold Kesler, died March 1864, of Buffalo, NY; Catharine, married Mr. Shwakert; Leopold, Loesa and Magdalina Kesler; - ; - ; 14

Leopold Kesler; 3 October 1864; Leopold Kesler, died March 1864, of Buffalo, NY; Catharine, married Mr. Shwakert; Frank, Loesa and Magdalina Kesler; - ; - ; 14

Loesa Kesler; 11 October 1854; Leopold Kesler, died March 1864, of Buffalo, NY; Catharine, married Mr. Shwakert; Frank, Leopold and Magdalina Kesler; - ; - ; 14

Magdalina Kesler; 1 January 1859; Leopold Kesler, died March 1864, of Buffalo, NY; Catharine, married Mr. Shwakert; Frank, Leopold and Loesa Kesler; - ; - ; 14

George C. Kessler; 28 October 1880; - ; - ; - ; PG George and Lena Kessler (born about 1822 and died about 1888), U- Andrew Kessler, U- Daniel Kessler, U- Charles Kessler; RE with George and Lena Kessler, the spelling Kesler and

Name; Date of Birth; Father; Mother; Siblings; Other Relatives; Notes; Box Number

Kessler interchanged throughout file, received money from estate of Frank Kessler; 14

Ada May Kester; about 1874; Charles W. Kester; - ; - ; - ; RE New Carlisle, Clark, Ohio; 48

Augustus F. Keyes; about 1862; - ; Rosanna H., of Portville, married Mr. Wright; - ; - ; received pension money; father died before December 1862; 75

Orson H. Keyes; 8 September 1893; Herbert Keyes; - ; Vernie Keyes; - ; mother died before October 1912; 14

Vernie E. Keyes; 18 June 1906; Herbert Keyes; - ; Orson Keyes; - ; mother died before October 1912; 14

Alice Kiernan; 2 April 1904; - ; - ; - ; U- M. W. Kiernan, A- Maria Slattery; - ; 48

Dora M. Kierstead; 2 May 1851; William R. Kierstead, died before July 1867; - ; - ; - ; received pension money, G- William N. Herrick; 75

Elizabeth F. Kimble; 14 October 1870; Byron Kimble; Cynthia, died October 1873; - ; PGF Charles Kimble, A- Phebe Southwick; - ; 14

Adelia Z. King; March 1823; Anson King, died before October 1841, of Burton (Allegany); Sophia; Sophia and Harriet King; - ; - ; 76

Charles E. King; 9 July 1830; - ; - ; Reuben King; - ; G- William King (of Yorkshire); 75

Harriet N. King; April 1831; Anson King, died before October 1841, of Burton (Allegany); Sophia; Sophia and Adelia King; - ; - ; 76

Mills M. King; 13 October 1876; Reuben V. King, in Washington, D. C.; Mary B.; - ; PGM Elizabeth A. King; RE Granville, Licking, Ohio 48

Nora E. King; 16 May 1893; - ; - ; Verna and Fred King; U- Amos B. Weast; father died about 1910 and mother died about 1904; 14

Reuben King; 9 July 1837; - ; - ; Charles King; - ; G- William King (of Yorkshire); 75

Name; Date of Birth; Father; Mother; Siblings; Other Relatives; Notes; Box Number

Sophia T. King; May 1829; Anson King, died before October 1841, of Burton (Allegany); Sophia; Harriet and Adelia King; - ; - ; 76

Verna Belle King; 12 October 1897; - ; - ; Nora and Fred King; U- Amos B. Weast; father died about 1910 and mother died about 1904; 14

Gertie Kingsley; 21 January 1868; - ; Augusta; - ; - ; - ;48

Nelson A. Kingsley; 2 April 1840; - ; Abi, married John Rust; Sarah Kingsley; PGM Orril Kingsley, PU Nelson S. Kingsley, PA Eliza A. Williams; - ; 75

Sarah H. Kingsley; 25 August 1838; - ; Abi, married John Rust; Nelson Kingsley; PGM Orril Kingsley, PU Nelson S. Kingsley, PA Eliza A. Williams; - ; 75

John Kinney; 27 April 1890; - ; - ; - ; U- James Butler; - ; 14

Lida Kinsey; 21 August 1906; - ; Minnie Prescott in 1926; - ; - ; - ; 48

Betsey E. Kinyon; 12 June 1837; - ; Lovisa M., married Mr. Prince; Lydia, Daniel and Lovisa Kinyon; - ; G- Halsey Prince; 75

Daniel M. Kinyon; 28 May 1845; - ; Lovisa M., married Mr. Prince; Lydia, Betsey and Lovisa Kinyon; - ; G- Halsey Prince; 75

Lovisa M. Kinyon; 12 June 1842; - ; Lovisa M., married Mr. Prince; Lydia, Betsey and Daniel Kinyon; - ; G- Halsey Prince; 75

Lydia Ann Kinyon; 13 July 1840; - ; Lovisa M., married Mr. Prince; Lovisa, Betsey and Daniel Kinyon; - ; G- Halsey Prince; 75

Frances Klink; 11 December 1911; foster father was Wm. C. Klink; foster mother was Mary; - ; - ; RE 210 N. 13th St., Olean; 48

Emily J. Klock; 3 August 1854; John F. Klock, of Conewango; - ; George Klock; - ; Manning Klock was her brother who died before August 1864, of Chautauqua County; 75

Helen Klock; 16 April 1910; - ; - ; Wilma Davis (W- of Edwin

Name; Date of Birth; Father; Mother; Siblings; Other Relatives; Notes; Box Number

Davis); HU Mr. Reed; - ; 47

Germonda Kluge; 19 May 1889; - ; - ; - ; BIL John K. Davis, of Marietta, Ohio; - ; 15

Anthony W. Knapp; 19 October 1850; - ; Emily; Carrie Knapp; - ; - ; 75

Carrie E. Knapp; 6 February 1855; - ; Emily; Anthony Knapp; - ; - ; 75

Cora E. Knight; January 1876; - ; Ellen; Bertha Knight Graves; - ; father died before February 1894; 14

Cordelia Knight; 12 February 1896; - ; - ; - ; second C- Myron E. Fisher; received money from estate of Daniel Knight; 48

Ralph Knight; 26 Februay 1884; - ; - ; - ; C- G. A. Stoneman; parents died before December 1901, received money from estate of A. D. and Jane Knight; 14

Anna Knoll; 4 July 1884; William Knoll, married 3 March 1897; Anastina, died October 1895; Hattie, Bessie, Edith and Henry Knoll; HU Mr. Hilliker; - ; 14

Bessie Knoll; 6 November 1889; William Knoll, married 3 March 1897; Anastina, died October 1895; Hattie, Anna, Edith and Henry Knoll; - ; - ; 14

Edith "Edie" Knoll; 12 January 1892; William Knoll, married 3 March 1897; Anastina, died October 1895; Hattie, Anna, Bessie and Henry Knoll; - ; - ; 14

Hattie Knoll; 8 December 1886; William Knoll, married 3 March 1897; Anastina, died October 1895; Edith, Anna, Bessie and Henry Knoll; - ; - ; 14

Henry Knoll; 9 June 1876; William Knoll, married 3 March 1897; Anastina, died October 1895; Edith, Anna, Bessie and Hattie Knoll; - ; - ; 14

Adella C. Knox; - ; - ; - ; Frederick Knox; - ; G- Andrew Knox (of Austin, Mower, Minnesota), heir of Mary A. Knox (died by 28 May 1873); 15

Anna Knox; March 1876; John W. Knox; Anne E.; George and James Knox; - ; G- Alexander Wentworth, no relation; 14

Frederick G. Knox:; - ; - ; - ; Adella Knox; - ; G- Andrew Knox

Name; Date of Birth; Father; Mother; Siblings; Other Relatives; Notes; Box Number

(of Austin, Mower, Minnesota), heir of Mary A. Knox (died by 28 May 1873); 15

Harriet Kober; - ; John Kober, died August 1860, of Great Valley; Anna, married Mr. Nichols; - ; - ; - ; 77

Adam Kohn; about 1855; - ; - ; Simon, John and Catherine Kohn; - ; G- Erastus Willard and an heir of Latham (?) and Catherine Kohn; 48

Catherine S. Kohn; about 1859; - ; - ; Simon, John and Adam Kohn; - ; G- Erastus Willard and an heir of Latham and Catherine Kohn; 48

John Kohn; 12 January 1860; - ; - ; Simon, Catherine and Adam Kohn; - ; G- Erastus Willard and an heir of Latham and Catherine Kohn; 48

Simon Kohn; about 1857; - ; - ; Catherine, John and Adam Kohn; - ; G- Erastus Willard and an heir of Latham and Catherine Kohn; 48

Frank Konklewski; 2 April 1903; - ; - ; Baldwin, Sopha and Thomas Konklewski; - ; - ; 48

Thomas Konklewski; 13 November 1900; - ; - ; Baldwin, Sopha and Frank Konklewski; - ; - ; 48

Anna Blanche Korb; about 1875; C. S. Courtright, of Gregory, Jewell, Kansas; - ; - ; - ; - ; 48

Daniel Perkins Kotts; 23 July 1898; Frederick A. Kotts; - ; - ; - ; heir of Margaret Z. Winters, papers from surrogate court of Lucas County, Ohio; 14

Norbert Krampf; about 1907; Joseph Krampf; Mary; - ; - ; received $50 for personal injury from Fred Forness; 14

Caroline Kraus; 25 March 1874; John Kraus, died before April 1889; Margaret, married Mr. Frendl/Frendall; - ; HU Mr. Lamb; G- James Campbell, no relationship; 48

Anton Krawczynski; about 1908; John Krawczynski, died 10 July 1909; Julia Bananski, lived in Lemburg, Austria; Bronislaw, Ladislaus and Mary Krawczynski; adopted by Michael Wiletowicz; - ; 14

Bronislaw Krawczynski; about 1901; John Krawczynski, died 10

Name; Date of Birth; Father; Mother; Siblings; Other Relatives; Notes; Box Number

**July 1909; Julia Bananski, lived in Lemburg, Austria; Anton, Ladislaus and Mary Krawczynski; RE Lemburg, Austria; - ; 14

Ladislaus Krawczynski; about 1909; John Krawczynski, died 10 July 1909; Julia Bananski, lived in Lemburg, Austria; Anton, Bronislaw and Mary Krawczynski; RE Lemburg, Austria; - ; 14

Mary Krawczynski; about 1907; John Krawczynski, died 10 July 1909; Julia Bananski, lived in Lemburg, Austria; Anton, Bronislaw and Ladislaus Krawczynski; RE Lemburg, Austria; AKA Maria Krawczynski ; 14

Adolph E. Krebs; 22 November 1900; William Krebs, Sr.; - ; William and Caroline Krebs; - ; RE 1917, Collins, Erie, NY 48

Caroline M. Krebs; 19 August 1896; William Krebs, Sr.; - ; William and Adolph Krebs; - ; RE 1917, Collins, Erie, NY 48

William H. Krebs, Jr.; 2 March 1899; William Krebs, Sr.; - ; Caroline and Adolph Krebs; - ; RE 1917, Collins, Erie, NY 48

Louise Willhelmina Krehl; 12 November 1882; Frederick Krehl; - ; - ; - ; - ; 48

Bertha Krencer; about 1899; Joseph Krencer; Freda Liechte, died 23 Jan 1905; Rose Krencer; MGM Barbara Liechte, U-John Liechte; indexed as Bertha Kreuzer; 14

Rose Krencer; about 1901; Joseph Krencer; Freda Liechte, died 23 Jan 1905; Bertha Krencer; MGM Barbara Liechte, U-John Liechte; indexed as Rose Kreuzer; 14

Helen Krepka; 18 February 1881; - ; Mary, died before July 1895, was Mary Fisher at time of her death; Edith Fisher; U-Joseph Burmaster/Bowmaster; received money from estate of grandfather. Albert Kerpka held mortgate on property and surname also spelled Kerpka; 14

William B. Krieger; 13 December 1903; - ; Addie B., married Mr. Ellis; - ; - ; RE 1924, in Berkley, Alameda, California; 48

Name; Date of Birth; Father; Mother; Siblings; Other Relatives; Notes; Box Number

John P. Kritter; 18 May 1889; Alfred Kritter; - ; - ; - ; - ; 48

Amelia J. Kruse; 18 June 1879; Henry Kruse; Mary; John and Dena Kruse; - ; - ;48

Dena M. Kruse; 15 August 1877; Henry Kruse; Mary; John and Amelia Kruse; - ; - ;48

Anna Kuehl; 17 November 1853; Gustavus Kuehl, died August 1872, of Olean; - ; Helen, Margaret, and Conrad Kuehl; U- Albert J. Kuehl; - ; 76

Conrad Kuehl; 11 June 1855; Gustavus Kuehl, died August 1872, of Olean; - ; Helen, Margaret, and Anna Kuehl; U- Albert J. Kuehl; - ; 76

Helen Kuehl; 31 May 1852; Gustavus Kuehl, died August 1872, of Olean; - ; Conrad, Margaret, and Anna Kuehl; U- Albert J. Kuehl; - ; 76

Margaret Kuehl; March 1859; Gustavus Kuehl, died August 1872, of Olean; - ; Conrad, Helen, and Anna Kuehl; U- Albert J. Kuehl; - ; 76

Joseph Kujawa; 5 February 1905; Frank Kujawa, died before 18 July 1924; Alezandria; Mary, Stephania, and Josephine Kujawa; - ; - ; 47

Josephine Kujawa; 6 March 1908; Frank Kujawa, died before 18 July 1924; Alezandria; Mary, Stephania, and Joseph Kujawa; - ; - ; 47

Mary Kujawa; 10 September 1903; Frank Kujawa, died before 18 July 1924; Alezandria; Josephine, Stephania, and Joseph Kujawa; - ; - ; 47

Stephania Kujawa; 19 June 1910; Frank Kujawa, died before 18 July 1924; Alezandria; Josephine, Mary, and Joseph Kujawa; HU Mr. Germack ; - ; 47

Joseph Kwiatowski; 4 May 1910; Frank Kwiatowski; - ; Leonard Kwiatowski; - ; - ; 48

Leonard Kwiatowski; 14 August 1907; Frank Kwiatowski; - ; Joseph Kwiatowski; - ; - ; 48

Bessie Kyler; about 1886; Ezra Kyler; - ; Mark, Tessie and Lloyd Kyler; - ; mother died before May 1899; 14

Name; Date of Birth; Father; Mother; Siblings; Other Relatives; Notes; Box Number

Lloyd Kyler; about 1890; Ezra Kyler; - ; Mark, Tessie and Bessie Kyler; - ; mother died before May 1899; 14

Mark E. Kyler; 7 October 1882; Ezra Kyler; - ; Lloyd, Tessie and Bessie Kyler; - ; mother died before May 1899; 14

Tessie Kyler; about 1888; Ezra Kyler; - ; Lloyd, Mark and Bessie Kyler; - ; mother died before May 1899; 14

George Franklin Kyser; 28 July 1873; - ; Susan, married Mr. Wright; Horace Kyser; PGF Horace Kyser (died April 1880, of Elma, Erie, NY); G-Manley A. Blakeslee, G- James F. Johnson; 48

Horace Erwin Kyser; 7 September 1875; - ; Susan, married Mr. Wright; George Kyser; PGF Horace Kyser (died April 1880, of Elma, Erie, NY); G-Manley A. Blakeslee, G- James F. Johnson; 48

Name; Date of Birth; Father; Mother; Siblings; Other Relatives; Notes; Box Number

L Surnames

Carrie Lacy; 16 August 1860; Wallace L. Lacy, died July 1864, of Hinsdale; Claire, of Hinsdale, married Mr. Willover; Francis and Lewis Lacy; MG Carlos and Permelia Lacy; G-Harlan Swift and received pension money; 76

Francis Lacy; 16 February 1858; Wallace L. Lacy, died July 1864, of Hinsdale; Claire, of Hinsdale, married Mr. Willover; Carrie and Lewis Lacy; MG Carlos and Permelia Lacy; G-Harlan Swift and received pension money; 76

Lewis Lacy; 21 December 1855; Wallace L. Lacy, died July 1864, of Hinsdale; Claire, of Hinsdale, married Mr. Willover; Carrie and Francis Lacy; MG Carlos and Permelia Lacy; G-Harlan Swift and received pension money; 76

Fanny H. LaFever; 27 December 1880; - ; Helen M.; - ; HU Mr. Rulison; father died by December 1892; received money from estate of Lewis LaFever; 15

Rena B. Laidlaw; 17 June 1889; Ulysses Crane, residence unknown; - ; Stanley and Elsie Crane; HU Gilbert Laidlaw; received money from estate of Elijah Chaffee; 40

Florence L. Lake; 22 October 1888; George W. Lake, died 20 March 1899; Eveline, married Mr. Babbitt by 1903; - ; - ; - ; 15

Nora B. Lake; 12 June 1870; Ezra B. Lake, died 9 December 1873; - ; - ; MG Seymour and Faithy Saxton, U- Henry C. Saxton, MU Perry Saxton (of Chautauqua County, NY), MU Seymour Saxton (of New Richmond, Wisconsin), MA Lara Seekens (of Lincoln, Wisconsin), MA Minerva Stafford (of Chautauqua County, NY), MA Jane Rublee (of Ellington, Chautauqua, NY), PU Lampson Lake (of Newtown, Connecticut), PA Mrs. Hard (of Sandy Hook, Connecticut); PA Hannah Hubbard (of NY City), cousins were Adelle, Horace and Melvin Saxton, Allison, Frank and Leroy Rublee, Ellen Smith, Orsell, Austin, Bertha, McClelland and Grant

Name; Date of Birth; Father; Mother; Siblings; Other Relatives; Notes; Box Number

Stafford; her father had owned a foundry and Nora resided with Henry Saxton in Ellington and Kennedy, NY; 29

E. Dema Lambert; about 1875; - ; - ; - ; U- Norman E. G. Cowen; - ; 49

John Lammie; 22 October 1892; - ; Ella, married Mr. Holmes; - ; - ; - ; 15

Clyde A. Lamper; 23 July 1890; Acta A. Lamper, lived in Jamestown; Nancy, died by May 1910; - ; - ; G- Samuel C. Henning, no relation; 15

Ilona Lamphere; 30 June 1828 or 1829; Silas Lamphere, died before February 1848; Mary Ann, of Ellicottville, married Mr. Potter; - ; - ; - ;77

Albert K. Langham; about 1901; - ; Ella K.; William Langham; - ; - ; 48

William L. Langham; 30 March 1896; - ; Ella K.; Albert Langham; - ; - ; 48

Lydia Langhans; 6 August 1893; - ; - ; Ruth Langhans; U- William Langhans; - ; 15

Ruth Langhans; 3 November 1895; - ; - ; Lydia Langhans; U- William Langhans; - ; 15

Bertha G. Langmade; 14 September 1869; - ; Maranda; Grace Langmade; - ; money from Stephen S. Langmade's estate; 29

Capitola J. Langmade; 11 April 1859; William F. Langmade, died before September 1876; - ; Emily and Nettie Langmade; - ; name also seen as Captolia, G- Heman Nickless; 29

Emily A. Langmade; about 1857; William F. Langmade, died before September 1876; - ; Capitola and Nettie Langmade; - ; G- Heman Nickless; 29

Grace A. Langmade; about 1870; - ; Maranda; Bertha Langmade; - ; money from Stephen S. Langmade's estate; 29

Nettie B. Langmade; about 1862; William F. Langmade, died before September 1876; - ; Capitola and Emily Langmade; - ; G- Heman Nickless; 29

Clive O. F. Larkin; 25 March 1875; - ; - ; - ; - ; - ; 49

Margaret Larkin; 13 December 1905; Thomas Larkin; Caroline;

Name; Date of Birth; Father; Mother; Siblings; Other Relatives; Notes; Box Number

- ; - ; RE 217 N. 1st St., Olean, legacy from Weltha A. Teller; 48

Gerald Latshaw; about 1895; - ; - ; - ; - ; needed guardian to enroll in National Guard; 49

Benton Lattin; 5 August 1885; - ; Grace, died before September 1901; Berton and Alice Lattin; - ; RE Cattaraugus in 1901, Oneonta by 1906, money from George Lattin's estate; 15

Berton Lattin; 5 August 1885; - ; Grace, died before September 1901; Benton and Alice Lattin; - ; RE Cattaraugus in 1901, Oneonta by 1906, money from George Lattin's estate; 15

E. Lucille Laughlin; 8 August 1909; Patrick J. Laughlin, died 21 January 1911; Katherine M.; James and Patrick Laughlin; - ; G- James Crowley; 67

Francis J. Laughlin; about 1907; Diamus B. Laughlin, died 13 July 1913; Catherine, of South Valley; Margaret and Mary Laughlin; - ; - ; 67

James Leo Laughlin; 17 July 1907; Patrick J. Laughlin, died 21 January 1911; Katherin; E. Lucille and Patrick Laughlin; - ; G- James Crowley; 67

Margaret J. Laughlin; about 1905; Diamus B. Laughlin, died 13 July 1913; Catherine, of South Valley; Francis and Mary Laughlin; - ; - ; 67

Mary E. Laughlin; about 1902; Diamus B. Laughlin, died 13 July 1913; Catherine, of South Valley; Francis and Margaret Laughlin; - ; - ; 67

Patrick J. Laughlin; 24 February 1911; Patrick J. Laughlin, died 21 January 1911; Katherin; E. Lucille and James Laughlin; - ; G- James Crowley; 67

Eveline Lauler; 6 July 1896; - ; Catherine; Joseph Lauler; - ; - ; 49

Joseph Lauler; 21 October 1899 or 1900; - ; Catherine; Eveline Lauler; - ; - ; 49

Doris E. Law; 24 January 1893; Ezra B. Law, died before 1907; - ; Reuben and Vernia Law; HU Mr. Leonard, married between 1909 and 1910; mother died before 1899, received

Name; Date of Birth; Father; Mother; Siblings; Other Relatives; Notes; Box Number

money from estate of Evaline Law; 15

Genevieve C. Law; 20 October 1894; - ; Sylvia A.; - ; - ; - ; 49

Reuben W. Law; about 1887; Ezra B. Law, died before 1907; - ; Doris and Vernia Law; - ; mother died before 1899, received money from estate of Evaline Law; 15

Vernia E. Law; about 1879; Ezra B. Law, died before 1907; - ; Reuben and Doris Law; HU Mr. Hooper; mother died before 1899, received money from estate of Evaline Law; 15

Polly Ann Lawrence; - ; Richard Lawrence, died October 1858, of Ellicottville; Harriet, of Pomfret, Chautauqua, NY; married Mr. Nichols; Reuben Lawrence and three other siblings; - ; RE Pomfret, Chautauqua, NY; 76

Reuben R. Lawrence; - ; Richard Lawrence, died October 1858, of Ellicottville; Harriet, of Pomfret, Chautauqua, NY; married Mr. Nichols; Polly Lawrence and three other siblings; - ; RE Mansfield; 76

Alfred Lawton; 3 September 1873; Peleg Lawton, died January 1878; Orrinda; Wilson and Ralph Lawton; - ; - ; 49

Cynthia J. Lawton; 27 March 1848; James Lawton, died before November 1866; - ; Emma Lawton; - ; G- Peter Oyer; 76

Emma Lawton; 2 September 1851; James Lawton, died before November 1866; - ; Cynthia Lawton; - ; G- Peter Oyer; 76

Ralph Lawton; 25 February 1877; Peleg Lawton, died January 1878; Orrinda; Wilson and Alfred Lawton; - ; - ; 49

Wilson Lawton; 24 November 1867; Peleg Lawton, died January 1878; Orrinda; Ralph and Alfred Lawton; - ; - ; 49

Florence A. Lay; - ; - ; Alice, married Mr. Chesner by 1901; Ruth Lay; - ; father died before January 1901, received money from estate of Edward Lay; 15

Ruth C. Lay; - ; - ; Alice, married Mr. Chesner by 1901; Florence Lay; - ; father died before January 1901, received money from estate of Edward Lay; 15

Bessie E. Le Blanc; 1 December 1885; Robert Le Blanc, of St. Bonaventure River, Canada; Ella, lived in Salamanca in December 1894; Charles and Blanch Le Blanc; - ; lived with

Name; Date of Birth; Father; Mother; Siblings; Other Relatives; Notes; Box Number

father; 15

Blanch Le Blanc; 15 February 1888; Robert Le Blanc, of St. Bonaventure River, Canada; Ella, lived in Salamanca in December 1894; Charles and Bessie Le Blanc; - ; lived with father; 15

Charles W. Le Blanc; 22 Mary 1884; Robert Le Blanc, of St. Bonaventure River, Canada; Ella, lived in Salamanca in December 1894; Blanch and Bessie Le Blanc; - ; lived with father; 15

George C. Le Roy; 13 July 1872; Simeon Le Roy; - ; Willard Le Roy; - ; - ; 48

Willard Le Roy; 27 March 1870; Simeon Le Roy; - ; George Le Roy; - ; - ; 48

John B. Leach; June 1881; John E. Leach; - ; - ; - ; - ; 49

Karl Leach; 12 May 1903; Albert Leach; Kathryn; - ; MGM Catherine Stewart, A- Sarah A. Collins; RE Pittsburgh, Allegheny, Pennsylvania; 48

Nettie Leach; about 1908; Ralph Leach; Bettie; - ; - ; - ; 48

Millard V. Learn; about 1893; Orlando C. Learn; - ; - ; - ; - ; 49

Nettie Learn; 3 January 1874; - ; Lydia; - ; HU Mr. Scott, married by 1892; - ; 15

Charles LeBarron; - ; - ; - ; - ; - ; there isn't anything in his envelope; 76

Robert Leckey; 31 January 1896; Robert Leckey, died before September 1910; - ; - ; - ; - ; RE by 1917, Jeannette, Westmoreland, Pennsylvania; 15

Edward W. Lee; 21 July 1859; William Lee, died February 1872, of Randolph; Anna E., died 29 April 1902; Elva and James Lee; - ; - ; 29

Elva A. Lee; 22 September 1865; William Lee, died February 1872, of Randolph; Anna E., died 29 April 1902; Edward and James Lee; - ; - ; 29

James B. Lee; 13 June 1862; William Lee, died February 1872, of Randolph; Anna E., died 29 April 1902; Edward and Elva Lee; - ; - ; 29

Name; Date of Birth; Father; Mother; Siblings; Other Relatives; Notes; Box Number

John Morril Lee; 1 August 1880; - ; - ; - ; U- James B. Lee; - ; 49

Lewis James Lee; 10 September 1895; - ; - ; - ; relatives were Mrs. Chas Simons, Grace W. Sweet, and W. C. Sweet; enlisted in Co. I., 3rd Regiment, NY, father died 6 August 1912 and mother died 29 April 1905; 67

William Oromel Leland; - ; Asa Leland, died before November 1841; - ; - ; relative was Harrison Leland; G- John Wilcox; 76

Lulu L. Lent; 6 March 1891; - ; Helen C., married Mr. Fellows; - ; - ; - ; 49

Reuben H. Lent; 15 March 1886; - ; Helen; - ; - ; - ; 49

Carrie E. Leon; 11 August 1871; Timothy Leon, died February 1874; Ann, married Mr. Drake; Daniel and John Leon; U- Daniel Leon, A- Elnora McLorey, A- Mary Darling, A- Ellen Corset; - ; 29

Daniel T. Leon; 18 February 1874; Timothy Leon, died February 1874; Ann, married Mr. Drake; Carrie and John Leon; U- Daniel Leon, A- Elnora McLorey, A- Mary Darling, A- Ellen Corset; - ; 29

John W. Leon; 24 January 1870; Timothy Leon, died February 1874; Ann, married Mr. Drake; Carrie and Daniel Leon; U- Daniel Leon, A- Elnora McLorey, A- Mary Darling, A- Ellen Corset; - ; 29

Dora Leonard; 12 August 1900; Melvin E. Leonard; - ; Flora, Satie, Stella, Leon and Eleanor Leonard; - ; - ; 49

Eleanor Leonard; 12 June 1903; Melvin E. Leonard; - ; Flora, Satie, Stella, Leon and Dora Leonard; - ; - ; 49

Flora Leonard; 22 September 1894; Melvin E. Leonard; - ; Eleanor, Satie, Stella, Leon and Dora Leonard; - ; - ; 49

Leon Leonard; 4 April 1893; Melvin E. Leonard; - ; Eleanor, Satie, Stella, Flora and Dora Leonard; - ; - ; 49

Norma A. Leonard; 2 March 1898; AF Milton A. Leonard; went by Louise Cann and lived in Roseville, OH; - ; - ; received money from estate of John R. Leonard; 49

Satie Leonard; 12 April 1896; Melvin E. Leonard; - ; Eleanor,

Name; Date of Birth; Father; Mother; Siblings; Other Relatives; Notes; Box Number

Leon, Stella, Flora and Dora Leonard; - ; - ; 49

Stella Leonard; 21 December 1898; Melvin E. Leonard; - ; Eleanor, Leon, Satie, Flora and Dora Leonard; - ; - ; 49

Cary M. Lewis; 25 June 1876; Nathan Lewis; Amanda; Myrtle Lewis; - ; - ; 49

Edward Lewis; 7 April 1889; Charles E. Lewis; - ; Paul Lewis; - ; - ; 49

Floyd Lewis; 18 April 1889; - ; - ; - ; - ; in same envelope as Forest Lewis, G- William Lewis; 15

Forest Lewis; 25 March 1885; - ; - ; - ; - ; in same envelope as Floyd Lewis, G- William Lewis; 15

Kitty Amelia Lewis; 26 September 1859; Alfred H. Lewis, died July 1863, of Freedom; Jane A., married Mr. Cheney; - ; PGM Sally Lewis, U- Jerome Lewis, U- Miles Lewis, U- Cary Lewis, A- Amelia White, A- Jerusha Lanckton, A- Mary Davis, A- Elizabeth Lewis; first G- Caleb Williston Kinney, only bond in envelope in box 76; 29 and 76

Laureat W. Lewis; June 1905; Laureat W. Lewis; - ; - ; - ; ; 15

Myrtle M. Lewis; 10 March 1870; Nathan Lewis; Amanda; Cary Lewis; HU Mr. Davis ; - ; 49

Paul C. Lewis; 19 November 1890; Charles E. Lewis; - ; Edward Lewis; - ; - ; 49

Stephen Stillman Lewis; 14 September 1897; Stanley E. Lewis, was in show business, AKA Stanley Huntley Lewis and Stillman E. Lewis; Carrie Reynolds; - ; MGF William E. Reynolds, 118 Coleman St., Olean; was in Military School in Staunton, Virginia; 48

Verna Lewis; 13 April 1882; Daniel E. Lewis; - ; - ; HU Brad H. Moody, MGF Cornelius C. K. B. Smith; received money from MGF's estate; 15

Charles Z. Lincoln; 5 August 1848; Pratt G. Lincoln, died before August 1863; - ; Mary Lincoln; - ; G- Lucius Lincoln and G- John Perkins; 76

Elizabeth F. Lincoln; 7 October 1882; - ; - ; - ; U- James G. Delamaster; mother died before 10 February 1902 ; 15

Name; Date of Birth; Father; Mother; Siblings; Other Relatives; Notes; Box Number

Mary A. Lincoln; 28 July 1846; Pratt G. Lincoln, died before August 1863; - ; Charles Lincoln; - ; G- Lucius Lincoln and G- John Perkins; 76

Mary Adaline Lincoln; 6 February 1887; F. E. Lincoln; - ; William Lincoln; - ; G- George Murray; 42

William Hugh Lincoln; 14 September 1880; F. E. Lincoln; - ; Mary Lincoln; - ; G- George Murray; 42

Einar E. Lind; 7 June 1901; Charles O. Lind; Josephine; - ; - ; - ; 48

Anna Link; 11 April 1842; Jacob Link, from Germany; Anna, died before February 1860, which was before family left Germany; Barbara and Jacob Link; - ; - ; 76

Barbara Link; 8 June 1839; Jacob Link, from Germany; Anna, died before February 1860, which was before family left Germany; Anna and Jacob Link; - ; - ; 76

Charles Edwin Linton; 22 April 1885; Edward Linton; - ; Fred and Joseph Linton; - ; - ; 15

Fred Thomas Linton; 21 January 1884; Edward Linton; - ; Charles and Joseph Linton; - ; - ; 15

Joseph J. Linton; 22 May 1888; Edward Linton; - ; Charles and Fred Linton; - ; - ; 15

Mary Elizabeth Lippart; about 1896; - ; Minnie, lived at 701 ½ E. State St., married Mr. Gale; - ; - ; - ; 67

Andrew Lippert; 12 July 1864; - ; - ; - ; - ; G- Frank Warters; 29

Beals E. Litchfield; 12 December 1823; Ensign Litchfield, died before February 1841; - ; - ; - ; G- Molly Litchfield, of Ellicottville; 77

Edward H. Litchfield; 5 April 1893; Eugene E. Litchfield; - ; William Litchfield; - ; received money from estate of William G. Fay; 15

William C. Litchfield; 10 August 1890; Eugene E. Litchfield; - ; Edward Litchfield; - ; money from William G. Fay's estate; 15

Ellen E. Little; 20 March 1909; Richard W. Little, of Lyndon; - ; - ; - ; - ; 67

Name; Date of Birth; Father; Mother; Siblings; Other Relatives; Notes; Box Number

Frances E. Little; 12 March 1847; Richard W. Little, died before March 1861; Mary Ann; William, Jane and Frederick Little; PGF William Little, of Lyndon; - ; 76

Frederick L. Little; 28 March 1854; Richard W. Little, died before March 1861; Mary Ann; William, Jane and Frances Little; PGF William Little, of Lyndon; - ; 76

Jane S. Little; 5 November 1851; Richard W. Little, died before March 1861; Mary Ann; William, Frederick and Frances Little; PGF William Little, of Lyndon; - ; 76

William C. Little; 15 April 1849; Richard W. Little, died before March 1861; Mary Ann; Jane, Frederick and Frances Little; PGF William Little, of Lyndon; - ; 76

Leola Lloyd; about 1899; William G. Lloyd; - ; Lysle Lloyd; - ; received money from estate of Cora Belle Lloyd; 15

Lysle Lloyd; about 1901; William G. Lloyd; - ; Leola Lloyd; - ; received money from estate of Cora Belle Lloyd; 15

Ethel L. Loader; 29 August 1889; - ; Addie O.; - ; - ; G- Oakley W. Chamberlain; 15

Alva O. Lockwood; 22 May 1907; - ; Jessie, of Ischua, married Mr. Lewis by 1925; - ; - ; received money from estate of Jacob Lockwood; 67

Sadie Loftus; 15 July 1900; John J. Loftus, of 329 Tompkins St., Olean; - ; - ; - ; - ; 48

Emerson S. Long; 1 March 1904; Andrew Long, died 25 November 1915; Mary Ellen, resided at 210 W. Green St.; Carl and Harold Long; - ; - ; 48

Harold A. Long; 10 June 1901; Andrew Long, died 25 November 1915; Mary Ellen, resided at 210 W. Green St.; Carl and Emerson Long; - ; - ; 48

Ralph Long; 21 October 1902; Charles Long; Frances; - ; - ; received money from estate of Sarah Arnold; 67

Alice Looney; 9 August 1894; - ; Mary; William Looney; - ; father died before June 1910; 15

William Looney; 28 March 1892; - ; Mary; Alice Looney; - ; father died before June 1910; 15

Name; Date of Birth; Father; Mother; Siblings; Other Relatives; Notes; Box Number

Lennie Loop; - ; - ; - ; Walter Loop; - ; - ; 16

Walter Loop; 27 September 1896; - ; - ; Lennie Loop; - ; - ; 16

Derrick V. C. Lord; 1901; Charles H. Lord, died before April 1902; Ethelyn L., of Perrysburg; Ellen and Mary Lord; - ; G- R. B. Van Schoonover; 67

Ellen E. Lord; about 1889; Charles H. Lord, died before April 1902; Ethelyn L., of Perrysburg; Derrick and Mary Lord; - ; G- R. B. Van Schoonover; 67

Mary E. Lord; about 1888 Charles H. Lord, died before April 1902; Ethelyn L., of Perrysburg; Derrick and Ellen Lord; - ; G- R. B. Van Schoonover; 67

Dellie Losee; 1861; - ; Jennette Ballard, married Mr. O'Brien; - ; PGF John A. Losee, MGF Garrison Ballard; received pension money; 76

Guy R. Lowden; 31 December 1877; James Lowden; Eloise Barton, died 8 February 1883; - ; PGF Charles Lowden, MGF Ralston S. Barton; - ; 49

Emerson Lowe; 6 May 1860; James Lowe; Almina Fuller, died before February 1864; - ; U- Asa Fuller, U- Charles Fuller; money from Chester Fuller's estate; RE 1881, Poweshiek County, Iowa; 29

Glenn H. Lowe; 8 April 1899; - ; - ; George Lowe, of Rochester, NY; - ; G- Henry Swartz, no relation; 49

Herman Lubberts; about 1890; - ; Mary; - ; - ; - ; 49

Frank L. Lucas; 11 February 1860; Theodore S. Lucas, died September 1864, of Townsend, Huron, Ohio; Pantha E., of Machias; Jennette Lucas; - ; - ; 76

Jennette E. Lucas; 5 May 1862; Theodore S. Lucas, died September 1864, of Townsend, Huron, Ohio; Pantha E., of Machias; Frank Lucas; - ; - ; 76

Berl Luce (Luceick, Lucek); 4 March 1883; Milford Luce; Augusta; - ; second C- Fred Herrick; parents were separated; 16

Charles H. Luce; 11 December 1855; John H. Luce, died October 1863, of Rushford, Allegany, NY; Caroline, of Randolph,

Name; Date of Birth; Father; Mother; Siblings; Other Relatives; Notes; Box Number

married Mr. Barnes; Clara and John Luce; - ; received pension money; 76

Clara J. Luce; 19 November 1860; John H. Luce, died October 1863, of Rushford, Allegany, NY; Caroline, of Randolph, married Mr. Barnes; Charles and John Luce; - ; received pension money; 76

Fred William Luce; 17 January 1858; Hiram H. Luce, died before March 1863; Marcena Adams; Phebe Luce; MG Henry and Belinda Adams, U- Franklin Luce, U- Lucius Luce, U- James Luce; - ; 76

Grace Luce; about 1886; - ; Mina; Orvis and Irwin Luce; HU Mr. Marsh, married by 1914; money from Fred Luce's estate; 67

Irwin Luce; about 1896; - ; Mina; Orvis and Grace Luce; - ; received money from estate of Fred Luce; 67

John H. Luce; 27 February 1864; John H. Luce, died October 1863, of Rushford, Allegany, NY; Caroline, of Randolph, married Mr. Barnes; Charles and Clara Luce; - ; received pension money; 76

Orvis M. Luce; 18 February 1903; - ; Mina; Irwin and Grace Luce; - ; AKA George Luce, money from Fred Luce's estate; 67

Phebe M. Luce; 11 February 1860; Hiram H. Luce, died before March 1863; Marcena Adams; Fred Luce; MG Henry and Belinda Adams, U- Franklin Luce, U- Lucius Luce, U- James Luce; - ; 76

Alice E. Luddington; about 1877; Alonzo H. Luddington; Ruth; Harvey, Ethel, Frank, Maude and Ernest Luddington; - ; - ; 49

Ernest G. Luddington; about 1888; Alonzo H. Luddington; Ruth; Harvey, Ethel, Frank, Maude and Alice Luddington; - ; - ; 49

Ethel B. Luddington; about 1882; Alonzo H. Luddington; Ruth; Harvey, Ernest, Frank, Maude and Alice Luddington; - ; - ; 49

Frank E. Luddington; about 1884; Alonzo H. Luddington; Ruth;

Name; Date of Birth; Father; Mother; Siblings; Other Relatives; Notes; Box Number

Harvey, Ernest, Ethel, Maude and Alice Luddington; - ; - ; 49
Harvey A. Luddington; about 1874; Alonzo H. Luddington; Ruth; Frank, Ernest, Ethel, Maude and Alice Luddington; - ; - ; 49
Maude M. Luddington; about 1886; Alonzo H. Luddington; Ruth; Frank, Ernest, Ethel, Harvey and Alice Luddington; - ; - ; 49
Molly Luntz; about 1910; Fred Watkins, abandoned family and lived in Dunkirk; - ; Ory Luntz; PGF and foster father was Isidor Luntz; received money from Cahen estate; 48
Ory Watkins Luntz; about 1909; Fred Watkins, abandoned family and lived in Dunkirk; - ; Molly Luntz; PGF and foster father was Isidor Luntz; money from Cahen estate; 48
Hattie V. Luther; 21 October 1873; - ; Mary A.; Jessie Luther; - ; - ; 16
Jessie L. Luther; December 1877; - ; Mary A.; Hattie Luther; - ; - ; 16
Christopher Luttman; 2 August 1889; Theodore Luttman, died 1892; Annie; Martha Luttman; - ; RE 1910, Chiapas, Mexico, Luttman's were from Lubeck, Germany and returned there; 15
Martha Luttman; 12 September 1892; Theodore Luttman, died 1892; Annie; Christopher Luttman; - ; Luttman's were from Lubeck, Germany and returned there; 15
Roger Cameron Lutz; 18 September 1911; Roger H. Lutz; - ; - ; relative was Frank Harrison Higgins; RE Paris, France, but attended school in US; 48
Beulah Lycett; 11 February 1898; Michael Lycett; Gertrude, married Mr. LeCour/LeLour; Kenneth Lycett; - ; - ; 49
Kenneth Lycett; 14 February 1907; Michael Lycett; Gertrude, married Mr. LeCour/LeLour; Beulah Lycett; - ; - ; 49
Anna Lynch; 20 October 1890; - ; went by Jennie E. North; - ; HU Robert Lynch; G- Edwin W. Smith; 49
Claude W. Lyons; 8 July 1870; - ; Lillian, married Charles R.. Gibson; - ; - ; parents divorced, father resided in Ohio; 49

Name; Date of Birth; Father; Mother; Siblings; Other Relatives; Notes; Box Number

Julia Lyons; 7 May 1861, in Humphrey; - ; Margurette, died before January 1877; - ; - ; G- Maria Lyons and G- Thomas Lyons; 75

Name; Date of Birth; Father; Mother; Siblings; Other Relatives; Notes; Box Number

M Surnames

Laura J. Macarty; - ; Thomas Macarty, died September 1862, of Hartford, Hartford, Connecticut; Susan, married Mr. Meloy; - ; - ; - ; 16

M. Edith MacColl; about 1881; William W. MacColl; - ; - ; - ; - ;17

Mary Ellen Mack; 6 July 1906; William P. Mack, of Randolph; - ; - ; A- Ella Mack, of 12 E. 4th St., Jamestown, Chautauqua, NY; RE 1927, in Beaumont, Jefferson, Texas; 69

May Mack; - ; - ; - ; - ; A- Mary C. Andrus; in same envelope as William Mack; 16

William Mack; - ; - ; - ; - ; A- Mary C. Andrus; RE Bradford, McKean, Pennsylvania, in same envelope as May Mack; 16

Miles B. Mackey; 29 July 1849; Conrad Mackey, died before 17 March 1868; Hannah, married Mr. Higbee; - ; - ; - ; 16

Beulah M. Mackmer; 23 June 1891; Albert Mackmer; Elizabeth C.; Frederick and Ralph Mackmer; PG Frederick and Rachel Mackmer; 51

Frederick W. Mackmer; 16 February 1894; Albert Mackmer; Elizabeth C.; Beulah and Ralph Mackmer; PG Frederick and Rachel Mackmer; 51

Ralph M. Mackmer; 29 January 1901; Albert Mackmer; Elizabeth C.; Beulah and Frederick Mackmer; PG Frederick and Rachel Mackmer; 51

Clare Maguire; 11 November 1894; - ; - ; - ; U- Michael P. Clare, RE 1915, Allegany County, Maryland, mother lived in Maryland; 52

Joseph E. Mahany; 12 June 1902; Cornelius Mahany; Catharine; Margaret Mahany; - ; - ; 50

Margaret G. Mahany; 30 August 1898; Cornelius Mahany; Catharine; Joseph Mahany; - ; - ; 50

Charles Mallery; 15 February 1894; - ; - ; Fred Mallery, resided 442 N. 10th St., Olean, NY; - ; father abandoned family; 50

Name; Date of Birth; Father; Mother; Siblings; Other Relatives; Notes; Box Number

Burt E. Mallory; 9 November 1888; - ; Anna M.; Ira, Lloyd, Cecil, Hazel, George, Malvina, Finice and Izola Mallory; - ; father died before February 1906, of Ischua; 76

Cecil Mallory; 4 May 1890; - ; Anna M.; Ira, Lloyd, Finice, Hazel, George, Malvina, Burt and Izola Mallory; - ; father died before February 1906, of Ischua; 76

Finice Mallory; 16 May 1899; - ; Anna M.; Ira, Lloyd, Cecil, Hazel, George, Malvina, Bert and Izola Mallory; - ; father died before February 1906, of Ischua; 76

George W. Mallory; 22 February 1896; - ; Anna M.; Ira, Lloyd, Cecil, Hazel, Finice, Malvina, Bert and Izola Mallory; - ; father died before February 1906, of Ischua; 76

Hazel Mallory; 16 May 1893; - ; Anna M.; Ira, Lloyd, Cecil, Finice, George, Malvina, Bert and Izola Mallory; HU Mr. Ferman; father died before February 1906, of Ischua; 76

Ira S. Mallory; 27 September 1885; - ; Anna M.; George Lloyd, Cecil, Hazel, Finice, Malvina, Bert and Izola Mallory; - ; father died before February 1906, of Ischua; 76

Izola Mallory; 20 January 1903; - ; Anna M.; Ira, Lloyd, Cecil, Finice, George, Malvina, Bert and Hazel Mallory; HU Mr. Smith; father died before February 1906, of Ischua; 76

Lloyd Mallory; 4 April 1885; - ; Anna M.; George Ira, Cecil, Hazel, Finice, Malvina, Bert and Izola Mallory; - ; father died before February 1906, of Ischua; 76

Malvina Mallory; 2 December 1897; - ; Anna M.; George Ira, Cecil, Hazel, Finice, Lloyd, Bert and Izola Mallory; - ; father died before February 1906, of Ischua; 76

Emma Malone; 30 January 1882 ; - ; - ; Mamie Malone; U- Henry Schulz, U- John Schultz, U- Christopher Schultz; received money from estate of Carl Schultz, G- James A. Napier, no relation; 50

Harry E. Malone; about 1905; - ; Celia, of Olean, died between 1907 and 1916; - ; A- Catherine Hart; - ; 68

James Malone; 3 March 1871; Andrew Malone, of Middlefield, Geauga, Ohio; Mary, died August 1881, of Salamanca;

Name; Date of Birth; Father; Mother; Siblings; Other Relatives; Notes; Box Number

Minnie Malone; - ; G- Oscar Senear, G- John J. Inman; 50

Mamie Malone; 17 November 1883; - ; - ; Emma Malone; HU Mr. Sill, U- Henry Schulz, U- John Schultz, U- Christopher Schultz; received money from estate of Carl Schultz, G- James A. Napier, no relation; 50

Minnie Malone; 4 July 1870; Andrew Malone, of Middlefield, Geauga, Ohio; Mary, died August 1881, of Salamanca; James Malone; - ; G- Oscar Senear, G- John J. Inman; 50

Catharine Maloney; about 1871; William Maloney; Catharine; James, Edward, Patrick, John, Margaret and William Maloney; - ; received money from estate of Eliza Howard, file also mentions Patrick, Timothy and John Howard; 51

Edward Maloney; about 1877; William Maloney; Catharine; James, Catharine, Patrick, John, Margaret and William Maloney; - ; received money from estate of Eliza Howard, file also mentions Patrick, Timothy and John Howard; 51

Elizabeth Maloney; 28 March 1899; Frank J. Duffy; Agnes; - ; HU Charles Maloney, died due to negligence of Erie R. R. County; G- P. S. Collins, no relation; 51

Frances M. Maloney; 24 May 1898; Patrick J. Maloney; - ; Virgil Maloney; - ; money from Mary Maloney's estate; 50

James Maloney; about 1873; William Maloney; Catharine; Edward, Catharine, Patrick, John, Margaret and William Maloney; - ; received money from estate of Eliza Howard, file also mentions Patrick, Timothy and John Howard; 51

John F. Maloney; about 1869; William Maloney; Catharine; Edward, Catharine, Patrick, James, Margaret and William Maloney; - ; received money from estate of Eliza Howard, file also mentions Patrick, Timothy and John Howard; 51

Margaret "Maggie" Maloney; about 1874; William Maloney; Catharine; Edward, Catharine, Patrick, James, John and William Maloney; - ; received money from estate of Eliza Howard, file also mentions Patrick, Timothy and John Howard; 51

Patrick Maloney; 29 October 1879; William Maloney;

Name; Date of Birth; Father; Mother; Siblings; Other Relatives; Notes; Box Number

Catharine; Edward, Catharine, Margaret, James, John and William Maloney; - ; received money from estate of Eliza Howard, file also mentions Patrick, Timothy and John Howard; 51

Virgil John Maloney; 3 June 1901; Patrick J. Maloney; - ; Frances Maloney; - ; money from Mary Maloney's estate; 50

William Maloney; about 1874; William Maloney; Catharine; Edward, Catharine, Margaret, James, John and Patrick Maloney; - ; received money from estate of Eliza Howard, file also mentions Patrick, Timothy and John Howard; 51

Mary C. Manchester; 15 August 1894; - ; - ; George A. Gabel; HU Roy G. Manchester; - ; 51

Annie S. Manley; - ; John Manley; Elizabeth; Laura Manley; - ; - ; 16

Laura B. Manley; - ; John Manley; Elizabeth; Annie Manley; - ; - ; 16

Bertha Mantenfall; about 1879; - ; Louisa, married Mr. Jockley; Mary Mantenfall; - ; last name also seen as Montenffel, received money from estate of Peter Mantenfall; 50

Mary Mantenfall; - ; - ; Louisa, married Mr. Jockley; Bertha Mantenfall; - ; last name also seen as Montenffel, received money from estate of Peter Mantenfall; 50

Alida Markham; 12 June 1875; - ; - ; - ; PGF Wm. J. Markham; first G- Henry Foote, second G- Frank M. Markham; 50

Ella Markham; 18 June 1874; - ; - ; - ; - ; G- Eugene A. Nash, G- William Howlett; 16

Ethel Markham; - ; - ; - ; - ; PGF Wm. J. Markham; first G- Henry Foote, second G- Frank M. Markham; 50

Frank D. Markham; about 1857; - ; - ; - ; - ; RE Howard County, Iowa, file mentions William Howlett; 16

Martha Markham; - ; - ; Marsha, married Mr. Straight and RE New Hudson, Allegany, NY; - ; - ; G- Silas Seely; 16

Rachel Markham; - ; - ; Lucretia; - ; - ; ; 16

John E. Maroney; 20 January 1888; - ; Bridget, of Carrollton; - ; - ; father died before March 1897, G- Frank J. Maroney,

Name; Date of Birth; Father; Mother; Siblings; Other Relatives; Notes; Box Number

received money from John J. Maroney, and W. H. Maroney (deceased brother); 73

Adelbert H. Marsh; 6 May 1833; Arba Marsh, died before January 1850; Artemisia; Anna Marsh; U- Orris Marsh; AKA Harvey Adelbert Marsh; 16

Anna Jane Marsh; February 1836; Arba Marsh, died before January 1850; Artemisia; Adelbert Marsh; U- Orris Marsh; - ; 16

Duane M. Marsh; 20 December 1844; Marshall Marsh, died by 5 September 1863; - ; Mary and Wellman Marsh; U- Orris Marsh; - ; 16

Emily P. Marsh; 29 June 1847; Nelson Marsh; Emily, married Mr. Smith between 1852 and 1856; Nelson Marsh; other relatives Permelia (wife of Emery Wood), Rosetta (wife of Henry Smith), Orpah (wife of George Banfield) and Susan (wife of Sylvester Sherwin); - ; 16

Harry E. Marsh; about 1894; - ; Hattie M.; Leon and Hattie Marsh; - ; received money from estate of Grace Marsh; 51

Hattie M. Marsh; about 1899; - ; Hattie M.; Leon and Harry Marsh; - ; received money from estate of Grace Marsh; 51

Mary Jane Marsh; 5 December 1847; Marshall Marsh, died by 5 September 1863; - ; Duane and Wellman Marsh; U- Orris Marsh; - ; 16

Nelson H. Marsh; 18 August 1850; Nelson Marsh; Emily, married Mr. Smith between 1852 and 1856; Emily Marsh; other relatives Permelia (wife of Emery Wood), Rosetta (wife of Henry Smith), Orpah (wife of George Banfield) and Susan (wife of Sylvester Sherwin); - ; 16

Robert E. Marsh; 8 October 1883; - ; - ; Walter Marsh; MG Levi and Mariah Goldborough (born about 1819), A- Mrs. Sanford H. Burger, GU J. M. Congdon, GU B. F. Congdon, GA Mrs. Susan B. Hazard; - ; 52

Walter G. Marsh; about 1880; - ; - ; Robert Marsh; MG Levi and Mariah Goldborough (born about 1819), A- Mrs. Sanford H. Burger, GU J. M. Congdon, GU B. F. Congdon, GA Mrs.

Name; Date of Birth; Father; Mother; Siblings; Other Relatives; Notes; Box Number

Susan B. Hazard; - ; 52

Wellman J. Marsh; 20 January 1846; Marshall Marsh, died by 5 September 1863; - ; Duane and Mary Marsh; U- Orris Marsh; - ; 16

Lucille Marshall; 6 October 1897; Edward Marshall; named Ada McDivitt at time of guardianship papers, married Mr. Ostrander; - ; GP Daniel and Alice McDivitt; AKA Lucille Marshall McDivitt, RE Smethport, McKean, Pennsylvania, parents divorced; 51

Julia E. Martin; 18 November 1878; - ; Adaline; - ; - ; - ; 50

Permina Martin; about 1855; Jesse Martin, died before 29 August 1859; - ; - ; MGM Lucy Baldwin, MA Mary Jane Baldwin; - ; 16

John Martina; 1 August 1860; John Martina, died before July 1867; Caroline Nolton; - ; MGF Martin Nolton, PU John Martina, PU Peter Martina; - ; 16

Kirby Martindale; about 1899; - ; Ida B. Burlingham; Roy Martindale; MGF Henry Burlingham; - ; 51

Roy E. Martindale; about 1888; - ; Ida B. Burlingham; Kirby Martindale; MGF Henry Burlingham; - ; 51

Florence A. Marvin; 7 April 1865; James B. Marvin; Hester A., died September 1867, of Hanover, Chautauqua, NY; - ; - ; - ; 16

Charles F. Mason; 20 September 1875; - ; - ; - ; - ; received money from estate of Mrs. L. Mason, of Knapps Creek and Charles' parents died and he had no relatives in state; 16

Mildred E. Mason; 1 October 1900; - ; Mina; Edgar Mason; - ; - ; 51

Mills Roy Mason; 1 October 1875; - ; - ; - ; U- James Kelsey, MU Charles Smith, MU Willard Smith, MU Stephen Smith, MA Mrs. Salisbury, A- Jane Kelsey, A- Emily Richardson; RE 16 Laurens St., Olean, mother died July 1882; 51

Myrtle Masoner; 27 May 1895; - ; Katharine, died before January 1911; - ; - ; - ; 52

Edward Mateson; 6 October 1858; - ; - ; - ; - ; G- Myron

Name; Date of Birth; Father; Mother; Siblings; Other Relatives; Notes; Box Number

Mateson, of Beaver Townsip, Clarion, Pennsylvania; 16

Edna May Mather; 3 May 1887; Emor Mather; - ; George Mather; HU Mr. Mallory; - ; 54

George Mather; 9 October 1884; Emor Mather; - ; Edna Mather; - ; - ; 54

Alfretta B. Matoon; 3 October 1883; - ; - ; - ; HU Mr. Hurd, married by July 1905; G- James Wilson, not related; 16

Mary H. M. Mattfeldt; about 1899; AF A. H. Mattfeldt; - ; - ; - ; RE Porcupine, Park, Montana 51

Alida Matthews; 29 December 1833; John Matthews, born before April 1844; Anne, married Mr. McCadden; Jane, Maria and Margery Matthews; - ; G- Bethuel McCoy (of Great Valley); 75

Jane Matthews; 5 March 1833; John Matthews, born before April 1844; Anne, married Mr. McCadden; Alida, Maria and Margery Matthews; - ; G- Bethuel McCoy (of Great Valley); 75

Margery Ann Matthews; 8 June 1829; John Matthews, born before April 1844; Anne, married Mr. McCadden; Alida, Maria and Jane Matthews; - ; G- Bethuel McCoy (of Great Valley); 75

Maria Matthews; 31 August 1831; John Matthews, born before April 1844; Anne, married Mr. McCadden; Alida, Jane and Margery Matthews; - ; G- Bethuel McCoy (of Great Valley); 75

Dacie Matthewson; 23 December 1898; Clinton Matthewson; - ; Dora Matthewson, Alfred Bond, and Angie Fuller; PGF Hale Matthewson, U- Henry Matthewson, U- Marvin Matthewson, MA Dora Starks; money from estate Ava Matthewson's estate; 51

Dora Matthewson; 23 July 1890; Clinton Matthewson; - ; Dacie Matthewson, Alfred Bond, and Angie Fuller; PGF Hale Matthewson, U- Henry Matthewson, U- Marvin Matthewson, MA Dora Starks; money from estate Ava Matthewson's estate; 51

Name; Date of Birth; Father; Mother; Siblings; Other Relatives; Notes; Box Number

Elida Mattoon; 21 September 1876; - ; - ; Florence M. Guest, (W- of Fred M. Guest), Jessie and Jennie Mattoon; - ; father abandoned family in 1884, mother died March 1891; 17

James Ward Mattoon; 6 July 1897; William T. Mattoon, died May 1913; Mary L., died 3 September 1913 in fire, which was caused from removing gasoline tank from house; William, Ida and Bernice Mattoon; C- Daniel L. Batsford; - ; 50

Jennie Mattoon; 23 November 1874; - ; - Florence M. Guest, (W- of Fred M. Guest), Jessie and Elida Mattoon; - ; father abandoned family in 1884, mother died March 1891; 17

Jessie Mattoon; 2 February 1873; - ; - Florence M. Guest, (W- of Fred M. Guest), Jennie and Elida Mattoon; - ; father abandoned family in 1884, mother died March 1891; 17

William H. Mattoon; 15 July 1900; William T. Mattoon, died May 1913; Mary L., died 3 September 1913 in fire, which was caused from removing gasoline tank from house; James, Ida and Bernice Mattoon; C- Daniel L. Batsford; - ; 50

Catherine Maulbetsch; about 1899; - ; Christine; George Maulbetsch; - ; - ; 51

George Maulbetsch; 31 July 1893; - ; Christine; Catherine Maulbetsch; - ; - ; 51

Clara V. Maxson; 14 November 1863; - ; Sarah A.; Charles T. Jones, in 1885 was in Montgomery County, Michigan; HU George Maxson; - ; 52

Edna M. Maxwell; about 1861; Joseph Maxwell, died 7 October 1864 in U. S. Army; Elizabeth P., married Ransom A. Chadwick; Henry Maxwell; MA Sarah Bissell; - ; 16

Henry L. Maxwell; about 1863; Joseph Maxwell, died 7 October 1864 in U. S. Army; Elizabeth P., married Ransom A. Chadwick; Edna Maxwell; MA Sarah Bissell; - ; 16

Clyde A. Maybee; 30 January 1885; Jeremiah Maybee, died 3 March 1888, of Kendall Creek, Foster Township, McKean, Pennsylvania; Alvira, in lunatic asylum at Warren, Pennsylvania; Myrtie and Frankie Maybee and Leona Meyer;

Name; Date of Birth; Father; Mother; Siblings; Other Relatives; Notes; Box Number

- ; - ; 52

Frankie Beatrice Maybee; about 1872; Jeremiah Maybee, died 3 March 1888, of Kendall Creek, Foster Township, McKean, Pennsylvania; Alvira, in lunatic asylum at Warren, Pennsylvania; Myrtie and Clyde Maybee and Leona Meyer; - ; - ; 52

Myrtie D. Maybee; about 1877; Jeremiah Maybee, died 3 March 1888, of Kendall Creek, Foster Township, McKean, Pennsylvania; Alvira, in lunatic asylum at Warren, Pennsylvania; Frankie and Clyde Maybee and Leona Meyer; HU Mr. Keene ; - ; 52

Christine D. Mayer; 20 August 1898; Rudolph C. Mayer; Elizabeth D.; Gretchen Mayer; - ; - ; 49

Gretchen P. Mayer; 21 May 1896; Rudolph C. Mayer; Elizabeth D.; Christine Mayer; - ; - ; 49

Mary Elizabeth McArthur; 17 August 1897; Frank McArthur; - ; Ward McArthur; - ; - ; 50

Plin S. McArthur; 21 November 1866; Thomas J. McArthur, died before 2 December 1885; Sarah A., married Mr. Warner; Thomas McArthur; - ; - ; 16

Thomas J. McArthur; 1 July 1870; Thomas J. McArthur, died before 2 December 1885; Sarah A., married Mr. Warner; Plin McArthur; - ; - ; 16

Ward Dewitt McArthur; 23 September 1899 Frank McArthur; - ; Mary McArthur; - ; - ; 50

Elizabeth McCaffery; about 1893; Charles McCaffery; - ; - ; - ; received money because of accident at Erie Railroad Crossing at the grade crossing near St. Bonaventure University, Allegany, on 24 September 1916; 17

Marie McCarty; about 1895; - ; - ; Ruth McCarty; U- Daniel McCarty; received money from estate of John J. McCarty; 50

Ruth McCarty; about 1897; - ; - ; Marie McCarty; U- Daniel McCarty; received money from estate of John J. McCarty; 50

Arthur G. McClellan; 19 September 1889; Wm. J. McClellan, died 24 December 1902, of Ellicottville; Kate; Joseph and

Name; Date of Birth; Father; Mother; Siblings; Other Relatives; Notes; Box Number

William McClellan; - ; RE 1910, at 5821 Douglass Ave., Pittsburgh, Pennsylvania; 50

Joseph Leo McClellan; 16 May 1893; Wm. J. McClellan, died 24 December 1902, of Ellicottville; Kate; Arthur and William McClellan; - ; - ; 50

William Claude McClellan; 21 August 1891; Wm. J. McClellan, died 24 December 1902, of Ellicottville; Kate; Arthur and Joseph McClellan; - ; - ; 50

Agnes McClelland; May 1855; David McClelland; - ; - ; - ; - ; 17

Margaret McClory; 29 August 1896; John McClory; Emily; Christopher McClory; - ; - ; 50

Benjamin McCluer; 8 May 1824; - ; - ; - ; - ; file mentions William M. Olden or Older of Livingston County, NY; 77

Caroline McCluer; 29 September 1826; Samuel McClure, died before March 1844; - ; Eunice and Frederick McClure; - ; G- James McClure, of Franklinville; 77

Eunice McCluer; 6 August 1828; Samuel McClure, died before March 1844; - ; Caroline and Frederick McClure; - ; G- James McClure, of Franklinville; 77

Emmaetta McClure; 6 November 1848; Ralph Evans; Harriett, died before 18 December 1866; - ; HU Henry H. McClure; - ; 17

Frederick McClure; 5 August 1825; Samuel McClure, died before March 1844; - ; Caroline and Eunice McClure; - ; G- James McClure, of Franklinville; 77

Will V. McCollister; - ; - ; - ; - ; - ; G- Mary McCollister; 17

Archie McDonald; about 1881; - ; Mary H.; Mabel and Hugh McDonald; - ; - ; 17

Edna B. McDonald; about 1897; W. W. McDonald; - ; - ; - ; - ; 17

Hugh McDonald; about 1877; - ; Mary H.; Mabel and Archie McDonald; - ; - ; 17

Mabel McDonald; about 1879; - ; Mary H.; Hugh and Archie McDonald; - ; - ; 17

Milton C. McDonald; about 1898; - ; Susie G.; Thomas

Name; Date of Birth; Father; Mother; Siblings; Other Relatives; Notes; Box Number

McDonald; - ; received insurance money on life of W. W. McDonald; 17

Thomas McDonald; about 1900; - ; Susie G.; Milton McDonald; - ; received insurance money on life of W. W. McDonald; 17

Merlie McElroy; 10 February 1880; - ; Jennie; - ; mother's C- David S. Abbott; - ; 17

John McFadden; 22 August 1896; - ; - ; Leo McFadden; A- Margaret Sharp (RE 942 N. Union St., Olean); received money from estate of Emma McFadden; 50

Leo McFadden; 22 January 1907; - ; - ; John McFadden; A- Margaret Sharp (RE 942 N. Union St., Olean); received money from estate of Emma McFadden; 50

Michael McGarvey; 24 January 1871; James McGarvey; - ; - ; - ; left legacy by brother; 16

Elizabeth Caroline McGavern; about 1889; - ; - ; - ; HU Clifford McGavern, BIL Clair S. McGavern; - ; 50

Arthur D. McGill; 8 June 1899; Arthur W. McGill, owned and operated blacksmith shop in Bradford; - ; Mary McGill; - ; married by December 1899; 17

Mary Celestine McGill; about 1908; Arthur W. McGill, owned and operated blacksmith shop in Bradford; - ; Arthur McGill; - ; AKA Celestine McGill, she attended convent by Sisters of Mercy of the Roman Catholic Church in Rochester; 17

Sadie McGinnis; 20 August 1893; John McGinnis, 1620 W. Henley St., Olean; Ellen; - ; - ; Sadie received money from damages against Mrs. Sartwell; 50

Belle McGuire; 6 November 1876; James H. McGuire died after 2 January 1894; - ; Sarah E. McGuire (married to W. E. Hazard) and Bertha McGuire; U- Daniel W. Horth; received money from life insurance for Flora E. McGuire and James H. McGuire; 17

Bertha McGuire; 21 August 1878; James H. McGuire died after 2 January 1894; - ; Sarah E. McGuire (married to W. E. Hazard) and Belle McGuire; HU Mr. Hunton, U- Daniel W. Horth; received money from life insurance for Flora E.

Name; Date of Birth; Father; Mother; Siblings; Other Relatives; Notes; Box Number

McGuire and James H. McGuire; 17

John Griscom McGuire; 12 April 1864; Thomas McGuire, died 18 June 1869 in Somerville, Middlesex, Massachusetts; Jane B., married Mr. Mead by June 1872; - ; - ; RE McMinnville, Warren, Tennessee in 1885; 16

Charles E. McIntosh; about 1909; Edgar A. McIntosh; - ; - ; - ; - ; 17

Anna "Annie" McIntyre; 11 November 1885; - ; - ; Arthur, Martin, and Frank McIntyre; - ; G- Shep L. Vibbard; 50

Arthur McIntyre; 7 November 1881; - ; - ; Anna, Martin, and Frank McIntyre; - ; boarded at The Randolph Home, G- Shep L. Vibbard; 50

Frank McIntyre; 8 May 1886; - ; - ; Anna, Martin, and Arthur McIntyre; - ; G- Shep L. Vibbard; 50

Martin McIrney; 27 November 1873; - ; Bridget; - ; - ; father died before February 1892; 54

Bernice F. McKay; 28 November 1889; John J. McKay, of Little Valley; Lulu A.; Roscoe and Francis McKay; HU Mr. Furlong, PGM Amelia McKay (of Salamanca); received money from estate of Richard J. McKay; 72

Daniel B. McKay; 27 February 1824; Silas McKay, died before September 1843; - ; Napoleon and Thomas McKay; relative was Sally McKay; G- Israel Day; 77

Francis C. McKay; 7 May 1885; John J. McKay, of Little Valley; Lulu A.; Roscoe and Bernice McKay; PGM Amelia McKay (of Salamanca); received money from estate of Richard J. McKay; 72

Napoleon B. McKay; 12 September 1826; Silas McKay, died before September 1843; - ; Daniel and Thomas McKay; relative was Sally McKay; G- Israel Day; 77

Roscoe J. McKay; 24 June 1887; John J. McKay, of Little Valley; Lulu A.; Francis and Bernice McKay; PGM Amelia McKay (of Salamanca); received money from estate of Richard J. McKay; 72

Thomas H. McKay; 3 July 1830; Silas McKay, died before

Name; Date of Birth; Father; Mother; Siblings; Other Relatives; Notes; Box Number

September 1843; - ; Daniel and Napolean McKay; relative was Sally McKay; G- Israel Day; 77

Anna M. McKernan; about 1882; - ; Joanna Moore; Mary, Thomas, Francis, James, Charles and Ellen McKernan; PU James McKernan, PU Francis McKernan, PU Thomas McKernan, PU Michael McKernan, MU Edward Moore; - ; 54

Charles McKernan; about 1878; - ; Joanna Moore; Mary, Thomas, Francis, James, Ellen and Anna McKernan; PU James McKernan, PU Francis McKernan, PU Thomas McKernan, PU Michael McKernan, MU Edward Moore; - ; 54

Ellen "Nellie" McKernan; about 1884; - ; Joanna Moore; Mary, Thomas, Francis, James, Charles and Anna McKernan; PU James McKernan, PU Francis McKernan, PU Thomas McKernan, PU Michael McKernan, MU Edward Moore; - ; 54

Francis Joseph McKernan; about 1875; - ; Joanna Moore; Mary, Thomas, Ellen, James, Charles and Anna McKernan; PU James McKernan, PU Francis McKernan, PU Thomas McKernan, PU Michael McKernan, MU Edward Moore; - ; 54

James Henry McKernan; about 1876; - ; Joanna Moore; Mary, Thomas, Ellen, Francis, Charles and Anna McKernan; PU James McKernan, PU Francis McKernan, PU Thomas McKernan, PU Michael McKernan, MU Edward Moore; - ; 54

Mary Frances McKernan; about 1873; - ; Joanna Moore; James, Thomas, Ellen, Francis, Charles and Anna McKernan; PU James McKernan, PU Francis McKernan, PU Thomas McKernan, PU Michael McKernan, MU Edward Moore; - ; 54

Thomas Edward McKernan; about 1874; - ; Joanna Moore; James, Mary, Ellen, Francis, Charles and Anna McKernan; PU James McKernan, PU Francis McKernan, PU Thomas

Name; Date of Birth; Father; Mother; Siblings; Other Relatives; Notes; Box Number

McKernan, PU Michael McKernan, MU Edward Moore; - ; 54

Hila E. McKibbin; about 1877; - ; - ; Edward McKibbin, of Punxsutawney; HU Roy Harris; received money from estate of Margaret McKibbin; 73

Agnes McKinley; 22 December 1876; - ; Agnes McClellan; Elizabeth and May McKinley; HU Robert Clements, PU Thomas McClellan ; - ; 54

Elizabeth "Libbie" McKinley; about 1879; - ; Agnes McClellan; Agnes and May McKinley; PU Thomas McClellan ; - ; 54

Hazel McKinley; about 1891; John McKinley; named Mrs. Lizzie Howey at time of guardianship papers; Henry McKinley; PGF Henry McKinley; RE Colorado Springs, El Paso, Colorado; 50

Henry W. McKinley; about 1889; John McKinley; named Mrs. Lizzie Howey at time of guardianship papers; Hazel McKinley; PGF Henry McKinley; RE Colorado Springs, El Paso, Colorado; 50

May McKinley; 6 November 1880; - ; Agnes McClellan; Agnes and Elizabeth McKinley; PU Thomas McClellan ; - ; 54

James M. McLaughlin, Jr.; 1878/1879; James M. McLaughlin. Sr.; Mary C., died December 1882, of Olean; - ; - ; estate of W. C. Carringer; 17 and 53

Mary E. McLaughlin; about 1883; - ; - ; - ; U- David Curry, of Olean; - ; 67

Arthur James McMahon; about 1894; - ; Mary J., married Mr. O'Toole; - ; - ; - ; 50

Genevieve McMahon; 7 March 1907; - ; - ; Helen G. McMahon (1923 RE 834 Main St., Jamestown) and HS M. Louise McMahon (1923 RE 759 President St, Brooklyn); - ; RE 1923 with Leo Scanlon at 65 Amm St., Bradford, Pennsylvania; 17

William Eugene McMahon; 9 May 1895; John H. McMahon, born about 1841, RE 109 N.6th St., Olean; - ; M. Louise McMahon (759 President St., Brooklyn) and Rose Egan (of

Name; Date of Birth; Father; Mother; Siblings; Other Relatives; Notes; Box Number

McDonald, Pennsylvania); - ; - ; 54

Emily McMaster; about 1838; - ; Jane; Susan, Wallace, Adalaide, and Ira McMaster; - ; file mentions that David McMaster Jr. is dead; 17

Susan McMaster; about 1841; - ; Jane; Emily, Wallace, Adalaide, and Ira McMaster; - ; file mentions that David McMaster Jr. is dead; 17

Wallace McMaster; 22 August 1845; - ; Jane; Emily, Susan, Adalaide, and Ira McMaster; - ; file mentions that David McMaster Jr. is dead; 17

Charlotte Ann McMillen; 18 July 1844; - ; Polly; Martha and John McMillen; - ; G- Selleck St. John; 17

John B. McMillen; 4 September 1842; - ; Polly; Martha and Charlotte McMillen; - ; G- Selleck St. John; 17

Martha Jane McMillen; 18 July 1844; - ; Polly; John and Charlotte McMillen; - ; G- Selleck St. John; 17

Frances Elizabeth McPherson; 3 April 1892; Wallace McPherson; - ; Roy McPherson; - ; - ; 50

Roy Vern McPherson; 25 March 1890; Wallace McPherson; - ; Frances McPherson; - ; - ; 50

Arthur McQuaid; 8 July 1895; Martin McQuaid; Rose A.; - ; - ; - ; 50

Margaret E. McStay; 28 May 1872; - ; - ; - ; HU Mr. Douglas (married 3 November 1892), MG William and Margaret Hamilton; Joseph Watson left her part of estate, RE In 1893, Pavilion, Genesee, NY; 17

Christina T. McVey; 25 May 1848; William McVey; Margaret; James, Susan, Arch., Margaret and Elizabeth McVey; BIL M. W. Bosworth; - ; 17

James Dow McVey; 22 March 1843; William McVey; Margaret; Christina, Susan, Arch., Margaret and Elizabeth McVey; BIL M. W. Bosworth; - ; 17

Susan McVey; 15 September 1841; William McVey; Margaret; Christina, James, Arch., Margaret and Elizabeth McVey; BIL M. W. Bosworth; - ; 17

Name; Date of Birth; Father; Mother; Siblings; Other Relatives; Notes; Box Number

Amy Anne Meacham; 15 December 1858; AF Jeremiah Meacham ; AM Rhoda L. died May 1876, of Little Valley; - ; HU Mr. Travis, biological father was Charles Schultz, of Dayton; she was an illegitimate child; 75

Harlan Meacham; 1 November 1877; Moses Meacham; - ; Henry and Le Roy Meacham; - ; - ; 17

Henry Meacham; 21 December 1879; Moses Meacham; - ; Harlan and Le Roy Meacham; - ; - ; 17

Le Roy Meacham; 26 October 1882; Moses Meacham; - ; Harlan and Henry Meacham; - ; - ; 17

Howard C. Meade; 26 April 1897; Henry G. Meade; Bertha Magner; - ; MGF Thomas J. Magner; RE Cuyahoga County, Ohio- 1707 E. 82nd St; 51

Cecelia Mele; 25 December 1908; Michael Bronold; - ; - ; HU Carl Mele; - ; 68

Nancy Melrose; 5 January 1858; James Melrose; - ; - ; MU Alexander Harvey, MA Elizabeth Morrison, MA Lydia Harvey, PU Ebenezer Melrose, PA Betsey Case; - ; 16

Helen Meridan; 16 July 1909; Jacob Meridan, of Allegany; Teresa; - ; - ; - ; 69

Rose Meridan; 30 June 1880; - ; - ; - ; - ; G- John Haber; 72

Charles Merkt; - ; Charles Merkt, died November 1901 in Tampiko, Mexico; - ; Edith Merkt; PA Cynthia Hamm; mother died in Texas after abandoning children; 50

Edith Irene Merkt; - ; Charles Merkt, died November 1901 in Tampiko, Mexico; - ; Charles Merkt; PA Cynthia Hamm; mother died in Texas after abandoning children; 50

Eldridge E. Merkt; September 1896; - ; - ; - ; U- Eugene Merkt; - ; 52

Eva M. Merow; 23 June 1889; - ; Estella D.; - ; HU Mr. Hout; - ; 10

Gertrude Merrick; 22 January 1907; - ; Ethel, married Mr. Young; - ; HU Mr. Longley; received money from Herron damage suit and father died before February 1920; 68

Albert James Merrill; 22 March 1903 in Dayton; Willie E.

Name; Date of Birth; Father; Mother; Siblings; Other Relatives; Notes; Box Number

Merrill; Hattie; - ; - ; - ; 50

Bernard W. Merrill; 30 January 1899; Frank M. Merrill; - ; - ; - ; - ; 51

Mertie Merrill; 18 October 1879; Henry S. Merrill, of Farmersville; - ; - ; - ; - ; 54

Minnie B. Merrill; 23 July 1871; - ; - ; Willie Merrill; - ; G- Edward E. Levining; 16

Harry V. Metcalf; about 1885; Leroy C. Metcalf; Ella K.; Raymond Metcalf; U- Charles Metcalf; - ; 17

Raymond F. Metcalf; 12 February 1887; Leroy C. Metcalf; Ella K.; Harry Metcalf; U- Charles Metcalf; RE 1900, Galveston, Galveston, Texas ; 17

Roxalana L. Metcalf; 24 February 1834; - ; - ; - ; - ; G- John B. Wood; 16

Julia Meyer; 27 May 1880; - ; Dorothea, married Mr. Ehman; - ; - ; received money from estate of C. Meyer; 16

Ellen S. Mighells; 3 June 1864; Florentine Mighells, died August 1875, of Randolph; Elizabeth H.; Sophronia, Marian, Elliott, Florentine and George Mighells, Louise R. Conley and Cordelia Dutcher; - ; - ; 52

Elliott C. Mighells; 27 October 1867; Florentine Mighells, died August 1875, of Randolph; Elizabeth H.; Sophronia, Marian, Ellen, Florentine and George Mighells, Louise R. Conley and Cordelia Dutcher; - ; - ; 52

Marian Eldora Mighells; 12 December 1865; Florentine Mighells, died August 1875, of Randolph; Elizabeth H.; Sophronia, Elliott, Ellen, Florentine and George Mighells, Louise R. Conley and Cordelia Dutcher; - ; - ; 52

Sophronia E. Mighells; 4 October 1862; Florentine Mighells, died August 1875, of Randolph; Elizabeth H.; Marian, Elliott, Ellen, Florentine and George Mighells, Louise R. Conley and Cordelia Dutcher; - ; - ; 52

Kenneth F. Miles; 19 April 1906; Arthur L. Miles, of 209 Court St., Little Valley; - ; - ; - ; mother died 9 May 1906; 69

Thomas Miles; about 1873; John Miles; Catherine, died before

Name; Date of Birth; Father; Mother; Siblings; Other Relatives; Notes; Box Number

August 27, 1883; - ; C- Edmond Donlin; - ; 52

Gilbert Milk; 7 November 1848; - ; - ; - ; - ; G- Harrison Judd; 16

Manly David Milk; about 1852; David Milk; - ; - ; PG John and Anna Milk, PU Martin Milk, PU John Milk, PU Benjamin Milk, PU George Milk, PU Giles Milk, PU Hiram Milk, PA Deborah Case, PA Mary Kinnicutt, MG John and Sophronia Kinnicutt, MU Leander Kinnicutt, MU John Kinnicutt, MU Lucius Kinnicutt, MA Matilda Hill, MA Adalissa Kinnicutt; - ; 16

Daisy Milks; 19 August 1887; - ; Rose; - ; - ; left legacy by Alexander Milks; 52

Horton Chester Milks; 9 December 1880; Jonathan Milks, died 17 April 1891, of New Albion; Jennie; Mina and Ruth Milks and Elizabeth Lion; - ; - ; 52

Manley K. Milks; 26 May 1880; Hiram Milks, died 23 January 1883, in Napoli; Martha; - ; - ; - ; 51

Olin R. Milks; 12 April 1881; - ; - ; Archie B. Milks; - ; received money from estate of Luther Milks; 52

Albert Miller; about 1862; - ; Ellen; Joseph, Clara, Hurbert, Charles and Nellie; - ; indexed as Albert Muller; 17

Cadelia Miller; 1849; Ansel Miller, died before 14 July 1848, of Lyndon; - ; Elizabeth and George Miller; PGF Thomas Miller; - ; 53

Charles Miller; about 1873; - ; Ellen; Joseph, Clara, Hurbert, Albert and Nellie; - ; indexed as Charles Muller; 17

Chrystole L. Miller; 12 June 1903/1904; - ; - ; David R. Miller, of Carrollton; - ; mother died and father was an invalid; 69

Clara Miller; about 1863; - ; Ellen; Joseph, Albert, Hurbert, Charles and Nellie; - ; indexed as Clara Muller; 17

Elizabeth Miller; about 1841; Ansel Miller, died before 14 July 1848, of Lyndon; - ; Cadelia and George Miller; PGF Thomas Miller; - ; 53

Elizabeth Mariah Miller; about 1827; Joseph H. Miller, died 20 April 1827, of Coldspring; Mariah, married Mr. Beardsley; - ; - ; G- Silas Miller, Peter Beardsley maintained Elizabeth;

Name; Date of Birth; Father; Mother; Siblings; Other Relatives; Notes; Box Number

77

Elma Miller; 5 September 1905; Peter Miller; Rose; Emeline and Thurman Miller; - ; - ; 51

Emeline Miller; 1 June 1894; Peter Miller; Rose; Elma and Thurman Miller; HU Mr. Learn; - ; 51

Frank J. Miller; 7 November 1875/1876; - ; Ellen Spaulding, died about 1882 in Wisconsin; - ; MA Bertha R. Dexter (wife of Marcus Dexter), MA Addie Harvey (wife of Oscar Harvey), MA Miranda Crooks, PU Asa Miller, PU James Miller, PA Mrs. Joseph Peaslee; G- Asa Cross, Frank had not lived with father since 1884, Father RE Wisconsin, Frank received money from estate of Eleanor Spaulding; 51

George Miller; about 1843; Ansel Miller, died before 14 July 1848, of Lyndon; - ; Cadelia and Elizabeth Miller; PGF Thomas Miller; - ; 53

Herman Miller; 7 January 1906; - ; - ; Martha and Bertha Gehrke and Frank Miller; BIL Fred Gehrke, of East Otto; both parents died before February 1924; 68

Howard J. Miller; 24 October 1900; - ; Mary B., of 902 W. Henley St., Olean; Walter Miller, Estella Gunder and Edna Miller; - ; - ; 69

Hurbert Miller; about 1864; - ; Ellen; Joseph, Clara, Albert, Charles and Nellie Miller; - ; indexed as Hurbert Muller; 17

Isabelle Miller; 24 May 1908; David Miller; Frances Anna, died 1 September 1924, she lived at 218 N. 15th St., Olean; - ; HU Mr. Thomas; RE 1929, in Buffalo, G- Wm. G. Wiedman; 69

Joseph Miller; about 1862; - ; Ellen; Clara, Albert, Hurbert, Charles and Nellie; - ; indexed as Joseph Muller; 17

Mary Grace Miller; - ; - ; - ; - ; - ;G- Chester F. Camp; 72

Myrtle Miller; 2 March 1904; - ; - ; - ; HU Harold DeForest, GM Amy Miller (born about 1849), U- Anson Miller; RE 1925, at 112 Coleman St., Olean; 69

Nancy E. Miller; 4 May 1861; Abram Miller, died July 1863 in Sheshequin, Bradford, Pennsylvania; Harriet E., married Mr. Hudson; Sarah and William Miller; - ; - ; 16

Name; Date of Birth; Father; Mother; Siblings; Other Relatives; Notes; Box Number

Nellie Miller; about 1874; - ; Ellen; Clara, Albert, Hurbert, Charles and Joseph; - ; indexed as Nellie Muller; 17

Sanford Miller; 19 February 1909; Leon Miller; - ; - ; - ; received money from estate of Mother; 51

Sarah E. Miller; 31 August 1856; Abram Miller, died July 1863 in Sheshequin, Bradford, Pennsylvania; Harriet E., married Mr. Hudson; Nancy and William Miller; - ; - ; 16

Thurman Miller; 21 February 1899; Peter Miller; Rose; Emeline and Elma Miller; - ; - ; 51

William A. Miller; 1 December 1858; Abram Miller, died July 1863 in Sheshequin, Bradford, Pennsylvania; Harriet E., married Mr. Hudson; Nancy and Sarah Miller; - ; - ; 16

Emma E. Mills; 6 February 1863; William J. Mills, died before 9 February 1880; - ; - ; - ; G- Charles K. Wright; 16

Ione B. Mills; 18 May 1879; Merrill Mills; - ; Jesse Mills; - ; G- Myron C. Hawley, no relation; 52

Jesse Mills; about 1886; Merrill Mills; - ; Ione Mills; - ; G- Myron C. Hawley, no relation; 52

Frank M. Miner; about 1882; Charles M. Miner, died before 31 July 1887; Lillian, married Mr. Gould; - ; - ; Charles Miner's will was probated in Madison County, NY, G-William H. Crandall, G- Jasper E. Smith; 52

Henry D. Miner; 13 April 1821; Jesse Miner, died before March 1837; - ; Thomas Miner; - ; G- Julius C. Miner; 77

Maxine E. Miner; 21 September 1904; Frank M., of Parkwood, Pennsylvania, deserted family about 1911; Nettie M., of 111 Wayne St., Olean; - ; - ; - ; 69

Thomas T. Miner; 4 March 1823; Jesse Miner, died before March 1837; - ; Henry Miner; - ; G- Julius C. Miner; 77

Carrie A. Mitchell; about 1867; John Mitchell; - ; Charles Mitchell; - ; - ; 51

Charles G. Mitchell; about 1869; John Mitchell; - ; Carrie Mitchell; - ; - ; 51

John Mitchell; about 1839; - ; - ; - ; - ; in same envelope as Margaret Mitchell, G- John McCready; 16

Name; Date of Birth; Father; Mother; Siblings; Other Relatives; Notes; Box Number

Margaret Mitchell; 16 January 1837 ; - ; - ; - ; - ; G- Richard Little, in same envelope as John Mitchell; 16

Elmer Bradford Moberg; 21 April 1911 in Brockton MA; Edgar E. Moberg died 1922 in Olean; Lena, married Mr. Appleton; - ; - ; Lena RE 114 Highland St., Brockton MA and Elmer received money from estate of Ada Moberg, which was shared with Helen Vaughn; 68

Clarence Mohr; about 1894; Andrew Mohr, died before May 1928; Julia, died before July 1910; Walter, Mary, Edward and Lucretia Mohr; - ; legacy from Walter Clare, of Allegany; 68

Edward Mohr; about 1900; Andrew Mohr, died before May 1928; Julia, died before July 1910; Walter, Mary, Clarence and Lucretia Mohr; - ; legacy from Walter Clare, of Allegany; 68

Lucretia Mohr; about 1897; Andrew Mohr, died before May 1928; Julia, died before July 1910; Walter, Mary, Clarence and Edward Mohr; - ; legacy from Walter Clare, of Allegany; 68

Mary (Loretta) Mohr; about 1910; Andrew Mohr, died before May 1928; Julia, died before July 1910; Walter, Lucretia, Clarence and Edward Mohr; - ; legacy from Walter Clare, of Allegany; 68

Walter Mohr; about 1895; Andrew Mohr, died before May 1928; Julia, died before July 1910; Mary, Lucretia, Clarence and Edward Mohr; - ; legacy from Walter Clare, of Allegany; 68

Cornelia Mong; 23 May 1902; - ; Anna, of Cattaraugus; Willson Mong; - ; father's residence was unknown; 68

Willson Mong; 27 July 1905; - ; Anna, of Cattaraugus; Cornelia Mong; - ; father's residence was unknown and Willson attended Univ. of Arkansas at Fayetteville, Ark; 68

Eloise Montgomery; about 1907; - ; Nellie, married Mr. Sylvester; - ; - ; RE Bradford, McKean, Pennsylvania; 50

Leroy Moon; 4 July 1851; - ; Mary, died before September 1869; Mary and Orville Moon; - ; G- Thomas Moon; 16

Name; Date of Birth; Father; Mother; Siblings; Other Relatives; Notes; Box Number

Mary Adel Moon; 18 October 1852; - ; Mary, died before September 1869; Leroy and Orville Moon; - ; G- Thomas Moon; 16

Orville Moon; 19 December 1854; - ; Mary, died before September 1869; Leroy and Mary Moon; - ; G- Thomas Moon; 16

Charles Knowlton Moore; 7 January 1861; Romanzo Moore, died by 14 April 1866; Eliza Rickards, died between 1866 and 1878; Edgar Moore; PGF Oliver Moore and MGF Nelson Rickards; 16

Edgar Moore; 27 January 1856; Romanzo Moore, died by 14 April 1866; Eliza Rickards, died between 1866 and 1878; Charles Moore; PGF Oliver Moore and MGF Nelson Rickards; 16

Emma Moore; 20 July 1849; Harlow E. Moore, died before June 1864; - ; - ; - ; G- John C. Green; 16

Richard J. Moore; about 1909; - ; Josephine G., of 118 N. 10th St., Olean; - ; - ; father died before September 1921; 69

Helen Moot; 12 April 1909; - ; Minnie, of Machias, married Mr. Prescott; - ; HU Mr. Ondra, married about 1928; RE 1931, Lowellville, Mahoning, Ohio, father died before October 1909; 69

Donald Moran; 1 July 1898; - ; Sarah; Sarto Moran; - ; - ; 51

Sarto Moran; 10 August 1903; - ; Sarah; Donald Moran; - ; - ; 51

Arthur Morgan; 23 August 1864; - ; Mary Williams; Henry Morgan; MGF Robert Williams, MU John Williams; second G- Daniel Lammie, no paternal relatives lived in NY state; 16

Christiana Fidelia Morgan; - ; Hiram Morgan, died before February 1865; Harriet C.; James, E. Atcelia, Cornelia, and Permelia Morgan, and Sarah C. Oaks; PU Henry Morgan, PA Almira Morgan, PA Eliza Campbell; - ; 75

Cornelia E. Morgan; 16 June 1847; Hiram Morgan, died before February 1865; Harriet C.; James, E. Atcelia, Christina, and Permelia Morgan, and Sarah C. Oaks; PU Henry Morgan, PA Almira Morgan, PA Eliza Campbell; - ; 75

Name; Date of Birth; Father; Mother; Siblings; Other Relatives; Notes; Box Number

E. Atcelia Morgan; 26 June 1845; Hiram Morgan, died before February 1865; Harriet C.; James, Cornelia, Christina, and Permelia Morgan, and Sarah C. Oaks; PU Henry Morgan, PA Almira Morgan, PA Eliza Campbell; - ; 75

Ernest Morgan; about 1890; William Morgan; - ; Philip Morgan; - ; received money from James Higgins' estate; 17

Henry Morgan; 12 April 1852; - ; Mary Williams; Arthur Morgan; MGF Robert Williams, MU John Williams; second G- Daniel Lammie, no paternal relatives lived in NY state; 16

Mary Isabel Morgan; 19 July 1860; Congdon Morgan, died before June 1867; Mercy, married Mr. Greene by August 1874; Mercy Morgan; HU Mr. Brewster, married by November 1881; RE November 1881, lived in Ellery, Chautauqua, NY, G- Emeline C. Durfee, second G- Alvin A. Hubbell (doctor), in 1869, she acquired interest in land by marriage of mother, by will of grandfather, which mentions gravestones for Newell Morgan; 16

Mercy "Delia" Adelia Morgan; 9 May 1851; Congdon Morgan, died before June 1867; Mercy, married Mr. Greene by August 1874; Mary Morgan; - ; G- Emeline C. Durfee, second G- Alvin A. Hubbell (doctor), in 1869, she acquired interest in land by marriage of mother, by will of grandfather, which mentions gravestones for Newell Morgan; 16

Permelia F. Morgan; 3 June 1849; Hiram Morgan, died before February 1865; Harriet C.; James, Cornelia, Christina, and E. Atcelia Morgan, and Sarah C. Oaks; PU Henry Morgan, PA Almira Morgan, PA Eliza Campbell; - ; 75

Philip Morgan; 14 October 1887; William Morgan; - ; Ernest Morgan; - ; received money from James Higgins' estate; 17

Ellen "Nellie" Moriarty; 22 February 1877; Michael Moriarty, Sr.; - ; John, Michael, Francis, Johanna and William Moriarty; - ; received pension money; 51

Francis "Frank" Moriarty; 30 May 1874; Michael Moriarty, Sr.; - ; John, Michael, Ellen, Johanna and William Moriarty; - ; received pension money; 51

Name; Date of Birth; Father; Mother; Siblings; Other Relatives; Notes; Box Number

Johanna Moriarty; 14 September 1879; Michael Moriarty, Sr.; - ; John, Michael, Ellen, Francis and William Moriarty; - ; received pension money; 51

Michael Moriarty, Jr.; 17/18 February 1869/1870; Michael Moriarty, Sr.; - ; John, Johanna, Ellen, Francis and William Moriarty; - ; RE 1891, Bradford, McKean, Pennsylvania, received pension money; 51

William Moriarty; 1 September 1881; Michael Moriarty, Sr.; - ; John, Johanna, Ellen, Francis and Michael Moriarty; - ; received pension money; 51

Herbert Morrill; January 1856; Franklin S. Morrill, died May 1863, of South Valley; Lucy, married Mr. Whitney by August 1868; Mary Morrill; - ; - ; 16

Mary Ella Morrill; 17 August 1860; Franklin S. Morrill, died May 1863, of South Valley; Lucy, married Mr. Whitney by August 1868; Herbert Morrill; - ; - ; 16

Ethel E. Morris; 28 March 1887; David Morris, died 23 December 1899; - ; - ; MGF James Sherman (of Wayne, Wayne, Michigan), PA Mary Griffith (wife of William Griffith), PA Anna Morgan, PA Harriet Hawks (wife of E. C. Hawks), PU William L. Morris (husband of Louisa), PU John W. Morris, PU Thomas B. Morris. PU Daniel Morris, MA Anna Clark (wife of Vincent Clark); mother died 28 March 1899; 16

James William Morris; 28 September 1886; - ; Hannah, insane and admitted to Providence Retreat in Buffalo; Julia Morris; U- John Crowley; - ; 16

Julia Morris; 26 April 1891; - ; Hannah, insane and admitted to Providence Retreat in Buffalo; James Morris; U- John Crowley; - ; 16

Richard Miles Morris; 22 November 1910; Charles D. Morris, lived at 119 Laurens St., Olean, and 1931 in NY City; Arminta; - ; - ; - ; 68

Clarence E. Morrison; 25 July 1892; William Morrison; Emma, of Franklinville; - ; - ; - ; 73

Name; Date of Birth; Father; Mother; Siblings; Other Relatives; Notes; Box Number

James Morrison; about 1896; Charles M. Morrison, died before 1906; Mary, married Mr. Brotherton; Maud and Lottie Morrison; U- Thomas Morrison, of Perrysburg; - ; 68

Lottie Morrison; about 1894; Charles M. Morrison, died before 1906; Mary, married Mr. Brotherton; Maud and James Morrison; U- Thomas Morrison, of Perrysburg; - ; 68

Maud Morrison; about 1899; Charles M. Morrison, died before 1906; Mary, married Mr. Brotherton; Lottie and James Morrison; U- Thomas Morrison, of Perrysburg; - ; 68

Agnes "Aggie" Townley Morton; 21 June 1872; Hugh Morton, died 25 July 1883; Agnes Townley, lived in River Falls, Wisconsin; DeForrest Morton, HB George Morton; HU Mr. White (married by 1884), MA Mary Lenhart, MA Sarah C. Whitney, MA Ann Perry, MU Frank Townley, PA Elizabeth Fobes; G- David H. Boller; 16

DeForrest Morton; 18 May 1874; Hugh Morton, died 25 July 1883; Agnes Townley, lived in River Falls, Wisconsin; Agnes Morton, HB George Morton; MA Mary Lenhart, MA Sarah C. Whitney, MA Ann Perry, MU Frank Townley, PA Elizabeth Fobes; G- David H. Boller; 16

H. Edith Morton; 13 February 1874; - ; - ; James and Robert Morton; U- Robert Morton Sr.; - ; 52

Guy F. Morton; 5 November 1893; - ; Anna; - ; - ; father died before June 1899, money from Nelson J. Morton's estate; 73

Horace G. Morton; 23 September 1864; - ; - ; Daniel Morton; BIL Isaac Baker; - ; 16

James J. Morton; 17 July 1876; - ; - ; H. Edith and Robert Morton; U- Robert Morton Sr.; - ; 52

Robert A. Morton; 8 February 1875; - ; - ; H. Edith and James Morton; U- Robert Morton Sr.; - ; 52

Lora J. Mosher; about 1874; - ; Betsey J.; Frank and Ara Mosher; - ; - ; 16

Lottie Mosher; about 1863; Thomas J. Mosher; Minerva; - ; - ; RE Wayne, Wayne, Michigan; special G- Andrew C. Adams, no relatives were in NY; 16

Name; Date of Birth; Father; Mother; Siblings; Other Relatives; Notes; Box Number

Patheria Mosher; 10 January 1850; Arctus P. Burroughs, died before 15 May 1868; - ; - ; - ; G- William P. Mosher; 16

John Moszak; - ; Peter Moszak, of Olean; - ; - ; - ; - ; 69

Charles P. Moulton; 1 November 1844; - ; Eglantine E. Washburn; - ; MU Charles P. Washburn, died 3 March 1853, left legacy to Charles; - ; 16

Alice Moyer; about 1861; John Moyer, died March 1865 in Allegany; Eunice S., married to Mr. Miller; Estella Moyer; - ; - ; 16

Estella Moyer; about 1860; John Moyer, died March 1865 in Allegany; Eunice S., married to Mr. Miller; Alice Moyer; - ; - ; 16

Geraldine Mudge; 26 November 1888; Charles Mudge, of Olean; Geraldine; Helen and Winifred Mudge; relative was Edwin H. Mudge (of Niagara County); G- Elroy D. Westbrook, received legacy from estate of Seldon J. Mudge; 73

Helen Louise Mudge; 26 August 1887; Charles Mudge, of Olean; Geraldine; Geraldine and Winifred Mudge; relative was Edwin H. Mudge (of Niagara County); G- Elroy D. Westbrook, Seldon J. Mudge left legacy; 73

Winifred Mudge; 17 March 1884; Charles Mudge, of Olean; Geraldine; Geraldine and Helen Mudge; HU Mr. Brett, relative was Edwin H. Mudge (of Niagara County); RE 1905, in Buffalo, G- Elroy D. Westbrook, Seldon J. Mudge left legacy; 73

Wilson Mudgett; 24 March 1817; - ; - ; - ; - ; file mentions Nathan Howe; 77

Clara Belle Mulcay; - ; - ; - ; Dora, Nora and John Mulcay; - ; G- Arthur Bedell, received money from Ellen Clark's estate; 73

John F. Mulcay; 12 June 1890; - ; - ; Dora, Nora and Clara Mulcay; - ; G- Arthur Bedell, received money from Ellen Clark's estate and lived with Mrs. Broderick; 73

Nora Mulcay; - ; - ; - ; Dora, Clara and John Mulcay; - ; G- Arthur Bedell, received money from Ellen Clark's estate; 73

John A. Mullin; 1 November 1900; James Mullin, died before

Name; Date of Birth; Father; Mother; Siblings; Other Relatives; Notes; Box Number

March 1921; May, of Ellicottville, married Mr. Ludwig; Theresa Mullin; - ; joined the US Army; 69

Theresa Mullin; 26 June 1907; James Mullin, died before March 1921; May, of Ellicottville, married Mr. Ludwig; John Mullin; - ; - ; 69

Alice Mildred Murphy; 14 January 1898; - ; Anna M.; - ; - ; RE Toledo, Lucas, Ohio, money from John J. Flohie's estate; 51

Blanche Murphy; 2 July 1879; - ; Marcella; Frank and Sarah Murphy; HU Mr. Taylor; received money from estate of James Murphy; 51

Daniel Murphy; about 1877; John Murphy, died before June 1896; Maggie, died before June 1896; John, Rose, James, and Mary Murphy; - ; G- Thomas Tray; 68

Frank Murphy; 12 December 1880; - ; Marcella; Blanche and Sarah Murphy; - ; money from James Murphy's estate; 51

James Murphy; about 1882; John Murphy, died before June 1896; Maggie, died before June 1896; John, Rose, Daniel, and Mary Murphy; - ; G- Thomas Tray; 68

Mary Murphy; about 1886; John Murphy, died before June 1896; Maggie, died before June 1896; John, Rose, Daniel, and James Murphy; - ; G- Thomas Tray; 68

Rose Murphy; about 1894; John Murphy, died before June 1896; Maggie, died before June 1896; John, Mary, Daniel, and James Murphy; - ; G- Thomas Tray; 68

Sarah Murphy; 29 August 1886; - ; Marcella; Blanche and Sarah Murphy; HU Mr. Smith; RE 1907, in Buffalo and received money from estate of James Murphy; 51

Bertha Murray; about 1883; - ; Margaret, of Allegany; Sara, Margarite and Ella Murray; - ; father died before March 1897; 73

Clifford Murray; - ; - ; - ; - ; - ; G- Anna Murray, in same envelope as Lena, Hayward, Novella and John Murray; 75

Ella Murray; about 1886; - ; Margaret, of Allegany; Sara, Margarite and Bertha Murray; - ; father died before March 1897; 73

Name; Date of Birth; Father; Mother; Siblings; Other Relatives; Notes; Box Number

Hayward Murray; - ; - ; - ; - ; - ; G- Anna Murray, in same envelope as Lena, Clifford, Novella and John Murray; 75

John Murray; - ; - ; - ; - ; - ; G- Anna Murray, in same envelope as Lena, Clifford, Novella and Hayward Murray; 75

Lena Murray; - ; - ; - ; - ; - ; G- Anna Murray, in same envelope as John, Clifford, Novella and Hayward Murray; 75

Margarite "Rita" Murray; about 1880; - ; Margaret, of Allegany; Sara, Ella and Bertha Murray; - ; father died before March 1897; 73

Mary Murray; 16 Sept 1875; John Murray; - ; Michael Murray; U- Timothy McCarthy; - ; 51

Michael Murray; 7 December 1873; John Murray; - ; Mary Murray; U- Timothy McCarthy; - ; 51

Novella Murray; - ; - ; - ; - ; - ; G- Anna Murray, in same envelope as John, Clifford, Lena and Hayward Murray; 75

Sara Murray; about 1882; - ; Margaret, of Allegany; Margarite, Ella and Bertha Murray; - ; father died before March 1897; 73

Adelaide "Addie" J. Myers; 12 May 1861; Aaron Myers; Mary, died before 17 August 1862, of Minnesota; Louisa, Olive and Arthur Myers; - ; RE New London, Waupaca, Wisconsin; 17

Arthur J. Myers; - ; Aaron Myers; Mary, died before 17 August 1862, of Minnesota; Louisa, Olive and Adelaide Myers; - ; - ; 17

Louisa M. Myers; - ; Aaron Myers; Mary, died before 17 August 1862, of Minnesota; Arthur, Olive and Adelaide Myers; - ; - ; 17

Olive E. Myers; - ; Aaron Myers; Mary, died before 17 August 1862, of Minnesota; Arthur, Louisa and Adelaide Myers; - ; - ; 17

Stephen J. Myers; 9 October 1893; Stephen Myers; - ; - ; - ; G- Albert L. Myers, received pension money; 18

Frank Myles; 7 April 1900; Frank Myles; Rose; Mary, James and Alice Myles; - ; Alice lived at 53 Maple St., Salamanca; 68

Clarence O. Myrick; 7 August 1884; John Myrick, died before

Name; Date of Birth; Father; Mother; Siblings; Other Relatives; Notes; Box Number

11 March 1889; Mary L., married Mr. Blowers between 1890 and 1891; John Myrick; - ; - ; 18

John S. Myrick; 15 June 1887; John Myrick, died before 11 March 1889; Mary L., married Mr. Blowers between 1890 and 1891; Clarence Myrick; - ; - ; 18

Name; Date of Birth; Father; Mother; Siblings; Other Relatives; Notes; Box Number

N Surnames

Ethel J. Napier; about 1882; Edward Napier; - ; - ; - ; G- James B. Lee, no relation; 56

Adaline Nash; 16 January 1836; Amos Nash, died before April 1850; Christiana McMillen, married Mr. Markham, of Dayton; Eugene, Victoria, Dewit, Silas, Emmet, and Corydon Nash; PGM Sally Nash, PU Dewitt Nash, PA Maranda Near, PA Emeline Strickland, MU William McMillen, MU Alden McMillen, MU Charles McMillen, MA Mary McMillen; G- Norman Allen; 57

Charles C. Nash; 6 May 1877; Adelbert Nash, moved to Michigan; Adell, born about 1859, died 1 October 1880, in Poland, her G- was Israel Alden; Perry Nash; - ; he either lived with Dewitt Nash or James Poland; 54

Clinton Nash: SEE DEWIT NASH

Corydon Nash; 16 November 1834; Amos Nash, died before April 1850; Christiana McMillen, married Mr. Markham, of Dayton; Eugene, Victoria, Dewit, Silas, Emmet, and Adelbert Nash; PGM Sally Nash, PU Dewitt Nash, PA Maranda Near, PA Emeline Strickland, MU William McMillen, MU Alden McMillen, MU Charles McMillen, MA Mary McMillen; G- Norman Allen; 57

Dewit Nash; 28 August 1841; Amos Nash, died before April 1850; Christiana McMillen, married Mr. Markham, of Dayton; Eugene, Victoria, Corydon, Silas, Emmet, and Adelbert Nash; PGM Sally Nash, PU Dewitt Nash, PA Maranda Near, PA Emeline Strickland, MU William McMillen, MU Alden McMillen, MU Charles McMillen, MA Mary McMillen; G- Norman Allen; 57

Emmet H. Nash; 15 July 1846; Amos Nash, died before April 1850; Christiana McMillen, married Mr. Markham, of Dayton; Eugene, Victoria, Corydon, Silas, Dewit, and Adelbert Nash; PGM Sally Nash, PU Dewitt Nash, PA

Name; Date of Birth; Father; Mother; Siblings; Other Relatives; Notes; Box Number

Maranda Near, PA Emeline Strickland, MU William McMillen, MU Alden McMillen, MU Charles McMillen, MA Mary McMillen; G- Norman Allen; 57

Eugene A. Nash; 30 March 1837; Amos Nash, died before April 1850; Christiana McMillen, married Mr. Markham, of Dayton; Emmet, Victoria, Corydon, Silas, Dewit, and Adelbert Nash; PGM Sally Nash, PU Dewitt Nash, PA Maranda Near, PA Emeline Strickland, MU William McMillen, MU Alden McMillen, MU Charles McMillen, MA Mary McMillen; G- Norman Allen; 57

Jane Nash: SEE VICTORIA NASH

Perry D. Nash; 15 March 1879; Adelbert Nash, moved to Michigan; Adell, born about 1859, died 1 October 1880, in Poland, her G- was Israel Alden; Charles Nash; - ; he either lived with Dewitt Nash or James Poland; 54

Silas C. Nash; 8 April 1843; Amos Nash, died before April 1850; Christiana McMillen, married Mr. Markham, of Dayton; Emmet, Victoria, Corydon, Eugene, Dewit, and Adelbert Nash; PGM Sally Nash, PU Dewitt Nash, PA Maranda Near, PA Emeline Strickland, MU William McMillen, MU Alden McMillen, MU Charles McMillen, MA Mary McMillen; G- Norman Allen; 57

Victoria Nash; 11 or 12 January 1839; Amos Nash, died before April 1850; Christiana McMillen, married Mr. Markham, of Dayton; Emmet, Silas, Corydon, Eugene, Dewit, and Adelbert Nash; PGM Sally Nash, PU Dewitt Nash, PA Maranda Near, PA Emeline Strickland, MU William McMillen, MU Alden McMillen, MU Charles McMillen, MA Mary McMillen; G- Norman Allen; 57

Beth L. Nelson; 30 April 1892; John Nelson, fought in Civil War; Lana, married Mr. Kelley; Frederick, Morris, Samuel and William Nelson; - ; G- James G. McMahon (died 15 Sept. 1909), received pension money; 57

Clara Nelson; 9 March 1883; Alexander Nelson; - ; - ; HU Elnathan Burlingham; RE 1906, in Jefferson County, TX and

Name; Date of Birth; Father; Mother; Siblings; Other Relatives; Notes; Box Number

her mother died 25 March 1884; 57

Eliza A. Nelson; 22 April 1847; Wilber A. Nelson, died before 16 April 1862; Margaret Oyer, married Chauncey Crumb; Wilber Nelson; MGF David Oyer, PA Aurora Kingman, PU Frank Nelson, MU Peter Oyer; - ; 57

Flora A. Nelson; 6 July 1878; - ; Emily P., of Hinsdale; Robert and Walter Nelson; - ; RE 1903, in Belfast, Allegany County, received money from estate of A. E. Nelson, and other heirs of A. E. Nelson's estate were Kate M. Allen and Mabel Grey; 57

Frederick C. Nelson; 14 June 1883; John Nelson, fought in Civil War; Lana, married Mr. Kelley; Beth, Morris, Samuel and William Nelson; - ; G- James G. McMahon (died 15 Sept. 1909), received pension money; 57

Marion J. Nelson; 29 September 1895; - ; Nellie Wood; Orrel Nelson; MGF Staley N. Wood; G- Nellie Nelson and G-Staley Nelson, money from A. T. Nelson's estate; 54

Morris E. Nelson; 21 July 1885; John Nelson, fought in Civil War; Lana, married Mr. Kelley; Beth, Frederick, Samuel and William Nelson; - ; G- James G. McMahon (died 15 Sept. 1909), received pension money; 57

Orrel N. Nelson; 14 November 1883; - ; Nellie Wood; Marion Nelson; MGF Staley N. Wood; G- Nellie Nelson and G-Staley Nelson, money from A. T. Nelson's estate; 54

Robert C. Nelson; 26 January 1882; - ; Emily P., of Hinsdale; Flora and Walter Nelson; - ; RE 1903, in Warren County, Pennsylvania, received money from estate of A. E. Nelson, and other heirs of A. E. Nelson's estate were Kate M. Allen and Mabel Grey; 57

Walter A. Nelson; - ; - ; Emily P., of Hinsdale; Flora and Robert Nelson; - ; RE 1894, in Bufalo, received money from estate of A. E. Nelson, and other heirs of A. E. Nelson's estate were Kate M. Allen and Mabel Grey; 57

Wilber D. Nelson; 19 December 1849; Wilber A. Nelson, died before 16 April 1862; Margaret Oyer, married Chauncey

Name; Date of Birth; Father; Mother; Siblings; Other Relatives; Notes; Box Number

Crumb; Eliza Nelson; MGF David Oyer, PA Aurora Kingman, PU Frank Nelson, MU Peter Oyer; - ; 57

Amos Nenno; 8 July 1888; - ; - ; Fred and Gertrude Nenno; C- Michael Nenno; money from Lewis Nenno's estate; 54

Charles J. Nenno; about 1877; - ; - ; Edward and M. W. Nenno, of Allegany; - ; - ; 56

Edward W. Nenno; about 1879; - ; - ; Charles and M. W. Nenno, of Allegany; - ; - ; 56

Fred J. Nenno; about 1885; - ; - ; Amos and Gertrude Nenno; C- Michael Nenno; money from Lewis Nenno's estate; 54

Gertrude Nenno; about 1890; - ; - ; Amos and Fred Nenno; C- Michael Nenno; money from Lewis Nenno's estate; 54

Ida Nesbit; 12 August 1875; - ; - ; - ; A- Mrs. William Mitchell; father RE in Kansas; 54

Isabell Nettleton; about 1847; - ; - ; - ; - ; G- Harmon Knickerbocker; 57

Frank Neugart; 24 August 1885; Berthold Neugart, died between 1897 and 1905; Mina; John Neugart and Minnie Shultz; BIL William C. Shultz; - ; 54

John Neugart; 24 June 1887; Berthold Neugart, died between 1897 and 1905; Mina; Frank Neugart and Minnie Shultz; BIL William C. Shultz; - ; 54

Joseph Nevarski; 19 October 1892; - ; - ; Eva Stachowiak; - ; - ; 54

Etta Newcomb; - ; David Newcomb, died 26 March 1893, of Dayton; Mary, married Mr. Ackerman; Freddie Newcomb; - ; received money from estate of John Newcomb; 57

Freddie Newcomb; 30 January 1889; David Newcomb, died 26 March 1893, of Dayton; Mary, married Mr. Ackerman; Etta Newcomb; - ; money from John Newcomb's estate; 57

George A. Newcomb; 30 March 1862; George Newcomb; Mary, married Mr. Ackerman; PGF Thomas Newcomb, PU Edwin Newcomb; received pension money; 56

Adelia Newman; 7 January 1893; - ; - ; Ira , Mary and Anna Newman; MGF Hiram Stimson, MU Charles Stimson, PU

Name; Date of Birth; Father; Mother; Siblings; Other Relatives; Notes; Box Number

Mansel Newman, A- Eunice Newman Ford (of Lyndon); - ; 57

Anna Newman; 24 November 1890/1891; - ; - ; Ira , Mary and Adelia Newman; MGF Hiram Stimson, MU Charles Stimson, PU Mansel Newman, A- Eunice Newman Ford (of Lyndon); - ; 57

Ira Newman; 3 December 1893; - ; - ; Anna , Mary and Adelia Newman; MGF Hiram Stimson, MU Charles Stimson, PU Mansel Newman, A- Eunice Newman Ford (of Lyndon); - ; 57

Mary Newman; 8 October 1899; - ; - ; Anna , Ira and Adelia Newman; MGF Hiram Stimson, MU Charles Stimson, PU Mansel Newman, A- Eunice Newman Ford (of Lyndon); - ; 57

Charles Newton; 30 December 1889; - ; - ; - ; U- Timothy Cunningham; - ; 54

Sophronia S. Newton; 26 November 1883; Milton Newton, died 11 December 1886; - ; - ; PGF Lyman Newton, A- Olive Godding, A- Sarah Jackson, A- Ellen Barnard, A- Martha Newton (wife of Myron), U- Charles Benson, U- Myron Newton; mother died 11 January 1884, G- Charles Lincoln, family Bible and family pictures part of inventoried items; 54

Charles B. Nichols; 14 January 1873; Richmond S. Nichols, of Ischua; - ; Robert and Grace Nichols; - ; received money from estate of Sarah E. Nichols, and life insurance money from Nellie Nichols; 55

Grace B. Nichols; 12 March 1874; Richmond S. Nichols, of Ischua; - ; Robert and Charles Nichols; - ; received money from estate of Sarah E. Nichols, and life insurance money from Nellie Nichols; 55

John G. Nichols; 30 August 1884; Orlando Nichols, of New Albion; - ; Nelson and Marietta Nichols; - ; received money from legacy left by Roxy Gilbey; 55

Marietta "Mattie" A. Nichols; 3 February 1879; Orlando Nichols, of New Albion; - ; Nelson and John Nichols; - ;

Name; Date of Birth; Father; Mother; Siblings; Other Relatives; Notes; Box Number

received money from legacy left by Roxy Gilbey; 55

Nelson S. Nichols; 11 August 1875; Orlando Nichols, of New Albion; - ; Marietta and John Nichols; - ; received money from legacy left by Roxy Gilbey; 55

Ray McKay Nichols; 24 October 1881; Hosea Nichols; - ; - ; - ; received money from estate of Richard McKay; 55

Robert R. Nichols; about 1880; Richmond S. Nichols, of Ischua; - ; Grace and Charles Nichols; - ; received money from estate of Sarah E. Nichols, and life insurance money from Nellie Nichols; 55

Amelia Nies; 15 April 1877; Christian F. Nies, died 29 January 1887, of Salamanca; Paulina; Pauline, Christian and Carl; - ; - ; 55

Carl Nies; 27 July 1882; Christian F. Nies, died 29 January 1887, of Salamanca; Paulina; Pauline, Christian and Amelia; - ; Carl died 20 September 1887 ; 55

Christian Nies; 27 June 1880; Christian F. Nies, died 29 January 1887, of Salamanca; Paulina; Pauline, Carl and Amelia; - ; - ; 55

Mabel M. Nies; 25 September 1900; Charles Nies; - ; Irving Nies; other relatives were Carl, Fred, Charles, and Christina Nies, Emma A. Peters, and Clara Rhodes; - ; 56

Pauline Nies; 20 October 1884; Christian F. Nies, died 29 January 1887, of Salamanca; Paulina; Christian, Carl and Amelia; - ; - ; 55

Clark H. Niles; about 1850; - ; - ; - ; - ; G- Lovina Niles; 57

Ethel M. Niles; 13 February 1905; Stephen Niles; Sarah, died 1916-1917; Howard Niles, HS Harriet Niles; relative was John Niles; money from estate of Charles P. Niles; 54

Herbert A. Niles; about 1906; - ; Annabelle; William Niles (born about 1903) Lucy Milks, and Eva Bartlett (born about 1900); - ; he attended American Trade School (869 Genesee St., Buffalo) to be mechanic; 54

Howard Niles; 13 January 1902; Stephen Niles; Sarah, died 1916-1917; Ethel Niles, HS Harriet Niles; relative was John

Name; Date of Birth; Father; Mother; Siblings; Other Relatives; Notes; Box Number

Niles; received money from estate of Charles P. Niles; 54

Margaret E. Niles; 31 October 1900; Gaylord Niles, of Salamanca; - ; - ; - ; money from estate of John Delp; 56

Charles M. Nix; 3 June 1894; - ; Malvina, of Lyndon; Eda Nix; - ; - ; 54

Eda M. Nix; 4 May 1899; - ; Malvina, of Lyndon; Charles Nix; - ; - ; 54

Eustace Paul Nolan; 20 September 1901; - ; - ; - ; A- Mary Priest, RE at 7171 Irving St., Olean; - ; 54

Clarence E. Noonan; about 1885; Patrick Noonan, of Four Mile; Mary; James, Harry and Frank Noonan; - ; - ; 54

Frank Noonan; about 1891; Patrick Noonan, of Four Mile; Mary; James, Harry and Clarence Noonan; - ; - ; 54

Harry S. Noonan; about 1890; Patrick Noonan, of Four Mile; Mary; James, Frank and Clarence Noonan; - ; - ; 54

James E. Noonan; about 1886; Patrick Noonan, of Four Mile; Mary; Harry, Frank and Clarence Noonan; - ; - ; 54

Anna Estelle North; - ; - ; - ; Edwin North; HU Mr. Lynch; G- Edwin W. Smith (died 26 September 1909), received money from estate of Anna Ingalls, Jennie North boarded the children; 56

Cora V. North; 5 October 1871; - ; - ; - ; - ; went by Cora Reed in May 1886, G- L. Elvira Reed; 57

Edwin S. North; - ; - ; - ; Anna North; - ; G- Edwin W. Smith (died 26 September 1909), received money from estate of Anna Ingalls, Jennie North boarded the children, Edwin was in Gowanda State Homeopathic Hospital at Collins, Erie, NY as incompetent person; 56

Elizabeth "Lizzie" E. Northrup; 23 September 1885; - ; Eva, married Mr. Titus; May and Jessie Northrup; - ; received money on life insurance of Moses Northrup (of Steuben County, NY); 57

Hiram R. Northrup; 22 April 1843; Lane Rounds Jr. died before May 1863; - ; - ; - ; file mentions Aaron Northrup; 57

Jessie M. Northrup; 26 April 1883; - ; Eva, married Mr. Titus;

Name; Date of Birth; Father; Mother; Siblings; Other Relatives; Notes; Box Number

May and Elizabeth Northrup; - ; received money on life insurance of Moses Northrup (of Steuben County, NY); 57

May N. Northrup; 23 April 1881; - ; Eva, married Mr. Titus; Jessie and Elizabeth Northrup; - ; received money on life insurance of Moses Northrup (of Steuben County, NY); 57

Alice Evelyn Norton; 7 July 1893; James Norton, died in Massachusetts about 1902; Nellie, married Clyton Schutts (1904 in Warren); - ; - ; RE 1901-1902, in Cleveland with Henry Donnelly, lived with Lawton's after 1904, AKA Alice Evelyn Lawton, James and Nellie separated 1896 in Buffalo, G- Merton Lawton and G- Maude Lawton; 57

Ivers J. Norton; 22 February 1897; - ; Elizabeth, of 811 W. Henley St., Olean; - ; - ; - ; 54

Agnes G. Norwood; about 1876; Fred Norwood, of Allegany; - ; Emma Norwood; - ; received legacy from Mary Phillips; 54

Emma D. Norwood; about 1881; Fred Norwood, of Allegany; - ; Agnes Norwood; - ; received legacy from Mary Phillips; 54

Araunah Nottingham; 9 May 1866; Jacob Nottingham, born about 1836; Electa, died about September 1886; Starl, Ned and Harry Nottingham; - ; G- Edward J. Liveridge; 54

Claude M. Nottingham; 7 March 1889; Solomon Nottingham died before January 1890; Elnora; Mabel Nottingham; - ; - ; 54

Harry P. Nottingham; 18 March 1884; Jacob Nottingham, born about 1836; Electa, died about September 1886; Starl, Ned and Araunah Nottingham; - ; G- Edward J. Liveridge; 54

Mabel Nottingham; 26 September 1887; Solomon Nottingham died before January 1890; Elnora; Claude Nottingham; - ; - ; 54

Ned Notthingham; 26 April 1878; Jacob Nottingham, born about 1836; Electa, died about September 1886; Starl, Harry and Araunah Nottingham; - ; G- Edward J. Liveridge; 54

Starl Nottingham; 1 November 1874; Jacob Nottingham, born about 1836; Electa, died about September 1886; Ned, Harry and Araunah Nottingham; - ; G- Edward J. Liveridge; 54

Name; Date of Birth; Father; Mother; Siblings; Other Relatives; Notes; Box Number

Edward R. Nourse; 29 March 1888; - ; Idella Robeson; Emma and Louise Nourse; MGF John Robeson; - ; 57

Emma Nourse; 29 September 1880; - ; Idella Robeson; Edward and Louise Nourse; MGF John Robeson; - ; 57

Guy W. Nourse; 23 September 1893; - ; - ; John H. Nourse; - ; received money from estate of Orrin Nourse; 57

Louise Nourse; 14 December 1881; - ; Idella Robeson; Edward and Emma Nourse; MGF John Robeson; - ; 57

Edwin M. Nutting; 8 September 1861; Edwin M. Nutting, died May 1862, of Conewango; - ; Eva and Ida Nutting; U- Martin Van Benson; G- Matilda Nutting; 57

Eva D. Nutting; 26 November 1856; Edwin M. Nutting, died May 1862, of Conewango; - ; Edwin and Ida Nutting; U- Martin Van Benson; G- Matilda Nutting; 57

Ida I. Nutting; 19 February 1855; Edwin M. Nutting, died May 1862, of Conewango; - ; Edwin and Eva Nutting; U- Martin Van Benson; G- Matilda Nutting; 57

Louise J. Nutting; 5 September 1848; - ; Melissa, married Mr. Wood; - ; - ; G- Lucien Nutting; 57

Mandana Nye; 7 March 1847; Lucas Luce, of New Albion; - ; - ; HU Samuel Nye; needed guardian for claim for bounty and pension for husband's death; 57

Name; Date of Birth; Father; Mother; Siblings; Other Relatives; Notes; Box Number

O Surnames

Grace Oakes; 8 October 1896; Jasper Oakes, died 11 May 1916; Alice; Jesse Oakes; HU Matthew Ganey, married 29 July 1916 ; - ; 44

Nellie A. Oakes; 24 April 1864; - ; Mary E.; - ; PGF Nichols Oakes; - ; 21

Gwendolyn Oakley; 10 August 1902; - ; Ada Blanche; Amanda Oakley Scott (died by 12 December 1919); HU Stanley Wasnick; RE 1920, in Chicago, Illinois ; 21

Caroline Oaks; 4 August 1896; - ; Ida, married Mr. Peraino; Ellie and Millie Oaks; HU Mr. Miller; - ; 21

Ellie Oaks; 23 August 1902; - ; Ida, married Mr. Peraino; Caroline and Millie Oaks; HU Mr. Preno; - ; 21

Millie Oaks; 16 May 1898; - ; Ida, married Mr. Peraino; Caroline and Ellie Oaks; HU Mr. Tuoto; - ; 21

Nellie May Oaks: born 3 May 1867; George R. Oaks, married after divorce; - ; - ; U- Seth Barnard; parents divorced and mother lived in Nebraska and remarried; 21

Ambrose O'Brien; 1898; - ; Bridget; James O'Brien; - ; - ; 22

Daisy E. O'Brien; 1 November 1871; Charles A. O'Brien; - ; Ida and Jennie O'Brien; HU Mr. Williams; received part of estate of Garrison Ballard; 22

Ida May O'Brien; 12 October 1866; Charles A. O'Brien; - ; Daisy and Jennie O'Brien; HU Mr. Burger; received part of estate of Garrison Ballard; 22

James O'Brien; about 1900; - ; Bridget; Ambrose O'Brien; - ; - ; 22

James R. O'Brien; 16 November 1880; James O'Brien; - ; - ; PGF John O'Brien (left legacy to James O'Brien), A- Margaret Fawley, U- David Roach, U- William Roach, U- Dennis O'Brien; - ; 22

Jennie O'Brien; 7 December 1875; Charles A. O'Brien; - ; Daisy and Ida O'Brien; - ; received part of estate of Garrison

Name; Date of Birth; Father; Mother; Siblings; Other Relatives; Notes; Box Number

Ballard; 22

John O'Brien; 9 May 1887; James "Simeon" O'Brien; - ; Sarah O'Brien; PGF Anthony O'Brien; RE Dennison, Ohio, John was an heir of Michael O'Brien, G- Zilla O'Brien; 21

Matthew J. O'Brien; 11 February 1866; Patrick O'Brien; - ; - ; MGF Patrick Dollard, died January 1873, of Humphrey; - ; 54

Richard O'Brien; - ; Stephen J. O'Brien; - ; - ; PGF John E. O'Brien; RE 1941, 78 Monticello Place, Buffalo, NY; 22

Sarah O'Brien; 21 August 1885; James "Simeon" O'Brien; - ; John O'Brien; PGF Anthony O'Brien; RE Dennison, Ohio, Sarah was an heir of Michael O'Brien, G- Zilla O'Brien; 21

Albert O'Dell; - ; Orrin O'Dell, died before March 1868; Amelia; Hellen Hall and Mary, Emma and Daniel O'Dell; - ; G- Silvertus McIntosh; 22

Emma O'Dell; 22 December 1854; Orrin O'Dell, died before March 1868; Amelia; Hellen Hall and Mary, Albert and Daniel O'Dell; HU Mr. Train ; G- Silvertus McIntosh; 22

Mary O'Dell; 14 April 1859; Orrin O'Dell, died before March 1868; Amelia; Hellen Hall and Emma, Albert and Daniel O'Dell; - ; G- Silvertus McIntosh; 22

Stephen Joseph O'Donnell; 12 May 1873; Cornelius O'Donnell, died September 1878, of St. Petersburgh, Clarion, Pennsylvania; Elizabeth, of Ellicottville. 1894, moved to Buffalo; William O'Donnell; other relatives were Elizabeth, Mary, and Archibald Vallelly; - ; 56

William John O'Donnell; November 1875; Cornelius O'Donnell, died September 1878, of St. Petersburgh, Clarion, Pennsylvania; Elizabeth, of Ellicottville. 1894, moved to Buffalo; Stephen O'Donnell; other relatives were Elizabeth, Mary, and Archibald Vallelly; - ; 56

Mildred A. Ohmer; about 1889; Mr. Harrington, died before January 1910; Georgia E.; Josephine, Myrtie, Carrie, and LaMott Harrington; - ; - ; 71

Clarence L. Oldham; 16 March 1890; Harvey Oldham; - ; - ; - ;

Name; Date of Birth; Father; Mother; Siblings; Other Relatives; Notes; Box Number

received money from estate of William Shicks; 22

Frances Olds; 10 December 1905; John Olds; Laura; Harriett Olds; - ; RE 3251 Eastwood Ave., Chicago, Illinois and received money from estate of F. C. Olds; 22

Harriett M. Olds; 27 September 1908; John Olds; Laura; Frances Olds; - ; RE 3251 Eastwood Ave., Chicago, Illinois and received money from estate of F. C. Olds; 22

Harvey O'Leary; 29 March 1882; - ; Mary; - ; - ; - ; 22

Bryan O'Mara; about 1881; Michael O'Mara, of Red Rock, McKean, Pennsylvania; - ; Michael, Ellen, John, Julia, Mary, and Catherine O'Mara; - ; mother owned property in Humphrey; 56

Catherine O'Mara; about 1888; Michael O'Mara, of Red Rock, McKean, Pennsylvania; - ; Michael, Bryan, Ellen, John, Julia, and Mary O'Mara; - ; mother owned property in Humphrey; 56

Ellen O'Mara; about 1873; Michael O'Mara, of Red Rock, McKean, Pennsylvania; - ; Michael, Bryan, Catherine, John, Julia, and Mary O'Mara; - ; mother owned property in Humphrey; 56

John O'Mara; about 1875; Michael O'Mara, of Red Rock, McKean, Pennsylvania; - ; Michael, Bryan, Catherine, Ellen, Julia, and Mary O'Mara; - ; mother owned property in Humphrey; 56

Julia O'Mara; about 1871; Michael O'Mara, of Red Rock, McKean, Pennsylvania; - ; Michael, Bryan, Catherine, Ellen, John, and Mary O'Mara; - ; mother owned property in Humphrey; 56

Mary O'Mara; about 1884; Michael O'Mara, of Red Rock, McKean, Pennsylvania; - ; Michael, Bryan, Catherine, Ellen, John, and Julia O'Mara; - ; mother owned property in Humphrey; 56

Michael O'Mara Jr.; about 1877; Michael O'Mara, of Red Rock, McKean, Pennsylvania; - ; Mary, Bryan, Catherine, Ellen, John, and Julia O'Mara; - ; mother owned property in

Name; Date of Birth; Father; Mother; Siblings; Other Relatives; Notes; Box Number

Humphrey; 56

Francis J. O'Meara; 25 April 1908; Patrick O'Meara; - ; Harry and Norman O'Meara; - ; - ; 55

Harry J. O'Meara; 15 November 1895; Patrick O'Meara; - ; Francis and Norman O'Meara; - ; - ; 55

Norman M. O'Meara; 13 August 1900; Patrick O'Meara; - ; Francis and Harry O'Meara; - ; - ; 55

Ida P. Oosterhoudt; about 1854; - ; - ; - ; - ; G- Emeline Oosterhoudt, in same envelope as William Oosterhoudt; 22

Mary Alice Oosterhoudt; 20 February 1881; Samuel F. Oosterhoudt; Louisa, of Olean; Samuel Oosterhoudt; PA Mary A. Allen; - ; 56

Samuel Arthur Oosterhoudt; 15 July 1876; Samuel F. Oosterhoudt; Louisa, of Olean; Mary Oosterhoudt; PA Mary A. Allen; AKA Arthur Samuel Oosterhoudt ; 56

William A. Oosterhoudt; about 1856; - ; - ; - ; - ; G- Emeline Oosterhoudt, in same envelope as Ida Oosterhoudt; 22

John O'Rourke; - ; Edward O'Rourke; - ; - ; - ; - ; 22

Leo Ortman; 10 May 1889; Step-father was John Volk; - ; - ;U- John Gold; RE 1911, in Galeton, Potter, Pennsylvania and mother left estate in Kalispell, Montana, where she and her husband, Mr. Volk, resided; 22

Adeline Osterstuck; 1 May 1858; William Osterstuck, died June 1866, while in the Civil War; Emeline Kimball, married Mr. Graham by August 1866; Angeline, Eveline, Mary and Warner Osterstuck; PGM Betsey Rumrill, PU George Osterstuck, PU John Osterstuck, PU Emery Osterstuck, PU Charles Osterstuck, PA Caroline Kimball, MG Eli and Sally Kimball, MU Ezra Kimball, MA Lorena or Lovina Stimpson; received pension; 22

Angeline Osterstuck; 4 November 1854; William Osterstuck, died June 1866, while in the Civil War; Emeline Kimball, married Mr. Graham by August 1866; Adeline, Eveline, Mary and Warner Osterstuck; PGM Betsey Rumrill, PU George Osterstuck, PU John Osterstuck, PU Emery

Name; Date of Birth; Father; Mother; Siblings; Other Relatives; Notes; Box Number

Osterstuck, PU Charles Osterstuck, PA Caroline Kimball, MG Eli and Sally Kimball, MU Ezra Kimball, MA Lorena or Lovina Stimpson; received pension; 22

Charles Linford Osterstuck; 20 December 1841; John Osterstuck; - ; - ; FL Lewis Rumrill; - ; 22

Eveline Osterstuck; 20 January 1860; William Osterstuck, died June 1866, while in the Civil War; Emeline Kimball, married Mr. Graham by August 1866; Adeline, Angeline, Mary and Warner Osterstuck; PGM Betsey Rumrill, PU George Osterstuck, PU John Osterstuck, PU Emery Osterstuck, PU Charles Osterstuck, PA Caroline Kimball, MG Eli and Sally Kimball, MU Ezra Kimball, MA Lorena or Lovina Stimpson; received pension; 22

Mary Osterstuck; 1 August 1861; William Osterstuck, died June 1866, while in the Civil War; Emeline Kimball, married Mr. Graham by August 1866; Adeline, Angeline, Eveline and Warner Osterstuck; PGM Betsey Rumrill, PU George Osterstuck, PU John Osterstuck, PU Emery Osterstuck, PU Charles Osterstuck, PA Caroline Kimball, MG Eli and Sally Kimball, MU Ezra Kimball, MA Lorena or Lovina Stimpson; received pension; 22

Warner Osterstuck; 12 September 1856; William Osterstuck, died June 1866, while in the Civil War; Emeline Kimball, married Mr. Graham by August 1866; Adeline, Angeline, Eveline and Mary Osterstuck; PGM Betsey Rumrill, PU George Osterstuck, PU John Osterstuck, PU Emery Osterstuck, PU Charles Osterstuck, PA Caroline Kimball, MG Eli and Sally Kimball, MU Ezra Kimball, MA Lorena or Lovina Stimpson; received pension; 22

Ette Osthaus; 3 April 1896; Carl Osthaus, of Conewango; - ; Johanna and Walter Osthaus; HU Andrew Westin; G- Jerome Crowley; 55

Johanna Osthaus; 22 January 1890; Carl Osthaus, of Conewango; - ; Ette and Walter Osthaus; HU Mr Westin; G- Jerome Crowley; 55

Name; Date of Birth; Father; Mother; Siblings; Other Relatives; Notes; Box Number

Walter Osthaus: about 1899; Carl Osthaus, of Conewango; - ; Johanna and Ette Osthaus; - ; Walter died 17 January 1917 at Fort Bliss, Texas, was a soldier and is buried in Conewango, G- Jerome Crowley; 55

James Ostrander; 28 May 1859; Andrew Ostrander, deserted family in Spring of 1864; went by Lany West; John, Nellie and Mary Ostrander; - ; received money from estate of John Ostrander and Andrew and Lany were never married according to file; 46

John Ostrander; 17 May 1857; Andrew Ostrander, deserted family in Spring of 1864; went by Lany West; James, Nellie and Mary Ostrander; - ; received money from estate of John Ostrander and Andrew and Lany were never married according to file; 46

Mary Ostrander; 12 April 1863; Andrew Ostrander, deserted family in Spring of 1864; went by Lany West; James, Nellie and John Ostrander; - ; received money from estate of John Ostrander and Andrew and Lany were never married according to file; 46

Nellie Ostrander; 27 March 1861; Andrew Ostrander, deserted family in Spring of 1864; went by Lany West; James, Mary and John Ostrander; HU Mr. Oyer ; received money from estate of John Ostrander and Andrew and Lany were never married according to file; 46

Anna D. Ostricker; 3 May 1900; Carl Stoeckel; Phoebe; - ; - ; Anna's HU died before 28 October 1919; 22

Mabel L. Otis; 20 April 1883; Sidney E. Morris; - ; - ; - ; - ; 22

Francis E. Oviatt; about 1877; Miles Oviatt, died November 1880, of Olean; Lucetta; - ; - ; - ; 55

Emma C. Owen; about 1866; Lemuel Owen died September 1871; Josephine, of Randolph; Flora, Jessie and Mabel Owen; - ; - ; 56

Flora J. Owen; about 1862; Lemuel Owen died September 1871; Josephine, of Randolph; Emma, Jessie and Mabel Owen; - ; - ; 56

Name; Date of Birth; Father; Mother; Siblings; Other Relatives; Notes; Box Number

Jessie B. Owen; about 1864; Lemuel Owen died September 1871; Josephine, of Randolph; Emma, Flora and Mabel Owen; - ; - ; 56

Mabel L. Owen; about 1865; Lemuel Owen died September 1871; Josephine, of Randolph; Emma, Flora and Jessie Owen; - ; - ; 56

Esther A. Owens; 5 October 1896; - ; Martha, of Freedom; Nina Owens; - ; - ; 56

Nina Owens; 11 October 1888; - ; Martha, of Freedom; Esther Owens; HU Mr. Ferguson, married by 1911; - ; 56

George W. Oyer; - ; Levi Oyer; Betsey Oyer, married John Vedder; John Oyer; MGF John P. Oyer, PGF George Oyer; - ; 22

John L. Oyer; 22 March 1848; Levi Oyer; Betsey Oyer, married John Vedder; George Oyer; MGF John P. Oyer, PGF George Oyer; - ; 22

Loretta L. Oyer; 28 April 1842; Horace Butler; Alzina; Lydia, Arthur, Jasper, Horace, and Olivia Butler; - ; - ; 2

Name; Date of Birth; Father; Mother; Siblings; Other Relatives; Notes; Box Number

P Surnames

Barbara Padlo; 15 June 1903; Joseph Padlo, of Olean; - ; - ; - ; - ; 63

Edward J. Page; 22 August 1881; - ; - ; - ; - ; G- Irving E. Worden, money from estate of John Page; 22

James R. Page; 20 July 1907; Joseph L. Page, died 2 December 1909, of Olean; Harriet C. Johnson, died 21 March 1911, of Olean; Jane Page; MGF Elisha Johnson (died 21 August 1915), U- Wilson R. Page (died 9 September 1922, of Olean), U- M. Tracy Page, PA Emma Smith, PA Fannie Tothill, C- Wilson K. Page; RE 220 N. 4th St., Olean; 64

Jane E. Page; 10 January 1906; Joseph L. Page, died 2 December 1909, of Olean; Harriet C. Johnson, died 21 March 1911, of Olean; James Page; MGF Elisha Johnson (died 21 August 1915), U- Wilson R. Page (died 9 September 1922, of Olean), U- M. Tracy Page, PA Emma Smith, PA Fannie Tothill, C- Wilson K. Page; attended school in Palo Alto, California; 64

Anna M. Palm; 10 February 1865; Andrew Palm, died May 1884; - ; Charles and James Palm; - ; G- Joseph H. Schaak, not related; 22

James Albert Palm; about 1868; Andrew Palm, died May 1884, of Persia; - ; Charles and Anna Palm; - ; G- John Kammerer; 56

Catherine Parbs; 1906; John Parbs, died about 1907; Mary, of Salamanca; - ; - ; - ; 63

Edna A. Parish; 17 September 1879; David L. Parish, died before November 1896; Mary R.; Smith Parish; - ; - ; 22

Arthur Parker; about 1876; - ; - ; Alice Dean; - ; G- Elizabeth Edwards; 56

Beulah Parker; 29 March 1885; John Parker; - ; Ernest, Ward and Wiley Parker; - ; - ; 46

Clifford Parker; 18 February 1898; - ; - ; - ; - ; G- James Dornan,

Name; Date of Birth; Father; Mother; Siblings; Other Relatives; Notes; Box Number

no relation; 56

Cora L. Parker; 25 September 1861; Ezra A. Parker, died 1863, of Erie County, Pennsylvania; Amy; S. Arvilla and Mira Parker; - ; G- John R. Townsend; 75

Emma F. Parker; 6 April 1858; James W. Parker, died before January 1864; Roxanna Skinner, married Samuel Hall; Flora and Urson Parker; PGM Eunice Parker, MGF Nathan Skinner (of Illinois), PU David Parker, MA Mrs. Daniel Perkins; received pension money; 75

Ernest Parker; 23 September 1879; John Parker; - ; Beulah, Ward and Wiley Parker; - ; - ; 46

Eva M. Parker; about 1856; Chauncey Parker, died 12 November 1866; Sarah C. Weir, died 23 November 1868; Mary and Willie Parker; HU Mr. Swetland, MGF John Weir, U- Asa Parker, C- Ellicott Parker, C- Emma Parker, C- Alice Parker, C- Albert Parker; G- Sidney S. Marsh (merchant and banker); 22

Flora A. Parker; 18 April 1860; James W. Parker, died before January 1864; Roxanna Skinner, married Samuel Hall; Emma and Urson Parker; PGM Eunice Parker, MGF Nathan Skinner (of Illinois) , PU David Parker, MA Mrs. Daniel Perkins; received pension money; 75

Leon Parker; 21 August 1896; Edwin Parker, of Olean; - ; - ; - ; - ; 56

Mabel J. Parker; 29 September 1863; - ; Permelia, of Perrysburg; - ; - ; father died before June 1862; 75

Mary Belle Parker; about 1860; Chauncey Parker, died 12 November 1866; Sarah C. Weir, died 23 November 1868; Eva and Willie Parker; MGF John Weir, U- Asa Parker, C- Ellicott Parker, C- Emma Parker, C- Alice Parker, C- Albert Parker; G- Sidney S. Marsh (merchant and banker); 22

Mira Parker; 8 May 1858; Ezra A. Parker, died 1863, of Erie County, Pennsylvania; Amy; S. Arvilla and Cora Parker; - ; G- John R. Townsend; 75

S. Arvilla Parker; 24 February 1860; Ezra A. Parker, died 1863,

Name; Date of Birth; Father; Mother; Siblings; Other Relatives; Notes; Box Number

of Erie County, Pennsylvania; Amy; Mira and Cora Parker; - ; G- John R. Townsend; 75

Urson Parker; 28 December 1851; James W. Parker, died before January 1864; Roxanna Skinner, married Samuel Hall; Emma and Flora Parker; PGM Eunice Parker, MGF Nathan Skinner (of Illinois), PU David Parker, MA Mrs. Daniel Perkins; received pension money; 75

Ward Parker; 7 October 1880; John Parker; - ; Beulah, Ernest and Wiley Parker; - ; - ; 46

Washington Parker; 17 February 1844; Heman Parker, died before May 1860; - ; William Parker; - ; G- William P. Crawford; 75

Wiley Parker; 23 April 1888; John Parker; - ; Beulah, Ernest and Ward Parker; - ; - ; 46

William Bradley Parker; 28 December 1841; Heman Parker, died before May 1860; - ; Washington Parker; - ; G- William P. Crawford; 75

Willie C. Parker; about 1857; Chauncey Parker, died 12 November 1866; Sarah C. Weir, died 23 November 1868; Eva and Mary Parker; MGF John Weir, U- Asa Parker, C- Ellicott Parker, C- Emma Parker, C- Alice Parker, C- Albert Parker; G- Sidney S. Marsh (merchant and banker); 22

Benjamin F. Parmeter; 5 March 1823; Osborn Parmeter, died before August 1841, of Moriah, NY; Lydia, married Mr. White; Gratia and Mary Parmeter; - ; G- Phineas White; 76

Gratia A. Parmeter; 2 April 1827; Osborn Parmeter, died before August 1841, of Moriah, NY; Lydia, married Mr. White; Benjamin and Mary Parmeter; - ; G- Phineas White; 76

Mary S. Parmeter; 31 October 1838; Osborn Parmeter, died before August 1841, of Moriah, NY; Lydia, married Mr. White; Benjamin and Gratia Parmeter; - ; G- Phineas White; 76

Clark Parrish; 20 February 1853; Marvin Parrish, died October 1864; Lucretia Lobdell, married Albert Burdick by May 1868; Leonard, John, and Orisy Parrish; PG Shubil and

Name; Date of Birth; Father; Mother; Siblings; Other Relatives; Notes; Box Number

Cynthia Parrish, MGF Peter Lobdell; received pension money; 22

Leonard B. Parrish; 17 December 1858; Marvin Parrish, died October 1864; Lucretia Lobdell, married Albert Burdick by May 1868; Clark, John, and Orisy Parrish; PG Shubil and Cynthia Parrish, MGF Peter Lobdell; received pension money; 22

Orisy Ann Parrish; 27 February 1861; Marvin Parrish, died October 1864; Lucretia Lobdell, married Albert Burdick by May 1868; Clark, John, and Leonard Parrish; PG Shubil and Cynthia Parrish, MGF Peter Lobdell; received pension money; 22

Rosetta L. Parrish; about 1857; - ; - ; - ; - ; G- Eliphalet Law; 22

Doris F. Raiber Parsons; 13 September 1907; - ; - ; - ; HU Howard C. Parsons, of 15 Washington St., Salamanca; - ; 63

Henry A. Parsons; 16 October 1835; - ; - ; - ; - ; G- Vine Yeomans; 75

Byron C. Patch; 6 August 1869; Abram Patch, died before February 1886; - ; HS Harriet Allen, HS Olive Patch; A- by marriage Judith Patch, U- John Robbins, U- Charles Robbins, U- Horace Robbins, C- Alson Patch; G- Amos Grantier, no relationship; 22

George Patch; - ; - ; - ; - ; MGF George Kelley, of Otto; father died before May 1864 (of Collins, Erie, NY), G- Edmond Palmer; George lived with Edmond Palmer; 75

H. Isabel Paton; 23 October 1875; - ; Mary L.; H. Janet Paton; - ; - ; 22

H. Janet Paton; 16 December 1878; - ; Mary L.; H. Isabel Paton; - ; - ; 22

Mildred L. Paton; about 1889; - ; Mary L.; Wilma Paton; - ; others mentioned in guardianship record were H. Jeannette Joy, Belle, Nettie and William Paton; 22

Wilma M. Paton; about 1891; - ; Mary L.; Mildred Paton; - ; others mentioned in guardianship record were H. Jeannette Joy, Belle, Nettie and William Paton; 22

Name; Date of Birth; Father; Mother; Siblings; Other Relatives; Notes; Box Number

Gordon Patterson; about 1911; James Patterson; Sophia; - ; - ; legacy left from Maggie Patterson; 63

Ida Patterson; - ; - ; Annie, of 599 Wildwood Ave, Salamanca; Grant, Walter, Genevieve, Violet and Annie Patterson; HU Mr. Brainard; RE 1928, in Belfast, Allegany, NY; 63

Lucy Jane Patterson; 11 March 1860; Nathaniel Patterson; - ; - ; HU Mr. Sessions, PGF Nathaniel Patterson Sr.; received pension money; 75

Josephine Pattituce; 5 November 1906; - ; - ; Vincent, Frank, Louis, Philomena, and Joseph Padlo, of Olean; - ; mother died December 1925 in Allegany; 63

Alice Pattyson; 13 August 1861; James H. Pattyson, died in Andersonville Prison; Mary C., married Mr. Warren; - ; U- Darius Pattyson; MA Dolly B. Herrick (wife of George), PU Russell Hubbard; G- John Warren; 75

Lyle Peabody; 2 September 1909; Charles Peabody, RE 64 Euclid Ave, Bradford, McKean, Pennsylvania; Minnie, died 15 August 1929, due to injuries from car accident, of Port Allegany, McKean, Pennsylvania; Wilma, Clyde and Raymond Peabody; - ; RE with Lillian Osborn; 63

Mary Virginia Pearce; 5 July 1909; Rounsville W. Pearce, died 5 or 6 December 1911, of Olean; Mary Virginia Taylorson, died 16 July 1909, of Olean; - ; PGM Mary Pearce (of Coudersport, Potter, Pennsylvania), MG William Arthur Taylorson and Margaret Taylorson (RE 523 N. 4th St., Olean), PU Benjamin I. Pearce (of William, Arizona), PA Nella Brown, PA Marjorie T. Pearce; William Taylorson was a conductor for the Penn RR County; 63

Arthur E. Pease; 20 April 1876; - ; Hattie Green, married Samuel Wright, she died before December 1886; Cora and Frank Pease; PGM Elsie Pease, MU Samuel Green, MU Theron Green, MU Frederick Green, MU Ora Green, PU Chauncey Pease, PU Samuel Pease, A- Martha Pease, A- Amanda Smith, A- Sarah Roberts, A- Mary Anne Hammond, GU Eben Sibley, GU Judson Sibley, GU Sherman Sibley, GA

Name; Date of Birth; Father; Mother; Siblings; Other Relatives; Notes; Box Number

Amanda Allen, GA Charlotte Boyle (W- of George S. Boyle); - ; 22

Cora M. Pease; 21 June 1875; - ; Hattie Green, married Samuel Wright, she died before December 1886; Arthur and Frank Pease; PGM Elsie Pease, MU Samuel Green, MU Theron Green, MU Frederick Green, MU Ora Green, PU Chauncey Pease, PU Samuel Pease, A- Martha Pease, A- Amanda Smith, A- Sarah Roberts, A- Mary Anne Hammond, GU Eben Sibley, GU Judson Sibley, GU Sherman Sibley, GA Amanda Allen, GA Charlotte Boyle (W- of George S. Boyle); - ; 22

Frank J. Pease; 19 March 1873; - ; Hattie Green, married Samuel Wright, she died before December 1886; Arthur and Cora Pease; PGM Elsie Pease, MU Samuel Green, MU Theron Green, MU Frederick Green, MU Ora Green, PU Chauncey Pease, PU Samuel Pease, A- Martha Pease, A- Amanda Smith, A- Sarah Roberts, A- Mary Anne Hammond, GU Eben Sibley, GU Judson Sibley, GU Sherman Sibley, GA Amanda Allen, GA Charlotte Boyle (W- of George S. Boyle); - ; 22

Eliza Peck; - ; Cyrus Peck, of Lee County, Iowa; - ; - ; - ; - ; 77

Dawson Peckham; 1 September 1900; Edwin Peckham, of Yorkshire; - ; - ; - ; - ; 63

Harold Peet; 10 July 1894; - ; - ; - ; PGF Abram A. Peet, Sarah Davidson; - ; 56

Thomas R. Peet; 6 March 1850; Thomas Peet, died before April 1864; Mary Williams, of Freedom, married Mr. Morgan; - ; PGF John Peet, MGF Robert Williams, PU Evan Peet, PU William Peet, PU David Peet, MU John Williams; - ; 75

Caleb M. Pelton; 30 May 1823; Tober Pelton, died before May 1840; - ; - ; - ; G- Solomon Prentiss; 77

Marjorie Pepperdine; 24 November 1892; - ; Chloe R.; - ; - ; - ; 22

Frederick Percival; 29 March 1880; - ; Nettie, married Mr. Benson, of Carrollton; James Percival; - ; received pension

Name; Date of Birth; Father; Mother; Siblings; Other Relatives; Notes; Box Number

money; 56

James G. Percival; 15 May 1882; - ; Nettie, married Mr. Benson, of Carrollton; Frederick Percival; - ; received pension money; 56

Francis Perkins; 17 August 1904; George Perkins, died 26 March 1908; Mabel, married Mr. Elmore; Harry Perkins; - ; - ; 23

Harry Perkins; 19 July 1903; George Perkins, died 26 March 1908; Mabel, married Mr. Elmore; Francis Perkins; - ; - ; 23

Lawrence Perkins; May 1908; Riley Perkins; Carrie; - ; - ; - ; 63

Mabel Perkins; 1 May 1886; - ; - ; - ; first HU George Perkins, killed in accident in Pennsylvania on 26 March 1908 (employed by the B. R. and P Railroad County), second HU Mr. Elmore, children were Harry and Francis Perkins; - ; 23

Mabel Grace Perrigo; 13 January 1905; - ; - ; - ; HU Mr. Allen; G- Flora Perrigo; 63

Edward M. Perrin; 10 October 1858; Hosea Perrin, died April 1865, of Erie, Erie, Pennsylvania; Eliza J., of Olean, married Mr. Scott; Mary and Hosea Perrin; - ; - ; 75

Hosea A. Perrin; 23 November 1862; Hosea Perrin, died April 1865, of Erie, Erie, Pennsylvania; Eliza J., of Olean, married Mr. Scott; Mary and Edward Perrin; - ; Hosea Jr. died 13 October 1867 ; 75

Mary A. Perrin; 25 August 1860; Hosea Perrin, died April 1865, of Erie, Erie, Pennsylvania; Eliza J., of Olean, married Mr. Scott; Edward and Hosea Perrin; - ; - ; 75

Charles "Charlie" S. Persons; 17 July 1858; Samuel Persons, died June 1870, of Yorkshire; Mary; Wilber Persons; - ; - ; 75

Wilber F. Persons; 24 November 1854; Samuel Persons, died June 1870, of Yorkshire; Mary; Charles Persons; - ; - ; 75

Aloysius Peter; 7 April 1879; Step-father was Benedict Zimmerman; - ; Catherine Peter; - ; - ; 56

Catherine Peter; 22 March 1883; Step-father was Benedict Zimmerman; - ; Aloysius Peter; - ; - ; 56

Clara Peters; 31 December 1911; Arthur H. Peters, of

Name; Date of Birth; Father; Mother; Siblings; Other Relatives; Notes; Box Number

Cattaraugus; - ; Frank Peters; - ; - ; 63

Frank Peters; 3 October 1909; Arthur H. Peters, of Cattaraugus; - ; Clara Peters; - ; - ; 63

Adda "Addie" J. Peterson; about 1865; Mr. Sanders; - ; - ; HU John Peterson; G- John H. Groves and G- George Keiser; 75

Harriet "Annette" Peterson; 17 May 1886; John Larson; Jennie; - ; - ; Harriet's HU died before March 1903; 22

Helena Peterson; 3 August 1902; George G. Peterson, died 1909; - ; - ; HU Mr. Bateman, U- Carl P. Peterson; - ; 57

Timothy H. Pettingell; 13 September 1864; - ; Mary Catharine, married Mr. Dockstader by October 1881; - ; - ; - ; 22

Joseph Pettit; 22 January 1840; Henry Pettit, died before January 1859; - ; - ; - ; G- Perry Pendleton; 75

Cedrick M. Petty; 20 June 1893; - ; Marcia; - ; - ; G- Rufus Petty; 22

Celia A. Pettys; 11 October 1896; Merritt A. Pettys, died 8 September 1906, of Olean, death due to negligence of Penn RR Company; Carrie, of Franklinville, married Mr. Thompson; Levi and Irma Pettys; A- Anna Smith, of Hinsdale; Merritt was married to someone else before marrying Carrie; 63

Irma M. Pettys; 13 November 1900; Merritt A. Pettys, died 8 September 1906, of Olean, death due to negligence of Penn RR Company; Carrie, of Franklinville, married Mr. Thompson; Levi and Celia Pettys; A- Anna Smith, of Hinsdale; Merritt was married to someone else before marrying Carrie; 63

Levi M. Pettys; 20 August 1894; Merritt A. Pettys, died 8 September 1906, of Olean, death due to negligence of Penn RR Company; Carrie, of Franklinville, married Mr. Thompson; Irma and Celia Pettys; A- Anna Smith, of Hinsdale; Merritt was married to someone else before marrying Carrie; 63

Charles H. Phelps; 7 December 1856; Cyrus Phelps, died before May 1874 in Cattaraugus County; Charlotte; Lucy Phelps; - ;

Name; Date of Birth; Father; Mother; Siblings; Other Relatives; Notes; Box Number

guardianship papers signed in Missouri; 23

Helen M. Phelps; - ; Benjamin C. Beach; Sarah, died before April 1917, of Elton; Blanch Anderson and Lewis Beach; HU McKinley Phelps; - ; 63

Lucy Phelps; 10 September 1859; Cyrus Phelps, died before May 1874 in Cattaraugus County; Charlotte; Charles Phelps; - ; guardianship papers signed in Missouri; 23

Daniel A. Phillips; 9 November 1856; Sylvenus Phillips, died August 1864, Company D, 179th Regiment, NY; Susan, married Mr. Payne, she died by 1886; Milo, John and William Phillips; - ; - ; 23

George E. Phillips; 8 May 1874; - ; Clara; - ; PGM Sarah B. Phillips; - ; 56

George W. Phillips; 21 November 1887; - ; Minnie, of Salamanca; - ; - ; - ; 56

John G. Phillips; 6 March 1859; Sylvenus Phillips, died August 1864, Company D, 179th Regiment, NY; Susan, married Mr. Payne, she died by 1886; Milo, Daniel and William Phillips; - ; - ; 23

Milo Phillips; 10 January 1861; Sylvenus Phillips, died August 1864, Company D, 179th Regiment, NY; Susan, married Mr. Payne, she died by 1886; John, Daniel and William Phillips; - ; - ; 23

Myrtle M. Phillips; about 1879; Jared Phillips; - ; - ; - ; Mary Phillips left legacy; 56

William H. Phillips; 14 May 1851; Sylvenus Phillips, died August 1864, Company D, 179th Regiment, NY; Susan, married Mr. Payne, she died by 1886; John, Daniel and Milo Phillips; - ; - ; 23

Clarence Phiney; - ; - ; - ; - ; - ; - ; 22

Alice Pierce; June 1856; - ; - ; - ; - ; G- Jane Snow, in same envelope with Lucinda Seneca and Eli Jimerson; 26

Caleb D. Pierce; - ; John Pierce, died June 1866, of Ischua; Mary; Patience, Hettie, Aldra (of Ischua), and Count Polasky Pierce; U- L. B. Pierce; G- George L. Winters; 75

Name; Date of Birth; Father; Mother; Siblings; Other Relatives; Notes; Box Number

Charles Pierce; 5 November 1847; - ; Sarah J., died before February 1866, married Mr. Brasted; - ; - ; G- John L. Perkins; 75

Elsie A. Pierce; 27 November 1861; - ; Clarissa; - ; HU Mr. Fuller; - ; 23

Fernando C. Pierce; 18 December 1878; Fernando C. Pierce, died April 1878; Mary J. Wright; - ; MGF George Wright (in Columbus, Ohio), U- Silas L. Wright, MA Lydia L. Hoover, MA Augusta Hoover, MA Sarah Wright; - ; 23

Hettie S. Pierce; - ; John Pierce, died June 1866, of Ischua; Mary; Patience, Caleb, Aldra (of Ischua), and Count Polasky Pierce; U- L. B. Pierce; G- George L. Winters; 75

James Frank Pierce: born 24 February 1900; Joseph Frank Pierce, died before August 1904; Emogene Lola Barton, died 1908; Richard Pierce; MGM Mary E. Barton (died about 1922), PGF James Pierce (of Malden, Massachusetts), A- Lottie Curtis; G- B. Frank Thomas, no relationship, received money from estate of James Pierce; 57

Minnie H. Pierce; about 1863; Nehemiah Pierce, died March 1873, of Springfield, Sangamon, Illinois; step-mother was Marcia, of Olean; - ; - ; - ; 75

Patience Pierce; - ; John Pierce, died June 1866, of Ischua; Mary; Caleb, Hettie, Aldra (of Ischua), and Count Polasky Pierce; U- L. B. Pierce; G- George L. Winters; 75

Paul L. Pierce; 26 December 1905; - ; Dolly; - ; - ; father deserted family and Paul's RE 1926, in Buffalo ; 63

Richard Fenn Pierce; 31 January 1904; Joseph Frank Pierce, died before August 1904; Emogene Lola Barton, died 1908; James Pierce; MGM Mary E. Barton (died about 1922), PGF James Pierce (of Malden, Massachusetts), A- Lottie Curtis; G- B. Frank Thomas; 57

Charles Pifer; 19 September 1860; Peter Pifer, died in service of war; Lucinda Bellows, married Levi Reynolds; Edward and Mary Etta Pifer; PGM Sophia Pifer, MGF Philip Bellows, PA Catharine Morris, PA Betsey Ann Lippart; - ; 23

Name; Date of Birth; Father; Mother; Siblings; Other Relatives; Notes; Box Number

Edward A. Pifer; 8 January 1855; Peter Pifer, died in service of war; Lucinda Bellows, married Levi Reynolds; Charles and Mary Etta Pifer; PGM Sophia Pifer, MGF Philip Bellows, PA Catharine Morris, PA Betsey Ann Lippart; - ; 23

Mary Etta Pifer; about 1852; Peter Pifer, died in service of war; Lucinda Bellows, married Levi Reynolds; Charles and Edward Pifer; PGM Sophia Pifer, MGF Philip Bellows, PA Catharine Morris, PA Betsey Ann Lippart; - ; 23

Alice L. Pitcher; 1 October 1848; - ; Laura C., of Randolph, married Mr. McCapes; Iona Pitcher; - ; G- Marcus Johnson, received pension money from brother's death; 75

Iona V. Pitcher; 5 July 1847; - ; Laura C., of Randolph, married Mr. McCapes; Alice Pitcher; - ; G- Marcus Johnson, received pension money from brother's death; 75

Fred Pixley; 18 May 1877; Orrin Pixley; - ; - ; - ; - ; 23

George H. Placher; 18 March 1887; James H. Placher, died before 10 October 1902 at San Isidrio, Philippines; - ; - ; PGM Mary Placher, of Olean; RE 1908, in Spring Valley, Fillmore, Minnesota and George's mother died May 1887 in Kearny County, Kansas ; 73

Mildred B. Plank; 17 November 1876; - ; - ; - ; - ; RE 1897 Hornellsville, Steuben, NY; 23

M. Florilla Plumb; 1 August 1833; - ; - ; - ; - ; G- Collen Lowe; 75

Ina J. Plummer; 10 March 1890; - ; - ; Lawrence, James and Susie Plummer; HU Mr. Herrick, U- Allen Williams (of Ischua), U- Nathan Williams; RE Ashland, Schuylkill, Pennsylvania and 1911, in Hinsdale, received money from estate of Simon R. Williams; 73

James W. Plummer; 1 May 1888; - ; - ; Lawrence, Ina and Susie Plummer; U- Allen Williams (of Ischua), U- Nathan Williams; RE Bradford, McKean, Pennsylvania, received money from estate of Simon R. Williams; 73

Lawrence Plummer; 23 October 1895; - ; - ; James, Ina and Susie Plummer; U- Allen Williams (of Ischua), U- Nathan

Name; Date of Birth; Father; Mother; Siblings; Other Relatives; Notes; Box Number

Williams; - ; 56

Susie A. M. Plummer; 16 May 1893; - ; - ; Lawrence, Ina and James Plummer; HU Mr. Degolia, U- Allen Williams (of Ischua), U- Nathan Williams; RE 1914, in Cuba, received money from estate of Simon R. Williams; 73

Maud Popple; about 1872; William Popple, left family in Yorkshire March 1875; Josephine; Willie Popple; MA Lottie Lincoln; - ; 56

Willie Popple; about 1874; William Popple, left family in Yorkshire March 1875; Josephine; Maud Popple; MA Lottie Lincoln; - ; 56

Alta M. Porter; 12 December 1877; - ; - ; - ; - ; received money from estate of Samantha Porter; 23

Anna G. Porter; 2 March 1862; Isaac G. Porter; - ; Edward, Henry, John and Mary Porter; - ; RE 1873, Porter, Rock, Wisconsin; 23

Edward A. Porter; 18 July 1864; Isaac G. Porter; - ; Anna, Henry, John and Mary Porter; - ; RE 1873, Porter, Rock, Wisconsin; 23

Henry I. Porter; 20 March 1861; Isaac G. Porter; - ; Edward, Anna, John and Mary Porter; - ; RE 1873, Porter, Rock, Wisconsin; 23

John Porter; 6 May 1854; Isaac G. Porter; - ; Anna, Henry, Edward and Mary Porter; - ; RE 1873, Porter, Rock, Wisconsin; 23

Mary W. Porter; 21 September 1855; Isaac G. Porter; - ; Anna, Henry, Edward and John Porter; - ; RE 1873, Porter, Rock, Wisconsin; 23

Ida A. Potter; - ; Gideon Potter, died before November 1866, of Company H., 21st Regt., Iowa Vol.; Catharine, of Portville, married David Chadwick; - ; - ; received pension money; 75

Louisa L. Powell; 2 April 1846; John L. Cross, of Great Valley; - ; - ; HU D. L. F. Powell, died January 1865; - ; 75

Marion Powers; 2 October 1909; - ; Kathryn, of 522 ½ W. State St., Olean; Edward and William Powers; - ; hurt in car

Name; Date of Birth; Father; Mother; Siblings; Other Relatives; Notes; Box Number

accident 22 September 1928 while riding with Lyle Elliott; 63

Albert P. Pratt; - ; John Pratt, died before November 1839, of Otto; - ; J. Hulda, M. Calvin, and Altna Pratt; - ; included with Weltha and other Blakely children's papers; 76

Alpha L. Pratt; 19 May 1859; Amos Pratt, died January 1867, of Ashford; Louisa Miller, of Ashford; Emily, Julia, and Judson Pratt; PGF John Pratt, MGF Henry Miller, PU Benjamin C. Pratt, PU Noah Pratt; - ; 75

Altna S. Pratt; - ; John Pratt, died before November 1839, of Otto; - ; J. Hulda, M. Calvin, and Albert Pratt; - ; included with Weltha and other Blakely children's papers; 76

Benjamin F. Pratt; 18 October 1894; - ; - ; Phoebe Pratt; - ; - ; 23

Clara Pratt; 3 October 1856; - ; Sally, of Napoli, married Mr. Burroughs; - ; - ; father died before July 1866; 75

Ella M. Pratt; about 1861; George B. Pratt, died May 1864, of Collins, Erie, NY; Clotilda M., of Gowanda, married Mr. Shack; Milton Pratt; - ; received pension money; 75

Emily L. Pratt; 29 March 1847; Amos Pratt, died January 1867, of Ashford; Louisa Miller, of Ashford; Alpha, Julia, and Judson Pratt; PGF John Pratt, MGF Henry Miller, PU Benjamin C. Pratt, PU Noah Pratt; - ; 75

Fannie Allegra Pratt; 5 December 1886; John W. Pratt, of Olean; - ; Mary Pratt; - ; attended College at Syracuse University; 73

J. Huldah Pratt; - ; John Pratt, died before November 1839, of Otto; - ; Altna, M. Calvin, and Albert Pratt; - ; included with Weltha and other Blakely children's papers; 76

Judson S. Pratt; 4 June 1862; Amos Pratt, died January 1867, of Ashford; Louisa Miller, of Ashford; Alpha, Emily, and Julia Pratt; PGF John Pratt, MGF Henry Miller, PU Benjamin C. Pratt, PU Noah Pratt; - ; 75

Julia Ann Pratt; 7 May 1850; Amos Pratt, died January 1867, of Ashford; Louisa Miller, of Ashford; Alpha, Emily, and Judson Pratt; PGF John Pratt, MGF Henry Miller, PU

Name; Date of Birth; Father; Mother; Siblings; Other Relatives; Notes; Box Number

Benjamin C. Pratt, PU Noah Pratt; - ; 75

M. Calvin Pratt; - ; John Pratt, died before November 1839, of Otto; - ; Altna, J. Huldah, and Albert Pratt; - ; included with Weltha and other Blakely children's papers; 76

Mary L. Pratt; about 1883; John W. Pratt, of Olean; - ; Fannie Pratt; - ; attended College at Syracuse University; 73

Milton Pratt; about 1859; George B. Pratt, died May 1864, of Collins, Erie, NY; Clotilda M., of Gowanda, married Mr. Shack; Ella Pratt; - ; received pension money; 75

Phoebe Pratt; 4 January 1891; - ; - ; Benjamin Pratt; HU Mr. Wilcox; - ; 23

Alice E. Prentice; about 1860; Simeon Prentice, died October 1863, of Lyndon; Mary L, married Mr. Niles; Edith Prentice; - ; RE Howell, Livingston, NY, G- Dewitt Stone; 75

Edith L. Prentice; about 1862; Simeon Prentice, died October 1863, of Lyndon; Mary L, married Mr. Niles; Alice Prentice; - ; RE Howell, Livingston, NY, G- Dewitt Stone; 75

Frances Prescack; 24 March 1893; - ; Irene, married Mr. Cribbs, of Sisterville, Tyler, West Virginia; Lizzie Presack; PGF Joseph Presack, A- Elizabeth Presack; RE 1914, in Rochester; 56

Lizzie Blanche Prescack; 14 February 1898; - ; Irene, married Mr. Cribbs, of Sisterville, Tyler, West Virginia; Frances Presack; HU Mr. Worfle, PGF Joseph Presack, A- Elizabeth Presack; RE 1914, in Rochester; 56

Mildred Prescott; 1 March 1908; Urban Prescott, died 18 June 1922; Lillian, died January 1926; Mrs. Robert Darling; father's C- Hubert Perry, other relatives were John, Jennings and Norton Prescott; G- Lincoln Vibbard (C- to Hubert Perry); 63

Emily Etta Preston; - ; - ; Seraph M. Johnson; Warren and Juliaetta Preston; MGF Parkman Johnson, MU Francis E. Johnson, MU Warren Johnson, PU Hiram Preston, MU Rossell Preston, MU Samuel Preston, MU Orrin Preston, G- Ira Browman; 75

Name; Date of Birth; Father; Mother; Siblings; Other Relatives; Notes; Box Number

Juliaetta Preston; 29 April 1844; - ; Seraph M. Johnson; Warren and Emily Preston; MGF Parkman Johnson, MU Francis E. Johnson, MU Warren Johnson, PU Hiram Preston, MU Rossell Preston, MU Samuel Preston, MU Orrin Preston, G- Ira Browman; 75

Warren Preston; - ; - ; Seraph M. Johnson; Juliaetta and Emily Preston; MGF Parkman Johnson, MU Francis E. Johnson, MU Warren Johnson, PU Hiram Preston, MU Rossell Preston, MU Samuel Preston, MU Orrin Preston, G- Ira Browman; 75

Eunice A. Prey; 15 August 1902; - ; Florence, married Elon Smith; - ; HU J. N. Henry, of 817 Main St., Olean; father died about 1917; 63

Dorr Price; 21 September 1842; Samuel Price, died before July 1862; - ; - ; - ; G- Ebenezer C. Price; 75

Elfie Price; 17 January 1875; Elbert Price, of Coldspring; - ; Hale, Merta, and Speda Price; - ; money from Albert Hale's estate; 56

Elizabeth D. Price; about 1856; David B. Price, died December 1864, of Randolph, served in Company B, 64th Regt., NY Vol., Sarah E. Bursee, of Randolph, married Mr. Gaffney; Lewis and George Price; MGF James Bursee, A- Jane Bursee, A- Mary Kelly; G- Robert D. Gould; 75

George R. Price; 6 July 1858; David B. Price, died December 1864, of Randolph, served in Company B, 64th Regt., NY Vol., Sarah E. Bursee, of Randolph, married Mr. Gaffney; Lewis and Elizabeth Price; MGF James Bursee, A- Jane Bursee, A- Mary Kelly; G- Robert D. Gould and G- Charles Adams; 23 and 75

Hale O. Price; 5 or 6 December 1876; Elbert Price, of Coldspring; - ; Elfie, Merta, and Speda Price; - ; received money from estate of Albert Hale; 56

Lewis Price; about 1858; David B. Price, died December 1864, of Randolph, served in Company B, 64th Regt., NY Vol., Sarah E. Bursee, of Randolph, married Mr. Gaffney; George and

Name; Date of Birth; Father; Mother; Siblings; Other Relatives; Notes; Box Number

Elizabeth Price; MGF James Bursee, A- Jane Bursee, A- Mary Kelly; G- Robert D. Gould; 75

Merta "Mertie" E. Price; 15 June 1879; Elbert Price, of Coldspring; - ; Elfie, Hale, and Speda Price; - ; received money from estate of Albert Hale; 56

Speda E. Price; 13 December 1880; Elbert Price, of Coldspring; - ; Elfie, Hale, and Merta Price; - ; received money from estate of Albert Hale; 56

Irma Priess; 15 July 1911; - ; - ; Henry and Hans Priess; - ; father died 16 April 1926, at Chicago; 63

Caroline "Carlie" E. Prosser; 29 March 1878; Michael Prosser, married Lizzie 9 February 1876, he died 18 September 1884 in Randolph; Lizzie Reeves; - ; MGF George Reeves (born about 1827), PGM Caroline Prosser; RE with Andrew Prosser, 1894, in Buffalo, 1892 in Salamanca; 56

Virginia Pullam; - ; Mr. Dean; - ; - ; - ; G- Weber; 5 and 8

Caroline Frances Putnam; 29 July 1826; Henry Putnam, died 21 June 1829 in Western, Worcester, Massachusetts; Eliza, of Farmersville; Eliza Putnam; - ; - ; 77

Eliza Ann Putnam; 13 April 1828; Henry Putnam, died 21 June 1829 in Western, Worcester, Massachusetts; Eliza, of Farmersville; Caroline Putnam; - ; - ; 77

Levi E. Putney; 21 November 1886; Edwin O. Putney; Sarah Arvilla, died August 1887; - ; MGM Amy Parker; RE 1908, in Forestville, Chautauqua, NY ; 23

Name; Date of Birth; Father; Mother; Siblings; Other Relatives; Notes; Box Number

Q Surnames

Clarence Quackenbush; March 1887; Frank Quackenbush, abandoned family; Emeline Phinney; MGF John Phinney, A- Mary J. Smith (married Mr. Johnson), A- Emma Olcutt, U- Eugene W. Phinney, U- Andrew Phinney; received money from estate of John Phinney; 56

Ella Quackenbush; 4 September 1876; David Quackenbush; Jane; Spencer Quackenbush; HU Mr. Lewis; RE 1897, Concord, Erie, NY, G- John L. Murphy, received money from estate of Rachel Spencer; 56

Spencer Quackenbush; 4 December 1882; David Quackenbush; Jane; Ella Quackenbush; - ; RE 1897, Concord, Erie, NY, G- John L. Murphy, received money from estate of Rachel Spencer; 56

Agnes Quigley; about 1879; James Quigley, of Olean; - ; Jane, Daniel and Mary Quigley; - ; - ; 58

Daniel Quigley; about 1876; James Quigley, of Olean; - ; Jane, Agnes and Mary Quigley; - ; - ; 58

Jane Quigley; about 1875; James Quigley, of Olean; - ; Daniel, Agnes and Mary Quigley; - ; - ; 58

Louis Bertrand Quigley; - ; - ; - ; - ; - ; G- Mary E. Tafel (RE 212 Park Pl, Brooklyn, NY) and Louis received money from estate of Eleanor Quigley; 58

Mary Quigley; about 1881; James Quigley, of Olean; - ; Daniel, Agnes and Jane Quigley; - ; - ; 58

Mary Quigley; 27 August 1911; John Quigley, of 108 ½ Coleman St., Olean; Clara; - ; - ; was in an auto accident 25 October 1930; 58

Catherine Quinn; about 1899; Thomas Quinn; - ; Frank and Mary Quinn; - ; Mary lived at 11 Allegany St., Salamanca; 58

Frank Quinn; about 1895; Thomas Quinn; - ; Catherine and Mary Quinn; - ; Mary lived at 11 Allegany St., Salamanca;

Name; Date of Birth; Father; Mother; Siblings; Other Relatives; Notes; Box Number

58
Robert J. Quinn; 18 December 1882; Michael Quinn, of Salamanca; - ; - ; - ; - ; 58

Name; Date of Birth; Father; Mother; Siblings; Other Relatives; Notes; Box Number

R Surnames

Ellen Rachford; 5 September 1875; Patrick Rachford, died March 1876, of Carrollton; Mary, died June 1882, she was committed to Gowanda Hospital in April 1881; - ; PU James Rachford, PU John Rachford; G- Levi H. Stevens; 73

Adam Raczkowsky; 4 December 1887; - ; Katherine, born about 1854, of Salamanca, didn't speak English well; - ; - ; RE 1908, in Buffalo, G- Joseph T. Myers, no relation; 73

George Herbert Ramsay; 17 August 1891; George E. Ramsay, of Olean; Kate; Florence Ramsay; - ; - ; 73

Florence M. Ramsay; 5 November 1882; George E. Ramsay, of Olean; Kate; George Ramsay; - ; - ; 73

Frank H. Ramsey; 17 June 1863; Silas Ramsey, died before March 1867; Jane M. Parish, of Olean; Silas Ramsey, HS Mary Ramsey, HB Sylvester Ramsey, HB William Ramsey, and HB George Ramsey; MGF Shubel Parish; had two other half-siblings; 76

George Ramsey; 65 August 1852; Silas Ramsey, died before March 1867; - ; Sylvester, William and Mary Ramsey plus two other siblings; HB Silas Ramsey, HB Frank Ramsey; - ; - ; 76

Mary Ramsey; 3 September 1848; Silas Ramsey, died before March 1867; - ; Sylvester, William and George Ramsey plus two other siblings; HB Silas Ramsey, HB Frank Ramsey; - ; - ; 76

Silas Ramsey; 1 January 1861; Silas Ramsey, died before March 1867; Jane M. Parish, of Olean; Frank Ramsey, HS Mary Ramsey, HB Sylvester Ramsey, HB William Ramsey, and HB George Ramsey; MGF Shubel Parish; had two other half-siblings; 76

Charles D. Randall; 24 November 1867; George Randall; - ; Lottie, Clinton, Helen, Cora and Daisy; MGM Muhaley Woodbury (born about 1812), U- Henry Woodbury; received

Name; Date of Birth; Father; Mother; Siblings; Other Relatives; Notes; Box Number

money from estate of Ruth Randall; 58

Clinton E. Randall; 22 March 1871; George Randall; - ; Lottie, Daisy, Helen, Charles and Cora Randall; MGM Muhaley Woodbury (born about 1812), U- Henry Woodbury; received money from estate of Ruth Randall; 58

Cora Randall; - ; George Randall; - ; Lottie, Clinton, Helen, Charles and Daisy; MGM Muhaley Woodbury (born about 1812), U- Henry Woodbury; received money from estate of Ruth Randall; 58

Daisy Randall; - ; George Randall; - ; Lottie, Clinton, Helen, Charles and Cora Randall; MGM Muhaley Woodbury (born about 1812), U- Henry Woodbury; received money from estate of Ruth Randall; 58

Edward Randall; 15 June 1859; Charles Randall; Ada Crosby; - ; MGF Nathan Crosby; in same envelope as Emma and Ida Crandall; 24

Elma Randall; 13 February 1863; Harvey Randall, died before January 1865; Jane Blair, married Mr. Curtis; George Randall; MGF William W. Blair; indexed as Edna Randall, received pension money; 76

Emma T. Randall; about 1858; Jacob Randall, died April 1868, of Wales, Erie, NY; Huldah Crosby; Ida T. Randall ; MGF Stephen Crosby; in same envelope as Edward Randall; 24

George Randall; 28 January 1859; Harvey Randall, died before January 1865; Jane Blair, married Mr. Curtis; Elma Randall; MGF William W. Blair; received pension money; 76

Helen D. Randall; 9 April 1876; George Randall; - ; Lottie, Daisy, Clinton, Charles and Cora Randall; MGM Muhaley Woodbury (born about 1812), U- Henry Woodbury; received money from estate of Ruth Randall; 58

Ida T. Randall; about 1856; Jacob Randall, died April 1868, of Wales, Erie, NY; Huldah Crosby; Emma Randall ; MGF Stephen Crosby; in same envelope as Edward Randall; 24

Lottie M. Randall; 19 February 1870; George Randall; - ; Helen, Daisy, Clinton, Charles and Cora Randall; MGM Muhaley

Name; Date of Birth; Father; Mother; Siblings; Other Relatives; Notes; Box Number

Woodbury (born about 1812), U- Henry Woodbury; received money from estate of Ruth Randall; 58

Edwin L. Ransom; 10 February 1856; Addison Ransom; Betsey; HB Alonzo R. Ransom; - ; in same envelope as Orrin C. Ransom; 24

Hiram Ransom; 19 September 1836; - ; - ; - ; - ; G- Truman Edwards; 76

Orrin C. Ransom; 7 August 1853; Orrin Ransom, died by August 1870; Betsey; Smith R. Ransom; - ; - ; 24

Smith S. Ransom; 16 December 1850; Orrin Ransom, died before 20 October 1866; - ; - ; - ; G- David Sanders; 18

Carrie F. Rathburn; about 1860; - ; Clarissa E., of Perrysburg, married Mr. Crow; - ; - ; father died May 1864, received pension money; 76

Allie M. Raub; 13 August 1878; O. J. Raub, of Abilene, Kansas; - ; - ; - ; - ; 73

Bessie Maxson Rauber; 23 May 1898; Barton J. Maxson, lived in Angelica; - ; - ; HU Albert Rauber, MGF A. J. Barnes (RE Mount View, California); RE 719 E. State St., Olean and mother died 5 July 1904; 75

John K. Ray; 8 June 1883; Daniel P. Ray; - ; - ; - ; - ; 74

Ada E. Razey; February 1855; Horace F. Razey; Mary J.; Charles, Chloe and Frances Razey; U- Lorenzo Razey; - ; 24

Charles F. Razey; 15 January 1851; Horace F. Razey; Mary J.; Ada, Chloe and Frances Razey; U- Lorenzo Razey; - ; 24

Chloe G. Razey; about 1853; Horace F. Razey; Mary J.; Ada, Charles and Frances Razey; U- Lorenzo Razey; - ; 24

Frances Anna Razey; about 1857; Horace F. Razey; Mary J.; Ada, Charles and Chloe Razey; U- Lorenzo Razey; - ; 24

Albertine H. Reasz; 7 September 1897; Willard L. Reasz, of Olean; Frances; Frank, Isabel, Catherine, and Edith Reasz; - ; - ; 58

Catherine I. Reasz; 24 October 1899; Willard L. Reasz, of Olean; Frances; Frank, Isabel, Albertine, and Edith Reasz; - ; - ; 58

Name; Date of Birth; Father; Mother; Siblings; Other Relatives; Notes; Box Number

Edith H. Reasz; 22 June 1901; Willard L. Reasz, of Olean; Frances; Frank, Isabel, Albertine, and Catherine Reasz; - ; - ; 58

Frank W. Reasz; 8 June 1895; Willard L. Reasz, of Olean; Frances; Edith, Isabel, Albertine, and Catherine Reasz; - ; - ; 58

Isabel L. Reasz; 1 January 1904; Willard L. Reasz, of Olean; Frances; Edith, Frankl, Albertine, and Catherine Reasz; - ; - ; 58

Ivan L. Reck; 27 July 1901; - ; Iva B., of Persia; - ; MGM Alice Burns, in Port Colborne, Welland, Ontario, Canada; - ; 58

Cora Villette Reed; October 1871; Emery V. Reed, died 30 December 1885; Elvira; Pearl Reed; - ; - ; 24

Pearl Reed; 13 September 1865; Emery V. Reed, died 30 December 1885; Elvira; Cora Reed; - ; - ; 24

Leonard Leo Reedy; 29 May 1909; Thomas Reedy, deceased by January 1926; - ; - ; - ; G- Hugh Cobb (died by 1930), RE 1928 with sister at 1454 Walbridge Ave., Toledo, Ohio and 1930 in Buffalo; 18

Eleanor "Ellen" Ann Reese; about 1862; Joshua Reese, died October 1875, of Freedom; Sarah; Esther Reese; PGF Thomas Reese, PA Mary Roberts (of Freedom); G- John Williams; 58

Esther "Hettie" E. Reese; about 1867; Joshua Reese, died October 1875, of Freedom; Sarah; Eleanor Reese; PGF Thomas Reese, PA Mary Roberts (of Freedom); G- John Williams; 58

Loyd V. Reeves; 11 December 1889; Clinton E. Reeves, died 21 April 1902; Edna E., of Steamburg, married Mr. Burr in 1904; - ; - ; father owned a store ; 73

Anna Reihm; 19 September 1849; Jacob Reihm, of Olean; - ; - ; - ; - ; 76

Fred Reilley; - ; George Reilly; - ; Lillie and George Reilley; - ; G- Edwin F. Hoy; 58

George Reilley; - ; George Reilly; - ; Lillie and Fred Reilley; - ;

Name; Date of Birth; Father; Mother; Siblings; Other Relatives; Notes; Box Number

G- Edwin F. Hoy; 58

Lillie Reilley; - ; George Reilly; - ; George and Fred Reilley; - ; G- Edwin F. Hoy; 58

Frederick Reitz; about 1868; John Reitz, died before August 1883; Catharine; Molly, Henry, Mary, John and Theodore Reitz; - ; - ; 24

Henry Reitz; about 1864; John Reitz, died before August 1883; Catharine; Molly, Frederick, Mary, John and Theodore Reitz; - ; - ; 24

John Reitz; about 1870; John Reitz, died before August 1883; Catharine; Molly, Frederick, Mary, Henry and Theodore Reitz; - ; - ; 24

Leona Reitz; 12 February 1895; - ; - ; Raymond Reitz; MGF Frederick W. Forness Sr.; - ; 18

Mary Reitz; about 1866; John Reitz, died before August 1883; Catharine; Molly, Frederick, John, Henry and Theodore Reitz; - ; - ; 24

Molly Reitz; about 1863; John Reitz, died before August 1883; Catharine; Mary, Frederick, John, Henry and Theodore Reitz; - ; - ; 24

Raymond Reitz; 29 March 1893; - ; - ; Leona Reitz; MGF Frederick W. Forness Sr.; - ; 18

Theodore Reitz; about 1873; John Reitz, died before August 1883; Catharine; Mary, Frederick, John, Henry and Molly Reitz; - ; - ; 24

Ida M. Remington; 4 March 1864; Seth W. Remington; - ; - ; MGF Samuel Webster; G- Stephen Remington; 24

Marcella B. Remington; 4 September 1903; - ; - ; Oramon, Robert and Ruth Remington; U- Heman E. Remington; received money from estate of Oramon I. Nash; 18

Oramon Remington; about 1892; - ; - ; Marcella, Robert and Ruth Remington; U- Heman E. Remington; Oramon died in the military 14 December 1918, money from Oramon I. Nash's estate; 18

Robert Remington; about 1900; - ; - ; Marcella, Oramon and

Name; Date of Birth; Father; Mother; Siblings; Other Relatives; Notes; Box Number

Ruth Remington; U- Heman E. Remington; received money from estate of Oramon I. Nash; 18

Ruth Remington; about 1893; - ; - ; Marcella, Oramon and Robert Remington; HU Mr. Lawson (married by 25 March 1919), U- Heman E. Remington; received money from estate of Oramon I. Nash; 18

William Renwick; - ; James F. Renwick, died in Military before July 1866; Jane, married Mr. Cook; - ; PGF Robert Renwick (of Oil City, Pennsylvania), MU Charles Toucy (of Binghamton); - ; 76

Lewis Retter; 15 Apri 1882; John Retter, of Ischua; - ; - ; MGF Henry Hill; G- Royal Litchfield, no relation; 58

John J. Reusch; about 1905; Michael Reusch, died 4 August 1909; Bertha; Margaret Reusch; PG John (died 7 February 1889) and Regina Reusch (remarried to Mr. Elsen); - ; 49

Margaret Reusch; about 1903; Michael Reusch, died 4 August 1909; Bertha; John Reusch; PG John (died 7 February 1889) and Regina Reusch (remarried to Mr. Elsen); - ; 49

Clara Louise Revett; 11 August 1874; - ; Mary, of Salamanca; Geneva Revett; - ; money from George Revett's estate; 58

Geneva Mary Revett; 15 October 1875; - ; Mary, of Salamanca; Clara Revett; - ; money from George Revett's estate; 58

Arthur W. Reynolds; 30 November 1893; - ; - ; Edward Reynolds (born about 1889 and RE 343 Normal Ave., Buffalo, NY) and Margaret Reynolds; - ; - ; 49

Charles A. Reynolds; 23 July 1873; Charles Reynolds, of Franklinville; Semantha; Mary Reynolds; - ; - ; 58

Emma J. Reynolds; 1 February 1860; Robert Reynolds, of Osawatomie, Miami, Kansas; Elizabeth; Ida, John and Roberta Reynolds; - ; - ; 24

Erma F. Reynolds; about 1899; James M. Reynolds; Alta Wexley; Lottie Miller and Richard Reynolds; MGF Alexander Wexley, (died before 2 February 1912, of Champaign, Illinois), James Reynolds' HS was Rose Butler; Erma's house burned 20 January 1915; 18

Name; Date of Birth; Father; Mother; Siblings; Other Relatives; Notes; Box Number

Esther E. Reynolds; 24 March 1903; Millard Reynolds; Bertha B.; - ; - ; G- Guy C. Ames; 18

Helen M. Reynolds; 12 May 1911; Elmer Reynolds; Mary; - ; - ; G- Dennis G. Reynolds; 18

Ida Reynolds; 5 October 1866; Robert Reynolds, of Osawatomie, Miami, Kansas; Elizabeth; Emma, John and Roberta Reynolds; - ; - ; 24

John C. Reynolds; 29 March 1865; Robert Reynolds, of Osawatomie, Miami, Kansas; Elizabeth; Emma, Ida and Roberta Reynolds; - ; - ; 24

Lillian Hornish Reynolds; 3 January 1901; - ; Myrtle Barnes was her name in August 1919; - ; HU Walter M. Reynolds, married by 18 August 1919; - ; 18

Margaret E. Reynolds; 3 September 1898; - ; - ; Edward Reynolds (born about 1889 and resided 343 Normal Ave., Buffalo, NY) and Arthur Reynolds; - ; - ; 49

Mary Adelia Reynolds; 27 December 1870; Charles Reynolds, of Franklinville; Semantha; Charles Reynolds; - ; - ; 58

Millard R. Reynolds; 22 September 1880; - ; Lovinia, of Franklinville; Lanie Pierce; - ; mentions Arthur J. Reynolds co-owned farms, money from estate of James Reynolds; 74

Millie Reynolds; 16 September 1861; Jacob Reynolds, died before 26 September 1864; Frances; - ; PG John and Permelia Reynolds, MGM Fanny Conrad; - ; 58

Richard W. Reynolds; about 1908; James M. Reynolds; Alta Wexley; Lottie Miller and Erma Reynolds; MGF Alexander Wexley, (died before 2 February 1912, of Champaign, Illinois), James Reynolds' HS was Rose Butler; Erma's house burned 20 January 1915; 18

Roberta J. Reynolds; 20 January 1862; Robert Reynolds, of Osawatomie, Miami, Kansas; Elizabeth; Emma, Ida and John Reynolds; - ; indexed under Robert Reynolds ; 24

Roy Reynolds; about 1893; - ; - ; - ; relative was James Reynolds, of Portville; G- Rufus Petty, received money from legacy from Yesley; 58

Name; Date of Birth; Father; Mother; Siblings; Other Relatives; Notes; Box Number

William Reynolds; 9 November 1868; - ; Callie, died February 1880; - ; PGM Pamelia Reynolds, PU Henry Reynolds, PU Dennis Reynolds; - ; 24

Hardy L. Rhoadhouse; 11 April 1873; - ; - ; Vernon (born about 1870) and Nelly (born about 1871) Rhoadhouse, of Randolph; - ; G- Charles Teny; 58

Jessamine Rhodes; 22 February 1903; George Rhodes; Addie; - ; - ; - ; 18

Silas Rhodes; 22 April 1886; Marcus Rhodes, of Dayton; - ; Merrill Rhodes; - ; - ; 58

Adele V. Rian; 25 August 1905; AF Nelson Rian; Mabel; - ; - ; - ; 18

Caroline Rice; 7 October 1836; Clark Rice, died before June 1847, of Farmersville; Emily; Lorette, Sally, Clark, and Mariet Rice; PU Charles Rice, PU William Rice; - ; 76

Clark Rice; 24 September 1838; Clark Rice, died before June 1847, of Farmersville; Emily; Lorette, Sally, Caroline, and Mariet Rice; PU Charles Rice, PU William Rice; - ; 76

Lorette Rice; about 1828; Clark Rice, died before June 1847, of Farmersville; Emily; Caroline, Sally, Clark, and Mariet Rice; PU Charles Rice, PU William Rice; - ; 76

Lottie L. Rice; 12 May 1867; - ; - ; - ; C- Clark Day; - ; 58

Mariet Rice; about 1830; Clark Rice, died before June 1847, of Farmersville; Emily; Caroline, Sally, Clark, and Lorette Rice; PU Charles Rice, PU William Rice; - ; 76

Minnie E. Rice; about 1886, of Olean ; - ; - ; - ; A- Lottie S. Tucker; parents died before February 1903; 73

Sally Rice; 21 February 1833; Clark Rice, died before June 1847, of Farmersville; Emily; Lorette, Mariet, Clark, and Caroline Rice; PU Charles Rice, PU William Rice; - ; 76

William Ellis Rice; about 1899; Elmer E. Rice; - ; - ; - ; received money from estate of Mary A. Jennings; 18

Addie M. Rich; 8 June 1905; Lynn W. Rich; - ; - ; - ; - ; 18

Lewis V. Rich; about 1880; Victor J. Rich, of Napoli; - ; Walter Rich; - ; - ; 74

Name; Date of Birth; Father; Mother; Siblings; Other Relatives; Notes; Box Number

Raymond H. Rich; 4 June 1908; Raymond J. Rich, died 1 April 1928; Bessie, died before her husband; Lillian Rich Johnson (of Bolivar) and Millicent Horth (of Erie); - ; - ; 18

Walter J. Rich; about 1886; Victor J. Rich, of Napoli; - ; Lewis Rich; - ; - ; 74

Helen R. Richards; 1 December 1872; John C. Richards, died September 1892, of Olean; - ; John Richards; - ; G- Charles Clark; 58

John B. Richards; 4 November 1874; John C. Richards, died September 1892, of Olean; - ; Helen Richards; - ; G- Charles Clark; 58

Millard Richards; about 1899; - ; Jennie; - ; - ; Millard was an illegitimate child and did not know where his father was; -

Beulah Richardson; about 1883; Leander C. Richardson; - ; - ; - ; indexed as Bulah Richardson, in same envelope as George Richardson; 18

George Richardson; about 1881; Henry Richardson; - ; - ; - ; received money from estate of Beaulah Ann Bristol, in same envelope as Beulah Richardson

Jennie Richardson; about 1898; - ; - ; Morris and Leander Richardson; - ; - ; 58

Morris Richardson; about 1894; - ; - ; Jennie and Leander Richardson; - ; - ; 58

Beulah Richey; about 1899; Hugh Richey, died 25 June 1914, cause of death was accident while working at sawmill, lived Keating Summit, Pennsylvania; Lola E., RE 311 North 1st St., Olean; Robert, Lela, Cecil, Pearl and Evelyn; - ; - ; 58

Cecil Richey; about 1903; Hugh Richey, died 25 June 1914, cause of death was accident while working at sawmill, lived Keating Summit, Pennsylvania; Lola E., RE 311 North 1st St., Olean; Robert, Lela, Beulah, Pearl and Evelyn; - ; - ; 58

Evelyn Richey; about 1907; Hugh Richey, died 25 June 1914, cause of death was accident while working at sawmill, lived Keating Summit, Pennsylvania; Lola E., resided at 311 North 1st St., Olean; Robert, Lela, Beulah, Pearl and Cecil; - ; - ; 58

Name; Date of Birth; Father; Mother; Siblings; Other Relatives; Notes; Box Number

Lela Richey; about 1901; Hugh Richey, died 25 June 1914, cause of death was accident while working at sawmill, lived Keating Summit, Pennsylvania; Lola E., RE 311 North 1st St., Olean; Robert, Evelyn, Beulah, Pearl and Cecil; - ; - ; 58

Pearl Richey; about 1905; Hugh Richey, died 25 June 1914, cause of death was accident while working at sawmill, lived Keating Summit, Pennsylvania; Lola E., RE 311 North 1st St., Olean; Robert, Evelyn, Beulah, Lela and Cecil; - ; - ; 58

Robert Richey; 17 March 1897; Hugh Richey, died 25 June 1914, cause of death was accident while working at sawmill, lived Keating Summit, Pennsylvania; Lola E., resided at 311 North 1st St., Olean; Pearl, Evelyn, Beulah, Lela and Cecil; - ; - ; 58

Elma O. Ridout; 5 October 1872 ; - ; Maria; Eva, Nellie, and Wesley Ridout; HU Mr. Ackler; second G- Peter Ackler, G- Frank D. Caneen (no relation), money from Nathan Ridout's estate; 33

Eva Ridout; 25 February 1875; - ; Maria; Elma, Nellie, and Wesley Ridout; HU Mr. Chapman; second G- Peter Ackler, G- Frank D. Caneen (no relation), received money from estate of Nathan Ridout; 33

Nellie Ridout; 26 November 1877; - ; Maria; Elma, Eva, and Wesley Ridout; HU Herbert Lawrence; second G- Peter Ackler, G- Frank D. Caneen (no relation), received money from estate of Nathan Ridout; 33

Wesley Ridout; 20 April 1882; - ; Maria; Elma, Eva, and Nellie Ridout; -; second G- Peter Ackler, G- Frank D. Caneen (no relation), received money from estate of Nathan Ridout; 33

Coral Riggs; about 1855; Lewis Riggs, died December 1862, of Franklinville; Eliza Ann; Miles, Franklin, L. S., and H. L. Riggs and Thankful Clarke, Laura Cummings, Mary E. Steele, Clara McNall, and Ann Phillips; - ; G- Nathan Weed; 58

Franklin Riggs; about 1858; Lewis Riggs, died December 1862, of Franklinville; Eliza Ann; Miles, Coral, L. S., and H. L. Riggs and Thankful Clarke, Laura Cummings, Mary E.

Name; Date of Birth; Father; Mother; Siblings; Other Relatives; Notes; Box Number

Steele, Clara McNall, and Ann Phillips; - ; G- Nathan Weed; 58

Miles Riggs; about 1861; Lewis Riggs, died December 1862, of Franklinville; Eliza Ann; Franklin, Coral, L. S., and H. L. Riggs and Thankful Clarke, Laura Cummings, Mary E. Steele, Clara McNall, and Ann Phillips; - ; G- Nathan Weed; 58

Harold J. Riley; 4 August 1903; James Riley; - ; - ; - ; - ; 24

Thomas J. Riley; 17 September 1900; James J. Riley, died before 23 August 1915; Mary C.; - ; - ; - ; 18

Gifford J. Rink; 19 May 1886; John Rink; Mina; - ; - ; in same envelope as Nellie Rink; 18

Nellie Rink; - ; - ; - ; - ; - ; in same envelope as Gifford J. Rink, but nothing in file contains her name; 18

Ella Mildred Ritchie; 13 August 1902; John Ritchie, of Ischua, died 2 January 1903; Bessie E. Nottingham, married Lambert Corthell in 1906; John Ritchie; HU Joe Lewis, MGF Wellington Nottingham; received pension money; 73

John Wellington Ritchie; 17 May 1898; John Ritchie, of Ischua, died 2 January 1903; Bessie E. Nottingham, married Lambert Corthell in 1906; Ella Ritchie; MGF Wellington Nottingham; received pension money; 73

John Ritter Jr.; about 1889; John W. Ritter, born about 1855; - ; Mary and Joseph Ritter; - ; received insurance money on life of Eva Ritter; 47

Joseph J. Ritter; 19 August 1895; John W. Ritter, born about 1855; - ; Mary and John Ritter; - ; received insurance money on life of Eva Ritter; 47

Mary Ritter; April 1892; John W. Ritter, born about 1855; - ; Joseph and John Ritter; HU Mr. Bathurst; received insurance money on life of Eva Ritter; 47

DeForest Riverburgh; 16 June 1882; - ; - ; - ; A- Carrie B. Purdy, of Olean; G- James W. Mulcay; 74

Albert E Robbins; 6 April 1843; Richard Robbins, died before February 1863; Mary, of Farmersville; Milton, Ellen, Esther,

Name; Date of Birth; Father; Mother; Siblings; Other Relatives; Notes; Box Number

Fred, Egbert, Richard, Mary and Frank Robbins; U- Peleg Robbins; - ; 76

Egbert W. Robbins; 6 April 1843; Richard Robbins, died before February 1863; Mary, of Farmersville; Milton, Ellen, Esther, Fred, Albert, Richard, Mary and Frank Robbins; U- Peleg Robbins; - ; 76

Frank Robbins; 22 October 1856; Richard Robbins, died before February 1863; Mary, of Farmersville; Milton, Ellen, Esther, Fred, Albert, Richard, Mary and Egbert Robbins; U- Peleg Robbins; - ; 76

Fred D. Robbins; 20 August 1854; Richard Robbins, died before February 1863; Mary, of Farmersville; Milton, Ellen, Esther, Frank, Albert, Richard, Mary and Egbert Robbins; U- Peleg Robbins; - ; 76

Mary E. Robbins; 11 August 1846; Richard Robbins, died before February 1863; Mary, of Farmersville; Milton, Ellen, Esther, Frank, Albert, Richard, Fred and Egbert Robbins; U- Peleg Robbins; - ; 76

Richard W. Robbins; 20 February 1849; Richard Robbins, died before February 1863; Mary, of Farmersville; Milton, Ellen, Esther, Frank, Albert, Mary, Fred and Egbert Robbins; U- Peleg Robbins; - ; 76

Winifred Robbins; 3 October 1872; Albert Robbins, of Farmersville; - ; - ; - ; 58

Harriet Roberts; 15 October 1856; Robert Roberts; - ; Katie, Mary, Owen and Willis Roberts; HU Mr. Pugh; - ; 25

Katie Roberts; 18 October 1867; Robert Roberts; - ; Harriet, Mary, Owen and Willis Roberts; - ; - ; 25

Margaret E. Roberts; 20 April 1902; Everel P. Roberts, died 1 January 1919; - ; - ; U- Thomas Farrell (RE 312 Henley St., Olean), RE Feb 1919, Sacred Heart Academy in Buffalo, NY and received legacy from will of Margaret Farrell; 19

Mary E. Roberts; 13 July 1860; Robert Roberts; - ; Harriet, Katie, Owen and Willis Roberts; - ; - ; 25

Owen W. Roberts; 27 May 1862; Robert Roberts; - ; Harriet,

Name; Date of Birth; Father; Mother; Siblings; Other Relatives; Notes; Box Number

Katie, Mary and Willis Roberts; - ; - ; 25

Willis Roberts; 15 November 1858; Robert Roberts; - ; Harriet, Katie, Mary and Owen Roberts; - ; - ; 25

Marjorie D. Robertson; about 1909; Whetten Robertson; Florence Ziegler, married Jesse Cole 27 December 1912, she died 5 May 1916; - ; MG Frank and Effie Ziegler, PA Mrs. Bessie Medley; Whetten and Florence divorced and Whetten's whereabouts were unknown; 19

Charles E. Robinson; about 1856; William Robinson; Catherine E., died 1858 in Ischua; - ; mother's GF was John Learn (he died Lansing, Tompkin, NY in 1867), U- Phalismen Snyder; - ; 76

James Robinson; about 1893; John Robinson, of Olean; - ; - ; - ; received money from estate of Elizabeth Robinson; 58

Jane Robinson; about 1848; - ; Jane, of Ellicottville; - ; - ; lived with Joseph Harrington and in same envelope with Lucy Maria Benson; 76

Jane Robinson: 21 by 24 September 1869; - ; - ; - ; HU Francis Morrison; RE Colden, Erie, NY; 2

Reuben W. Robinson; 2 November 1867; Horace Robinson, died 8 January 1882; Eunice; - ; - ; received money from estate of Mary Robinson; 24

Adrial A. Rodgers; 22 or 23 August 1861; Augustus Rodgers, died June 1864; Maria D., married Byron G. Mackey and she died December 1869; - ; - ; G- William Mackey; 24

Albert A. Roff; - ; Lysander Roff, died July 1864, of Ossian, Livingston, NY; Mary A. France, married Mr. Mead; Della Roff; MG George and Fanny France; - ; 76

Della Roff; - ; Lysander Roff, died July 1864, of Ossian, Livingston, NY; Mary A. France, married Mr. Mead; Albert Roff; MG George and Fanny France; - ; 76

Leo C. Rogers; 14 November 1886; - ; Ada, of Mansfield, married Mr. Cox and then married Mr. Russell; Oma Rogers; - ; G- Lafayette "Fayette" Rogers, received money from estate of Isaac P. Rogers; 73

Name; Date of Birth; Father; Mother; Siblings; Other Relatives; Notes; Box Number

Oma D. Rogers; 15 September 1890; - ; Ada, of Mansfield, married Mr. Cox and then married Mr. Russell; Leo Rogers; - ; G- Lafayette "Fayette" Rogers, received money from estate of Isaac P. Rogers; 73

Catherine Rohan; - ; - ; - ; - ; - ; papers state that Johanna Shay Rohan was given money for Dower, in same envelope with William, Mary, Johanna, Nancy, Ellen and John Rohan; 75

Ellen Rohan; - ; - ; - ; - ; - ; papers state that Johanna Shay Rohan was given money for Dower, in same envelope with William, Mary, Johanna, Nancy, Catherine and John Rohan; 75

Johanna Rohan; - ; - ; - ; - ; - ; papers state that Johanna Shay Rohan was given money for Dower, in same envelope with William, Mary, Ellen, Nancy, Catherine and John Rohan; 75

John Rohan; - ; - ; - ; - ; - ; papers state that Johanna Shay Rohan was given money for Dower, in same envelope with William, Mary, Ellen, Nancy, Catherine and Johanna Rohan; 75

Mary Rohan; - ; - ; - ; - ; - ; papers state that Johanna Shay Rohan was given money for Dower, in same envelope with William, John, Ellen, Nancy, Catherine and Johanna Rohan; 75

Nancy Rohan; - ; - ; - ; - ; - ; papers state that Johanna Shay Rohan was given money for Dower, in same envelope with William, John, Ellen, Mary, Catherine and Johanna Rohan; 75

William Rohan; - ; - ; - ; - ; - ; papers state that Johanna Shay Rohan was given money for Dower, in same envelope with Nancy, John, Ellen, Mary, Catherine and Johanna Rohan; 75

John Rojek; 3 December 1898; Joseph Rojek; Maggie, of Salamanca; - ; - ; moved back to Poland after death of mother, G- Sophia Graczyjk; 18

Daisy Rondoll; - ; - ; - ; - ; - ; G- Henry Woodbury, received money from estate of Ruth Rondoll, in file, states Clinton Rondoll (possibly Randall) turned 21 about 1873; 73

Edith M. Rood; 30 September 1907; Herbert F. Rood, died before September 1920; Anna, married Mr. Rich; Evelyn

Name; Date of Birth; Father; Mother; Siblings; Other Relatives; Notes; Box Number

Rood; - ; - ; 24

Evelyn F. Rood; 7 December 1901; Herbert F. Rood, died before September 1920; Anna, married Mr. Rich; Edith Rood; - ; - ; 24

Emma Francelia Root; - ; - ; - ; Nancy Root, Melissa (W- of Jerome Allen) and Hannah J (W- of Amos Allen); U- George W. Harvey, U- Nelson A. Vandyke; - ; 76

Nancy Angelia Root; - ; - ; - ; Emma Root, Melissa (W- of Jerome Allen) and Hannah J (W- of Amos Allen); U- George W. Harvey, U- Nelson A. Vandyke; - ; 76

Ruth A. Ropps; 1 September 1886; George Ropps, of East Randolph; - ; - ; GGM Ruth Gardner; - ; 74

Carolyn C. Rosen; 4 June 1892; - ; - ; Louise Rosen; - ; parents died before January 1912; 74

James Francis Rosenberry; 3 November 1881; Thomas Rosenberry, of Red House; - ; Richard Rosenberry; - ; G- Isaac Winship, received legacy from Sarah Rosenberry; 74

Richard R. Rosenberry; 28 August 1883; Thomas Rosenberry, of Red House; - ; James Rosenberry; - ; G- Isaac Winship, received legacy from Sarah Rosenberry; 74

Joseph Rosenfield; 25 December 1894; - ; - ; - ; - ; parents RE Vladislawob, Russia, needed guardian to enlist in Army, G- Henry Ford, no relation; 58

Clara Ross; 18 April 1875; - ; Ella, married Mr. Coolidge; Floyd Ross; - ; received pension money; 58

Earl D. Ross; about 1888; Asa Ross, died before April 1899; Florence A., of Gowanda, married Mr. Dawson; - ; - ; - ; 74

Floyd Ross; - ; - ; Ella, married Mr. Coolidge; Floyd Ross; - ; received pension money; 58

Franklin Ross; 27 June 1834; - ; - ; - ; - ; G- Nelson Herrick; 76

John C. Ross; about 1842; - ; - ; - ; BIL Bryant Brown; - ; 76

Mildred B. Ross; 17 November 1876; Walter Ross, of Leon; - ; - ; HU Mr. Plank; - ; 58

Margaret Rotschky; 15 January 1858; Gottfried Rotschky, of Allegany; Frederica Teresa, died before August 1866; Mary

Name; Date of Birth; Father; Mother; Siblings; Other Relatives; Notes; Box Number

and Sophia Rotschky; - ; - ; 76

Mary P. Rotschky; 24 March 1859; Gottfried Rotschky, of Allegany; Frederica Teresa, died before August 1866; Margaret and Sophia Rotschky; - ; - ; 76

Sophia Susannah Rotschky; 13 November 1853; Gottfried Rotschky, of Allegany; Frederica Teresa, died before August 1866; Margaret and Mary Rotschky; - ; - ; 76

John Rowland; 30 August 1849; John Rowland, died before May 1865; - ; - ; - ; G- John McCoy; 76

Charles Royan; about 1863; - ; Anna, died January 1875; Anna Strohuber, Leo and Julia Erhard, and Josephine Royan ; MU Augus Hallers, MU Charles Hallers; G- George Strohuber, received pension; 24

Josephine Royan; 5 November 1864; - ; Anna, died January 1875; Anna Strohuber, Leo and Julia Erhard, and Charles Royan ; MU Augus Hallers, MU Charles Hallers; G- George Strohuber, received pension; 24

William H. Royce; 13 December 1850; Horace M., died before April 1861; Almira Johnson; - ; MG Jacob and Maria Johnson, U- Hiram Royce, PA Helen Hicks (W- of Jefferson Hicks), MA Eliza Searl (W- of Justin Searl); - ; 76

Dorothy Ruf; - ; Louis F. Ruf, of Olean; - ; - ; - ; received money from estate of E. J. Sunderlin; 58

Jennie O. Rugg; 18 June 1875; W. Wilson Rugg, of Olean; - ; - ; - ; - ; 74

Seymour Salisbury Rugg; 9 August 1894; Charles L. Rugg, of Olean; - ; - ; - ; RE 1915, in Randolph; 58

Gretchen Rulison; 9 June 1903; John H. Rulison; Fannie, of Olean; - ; - ; parents were divorcing; 58

David Rundell; 6 January 1886; - ; - ; - ; distant relative was Cyrus W. Ingersoll; - ; 26

Richard C. Runyon; 1 October 1910; C. A. Runyon; Lydia; - ; - ; - ; 24

Edith Ruple; 19 October 1884; - ; Mary, of South Valley, married Mr. Laughlin; - ; - ; - ; 74

Name; Date of Birth; Father; Mother; Siblings; Other Relatives; Notes; Box Number

Calvin Rush; - ; - ; Roxana Pratt; Jacob, Mary and Sabelia Rush; MG Darius and Jennett Pratt, U- Poltus Rush; - ; 76

Jacob Rush; - ; - ; Roxana Pratt; Calvin, Mary and Sabelia Rush; MG Darius and Jennett Pratt, U- Poltus Rush; - ; 76

Mary J. Rush; - ; - ; Roxana Pratt; Calvin, Jacob and Sabelia Rush; MG Darius and Jennett Pratt, U- Poltus Rush; - ; 76

Sabelia Rush; - ; - ; Roxana Pratt; Calvin, Jacob and Mary Rush; MG Darius and Jennett Pratt, U- Poltus Rush; - ; 76

Cordelia Adell Rust; about 1850; - ; - ; - ; PA Cordelia Hyde (W- of Reuben Hyde), GM Huldah Venables; - ; 24

Catherine L. Ryan; 23 June 1879; - ; Mary A., of Carrollton; Francis and Mary Ryan; - ; father died before June 1897; 74

Francis "Frank" L. Ryan; 9 November 1883; - ; Mary A., of Carrollton; Catherine and Mary Ryan; - ; father died before June 1897; 74

Mary E. Ryan; 27 March 1877; - ; Mary A., of Carrollton; Catherine and Francis Ryan; - ; father died before June 1897; 74

Michael Ryan; 15 February 1877; William Ryan, of Carrollton; - ; Patrick and William Ryan; - ; - ; 74

Patrick Ryan; 9 March 1881; William Ryan, of Carrollton; - ; Michael and William Ryan; - ; - ; 74

William Ryan; 15 December 1878; William Ryan, of Carrollton; - ; Michael and Patrick Ryan; - ; - ; 74

Name; Date of Birth; Father; Mother; Siblings; Other Relatives; Notes; Box Number

S Surnames

Frederick Sacket; - ; John H. Sacket; - ; Garry, John, and W. Gilmore Sacket; - ; file mentions Jonathon Sacket (died July 1869, of Seneca Falls, Seneca, NY); 25

Garry V. Sacket; - ; John H. Sacket; - ; Frederick, John, and W. Gilmore Sacket; - ; file mentions Jonathon Sacket (died July 1869, of Seneca Falls, Seneca, NY); 25

John H. Sacket Jr.; 20 May 1856; John H. Sacket; - ; Frederick, Garry, and W. Gilmore Sacket; - ; file mentions Jonathon Sacket (died July 1869, of Seneca Falls, Seneca, NY); 25

W. Gilmore Sacket; - ; John H. Sacket; - ; Frederick, Garry, and John Sacket; - ; file mentions Jonathon Sacket (died July 1869, of Seneca Falls, Seneca, NY); 25

Harriet B. Sackrider; 6 March 1882; Daniel A. Sackrider; - ; - ; - ; - ; 19

Ann Salisbury; - ; - ; - ; - ; - ; file mentions Lorentus Salisbury, in same envelope with Cyrus, Jane, Jenette and Maryon Salisbury; 77

Cyrus B. Salisbury; - ; - ; - ; - ; - ; file mentions Lorentus Salisbury, in same envelope with Ann, Jane, Jenette and Maryon Salisbury; 77

Frank Boyd Salisbury; about 1868; Foster B. Salisbury, died September 1871, of Humphrey; Elizabeth Thomas; Barnard Salisbury; MU Charles Thomas, MU Shepard Thomas, MA Janet Thomas; - ; 62

Jane S. Salisbury; about April 1842; - ; - ; - ; - ; file mentions Lorentus Salisbury, in same envelope with Ann, Cyrus, Jenette and Maryon Salisbury; 77

Jenette Salisbury; born 14 January 1844; - ; - ; - ; HU Mr. Babcock; file mentions Lorentus Salisbury, in same envelope with Ann, Cyrus, Jane and Maryon Salisbury; 77

Mable Salisbury; 1 August 1881; - ; Lavancha; - ; - ; - ; 61

Maryon Salisbury; - ; - ; - ; - ; - ; file mentions Lorentus

Name; Date of Birth; Father; Mother; Siblings; Other Relatives; Notes; Box Number

Salisbury, in same envelope with Ann, Cyrus, Jane and Jenette Salisbury; 77

Etta Sanderson; 7 October 1871; - ; - ; - ; HU Mr. Walton, GM Sylvia Crane; RE 1892, in Rochester, Monroe, NY, G- Thomas Mitchell, no relation; 26

Edna Sandstone; 25 May 1909; - ; Hannah, married Mr. True by September 1918; - ; PGF Henry Sandstone; Henry Sandstone adopted Edna, G- Charles H. Sandstone; 26

Adda J. Saunders; 5 November 1864; Hezekiah Saunders, died before April 1868; Julia; - ; - ; G- John Graves; 25

Walter B. Saunders; 13 May 1859; - ; - ; - ; - ; G- Nelson Saunders; 25

Elizabeth Savage; about 1892; - ; Elizabeth, died before 17 June 1909; Frank, Marguerite, Nellie and Patrick Savage, and Katherine Brundage; HU Mr. Rounds; father died May 1901; 59

Frank Savage; about 1895; - ; Elizabeth, died before 17 June 1909; Elizabeth, Marguerite, Nellie and Patrick Savage, and Katherine Brundage; - ; father died May 1901; 59

Marguerite Savage; about 1899; - ; Elizabeth, died before 17 June 1909; Elizabeth, Frank, Nellie and Patrick Savage, and Katherine Brundage; - ; father died May 1901; 59

Nellie Savage; about 1889; - ; Elizabeth, died before 17 June 1909; Elizabeth, Frank, Marguerite and Patrick Savage, and Katherine Brundage; - ; father died May 1901; 59

Patrick Savage; 21 May 1893; - ; Elizabeth, died before 17 June 1909; Elizabeth, Frank, Marguerite and Nellie Savage, and Katherine Brundage; - ; father died May 1901; 59

Albert Henry Saxton; 19 July 1822; Henry Saxton, died before May 1838; - ; Walter, Hannah, Baker, Frederick and Ebenzer Saxton; other relatives were Ruth Dixon and Daniel Dixon; G- Lucy Saxton; 76

Baker Leonard Saxton; 24 July 1825; Henry Saxton, died before May 1838; - ; Walter, Hannah, Albert, Frederick and Ebenzer Saxton; other relatives were Ruth Dixon and Daniel Dixon;

Name; Date of Birth; Father; Mother; Siblings; Other Relatives; Notes; Box Number

G- Lucy Saxton; 76

Ebenezer F. Saxton; 4 June 1832; Henry Saxton, died before May 1838; - ; Walter, Hannah, Albert, Frederick and Baker Saxton; other relatives were Ruth Dixon and Daniel Dixon; G- Lucy Saxton; 76

Emma Mary Saxton; 5 August 1884; Henry B. Saxton, died 23 October 1891; Mary Lauretta Reynolds, married Mr. Northrup by 20 October 1905; Florence and William Saxton; PGM Mariette Saxton, MGM Catharine Reynolds, A- Florence E. Saxton, U- John Reynolds, A- Katie Lawler, U- William Reynolds; - ; 19

Florence Anna Saxton; 1 June 1879; Henry B. Saxton, died 23 October 1891; Mary Lauretta Reynolds, married Mr. Northrup by 20 October 1905; Emma and William Saxton; HU Mr. Canfield (married before 2 October 1900), PGM Mariette Saxton, MGM Catharine Reynolds, A- Florence E. Saxton, U- John Reynolds, A- Katie Lawler, U- William Reynolds; RE 1900, in Syracuse, NY ; 19

Florence Eveline Saxton; 31 October 1856; Leonard B. Saxton, died 30 July 1864; - ; Henry Saxton; - ; - ; 26

Frederick Saxton; 2 Dec 1897/1909; Fred J. Saxton, of Onoville; - ; Genevieve Saxton; - ; - ; 61

Frederick A. Saxton; 13 June 1826; Henry Saxton, died before May 1838; - ; Walter, Hannah, Albert, Ebenezer and Baker Saxton; other relatives were Ruth Dixon and Daniel Dixon; G- Lucy Saxton; 76

Genevieve Saxton; 4 May 1893/1907; Fred J. Saxton, of Onoville; - ; Frederick Saxton; HU Mr. Cooper; attended school in Corydon ; 61

Hannah L. Saxton; 15 December 1823; Henry Saxton, died before May 1838; - ; Walter, Frederick, Albert, Ebenezer and Baker Saxton; other relatives were Ruth Dixon and Daniel Dixon; G- Lucy Saxton; 76

Henry B. Saxton; 17 May 1857; Leonard B. Saxton, died 30 July 1864; - ; Florence Saxton; - ; - ; 26

Name; Date of Birth; Father; Mother; Siblings; Other Relatives; Notes; Box Number

Walter Saxton; 12 March 1830; Henry Saxton, died before May 1838; - ; Hannah, Frederick, Albert, Ebenezer and Baker Saxton; other relatives were Ruth Dixon and Daniel Dixon; G- Lucy Saxton; 76

William Leonard Saxton; 10 November 1886; Henry B. Saxton, died 23 October 1891; Mary Lauretta Reynolds, married Mr. Northrup by 20 October 1905; Florence and Emma Saxton; PGM Mariette Saxton, MGM Catharine Reynolds, A- Florence E. Saxton, U- John Reynolds, A- Katie Lawler, U- William Reynolds; - ; 19

Laura Scheier; 2 May 1898; - ; - ; Theresa Scheier; U- Joseph Meier/Myer; RE 1920, in Canton, Starke, Ohio; 59

Theresa Scheier; 1 October 1899; - ; - ; Laura Scheier; U- Joseph Meier/Myer; - ; 59

Mary Schindler; - ; - ; - ; - ; - ; GGM left estate to Mary; 19

Frederick Schlittler; 17 August 1881; - ; Elizabeth, married Mr. Yewdell by July 1897; George and William Schlittler; A- Amelia Hoffman; - ; 19

George Schlittler; - ; - ; Elizabeth, married Mr. Yewdell by July 1897; Frederick and William Schlittler; A- Amelia Hoffman; - ; 19

William Schlittler; - ; - ; Elizabeth, married Mr. Yewdell by July 1897; Frederick and George Schlittler; A- Amelia Hoffman; - ; 19

John C. Schlosser; about 1904; - ; Frances; Joseph and Theodore Schlosser; - ; - ; 20

Joseph L. Schlosser; about 1905; - ; Frances; John and Theodore Schlosser; - ; - ; 20

Theodore Schlosser; about 1910; - ; Frances; John and Joseph Schlosser; - ; - ; 20

Emma Schmalz; about 1869; John Schmalz, from Germany; Mary, German speaking; Michael, Jennie and Gotlieb Schmalz; - ; - ; 60

Jennie Schmalz; about 1870; John Schmalz, from Germany; Mary, German speaking; Michael, Emma and Gotlieb

Name; Date of Birth; Father; Mother; Siblings; Other Relatives; Notes; Box Number

Schmalz; - ; - ; 60

Michael Schmalz; about 1865; John Schmalz, from Germany; Mary, German speaking; Jennie, Emma and Gotlieb Schmalz; - ; - ; 60

Arthur Schnell; 8 September 1909; - ; Delia J.; Edwin, Violetta, Irene, Norbert and Erwin Schnell; - ; money from F. H. Schnell estate's; 20

Edwin J. Schnell; 5 April 1898; - ; Delia J.; Arthur, Violetta, Irene, Norbert and Erwin Schnell; - ; received money from F. H. Schnell estate; 20

Erwin Schnell; 19 July 1895; - ; Delia J.; Arthur, Violetta, Irene, Norbert and Edwin Schnell; - ; received money from F. H. Schnell estate; 20

Irene Schnell; 14 August 1904; - ; Delia J.; Arthur, Violetta, Erwin, Norbert and Edwin Schnell; - ; received money from F. H. Schnell estate; 20

Norbert Schnell; 7 May 1907; - ; Delia J.; Arthur, Violetta, Erwin, Irene and Edwin Schnell; - ; received money from F. H. Schnell estate; 20

Violetta M. Schnell; 5 June 1900; - ; Delia J.; Arthur, Norbert, Erwin, Irene and Edwin Schnell; - ; received money from F. H. Schnell estate; 20

Edward J. Schnepel; 12 May 1876; George H. Schnepel, died 31 December 1883; Mary E., married Mr. Graff; - ; - ; - ; 26

Helen B. Schnepel; 3 May 1904; Edward J. Schnepel, died 19 March 1909 at Phoenix, Arizona; - ; - ; HU Irving Galuska, GU Charles Schnepel (died October 1925), GU John Schnepel (died 1922), GA Hannah Bedell; file mentions George H. Schnepel; 61

Burdette Scholl; 13 December 1902; - ; Mamie, of Allegany; Catherine and Gilbert Scholl; - ; father died 21 April 1905; 59

Catherine Scholl; 9 February 1897; - ; Mamie, of Allegany; Burdette and Gilbert Scholl; - ; father died 21 April 1905; 59

Gilbert Scholl; 19 April 1899; - ; Mamie, of Allegany; Burdette

Name; Date of Birth; Father; Mother; Siblings; Other Relatives; Notes; Box Number

and Catherine Scholl; - ; father died 21 April 1905; 59

Alice Schoonover; about 1906; - ; Nellie, of Ashford; - ; - ; - ; 60

Olive L. Schott; 3 July 1904; John Buckles; Elizabeth; - ; HU Walter W. Schott; - ; 26

John Schuler; 9 August 1886; Philip Schuler, died 20 May 1898; Julia, RE Marion County, West Virginia, in 14 September 1903; Nicholas Schuler; - ; - ; 19

Nicholas Schuler; 23 August 1882; Philip Schuler, died 20 May 1898; Julia, RE Marion County, West Virginia, in 14 September 1903; John Schuler; - ; - ; 19

Emma J. Schults; 30 July 1893; - ; - ; - ; - ; was bound to George W. Schults by Poor Authorities of Allegany County; 60

Minnie Neugart Schultz; 27 May 1876; Bart. Neugart; - ; - ; HU Mr. Schultz, married before 26 May 1897; - ; 19

Mary Schuster; 11 Dec 1908; - ; Emma; - ; - ; RE 1929, in Buffalo, file mentions John A. Schuster; 61

Clifton W. Schutt; about 1894; - ; Mary; L. D. V. and Ethel Schutt; U- Fred Schutt; money from John Schutt's estate; 58

Ethel R. Schutt; about 1892; - ; Mary; L. D. V. and Clifton Schutt; U- Fred Schutt, money from John Schutt's estate; 58

Helen Schutt; 12 Sept 1910; - ; Mary, married Mr. Applebee; - ; HU Mr. Frost; father died before July 1909 and received money from estate of Adah Boller; 61

L. D. V. Schutt; 4 March 1896; - ; Mary; Ethel and Clifton Schutt; U- Fred Schutt; money from John Schutt's estate; 58

Victoria Schwalb; about 1889; - ; - ; Anthony Schwalb; - ; - ; 60

Anna L. Scobey; 3 November 1886; - ; Hannah; Ruth Scobey; - ; RE 1908, Hazelhurst, Pennsylvania; 1910, in NY City and G-Fred Eckhart; 19

Ruth C. Scobey; 18 May 1889; - ; Hannah; Anna Scobey; - ; G-Fred Eckhart; 19

Ellen Louise Scofield; 26 May 1892, of Allegany; Willis J. Scofield, died 25 November 1907; Sarah; - ; - ; received money from estate of Ellen L. Smith; 59

Burt Scott; 17 or 30 January 1872; - ; - ; Frankie Groat; BIL

Name; Date of Birth; Father; Mother; Siblings; Other Relatives; Notes; Box Number

Frank Groat; first G- O. P. Scott, third G- John Oyer (his friend); 61

Elwin Charles Scott; 29 June 1897; Charles J. Scott, died before December 1910; Nettie A., of Humphrey, married Mr. Collie; Zer Scott; A- Myra E. Lexer; G- Frank J.Lexer; 59

Mildred Scott; 16 March 1867; - ; Elizabeth, of Olean; John and Sarah Scott; - ; - ; 60

Zer Allen Scott; 12 February 1895; Charles J. Scott, died before December 1910; Nettie A., of Humphrey, married Mr. Collie; Elwin Scott; A- Myra E. Lexer; G- Frank J. Lexer; 59

Elizabeth "Lizzie" L. Scudder; 7 June 1868; Alvin Scudder; Lodema Fenton, died 17 September 1868; - ; MGF John F. Fenton (died 11 September 1869). GU William H. H. Fenton (died 4 July 1887, of Carroll, Chautauqua, NY); money from estate of Reuben Fenton (died 25 August 1885); 29

Genevieve Scudder; 11 January 1868; Samuel Scudder, died before 8 October 1883; Amanda; - ; - ; - ; 29

Ralph Searl; 16 May 1877; - ; - ; Frank Searl; - ; file mentions paid for digging of grave on 20 May 1894, and paid for cemetery lot on 25 June 1894; 19

Mary Lennett Searle; 7 March 1910; Theodore Searl; - ; Roberta, Theodore, and William Searl; HU Mr. Wade; G- Florence A. Searl, Mary L. Adams left money to children; 20

Roberta Searle; 13 May 1905; Theodore Searl; - ; Mary, Theodore, and William Searl; - ; G- Florence A. Searl, Mary L. Adams left money to children; 20

Theodore A. Searle; - ; Theodore Searl; - ; Mary, Roberta, and William Searl; - ; G- Florence A. Searl, Mary L. Adams left money to children; 20

William A. Searle; 10 June 1906; Theodore Searl; - ; Mary, Roberta, and Theodore Searl; - ; G- Florence A. Searl, Mary L. Adams left money to children; 20

Dorothy C. Searles; 3 June 1848; George Searles; - ; John, Harmon and Eliza Searles; other relative was Adam Dockstader Jr.; heir of Dennis Searles; 26

Name; Date of Birth; Father; Mother; Siblings; Other Relatives; Notes; Box Number

Eliza H. Searles; 13 March 1839; George Searles; - ; John, Dorothy and Harmon Searles; HU Stillman Hodgeman, other relative was Adam Dockstader Jr.; heir of Dennis Searles; 26

Harmon D. Searles; 30 April 1842; George Searles; - ; John, Dorothy and Eliza Searles; other relative was Adam Dockstader Jr.; heir of Dennis Searles; 26

Charlie R. Sears; 22 June 1866; Delevan Sears, died 23 March 1869; Lucy, married Riley Baker; Clarence Sears; PG Resolved (left legacy) and Eliza Sears, A- Albina Sears, A- Eliza Stewart, (W- of Elisha Stewart), U- James Spencer; RE 1887, in Culbertson, Hitchcock, Nebraska; 26

Clarence S. Sears; - ; Delevan Sears, died 23 March 1869; Lucy, married Riley Baker; Charlie Sears; PG Resolved (left legacy) and Eliza Sears, A- Albina Sears, A- Eliza Stewart, (W- of Elisha Stewart), U- James Spencer; - ; 26

William H. Seeker; 18 April 1863; - ; Runette, of Dayton, married Leander Pierce 18 September 1867; - ; - ; father died 1862, all paternal relatives lived in Chautauqua County; 75

Manley A. Seekins; - ; Martin V. Seekins, died June 1862, of Ellington, Chautauqua, NY; - ; Monroe and Martin Seekins; U- Alfred B. Price, other relatives were Mattiah H., Lucinda and Emma F. Price; received pension money; 26

Martin V. Seekins; - ; Martin V. Seekins, died June 1862, of Ellington, Chautauqua, NY; - ; Monroe and Manley Seekins; U- Alfred B. Price, other relatives were Mattiah H., Lucinda and Emma F. Price; received pension money; 26

Monroe Seekins; - ; Martin V. Seekins, died June 1862, of Ellington, Chautauqua, NY; - ; Martin and Manley Seekins; U- Alfred B. Price, other relatives were Mattiah H., Lucinda and Emma F. Price; received pension money; 26

Laura Senear; - ; - ; - ; - ; money from Jesse J. Senear's estate ; 19

Lucinda Seneca; March 1855; - ; - ; - ; - ; G- Jane Snow, in same envelope with Alice Pierce and Eli Jimerson; 26

Henry L. Sessions; 16 January 1854; Albert Sessions; - ; John

Name; Date of Birth; Father; Mother; Siblings; Other Relatives; Notes; Box Number

and Martha Sessions; PG Israel and Sophia Sessions, MGF Brightman Brooks; received pension money, G- William Henderson Cady, file mentions Roquel N. Rogers; 26

John B. Sessions; 14 December 1857; Albert Sessions; - ; Henry and Martha Sessions; PG Israel and Sophia Sessions, MGF Brightman Brooks; received pension money, G- William Henderson Cady, file mentions Roquel N. Rogers; 26

Martha E. Sessions; - ; Albert Sessions; - ; Henry and John Sessions; PG Israel and Sophia Sessions, MGF Brightman Brooks; received pension money, G- William Henderson Cady, file mentions Roquel N. Rogers; 26

Mary Belle Sessions; 13 December 1888; Henry L. Sessions; Edna; - ; - ; RE 1906, in Buffalo, money from Mary Mitchell's estate ; 19

Henry Setoff; 26 June 1856; Louis Setoff, died before July 1870; - ; - ; - ; G- Frederick Dietz; 75

Alphonse Seyller; 10 Dec 1905; Julius Seyller, of Olean; - ; Louise Seyller ; - ; - ; 61

Louise Seyller; 29 March 1907; Julius Seyller, of Olean; - ; Alphonse Seyller ; - ; - ; 61

May B. Seymour; 12 March 1869; - ; Mina; - ; - ; father lived in Santa Ana, California, parents divorced September 1881; 61

George E. Shafer; 20 August 1861; - ; - ; - ; - ; G- Henry M. Seymour; 26

Oren R. Shaffner; 25 August 1902; Eugene Shaffner; - ; - ; - ; RE 1923, in Arcade ; 61

Aggie Shannon; 26 June 1884; James W. Shannon, died by 15 December 1895; Ella; Bessie Shannon; - ; - ; 19

Alice Shannon; 21 December 1861; Truman S. Shannon, died before 26 March 1867, served in Company K, 154th Regt.; Emily, married Mr. Rugg; - ; PG Samuel and Eliza Shannon, C- Eugene R. Hulbert (of Argo, Brookings, Dakota); - ; 25

Bessie Shannon; 2 July 1885; James W. Shannon, died by 15 December 1895; Ella; Aggie Shannon; - ; - ; 19

George D. Sharp; 1 July 1863; - ; Mary E., married Mr. Wheat;

Name; Date of Birth; Father; Mother; Siblings; Other Relatives; Notes; Box Number

- ; - ; - ; Stephen Bennet of Waverly, Tioga, NY, was appointed G- in the Tioga County Surrogate Court, John Boardman was also appointed G-; 26

Cladius W. Shattuck; May 1877; Lewis Shattuck, died 25 April 1879; Mary E., married Mr. Tafel; Lewis Shattuck; - ; RE September 1896, attended Department of Law at Yale; 19

Lewis E. Shattuck; about 1875; Lewis Shattuck, died 25 April 1879; Mary E., married Mr. Tafel; Cladius Shattuck; - ; RE September 1896, - ; 19

Adell S. Shaw; 25 October 1862; Cortland H. Shaw, died December 1880; Emma; Herbert, Nellie and Hamlin Shaw; - ; - ; 26

Hamlin F. Shaw; 11 February 1861; Cortland H. Shaw, died December 1880; Emma; Herbert, Nellie and Adell Shaw; - ; - ; 26

Irene Shaw; 14 February 1892; William B. Shaw; - ; Leo Shaw; HU Mr. Finn, married by 17 February 1913; - ; 19

Leo Shaw; 13 August 1888; William B. Shaw; - ; Irene Shaw; - ; - ; 19

Nellie G. Shaw; 30 March 1870; Cortland H. Shaw, died December 1880; Emma; Herbert, Hamlin and Adell Shaw; - ; - ; 26

Orlo J. Shean; 16 November 1869; John Shean; - ; - ; - ; Orlo died 1 June 1893, at Randolph, of Consumption; 60

Sarah E. Shear; - ; - ; - ; - ; - ; G- Grant Bailey, other minors listed in file were Libbie Shear Bailey and Emma Shear, H. J. Trumbull was administrator of estate; 62

Zilla Shedd; 3 October 1891; John B. Shedd, of Napoli; - ; - ; - ; received money from legacy from Amelia Hodges; 58

Lawrence Sheehan; 22 March 1908; Michael Sheehan, of Salamanca; - ; Mildred Sheehan; A- Edith Layton, A- Minnie Hatsaver, A- Maud Reed; mother died 3 Jan 1913; 61

Mildred Sheehan; 23 Feb 1906; Michael Sheehan, of Salamanca; - ; Lawrence Sheehan; A- Edith Layton, A- Minnie Hatsaver, A- Maud Reed; mother died 3 Jan 1913; 61

Name; Date of Birth; Father; Mother; Siblings; Other Relatives; Notes; Box Number

Mary Shehen; 17 May 1846; John Shehan, died before January 1863; - ; - ; - ; G- Erastus Willard; 75

Clyde C. Sheldon; about 1911; Leslie W. Sheldon; Ruby A., married Mr. Irish; - ; - ; RE 1926, in Grand Rapids, Michigan; 25

Leverett S. Shepard; August 1827; Chandler Shepard, died before November 1836, of Perrysburg; - ; Luther and Sarah Jane Shepard; U- Luther Gibbs; - ; 77

Luther G. Shepard; 10 September 1823; Chandler Shepard, died before November 1836, of Perrysburg; - ; Leverett and Sarah Jane Shepard; U- Luther Gibbs; - ; 77

Sarah Jane Shepard; June 1829; Chandler Shepard, died before November 1836, of Perrysburg; - ; Leverett and Luther Shepard; U- Luther Gibbs; - ; 77

Fred A. Sherlock; 18 October 1883; - ; Amarette; - ; - ; - ; 19

Grace M. Sherlock; December 1868; - ; - ; - ; HU Judson Sherlock, of Franklinville; - ; 62

Jay Sherlock; 24 April 1887; Judd M. Sherlock, of Olean; - ; John Sherlock; PGF Sylvester R. Sherlock; RE 1906, Seattle, King, Washington; 72

John Lee Sherlock; 25 January 1885; Judd M. Sherlock, of Olean; - ; Jay Sherlock; PGF Sylvester R. Sherlock; RE 1906, lived in Seattle, King, Washington; 72

Bennie Sherman; 20 March 1878; - ; Dora, of Otto, married Mr. Foster; Orlo Sherman; - ; received pension money; 60

Edward M. Sherman; 16 December 1829; Theodorus S. Sherman, died before September 1846; - ; Latusia Sherman; - ; file mentions Selana M. Sherman of Yorkshire; 76

Latusia Sherman; - ; Theodorus S. Sherman, died before September 1846; - ; Edward Sherman; - ; file mentions Selana M. Sherman of Yorkshire; 76

Orlo Sherman; 9 April 1885; - ; Dora, of Otto, married Mr. Foster; Bennie Sherman; - ; received pension money; 60

Nellie Sherry; 10 January 1885; - ; - ; Margaret, James, Anna, Peter and Will Sherry; - ; - ; 19

Name; Date of Birth; Father; Mother; Siblings; Other Relatives; Notes; Box Number

Caroline Shields; 4 April 1858; George Shields, died before 21 July 1866; Christina, married Mr. Gibson; George, Henry and John Shields; - ; - ; 25

George Shields; 13 October 1856; George Shields, died before 21 July 1866; Christina, married Mr. Gibson; Caroline, Henry and John Shields; - ; - ; 25

Henry Shields; 15 October 1861; George Shields, died before 21 July 1866; Christina, married Mr. Gibson; Caroline, George and John Shields; - ; - ; 25

John Shields; 4 February 1860; George Shields, died before 21 July 1866; Christina, married Mr. Gibson; Caroline, George and Henry Shields; - ; - ; 25

Mary Shingler; 9 October 1894; John L. Shingler; - ; - ; MGF Joseph Wartz/Wurtz, of Wyandale, Erie, NY; - ; 60

Doris J. Shipman; about 1906; - ; Lizzie A., married Mr. Collins; - ; - ; parents divorced; 58

Isaac K. Shippy; 13 October 1848; - ; - ; Kate, Sarah and Seville Shippy; other relatives were Rosell and Charlotte Shippy, and Gertrude Springer; Alfred was a brother who died before July 1862; 26

Sarah Shippy; 5 March 1842; - ; - ; Kate, Isaac and Seville Shippy; other relatives were Rosell and Charlotte Shippy, and Gertrude Springer; Alfred was a brother who died before July 1862; 26

Seville Shippy; 5 November 1845; - ; - ; Kate, Isaac and Sarah Shippy; other relatives were Rosell and Charlotte Shippy, and Gertrude Springer; Alfred was a brother who died before July 1862; 26

Keziah A. Shirline; - ; Henry A. Shirline, died before 5 December 1856; - ; - ; - ; G- Lewis P. Wheeler, indexed as Heziah Shirline; 26

Louise H. Shoemaker; - ; - ; Millie E.; - ; - ; - ; 19

Brady Shoff; 15 December 1911; Clair John Shoff, died 25 January 1928; step-mother was Lucille; Elizabeth Shoff, Ruth Adams, and Marion Miller (W- of Max Miller); BIL

Name; Date of Birth; Father; Mother; Siblings; Other Relatives; Notes; Box Number

Kenneth W. Barnes, other relative was Grace Seibert; - ; 20

Elizabeth Shoff; 24 May 1910; Clair John Shoff, died 25 January 1928; step-mother was Lucille; Brady Shoff, Ruth Adams, and Marion Miller (W- of Max Miller); BIL Kenneth W. Barnes, other relative was Grace Seibert; - ; 20

Ella F. Shorts; 2 February 1885; - ; - ; Edith and Willie Farnum; - ; G- A. D. Bedell, in same envelope with Jennie, Gertrude, Maude, Edith, Willie and Ellen Farnum; 42

Clara Shroeder; born about 1887; Leo Shroeder, of Olean; - ; Julia, Louisa, Deana, Grace and Samuel Shroeder; - ; - ; 60

Daniel C. Shroeder; 28 July 1895; Leo C. Shroeder; Mary; - ; - ; RE 1016 Washington St., Olean and Daniel lost his right foot above the ankle due to an accident while working for the Erie Railroad Company; 28

Deana Shroeder; about 1881; Leo Shroeder, of Olean; - ; Julia, Louisa, Clara, Grace and Samuel Shroeder; - ; - ; 60

Grace Shroeder; about 1883; Leo Shroeder, of Olean; - ; Julia, Louisa, Clara, Deana and Samuel Shroeder; - ; - ; 60

Julia Shroeder; 21 July 1876; Leo Shroeder, of Olean; - ; Grace, Louisa, Clara, Deana and Samuel Shroeder; - ; - ; 60

Louisa Shroeder; 3 January 1878; Leo Shroeder, of Olean; - ; Grace, Julia, Clara, Deana and Samuel Shroeder; - ; - ; 60

Samuel Shroeder; about 1889; Leo Shroeder, of Olean; - ; Grace, Julia, Clara, Deana and Louisa Shroeder; - ; - ; 60

Ella L. Shultes; about 1866; Henry Shultes, died March 1872; Emma; Ida Shultes; - ; - ; 25

Ida M. Shultes; about 1870; Henry Shultes, died March 1872; Emma; Ella Shultes; - ; - ; 25

Minnie Straight Sibley; - ; - ; - ; - ; - ; - ; 19

Cora E. Sigman; 4 October 1893; John H. Sigman; Laura Maria, died before 18 March 1918; - ; - ; G- Andrew F. Sigman (died 20 November 1913), second G- Alice Sigman (widow of Andrew Sigman), money from Albert Sigman estate; 19

F. Irving Sigman; 11 January 1889; John W. Sigman; - ; - ; U- Andrew F. Sigman; - ; 74

Name; Date of Birth; Father; Mother; Siblings; Other Relatives; Notes; Box Number

Ruth B. Sigman; 22 April 1892; John H. Sigman, of Cattaraugus; Laura Maria, of Cattaraugus; - ; U- Albert J. Sigman, died before April 1909; G- Alice Sigman, of New Albion; 74

Sylvia D. Sigman; 20 November 1899; John H. Sigman, of New Albion; - ; - ; HU Earl Baird, G- Catherine Pfleuger (died 7 March 1918, of New Albion, left legacy); also received money from estate of Albert Sigman, RE 1921, in Westfield, Chautauqua, NY; 1919, Columbia, Warren, Pennsylvania; 59

Clare Sill; 19 March 1895; - ; Minnie Reynolds; Clyde and Ona Sill; - ; G- Floyd Hogg (not related), G- Franklin Willard (died 3 January 1911); 60

Clyde Sill; about 1891; - ; Minnie Reynolds; Clare and Ona Sill; - ; G- Floyd Hogg (not related), G- Franklin Willard (died 3 January 1911); 60

Ona Sill; about 1888; - ; Minnie Reynolds; Clare and Clyde Sill; - ; G- Floyd Hogg (not related), G- Franklin Willard (died 3 January 1911); 60

George Dewey Silverheels; 8 August 1898; - ; Lillie, of Perrysburg; Lawrence Silverheels; - ; G- Ethel Bertha Dockstader, received pension money; 59

Lawrence O. Silverheels; 20 June 1896; - ; Lillie, of Perrysburg; George Silverheels; - ; G- Ethel Bertha Dockstader, received pension money; 59

Etta Simmons; 10 May 1870; Seth Simmons, died May 1885, of Great Valley; Rose Chamberlain, married Mr. Milks; Seth, Lola and Loretta Simmons; MGF Henry Chamberlain, A- Harriet Green, A- Sarah Morton, A- Mary Calkins; AKA Etta Milks, G- Wilson Howe, no relation; 62

Frederick Simmons; 4 June 1861; Richard Simmons, died before June 1879; - ; William Simmons; - ; G- Jerome Higbee; 25

Ida Simmons; 17 December 1876; - ; - ; - ; - ; RE 1897, in Springville, Erie, NY, G- Hudson Waite, received money from estate of Adam Simmons; 20

Lola Simmons; 26 October 1878; Seth Simmons, died May 1885, of Great Valley; Rose Chamberlain, married Mr. Milks; Seth,

Name; Date of Birth; Father; Mother; Siblings; Other Relatives; Notes; Box Number

Etta and Loretta Simmons; HU William McArthur (married 20 April 1897), MGF Henry Chamberlain, A- Harriet Green, A- Sarah Morton, A- Mary Calkins; RE 1898, at 74 Howell St., Buffalo, NY, G- Wilson Howe, no relation; 62

Loretta M. Simmons: 26 October 1878; Seth Simmons, died May 1885, of Great Valley; Rose Chamberlain, married Mr. Milks; Seth, Etta and Lola Simmons; MGF Henry Chamberlain, A- Harriet Green, A- Sarah Morton, A- Mary Calkins; G- Wilson Howe, no relation; 62

Seth J. Simmons; 9 June 1874; Seth Simmons, died May 1885, of Great Valley; Rose Chamberlain, married Mr. Milks; Loretta, Etta and Lola Simmons; MGF Henry Chamberlain, A- Harriet Green, A- Sarah Morton, A- Mary Calkins; G- Wilson Howe, no relation; 62

William Simmons; about 1859; Richard Simmons, died before June 1879; - ; Frederick Simmons; - ; G- Jerome Higbee; 25

Harry Cotton Simons; 30 April 1891; Charles E. Simons, of Great Valley; - ; - ; - ; first G- William H. Crandall (died 5 February 1905), second G- M. K. Harrison (no relation); 72

Harry L. Simons; - ; - ; - ; - ; - ; in envelope with Helen Elizabeth Simons, but nothing in the file mentions him; 26

Helen Elizabeth Simons; 26 February 1909; - ; - ; - ; - ; G- Dora R. Simons, in envelope with the name Harry L. Simons; 26

William H. Sirline; 24 May 1867; Charles Sirline; - ; - ; - ; - ; 26

Ada Sisson; about 1906; AF Rev. C. W. Batchelder; - ; Clara, Helen, Mamie and Elmer Sisson; MGF Clark Frank, of 1125 W. Henley St., Olean; AKA Ada Batchelder (was adopted on 13 May 1909); 59

Adell T. Sisson; - ; Henry Sisson, died January 1864, in Collins, Erie, NY; Malvina, married Mr. Darbee; - ; HU Adelbert Nash and their children were Charles and Perry Nash, of Dayton; G- Israel Alden, received pension money; 57

Clara Sisson; about 1894; - ; - ; Ada, Helen, Mamie and Elmer Sisson; MGF Clark Frank, of 1125 W. Henley St., Olean; - ; 59

Name; Date of Birth; Father; Mother; Siblings; Other Relatives; Notes; Box Number

Elmer Sisson; about 1902; - ; - ; Ada, Helen, Mamie and Clara Sisson; MGF Clark Frank,of 1125 W. Henley St., Olean; - ; 59

Helen Sisson; about 1897; - ; - ; Ada, Elmer, Mamie and Clara Sisson; MGF Clark Frank,of 1125 W. Henley St., Olean; - ; 59

Mamie Sisson; about 1899; - ; - ; Ada, Elmer, Helen, and Clara Sisson; MGF Clark Frank,of 1125 W. Henley St., Olean; - ; 59

Burt Henry Skeels; 26 July 1860; Luther Skeels, died January 1870, of Wellsville, Allegany, NY; - ; Daniel and Alsina Skeels; U- John Howlett; - ; 26

Daniel E. Skeels; 14 September 1862; Luther Skeels, died January 1870, of Wellsville, Allegany, NY; - ; Burt and Alsina Skeels; U- John Howlett; Daniel died 26 December 1875; 26

Evelyn Margaret Skinner; 15 March 1908; Archie Skinner, of Chicago, Illinois was employed as air brake inspector for Santa Fe RR; Ethel, abandoned Evelyn in April 1914; - ; PGM Anna Skinner (born about 1856, lived 109 S. 2nd St., Olean); parents separated 5 January 1914, had lived in Chicago; 60

Alida B. Slater; 16 May 1898; Levi Slater; - ; John Slater; HU Mr. Rice; received money from estate of Georgia Slater; 61

John Clarence Slater; 30 August 1900; Levi Slater; - ; Alida Slater; - ; received money from estate of Georgia Slater; 61

Andrew Slattery; about 1888; John Slattery; - ; Matthew and Michael Slattery; - ; - ; 20

Matthew Slattery; about 1886; John Slattery; - ; Andrew and Michael Slattery; - ; - ; 20

Michael V. Slattery; about 1893; John Slattery; - ; Andrew and Matthew Slattery; - ; - ; 20

Celia M. Slawson; March 1883; Newton S. Slawson, died 21 April 1883, of Perrysburg; Rose C.; Minnie and William Slawson; PGF Silus N. Slawson; - ; 60

Name; Date of Birth; Father; Mother; Siblings; Other Relatives; Notes; Box Number

Minnie R. Slawson; 12 January 1865; Newton S. Slawson, died 21 April 1883, of Perrysburg; Rose C.; Celia and William Slawson; PGF Silus N. Slawson; - ; 60

William "Willie" N. Slawson; 26 May 1873; Newton S. Slawson, died 21 April 1883, of Perrysburg; Rose C.; Celia and Minnie Slawson; PGF Silus N. Slawson; - ; 60

Ansel P. Slocum; 24 October 1866; Henry Slocum, died before October 1881; Elizabeth; Georgia Slocum; - ; - ; 62

Etta J. Slocum; 18 December 1868; Albert Slocum, died before 1882; Sarah, RE Michigan; Gilbert Slocum; U- Almanzo B. Slocum, and other relatives were Mary, Jersey, and Henry Slocum and Amelia Straight; - ; 62

Georgia A. Slocum; 30 January 1861; Henry Slocum, died before October 1881; Elizabeth; Ansel Slocum; - ; RE 1882, in Oswego County, NY ; 62

Gilbert M. Slocum; about 1870; Albert Slocum, died before 1882; Sarah, RE Michigan; Etta Slocum; U- Almanzo B. Slocum, and other relatives were Mary, Jersey, and Henry Slocum and Amelia Straight; - ; 62

Harley J. Slocum; - ; - ; - ; Henry Slocum; - ; G- Susan Feeney, no relation; 20

Henry A. Slocum; - ; - ; - ; Harley Slocum; - ; G- Susan Feeney, no relationship; 20

Henry P. Slocum; about 1837; Willard Slocum, died before April 1845; - ; Sylvia and Abner Slocum; - ; G- Ruth Slocum; 77

Sylvia Ann Slocom; about 1826; Willard Slocum, died before April 1845; - ; Henry and Abner Slocum; - ; G- Ruth Slocum; 77

Adeline S. Slover; 4 July 1834; James Slover, died before December 1850, of Machias; Anna; John Slover; - ; - ; 75

John Slover; 31 January 1832; James Slover, died before December 1850, of Machias; Anna; Adeline Slover; - ; - ; 75

Addie E. Smith; 1 November 1901; Lloyd D. Smith; - ; Percy and Jennie Smith; - ; RE 1921, in Battle Creek, Michigan, received legacy from Addie Y. McClure and money from

Name; Date of Birth; Father; Mother; Siblings; Other Relatives; Notes; Box Number

estate of Ella R. Smith; 60

Alice Smith; 21 May 1894; - ; Ida, married Mr. Oakes, of Red House; - ; - ; - ; 59

Alpha D. Smith; 24 October 1842; - ; Betsey, RE Erie County, Pennsylvania; Silvester, Mary, Elizabeth, Sarahett, and Desdemona Smith; - ; G- William H. Robinson; 25

Anson M. Smith; 2 February 1900; - ; Bessie A., of Salamanca; Frances and Grace Smith; - ; - ; 59

Arthur H. Smith; 29 June 1894; - ; - ; - ; A- Bessie M. Neuman; - ; 59

Arthur K. Smith; 3 March 1851; David E. Smith, died before February 1866; - ; - ; U- Nathaniel Smith; G- Elijah P. Smith (of Evans, Erie, NY); 75

Athalene M. Smith; about 1887; Andrew J. Smith; - ; Earl, Jane, Helen and Marguerite Smith; - ; AKA M. Athalene Smith, received money from Henrietta Smith's estate; 20

Clyde Z. Smith; about 1886; Z. W. Smith, lived in Neola, Greenbrier, West Virginia by January 1909; - ; Mary and Minnie Smith; - ; - ; 20

Cora Smith; about 1873; - ; - ; Nora, Matie, Emory, Viola and Grover Colf; - ; G- Andrew B. Neff, received money from estate of Delevan Colf, in same envelope as Colf children; 38

Daisy B. Smith; 8 August 1875; Chester Smith, of Ashford; - ; Emery, Wilma and Leena Smith; GM Louisa Bond, A- Mrs. Henry House; - ; 62

Desdemona T. Smith; 5 October 1847; - ; Betsey, residing in Erie County, Pennsylvania; Silvester, Mary, Elizabeth, Sarahett, and Alpha Smith; - ; G- William H. Robinson; 25

Doris Smith; 23 July 1903; Ray G. Smith, of Mansfield; - ; - ; - ; Ray adopted son of Willis P. Smith; 59

Earl Smith; 9 September 1890; - ; Lucy A., of Machias; May, Ralph and Elva Smith; - ; - ; 59

Earl R. Smith; about 1885; Andrew J. Smith; - ; Athalene, Jane, Helen and Marguerite Smith; - ; received money from Henrietta Smith's estate; 20

Name; Date of Birth; Father; Mother; Siblings; Other Relatives; Notes; Box Number

Edwin B. Smith; 23 January 1859; James H. Smith, died November 1863; Euphernia A. Burdick, married Mr. Miller; - ; MG Abel and Lucy Burdick; - ; 25

Elizabeth Smith; 31 March 1845; - ; Betsey, resided in Erie County, Pennsylvania; Silvester, Mary, Desdemona, Sarahett, and Alpha Smith; - ; G- William H. Robinson; 25

Elva M. Smith; 22 October 1894; - ; Lucy A., of Machias; May, Ralph and Earl Smith; - ; - ; 59

Emery J. Smith; 27 September 1873; Chester Smith, of Ashford; - ; Daisy, Wilma and Leena Smith; GM Louisa Bond, A- Mrs. Henry House; - ; 62

Emma L. Smith; 12 October 1868; - ; Charlotte E.; Nellie Smith; HU Mr. Crowell (married January 1889) ,GGF Augustine Smith (died before 12 February 1887, his will was probated in Erie County, NY); money from S. W. Smith's estate; 29

Flora Smith; 2 June 1860; Hiram A. J. Smith, died by 26 June 1867, was a Private in County H, 154th Regiment; - ; Isaac, Lucy and Jefferson Smith; MU Goodwin Staples, PU Sylvester Grover, A- Abigail R. Grover; mother died Spring of 1867; 26

Frances C. Smith; 25 July 1893; - ; Bessie A., of Salamanca; Anson and Grace Smith; HU Mr. Oakes; - ; 59

Frederick Smith; 18 February 1858; Henry Smith; Caroline, married Mr. Wilter; Henry, Matilda, Louisa and Lewis Smith; MA Mary Cook (W- of John Cook); received pension money; 26

George L. Smith; about 1873; William A. J. Smith, of Olean; - ; Ida and Goldie Smith; - ; - ; 60

George M. Smith; about 1876; Monroe Smith; - ; - ; U- Fred Smith; - ; 60

Glennie O. Smith; 4 October 1885; - ; Ophelia; - ; HU Mr. Ditcher; received money from estate of Harlan W. Smith; 20

Goldie F. Smith; about 1877; William A. J. Smith, of Olean; - ; Ida and George Smith; - ; - ; 60

Name; Date of Birth; Father; Mother; Siblings; Other Relatives; Notes; Box Number

Grace A. Smith; 4 February 1905; - ; Bessie A., of Salamanca; Anson and Frances Smith; - ; - ; 59

Grace W. Smith; 30 September 1872; - ; - ; - ; second C- David Steele; - 26

Harold C. Smith; 24 July 1900; - ; - ; - ; other relatives were Russell R. Smith and Wilma B. Smith; received money from estate of J. J. Smith; 59

Helen Boyd Smith; about 1892; Andrew J. Smith; - ; Athalene, Earl, Jane and Marguerite Smith; - ; received money from Henrietta Smith's estate; 20

Henry Smith; 18 March 1856; Henry Smith; Caroline, married Mr. Wilter; Frederick, Matilda, Louisa and Lewis Smith; MA Mary Cook (W- of John Cook); received pension money; 26

Henry W. Smith; 13 June 1885; - ; - ; - ; - ; G- Charles Winship, received money from estate of Royal Smith; 20

Ida Grace Smith; 37 June 1891; - ; - ; Jessie Smith; - ; G- Julia K. Smith; 60

Ida M. Smith; about 1877; William A. J. Smith, of Olean; - ; Goldie and George Smith; - ; - ; 60

Isaac J. Smith; - ; Hiram A. J. Smith, died by 26 June 1867, was a Private in County H, 154th Regiment; - ; Flora, Lucy and Jefferson Smith; MU Goodwin Staples, PU Sylvester Grover, A- Abigail R. Grover; RE 1869, Chautauqua County and mother died Spring of 1867; 26

Jane Celia Smith; about 1889; Andrew J. Smith; - ; Athalene, Earl, Helen and Marguerite Smith; - ; AKA Celia Jane Smith, received money from Henrietta Smith's estate; 20

Jefferson Smith; 1 July 1857; Hiram A. J. Smith, died by 26 June 1867, was a Private in County H, 154th Regiment; - ; Flora, Lucy and Isaac Smith; MU Goodwin Staples, PU Sylvester Grover, A- Abigail R. Grover; mother died Spring of 1867; 26

Jennie Smith; 16 March 1904; Lloyd D. Smith; - ; Percy and Addie Smith; HU Carl Schaffer, married October 1923; RE 25 Pine St., Salamanca, received legacy from Addie Y.

Name; Date of Birth; Father; Mother; Siblings; Other Relatives; Notes; Box Number

McClure and money from estate of Ella R. Smith; 60

Jennie E. Smith; 14 July 1869; Edwin Smith; - ; - ; HU Mr. North; - ; 25

Jessie Smith; 11 January 1884; - ; - ; - ; HU Mr. Damon; G- Charles Winship, money from estate of Royal Smith; 20

Jessie Edwin Smith; 18 July 1893; - ; - ; Ida Smith; - ; G- Julia K. Smith; 60

Leena M. Smith; 4 October 1879; Chester Smith, of Ashford; - ; Daisy, Wilma and Emery Smith; GM Louisa Bond, A- Mrs. Henry House; - ; 62

Leroy Smith; 17 November 1883; Edwin B. Smith; - ; - ; - ; G- Ben Green, no relation; 20

Lewis Smith; 12 November 1861; Henry Smith; Caroline, married Mr. Wilter; Frederick, Matilda, Louisa and Henry Smith; MA Mary Cook (W- of John Cook); received pension money; 26

Louisa Smith; 9 September 1859; Henry Smith; Caroline, married Mr. Wilter; Frederick, Matilda, Lewis and Henry Smith; MA Mary Cook (W- of John Cook); received pension money; 26

Lucy Smith; 26 July 1853; Hiram A. J. Smith, died by 26 June 1867, was a Private in County H, 154th Regiment; - ; Flora, Jefferson and Isaac Smith; MU Goodwin Staples, PU Sylvester Grover, A- Abigail R. Grover; mother died Spring of 1867; 26

Lynne J. Smith; 30 September 1899; - ; Flora, of New Albion, married Fred E. Bates; - ; - ; received money from estate of James R. Smith; 59

Marguerite L. Smith; about 1894; Andrew J. Smith; - ; Athalene, Earl, Helen and Jane Smith; - ; received money from Henrietta Smith's estate; 20

Mary L. Smith; about 1889; Z. W. Smith, lived in Neola, Greenbrier, West Virginia by January 1909; - ; Clyde and Minnie Smith; - ; - ; 20

Mary P. Smith; 19 July 1837; - ; Betsey, resided in Erie County,

Name; Date of Birth; Father; Mother; Siblings; Other Relatives; Notes; Box Number

Pennsylvania; Silvester, Elizabeth, Desdemona, Sarahett, and Alpha Smith; - ; G- William H. Robinson; 25

Matilda Smith; 8 July 1851; Henry Smith; Caroline, married Mr. Wilter; Frederick, Louisa, Lewis and Henry Smith; MA Mary Cook (W- of John Cook); received pension money; 26

May B. Smith; 16 August 1888; - ; Lucy A., of Machias; Elva, Ralph and Earl Smith; - ; - ; 59

Millie Smith; 12 May 1884; - ; - ; - ; - ; G- William H. Ruckh; 20

Minnie E. Smith; about 1875; Z. W. Smith, lived in Neola, Greenbrier, West Virginia by January 1909; - ; Clyde and Mary Smith; - ; - ; 20

Nellie L. Smith; 18 November 1866; - ; Charlotte E.; Emma Smith; GGF Augustine Smith (died before 12 February 1887, his will was probated in Erie County, NY)); money from S. W. Smith's estate; 29

Norman M. Smith; about 1856; - ; - ; - ; - ; G- Adeline Smith; 26

Ora Smith; about 1889; - ; Ettie; Rolla and Otis Smith; PGF Adam Smith; - ; 62

Otis Smith; about 1889; - ; Ettie; Rolla and Ora Smith; PGF Adam Smith; - ; 62

Percy A. Smith; 2 July 1899, of Great Valley; Lloyd D. Smith; - ; Jennie and Addie Smith; - ; received legacy from Addie Y. McClure and money from estate of Ella R. Smith; 60

Ralph L. Smith; 27 March 1902; - ; Lucy A., of Machias; Elva, May and Earl Smith; - ; - ; 59

Roger M. Smith; 16 November 1885; - ; - ; - ; U- Albert C. White, of Pomfret, Chautauqua, NY; Marvin E. Smith signed waiver giving up rights for guardianship; 74

Rolla Smith; about 1883; - ; Ettie; Otis and Ora Smith; PGF Adam Smith; - ; 62

Samuel E. Smith; 25 September 1879 ; John B. Smith, born about 1846, was a druggist; - ; - ; MGF Samuel Oosterhoudt, left Samuel shares of stock; - ; 20

Sarahett (Saryette) Smith; 1 October 1840; - ; Betsey, resided in Erie County, Pennsylvania; Silvester, Elizabeth,

Name; Date of Birth; Father; Mother; Siblings; Other Relatives; Notes; Box Number

Desdemona, Mary, and Alpha Smith; - ; G- William H. Robinson; 25

Silvester C. Smith; 1 May 1833; - ; Betsey, resided in Erie County, Pennsylvania; Alpha, Mary, Elizabeth, Sarahett, and Desdemona Smith; - ; G- William H. Robinson; 25

William A. Smith; 6 August 1876; - ; Emma, of New Albion; - ; - ; - ; 60

Wilma Smith; 3 June 1877; Chester Smith, of Ashford; - ; Daisy, Leena and Emery Smith; GM Louisa Bond, A- Mrs. Henry House; - ; 62

Elma Smyth; - ; - ; - ; - ; - ; - ; 60

Emma Sniter (Snider); 14 April 1852; Joseph Snider, died before December 1866; - ; - ; - ; G- Andrew Hirt; 75

Samantha C. Snow; November 1850; - ; - ; - ; - ; G- Charles Danley; 75

Augustus Snyder; about 1892; Homer Snyder; - ; Clyne, Elva and Esther Snyder; - ; - ; 20

Clyne Snyder; about 1893; Homer Snyder; - ; Augustus, Elva and Esther Snyder; - ; - ; 20

Elva Snyder; about 1903; Homer Snyder; - ; Augustus, Clyne and Esther Snyder; - ; - ; 20

Esther Snyder; about 1896; Homer Snyder; - ; Augustus, Clyne and Elva Snyder; - ; - ; 20

Eugene G. Snyder; 23 June 1867; Eugene E. Snyder, died 20 March 1867; Hellen M.; - ; GGF John Learn; - ; 25

Inez Pearl Snyder; 23 March 1899; - ; - ; - ; HU Merl G. Snyder, died in WWI, before April 1919; RE with A. W. Snyder, 22 Hancock St., Salamanca, parents RE 21 Hawley Ave, Bradford, G- John Walrath, no relation; 59

Wayland Snyder; 30 March 1910; - ; - ; Marie and Mildred Frost and Robert, Carl and Lynn Synder; - ; father died before July 1929, G- Leslie Ransom, neighbor; 61

John Sobkowiak; about 1881; - ; Anna, married Mr. Forman; Stanislaws, Victoria, Zelka, and Wladislaw Sobkowiak; - ; G- Charles Nies; 62

Name; Date of Birth; Father; Mother; Siblings; Other Relatives; Notes; Box Number

Stanislaws Sobkowiak; about 1874; - ; Anna, married Mr. Forman; John, Victoria, Zelka, and Wladislaw Sobkowiak; - ; G- Charles Nies; 62

Victoria Sobkowiak; about 1876; - ; Anna, married Mr. Forman; John, Stanislaws, Zelka, and Wladislaw Sobkowiak; - ; G- Charles Nies; 62

Wladislaw Sobkowiak; about 1883; - ; Anna, married Mr. Forman; John, Stanislaws, Zelka, and Victoria Sobkowiak; - ; G- Charles Nies; 62

Zelka Sobkowiak; about 1879; - ; Anna, married Mr. Forman; John, Stanislaws, Wladislaw, and Victoria Sobkowiak; - ; G- Charles Nies; 62

Clara Solarek; - ; Edward Solarek; Katherine Prebynske, married Martin Kasprick, she died 13 April 1922 in Lackawanna, Erie, NY; Harry Solarek; MGM Michaelino Prebynske, MA Frances Stanick; Martin Kasprick died 16 May 1921 while in the employ of S. Buffalo RR County, G- Anthony Prebynske, parents divorced 8 April 1913; 60

Harry Solarek; 20 May 1907; Edward Solarek; Katherine Prebynske, married Martin Kasprick, she died 13 April 1922 in Lackawanna, Erie, NY; Clara Solarek; MGM Michaelino Prebynske, MA Frances Stanick; Martin Kasprick died 16 May 1921 while in the employ of S. Buffalo RR County, G- Anthony Prebynske, parents divorced 8 April 1913; 60

Charlotte A. Sommer; 26 December 1905; Edward L.Sommer, of Olean; Hattie M.; - ; - ; - ; 61

Eugene F. Southwick; 21 Dec 1850; Frank B. Southwick, of Leon, died before Aug 1869; - ; - ; - ; G- Abiah E. Southwick; 62

Elbert E. Sowl; 1 July 1901; Elbert J. Sowl, died 6 September 1912 in Salamanca; Anna Belle O'Donnell, of Salamanca; John Sowl and Claudia S. Wagner; A- Ellen Crandall, A- Elizabeth O'Donnell, A- Sarah Hutchinson, A- Blanche B. Moore, A- Ira M. Brennanan, U- Benjamin E. O'Donnell; RE 32 Clinton St., Salamanca; 59

Name; Date of Birth; Father; Mother; Siblings; Other Relatives; Notes; Box Number

John O'Donnell Sowl; 5 May 1903; Elbert J. Sowl, died 6 September 1912 in Salamanca; Anna Belle O'Donnell, of Salamanca; Elbert Sowl and Claudia S. Wagner; A- Ellen Crandall, A- Elizabeth O'Donnell, A- Sarah Hutchinson, A- Blanche B. Moore, A- Ira M. Brennanan, U- Benjamin E. O'Donnell; RE 32 Clinton St., Salamanca; 59

Orson Spark; about 1874; David Spark, of New Albion; - ; - ; - ; - ; 62

Almon W. Spaulding; 13 November 1832; - ; - ; - ; - ; G- Ryland Spaulding; 25

Harry E. Spaulding; 24 July 1871; William H. Spaulding; Eliza J.; Preston Spaulding; - ; - ; 27

Lutie Spaulding; about 1873; L. H. Spaulding, died September 1878, of Otto; Alice; - ; U- Chester Soule, U- John Strickland, U- Owen Losee, U- H. P. Spaulding, A- Lucy Soule, A- Clara Strickland, A- Augusta Losee, A- Mary Stebbins, A- Bertha Stebbins; - ; 60

Preston D. Spaulding; 10 September 1867; William H. Spaulding; Eliza J.; Harry Spaulding; - ; - ; 27

Sarah A. Spears; 23 December 1848; Ezra Spears, died before January 1864; Amy J., died before January 1864; - ; - ; G- Myron M. Parker, in same envelope with William Jay Sprague; 27

Clara Belle Spencer; 2 January 1892; - ; - ; Floyd Spencer; U- Geo. W. Hotchkiss, U- Harrison Hotchkiss, C- Cassie McCovey; - ; 21

Doris Rita Spencer; about 1916; - ; Anna M., married Ralph O. Mullin; James Spencer; - ; - ; 20

Earl B. Spencer; - ; Burton M. Spencer, died before 1890; Della, RE Bath in 1891; Isabel Spencer; - ; G- Stephen J. Spencer; 62

Floyd Spencer; 12 May 1884; - ; - ; Clara Spencer; U- Geo. W. Hotchkiss, U- Harrison Hotchkiss, C- Cassie McCovey; - ; 21

Isabel Spencer; - ; Burton M. Spencer, died before 1890; Della, RE Bath in 1891; Earl Spencer; - ; G- Stephen J. Spencer; 62

Name; Date of Birth; Father; Mother; Siblings; Other Relatives; Notes; Box Number

James Spencer; 4 December 1900; - ; Anna, of Salamanca; John Spencer; - ; father died 8 January 1907; 59

James Francis Spencer; about 1911; - ; Anna M., married Ralph O. Mullin; Doris Spencer; - ; - ; 20

John Spencer; 4 December 1900; - ; Anna, of Salamanca; James Spencer; - ; father died 8 January 1907; 59

Lewis James Spencer; 5 December 1896; - ; Marion; - ; PGF Jacob K. Spencer, left part of estate for Lewis; - ; 20

Maggie E. Spencer; 14 April 1877; Azarah Spencer, he first lived in Oregon, then transferred the guardianship to NY, and then moved to Doniphan County, Kansas by May 1894; Mary W. Beck; Omer Spencer; HU Mr. Townsend; received money from estate of John Beck; 20

Omer W. Spencer: born August 1879; Azarah Spencer, he first lived in Oregon, then transferred the guardianship to NY, and then moved to Doniphan County, Kansas by May 1894; Mary W. Beck; Maggie Spencer; - ; received money from estate of John Beck; 20

Anna Spiesman; about 1896; - ; Mary; Harry, Matthew and Theresa Spiesman; - ; GF in Germany left money to Mary's husband; 20

Harry Spiesman; about 1894; - ; Mary; Anna, Matthew and Theresa Spiesman; - ; GF in Germany left money to Mary's husband; 20

Matthew Spiesman; about 1897; - ; Mary; Anna, Harry and Theresa Spiesman; - ; AKA Mathias Spiesman, GF in Germany left money to Mary's husband; 20

Theresa Spiesman; about 1901; - ; Mary; Anna, Harry and Matthew Spiesman; - ; GF in Germany left money to Mary's husband; 20

Willard Spoor; 27 July 1854; Abram Spoor, died before 21 June 1870; - ; - ; - ; G- Joseph A. Jewell; 27

Dulcenia Sprague; 13 or 30 October 1857; Henry Sprague, died before January 1864; Lois, married Mr. Slawson; Lorenzo Sprague; - ; G- George Beebe; 27

Name; Date of Birth; Father; Mother; Siblings; Other Relatives; Notes; Box Number

Henry W. Sprague; 4 August 1866; - ; - ; - ; U- Christopher L. Sprague; - ; 27

Lorenzo D. Sprague; 16 January 1848; Henry Sprague, died before January 1864; Lois, married Mr. Slawson; Dulcenia Sprague; - ; G- George Beebe; 27

William Jay Sprague; 1 January 1852; William Sprague; Amy J., died before January 1864; - ; PGF Arthur Sprague, U- Delos W. Sprague; G- Myron M. Parker; William lived with William Cooper (overseer of Poor), in same envelope with Sarah A. Spears; 27

Harold Spraker; - ; William Spraker Sr, first W- Susan E., who died August 1886; Phebe Hall, married 12 August 1886; William Spraker, HB Clarence Spraker, HB George Spraker, HS Lois Carr; - ; - ; 58

William Spraker; - ; William Spraker Sr, first W- Susan E., who died August 1886; Phebe Hall, married 12 August 1886; Harold Spraker, HB Clarence Spraker, HB George Spraker, HS Lois Carr; - ; - ; 58

Harriet Spreator; about 1873; - ; Catharine; - ; - ; - ; 62

Catherine M. Spring; about 1871; Samuel Spring, died July 1875; Ellen; Alfred, Samuel, Ellen, George and Levi Spring; - ; - ; 27

Ellen M. Spring; about 1868; Samuel Spring, died July 1875; Ellen; Alfred, Samuel, Catherine, George and Levi Spring; - ; - ; 27

George E. Spring; 27 October 1859; Samuel Spring, died July 1875; Ellen; Alfred, Samuel, Catherine, Ellen and Levi Spring; - ; - ; 27

Levi T. Spring; 28 June 1854; Samuel Spring, died July 1875; Ellen; Alfred, Samuel, Catherine, Ellen and George Spring; - ; - ; 27

Samuel A. Spring; about 1862; Samuel Spring, died July 1875; Ellen; Alfred, Levi, Catherine, Ellen and George Spring; - ; - ; 27

Charles W. Stacy; 15 July 1867; William H. Stacy, died

Name; Date of Birth; Father; Mother; Siblings; Other Relatives; Notes; Box Number

November 1869, of Yorkshire; Carrie A., married J. S. Roupe by 1876; Jennie Stacy; PGF William B. Stacy, MGM Parmelia Hadley; Charles died 22 August 1880; 62

Jennie B. Stacy; 22 July 1869; William H. Stacy, died November 1869, of Yorkshire; Carrie A., married J. S. Roupe by 1876; Charles Stacy; PGF William B. Stacy, MGM Parmelia Hadley; - ; 62

Herman Nelson Stadler; about 1897; Leonard A. Stadler, of Machias and Mansfield; - ; - ; - ; Hattie Nelson left legacy; 59

Elsie M. Stady; 9 January 1891; Fred Stady, of Machias; - ; - ; - ; - ; 59

Adella L. Stanley; 10 February 1860; Isaac C. Stanley, died 14 April 1875; Juliaette; Luther, Joseph, Ellen, and Addison Stanley; - ; - ; 25

Lucy Stanley; 29 May 1836; - ; - ; - ; - ; G- Joseph Weeden; 75

Frances Loretta Stapleton; 20 February 1890; - ; Mary A, of Salamanca; - ; - ; father died before February 1902; 74

Eugene Starks; - ; - ; Eliza; Sarah Starks; - ; - ; 25

Pearl Starks; 19 December 1890; - ; - ; - ; - ; G- Jennie Starks

Sarah Starks; - ; - ; Eliza; Eugene Starks; - ; - ; 25

ElRoy Starkweather; - ; William Starkweather, died before September 1866; Lucinda Shepard, married Mr. Rodgers; - ; MGF Thomas B. Shepard; received pension money; 27

Georgia M. Starr; about 1883; - ; Maria E., of Allegany; - ; - ; father died before November 1894 ; 61

Francis D. Stebbins; - ; Silvanus Stebbins; - ; Lyman Stebbins; - ; - ; 77

Lyman H. Stebbins; - ; Silvanus Stebbins; - ; Francis Stebbins; - ; - ; 77

Ella Steel; 20 November 1891; Jacob Steel, of Harmony, Butler, Pennsylvania; - ; Myrtle Steel; HU Mr. Boser; GM Pauline (Paulena) Brandel; - ; 21

Myrtle Steel; 6 December 1893; Jacob Steel, of Harmony, Butler, Pennsylvania; - ; Ella Steel; HU Mr. Hamilton; GM Pauline (Paulena) Brandel; - ; 21

Name; Date of Birth; Father; Mother; Siblings; Other Relatives; Notes; Box Number

Melvin C. Steffenhagen; 26 October 1906/1907; Frank R. Steffenhagen, of West Valley; - ; - ; MGF Truman D. Blowers; - ; 61

Alfred F. Steiger; 1 July 1904; - ; Amelia, born about 1874, of Olean; married Mr. Gagliardo; Erik J. Steiger; - ; - ; 61

Mary A. Stein; 21 July 1882; Mr. Camp, died 1 February 1897; Emma V., of Franklinville, married Mr. Sayles; Flora Camp; HU Frank Stein; received money from estate of Mary Mitchell, of Machias; 71

William Arlington Stephen; 12 December 1902; William Stephen, died 12 January 1913; Anne, of Olean; - ; - ; - ; 61

Warner D. Stetson; 8 May 1892; - ; - ; - ; - ; G- John M. Gena, needed guardian to enlist in Nat'l Guard; 60

Carol Young Stevens; 30 July 1878; David Stevens; Louise Young; David, Horace and Lawrence Stevens; - ; received money from estate of Helen Young Bailey; 61

David Louis Stevens; 18 June 1871; David Stevens; Louise Young; Carol, Horace and Lawrence Stevens; - ; received money from estate of Helen Young Bailey, RE 1892, Ironwood, Michigan; 61

Horace Jared Stevens; 5 January 1866; David Stevens; Louise Young; Carol, David and Lawrence Stevens; - ; RE 1887, in Ishpeming, Marquette, Michigan, received money from estate of Helen Young Bailey; 61

Lawrence P. Stevens; 17 September 1868; David Stevens; Louise Young; Carol, David and Horace Stevens; - ; RE 1891, in Ironwood, Michigan, received money from estate of Helen Young Bailey; 61

Madge Stevens; 28 January 1899; William H. Stevens; Lottie D.; Mary, Nancy and Ruth Stevens; - ; - ; 21

Mary Stevens; 20 January 1896; William H. Stevens; Lottie D.; Madge, Nancy and Ruth Stevens; - ; - ; 21

Nancy Stevens; 28 January 1902; William H. Stevens; Lottie D.; Madge, Mary and Ruth Stevens; HU Mr. Whitcomb ; - ; 21

Olin Stevens; 23 July 1909; Carol Y. Stevens; Inez; - ; - ; - ; 29

Name; Date of Birth; Father; Mother; Siblings; Other Relatives; Notes; Box Number

Raymond H. Stevens; 4 May 1901; Fred Stevens; Anna Blowers; - ; MGF Truman D. Blowers; - ; 61

Ruth Stevens; 9 August 1908; William H. Stevens; Lottie D.; Madge, Mary and Nancy Stevens; - ; - ; 21

Cora M. Stevenson; 16 March 1883; David Stevenson, died before July 1891; Angeline, of Humphrey, married Mr. Ball 20 March 1890; Frank, Joseph, Ella, William, James and David Stevenson; other relatives were Charles L. Tanner, George W. Tanner, and Mary W. Halladay; G- Wm. Morton (no relation), received pension money; 74

David C. Stevenson; 26 June 1885; David Stevenson, died before July 1891; Angeline, of Humphrey, married Mr. Ball 20 March 1890; Frank, Joseph, Ella, William, James and Cora Stevenson; other relatives were Charles L. Tanner, George W. Tanner, and Mary W. Halladay; G- Wm. Morton (no relation), received pension money; 74

Ella L. Stevenson; 30 January 1877; David Stevenson, died before July 1891; Angeline, of Humphrey, married Mr. Ball 20 March 1890; Frank, Joseph, David, William, James and Cora Stevenson; other relatives were Charles L. Tanner, George W. Tanner, and Mary W. Halladay; G- Wm. Morton (no relation), received pension money; 74

Frank J. Stevenson; 27 May 1871; David Stevenson, died before July 1891; Angeline, of Humphrey, married Mr. Ball 20 March 1890; Ella, Joseph, David, William, James and Cora Stevenson; other relatives were Charles L. Tanner, George W. Tanner, and Mary W. Halladay; G- Wm. Morton (no relation), received pension money; 74

James H. Stevenson; 31 March 1881; David Stevenson, died before July 1891; Angeline, of Humphrey, married Mr. Ball 20 March 1890; Ella, Joseph, David, William, Frank and Cora Stevenson; other relatives were Charles L. Tanner, George W. Tanner, and Mary W. Halladay; G- Wm. Morton (no relation), received pension money; 74

Joseph C. Stevenson; October 1874; David Stevenson, died

Name; Date of Birth; Father; Mother; Siblings; Other Relatives; Notes; Box Number

before July 1891; Angeline, of Humphrey, married Mr. Ball 20 March 1890; Ella, James, David, William, Frank and Cora Stevenson; other relatives were Charles L. Tanner, George W. Tanner, and Mary W. Halladay; G- Wm. Morton (no relation), received pension money; 74

William P. Stevenson; 10 March 1879; David Stevenson, died before July 1891; Angeline, of Humphrey, married Mr. Ball 20 March 1890; Ella, James, David, Joseph, Frank and Cora Stevenson; other relatives were Charles L. Tanner, George W. Tanner, and Mary W. Halladay; G- Wm. Morton (no relation), received pension money; 74

Ella S. Stewart; 18 September 1853; Anson Stewart, died before 21 August 1873; - ; - ; - ; G- William W. Henry; 27

Eva Stewart; 22 December 1857; step-father was Alpheus Wright; - ; Frances, Ira and Joseph Stewart; PA Amanda Haynes (W- of Daniel Haynes); paternal half-aunts Louis Bump (wife of Harly Bump) and Anna Clark, C- James Haynes, C- Ann Eliza Haynes, C- Lewis Bump, C- Sally Bump; G- Hiram Thorton, received money from estate of Allen Stewart, Alonzo R. Thorton (BIL of one of the parents); 27

Fenton M. Stewart; about 1892; Joseph T. Stewart; - ; Wesley Stewart; - ; - ; 21

Frances Adela Stewart; 15 December 1847; step-father was Alpheus Wright; - ; Eva, Ira and Joseph Stewart; PA Amanda Haynes (W- of Daniel Haynes); paternal half-aunts Louis Bump (wife of Harly Bump) and Anna Clark, C- James Haynes, C- Ann Eliza Haynes, C- Lewis Bump, C- Sally Bump; G- Hiram Thorton, received money from estate of Allen Stewart, Alonzo R. Thorton (BIL of one of the parents); 27

Ira Wellington Stewart; 28 May 1849; step-father was Alpheus Wright; - ; Eva, Frances and Joseph Stewart; PA Amanda Haynes (W- of Daniel Haynes); paternal half-aunts Louis Bump (wife of Harly Bump) and Anna Clark, C- James

Name; Date of Birth; Father; Mother; Siblings; Other Relatives; Notes; Box Number

Haynes, C- Ann Eliza Haynes, C- Lewis Bump, C- Sally Bump; G- Hiram Thorton, received money from estate of Allen Stewart, Alonzo R. Thorton (BIL of one of the parents); 27

Joseph Stewart; 17 March 1851; step-father was Alpheus Wright; - ; Eva, Frances and Ira Stewart; PA Amanda Haynes (W- of Daniel Haynes); paternal half-aunts Louis Bump (wife of Harly Bump) and Anna Clark, C- James Haynes, C- Ann Eliza Haynes, C- Lewis Bump, C- Sally Bump; G- Hiram Thorton, received money from estate of Allen Stewart, Alonzo R. Thorton (BIL of one of the parents); 27

Letha M. Stewart; 4 September 1906 ; - ; - ; - ; A- Sarah A. Collins, other relatives were Leo Stewart and Catherine Stewart; she lived with dad and step-mom, of Olean; 61

Marion Albertson Stewart; 22 February 1906; Joseph Stewart, lived at 207 E. Green St., Olean; - ; - ; - ; - ; 61

Wesley A. Stewart; about 1894; Joseph T. Stewart; - ; Fenton Stewart; - ; - ; 21

August Stier; 23 May 1885; - ; - ; John Stier; - ; - ; 21

Frederick Stillman; 20 March 1909; Thomas Stillman, married to Ina (McClure) Woolheiser on 11 June 1907 by Rev. Conrad at Arcade; Ina McClure, she abandoned the family with Wal Church, she died 18 June 1910; Marie Stillman; MG Nelson and Della McClure, PA Mary Meacham; - ; 59

Marie Stillman; 29 December 1910; Thomas Stillman, married to Ina (McClure) Woolheiser on 11 June 1907 by Rev. Conrad at Arcade; Ina McClure, she abandoned the family with Wal Church, she died 18 June 1910; Frederick Stillman; MG Nelson and Della McClure, PA Mary Meacham; - ; 59

Henry G. Stilwell; 15 April 1856; Lewis E. Stillwell; - ; Horace Stillwell; - ; - ; 27

Horace L. Stilwell; 17 July 1859; Lewis E. Stillwell; - ; Henry Stillwell; - ; - ; 27

Jennie B. Stimson; 20 June 1895; Harvey A. Bishop; Mabel M.; - ; HU J. Edward Stimson; RE at 626 ½ Kittaning Ave.,

Name; Date of Birth; Father; Mother; Siblings; Other Relatives; Notes; Box Number

Olean; 60

Ludwig Stoll; 7 March 1891; - ; Elizabeth, of Little Valley; - ; - ; - ; 72

Anson Stone; - ; - ; - ; - ; - ; in same envelope as Olive, Esther and Johnstone Stone; 20

Bradley L. Stone; - ; - ; - ; - ; - ; in same envelope as Eunice Stone; 20

Esther Stone; - ; - ; - ; - ; - ; in same envelope as Olive, Anson and Johnstone Stone; 20

Eunice Stone ; - ; - ; - ; - ; - ; in same envelope as Bradley Stone; 20

Gertie E. Stone; 29 August 1876; Sidney D. Stone; - ; - ; HU Mr. Bishop ; - ; 21

Johnstone Stone; - ; - ; - ; - ; - ; in same envelope as Olive, Anson and Esther Stone; 20

Lora Falk Stone; 18 March 1902; Mr. Falk; - ; Georgia Hall, Edith A. Sandy, and Florence F. Hagerdon; HU Wilber Stone, of Dayton; - ; 61

Mary Blanche Stone; Octobetr 1873; - ; - ; HS Lena Stone; U- Timothy Wilcox (of Leon), other relatives were Martha Frink, P. F. P. Crooken, Doris D. Penhollow; father died 11 November 1885 (of Milwaukee, Wisconsin), received money from estate of Burney Stone; 62

Minnie M. Stone; 10 October 1861; John S. Stone, died before September 1864; Frances D., married Mr. Locke; - ; - ; received pension money; 27

Olive Stone; - ; - ; - ; - ; - ; in same envelope as Johnstone, Anson and Esther Stone; 20

Ralph L. Stone; 7 June 1906; Anson Stone Jr.; Anna B., died 13 June 1925 in Mansfield; Ross Stone; - ; - ; 26

Ross A. Stone; 12 October 1908; Anson Stone Jr.; Anna B., died 13 June 1925 in Mansfield; Ralph Stone; - ; - ; 26

Alexander J. Stothard; about 1880; - ; - ; Annie, Mary, Euphemia, William, James and Sarah Stothard; A- Anna Murphy and MA Mary Crowley; - ; 62

Name; Date of Birth; Father; Mother; Siblings; Other Relatives; Notes; Box Number

Annie G. Stothard; about 1875; - ; - ; Alexander, Mary, Euphemia, William, James and Sarah Stothard; A- Anna Murphy and MA Mary Crowley; - ; 62

Euphemia G. Stothard; about 1878; - ; - ; Alexander, Mary, Annie, William, James and Sarah Stothard; A- Anna Murphy and MA Mary Crowley; - ; 62

James S. Stothard; about 1886; - ; - ; Alexander, Mary, Annie, William, Euphemia and Sarah Stothard; A- Anna Murphy and MA Mary Crowley; - ; 62

Mary C. Stothard; about 1877; - ; - ; Alexander, James, Annie, William, Euphemia and Sarah Stothard; A- Anna Murphy and MA Mary Crowley; - ; 62

Sarah Stothard; about 1888; - ; - ; Alexander, James, Annie, William, Euphemia and Mary Stothard; A- Anna Murphy and MA Mary Crowley; - ; 62

William L. Stothard; about 1881; - ; - ; Alexander, James, Annie, Sarah, Euphemia and Mary Stothard; A- Anna Murphy and MA Mary Crowley; - ; 62

Ailen Stowell; about 1884; Calvin S. Stowell, died August 1892; Sarah W.; Louis, Fannie, Calvin, Fredrick, and Grace Stowell; - ; - ; 21

Calvin S. Stowell; about 1889; Calvin S. Stowell, died August 1892; Sarah W.; Louis, Fannie, Ailen, Fredrick, and Grace Stowell; - ; - ; 21

Fannie Stowell; about 1881; Calvin S. Stowell, died August 1892; Sarah W.; Louis, Calvin, Ailen, Fredrick, and Grace Stowell; - ; - ; 21

Fredrick Stowell; about 1892; Calvin S. Stowell, died August 1892; Sarah W.; Louis, Calvin, Ailen, Fannie, and Grace Stowell; - ; - ; 21

Grace Stowell; about 1887; Calvin S. Stowell, died August 1892; Sarah W.; Louis, Calvin, Ailen, Fannie, and Fredrick Stowell; - ; - ; 21

Louis W. Stowell; about 1877; Calvin S. Stowell, died August 1892; Sarah W.; Grace, Calvin, Ailen, Fannie, and Fredrick

Name; Date of Birth; Father; Mother; Siblings; Other Relatives; Notes; Box Number

Stowell; - ; - ; 21

Allen G. Straight; 21 July 1883; Charles D. Straight; Mabel; Emily Straight; - ; - ; 21

Emily Straight; 2 August 1885; Charles D. Straight; Mabel; Allen Straight; - ; - ; 21

John R. Straight; 25 October 1882; Charles B. Straight, died 23 March 1884; Jennie M.; - ; - ; - ; 21

Laura A. Strait; 12 October 1873; - ; - ; - ; - ; - ; 21

Dan Allen Strickland; 1 May 1849; Walter H. Strickland; - ; John and Laura Strickland; - ; money from estate of Dan Allen; 21

John Platt Strickland; 23 June 1846; Walter H. Strickland; - ; Dan and Laura Strickland; - ; money from estate of Dan Allen; 21

Laura Ann Strickland; 6 November 1844; Walter H. Strickland; - ; Dan and John Strickland; HU Mr. Smith; money from estate of Dan Allen; 21

Frank D. Stringham; 9 Dec 1872; - ; Maria Poor; - ; MGF Franklin Poor; RE Topeka, Shawnee, Kansas; 61

Abigail Strong; 29 June 1840; David Strong, of Randolph; - ; Romeo and Mary Strong; MGF Joseph Stanley, PGF Clement Strong; PU Azael Losee, MU Isaac Stanley, MU Harris Aldrich, MU Orange Abbey, MU Orlando Fisher; - ; 75

Adner E. Strong; - ; - ; - ; - ; - ; G- David Whipple and Kane County, Illinois, has probate records for estate; 76

Bertha M. Strong; 12 October 1866; - ; Helen G.; - ; - ; - ; 49

Mary Strong; 1 August 1843; David Strong, of Randolph; - ; Romeo and Abigail Strong; MGF Joseph Stanley, PGF Clement Strong; PU Azael Losee, MU Isaac Stanley, MU Harris Aldrich, MU Orange Abbey, MU Orlando Fisher; - ; 75

Olive E. Strong; 30 September 1890; - ; Emeline, of Farmersville; - ; HU Mr. Roblee, married about 1909; father died before June 1899 and received money from estate of Wallace Strong; 72

Name; Date of Birth; Father; Mother; Siblings; Other Relatives; Notes; Box Number

Romeo D. Strong; 24 April 1836 ; David Strong, of Randolph; - ; Mary and Abigail Strong; MGF Joseph Stanley, PGF Clement Strong; PU Azael Losee, MU Isaac Stanley, MU Harris Aldrich, MU Orange Abbey, MU Orlando Fisher; - ; 75

Franklin Strope; 5 March 1856; Levi W. Strope, died March 1867, of Persia; step-mom was Betsey; Frederick and Eveline Strope; - ; G- Frank A. Newell; 75

Frederick J. Strope; 30 January 1854; Levi W. Strope, died March 1867, of Persia; step-mom was Betsey; Franklin and Eveline Strope; - ; G- Frank A. Newell; 75

Adeline Struble; 25 April 1899; William Struble, died 19 March 1904, of Olean; Bessie B., married Mr. Irish, RE 1925 in Ft. Meade, Polk, Florida; Paul and Robert Struble; AF Arthur Bailey, A- Nellie Harter, A- Bertha Keeler; AKA Adeline Bailey, adopted on 11 November 1904; 59

Paul Struble; 12 July 1901; William Struble, died 19 March 1904, of Olean; Bessie B., married Mr. Irish, RE 1925 Ft. Meade, Polk, Florida; Adeline and Robert Struble; A- Nellie Harter, A- Bertha Keeler; - ; 59

Robert Clarence Struble; 23 April 1903; William Struble, died 19 March 1904, of Olean; Bessie B., married Mr. Irish, RE 1925 Ft. Meade, Polk, Florida; Adeline and Paul Struble; A- Nellie Harter, A- Bertha Keeler; - ; 59

Cora V. Stuart; 22 November 1849; William H. Stuart; Barbara A., died October 1862; Glenn and Maud Stuart; - ; - ; 27

Glenn Douglas Stuart; 15 February 1859; William H. Stuart; Barbara A., died October 1862; Cora and Maud Stuart; - ; - ; 27

Maud Sibyl Stuart; 29 September 1860; William H. Stuart; Barbara A., died October 1862; Cora and Glenn Stuart; - ; - ; 27

Florence Sullivan; 8 September 1897; - ; Josie, RE 628 E. State St., Salamanca; - ; - ; father died 7 November 1916 ; 60

Leonard D. Sullivan; about 1911; Dennis J. Sullivan; - ; - ; - ;

Name; Date of Birth; Father; Mother; Siblings; Other Relatives; Notes; Box Number

was hit by a car driven by Edward B. Vreeland on 11 June 1922; 25

Margaret Sullivan; 28 June 1886; Mr. McMahon; - ; - ; HU Jerry H. Sullivan; money from Edward McMahon's estate; 27

Thomas J. Sullivan; 6 February 1889; Michael Sullivan; - ; - ; - ; - ; 21

Leo J. Sumner; 24 February 1894; Joseph Callihan, of Machias; Etta Sumner, RE Columbia Station, Lorain, Ohio; - ; AF and MU George Sumner, AM Rosa Baker (died April 1908 in Machias), adopted MU Arunah Baker; Leo was adopted in Lorain County, Ohio on 21 March 1899, parents divorced and at the time lived in Ohio; 59

Ettie M. Sutherland; 16 May 1870; William H. Sutherland, crippled soldier; Mary J.; William and Hewitt Sutherland; - ; G- John Hacket, no relation; 60

Hewitt "Hugh" Sutherland; 10 March 1874; William H. Sutherland, crippled soldier; Mary J.; William and Ettie Sutherland; - ; G- John Hacket, no relation; 60

Inez G. Sutherland; 10 October 1900; William A. Sutherland; - ; Vera Sutherland; - ; G- Carrie Sutherland; 61

Ralph Sutherland; 5 January 1900; Fred Crook, died 1917, Isabella Sutherland, died 2 December 1919; George and Frank Crook; step-father was Herman Gilbert (married Isabella 27 December 1918 in Allegany), MG (adopted Isabella) Edward and Mary Elizabeth Sutherland. Isabella indentured to them 1878, they legally adopted Isabella, PG Charles and Mina Crook, GA Harriet Adsit, GU Alfred Swift, GU Volorous Swift; born after marriage of Fred and Isabella Sutherland, Mary E. Sutherland died 27 April 1920 in Limestone; 53

Vera H. Sutherland; 15 April 1897; William A. Sutherland; - ; Inez Sutherland; - ; RE 1918, in Grand Rapids, Michigan, G- Carrie Sutherland; 61

William A. Sutherland; 26 May 1872; William H. Sutherland, crippled soldier; Mary J.; Hewitt and Ettie Sutherland; - ; G-

Name; Date of Birth; Father; Mother; Siblings; Other Relatives; Notes; Box Number

John Hacket, no relation; 60

Veronica Agnes Sutter; 20 January 1899; George Sutter, of 1301 W. Sullivan St., Olean; - ; - ; - ; - ; 59

Gertrude Swain; 1 March 1844; John Marvin Swain, died before August 1860; - ; Helen Swain; - ; G- Edwin C. Durfee; 75

Helen Swain; 22 June 1846; John Marvin Swain, died before August 1860; - ; Gertrude Swain; - ; G- Edwin C. Durfee; 75

Blanch Pearl Swartz; about 1887; Francis Swartz, died 12 January 1890; Hattie, married Mr. Carr before 1892; Elenora and Peter Swartz; - ; - ; 21

Elenora M. Swartz; about 1885; Francis Swartz, died 12 January 1890; Hattie, married Mr. Carr before 1892; Blanch and Peter Swartz; - ; - ; 21

Elmer W. Swartz; 30 May 1861; William Swartz, died December 1861; Mary P., married Mr. Bradford by October 1871; Ida Swartz; - ; - ; 25

Harold Swartz; about 1899; - ; - ; - ; PGM Katherine Swartz; mother was in Gowanda Hospital; 61

Ida Jane Swartz; 19 August 1857; William Swartz, died December 1861; Mary P., married Mr. Bradford by October 1871; Elmer Swartz; - ; - ; 25

Marion I. Swartz; 3 April 1900; Ralph, RE 518 1st Ave, Olean; Frankie; - ; - ; - ; 60

Ada L. Sweet; 22 June 1880; Edgar Sweet, died March 1890, of Lander, Warren, Pennsylvania; Alice, married Charles Rowland; Alice, William, Lizzie and Mary Sweet; - ; - ; 61

Alice May Sweet; 25 February 1885; Edgar Sweet, died March 1890, of Lander, Warren, Pennsylvania; Alice, married Charles Rowland; Ada, William, Lizzie and Mary Sweet; - ; - ; 61

William Edgar Sweet; 20 May 1888; Edgar Sweet, died March 1890, of Lander, Warren, Pennsylvania; Alice, married Charles Rowland; Ada, Alice, Lizzie and Mary Sweet; - ; - ; 61

Blanche S. Sweitzer; 14 March 1871; - ; Caroline, born about

Name; Date of Birth; Father; Mother; Siblings; Other Relatives; Notes; Box Number

1830 (last name was Reed in 1890); - ; HU George G. Sweitzer, died January 1890, had a child; father went to Wyoming Territory, G- Nicholas Franchot; 60

Douglas Swift; 26 April 1892; George H. Swift; Lucy E.; - ; U- Simon P. Swift; - ; 60

Leslie Swift; 4 June 1897; John Poole, lived in Oramel; - ; - ; - ; mother lived with man named Hunywood, G- Harry Richardson; 60

Name; Date of Birth; Father; Mother; Siblings; Other Relatives; Notes; Box Number

T Surnames

Asher A. Talbot; 31 January 1878; Stephen Talbot, died before 1884, of Franklinville; Roxanna, married George B. Matteson; Bessie and William Talbot; - ; received real estate located in Sylvester, Michigan; 63

Bessie A. Talbot; 11 July 1868; Stephen Talbot, died before 1884, of Franklinville; Roxanna, married George B. Matteson; Asher and William Talbot; HU Mr. Pinney ; received real estate located in Sylvester, Michigan; 63

William M. Talbot; 27 Mary 1865; Stephen Talbot, died before 1884, of Franklinville; Roxanna, married George B. Matteson; Asher and Bessie Talbot; - ; received real estate located in Sylvester, Michigan; 63

Harold Leslie Tapp; 10 February 1907; William J. Tapp, of Portville; Parma Belle; William, Margaret and Theodore Tapp; step-mother was Carrie L. Tapp; - ; 62

Margaret Elizabeth Tapp; 29 July 1905; William J. Tapp, of Portville; Parma Belle; William, Harold and TheodoreTapp; step-mother was Carrie L. Tapp; - ; 62

Theodore Leland Tapp; about 1910; William J. Tapp, of Portville; Parma Belle; William, Harold and Margaret Tapp; step-mother was Carrie L. Tapp; - ; 62

William Wayne Tapp; 19 March 1903; William J. Tapp, of Portville; Parma Belle; Theodore, Harold and Margaret Tapp; step-mother was Carrie L. Tapp; - ; 62

F. Grace Tarbox; 4 April 1877; Luther W. Tarbox, died 23 October 1891, in Dayton; Alice, married Millard Hinman; Irving and Luther Tarbox; - ; - ; 30

Grace R. Tarbox; - ; - ; - ; - ; - ; G- Giles Johnson; 63

Irving A. Tarbox; 26 October 1873; Luther W. Tarbox, died 23 October 1891, in Dayton; Alice, married Millard Hinman; F. Grace and Luther Tarbox; - ; - ; 30

Luther "Willie" William Tarbox; 26 July 1879; Luther W.

Name; Date of Birth; Father; Mother; Siblings; Other Relatives; Notes; Box Number

Tarbox, died 23 October 1891, in Dayton; Alice, married Millard Hinman; F. Grace and Irving Tarbox; - ; - ; 30

Stephan A. Tatar; 25 March 1905; Stephen Tatar, of Lebanon, Pennsylvania; - ; - ; - ; needed guardian for a lawsuit against Spero Krusos because of an automobile accident that happened 1 September 1924; 62

John Tatsis; about 1919; Gust Tatsis; - ; - ; - ; RE 11 E. State St., Salamanca; 30

Athalinda Ann Taylor; 23 November 1861; Benjamin F. Taylor, died before July 1866 while in service of the Army; Amie I. Warner, married Mr. Babcock; - ; PG Asahel and Mary Taylor, MGF Alpheus Warner; - ; 30

Charles Taylor; - ; - ; - ; Ruth Taylor; - ; Estella McAuliffe's will stated that the children's G- should be Clara Garr; 61

Cora A. Taylor; about 1864; - ; - ; - ; U- Joseph Lingenfelter; father in Michigan ; 63

Edwin L. Taylor; 6 Apr 1878; Emory Taylor, of Jamestown, left family when Edwin was baby; Sylvia Kellogg, of Leon; - ; MGF Edwin A. Kellogg (died 8 February 1892), U- Albert Kellogg; - ; 61

Emma Taylor; 25 March 1866; J. M. Bargy; - ; Sylvanus, Mary, Minnie and Devillo Bargy; HU James Taylor, A- Emily Millhollen, U- Devello Bargy; - ; 37

Franklin W. Taylor; 7 December 1869; Ira C. Taylor; Virginia; - ; GM Mrs. L. Wasson, A- Mrs. C. H. Rockwood; parents divorced 24 April 1876 (in Erie, Erie, Pennsylvania,) received money from estate of Sam Taylor (of Hudson, Bates, Missouri), file mentions Lewella Brooks Hubbard, child of James Brooks; 63

Ruth Taylor; - ; - ; - ; Charles Taylor; - ; Estella McAuliffe's will stated that the children's G- should be Clara Garr; 61

Mary Jane Ten Broeck; - ; - ; - ; - ; - ; G- Jonas K. Button; 30

Edwin C. Terhune; 16 October 1899; Edwin R. Terhune; Genevieve; - ; - ; Mary L. Adams left legacy; 62

Amy Belle Terry; 3 December 1886; William Terry; Arabella

Name; Date of Birth; Father; Mother; Siblings; Other Relatives; Notes; Box Number

"Belle"; - ; HU G. L. Robson, U- James Morris, of Franklinville; - ; 61

Charles Monroe Thayer; 11 March 1853; William Thayer; Ann E. Swarthout; Martha and Rosina Thayer; MGF Oakley Swarthout, PGF Daniel W. Thayer, PU Jacob Thayer, PU Amariah Thayer, PU George Thayer, PU Daniel Thayer, PA Phebe (W- of Oakley Swarthout), PA- Mercy Swarthout, PA Laura (W- of Daniel Hoyt), MU Alexander Swarthout, MU John Swarthout, MA Martha (W- of Milo Meacham), MA Jane Swarthout; AKA Monroe Thayer; 30

Martha Jane Thayer; 28 March 1850; William Thayer; Ann E. Swarthout; Charles and Rosina Thayer; HU Mr. Ball, MGF Oakley Swarthout, PGF Daniel W. Thayer, PU Jacob Thayer, PU Amariah Thayer, PU George Thayer, PU Daniel Thayer, PA Phebe (W- of Oakley Swarthout), PA- Mercy Swarthout, PA Laura (W- of Daniel Hoyt), MU Alexander Swarthout, MU John Swarthout, MA Martha (W- of Milo Meacham), MA Jane Swarthout; AKA Monroe Thayer; 30

Rosina "Rose" Thayer; 18 February 1856; William Thayer; Ann E. Swarthout; Charles and Martha Thayer; HU Mr. Reynolds, MGF Oakley Swarthout, PGF Daniel W. Thayer, PU Jacob Thayer, PU Amariah Thayer, PU George Thayer, PU Daniel Thayer, PA Phebe (W- of Oakley Swarthout), PA- Mercy Swarthout, PA Laura (W- of Daniel Hoyt), MU Alexander Swarthout, MU John Swarthout, MA Martha (W- of Milo Meacham), MA Jane Swarthout; AKA Monroe Thayer; 30

William W. Thayer; - ; Lemuel Thayer, died before October 1833; - ; - ; - ; G- William Wilcox; 77

Ellen Theimer; 12 March 1859; Christian Theimer, died October 1864; Catharine, married Mr. Boehler; Pauline Theimer; - ; - ; 25

Pauline Theimer; 25 May 1861; Christian Theimer, died October 1864; Catharine, married Mr. Boehler; Ellen Theimer; - ; - ; 25

Harry E. Thomas; 21 June 1881; Edgar Thomas; - ; - ; - ;

Name; Date of Birth; Father; Mother; Siblings; Other Relatives; Notes; Box Number

received money from estate of Mary A. Thomas; 62

Mary Meech Thomas; 13 November 1878; Melvin Meech, born - about 1832, died 3 or 4 May 1889; Ida Brooks, born about 1861, married Charles LaPoint in June 1889; HU Morris Thomas, PA-Minerva Meech Smith (married Mr. Jenks), A- Sarah Wells, A- Evaline Howell, MU Emmett B. Brooks; Ida Brooks mother died 3 December 1886 in Marseille, NY, Melvin Meech's mom died about 1862, Melvin's dad died about 1876. Ida Brooks had a daughter, Jennie, who was the daughter of Philetus Cook. Ida and Philetus weren't married. The child was placed in the Utica Asylum and bound out to a family with last name of Foster. Philetus Cook's father is Alonzo Cook. Melvin Meech and Ida Brooks were married by Edwin Bush; 50

Frank H. Thompson; 29 April 1857; Welcome A. Thompson, died July 1865, of Granville, Washington, NY; Rachel J., married Mr. Dewey; Fred Thompson; other relatives were Emeline Pierce and Millard Hinman; received pension money; 30

Fred W. Thompson; 29 June 1861; Welcome A. Thompson, died July 1865, of Granville, Washington, NY; Rachel J., married Mr. Dewey; Frank Thompson; other relatives were Emeline Pierce and Millard Hinman; received pension money; 30

Jennie E. Thompson; 2 January 1880; - ; - ; Lewis Thompson; U- Archibald Thompson, A- Isabella Fuller, A- Louisa Clark (W- of John R. Clark), A- Jennie Hooper (wife of Grant Hooper), MGF Lewis Watson; received money from estate of Mary Thompson; 28

Lauren Thompson; 8 February 1841; John B. Thompson, died before January 1860; - ; - ; - ; G- Heman G. Button; 30

Lewis W. Thompson; 8 October 1876; - ; - ; Jennie Thompson; U- Archibald Thompson, A- Isabella Fuller, A- Louisa Clark (W- of John R. Clark), A- Jennie Hooper (wife of Grant Hooper), MGF Lewis Watson; RE, 1897 in Rochester, received money from estate of Mary Thompson; 28

Name; Date of Birth; Father; Mother; Siblings; Other Relatives; Notes; Box Number

Faith T. Thorne; 9 February 1909; Sanford H. Thorne; Anna; Rhea Thorne; GM Annie Kurtzhalts, of Olean; - ; 62

Rhea H. Thorne; 15 October 1900; Sanford H. Thorne; Anna; Faith Thorne; GM Annie Kurtzhalts, of Olean; - ; 62

Anna Thorton; - ; - ; - ; George and Thomas Thorton; - ; G-Sarah Thorton, of Lyndon; 63

Eleanor E. Thorton; 14 October 1849; Samuel Thorton, died before April 1861; - ; Ernest, Marion and Lucina Thorton; MG Stephen and Aceneth Langmade, PGM Eleanor Thorton, U- Richard B. Thorton, U- Nathan Langmade, U- Whitman Langmade, A- Miranda Langmade, A- Phebe Pierce, A- Lucy E. Smith, A- Sally Bailey; - ; 30

Ernest M. Thorton; 9 July 1858; Samuel Thorton, died before April 1861; - ; Eleanor, Marion and Lucina Thorton; MG Stephen and Aceneth Langmade, PGM Eleanor Thorton, U- Richard B. Thorton, U- Nathan Langmade, U- Whitman Langmade, A- Miranda Langmade, A- Phebe Pierce, A- Lucy E. Smith, A- Sally Bailey; - ; 30

George Thorton; - ; - ; - ; Anna and Thomas Thorton; - ; G-Sarah Thorton, of Lyndon; 63

Joseph A. Thorton; - ; - ; - ; George and Anna Thorton; - ; G-Sarah Thorton, of Lyndon; 63

Lucina Thorton; 13 June 1846; Samuel Thorton, died before April 1861; - ; Ernest, Marion and Ernest Thorton; MG Stephen and Aceneth Langmade, PGM Eleanor Thorton, U- Richard B. Thorton, U- Nathan Langmade, U- Whitman Langmade, A- Miranda Langmade, A- Phebe Pierce, A- Lucy E. Smith, A- Sally Bailey; - ; 30

Marion F. Thorton; 15 February 1842; Samuel Thorton, died before April 1861; - ; Ernest, Lucina and Ernest Thorton; MG Stephen and Aceneth Langmade, PGM Eleanor Thorton, U- Richard B. Thorton, U- Nathan Langmade, U- Whitman Langmade, A- Miranda Langmade, A- Phebe Pierce, A- Lucy E. Smith, A- Sally Bailey; - ; 30

Donald Thrall; 19 December 1895; Stephen Thrall; Nellie;

Name; Date of Birth; Father; Mother; Siblings; Other Relatives; Notes; Box Number

Virginia and Mary Thrall; PA Mina Linderman , PA Effie Alsmorth; RE Lakeville, Connecticut; 30

Mary Thrall; 13 May 1899; Stephen Thrall; Nellie; Virginia and Donald Thrall; PA Mina Linderman , PA Effie Alsmorth; RE Lakeville, Connecticut; 30

Virginia Thrall; 19 December 1895; Stephen Thrall; Nellie; Mary and Donald Thrall; PA Mina Linderman, PA Effie Alsmorth; RE Lakeville, Connecticut; 30

Frank A. Ticknor; 13 May 1847; William Ticknor, died before November 1865; - ; Olive Ticknor; - ; G- DeForest N. Parker; 30

Olive M. Ticknor; 4 March 1845; William Ticknor, died before November 1865; - ; Frank Ticknor; - ; G- DeForest N. Parker; 30

Elizabeth A. Tietz; 10 December 1889; - ; - ; Emma, Mary, Viola and Ernest W. Tietz; - ; - ; 62

Emma Tietz; 4 Jan 1895; - ; - ; Elizabeth, Mary, Viola and Ernest W. Tietz; - ; - ; 62

Mary M. Tietz; 10 September 1892; - ; - ; Elizabeth, Emma, Viola and Ernest W. Tietz; - ; - ; 62

Viola C. Tietz; about 1906; - ; - ; Elizabeth, Emma, Mary and Ernest W. Tietz; - ; - ; 62

George D. Timmerman; - ; John D. Timmerman, soldier; Caroline, married Joel Ewing; - ; - ; received pension money; 30

Hazel Timmerman; 28 May 1906; George Timmerman, died 22 June 1923, in Jamestown; - ; Ruby Timmerman, HB Robert Timmerman, HB Cary Timmerman; HU Norval Halstead; file mentions Muriel P. Timmerman (died about 1913), G- Eliza Yaw; 10

Ruby J. Timmerman; 25 October 1907; George Timmerman, died 22 June 1923 at WCA Hospital, Jamestown; Muriel, died about 1913; Hazel Timmerman Halstead, HB Robert Timmerman, HB Cary Timmerman; MA Eliza Yaw, HU Mr. Cullis; RE 101 Atlantic St., Salamanca 29

Name; Date of Birth; Father; Mother; Siblings; Other Relatives; Notes; Box Number

Joanna Tingue; 4 March 1861; Peter Tingue; Mary Ann, of New Albion; Peter and Will Tingue; HU Mr. Spink, married about 1883; - ; 63

Peter A. Tingue; 27 October 1861; Peter Tingue; Mary Ann, of New Albion; Joanna and Will Tingue; - ; - ; 63

Will O. Tingue; 26 April 1860; Peter Tingue; Mary Ann, of New Albion; Joanna and Peter Tingue; - ; - ; 63

James J. Tinkcorn; - ; - ; Mary A. Vallely, of Findlay, Hancock, Ohio, married Mr. Pollard; John Tinkcorn; MGF James L. Vallely; - ; 62

John "JJ" J. Tinkcorn; - ; - ; Mary A. Vallely, of Findlay, Hancock, Ohio, married Mr. Pollard; James Tinkcorn; MGF James L. Vallely; RE 1916, in Bloomdale, Wood, Ohio; 62

Ida E. Titus; 15 November 1877; - ; - ; - ; distant relation by marriage was John Volk; - ; 62

Nellie Titus; about 1851; Starr Titus, died before 31 May 1860; - ; Sarah and Stephen Titus; - ; G- Ira Titus; 30

Sarah P. Titus; about 1853; Starr Titus, died before 31 May 1860; - ; Nellie and Stephen Titus; - ; G- Ira Titus; 30

Stephen Titus; about 1849; Starr Titus, died before 31 May 1860; - ; Nellie and Sarah Titus; - ; G- Ira Titus; 30

Leo Tobin; 26 November 1898; Carthage Tobin, RE 1105 N. Union St., Olean; Bridget; Loretta and Louise Tobin, Ella Callahan, Margaret Ostrander, Anna Matilda Timmerman, Ruth Tobin Hahn; - ; first G- Patrick Shea, second G- Mary Shelehan; 62

Loretta Tobin; about 1902; Carthage Tobin, RE 1105 N. Union St., Olean; Bridget; Leo and Louise Tobin, Ella Callahan, Margaret Ostrander, Anna Matilda Timmerman, Ruth Tobin Hahn; - ; first G- Patrick Shea, second G- Mary Shelehan; 62

Louise Tobin; about 1897; Carthage Tobin, RE 1105 N. Union St., Olean; Bridget; Leo and Loretta Tobin, Ella Callahan, Margaret Ostrander, Anna Matilda Timmerman, Ruth Tobin Hahn; - ; first G- Patrick Shea, second G- Mary Shelehan; 62

Clara B. Tompkins; 18 February 1872; Rempson D. Tompkins;

Name; Date of Birth; Father; Mother; Siblings; Other Relatives; Notes; Box Number

Martha E.; - ; - ; - ; 30

John E. Tompkins; 12 June 1905; Harry E. Tompkins; - ; Norman Tompkins; - ; RE 209 N. 6th ST., Olean; 30

Hawley Tooley; 13 or 30 February 1842; - ; Julia Ann Sikes, of Otto; James and Salina Tooley; MGF Shadiak Sikes, U-Hiram Sikes, U- Stephen Sikes, U-Caleb Sikes; - ; 77

James E. Tooley; 12 November 1837; - ; Julia Ann Sikes, of Otto; Hawley and Salina Tooley; MGF Shadiak Sikes, U-Hiram Sikes, U- Stephen Sikes, U-Caleb Sikes; - ; 77

Merrill E. Tooley; 26 April 1865; James E. Tooley, died October 1872, of East Otto; Lura, married Mr. Kelsey; - ; - ; RE 1878, in Alexander, Genesee, NY, 1886, in Bennington, Wyoming, NY; 30

Salina Tooley; 27 July 1838; - ; Julia Ann Sikes, of Otto; Hawley and James Tooley; MGF Shadiak Sikes, U- Hiram Sikes,U- Stephen Sikes, U-Caleb Sikes; - ; 77

Laura Mae Torrey; 6 December 1901; Seymour B. Torrey; - ; HS Naoma Torrey; - ; - ; 30

Naoma Cecille Torrey; 13 January 1896; Seymour B. Torrey; - ; HS Laura Torrey; - ; - ; 30

Emily J. Tothill; 10 April 1903; Edward M. Tothill; - ; - ; - ; received money from the estate of Fanny D. Tothill; 30

Alva Rue Tousey; 22 April 1889; - ; - ; Marcia and Lillis Tousey; - ; went by the first name Rue, received money from estate of Ruth J. Tousey; 30

Lillis S. Tousey; 1 January 1892; - ; - ; Marcia and Alva Tousey; - ; received money from estate of Ruth J. Tousey; 30

Gordon B. Towers; 12 June 1900; - ; Rebecca; - ; U- Clair Andrews/Andrus; E. C. Ferguson is who money was given to for the casket and embalming of Rebecca Towers. Frank L. Pritchard, of Conewango, dug grave; 62

Madelin R. Towne; 9 March 1898; - ; - ; - ; C- by marriage Fred T. Bush; RE Dayton NY ; 62

Jessie May Towns; - ; Oscar Towns, died before September 1866, while in Company D., 10th Regiment, NY State

Name; Date of Birth; Father; Mother; Siblings; Other Relatives; Notes; Box Number

Volunteers; Emma J., married Mr. Hering; Oscar Towns; - ; - ; 30

Oscar Elmer Towns; - ; Oscar Towns, died before September 1866, while in Company D., 10th Regiment, NY State Volunteers; Emma J., married Mr. Hering; Jessie Towns; - ; - ; 30

Wicenty Trace; 22 July 1889; - ; - ; - ; - ; father in Austria or Poland, G- John Jonak (no relation), needed guardian for marriage application; 62

Henry Trommer; 14 February 1899; - ; Clara, married Mr. Labuhn; William Trommer; - ; - ; 30

William Trommer; 6 May 1897; - ; Clara, married Mr. Labuhn; Henry Trommer; - ; - ; 30

Marshall G. Trowbridge; 21 July 1883; - ; Marion, married Mr. Hedding; - ; - ; - ; 62

Emma W. Tucker; 13 September 1869; Albert Tucker, of Roulette, Potter, Pennsylvania; Sarah A., of Olean; - ; - ; RE 12 Laurel Ave., Olean; 62

Eliza M. Tuggie; 1 May 1874; AF David Bell, died before 11 March 1891; AM Laurice, died before 11 March 1891; - ; HU Mr. Rockwell; AKA Lizzie Bell ; 37

Marian Turner; 20 August 1909; Bery Turner; Zella I., died 14 December 1921, lived N. 13th St.; William C. Turner, 1923, in Chicago, Cook, Illinois; and 1927 was in East Orange, New Jersey; - ; she was in epileptic, who was an inmate at the Dixon State Hosp., Dixon, Illinois, stated she was "normal minded epileptic", also in a reform school as she ran away and was found in the County Hospital; 64

Morris Turner; 31 July 1866; James Turner; - ; - ; - ; name also seen as Maurice, received money from will of Major Macapes; 30

Minnie D. Twomley; 8 July 1874; AF Lyman Twomley, AM Urania, died 5 September 1889; - ; - ; she was taken from the "American Female Guardian Society" of NY City on 30 November 1877, and was adopted May 1888; 30

Name; Date of Birth; Father; Mother; Siblings; Other Relatives; Notes; Box Number

Albert Roscoe Tyler; 23 February 1876; - ; Jennie; - ; U- Adelbert Ewell; father died before March 1889; 63

Teresa Tyma; 12 August 1896; - ; - ; - ; - ; G- Maciej Tyma, of Buffalo, had real estate in Marcikowo Gorne, Germany; 30

Albert Tyrer; August 1863; - ; - ; - ; - ; G- Everett Fisher; 30

Myrtie H. Tyrer; 3 February 1867; Levi W. Harmon; - ; - ; - ; RE 1888, Pike, Wyoming, NY; 30

Name; Date of Birth; Father; Mother; Siblings; Other Relatives; Notes; Box Number

U Surnames

Charles Ulmschnieder; - ; Matthias Ulmschnieder, of Olean; - ; Rose, Mary, Emma, Ida and Louisa Ulmschnieder; - ; mother died before October 1903; 70

Emma Ulmschnieder; - ; Matthias Ulmschnieder, of Olean; - ; Rose, Mary, Charles, Ida and Louisa Ulmschnieder; - ; mother died before October 1903; 70

Ida Ulmschnieder; - ; Matthias Ulmschnieder, of Olean; - ; Rose, Mary, Charles, Emma and Louisa Ulmschnieder; - ; mother died before October 1903; 70

Louisa Ulmschnieder; - ; Matthias Ulmschnieder, of Olean; - ; Rose, Mary, Charles, Emma and Ida Ulmschnieder; - ; mother died before October 1903; 70

Mary Ulmschnieder; - ; Matthias Ulmschnieder, of Olean; - ; Rose, Louisa, Charles, Emma and Ida Ulmschnieder; - ; mother died before October 1903; 70

Rose Ulmschnieder; - ; Matthias Ulmschnieder, of Olean; - ; Mary, Louisa, Charles, Emma and Ida Ulmschnieder; - ; mother died before October 1903; 70

Anna F. Utley; 28 August 1882; Rodney Utley; Electa; - ; HU Mr. Phillips, married by 1901, U- E. Oscar Wilson; - ; 67

John Utrich; 11 March 1856; Joseph Utrich, died before October 1866; - ; George, Louisa, and Joseph Utrich; - ; - ; 30

Joseph Utrich; 26 May 1851; Joseph Utrich, died before October 1866; - ; George, Louisa, and John Utrich; - ; - ; 30

Louisa Utrich; 16 December 1849; Joseph Utrich, died before October 1866; - ; George, Joseph, and John Utrich; - ; - ; 30

Name; Date of Birth; Father; Mother; Siblings; Other Relatives; Notes; Box Number

V Surnames

Helen Valentine; 18 September 1908; Harry Valentine, died before March 1927; Ruth; - ; - ; - ; 70

Mina Josephine Valiante/Valiquette; about 1892; foster father was Louie St. Louis; - ; - ; HU Mr. Saar; RE of parents unknown, Mina RE 1913, in Clinton County, NY, G- James P. Casey; 45

Alexander Vallance; 18 November 1860; Robert Vallance, died before February 1867; - ; Margaret Vallance; PG Alexander and Margaret Vallance, U- James Vallance; - ; 32

Margaret Vallance; 3 April 1857; Robert Vallance, died before February 1867; - ; Alexander Vallance; PG Alexander and Margaret Vallance, U- James Vallance; - ; 32

George Valley; about 1901; Paul Valley, Sr., of Olean; - ; Joseph, Paul, Mary and Harry Valley; - ; - ; 70

Harry Valley; August 1900; Paul Valley, Sr., of Olean; - ; Joseph, Paul, Mary and George Valley; - ; - ; 70

Joseph Valley; about 1899; Paul Valley, Sr., of Olean; - ; Harry, Paul, Mary and George Valley; - ; - ; 70

Mary Valley; September 1904; Paul Valley, Sr., of Olean; - ; Harry, Paul, Joseph and George Valley; - ; - ; 70

Paul Valley; 29 July 1897; Paul Valley, Sr., of Olean; - ; Harry, Mary, Joseph and George Valley; - ; - ; 70

Carrie B. Van Dewater; 17 May 1843; - ; - ; - ; - ; in same envelope with Ida Van Dewater; 32

Ida Mary Van Dewater; - ; - ; - ; - ; - ; in same envelope with Carrie Van Dewater; 32

Marie Van Dewater; 24 September 1892; - ; Nellie, of Machias; - ; - ; money from estate of Wm. J. Van Dewater; 64

Ernest D. Van Etten; 25 February 1869; - ; Mariam O., died November 1880; Horton Van Etten; - ; - ; 32

Horton Van Etten; 29 May 1864; - ; Mariam O., died November 1880; Ernest Van Etten; - ; - ; 32

Name; Date of Birth; Father; Mother; Siblings; Other Relatives; Notes; Box Number

May Van Marter; about 1898; - ; Frances, of Great Valley; - ; - ; G- Wm. H. Folts, Peter Kobinksi and wife adopted May, then the order was lifted because Peter and his wife divorced; 64

Abram Van Rensselaer; 1 January 1849; Abram L. Van Rensselaer; - ; Minerva and Phillip Van Rensselaer; MGF William Caswell, MU David Caswell; - ; 30

Minerva Van Rensselaer; September 1856; Abram L. Van Rensselaer; - ; Abram and Phillip Van Rensselaer; MGF William Caswell, MU David Caswell; - ; 30

Phillip P. Van Rensselaer; December 1848; Abram L. Van Rensselaer; - ; Abram and Minerva Van Rensselaer; MGF William Caswell, MU David Caswell; - ; 30

Clara Ann Van Rensselear; 3 February 1870; Phillip P. Van Rensselear, abandoned daughter June 1872; Sophia, died 8 February 1870, of Randolph, file states Clara was born same day her mother died; HS Henrietta Williams (Sophia is also her mother and Henrietta was born about 1857), MA Mary McDegraus, MA Sarah Ann Hunt, MA Caroline Gray, MA Mary Eliza Gray, MA Jane Finley, MA Zillah Lilly, MA Rebecca Terry; MU George Van Syckle, PG Abram L. and Clarissa Van Rensselear. Clara's daughter was Mrs. Florence Weems (in 1930, resided at Astoria, Long Island, New York), another, or same daughter, is Mrs. Henry J. Phillips (of Flushing, New York); G- Clarissa A. Van Rensselear; 64

George E. Vangilder; about 1864; Abram Vangilder, died 12 May 1864, of Coldspring; - ; Milton and William Vangilder; U- Rufus A. Freeman; G- Adeline B. Brown; 76

Milton R. Vangilder; about 1857; Abram Vangilder, died 12 May 1864, of Coldspring; - ; George and William Vangilder; U- Rufus A. Freeman; G- Adeline B. Brown; 76

William A. Vangilder; about 1862; Abram Vangilder, died 12 May 1864, of Coldspring; - ; George and Milton Vangilder; U- Rufus A. Freeman; G- Adeline B. Brown; 76

Addison E. Varnum; April 1845; Michael Varnum; - ; Ann

Name; Date of Birth; Father; Mother; Siblings; Other Relatives; Notes; Box Number

Varnum; - ; received money from the Collins; 30

Ann Varnum; October 1843; Michael Varnum; - ; Addison Varnum; - ; received money from the Collins; 30

Alice Vedder; - ; John A. Vedder, died April 1870; Betsey; Rachel and Mary Vedder; U- Comodore P. Vedder; - ; 32

Mary E. Vedder; - ; John A. Vedder, died April 1870; Betsey; Rachel and Alice Vedder; U- Comodore P. Vedder; - ; 32

Rachel Vedder; 12 July 1844; John A. Vedder, died April 1870; Betsey; Mary and Alice Vedder; U- Comodore P. Vedder; - ; 32

Sylvanus N. Vedder; 2 October 1860; - ; Jennie Hanson, married Mr. Davenport; - ; PGM Polly Frank, MGM Catharine Hanson, MU Richard Hanson, MU George Hanson; G- Comodore Vedder; 30

Irene Vena; 21 May 1911; Anthony Vena, was a grocer, of 404 Wayne St; Carmella; - ; - ; money due to accident that occurred on 26 October 1930 with John C. Looker; 70

Ellen Venburg; 15 February 1893; - ; Mary H., of Portville; Florence Venburg; - ; file also mentions Peter and Paul Venburg; 64

Florence O. Venburg; 22 March 1896; - ; Mary H., of Portville; Ellen Venburg; - ; file also mentions Peter and Paul Venburg; 64

Cora Bell Very; 22 September 1877; Elijah Very, of Portville; - ; Martha Very; - ; G- William B. Merse, no relationship; 64

Martha Ellen Very; 23 January 1881; Elijah Very, of Portville; - ; Cora Very; HU Mr. Coss, married 1898 ; G- William B. Merse, no relationship; 64

Jessie E. Vickery; 27 May 1873; John Vickery, died 25 April 1890; Clotilda "Eva"; Grace Griffeth; HU Mr. Remington; - ; 33

Vitale Viglo; 4 July 1900; - ; - ; - ; - ; parents were in Italy and long time friend was Anthony Monteleone; 70

Bertha M. Vincent; 27 January 1871; Oscar Vincent, died February 1876, of Leon; - ; - ; HU E. C. Hurlburt, married

Name; Date of Birth; Father; Mother; Siblings; Other Relatives; Notes; Box Number

about 1890, MG Ahimaz and Lovina Easton, PGM Lydia Vincent; G- William J. Easton; 64

Charles Vining; 16 August 1849; David Vining, died before August 1865; Hannah, died before August 1865; - ; - ; G- John Kinnicutt; 30

Charles F. Vinton; 6 October 1859; Charles B. Vinton, died November 1859, of Ellicottville; Caroline, married Mr. Oaks; - ; PGF Lathrop Vinton, died before 23 May 1870; - ; 30

Fred Vollmer, Jr.; 6 October 1881; - ; Annie C.; - ; - ; - ; 67

Charles G. Vreeland; 17 July 1878; - ; Anna M., of Salamanca; - ; - ; - ; 70

Name; Date of Birth; Father; Mother; Siblings; Other Relatives; Notes; Box Number

W Surnames

Evelyn Wade; 8 April 1898; - ; Lena, of Olean, married Mr. Galbraith; - ; - ; received legacy from GA; 65

Florence P. Wade; 18 April 1900; - ; - ; - ; - ; received money from estate of Amanda Scott, lived with Edwin Coldrock, Florence's RE Joplin, Jasper, Missouri; 70

Mary E. Wadsworth; 17 September 1878; J. C. Sanders; Cora; - ; U- Jay Sanders; - ; 32

Cortland I. Waite; 27 September 1909; - ; Nellie G.; - ; - ; RE 1928, attended Syracuse University; 35

Edward Everett Waite; 21 December 1909; - ; - ; - ; GU William P. Martin; RE with Nettie and Lawrence Fries. In 1928, attended Cornell University in Ithaca, mother died 6 September 1926, file states that Ida M. Waite is deceased; 35

Gertie Waite; 17 June 1871; - ; - ; - ; HU Mr. Trepus; RE 1892, in Boyceville, Wisconsin, G- Julius Edwards; 65

Thirza J. Waite; 3 January 1870; George Waite; - ; - ; - ; - ; 32

Avaline E. Wakefield; about 1847; - ; - ; - ; - ; G- Silas H. Seymour (of Poland, Chautauqua, NY), in envelope with Mary Wakefield; 32

Mary Jane Wakefield; about 1848; - ; - ; - ; - ; G- Silas H. Seymour, of Poland, Chautauqua, NY, in envelope with Avaline Wakefield; 32

Shirley A. Wakefield; 16 November 1902; Edwin J. Hull; Lottie; - ; - ; - ; 66

Florence L. Wakelee; about 1889; John H. Wakelee, of Olean; - ; - ; - ; G- Anna Wakelee; 69

Lela Wakely; about 1862; Henry Wakely, died September 1870; Cornelia "Dolly"; Martha and Walter Wakely; - ; Lela died by 2 March 1886; 32

Martha Wakely; about 1867; Henry Wakely, died September 1870; Cornelia "Dolly"; Lela and Walter Wakely; HU Mr. McKern; - ; 32

Name; Date of Birth; Father; Mother; Siblings; Other Relatives; Notes; Box Number

Walter H. Wakely; abot 1869; Henry Wakely, died September 1870; Cornelia "Dolly"; Lela and Martha Wakely; - ; - ; 32

Ada M. Waldo; 5 March 1865; Henry Olcutt, died before September 1882; - ; - ; - ; G- Elgene W. Read, no relation; 33

Ida May Waldron; 7 July 1889; - ; - ; Otis Waldron; - ; - ; 32

Roy W. Waldron; about 1883; Robert H. Waldron; Emma E.; - ; PGM Lucy Lathom (died 13 April 1894), PU George M. Wilhelm (died 14 December 1900), PA Sarah E. McNinch, PA Jenny Ovenshire, cousins were Walter, Arthur and Loise Wilhelm, Nellie and Lee McNinch, and Olive Waldron; Roy died November 1898 at Westfield, Chautauqua, NY; 31

Janice A. Walker; 18 December 1906; - ; L. Jane, of Olean; Preston Walker; - ; father died before September 1913; 70

Preston M. Walker; 8 May 1900; - ; L. Jane, of Olean; Janice Walker; - ; father died before September 1913; 70

Elizabeth Howard Wallace; 28 October 1906; - ; Georgia, died before 13 September 1924; - ; A- Hazel Grow (of Albany, NY), and other relatives were Frank Howard and Beatrice Wells; Elizabeth lived with Hazel; - ; 35

Oscar C. Waller; about 1867; - ; Jeannette, of Little Falls, Morrison, Minnesota, married Mr. Murphy; - ; - ; - ; 66

Alice Walrad; 3 July 1858; James C. Walrad, died October 1863, in Perrysburg; Sophronia Hinds, died 27 September 1867, in Perrysburg; Jane Walrad; MGF Charles Hinds; needed guardian to receive pension money; 32

Jane Walrad; 6 March 1862; James C. Walrad, died October 1863, in Perrysburg; Sophronia Hinds, died 27 September 1867, in Perrysburg; Alice Walrad; MGF Charles Hinds; needed guardian to receive pension money; 32

Jane Walsh; about 1876; - ; - ; Mary, Margaret, John, Timothy, James, and Daniel Walsh; - ; father died 6 April 1890; 64

Margaret Walsh; October 1878; - ; - ; Mary, Jane, John, Timothy, James, and Daniel Walsh; - ; father died 6 April 1890; 64

Mary Walsh; about 1873; - ; - ; Margaret, Jane, John, Timothy,

Name; Date of Birth; Father; Mother; Siblings; Other Relatives; Notes; Box Number

James, and Daniel Walsh; - ; father died 6 April 1890; 64

Frank Ward; 16 March 1876; - ; Anna, married Mr. Holton; - ; C- Charles M. Ward; RE Indianapolis, Marion, Indiana; 31

O. Donald Ward; 24 January 1901; James Ward, died 9 May 1904, of Dayton; Minnie, married Mr. Wiggie before May 1909; - ; - ; - ; 65

Samuel Ward; 12 January 1903; - ; - ; - ; - ; only one guardian report in envelope; 76

Henry Clare Waring; 28 April 1876; Henry W. Waring; - ; - ; - ; G- Charles W. Phillips (not related), G- James Waring; 31

William R. Waring; about 1856; George Waring, died before May 1876; - ; - ; - ; G- John Waring; 33

Edwin Alphius Warner; 4 May 1871; Alpheus Warner, died 18 September 1872, of Lyndon; Charlotte; Perry, Alonzo, Riley, Ellen and Louisa Warner; and Aniss Babcock; - ; - ; 66

Emma H. Warner; about 1866; - ; Carrie E., of Conewango; Lizzie and Willie Warner; U- Seth Thompson; received money from estate of Wm. Warner; 65

Lizzie M. Warner; about 1868; - ; Carrie E., of Conewango; Emma and Willie Warner; U- Seth Thompson; received money from estate of Wm. Warner; 65

Mary Louesa Warner; about 1854; - ; - ; - ; - ; G- Nathan F. Weed/Wood; 32

Willie C. Warner; about 1871; - ; Carrie E., of Conewango; Emma and Lizzie Warner; U- Seth Thompson; received money from estate of Wm. Warner; 65

Charles Warren; 25 February 1884; Jerome Warren; Mary; - ; - ; received $350 from Supreme Court Case against Vacuum Oil County for injury to Charles; 69

Carl Washburn; 23 October 1873; - ; Amelia; - ; - ; received legacy from John Shum; 31

Clarence S. Washburn; November 1856; Howland Washburn, died 1864; - ; Melvin, Daniel and Martha Washburn; - ; G- Quarteus Rust; 32

Daniel M. Washburn; - ; Howland Washburn, died 1864; - ;

Name; Date of Birth; Father; Mother; Siblings; Other Relatives; Notes; Box Number

Melvin, Clarence and Martha Washburn; - ; G- Quarteus Rust; 32

Martha L. Washburn; - ; Howland Washburn, died 1864; - ; Melvin, Clarence and Daniel Washburn; - ; G- Quarteus Rust; 32

Pearl Wasson; 20 October 1886; Wallace Wasson, of Ashford; - ; - ; - ; - ; 65

Polina J. Wasson; 6 February 1865; - ; - ; Annice E., W- of Laurentine Miller; - ; - ; 66

Hattie D. Waters; 12 July 1875; Henry D. Waters, of Conewango; - ; - ; - ; received money from Hattie L. Meighs, Margaret Stiles also mentioned in file; 65

John H. Waters; 25 June 1907; - ; - ; Lee Waters; other relatives were Fred, Roy and Bert Waters; - ; - ; 35

Mary Jane Waters; 19 May 1847; James Caine; - ; - ; - ; G- George W. Clark; 32

Diana F. Watkins; 19 October 1850; - ; - ; - ; - ; Watkins is her married last name, G- Chauncey Snow; 32

Amelia Watson; 23 October 1840; - ; - ; - ; - ; G- Jacob Watson, file mentions Lovina Watson; 77

Isabella Watson; about 1864; Edward Wallace Watson, of Salamanca; - ; - ; - ; money from Mary Harvey's estate; 64

Walter D. Watson; 25 January 1874; - ; - ; - ; - ; G- Clarence Ewell; 64

James Edmond Watts; 23 July 1895; - ; Aria B., of Olean; - ; A- Jennie B. Oakleaf, cousins were James, Edward and Marion Oakleaf; father died 27 March 1907 ; 66

Evelyn M. Waxell; 13 March 1909; - ; - ; - ; HU Mr. Chaffee, MA Allie M. Frank, A- Nellie Newton; parents divorced, father died and mother's whereabouts unknown; 35

John L. Weast; 5 June 1866 ; - ; Sally; - ; - ; - ; 33

Claude Raymond Weaver; - ; Charles F. Weaver, died before April 1919; Katherine M., of 313 Irving St., Olean, married Mr. Williams before March 1926; - ; - ; received money from oil produced on Mosher Lease in Foster Township,

Name; Date of Birth; Father; Mother; Siblings; Other Relatives; Notes; Box Number

McKean, Pennsylvania; 70

Gertrude E. Weber; 1 March 1888; Frank Joslin, worked for railroad; Elizabeth M., RE 710 Washington St., Olean; - ; HU Henry C. Weber, died before 8 October 1907, from Olean; - ; 32

Annis Webster; 3 June 1840; - ; - ; Herme A. Cox, Lucy, Levi, Eveline, Julia, and Warren Webster; BIL Matthew Cox; G-Elisha Eddy; 33

Carlisle E. Webster; 9 February 1888; Edward R. Webster; Julia C.; - ; - ; parents did not live together, Carlisle lived with his father; 32

Eveline Webster; 6 May 1843; - ; - ; Herme A. Cox, Lucy, Levi, Annis, Julia, and Warren Webster; BIL Matthew Cox; G-Elisha Eddy; 33

Julia E. Webster; 17 January 1838; - ; - ; Herme A. Cox, Lucy, Levi, Annis, Eveline, and Warren Webster; BIL Matthew Cox; G- Elisha Eddy; 33

Levi C. Webster; 6 September 1845; - ; - ; Herme A. Cox, Lucy, Julia, Annis, Eveline, and Warren Webster; BIL Matthew Cox; G-Elisha Eddy; 33

Lucy E. Webster; 8 May 1850; - ; - ; Herme A. Cox, Levi, Julia, Annis, Eveline, and Warren Webster; BIL Matthew Cox; G-Elisha Eddy; 33

Vivian Weeks; about 1902; - ; - ; HB J. Grant Weeks, of Salamanca; - ; parents died before June 1906; 76

Anna Weiser; 21 August 1888; Joseph Weiser, died 11 May 1904; Theresa, lived at 310 South 8th St., Olean; Joseph, Herman, Emma and Clara Weiser; - ; - ; 65

Clara Weiser; about 1896; Joseph Weiser, died 11 May 1904; Theresa, lived at 310 South 8th St., Olean; Joseph, Herman, Emma and Anna Weiser; - ; - ; 65

Emma Weiser; about 1894; Joseph Weiser, died 11 May 1904; Theresa, lived at 310 South 8th St., Olean; Joseph, Herman, Clara and Anna Weiser; - ; - ; 65

Herman Weiser; about 1892; Joseph Weiser, died 11 May 1904;

Name; Date of Birth; Father; Mother; Siblings; Other Relatives; Notes; Box Number

Theresa, lived at 310 South 8th St., Olean; Joseph, Emma, Clara and Anna Weiser; - ; - ; 65

Joseph Weiser; 24 February 1890; Joseph Weiser, died 11 May 1904; Theresa, lived at 310 South 8th St., Olean; Herman, Emma, Clara and Anna Weiser; - ; - ; 65

Jacob Weiss; - ; John Weiss, died before 2 May 1865; Elizabeth, died before 2 May 1865, of Tonawanda; Magdalina Weiss; C- Nicolas Lang; - ; 32

Magdalina Weiss; 19 May 1853; John Weiss, died before 2 May 1865; Elizabeth, died before 2 May 1865, of Tonawanda; Jacob Weiss; C- Nicolas Lang; - ; 32

Bridget Welch; - ; John Welch, died 14 June 1879, of Salamanca; Ellen; Mary, John, Nellie, Patrick and Lizzie Welch; PA Mary Ellen Welch, PA Kate Birmingham; G- Charles Gallagher; 66

James E. Welch; about 1903; - ; step-mother was Gertrude, of Franklinville, married Mr. Jones; Raymond and Margaret Welch; - ; father died 6 June 1918; 70

John Welch; about 1862; John Welch, died 14 June 1879, of Salamanca; Ellen; Mary, Bridget, Nellie, Patrick and Lizzie Welch; PA Mary Ellen Welch, PA Kate Birmingham; G- Charles Gallagher; 66

Lizzie Welch; - ; John Welch, died 14 June 1879, of Salamanca; Ellen; Mary, Bridget, Nellie, Patrick and John Welch; PA Mary Ellen Welch, PA Kate Birmingham; G- Charles Gallagher; 66

Margaret Welch; about 1908; - ; step-mother was Gertrude, of Franklinville, married Mr. Jones; Raymond and James Welch; - ; father died 6 June 1918, Margaret was burned on or before 1 May 1925; 70

Mary Welch; about 1860; John Welch, died 14 June 1879, of Salamanca; Ellen; Lizzie, Bridget, Nellie, Patrick and John Welch; PA Mary Ellen Welch, PA Kate Birmingham; G- Charles Gallagher; 66

Nellie Welch; about 1863; John Welch, died 14 June 1879, of

Name; Date of Birth; Father; Mother; Siblings; Other Relatives; Notes; Box Number

Salamanca; Ellen; Lizzie, Bridget, Mary, Patrick and John Welch; PA Mary Ellen Welch, PA Kate Birmingham; G- Charles Gallagher; 66

Patrick Welch - ; John Welch, died 14 June 1879, of Salamanca; Ellen; Lizzie, Bridget, Mary, Nellie and John Welch; PA Mary Ellen Welch, PA Kate Birmingham; G- Charles Gallagher; 66

Raymond P. Welch; about 1909; - ; step-mother was Gertrude, of Franklinville, married Mr. Jones; Margaret and James Welch; - ; father died 6 June 1918, Raymond was married before July 1925; 70

Ulie Ambrose Welch; about 1884; - ; Rose, of Allegany, married Mr. McQuaid; - ; - ; - ; 65

Harry D. Weldon; 1 February 1897; - ; step-mother was Emma; HB Howard K. Weldon; PU Frank Weldon, PU Herbert Welden, PU George Welden, PA Mrs. C. H. Hammer; RE with A- on River St., Olean, father died January 1912, received money from estate of David Clarkson; 31

Sophia Weller; 24 June 1861; John Weller, died before April 1866; - ; - ; MGF Christian Hartung, PU Godfried Weller (in the Lunatic Asylum in Utica); - ; 32

John Wellnhofer; about 1875; - ; Theresa, of Salamanca; Mary, Leonard, and Peter Wellnhofer; - ; - ; 65

Leonard Wellnhofer; about 1874; - ; Theresa, of Salamanca; Mary, John, and Peter Wellnhofer; - ; - ; 65

Mary Wellnhofer; about 1872; - ; Theresa, of Salamanca; Leonard, John, and Peter Wellnhofer; - ; - ; 65

Peter Wellnhofer; about 1877; - ; Theresa, of Salamanca; Leonard, John, and Mary Wellnhofer; - ; - ; 65

Alice Wells; about 1851; - ; Rebecca Parsell; Sophronia and Clarinda Wells, HB Franklin Wells; MU John Parsell, MU Warren Parsell, MU Worden Parsell, MA Lucy Randall (W- of Elisha Randall), MA Corilla Parsell, PU William Wells; - ; 33

Ceila Alena Wells; 1 October 1882; - ; - ; - ; U- Charles Metcalf;

Name; Date of Birth; Father; Mother; Siblings; Other Relatives; Notes; Box Number

- ; 69

Clarinda Wells; about 1849; - ; Rebecca Parsell; Sophronia and Alice Wells, HB Franklin Wells; MU John Parsell, MU Warren Parsell, MU Worden Parsell, MA Lucy Randall (W- of Elisha Randall), MA Corilla Parsell, PU William Wells; - ; 33

Ellen A. Wells; 21 September 1846; Luther Wells; - ; Hannah Wells; - ; G- Dexter Mills, file mentions an Almira Wells Merrill, born about 1845; 33

Evelyn M. Wells; 13 November 1910; John Wells; Bernice, married Mark Luce; - ; MG Frank L. and Emeline S. Pickup; - ; 70

George W. Wells; 30 April 1840; Gershon Wells, died before May 1853; step-mother was Rebecca; - ; GM Ruth Blakesley, U- William Wells; - ; 33

Hannah A. Wells; 27 March 1845; Luther Wells; - ; Ellen Wells; - ; G- Dexter Mills, file mentions an Almira Wells Merrill, born about 1845; 33

Jenny Wells; 20 March 1859; Albert Dye, died before May 1866, he was a Sgt. In Company K, 64th Regiment; Lucinda Hodge; - ; MG Abraham and Rebecca Hodge, PU Champion Wells, PA Sarah Wood; - ; 32

Peter Wells; 26 October 1849; - ; - ; - ; - ; G- Franklin E. Ramsey; 32

Sophronia Wells; about 1844; - ; Rebecca Parsell; Clarinda and Alice Wells, HB Franklin Wells; MU John Parsell, MU Warren Parsell, MU Worden Parsell, MA Lucy Randall (W- of Elisha Randall), MA Corilla Parsell, PU William Wells; - ; 33

Erwin H. Wentz; 22 February 1879; Louis or Lewis Wentz, died 5 July 1890, in collision near Jamestown on NYP and O RR; - ; Ramel Wentz; MGF Curtis Harding (died 3 May 1892), U- John Wentz, U- Frank Harding, U- Rady Harding, U- Jacob Wentz, U- Charles Wentz, U- George Wentz, A- Effa Burbank, A- Emma Jeffords, A- Carrie Owen, A- Carrie

Name; Date of Birth; Father; Mother; Siblings; Other Relatives; Notes; Box Number

Harding; A- Sarah Wentz (W- of John Wentz); mother died about October 1884, RE 1900, in Youngstown, Ohio, received family books and family pictures; 65

Ramel A. Wentz; 1 January 1884; Louis or Lewis Wentz, died 5 July 1890, killed in collision near Jamestown on NYP and O RR; - ; Erwin Wentz; MGF Curtis Harding (died 3 May 1892), U- John Wentz, U- Frank Harding, U- Rady Harding, U- Jacob Wentz, U- Charles Wentz, U- George Wentz, A- Effa Burbank, A- Emma Jeffords, A- Carrie Owen, , A- Carrie Harding; A- Sarah Wentz (W- of John Wentz); mother died about October 1884, RE 1905, in Elyria, Lorain, Ohio, received family books and family pictures and Ramel was kidnapped by Sarah Blair who owned a hotel where the family stayed before Lewis was killed; 65

Herbert A. Werich; 26 May 1896; - ; - ; - ; - ; RE 1917, in Buffalo, G- John Werich; 64

Clarence Wescott; - ; - ; - ; - ; - ; in same envelope with Grace Wescott; 32

Clark Wescott; 13 May 1855; Anthony Wescott, died January 1865; Sally, married Mr. Livermore; Flora, George, Edwin and Joseph Wescott; - ; received pension money; 33

Edwin E. Wescott; 13 March 1860; Anthony Wescott, died January 1865; Sally, married Mr. Livermore; Flora, George, Clark and Joseph Wescott; - ; received pension money; 33

Flora Ann Wescott; 16 April 1853; Anthony Wescott, died January 1865; Sally, married Mr. Livermore; Edwin, George, Clark and Joseph Wescott; - ; received pension money; 33

George R. Wescott; 23 July 1857; Anthony Wescott, died January 1865; Sally, married Mr. Livermore; Edwin, Flora, Clark and Joseph Wescott; - ; received pension money; 33

Grace Wescott; - ; - ; - ; - ; - ; in same envelope with Clarence Wescott; 32

Joseph A. Wescott; 5 October 1862; Anthony Wescott, died January 1865; Sally, married Mr. Livermore; Edwin, Flora, Clark and George Wescott; - ; received pension money; 33

Name; Date of Birth; Father; Mother; Siblings; Other Relatives; Notes; Box Number

Clifford B. West; 18 February 1907; - ; Lela, died 20 August 1913, married Perry Evans; HS Norma Evans; - ; father died before September 1913 ; 70

Fred West; 9 November 1895; Minard E. West; - ; Minard Jr., and Walberga West; U- James West, Jr., of West Valley; - ; 64

Minard West, Jr.; 30 December 1893; Minard E. West; - ; Fred and Walberga West; U- James West, Jr., of West Valley; - ; 64

Sheldon West; 20 December 1911; Ernest West; - ; Willard West; - ; received money from estate of Jennie L. West; 35

Walberga West; 10 June 1897; Minard E. West; - ; Fred and Minard Jr. West; U- James West, Jr., of West Valley; - ; 64

Willard West; 26 November 1909; Ernest West; - ; Sheldon West; - ; received money from estate of Jennie L. West; 35

John Westerlind; - ; - ; - ; - ; U- John K. Ahlquist, RE 116 N. 2nd St., Olean; parents RE Westby, Gotland, Sweden, needed guardian to get employment with Pennsylvania Railroad County; 32

Albert Westfall; about 1885; - ; Sophia, died 20 May 1895 in Ashford; Augusta Plutz, Louisa Highman, Martin, Allen, Herman, and Lewis Westfall; - ; - ; 32

Martin Westfall; about 1884; - ; Sophia, died 20 May 1895 in Ashford; Augusta Plutz, Louisa Highman, Albert, Allen, Herman, and Lewis Westfall; - ; - ; 32

Dora Westphall; 22 March 1859; - ; - ; - ; - ; G- Sophia Sackrider; 32

Eugene Wetherly; 29 June 1851; Henry Wetherly, died before June 1858; Mirinda Holmes, married Mr. Freeman; George Wetherly; MGF Samuel Holmes, A- Polly Blood; G- Buel Smith; 32

George R. Wetherly; 24 January 1849; Henry Wetherly, died before June 1858; Mirinda Holmes, married Mr. Freeman; Eugene Wetherly; MGF Samuel Holmes, A- Polly Blood; G- Buel Smith; 32

Name; Date of Birth; Father; Mother; Siblings; Other Relatives; Notes; Box Number

Eugene Whaley; 10 July 1879; Charles E. Whaley; - ; Guy Whaley; - ; - ; 32

Guy Whaley; 5 March 1883; Charles E. Whaley; - ; Eugene Whaley; - ; - ; 32

John Robert Whalon; 16 May 1892; - ; - ; - ; A- Sarah Garing, of Ellicottville, wife of J. C. Garing; also indexed under John Whalen and father RE Indiana and left when John was 3 months old; 31 and 65

Carroll Wheaton; about 1909; John Stewart Wheaton, died 17 November 1913, of Hinsdale; Rose A., married Mr. Hunt; Mark, Neva and Roy Wheaton; - ; - ; 70

Earl Wheaton; 28 November 1881; Samuel Wheaton; Mary, died before 30 April 1901; L. S. Wheaton; - ; - ; 35

Mark S. Wheaton; about 1900; John Stewart Wheaton, died 17 November 1913, of Hinsdale; Rose A., married Mr. Hunt; Carroll, Neva and Roy Wheaton; - ; - ; 70

Neva A. Wheaton; about 1901; John Stewart Wheaton, died 17 November 1913, of Hinsdale; Rose A., married Mr. Hunt; Carroll, Mark and Roy Wheaton; - ; - ; 70

Roy S. Wheaton; about 1903; John Stewart Wheaton, died 17 November 1913, of Hinsdale; Rose A., married Mr. Hunt; Carroll, Mark and Neva Wheaton; - ; - ; 70

Ella Whedon; about 1865; - ; - ; - ; HU Fred A. Whedon (died before 1884), FIL Charles A. Whedon; parents RE in McKean County, Pennsylvania; 64

Glenn Wheeler; about 1893; - ; Nettie, of Olean; - ; - ; - ; 65

Lyman C. Wheeler; 15 November 1851; Warren Wheeler, died before September 1863; Elitha; Ruel and Semantha Wheeler; PGM Rhoda Wheeler; - ; 32

Mary Ann Wheeler; 27 November 1867; - ; Catherine; - ; HU Mr. McAuliffe; money from estate of Roger Ryan; 33

Melissa Wheeler- ; Benjamin Wheeler, died September 1856, of Great Valley; - ; - ; PGF John Wheeler, PU George Wheeler, MA Mrs. Moses Chamberlain; - ; 32

Ruel J. Wheeler; 8 May 1859; Warren Wheeler, died before

Name; Date of Birth; Father; Mother; Siblings; Other Relatives; Notes; Box Number

September 1863; Elitha; Lyman and Semantha Wheeler; PGM Rhoda Wheeler; - ; 32

Semantha M. Wheeler; 3 June 1848; Warren Wheeler, died before September 1863; Elitha; Lyman and Ruel Wheeler; PGM Rhoda Wheeler; - ; 32

Lucy Whelan; 4 October 1902; Fenton Whelan, RE in Pennsylvania; - ; - ; GM Hattie J. Whelan; - ; 31

Elizabeth Whipple; 31 January 1911; Burdette Whipple, attorney, 32 Park Ave, Salamanca; Laura Vreeland; - ; MG Mr. & Mrs. E. B. Vreeland, PGF James S. Whipple, U- Edward P. Vreeland, U- Dr. W. W. Whipple; - ; 35

Emeline Whipple; about 1857; - ; - ; - ; - ; in same envelope with Morgan and Fred Whipple, G- Clarissa Whipple; 33

Ethan A. Whipple; 27 September 1862; - ; Belinda; Lydia McMillan; U- Theron Whipple, U- Samuel Whipple; RE 1885, in Keating, McKean, PA, G- Isaac Winship; 32

Fred Whipple; about 1857; - ; - ; - ; - ; in same envelope with Morgan and Emeline Whipple, G- Clarissa Whipple; 33

Morgan Whipple; about 1854; - ; - ; - ; - ; in same envelope with Fred and Emeline Whipple, G- Clarissa Whipple; 33

Willis W. Whipple; August 1858; - ; Martha A., married Mr. Oaks; - ; - ; received pension money; 33

Franklin A. Whitcomb; 25 March 1858; Newell Whitcomb, died before April 1866; - ; Oren, Newell and William Whitcomb; MGM Susanah Wright, MU Seth Wright, MU Lyman Wright, MA Rachel Wright, MA Eliza Wright, U- Sanford Wright; - ; 32

Newell E. Whitcomb; 23 June 1862; Newell Whitcomb, died before April 1866; - ; Oren, Franklin and William Whitcomb; MGM Susanah Wright, MU Seth Wright, MU Lyman Wright, MA Rachel Wright, MA Eliza Wright, U- Sanford Wright; - ; 32

Oren E. Whitcomb; 14 March 1853; Newell Whitcomb, died before April 1866; - ; Newell, Franklin and William Whitcomb; MGM Susanah Wright, MU Seth Wright, MU

Name; Date of Birth; Father; Mother; Siblings; Other Relatives; Notes; Box Number

Lyman Wright, MA Rachel Wright, MA Eliza Wright, U- Sanford Wright; - ; 32

William E. Whitcomb; 22 February 1864; Newell Whitcomb, died before April 1866; - ; Newell, Franklin and Oren Whitcomb; MGM Susanah Wright, MU Seth Wright, MU Lyman Wright, MA Rachel Wright, MA Eliza Wright, U- Sanford Wright; - ; 32

Calvin W. White; 29 July 1872; Henry White; Harriet G., of Olean; Henry White, Jr.; - ; - ; 65

Charles E. White; - ; Edmund C. White, died before June 1901; Margaret; William, Margaret, Robert and Wilbur White; - ; - ; 35

Edith L. White; 6 February 1873; Henry K. White; - ; Earl White; - ; Harvey Smith left legacy, and money from estate of Sarah White; 31

Ellinora White; - ; Richard White, died before November 1846; - ; George and Hannah White; - ; - ; 77

George W. White; - ; Richard White, died before November 1846; - ; Ellinora and Hannah White; - ; - ; 77

Hannah White; - ; Richard White, died before November 1846; - ; Ellinora and George White; - ; - ; 77

Henry White, Jr.; January 1881; Henry White; Harriet G., of Olean; Calvin White; - ; - ; 65

Manly C. White; about 1846; Joel C. White, of Persia; stepmother was Mary A.; Wesley White; PGF Truman White; G- Almer White; 33

Margaret E. White; - ; Edmund C. White, died before June 1901; Margaret; William, Charles, Robert and Wilbur White; - ; - ; 35

Robert B. White; - ; Edmund C. White, died before June 1901; Margaret; William, Charles, Margaret and Wilbur White; - ; - ; 35

Sarah L. White; 11 September 1830; - ; - ; - ; - ; G- Luke White; 33

Theron R. White; 25 June 1906, in Clarion, Pennsylvania;

Name; Date of Birth; Father; Mother; Siblings; Other Relatives; Notes; Box Number

Charles Henry White; Arvilla B., married James P. Kelly. She died 26 October 1925 and RE 193 Elm St., Salamanca, NY; - ; - ; Theron's parents divorced 31 Aug. 1909 in Clarion, Pennsylvania; 35

Wesley L. White; about 1842; Joel C. White, of Persia; stepmother was Mary A.; Manly White; PGF Truman White; G-Almer White; 33

Wilbur G. White; - ; Edmund C. White, died before June 1901; Margaret; William, Charles, Margaret and Robert White; - ; - ; 35

William C. White; - ; Edmund C. White, died before June 1901; Margaret; Wilbur, Charles, Margaret and Robert White; - ; - ; 35

Agnes L. Whitford; 7 March 1879; - ; Ella H., of E. Otto, married Mr. Hardy; Inez Whitford; HU Elbridge Witter, of Andover, U-in-law was William Schwenk; father died before November 1897; 69

Alice Maria Whitford; 22 April 1870; Rufus Whitford, died before 30 January 1871; - ; Charles Whitford; HU Mr. Schwenk, U- Elias Whitford; - ; 33

Charles B. Whitford; 20 December 1856; Rufus Whitford, died before 30 January 1871; - ; Alice Whitford; U- Elias Whitford; - ; 33

Inez H. Whitford; 19 December 1889; - ; Ella H., of E. Otto, married Mr. Hardy; Agnes Whitford; U-in-law was William Schwenk; father died before November 1897; 69

Jennie Whitford; 9 October 1854; - ; - ; - ; - ; G- Austin Morris; 33

Gladys Elliott Whiting; 10 October 1893; Robert M. Elliott; - ; Cecile A. Elliott; - ; - ; 36

Mary Adel Whiting; 24 November 1862; - ; - ; - ; - ; G- Flora Peet; 33

Almond Eugene Whitlock; - ; Theodore Whitlock, died February 1864; - ; Emily and Katie Whitlock; MGF Sidney Newell; in same envelope as Mary and Moselia Whitlock; 32

Name; Date of Birth; Father; Mother; Siblings; Other Relatives; Notes; Box Number

Bessie Whitlock; 5 December 1893; Wallace McPherson; Floris Drown; Ray and Frances McPherson; HU Allison Mathias, MGF Elbridge Drown (died 12 September 1904), U- Peter M. Drown; name at birth was Jessie McPherson, Eugene and Hattie Whitlock adopted her in 1894; 35

Emily Whitlock; - ; Theodore Whitlock, died February 1864; - ; Almond and Katie Whitlock; MGF Sidney Newell; in same envelope as Mary and Moselia Whitlock; 32

Katie Ann Whitlock; - ; Theodore Whitlock, died February 1864; - ; Almond and Emily Whitlock; MGF Sidney Newell; in same envelope as Mary and Moselia Whitlock; 32

Mary Alice Whitlock; 2 December 1862; Spencer Whitlock, died while in service of United States; Julia Ann Lockie; Moselia Whitlock; HU Mr. Clark, PGF Benazah Whitlock, MGF Andrew Lockie, MU James Lockie, PU John Whitlock; G- S. S. Cole, in same envelope with Emily, Katie and Almond Whitlock; 32

Moselia A. Whitlock; - ; Spencer Whitlock, died while in service of United States; Julia Ann Lockie; Mary Whitlock; PGF Benazah Whitlock, MGF Andrew Lockie, MU James Lockie, PU John Whitlock; G- S. S. Cole, in same envelope with Emily, Katie and Almond Whitlock; 32

H. Logan Houk Whitman; 25 April 1894; F. J. Whitman; - ; - ; - ; - ; 65

Zoe E. Whitman; 15 July 1896; George Whitman; - ; - ; - ; - ; 31

Alice Whitmer; 24 November 1891; - ; Christina, of Great Valley; Milford Whitmer, and two others; - ; - ; 65

Milford H. Whitmer; 20 December 1896; - ; Christina, of Great Valley; Alice Whitmer, and two others; - ; - ; 65

Fannie A. Whitney; 19 April 1891; Charles Whitney; Sarah; Clara Maher; - ; - ; 65

Lee A. Whitney; 14 November 1873; - ; - ; - ; U- John Parker, U- Charles E. Whitney; parents lived in Pennsylvania, Lee was injured at a RR crossing in NY; 35

Mary "Gertie" Gertrude Whittier; 23 December 1881 in

Name; Date of Birth; Father; Mother; Siblings; Other Relatives; Notes; Box Number

Pennsylvania; J. F. Whittier, born in Maine; Mary E., born in Maine, died December 1892 in Seattle, Washington; Charles and Frank Leroy Whittier; - ; G- William H. Crandall (died 5 February 1905), Mary died 27 October 1900 in San Diego, California, and is buried in the GAR Cemetery, San Diego. The cause of death was general tuberculosis, she lived 1917 F. St., San Diego, California at time of her death. Ann Whittier left legacy; 31

Augustus Whitton; about 1887; James E. Whitton; Clara J., of Olean, married Mr. MacDonald, about 1906; James and William Whitton; - ; - ; 65

Catherine Whitton; 19 April 1910; - ; Charlotte C., of Olean, married Mr. Allan; - ; - ; father died before April 1922; 70

Ethel A. Whitton; 3 July 1892; - ; Eva B.; Gertrude Whitton; HU Mr. Dineen; money from estate of Thomas Whitton; 33

Gertrude Whitton; 21 September 1889; - ; Eva B.; Ethel Whitton; - ; money from estate of Thomas Whitton; 33

James M. Whitton; about 1885; James E. Whitton; Clara J., of Olean, married Mr. MacDonald, about 1906; Augustus and William Whitton; - ; - ; 65

Thomas Whitton, Jr.; 31 July 1886; - ; Eva; - ; - ; - ; 35

William Whitton; about 1900; James E. Whitton; Clara J., of Olean, married Mr. MacDonald, about 1906; Augustus and James Whitton; - ; - ; 65

Martin Wholeben; about 1883; Martin Wholeben, Sr.; Maggie, died June 1892; Phillip and William Wholeben; PGM Sophia Wholeben; RE 1907, 308 Park St., Warren, Pennsylvania; 31

Phillip Wholeben; 4 May 1886; Martin Wholeben, Sr.; Maggie, died June 1892; Martin and William Wholeben; PGM Sophia Wholeben; - ; 31

William "Willie" Wholeben; about May 1892; Martin Wholeben, Sr.; Maggie, died June 1892; Martin and Phillip Wholeben; PGM Sophia Wholeben; RE 1907, 308 Park St., Warren, Pennsylvania; 31

Fred A. Wichert; 22 March 1903; - ; - ; Charles and William

Name; Date of Birth; Father; Mother; Siblings; Other Relatives; Notes; Box Number

Wichert; A- Louise Gratz; father died before December 1921, G- Hugh A. Cobb, Fred lived with Theodore Gratz and Agnes Wilson; 71

William T. Wichert; 12 October 1909; - ; - ; Charles and Fred Wichert; A- Louise Gratz; father died before December 1921, G- Hugh A. Cobb, William lived with Theodore Gratz and Agnes Wilson; 71

Harry Wicker; 7 July 1859; Henry Wicker; - ; Susie Wicker; - ; left legacy by Henry Wicker (of NY City, NY, died 1865 or 1866); 32

Susie C. Wicker; 22 July 1862; Henry Wicker; - ; Harry Wicker; - ; left legacy by Henry Wicker (of NY City, NY, died 1865 or 1866); 32

Harley A. Wickham; 11 August 1861; Lucius Wickham, died September 1870, of Persia; - ; - ; A- Sarah Rice; received money from estate of Waity Southwick; 31

Dorothy H. Wickwire; - ; - ; Eliza, married Mr. Holland; Ruth Wickwire; - ; Wallace M. Wickwire left legacy; 35

Ruth P. Wickwire; - ; - ; Eliza, married Mr. Holland; Dorothy Wickwire; - ; Wallace M. Wickwire left legacy; 35

Mary Widrig; 30 July 1891; Henry Gerwitz; Mary; - ; HU Fred E. Widrig, of Mansfield ; - ; 65

Florence Wilber; 3 January 1903; Albert C. Wilber; Pearl, married Mr. McIntoch; Vivian Wilber; A- Luella J. Bozard; received money from estate of Orrin S. Bennett; 65

Fred G. Wilber; 1 January 1866; - ; - ; Charles A. Wilber; - ; G- Charles H. Miller, no relation; 33

Helen Wilber; about 1902; Mark W. Wilber, of Chicago; Nellie; Ruth, Robert and Nellie Wilber; - ; G- Alanson S. Courter, friend of family; 65

Nellie Wilber; 5 October 1904; Mark W. Wilber, of Chicago; Nellie; Ruth, Robert and Helen Wilber; HU Mr. Mahoney ; G- Alanson S. Courter, friend of family; 65

Robert Wilber; 1 July 1900; Mark W. Wilber, of Chicago; Nellie; Ruth, Nellie and Helen Wilber; - ; G- Alanson S.

Name; Date of Birth; Father; Mother; Siblings; Other Relatives; Notes; Box Number

Courter, friend of family; 65

Ruth Wilber; about 1897; Mark W. Wilber, of Chicago; Nellie; Robert, Nellie and Helen Wilber; - ; G- Alanson S. Courter, friend of family; 65

Vivian Wilber; 27 July 1901; Albert C. Wilber; Pearl, married Mr. McIntoch; Florence Wilber; A- Luella J. Bozard; received money from estate of Orrin S. Bennett; 65

Allina J. Wilcox; 14 July 1858; Hiram Wilcox, died before February 1865 in service of United States; Dorlesca A., married Mr. Ames; - ; - ; - ; 32

Helen J. Wilcox; 14 April 1896; - ; Ella S.; - ; - ; - ; 31

Lizzie Wilcox; 4 July 1852; - ; - ; - ; HU Frank Wilcox; - ; 32

Roy O. Wilder; 24 August 1893; - ; - ; - ; U- Elmer S. Dewitt; - ; 35

Fanny Wildrick; about 1886; - ; Sophronia, of Portville; Helen Wildrick; - ; - ; 65

Helen M. Wildrick; about 1889; - ; Sophronia, of Portville; Fanny Wildrick; - ; - ; 65

Grace M. Wiley; 10 August 1876 or 1877; - ; Martha; Lynn Wiley; HU Mr. Barnes ; - ; 33

Lynn C. Wiley; 28 November 1879 or 1880; - ; Martha; Grace Wiley; - ; RE 1908, Crawford County, Illinois ; 33

Roy W. Wilhelm; - ; - ; - ; - ; - ; G- George M. Wilhelm, Lucy Latham left legacy and Roy is an heir of Roy W. Waldron; 35

Arthur B. Wilkinson; 16 December 1878; Henry J. Wilkinson, of Chili, Monroe, NY; Lizzie Bradnack, of Little Valley; Edith Wilkinson; MGF Rev. J. R. Bradnack (of Little Valley, Reverend of Congregational Church), parents married 19 March 1878, resided together until January 1881; 66

Edith Wilkinson; 28 December 1879; Henry J. Wilkinson, of Chili, Monroe, NY; Lizzie Bradnack, of Little Valley; Arthur Wilkinson; MGF Rev. J. R. Bradnack (of Little Valley, Reverend of Congregational Church), parents married 19 March 1878, resided together until January 1881; 66

Clare Willard; - ; - ; - ; - ; - ; G- Harriet Willard and received

Name; Date of Birth; Father; Mother; Siblings; Other Relatives; Notes; Box Number

money from estate of Erastus Willard; 65

Doris L. Willard; about 1908; - ; - ; Herbert Willard; HU Mr. Spindler, A- Ida Beers; - ; 66

Dorothy Willard; about 1897; Clare Willard, of Allegany; F. Estelle; Robert and Virginia Willard; - ; - ; 70

Herbert O. Willard; 4 June 1910; - ; - ; Doris Willard, A- Ida Beers; - ; 66

Robert Willard; about 1906; Clare Willard, of Allegany; F. Estelle; Dorothy and Virginia Willard; - ; - ; 70

Virginia Willard; about 1903; Clare Willard, of Allegany; F. Estelle; Dorothy and Robert Willard; - ; - ; 70

Agnes Williams; 10 January 1893; James Williams, of 615 Queen Anne Ave., Seattle, Washington; Emma; - ; U- Nathan R. Williams; boarded with Felton Kenfield; 65

Bertha Williams; 15 June 1891; - ; May, of Olean; James Williams; - ; father lived in Syria, RE with Seid Zoghibe family. Her mother wanted her to marry Moses, and had her committed to the State Ind. School at Rochester; 65

Chauncey Williams; 29 December 1849; Ralph Williams, died before December 1863; - ; - ; MGF Daniel Davis; - ; 33

Douglas D. Williams; 4 July 1893; - ; - ; - ; C- Lola Parker (raised by Douglas's parents), A- Susie O'Donnell; - ; 33

Fred D. Williams; about 1853; Lauren E. Williams, died 20 August 1871; - ; - ; U- George A. Williams; - ; 75

Gillett Decker Williams; 8 June 1910, in Olean; Allen B. Williams, lived 130 S. Barry St., Olean; - ; Marian, Eleanor, Myron and Friend Williams; PGF Allen I. Williams; - ; RE 2741 Proctor Ave., Port Arthur, Texa ; 66

Helen I. Williams; 3 October 1886; - ; - ; - ; PGF William W. Williams; money from estate of John P. Williams; 35

Henrietta Williams; 9 May 1856; - ; known as Sophia Van Rensselaer at time of death in February 1870; HS Ann Van Rensselaer, born February 1870; U- George W. Van Syckle; - ; 33

Herman B. Williams; about 1888; - ; Martha A.; Lena Williams;

Name; Date of Birth; Father; Mother; Siblings; Other Relatives; Notes; Box Number

- ; father was found to be incompetent and was kept at Gowanda State Hospital and Herman received money from Delos William estate; 65

Ida Williams; 12 December 1877; Fred D. Williams; - ; L. Eugene Williams; HU Mr. Bennett; received money from estate of Henrietta C. Williams; 31

Imogene Williams; 29 May 1893; M. D. Williams; - ; - ; - ; - ; 65

John W. Williams; 7 August 1861; George Williams, died August 1864, of Port Byron, Cayuga, NY; Jane, married George Parker; Sarah Williams; - ; George Parker died before 4 March 1869, G- Herman Ingersoll; 33

Joshua D. Williams; 31 December 1864; Thomas Williams, died August 1870, of Freedom; Margaret; Thomas Williams; - ; - ; 33

L. Eugene Williams; 27 December 1875; Fred D. Williams; - ; Ida Williams; - ; money from Henrietta C. Williams's estate; 31

Lena M. Williams; 9 July 1889; - ; - ; Lloyd Williams; - ; - ; 35

Lena M. Williams; about 1890; - ; Martha A.; Herman Williams; - ; father was found to be incompetent and was kept at Gowanda State Hospital and she received money from Delos William estate; 65

Lloyd P. Williams; 11 September 1885; - ; - ; Lena Williams; - ; - ; 35

Louise Williams; 13 September 1907; - ; - ; Sophia Williams; U- Oliver J. Williams, U- Henry Elling, PGF Almon Williams, MGF Chris Elling; parents died before October 1917 and received money from estate of Simeon Williams; 70

Lucille Williams; - ; Frank Williams; Carrie B.; - ; - ; - ; 35

Martin Williams; about 1860; Levi Williams, died before October 1863, of Company K, 57th Regt., Pennsylvania; - ; - ; A- Mary Jemison; 76

Mary "Minnie" C. Williams; 19 September 1871; John Williams; - ; - ; - ; money from estate of Wm. E. Williams; 33

Mary L. Williams; 21 September 1877; J. Wayland Williams,

Name; Date of Birth; Father; Mother; Siblings; Other Relatives; Notes; Box Number

died October 1879; Mary E. Crumb, died April 1881; - ; MGF Chauncey S. Crumb, A- Mrs. Robert Wallace; paternal relatives lived in Wisconsin; 31

Nellie Williams; 17 October 1881; John L. Williams; - ; - ; - ; - ; 35

Robert Devee Williams; about 1907; John Williams, died before October 1919; A. Laura, of Portville; - ; - ; - ; 70

Sarah L. Williams; 26 January 1859; George Williams, died August 1864, of Port Byron, Cayuga, NY; Jane, married George Parker; John Williams; HU Mr. Brown; George Parker died before 4 March 1869, G- Herman Ingersoll; 33

Sophia Williams; 7 October 1903; - ; - ; Louise Williams; HU Mr. Mix, U- Oliver J. Williams, U- Henry Elling, PGF Almon Williams, MGF Chris Elling; parents died before October 1917, money from estate of Simeon Williams; 70

Thomas Williams; 3 July 1857; Thomas Williams, died August 1870, of Freedom; Margaret; Joshua Williams; - ; - ; 33

William Williams; 7 August 1861; - ; Jane, married Mr. Spencer; - ; - ; G- Herman Ingersoll, received pension money; 75

Albert C. Willis; 13 May 1881; Daniel Willis, died 12 September 1896; Loretta, married Mr. Brown September 1902; Josie and Sarah Willis; PG Chauncey (died 24 January 1894), and Polly Willis, C- Cora A. Ethridge; - ; 31

Carrie L. Willis; 4 January 1886; Hezeriah Willis, died 26 April 1904; - ; Leroy Willis; - ; - ; 74

Josie Lucille Willis; 22 Ocotber 1895; Daniel Willis, died 12 September 1896; Loretta, married Mr. Brown September 1902; Albert and Sarah Willis; HU Mr. Larson, PG Chauncey (died 24 January 1894), and Polly Willis, C- Cora A. Ethridge; - ; 31

Leroy H. Willis; 30 June 1883; Hezeriah Willis, died 26 April 1904; - ; Carrie Willis; - ; - ; 74

Sarah J. Willis; 18 February 1894; Daniel Willis, died 12 September 1896; Loretta, married Mr. Brown September 1902; Albert and Josie Willis; HU Claude L. Austin (married

Name; Date of Birth; Father; Mother; Siblings; Other Relatives; Notes; Box Number

May 1903), PG Chauncey (died 24 January 1894), and Polly Willis, C- Cora A. Ethridge; - ; 31

Helen Cecelia Willock; 7 June 1907; AF Abram Mabee; - ; - ; HU Mr. Smith, A- Helen C. Scotland (of Ashford, single), C- Edward E. Best; parents died before December 1917. File mentions she was "colored", her mom was a "Barbadoes Negro" and met her father at a Masquerade ball. Her mother was a descendant of one of Mabee's brothers or sisters; 70

Annis Willson; 14 February 1890; AF Urbern Willson; - ; - ; - ; - ; 35

Jessie Guy Willson; 24 December 1885; Norman C. Wilson; went by Sarah Hayden Wilson at time of death, died 23 April 1888; - ; A- Mrs. T. H. B. Rogers; RE 1908, Cleveland, Cuyahoga, Ohio, last name also seen as Wilson ; 31

Alburtus L. Wilson; - ; - ; Louisa, married April 1863; - ; - ; G- Heber Weatherly, his Grandpa Wilson adopted him in 1856, file mentions Elzora (born about 1838) and Buel Wilson (died 22 March 1858) sharing the estate; 75

Donald D. Wilson; 14 August 1902; Claude L. Wilson; Gertrude D. Darrin; - ; MGF Adelbert E. Darrin, of Little Valley; G- Ray Wilson; 66

George Henry Wilson; 29 July 1876; George Wilson, died before December 1889; Mary, of Portville; Pearl Wilson; - ; - ; 64

George Merle Wilson; 31 October 1876; - ; Lucina E., married Mr. Farrar; - ; - ; - ; 35

Irma M. Wilson; 14 January 1909; - ; Sarah, of 1102 Clayton St., Denver, Colorado; - ; - ; received money from Leander S. Wright estate and father died before 1910; 70

Luria E. Wilson; 20 April 1894; Luther P. Wilson; - ; Lynn and Maude Wilson; - ; - ; 35

Lynn A. Wilson; 24 February 1880; Luther P. Wilson; - ; Luria and Maude Wilson; - ; - ; 35

Maude L. Wilson; 11 January 1884; Luther P. Wilson; - ; Luria and Lynn Wilson; HU Mr. Tuttle ; - ; 35

Pearl Alena Wilson; 23 March 1882; George Wilson, died before

Name; Date of Birth; Father; Mother; Siblings; Other Relatives; Notes; Box Number

December 1889; Mary, of Portville; George Wilson; - ; - ; 64

Reid Wilson; 3 December 1889; - ; - ; - ; - ; in envelope with Sarah Wilson; 35

Sadie I. Wilson; - ; J. H. Wilson; - ; - ; - ; - ; 35

Sarah I. Wilson; - ; - ; - ; - ; - ; in envelope with Reid Wilson; 35

Speedy D. Wilson; 14 August 1859; Henry S. Wilson; - ; - ; HU Mr. Hale, GF Luther Powell; - ; 10

Howard Wiltse; 6 May 1901; - ; Eva Keller; - ; MGF George B. Keller; George's will was probated in Allegany County, NY; - ; 35

Hattie Wimple; about 1870; Charles T. Wimple, died March 1875, of Little Valley; Emma Marsh; Willie Wimple; PGF Henry Wimple (of Mexico, Oswego, NY), MGF Reuben Marsh, MA Virginia Marsh, PGA Harriet Morgan, PGA Pamelia Campbell, PGA Christiana Berry; - ; 64

Willie Wimple; about 1873; Charles T. Wimple, died March 1875, of Little Valley; Emma Marsh; Hattie Wimple; PGF Henry Wimple (of Mexico, Oswego, NY), MGF Reuben Marsh, MA Virginia Marsh, PGA Harriet Morgan, PGA Pamelia Campbell, PGA Christiana Berry; - ; 64

Caroline Winchell; 1 May 1860; James Winchell, died 9 July 1871, of Lyndon; Lydia; Jacob, Miranda, Ellen and Henry Winchell; HU Mr. Adams ; - ; 33

Ellen M. Winchell; 14 January 1863; James Winchell, died 9 July 1871, of Lyndon; Lydia; Jacob, Miranda, Caroline and Henry Winchell; HU Mr. Dye ; - ; 33

Henry Frank Winchell; 14 September 1843; James Winchell, died 9 July 1871, of Lyndon; Lydia; Jacob, Miranda, Caroline and Ellen Winchell; - ; - ; 33

Jacob Winchell; - ; James Winchell, died 9 July 1871, of Lyndon; Lydia; Henry, Miranda, Caroline and Ellen Winchell; - ; - ; 33

Miranda Winchell; 7 August 1857; James Winchell, died 9 July 1871, of Lyndon; Lydia; Henry, Miranda, Caroline and Ellen Winchell; HU Mr. Jenkins; - ; 33

Name; Date of Birth; Father; Mother; Siblings; Other Relatives; Notes; Box Number

Joseph J. Wind; 3 April 1892; - ; - ; Anna Wind, RE 512 N. 8th St., Olean; needed guardian to work for Penn RR County; 65

Clifford Wing; about 1904; - ; Mae E., of Olean; Pauline Wing; - ; father died before August 1905; 70

Pauline A. Wing; about 1900; - ; Mae E., of Olean; Clifford Wing; - ; father died before August 1905 ; 70

Esther Winship; 24 July 1839; - ; - ; - ; - ; G- Charles Winship, in same envelope as Isaac, Joseph and Truman Winship; 33

Isaac Winship; 15 October 1835; - ; - ; - ; - ; G- Charles Winship, in same envelope as Esther, Joseph and Truman Winship; 33

Joseph Winship; 1 September 1833; - ; - ; Nathan and Truman Winship; in same envelope with Isaac and Esther Winship; 33

Truman Winship; 26 September 1837; - ; - ; Nathan and Joseph Winship; in same envelope with Isaac and Esther Winship; 33

Anna M. Wiser; 8 September 1881; Henry B. Wiser, died 1 September 1891; Catherine H.; Elmer Wiser; MGM Hannah J. Barton, MA Susan Henry, MA Eunice Henry; G- Wm. H. Crandall (died 5 February 1905); 31

Elmer E. Wiser; 13 January 1887; Henry B. Wiser, died 1 September 1891; Catherine H.; Anna Wiser; MGM Hannah J. Barton, MA Susan Henry, MA Eunice Henry; G- Wm. H. Crandall (died 5 February 1905); 31

Aileen Witherell; 1 February 1908; Robert L. Witherell, of 419 King St., Olean NY; Ethel, died 16 October 1926; Robert Witherell, Jr.; HU Richard B. Andrews, married 19 February 1927, in Erie, Pennsylvania ; RE 1927, in Erie, Erie, Pennsylvania; 66

Doris Witherell; 19 February 1901; Roy Witherell, of Jamestown, Chautauqua, NY; - ; Musetta Witherell; GM Margaret Petty; - ; 70

Musetta Witherell; about 1903; Roy Witherell, of Jamestown, Chautauqua, NY; - ; Doris Witherell; GM Margaret Petty; - ; 70

Name; Date of Birth; Father; Mother; Siblings; Other Relatives; Notes; Box Number

Robert L. Witherell, Jr.; 29 July 1911; Robert L. Witherell, of 419 King St., Olean NY; Ethel, died 16 October 1926; Aileen Witherell, Jr.; - ; - ; 66

Leroy E. Witter; about 1904; - ; Gertrude, of Hinsdale; Jay, Rufus and Myrtle Witter; - ; father died before March 1911; 70

Myrtle D. Witter; about 1908; - ; Gertrude, of Hinsdale; Jay, Rufus and Leroy Witter; - ; father died before March 1911; 70

Rufus G. Witter; about 1906; - ; Gertrude, of Hinsdale; Jay, Myrtle and Leroy Witter; - ; father died before March 1911; 70

Henrietta M. Wolf; 5 November 1910; - ; - ; Virginia R. Wolf; U- Frank F. Wolf; - ; 66

Rose Wolf; about 1887; - ; Anna; - ; - ; - ; 35

Burdena C. Wolfe; 21 July 1892; - ; - ; - ; HU Edward R. Wolfe, lived at 305 W. Green St., Olean; - ; 65

Bessie H. Wolford; 8 June 1888; - ; - ; - ; U- Frank D. Hicks; - ; 35

Bessie F. Wood; 19 September 1886; George N. Wood, died September 1887; Nellie B., married Mr. Hiester, in Denver, Colorado; Mildred and Genevieve Wood; HU Mr. Kelly; - ; 31

Elbert F. Wood; about 1856; Gabriel J. Wood; Melissa, died March 1867; Ellsworth Wood; - ; G- Lucien Nutting; 33

Ellsworth Wood; about 1862; Gabriel J. Wood; Melissa, died March 1867; Elbert Wood; - ; G- Lucien Nutting; 33

Emery W. Wood; 5 August 1880; - ; Mattie, married Mr. Edwards; Nellie Wood; - ; money from estate of Wm. H. Wood; 31

Ethel Wood; 2 October 1893; - ; - ; Hazel Wood; MGF William A. Mills; - ; 35

Genevieve C. Wood; 11 June 1881; George N. Wood, died September 1887; Nellie B., married Mr. Hiester, in Denver, Colorado; Bessie and Mildred Wood; - ; - ; 31

Name; Date of Birth; Father; Mother; Siblings; Other Relatives; Notes; Box Number

Hazel Wood; 10 April 1892; - ; - ; Ethel Wood; HU Mr. Hartman, MGF William A. Mills; - ; 35

Lee J. Wood; 23 December 1866; James Frank Wood, of Great Valley; - ; - ; MGF Job L. Bates; - ; - ; 35

Maria Wood; 12 April 1851; Gilbert Wood, died before June 1866; - ; - ; - ; G- Josiah Perry; 32

Marthaette Wood; about 1863; Daniel Wood, died March 1870, of Yorkshire; - ; - ; MGF Jonah Phillips, U- Delos Phillips, PA Maria Harvey (W- of Nathan Harvey), PA Amy Nourse; G- Moses Houghtaling; 33

Mildred B. Wood; 2 June 1884; George N. Wood, died September 1887; Nellie B., married Mr. Hiester, in Denver, Colorado; Bessie and Genevieve Wood; - ; - ; 31

Nellie F. Wood; 28 December 1878; - ; Mattie, married Mr. Edwards; Emery Wood; - ; money from estate of Wm. H. Wood; 31

Thomas E. Wood; 5 January 1873; Thomas J. Wood, died April 1862, of Freedom; Mary E.; - ; GGF Charles Wilkin; - ; 33

Ira Woodard; 23 May 1850; Ephraim Woodard, died before 13 December 1867; - ; - ; - ; G- James Whiting; 32

Jenette Woodard; 15 September 1830; Ara Woodard, died before November 1846; - ; William Woodard; - ; G- William Fisher; 77

William Woodard; 16 November 1831; Ara Woodard, died before November 1846; - ; Jenette Woodard; - ; G- William Fisher; 77

Georgia A. Woodin; 26 April 1870; Eri Woodin, died April 1878, of Perrysburg; Harriet, married Frank Taylor; Mary and William Woodin; - ; - ; 66

Homer E. Woodin; - ; William Woodin, died before July 1864; Abi Derby; Tharecia Woodin; PGF Homer Woodin, MGF Elisha Derby; - ; 32

Mary D. Woodin; 12 January 1868; Eri Woodin, died April 1878, of Perrysburg; Harriet, married Frank Taylor; Georgia and William Woodin; - ; - ; 66

Name; Date of Birth; Father; Mother; Siblings; Other Relatives; Notes; Box Number

Tharecia V. Woodin; - ; William Woodin, died before July 1864; Abi Derby; Homer Woodin; PGF Homer Woodin, MGF Elisha Derby; - ; 32

William L. Woodin; 20 January 1873; Eri Woodin, died April 1878, of Perrysburg; Harriet, married Frank Taylor; Georgia and Mary Woodin; - ; - ; 66

Bertha Woodmansee; about 1868; - ; - ; George Woodmansee; - ; G- Albert Eddy, no relationship; 65

Amelia M. Woodruff; 25 November 1851; Henry S. Woodruff, died October 1865, of Franklinville; Maryette, married Mr. Woodworth; Angelette, Kate and Frank Woodruff; HU Mr. Wasson, U- Austin Woodruff; - ; 32

Angelette Woodruff; 26 November 1855; Henry S. Woodruff, died October 1865, of Franklinville; Maryette, married Mr. Woodworth; Amelia, Kate and Frank Woodruff; HU Mr. McLane, U- Austin Woodruff; - ; 32

Frank Woodruff; 25 November 1854; Henry S. Woodruff, died October 1865, of Franklinville; Maryette, married Mr. Woodworth; Amelia, Kate and Angelette Woodruff; U- Austin Woodruff; - ; 32

Kate Woodruff; 8 May 1861; Henry S. Woodruff, died October 1865, of Franklinville; Maryette, married Mr. Woodworth; Amelia, Frank and Angelette Woodruff; U- Austin Woodruff; - ; 32

Ulyssis Grant Woodruff; 8 April 1864; Franklin Woodruff, died June 1864, of Humphrey; Louisa, married Mr. Whitcomb; - ; PGF Charles Woodruff, MGM Sarah Wheeler, distant C- George Calvin De Golia; G- Frederick Wright (died 12 April 1883), received pension money; 32

William Wilson Woods; 5 October 1842; William Woods; - ; - ; - ; - ; 32

Charles J. Woodworth; 25 October 1855; - ; - ; - ; - ; RE 1880, in Oneonta, Otsego, NY and G- Elisha J. Sexton; 32

Jennie M. Woodworth; 13 October 1882; - ; - ; - ; U- George K. Marsh, A- Mrs. Orrin A. Tompkins (died 11 June 1907); - ;

Name; Date of Birth; Father; Mother; Siblings; Other Relatives; Notes; Box Number

35

Frank V. Worden; 18 April 1892; - ; Minnie A., of Delevan; George and Ruby Worden; - ; father died before June 1908; 72

George D. Worden; 10 July 1898; - ; Minnie A., of Delevan; Frank and Ruby Worden; - ; father died before June 1908; 72

Ruby R. Worden; 23 January 1893; - ; Minnie A., of Delevan; Frank and George Worden; - ; father died before June 1908; 72

Carl D. Worthington; 29 January 1867; Randolph Worthington; - ; - ; - ; - ; 33

Gertrude Worthington; 18 August 1862; Sylvester Worthington; - ; - ; PGF Squire Worthington, U-Henry Worthington, U-Hosea T. Holmes, U- Cicero Holmes, HU Mr. Elwell; RE 1884, Rushford, Allegany, NY 32

Catherine Woyan; 16 April 1854; John Woyan, died before February 1871; - ; - ; - ; G- Calvin Stowell; 32

Alice V. Wright; 21 January 1857; Harvey G. Wright, died before 22 August 1863; Luna M., married Mr. Atkison; - ; GM Ruth Pickett, U- Edwin Carrington; - ; 32

Harold A. Wright; 29 March 1893; - ; Mary A., lived 113 South 4th St., Olean; - ; - ; - ; 65

Myrtle J. Wright; 27 April 1859; - ; Cordelia J., married Mr. Dutcher; - ; - ; - ; 32

Sherman Wright; 20 August 1831; - ; - ; - ; - ; G- Simeon Beebe; 33

Warren J. Wright; 25 January 1887; - ; - ; - ; - ; G- Howard Wright; 35

Zabin Wright; 11 February 1882; - ; - ; - ; - ; G- Howard Wright; 35

Lewis E. Wulff; 6 February 1906; Gustave C. Wulff, of Orlando, Mansfield, NY; Emma; - ; - ; - ; 70

Name; Date of Birth; Father; Mother; Siblings; Other Relatives; Notes; Box Number

Y Surnames

Frank M. Yager; 16 November 1872; David Yager; - ; Glenn Yager; MG Augustus and Dora Hasper (of Ellicottville), U- John Hasper, U- Ed. Hasper, A- Lena Harson, (W- of James Harson); - ; 68

George Yager; 10 November 1880; - ; - ; - ; - ; G- John Stady (no relation), received money from estate of John Yager, W. H. Proctor was undertaker listed, J. L .West was the clergyman listed; 67

Glenn Yager; 3 September 1873; David Yager; - ; Frank Yager; MG Augustus and Dora Hasper (of Ellicottville), U- John Hasper, U- Ed. Hasper, A- Lena Harson, (W- of James Harson); Glenn lived with Lena and James Harson ; 68

John Yaw; 25 December 1880; Charles Yaw, died before December 1890; Emily; - ; - ; G- W. H.. Crandall; 67

Abigail York; 24 November 1907; - ; - ; Mary York; PGM Catherine York, of Olean; parents died before April 1908; 68

Mary Catherine York; 24 November 1907; - ; - ; Abigail York; PGM Catherine York, of Olean; parents died before April 1908; 68

James C. Young; 18 February 1903; C. Verne Young, of New Albion; - ; Muriel Young; - ; Catharine Young left legacy; 76

Muriel J. Young; 7 July 1907; C. Verne Young, of New Albion; - ; James Young; HU Mr. Peterson, married about 1926; Catharine Young left legacy; 76

John J. Youngs, Jr.; 7 January 1883; - ; Lizzie, of Ashford; - ; - ; - ; 68

Name; Date of Birth; Father; Mother; Siblings; Other Relatives; Notes; Box Number

Z Surnames

Genevieve Zaph; 26 February 1897, in Allegany; John Zaph, died 24 March 1917, in Allegany; Anna, died 17 March 1917 in Allegany; Eva Zaph Pauly, Anna Zaph Jobe, Lettie Hotchkiss, John Zaph, and Margaret Zaph Mohr; - ; G-Clarence Jobe; 59

Marvalons Zeluff; about 1880; - ; Catharine, of Carrollton; - ; - ; - ; 67

George E. Zimbar; 28 October 1908; Matthew Zimbar, of 121 Merden St., Salamanca; - ; - ; other relatives were Frances and Mary Zimbar; James Ryan left legacy; 68

Herman Peter Zingg; 19 February 1893; - ; Ella K., of Great Valley; - ; - ; - ; 68

Agnes Zinn; 27 April 1908; Albert Zinn; Estella, lived 350 Wildwood Ave., Salamanca; - ; - ; Benjamin Whipple left legacy; 67

ABBEY Carlia 121, Cornelius 1, James 1, Orange 303-304, Sarah 1
ABBOTT David S.195, Evan C. 1, Joseph 1, Mary E. 1
ABRAMS William M. Jr. 55
ABUILE Edward 15
ACHENBACH Frederick 1, Lena 1, Martin 1
ACKERMAN Mr. 218
ACKLER Elma O. 1, Henry 93, Lemuel 1, Mr. 260, Peter 1, 260
ACKLEY Elzina 1, John S. 1, Mabel 1
ADAMS A. Clark 53, Addie H. 1-2, Andrew 53, 209, Belinda 181, Carrie 1-2, Charles 247, Douglas 1, Edward 75, G. 1-2, Genevieve 123, Henry 181, James 1-2, Joel R. 1, Louisa C. 1, Marcena 181, Mary 275, 310, Minnie 1, Mittie 1, Mr. 66, 347, Percy 2, Phillips 1, Ruth 280-281
ADSIT Anna 2, Harriet 67-68, 305, Seldon 2
ADYE Frederick 2
AHLQUIST John 334
AKERS Candis 2, Inez 2
AKINS Edward 2
ALDEN David S. 2, Glenn 2, Israel 215-216, 283, M. Belle 2, Mary 2
ALDRICH Cloe 21-22, Emma 114, Harris 18, 303-304
ALEXANDER Carrie 3, Franklin 2-3, John 2-3, Mary 2-3, Stephen 2-3
ALGER Olive R. 3, Webster 3
ALLAN Mr. 340
ALLEN Acel 3, Amanda 238, Amos 265, Annette 3-4, Constant 145, Dan 303, Dascum 3, Edward 4, Eliza 3-4, Ethel 3, Eugene 3, Frances 3, Grace 3, Hannah 265, Harmony 4, Harriet 236, Henry 132, Jane 59, Jerome 265, John 59, Jonathan B. 149, Jonathan 3-4, Julia 3-4, Kate 217, Lois 3, Loyal 3, Luther 3, Mary Ann , Mary 228, Melissa 265, Mr. 239, N. Boyd 3, Newton 3, Norman 3-4, 149, 154, 215-216, Peter 3, Rowanna 3-4, Samuel 3
ALSMORTH Effie 314
AMES Angie 4, Guy 34, 257, Henry 4, Howard 4, Lois 4, Mr. 102,342, Victor 78, William 4
AMIDON Calvin 4
AMSBRY Mary 65
AMSDELL Bertie 4, Charles 4, Harmon 4, Matilda 4, Nettie 4
ANDERSON Blanch 241, Clarence 4, Grace 5, Hilda 5, Otto 5
ANDREWS Clair 316, Claude 5, Edwin 5, Frank 5, Jennie 5, Richard 348, Ruth 5, Walter 21
ANDRUS Clair 316, Mary 185
ANGLE Nicholas 136
ANNIS Nancy 141
ANSLEY George 49
ANTHONY Lena 5
APPLEBEE Andrew 87, Mr. 274
APPLETON Mr. 205
ARCHER Allen 54, Benson 33, Bertha 5, Carrie 5, Hannah 53, John 5, 54, Mary 5, Reuben 33, 48, Roy 5
ARMSTRONG Claude 127
ARNOLD Ambrose 5-6, Armenia 6, Calista 5-6, Caroline 5-6, Delevan 6, Dennis 6, Emeline 5-6, Ephraim 5-6,95, Fanny 5-6, Francis 5-6, George 5, Grace 13, Horace 6, Jane 6, Julia 6, Lewis 6, Lucy 6, Orrin 5, Samuel 6, Sarah 179, Susan 5,153, Wesley 5-6, William 5-6,95
ARRANTS James 6, Susan 6, Thomas 6, William 6
ASHDOWN Mary 75
ASHLEY Harmon 6, Luella 6
ATKINSON Mr. 352
ATWELL Julia M. 6
ATWOOD Theresa 6
AUSTIN Alfred 35-36, Claude 345, E. 7, Edna 7, Elizabeth 7,95,

Georgianna 7, Henry 7, Lucretia 7, Marvin 16, Rhoda 7
AXTELL Louisa 7, Theodore 7
AYER Alfred 24
AYLESWORTH Cora 7, Dora 7, Electa 7, Emmet 7, Frank 7, Marcus 7, Maria 7, Victor 7
BABBITT Mr. 35,171
BABCOCK Annis 327, Horace 9, Katharine 9, Louis 9, Mary 9,68-69, Mr. 269, 310
BABINGER Leo 9, Louise 9, Minnie C. 9
BACHELDOR Ada 9
BACON Alice 9, Almon 9, Chloe 9, Fred 9, Harry 9, Lodema 9, Mr. 38, Myrtle 9, Penuel 9, Rolland 9, William 9, May 9
BAILEY Adeline 304, Andrew 72-73, Arthur 304, Deborah 70, Grant 9,278, Helen 297, James 72-73, Libbie 9,278, Sally 313
BAILLET John 156-157
BAIRD Charles 10, Earl 282, George 10, John 10, Rose 10, Sarah 10
BAKER Adorah 10-11, Arunah 10-11,305, Augustus 10-11, Clara 10, Daniel 110, Dorothy 10, Edwin 102, Elizabeth 10-11, Florence 10, Frances 10-11, Francis 10-11, Henrietta 10-11, Isaac 209, Iva 10, J. A. 10, James 10, Julian 10-11, Loren 11, Marietta 10-11, Marsena 11, Mary 10, Nellie 10-11, Netta 10, Rensselaer 10-11, Riley 276, Rosa 305, Rosalinda 10-11, Sally 71-73, W. Scott 10
BALDWIN Lucy 190, Mary Jane 190
BALL Ella 11, Mr 298-299, 311
BALLARD Charles 11, Garrison 180,225-226, George 11, Helen 11, Henry 11, Jennette 180, Sarahette 11
BANANSKI Julia 167-168
BANFIELD George 189, Orpah 189

BANSON Margaret 100
BARBER Ben 11, Dominick 11, Glenn 11, Josephine 11, Mary 11, Mr. 3,11, William 131
BARGY Devillo 11,310, J. M. 11,310, Mary 11, 310, Minnie 11, Minnie 310, Sylvanus 11, 310
BARHITE Charles 12, Elva 12, Fay 12, Helen 12, Janice 12, Welcome 12
BARKER Ellen 12, Isabell 12, Josephine 12, Marshall 12, Mr. 72, Theodore 12
BARNARD Ellen 219, Seth 225
BARNES A. J. 253, Carl 12, Clark 12, Eva 12, John 12, Kenneth 281, Maud 12, Mr. 181,342, Myrtle 257, Rose 12
BARNHART Henrietta 121
BARRET Asher 12, Emily 54, Frank 12-13, Ida 12-13, James 12-13, Leo 12-13, Mark 12-13, Martin 12-13, Mary 12-13, Simeon 54, Thomas 12-13, William 90
BARSE Archibald 13, Estella 13, Flora 13, Rosa 13, Sabina 13
BARTELT Alvina 13, Arthur 13
BARTHOLOMEW Ira 126
BARTLETT Belle M. 14, Daniel 13, Edward 13, Eva 220, Franc 13, Frank 13,49, Harriet 13, Phoebe 13, Willis 14
BARTON Eloise 180, Emogene Lola 242, Hannah 348, Mary 242, Ralston 180
BASSINGER Anthony 14, Fred 14, Mary 14, Paul 14, Peter 14, Peter 14, Rosa 14, William 14
BATCHELDER Ada 283, C. W. 283
BATEMAN Mr. 240
BATES Fred 289, Job 350, Mr. 137, Samuel 15
BATHURST Mr. 261
BATSFORD Daniel 192
BATT Volney 41, William 41
BATTLES Lizzie 15, Mildred 15,

Reva 15
BAXTER Edward 15, John L. 59-60, John T. 82, Norman 15, Richard 15, William 58
BAZO John 139
BEACH Arlene 15, Arlene 15, Benjamin 241, Edith 15, Edwin 15, Esther 15, Ethan 15, Lewis 241, Millard 15, Nellie 15, Ora 15, Orlando 15, Oscar 83, Robert 15, Roberta 15, Sarah 241, William 15
BEAN Cora 15, Lynn 11
BEARDSLEY Charles 16, Fred 15, George 81, Mr. 202, Peter 202
BEATTIE Mr. 133
BECK John 294, Mary 294
BECKER Alley 16, Harriet 16, Helen 16, Herbert 16, Howard 16, Louise 16, Madeline 16, Mr. 16, William 16
BECKMAN Charles 16, Louisa 16, Robert 16
BECKWITH Blanche 16-17, George 16-17, Hannah 38-39, Harlow 16-17, Luther 16, Orrin 16-17, Rachel 16-17, Simon 38-39, Stella 16-17
BEDELL A. D. 99,281, Allie 109, Arthur 53,210, Hannah 273
BEEBE Daniel 17, Ellen 17, George 294-295, Henry 17, Orson 17, Orvis 17, Roland 17, Simeon 352
BEECHER Ann 35, Mark 136, W. H. 34, William 35
BEEMAN Esther 17, Fred 17
BEERS Ida 343
BELL David 317, Edna 17, Edwin 132, Eva 17, Laurice 317, Lizzie 317, Ralph 17
BELLOWS Lucinda 242-243, Philip 242-243
BENDER Conrad 35-36, Rosina 35-36
BENHAM Mr. 105
BENNEHOFF Effie 17, R. Lyle 17
BENNETT Clara 18, David 18, Fanny 18, Jemima 18, Maria 17, Mary 17-18, Mr. 344, Oliver 17, Orrin 28,341-342, Polly 18, Stephen 278, Thomas 17, Wallace 17
BENSON C. A. 70, Charles 219, John G. 18, Lucy 263, Mr. 26,238-239
BENT Betsey 18-19, Diana 18-19, Hartwell 18-19, Helen 18, Henrietta 18, Horace 18-19, Melvina 18-19
BENTLEY Burr 19, Luman 119, Stephen 19
BERES Stephen 120
BERRY Alexander 19, Caroline 19-20, Christiana 19,347, Henrietta 19, Henry 19-20, Herbert 19-20, Horatio 19, Imogene 19-20, L.P. 19, Leona 19-20, Louisa 19-20, William 19
BESECKER Lena 20
BESSEY Anna 95
BEST Edward 346
BETTINGER Frank 20, Nicholas 20, Sarah 20
BEVERLY Margaret 20
BEWLEY Mr. 44
BIERNS Mary 138
BIRMINGHAM Kate 330-331
BISHOP Ellen 20, Florilla 63, George 20, Harriston 20, Harvey 300, Henry 20, Louisa 20, Mabel 300, Mr. 301, Sarah 20, 192
BIXBY Barnes 20, James 46
BLACKMER Elizabeth 20, Henry 20, Levi 20, Sarah 20
BLACKMERE Henry 101
BLACKWELL Bertha 20-21, Florence 20-21, Harry 20-21, Howard 20-21, Joseph 20-21, Morris 20-21, Robert 20-21
BLAIR Jane 252, Lydia 57, William 252
BLAKE Alice 21, Elmer 21, Maud 21
BLAKELY SEE PAGE 245, Fanny 21-22, Harriet 21, Harry 21, Hiram

21, Justus 21, Otsey 21, Weltha 21
BLAKESLEE Manley 170
BLAKESLEY Ruth 332
BLANCHARD A. D. 22, Cornelius 22, 29, Eliza 152, Emma 29, Erma 22, Florence 22, Harrie 22, Harry 22, Hattie 22, Hiram 152, Jamerson 140, Lynn 22, Marsevan 22, 29, Nellie 22, Solotus 22, 29, 152, Tamasin 152, Tamerson 22, 29, Washington 22,29
BLEMUSTER Martin 22, B
BLISS Lucius 22, Lydia 22, Mary 22, S. M. 42
BLITON Lloyd 22, Margaret 22, Nellie 22, Rupert 22
BLOCK Mary 22, Mr. 138
BLODGET Harrison 75
BLOOD Irwin 22, Lucia 22, Polly 334
BLOSSOM Earl 23, Elmer 23, Ernest 23, Eugene 23, Leota 23
BLOWERS Addie 23, Amba 23, Andrew 23, Anna 298, Annis 23, Charlotte 23, Clark 23, Hassan 23, Huldah 23, Mary 23, Matilda 23, Mr. 213, Omer 23, Phebe 23, Silas 23, Smith 23, Truman 297- 298, William 23
BOARDMAN Arminta 24, 146, Edwin 24, Jerome 24, John 278, Lee 24, Nellie 24, Solomon 24, Thomas 24
BOBERG William 24
BOCKMIER Avena 24-25, Clare 24-25, Conrad 24, John 24-25, Mr. 130, Rheinhart 24-25, Rosa 24, William 24
BOEHLER Mr. 311
BOLANDER Charles 25, Lana 25, Mary 25, William 25
BOLLER Adah 274, David 209
BOND Alfred 25, 191, Angie 25, Daniel 110-111, Eliza Ann 68, Louisa 286-287, 289, 291, Marshall 68, Perry 25, Warren 25

BONESTEEL Almon 90, Reuben 25
BOORN Maria 92
BOOTH Beatrice 25, Charlotte 25, Lucy 25, Mildred 25, Vance 25, Virgil 25
BORDEN Andrew 145, Elizabeth 25, George 26, Henrietta 66, James 66, 92
BOSER Henry 26, Lena 26, Mr. 296
BOSWER Mr. 40
BOSWICK Mr. 82
BOSWORTH M. W. 199
BOUTELL Charles 26, Clark 26, Cynthia 26, Jannette 26
BOUTELLE Calvin 26, Clark 26
BOUTON Clarissa 26, Lewis 26, 120
BOWEN Charles 26-27, Effie 26-27, Ernest 26-27, Ethel 27, Frank 27, George 27, Hattie 26-27, Hector 26, Jesse 27, Judson 26, Lawrence 27, Leonard 26-27, Luzerne 26, Susan 26-27, Victor 27, William 26
BOWMASTER Joseph 168
BOYCE Mary 147
BOYINGTON Emeline 68-69
BOYLE Charlotte 238, Edward 27, George 238, Hattie 27, Margaret 27, Mary 27, Nellie 27, Peter 27, William 27
BOZARD Alphonzo 28, Beatrice 28, Clifford 27, Eva 27-28, Luella 28, 341, 342, Truman 28
BRADFORD Dorothy 146, Mr. 306
BRADLEY Aditha 28, Alvin 28, Eliza 28, John 28, Levi 28, Lydia 28, Samuel 28, Watia 28
BRADNACK J.R. 342, Lizzie 342
BRADT Edna 28, Hazel 28, J. N. 28
BRAINARD Mr. 237
BRAND Anna 28-29, David 28-29, Gladys 28-29, Lois 28-29, Mr. 29, Richard 28-29
BRANDEL Frederick 29, John 29, Paulena 29, Pauline 296, Robert 29
BRASTED Mr. 242, Rebecca 4

BRENNANAN Ira 292-293
BRENNER Hilda 5
BRETT Mr. 210
BREWSTER Mr. 207
BRIDENBAKER Floris 29, Pearl 29, William 29
BRISSEE Adda 29
BRISTON Beulah 259
BRODERICK Armenia 30, Catharine 29-30, Elizabeth 29- 30, Ellen 29-30, Maggie 29-30, Mary 29-30, Michael 29-30, Mrs. 210, Rose 29-30, Thomas 29-30
BRONOLD Michael 200
BROOKS Brightman 277, Carl 30, Clara 117, Emmet 312, Helen 64, Ida 312, James 310, Lewella 310, P. M. 54
BROTHERS Mary 30
BROTHERTON Mr. 209
BROW Mabel 49
BROWMAN Ira 246-247
BROWN Achsah 31-32, Adeline 322, Albert 30-33, Alfred 31, Allan 32, Alton 32, Archibald 31, 33, Arthur 30-33, Asher 21, Bryant 265, Caleb 38, Carl 31, Carrie 31- 33, Charles 30-32, 143, D. Alton 33, Daniel 31, 100, 104, David 32, David Edwin 31, David M. 151, Dean 31, Delila 32, Edith 32, Effa 31, Elizabeth 32, Ellen 30-32, Ellis 31, 33, Emily 66, Eva 31, Ezra 31, Florence 151, Florian 32, Francis B. 115-116, Franklin 19, G. W. 64, George 31, 33, Grace E. 33, Grace 30-32, Gracie 32-33, Harry 32-33, Harvey 31, 33, Henry 30-32, Horace 104, James 30-33, John 33, Leslie 32- 33, Lillian 30-32, Lizzie 5, Louisa 33, Lyman 30-32, Lynn 31-33, Margaret 114, Marilda 32, Mary L. 33, Mary 31, Merrill 31, 33, Mr. 17, 93, 345, N. S. 30-33, Nancy 31, Nathaniel 31, Nella 237, Nettie 31, Olive 30-32, Perry 13, Peter 31, Robert 32, Ruby 32, Silas 32, Thos. 33, Victor 32, Wallace 33, Warren Leroy 32
BRUCE Charles 33
BRUNDAGE Katherine 270
BRUSHINGHAM Timothy 33
BRYANT Cordelia 33, Isaac 33
BUCHER Jacob 33, William 33
BUCK Abigail 33, Louisa 33
BUCKLES Elizabeth 274, John 274
BUFFIN Nina 33, William 93
BUFFINGTON Florence 33-34, Frances 34, Helen 33-34, S. Arline 33-34, William 33-34
BUGSBEY Jane 34, Sarah 34
BULL Bernice 34, Fayette 34, Henry 34, Perus 34, Wallace 34, William 34
BULLOCK Anna 34, Cady 34, Charles 34, Della 53, George 53, Luella 34, Marcia 34, Milton 34, Mr. 160, Orrin 34
BUMP Harley 299-300, Lewis 299-300, Louis 299-300, Sally 299-300
BUNCE Hamilton 155, Sanford 34
BURBANK Effa 332-333
BURCH Mr. 34
BURDICK Abel 287, Albert 235-236, Euphernia 287, Lucy 287, Nellie 35, Samuel 35, Silas 21-22
BURDITT William 35
BURGER Alexander 35, Mr. 225, Sanford 189
BURKHALDER Christine 35, Lucile 35, Nicholas 35
BURKHALTER Emma 35, George 35, Henry 35, Louisa 35, Nicholas 35
BURLESON Owen 125
BURLINGAME Adel 36, Emeline 35-36, Fred 36, George 35-36, Hannah 35-36, Ira 35-36, Isabelle 35-36, John 35-36, May 35-36, Philo 35-36, Walter 35-36
BURLINGHAM Amos 36, Beatrix 37, Charles 36-37, Elnathan 36-

37, 216, Emma 36-37, Henry 190, Ida 190, Margaret 36-37, William 36-37
BURMASTER Joseph 103, 168
BURNS Alice 254, Eurnice 75
BURR Grace 34, James 34, Mr. 254, Stephen 34
BURRELL Jerry 37, Laurie 37, William 37
BURRILL David 37
BURROUGHS Arctus 37, 210, Mr. 245, Susan 37
BURSEE James 247-248, Jane 247-248, Sarah 247
BURT Hezekiah 37, 146
BURTON Beatrice 37, Charles 37, Lillian 37
BURY Iona 37, William 37
BUSEKIST John 37
BUSH Edwin 312, Fred 316, Julia 38
BUSHINGHAM Margret 33
BUSLEY Ann 70
BUSSLER Augustus 149
BUTCHER Franklin 153-154, Fred 48, Mr. 45
BUTLER Alvin 38, Alzina 38, 231, Arthur 38, 231, Donald 38, Elizabeth 38, Henrietta 38, Horace 38, 231, James 165, Jasper 38, 231, Joseph 38, Lillian 38, Louisa 38, Lydia 38, 231, Maria 38, Mr. 10, Olivia 38, 231, Patrick 38, hebe 47, Rose 256-257, Seneca 38, Thomas 147, Wilder 38
BUTTERFIELD Morris 27
BUTTON Caroline 39, Charles 38-39, David 38, Harriet 39, Harvey 38-39, Heman G. 86, Heman 10-11, 38-39, 312, Horace 39, Jane 39, Jesse 38-39, Jonas K. 52, Jonas 38-39, 100, 310, Leon 39, Louise 39, Lucetta 38-39, Lyman 38-39, Margaret 39, Mr. 41, Naomi 38-39, Peter 39, Polly 38-39, Reuben 38-39, Sophia 38-39
BUTTS Mr. 140

BUXTON Charles 39-40, 80, Clarence 40, John 40
BYRNE Jeannette 40, Paul 40, Peter 40, Robert 40
BYRON Augusta 40, Augustus 40, Emma 40, John 40, Nellie 40
CABLE George 78
CADY Alice 41, Betsey 41, Carlina 41, John 41, Josiah 41, Melissa 41, William Henderson 277
CAGWIN Alexander 41, C. Hellen 41, C. J. 52, Charles 41, Florence 41, Helen 81, Isaac 41, James 81, Jane 41, Jessie 41, Louisa 81
CAHEN See page 182
CAIN Seth 41
CAINE James 328
CALKINS George 41
CALKINS Mary 282-283, Sally 41, Thomas 41
CALLAHAN Ella 315
CALLIHAN Joseph 305
CAMP Austin 41, Chester 203, Emma 42, 297, Flora 297, Jennie 1, Mr. 297, Welcome 29
CAMPBELL Adeline 42, Bertha 42, harles 42-43, Dewitt 42-43, Edna 2, Eliza 206-207, Harry 42-43, Howe 42, James 167, Lizzie 42, Martha 42, Pamelia 347, Ruth 42, William 42
CANEEN Frank 260, Thomas 63
CANFIELD C. Porter 43, Cornelius 43, Fanny 43, George 43, Henry 43, Lucy 43, Minnie 43, Mr. 127, 271, Porter 43, Samuel 43, Sylvester 43
CANN Louise 176
CAPRON Benjamin 43, Ephraim 43, Joseph 43
CARBACH Gertrude 43
CARD Flora 43, Jay 43, John 43, Mabel 51, Mr. 51, William H. 43
CARLBERG Christina Marie 44, George 44, Grace 43-44, Lula 43-44, Mildred 44

CARLING Ada 44, Alonzo 44, Alvinah 44, Emeline 44, Lovina 44, Mildred 44, Samuel 44
CARLISLE Ella 65
CARLS Cleatus 44-45, Florence 44-45, J. J. 44-45, John 24, 44-45, Kenneth 44-45, Lewis 44, Mary 44-45
CARLSON Benjamin 45, Millie 45, Tillie 45
CARMATZ Ida 45, Lewis 45, Sylvia 45, William 45
CARPENTER Arthur 155, Charles 45, 155, Eliphalet 109, Floyd 45, James 45, Jane 45, John 45, Lee 45, Nelson 45, Sally 45, Stephen 45
CARR Betsey 68-69, Daniel 68-69, Hazel 45, Lois 295, Mary E. 45, Mr. 306, William 45
CARRIER Adel 46, Alice 45-46, Carrie 45-46, Frances 45-46, Grace 45-46, Lucy 45-46, Mr. 25, Sarrah 45-46, Timothy 45-46
CARRINGER W. C. 198
CARRINGTON Edwin 352
CARROLL Daniel 46, John 46, Julia 46, Lawrence 46, Margaret 46, Mary 46, Myrtle 46
CARTER Cleveland 46
CARTHELL Mr. 26
CARTWRIGHT Charles 47, Levi 47, Mary 47
CARVER Rebecca 117
CARY George 135, Josiah 47, Phebe 47, Susan 47, William 47
CASE Betsey 200, Dean 47, Deborah 162-163, 202, Edward 47, Elliott 47, Emerson 47, Maude 47, Theresa 47
CASEY Carrie 47-48, Charles 90, Dennis 47-48, Edmond 47-48, Francis 47-48, James 131, 321 John 47-48, Mariah 47-48, Marion 47-48, Martha 90, Susie 90
CASWELL Calvin 48, Charles 48, Darwin 48, David 322, Lora 48, Media 48, Merl 48, Orlinda 48, Sylvester 48, Thomas 48, Warren 48, William 322
CAUGHLIN Patrick 48
CHADWICK David 244, Ransom 192
CHAFFEE Elijah 66-67, 171, Ida 49, Mr. 134, 328, William 49
CHAMBERLAIN Almira 49, Anna 49, Charles 34, 49, Emily 49, Emma 49, Fred 49, George 49, Harriet 49, Henry 49, 282, 283, Lucy 49, Moses 335, Oakley 179, Rose 282, Roy 49, Verna 49, William A. 49, Willis 49
CHAMBERLIN C. Huested 49, C. J. 62, Emma 49, George 49, Henry 49, Huldah 62, Patience 49, Wales 62
CHAMBERS Mr. 49, Oliver 49
CHAMPLAIN Matilda 37
CHAMPLIN Elizabeth 50, John B. 50, Hannah 50, Lydia 50, Pauline 50
CHANDLER Charles 50, Clarence 50, Roy 50
CHAPIN Albert 50, Fearette 50, Frank 50, Lois 50, Nancy 50, Welcome 50
CHAPMAN Ara 51, Daniel 51, Emory 51, Frank 51, Hattie 51, Matilda 51, Myron 51, Rathbun 51, Rhoda 51, Townsend 51, Welcome 51
CHARLESWORTH Charles 16-17, Deliah 94
CHASE Horace 51, James 51, Maria 51, Mr. 156-157
CHEEK George 82
CHEESEMAN Carrie 51-52, Charlie 51-52, Charlotte 81, Louis 51-52, Mary E. 51-52, Morris 81, Nellie 51-52, Rollin 51-52
CHENEY Lyman 52, Monroe 52, Mr. 177
CHESNER Mr. 174
CHILDS John C. 52, Sarah W. 52

CHITTENDON Hazel 52, Jared 52, Louis 52, Marion 52, Robert 52
CHURCH Mark 50, Mary 49, Nelson 52, Wal 300
CHURCHILL Frank 52
CIPLES Abigail 100, Mr. 100
CLARE Michael 185, Walter 205
CLARK Andy 53, Anna 208, 299-300, Asahel 53, Bertha May 53, Charles 259, Clarissa 53, Ellen 53, 210, Ephraim 57, Francis B. 53, Frank 53, George 328, Georgia 53, Georgie 53, Jane 53, John B. 57, John R. 312, John 53, Lila 53, Lorena 53, Louisa 312, Lucius 53, M. Lena 53, Mary 57, Morris 53, Mr. 121, 339, Orin 54, Vincent 208, Warner 57, William 53
CLARKE Thankful 260-261
CLARKSON David 331
CLARY James 115
CLAUSEN Minerva 54
CLAWSON Julia 54
CLEMENTS Cora 54, Robert 198
CLEVELAND Juliette 54
CLINE Ann 105, John W. 105
CLOUGH Adella 54, Amyra 54, Lester 54
COAST Bessie 54, Emilie 54, Fleming 54, J. Weston 54, John 54, John Weston 54, Mary 54, Mary Gladys 54
COBB Hugh 254, 341
COE Mr. 41
COFFEY Winifred G. 54
COGSWELL John L. 54, Mason 54, Perry 54
COHEN Betsey 55, Fannie 55, Israel 54-55, Louis 54, Michael 54-55, Mollie 54-55, Samuel 54-55
COIT Gordon 70
COLBURN David 119, Helen 55, Josiah 55
COLBY Eda 42, M. D. 42
COLDRICK Edwin 325
COLE Ada 56, Alzera 55-56, Americus 55-56, Anna Maria 55-56, Arthur 56, Asahel 55-56, Caroline 43, Charles 43, Daniel 55-56, Elizabeth 56, Ellen 55-56, George 55-56, Gerald 56, Hannah 55-56, Jesse 263, Joseph 55-57, Lelie 55-56, Maryan 55-56, Maurice 56, Myrtal 55-56, Nancy 55-56, Richard 55-56, S. S. 339, Sally 55-56, Theodore 55, Truman 55-56, William 55-56
COLEMAN E. G. 57, Marjorie 57
COLF Albert 57, Altie 57, Delevan 57-58, 286, Edie 57, Emma 58, Emory 55-56, 286, Erastus 57, Grover 57-58, 286, Herbert 57-58, Jehiel 57, John D. 57, Matie 57, 286, Nora 57-58, 286, Viola 57-58, 286
COLLIE Mr. 275
COLLINS See Page 323, Daniel 58, Jeanne 58, John 58, Josephine 58, Lola 58, Mary 58, Mr. 280, P. S. 187, Robert 58, Sarah 300, Sarah A. 175, Timothy 58, Wm. 41
COLVIN Alma 58-59, Barton 58-59, George 11, Iona 59, Laura 11, Marvin 59, Morris 59, Susan 11
COLWELL Adaline 40
COMPETIRO Joseph 59
COMSTOCK James 136
CONDON John 59, Johnanna 59, Margaret 59, Mary 59, Nellie 59, William 59
CONE Amanda 28
CONGDON B. F. 189, Darwin 128-129, J. M. 189
CONHISER Caroline 60, Frank 60
CONKLIN Alice 60, Emma 54, Emory 60, Martha 141, Mary 60, Mary A. 110, Millard 60, 110, Zachary 60, 110
CONKLING Samuel 60
CONLEY Louise R. 201
CONNELL Bertha 60, Blanche 60, Eunice 60, Frances 60, Gertrude

61, James 60-61, John 60-61, Lawrence 60-61, Margaret 60, Martin 60-61, Mary 60-61, Mayme 60-61, Owen 60, Peter 60
CONNORS Benjamin 61-62, Bessie 62, Charles 61-62, Edward 61-62, Emma 61-62, Gertrude 61-62, James 61-62, Jessie 61-62, Lawrence 61-62, Margaret 61-62, Maria 61-62, Michael 62, Rose 61-62, Susan 61-62
CONRAD Charles 62, Elva 62, Fanny 257, H. J. 62, Oristus 28, Rev. 300, Wallace 62
COOK Alonzo 312, Jennie 312, John 287, 289-290, Mary 287, 289-290, Mr. 256, Philetus 312
COOKINGHAM Cora 62, Walter J. 62
COOL Mr. 83
COOLEY Adell 142, Ebenezer 142, Oliver 142, William H. 62
COOLIDGE Mr. 265
COON Nathan L. 23, Oliver 143
COONEY Mary C. 62, Michael J. 62
COOPER Abigail 63, Benjamin 1, Christiana 63, Elish 63, Emma Jane 63, George 63, Harvey 63, Margaret 63, Mr. 271, Polly 63, Rebecca 63, Silas 62-63, Sylus 63, William 295
COOT Ellen 63, Jennie 63, Mary 63, Nettie 63
CORBETT Emma 63, Paul 63, Shirley 63
CORKINS Julia 63, Patrick 63
CORMYA Frank 63
CORNELL Sadie 151
CORNWELL Charles 63, Elizabeth 63
CORSAW Devillo 63, Sarah 63
CORSET Ellen 176
CORSETT Carrie 64, Ellen 64, Lincoln 64
CORTHELL Lambert 261
COSS Charles 64, Helen 64

COSTELLO Claude 64, Esther 64, George 64, Ida 64, John 64, Marion 64, Mildred 64
COSTIGAN John 61-62
COTRAEL Carlton 64, Ellen 64, Hiram 64, Jonathan 64, Mary 64
COTTON Charles 64, Mariah 64
COUNCILMAN Andrew 64, Ira 64, John 64
COURTER Alanson 341-342
COURTRIGHT C. C. 167, Reba 65, William 64
COUSE Asa 30
COUSINS Albert 65, Paul 65
COVERT Almira 65, Anthony 65, Glenn 65, John 65, Leo 65
COWEN Anna 65, John 2, Norman 12, 172
COWLEY Horace 65, Orlo 65
COX Augusta 65, Ethel 65, Fred 65, Herme 329, Howard 65, Lloyd 65, Matthew 329, Mr. 263-264, Polly 41
COXES Augusta 82
CRADDUCK Alice 66, Fred 66
CRAM Burt 66, Eva 66, Harry 66, Henry 66
CRAMER Marie 58
CRANCE Lorenzo 66
CRANDALL Clea 66, Curtis 66, Ellen 292-293, Emma 252, Frank 66, Guy 66, Harvey 66, Ida 252, Jessie 66, Lemuel 66, Loretta 66, Mr. 71, 145, Mrs. 140, Orville 66, W. H. 353, William 21-22, 204, 283, 340, Wm. 348
CRANE Alex 66, Elsie 66, 171, Julia 66, Mr. 270, Stanley 66, 171, Ulysses 66, 171
CRANNELL Bertha 67, Luther 67
CRAWFORD Bridget 67, Ellen 67, Isabelle 67, James 67, John 67, Loretta 67, Margaret 67, Mary 67, William 235
CRIBBS Mr. 246
CROKER Annie 67, Daniel 67
CROMIE Edith 32

CRONIN Rosalie B. 90
CROOK Charles 67-68, 92, 305, Cyrenia 68, Frank 67, 305, Fred 67, 305, George 67-305, Martha 92, Mina 67-68, 305
CROOKEN P. F. 301
CROOKS Miranda 203
CROSBY Ada 252, Horatio 68, Huldah 252, Miranda 68, Nathan 252, Stephen 252
CROSGROVE Mr. 108-109
CROSS Almira 68-69, Amanda 68, Asa 68-69, 203, Cora 69, Derdick 68-69, Ella 68-69, Eva 68-69, Francis 68-69, Garwood 68-69, George 68-69, Gertrude 69, Hawley 69, Hilda 69, Isaiah 68-69, John 244, Lizzie 69, Luther 68, Reuben 68, Stephen 68, William H. 68-69
CROTZER Albert 101, Fannie 101
CROW Mr. 10, 253
CROWELL Mr. 287
CROWLEY Asahel 136, James 173, Jane 69, Jerome 229-230, John 208, Mary 301-302, Melvin 101, Rodney 69
CRUMB Chauncey 70, 217-218, 345, Chiles 70, Culver 69, Kingsley 70, Mary 69, 345, Olive 70, Sylvia 70
CUIT Roger 70
CULLEN Hattie 70, Joseph 70, Lucy 70, Montreville 70, Samuel 70
CULLINAN Margaret 70, Mary 70, Sara 70, Theresa 70
CULLIS Mr. 314
CULVER Cary 70, Julia 64, Lelia 64, Lyman 70, Mary 70, Sarah 70
CUMMING Joseph 71
CUMMINGS Laura 260-261, Leonard 71, Philander 71, Sarah 71
CUNNINGHAM Timothy 219
CURRIE Agnes 71, Alexander 71, Andrew 71, Ella 71, Hazel 71, James 71, Olive 71, Roy 71, William 106
CURRY David 46, 198, Mary 71, Richard 71, Sarah 46
CURTINDALL Libbie 55-56
CURTIS Abiah 72-73, Amelia 71-73, Byron 73, Catharine 72, Elliott 72, Elmina 72, Expenance 6, Helen 73, Henry 72, Joseph 71-73, Leslie 72, Logan 72, Lottie 242, Margaret 72, Mary 72-73, Mr. 44, 252, Rensselaer Leigh 72-73, Ruth 72, Smith 71- 73, Susan 71-72, Thomas 72, Waldo 15, 72, William 71-73, Willie 72
CURTISS Elliott 15
CYENER Alice 73
CYZMANOWSKI Alexander 82
DAKE Mr. 21, Pearl 131
DALEY Erastus 129
DAMON Ada 75, Amelia 155-157, Axy 18, Cary 75, Daniel 75, Edmund 75, Emeline 75, Emma 75, Henry 75, Hiram 75, Lyman 75, Martin 75, Melvina 75, Minnie 75, Mr. 289, Myra 75, Ralph 75, William H. 156-157
DANA Frank 75-76, George 75-76, Ivy 75-76, Kate 75-76, Lawrence 75-76, Minnie 75-76, Stewart 75-76, Susie 75-76, Warner 75-76
DANIELS Emily 97, Ethern 76, Joseph 97, Samuel 97
DANLEY Charles 110, 291
DARBEE Anna 76, Azariah 76, George 76, Gladys 76, Hoyt 76, Mary 94, Mr. 283, Willie 76
DARLING Clara 76, George 76, John L. 76, Judson 76, Loraine 76, Lovina 76, Mary 176, Robert 76, 246
DARRING Adelbert 346, Gertrude 346
DAVENPORT Mr. 323
DAVID Daniel 343, Edwin F. 55
DAVIDSON Mr. 71, Sarah 238
DAVIES Alfred 77, Carl 77, David

77, 95, Gladys 77, John 77, Maurice 77, Morris 77, Norman 77, Rena 77
DAVIS Adelbert 77, Angeline 115, Benjamin 77-78, Charles 115, Clarence 78, Daniel 78, Edwin 56, 165-166, Emory 77, Fred 20, 77, Harry 77, Hiram 78, John F. 128, 129, John K. 166, Julia 38, Lyman 77-78, Mary 177, Mary E. 77-78, Mary J. 53, Mildred 105, Mr. 177, Sarah 77, Thomas 77, William 78, Wilma 165
DAWLSEY Archie 78, Beulah 78, John 78, Rose 78
DAWSON Alexander 78, Henry 78, James 78, Mary 78, Mayme 60-61, Mr. 265
DAWTON Welcome J. 138
DAY Anna 78-79, Asahel 78, Catherine 79, Charles 78-79, Clark 258, Flora 78-79, Georgia 78-79, Harriet 78-79, Hartson 78-79, Ida 78, Israel 196, Leroy 78, Louisa Ann 139, Lucy 78-79, Mary J. 78, Morgan 78-79, Mr. 110, Myrtle 78, Reuben 78, Salmon 78-79, William 78-79, William A. 121, William A., Sr. 78-79, William T. 78
DE GOLIA George Calvin 351
DEAN Alice 233, Edith 79, Euretta 79, Henry 161, Merwin 79, Mr. 248
DECHOW Frederick 79, William 79
DEFOREST Harold 203
DEGOLIA Mr. 244
DEIBLER See Page 79
DEITER Frank 81
DEITT Christian 138
DELAMASTER James 177
DELANEY Marguerite 79, Michael 79
DELMAGE Cora 79, Floyd 79, John 79, Sheldon 79
DELP John 221
DEMING Esther 90, Sally 90
DEMMING Joseph 90, Thomas 90
DEMMON Abel 43, Enos 79, Mertie 79, Mr. 15
DEMPSEY Raymond M. 79
DENNING Henry 97
DERBY Abi 350-351, Elisha 350-351
DEREMER Jonathan 118
DERMONT Emegene 80, Ralph 80, Ray 80, William 80
DEVEREUX Ellen 80, Mary 80
DEWEY Alanson 80, Hannah 80, John 80, Mr. 312, Theodore 59
DEWITT Chloe 80, Clarence 80, Clinton 80, Elmer 342, Florett 80, Mary 80
DEXTER Bertha 203, Henry 80, Jennie 80, Marcus 203, Norman 80
DEYOE Edna 80-81, Flora 80-81, Leona 80-81, Velma 80
DIBBLE Benedict 81, Daniel 81, Mason 81
DIBBLER See Page 79
DIBLER Esther 79, Joseph 79, Nathan 79, Sylvester 79, William 79
DICKSON Anna 81, Weldon 81
DIDAS Bessie 81, John 81, Kathleen 81, Mary 81
DIDCOCK H. D. 133
DIETER George 81
DIETZ Frederick 277
DILTS Gilbert 81, Lillian 81, Lydia 81, William 81
DINAN John 81, Michael 81
DINDER Ernest 81
DINEEN Mr. 340
DITCHER Bernice 82, Christopher 82, Edna 82, Glenn 82, LaVern 82, Mr. 287, Ralph 82
DIVER Anna 82, Jane 82, John 82, William 82
DIXON Andrew 82, Daniel 270-272, Ruth 270-272, Thomas 82, William 82
DOBKOWSKI John 82
DOCKSTADER Adam 131, 275-

276, Ethel Bertha 282, Mr. 240
DODGE Almon 83, C. I. 82, Eliza Ann 83, Horace 83, Lottie 82-83, Mr. 65, Myra 82-83, Myron 82-83, Ruth 82-83
DOLLARD Anastatia 83, Jane 83, Matthew 83, Myrtle 20, Patrick 226
DOLLEY Eliza 85
DONALDSON Daniel 83, Jennie 83, John 83, Laura 83, Lydia 83, Viola 83
DONEGAN James 83-84, 127, Jerry 83-84, 127, John 83-84, 127, Mary 83-84, 127, Thomas 83-84, 127
DONLIN Edmond 202
DONNELLAN Francis 84, Margaret 84, Michael 84
DONNELLY Henry 222, John 84, Mary 84
DONOVAN Aileen 84, Catherine 84, Daniel 84, James 84, Mr. 59, William 84
DOOLEY Jeremiah 85, Mary 85, Richard 85, William 85
DORNAN James 233
DORR Frank 85, Fred 85, Frederick 85, Henry 85, John, Jr. 85, Lottie 85, Mary 85
DORT Leon 62
DOTY Mr. 154
DOUGHERTY Alfred 85
DOUGLAS Mr. 199
DOW John 27
DOWD T. H. 70
DOYLE Junie 85, Thomas 85
DRAKE G. W. 72, Mr. 176
DRAPER Florence 85, Lois 85
DRAYER Emerson 85, Frederick 85, Henry 85, Hubert 86, John 86, Minnie 85, Theodore 86, William 85
DREAVER Clark 86, Sarah 86, William 86
DREPENSTED Walter 137
DREPPENSTEAD Henry 86

DRISCOLL Arthur 86, 160, James 86, 160, John 86, 160, Mr. 109, Sarah 86, 160, William 86, 160
DROWN Elbridge 339, Floris 339, Harriet 86, Lillian 86, Nancy 41, Oliver 86, Peter 78, 339, May 86
DUFFY Frank 187, Marguerite 86
DUKE Emily 87, J. Hanford 87, Joseph 87, Myron 87
DULIAN Joseph 87, Louis 87, Rose 87
DUNBAR Alice 87, Arthur 87
DUNCAN Addie 87, Katherine 108-109
DUNLAVEY John 87, Margaret 87
DUNN Alice 87, Patrick 87
DURAN Michael 130
DURFEE Edwin 306, Elmer 87, Emeline 207, Mary 87
DUSENBERRY Duncan 88, Edgar 87-88, Helen 87-88, William 87-88
DUTCHER Cordelia 201, Mr. 352
DUTTON Berlin 88, Franklin 88, Gertrude 88, Harriet 88, James 88, Joseph 88, Margaret 88, Mary 88, Peter 88, Ransom 88, Thomas 88
DYE Albert 332, Mason 88, Mr. 103, 347, Nathan 88
EARL Adeline 89, Alfred 89, Ann 89, Frederick 89, Lewis 89, Thomas 89, William 89
EASTERLY Bertha 89, Henry 89, Huldah 89, Lodema 21, Price 89
EASTMAN John 89, Norman 89, Orville 97, William 89
EASTON Ahimaz 324, Ellen 89-90, Hazel 89-90, Lovina 324, Lurilla 21, Nina 89-90, Ruby 89, William 324
EATON Emma 90, George 65, Tappan 90
EBERHARDT Lizzie 90
ECKHART Fred 274
EDDY Albert 351, Elisha 329, Elvira 90, Enos 90, 131, John 127 Lorin 90

EDEL Catherine 90, Dorothy 90, Lillian 90, Mr. 36
EDICK Andrew 90
EDMONDS Fred 90
EDMUNDS Austin 90, Burrett 91, Chester 90-91, Ellen 90-91, Emily 90-91, Jane 90-91, Ruth 90, Salem 90
EDWARDS Alice 91, Elizabeth 233, Julius 325, Mr. 349-350, Truman 253
EELLS William 91
EGAN Rose 198
EGLINGTON Eliza 91, Florence 91
EHMAN Frank 91, Iva 91, Laurena 91, Lorena 91, Mr. 201
EISERT Anna 91, Coletta 91, George 91, Rose 91
ELDRIDGE Clara 92, Daniel 92, Francis 92, Lemuel 92, Ophelia 92
ELLING Chris 344-345, Henry 344-345
ELLIOTT Cecile 338, David 92, Lyle 245, Margaret 92, Robert 92, 338
ELLIS Eleanor 103, Elizabeth 92, Giles 92, Henry 92, John 92, Mr. 70, 168, Reuben 92, Will 92, William 92
ELLITHORPE Millard 92
ELLWOOD Mr. 109
ELMORE Mr. 239
ELSEN Mr. 256
ELWELL Ettie 93, Josiah 93, Michael 92, Mr. 77, 352
ELY Caroline 93, William 93
EMERSON Clara 93, Lovinia 93, Lowell 93, Sarah 93, William 93
ENDERS Alfred 33, 93, Celia 33, 93-94, Charles 33, 93-94, Isabella 33, 93-94, Louis 33, 93-94, Mildred 93-94, Nina 33, 93-94, William 33, 93
ENGBLOM Berger 94, Frank 94
ENGLISH Mr. 98
ENOS Silas 94
ERHARD Julia 266, Leo 266

ERHART Emma 94, Grace 94, Julia 94, Leo 94, Lewis 94, Mary 94
ERNEST Christina 94, Leslie 94, William 94
ESSENA Hedley 94
ESSEX Cyrenius 94, Lavantia 94
ETHRIDGE Cora 345-346
EVANS David 95, Elizabeth 95, Frank 95, Fred 95, Harriett 194, Harry 95, Irene 95, John 95, Mamie 95, Mary 95, Morris 95, Norma 334, Perry 334, Ralph 194, Ruth 95, Sarah 95, William 95, Wm. 95
EVENS Betsey 95, Eleanor 95, Evander 95, Francis 95, Sylvester 95
EVERTS Orsemus 95
EWELL Adelbert 318, Clarence 328
EWING Joel 314
FAILING Allen 97, Charles 97, Emily 97
FAIRBANKSs Eleazer 90, Lavaca 90, Walter 43
FAIRCHILD Bertha 97, Bruce 97, Florence 97, Fred 97, James H. 97, James W. 97, Lewis 97, M. D. 97, Mary 97, Nellie 97, Robert 97, Rosalia 97, Rose 97
FALCONER Charles 97, Elizabeth 97
FALK Mr. 301
FANCHER Charles 98, John 98, Lynn 98
FARLEY Ann 98, Frank 98, Georgiana 98, Harry 98, Julia 98, Kathryn 98, Leon 98
FARNUM A. H. 98, David 45-46, Edith 98-99, 281, Ellen 98-99, 281, Gertrude 98-99, 281, Jennie 98-99, 281, Josephine 98, Lefa 45-46, Maude 98-99, 281, Willie 98-99, 281
FARRAR Aleanzor 42, Mr. 346, Royal 99
FARRELL Margaret 262, Thomas 262

FARRINGTON Edward 99, Ellen 99, F. Vernal 99, Forrest 99, Harry 99, Howard 99, Sarah 99
FARWELL Abram 99, Catharine 118, Daniel 99, Elizabeth 99, Eugene 99, John 118, Mabel 99, Maria 118, Samuel 118
FAWLEY Margaret 225
FAY Cyrus 99, Ellen 99, Emerson 76, Warren 99, William 178
FEE Albert 100, Catherine 100, Charles 100, Eugene 100, James 100, Nellie 100, Owen 100
FEEHAN Florence 19, Frank 19
FEENEY Susan 285
FEGLEY Clara 100, Jesse 100, Jessiah 100, Lena 100
FELCH Eli 31, 100, George 100, John 100, Mary 100, Perry 100, Sullivan 100
FELLOWS Francis 100, 141, Mr. 176
FELT Addie 100, Agnes 100, Clement 100, Coletta 100, John 100, Mr. 100
FELTON See page 134
FENTON Annie 101, Bridget 101, Charles 101, George 101, John 275, John A. 101, Joseph 101, Lodema 275, Mary 101, Reuben 101, 275, Rill 101, Seth 101, William 101, 275
FERGUSON E. C. 316, Mr. 231
FERRARA Mr. 136
FERRIN Mr. 111
FERRY Jane 10
FEUTCHER Charles 101, Fred 101
FIE William 101
FIELDEN Mr. 85
FINCH Hanley 119
FINDLAY John 102
FINGERLOS Albert 102, Arthur 102, Clara 102, Clinton 102, Fred 102, George 102, Ina 102, Wm. 102
FINLEY Jane 102, 322
FINN Delia 102, Edward 102, Mary 102, Mr. 278, Richard 102

FIRMAN Harrison 102
FISCHER Alta 102
FISH Emma 102, George 102, Harrison 102, Herbert 102, Jennie 102, M. Herrick 102, Rosaltha 102, William 102
FISHER Alice 72-73, Anna 103, Caroline 103, Catherine 103, Charles 103, Clara May 103-104, Edith 168, Eva 103, Everett 72-73, 318, George 102, Harmon 103, Harvey 103, Isaac 72-73, Jacob 103, Joel 103-104, John 103, Leon 104, Mary 168, Montrose 103, Mr. 47, Myron 166, Nancy H. 103, Nancy 103, Nina 104, Orlando 303-304, Otis 103-104, Rebecca 72-73, Samuel 103, Silas 72-73, William 350, Zana 103-104
FISK Betsey 104, Merle 104
FITCH Adda 104, Asaph 104, Athalia 81, Caroline 104, Emma 104, Frank 104, George 104, Laura 104, Margaret 75
FITTS Ephraim 22
FITZGERALD Anna 104-105, Bridget 104-105, Edward 104-105, Helen 104, Mary 104-105, Michael 104-105, Nicholas 105, Owen 105
FITZPATRICK Emma 157, Malachy 105, Mary 105
FLAGG David 94, Irma 105, Mary 107, Mr. 107, William 105
FLECKENSTEIN Frank 25, Lena 25
FLOHIE John 211
FLOWERS George 76, Mary 76
FLYTE Alfred 105, George 105, Jacob 105
FOBES Amanda 105, Edward 105, Elizabeth 209, Frederick 105, George 105, Mary 105, Walter 105
FOLTS George 142, Jeremiah 105, Timothy 106, Wm. 322
FOLTZ Timothy 106
FOOTE Heli 106, Henry 106, 188, Larmon 106, Lucius 106, Mary

106, Prosper 106, Ransford 106, Rufus 106, William 106
FORD Duane 106, Elizabeth 106-107, Eunice 219, Freda 106, Henry 265, Kenneth 106, Millard 106, Patrick 106, Sylvester 90, Victor 106, William 106
FORESTER David 107
FORMAN Mr. 291-292
FORNESS Frederick 255
FOSKET Mary R. 107
FOSTER Albert 107, Burt 107, Jennie 312, Mr. 279, Rachel 107
FOX Anna 107-107, Caroline 107, Charles 107-108, Chauncey, Jr. 6, Eleanor 107, Elizabeth 107, Emily 107, Eunice 107, George 101, 107, Laura 107, Marion 107, Mary 108 Paul 107, Richard 107-108, Theresa 108, William 107-108
FRAME Anna 108, Herman 108, Irene 108, Rena 108
FRANCE Dorothy 108, Fanny 263, George 108, 263, Howard 108, Mary 263
FRANCHOT Annie 108, N. V. V. 108, Nicholas 307
FRANK Abram 108, Alice 109, 328, Allie 328, Almira 23, Almon 108, Bert 108, Candis 109, Clark 283-284, Ellen 109, Eveline 80, Ezra 23, 109, Fred 109, Goldie 109, Henry 23, 109, Hiram 23, Jacob 23, 108, Mary Ann 108, Mildred 108, Mr. 2, 80, 127, 159, Polly 323, Reuben 23, Sarah 108, Solomon 108
FRANTS Edward 105, Maryette 105
FRANZEN Andrea 151
FRARY Alice 68-69
FREEL Anna 109, Michael 109
FREELAND James 118
FREEMAN Caleb 109, Hiram 109, Melissa 109, Mr. 334, Phineas 109, Rufus 322
FRENCH Francis 109, George 109, Guy 109, Iris 109, Jessimyne 109, Leland 109, Linus 109, Mary 109
FRENDALL Mr. 167
FRENDL Mr. 167
FRIEL Margaret 110, Patrick 110
FRIER Clarence 110, Florence 110, Ida 110
FRIES Lawrence 325, Nancy 325
FRINK Martha 301
FRITZ Harry 110, John 110
FROSE Marie 291, Mildred 291, Mr. 274
FULLAM Mr. 79
FULLER Adelaide 110, Almina 180, Angie 151, 191, Ann 110, Asa 180, Augusta 110-111, Benjamin 110, Catherine 110-111, Charles 180, Chester 180, Clara 110, Cora 111, Edgar 60, Floy Ruth 110, Forrest 110, Henry 110, Isabella 312, John 110, Mr. 242, Taylor 110, Wilma 110
FURLONG Allie 111, Lelia 111, Mr. 196, William 111, Wm. C. 111
GABEL George 113, 188
GADZIK Andrew 113, Emil 113, Irene 113, Margaret 113, Rudolph 113
GAENSSLER Albert 113, Albul 113, Frances 113, Harmony 113, Henry 113
GAFFNEY Mr. 247
GAGE Bernard 113, Charles 93, Emma 113, Fern 113, Floyd 113, Fred 113, J.W. 113, Ora 113, Ruth 113, Van Norman 113
GAGLIARDO Mr. 297
GALBRAITH Mr. 325
GALE Mr. 178
GALIGAR Andrew 83, Mary 83
GALLAGHER Charles 114, 330-331, Francis 114, Ralph 114
GALLETS Jacob 114
GALLOWAY Agnes 106, Charles 114, George 106, Jacob 106
GALLUP Fred 122, James 122

GALUSKA Irving 273
GANEY Matthew 225
GARDNER Augusta 114, Carrie 114, Decatur 114, F. Ross 114, George D. 114, John C. 146, JohnT. 114, Julia 114, Lorena 114, Lucretia 10, Luella 114, Ruth 265, Veeder 114, Viola 114
GARING J. C. 335, Sarah 335
GARR Clara 310, Julius 128
GARVEY Ella 114
GARWOOD Rebecca 114, William 114
GASKILL Winnifred 115
GAVIN Anthony 115, Cornelius 115, Hattie 115, James 115, Mr. 15, William 150
GAY Frank 115
GAYTON Nora 117
GEARY Ellen 115, Laura 115, Thomas 115
GEHRKE Bertha 203, Fred 203, Martha 203
GEISE Cynthia 115, Frances 115, Mr. 24, Rosa 115, Veronica 115
GEISSER Agnes 115, Anna 115, Mary 115
GENA John 297
GEORGE Adams 2
GEPHARD Mary 10
GERAN Michael 116
GERBER Emma 14
GERGEL Thomas 116
GERGLEY Anna 116, Ernest 116, John 116, Julia 116, Mary 116
GERMACK Mr. 169
GERMAN Mr. 31
GERRINGER Adam 116, Amelia 116, Gladys 116, Lucille 116, Marion 116, Mary 116
GERWITE May 131
GERWITZ Henry 341, Mary 341, Mr. 83
GEUDEN Anna 117, John 117, Lena 116
GEUDER Anna 116, Arthur 117, Edward 117, George 116, John 116
GIBBS Anna 11, Luther 279
GIBBY Albert 117, Charles 117, Cora 117, Joseph 117, Thomas 117, William 117
GIBSON Abigail 47, Alonzo 117, Charles 182, Mr. 280, Nathan 117, Nehemiah 117, William 117
GIFFORD Elizabeth 34
GILBERT Charles 117, Edward 117, Fred 14, 117, Herman 67, 305, Marin 117, Will 117
GILBEY Roxy 219-220
GILES Alice 118, Cyrus 117-118, John 117-118, Jonathan 117
GILLET Catharine 118, Melvin 118, Sarah 118
GILLIAT John 118, Rachael 118, Robert 118, Ruth 118, Thomas 118
GILLIGAN Catherine 118, Dennis 118
GILLMASTER Mr. 101
GINADER John 118
GLEASON Amanda 118, Ele 22, Ira 118, Jane 118, Maria 118, Mary Ann 118, Mr. 22
GODDING Asa 119, Levi 119, Mary 119, Matilda 119, Olive 219, Sabra 119
GODFREY Dolly 119, I. M. 119, Jennie 119, Lillian 119, Silas 119
GOLD Henry 37
GOLDBOROUGH Levi 189, Mariah 189
GOLTZ Frederick 119
GOOD Martha 119, Mr. 154
GOODALE Martha 129
GOODEMOTE Allen 119, Charity 119, David 119, Mary Ann 119, Philip 119
GOODEN Charles 119, Clara 119 Harold 119
GOODFORD George 120, Helen 120, John 120, William 120
GOODMAN Irene 78
GOODRICH Arthur 120, Ellen 120, Elton 120, George 120, Orestus 120,

Sarah 120, Zenas 120
GOODSELL Charles 120, Helen 120, Loryne 120, Mildred 120
GORDAN Isaac 120, Willard 120
GORDON Anne 121, Elizabeth 121, John 120-121, Nellie 121, Walter 121
GOULD Amelia 121, Arden 121, Elsie 121, Margaret 121, Minerva 121, Mr. 204, Robert 247-248, William 121
GRACZYJK See Page 264
GRAFF Mr. 273
GRAHAM Mr. 228-229, Sarah 30-33
GRANTIER Amos 236
GRATZ Louise 341, Theodore 341
GRAVES Bertha 166, Charles 125, John 270, Mabel 121
GRAY Caroline 322, Clarissa 43, David 121, Hannah 121, Julia 120, Mary 322
GREELEY Alice 12
GREEN Albert 121, Almina 88, Anna 110, Ben 289, Eliza 81, Eunice 97, F. M. 82, Frank 121, Frederick 237-238, Freeman 121, Harriet 282-283, Hattie 237-238 Hiram 81, James 81, John 206, Joseph 46, Louisa 121, Martha 121, Mary 81, Niles 121, Nora 121, Ora 237-238, Samuel 237-238, Theron 237-238
GREENE Edwin 140, Ida 29, Mr. 207
GREINER Laura 121
GREY Josephine 120, Mabel 217, Mr. 44
GRIERSON Helen 122, Ray 122
GRIFFETH Grace 323
GRIFFIN Genevieve 122, Ilene 122, James 160, John 160, Marie 122
GRIFFITH Helen 113, Mary 208, William 208
GRIFFITHS Alberta 122, Catherine 122, Gertrude 122, Phillip 122
GRIMELLS Lovinda 66
GRIMES Caroline 122, Eugene 122, Grace 122, Hannah 122, James 122
GRINER See Greiner, Philip 35, 121
GRISWOLD Caroline 122, Edwin 122, Jerome 122, Sylvia 43
GROAT Charles 122, Earl 122, Frank 122, 275, Frankie 274, Jasper 122, John 122
GROSE Mr. 142
GROVER Abigail 287-289, Frank 123, Gustavius 123, Sylester 288-289
GROVES John 240
GROW Hazel 326
GROWN Archibald 32
GUENTHER Henry 125, Susan 125
GUEST Florence 192, Fred 192
GUILD Charles 123, Emma 123, Fred 123, Mary 123, William 123
GUNDER Estella 203
GUNNISON Genevieve 123
GUTHRIE Carrie 123, Cora 123, Leslie 123
GUY Laura 123, Lydia 123, Timothy 123
HAASE August 125, Carrie 125
HABER John 200
HABERLY Elnora 125, Fred 125
HACKET John 305
HACKETT George 125
HADAWAY Alfred 125, Charlotte 125, Irena 125, James 125
HADLEY Frederick 77-78, Hartwell 125, Herbert 125, Jessie 77-78, Nathan 125, Palmer 125, Parmelia 296
HAGERDON Florence 301
HAHN Daniel John 125, Ruth 315
HAIGHT Frank 125, Joseph 125
HAIRE Ella 126, Margaret 125
HALE Albert 247, Albert 248, Edson 126, Edwin 126, Martha 126, Mr. 347, Nathaniel 126, Sylvia 126
HALEY Caroline 126, Thomas 126
HALL Alexander 127, Allie 126-127, Artell 126, Artimus 127, Azariah 126, Bert 127, Charles 126-127,

Clarence 126-127, Clarissa 4, Delbert 46, Elmer 127, Floyd 126, Frances 127, Georgia 301, Gladys 126-127, Hellen 226, Irving 126, Lawrence 126-127, Lemuel 140, Lilly 19, Marion 126, Mildred 126, Mr. 41, 45, 154, Nellie 126, Phebe 295, Rachael 126, Samuel 234-235, William 4, 126
HALLADAY Mary 298-299
HALLERS August 266, Charles 266
HALPIN Sarah 127, William 127
HALSEN Edward 127
HALSTEAD Norval 314
HAMILTON Charles 127, Ira 127, Lucinda 127, Margaret 199, Samuel 127, William 127, 199
HAMM Cynthia 200
HAMMER C. H. 331
HAMMOND Mary 238, Mary Anne 237
HANDRAHAN Catharine 83-84
HANLEY Alta 127, Carrie 127, George W. 127
HANNAGEN Clyde 128, Etta 128, James 128, Mary 128
HANNEGAN Annie 128, George 128, Martha 128, Mary Ellen 128, Mina 128
HANNIFAN George M. 128
HANRATTY J. T. 33
HANSON Catharine 323, George 323, Jennie 323, Luella 128, Richard 323
HARBECK Clara 128, Eliza 128, Frederick 128, Roscoe 128, Victor 128
HARD Mrs. 171
HARDING Carrie 333, Curtis 332-333, Frank 332-333, Rady 332-333
HARDY Mr. 22, 338
HARE Albert 129, Benjamin 128-129, Ethel 128-129, Ida 128-129, Maria 128-129, Millard 128-129, Mr. 63, Thomas 128-129
HARKNESS Florence 129, Frances 129, Joseph 129, William 129
HARMON Flora 85, Levi 318, Lovina 139, Rowland 38
HARNING Sophia 129
HARNS Iola 129, Libbie 129, Theodore 129-130
HARRINGTON Carrie 130, 226, Georgia 130, 226, Horace 50, Joseph 18, 263, Josephine 130, 226, LaMott 130, 226, Mr. 226, Myrtie 130, 226
HARRIS Roy 198
HARRISON Charles H. 130, G. Wilks 130, Joseph 130, M. K. 283, Susan 130
HARSON Flora 130, James 353, Julius 130, Lena 353
HART Catherine 186
HARTER Nellie 304
HARTLEY Mary 130
HARTMAN Mr. 350
HARTUNG Catherine 130, Christian 331, John 130, Joseph 130, Sophia 130
HARTWIG Caroline 130, Frank 130, Harriet 130
HARVEY Addie 203, Alexander 200, Alfred 131, George 265, Ida 131, John 131, Kate 131, Linnie 11, Lydia 200, Maria 350, Mary 131, 328, Mr. 141, Nathan 350, Oscar 203
HASKINS Mr. 7
HASLEY Jefferson 125
HASPER Augustus 353, Dora 353, Ed. 353, John 353
HATCH Mary 72
HATSAVER Minnie 278
HATZELL Carl C. 131, Emily 131, Robert 131, William 131
HAWKINS Arthur 131, Betsey 131, Elijah 131, John 65, Lorenzo 131, Mary 131, Orson 131, Roxana 131, William 65, Willie 131
HAWKS E. C. 208, Harriet 208
HAWLEY Alonzo 131-132, Aretus 132, Caroline 131-132, Frances

131-132, Frederick 131-132, Horace E. 131, Jesse D. 132, Jonathan 131-132, Lucy 131, Myron 204
HAYDEN Asenath 132, Augustine 132, Augustus 132, Ebenezer 132, Edward 132, Lucretia 132
HAYES Eva K. 132
HAYNES Amanda 299-300, Ann 300, Ann Eliza 299, Daniel 299-300, James 299-300, Sterling 132
HAYS Carrie 132, Frankie 132, Lena 132, Mary Jane 132
HAZARD Arthur 132, Joseph 79, 132, Susan 132, 189-190, Theodore 132, W. E. 195, William H. 32, Willie 132
HAZZARD Helen M. 132
HEATH Barbara 123, Charles 133, Henry 133
HEDDEN John 31-32, Sarah 31-32, William 31, 33
HEDDING Mr. 317
HEHIR Agnes 133, Edward 133, Ethel 133, Mary 133, William 133
HELMS Alberta 133, Benson 133, China 133, Daisy 133, Emma 133, Mark C. 133, Mary 133, Olive E. 133, Verland 133
HELSER Charles 133, Francis 133, Joseph 133, Moneyck 133, Thomas 133
HELVERING Kathryn 133
HENDERSHOT Agnes 138
HENDERSON Mary A. 133
HENNESEY Ann 133-134, Julia 134, Mary 133, Mary Ann 134, Rebecca 133-134, Timothy 133
HENNESSY Catherine 134, James 134, Mary 134
HENNING Samuel C. 172
HENRY Ann 134, Carlisle 134, Elmer 134, Eunice 348, George 53, Hollice 134, Irene 134, J. N. 247, Joseph 134, Katherine 134, Lena 134, Lewis 134, Lula 134, Nellie 134, Perry 134, Susan 348, Vincent 134, William 299
HERING Mr. 317
HERMANCE Sophia 55-56
HERRICK Belle 134, 157, Dolly 237, Fred 180, George 237, Glenn 135, John 135, Marian 135, Marvin 135, Mary 135, Mr. 243, Nelson 265, Paul 135, Rachel 141, Stephen 135, Virginia 135, William 164, Willie 135
HERRON See Page 200
HEVENOR Charles 135, Charlotte 135, Edward 135, Harvey 135, William 135
HICKEY Margaret 135, Nicholas 115
HICKS Frank 349, Helen 266, J Jefferson 266
HIESTER Mr. 349-350
HIGBEE David 109, Jerome 283, Mary Ann E. 109, Mr. 185
HIGGINS Frank Harrison 182, James 139, 207, Kate 135
HIGHMAN Louisa 334
HILDUM Charles 135
HILL Addie 136, Alice 136, Alma 136, Clarise 136, Delevan 136, Elizabeth 136, Ellen 78, Henrietta 136, Henry 256, L. D. 136, Leroy 136, Levi 136, Mary R. 136, Matilda 202, Max 136, Millen 78, Ray 136, Sidney 136
HILLEBERT Eleanor 136, Mary 136, Nelson 136, Warren 136
HILLENBRAND John 69
HILLIKER Mr. 166
HILLMILLER Regina 136
HINDS Arthur 18, Charles 326, Sophronia 326
HINMAN Abigail 66, Alfred 137, Alice 66, Anna 137, Anson 137, Benjamin 137, Byron 66, DeForest 137, Elizabeth 137, Francis 66, Franklin 66, Hoyt 137, Imogene 66, Jennie 137, Mabel 137, Manley 137, Mary 137, Matilda 66, Millard 309-

310, 312, Richard 66, Truman 66
HINZE Bert 137, Dorothy 137, John 137, Matilda 137
HIRT Andrew 24, 291
HITCHCOCK Amelia 138, Charles Eugene 138, Edward 137, Elsie 137, Emma 138, George 137, Henry 138, Jane 137, Jos. 137-138, Ruth 137-138, Wesley 133, William 138
HOAG Morris 138, William C. 153
HOAKER Frederica 138, Lawrence 138
HODGE Abraham 332, Lucinda 332, Rebecca 332
HODGEMAN Stillman 276
HODGES Amelia 278, Fred 138, Halla 138, Jerome 138, Laura 138
HODSON Clara B. 138
HOFER Susana 78
HOFFMAN Amelia 272
HOFFMIRE Emma 138
HOGAM Clara 138, Margaret 144-145, Martin 138, Mary 160, Mr. 114, William 138
HOGG Anna 138, Ethel 138, Floyd 282, Mina 138
HOLBROOK Helen 138-139, Jessie 139, Mac 138-139, Martin 138-139, Orpha 138-139, Rollin 138-139
HOLDRIDGE Price 72, Zina 15, 28, 72
HOLLAND Amelia 139, Lott 139, Mr. 341, Nathaniel 139
HOLLIS Mr. 98
HOLLISTER Elihu 139, Harlin 139, Homer 137, John 139, Major 139, Mr. 20, Robert 139
HOLMES Alma 139, Blanche 139, Burnom 139, Burton 139, Cicero 352, Delos 139, Ernest 140, Hervey 139, Hosea 352, Marcia 140, Mark 108, Mayme 139, Mirinda 334, Mr. 172, Nina 139, Philetus 140, Samuel 334, Sylvester 139
HOLT Manley 42
HOLTON Mr. 327
HOLZWARTH Andrew 140, Christian 140, Elizabeth 140, Laura 140
HOMER Emma 140, Jacob 140, Lena 140
HOOKER Stephen 140, William 140
HOOPER Cye 140, Edith 140, Grant 312, Jennie 312, Jessie 140, Mr. 174
HOOVER Augusta 242, Lydia 242
HOPKINS Dora 77-78, Mr. 22, Sally 75, William 38
HOPPING Wm. 3
HORNBLOWER W. G. 17
HORNING William 140
HORTH Ada 141, Alexander 141, Benjamin 141, Cassie 141, Daniel 195, De Hart 140, Eleanor 141, Frances 140, Francis 100, George 140-141, Hiram 141, Ida May 141, Lydia 141, Marcus 141, Mark 141, Millicent 259
HORTON Albert 141, Angeline 141, Dulcina 141, Edward 141, John 141, Stephen 53, William 141
HOTCHKISS Addison 141, Amanda 141, Asahel 141, Geo. 293, Harrison 293, John 141, Lettie 355, Rachel Amanda 141
HOTTON Esther 141, Harold 141, Louis 141, Nicholas 141
HOUCK Ellen 140, Florence 143, George W. 143
HOUGHTAILING Alvah 142, Bird 142, Budd 142, Burton 142, John 142
HOUGHTALING Bird 142, Blanche 142, Guy 142, Moses 350, Rose 142
HOUSE Henry 286-287, 289-291
HOUT Mr. 200
HOW Laura 21-22
HOWARD Blanche 142, Claude 142, Clide 142, Cora 142, Earl 142, Eliza 47, 187-188, Emeline 145, Ernest 142, Frank 326, Grace 142,

Henry 145, John 187-188, Patrick 187-188, Plara 47, Roderick 142, Sarah 99, Timothy 187-188, William 142
HOWE Arlie 142, Charlotte 142, Dean 152, J. M. 142, Matilda 143, Nathan 210, Victor 143, Victoria 143, Wilson 282-283
HOWELL Evaline 312
HOWEY Lizzie 198
HOWLETT John 284, William 188
HOXIE Etta 143
HOY Edwin 254-255
HOYT Daniel 311, Laura 311
HUBBARD Blanche 2, 143, Clarence 143, Ella 143, Emmett 143, Esther 143, Ethel 143, Florence 143, Grace 143, Hannah 171, Irene 88, Jemima 143, Leola 143, Lewella 310, Manley 143, Mark 143, Miner 143, Ralph 143, Russell 143, 237, Walter 137, 143
HUBBELL Alvin 207, Wesley 143
HUDSON Mr. 203-204
HUFF Lenora 143
HUGGINS Charles 144, Elizabeth 144, Elmore 144, Emma 144
HUGHES Anna 144-145, Dorothea 144-145, Ellen 144, George 144, J. Les 144-145, James 144, John 144-145, Katherine 144-145, Margaret 144-145, Mary 144-145, Mrs. 161, Theresa 144-145, William 144
HUGHEY Claude 145, George 145, Guy 145, Neil 145
HUGHS John 48
HULBERT Eugene 277, Henry 147
HULL Edwin 325, Lottie 325, Samuel 145
HUMES Eleanor 145, Jackson 145
HUMPHREY Eliza 145, Seymour 145
HUNGTINTON Lafayette 146
HUNT Anna 146, Frances 145, Hiram 145, Loretta 145, Mariette 145, Mr. 335, Sarah 322, William 66, 145

HUNTINGTON Arnold 146, David 146, Emily 146, George 146, Henry 146, Horace 146, Maria 146, Monroe 146, Nancy 146, Rachel 146
HUNTLEY DeRoy 146
HUNTON Cora 146, Elbridge 146, Eugene 146, John 146, Nellie 146, Susan 146
HUNYWOOD Mr. 307
HURD Ashahel 146-147, Clarence 147, Ellen 146, Francis 147, Madellon 147, Mr. 191, Nelson 147, Philander 147, Rebecca 146-147
HURLBERT Annie 147, Earl 147, George 147, John 147, Lee 147, Mildred 147
HURLBURT E. C. 323
HURLEY Anna 134, Hannah 134, Jerry 147, Mary 134, Nora 147, Timothy 134
HUTCHINSON Sanford 147, Sarah 292-293
HUYCK Wilbur 148
HYDE Cordelia 267, Mr. 82, Reuben 267
INGALL Anna 221
INGERSOLL Cyrus 90, 149, 266, Francis 3-4, 149, Harlow 149, Harmon 149, Herman 344-345, John 149, Josephus 149, Laura 3-4, Lovica 149, Mr. 33
INMAN Cora 149, John 149, 187, Lowell 149, Lynn 149, Mr. 64
IRISH Charles 149, Mr. 279, 304, R. Henry 149, Simon 149
IRWIN Bernice 149-150, Bruce 149-150, Flora 149-150, Marian 149-150, Thomas 149, Wm. 149-150
ISAMAN De Vere 150, George 45, 150, Lyman 150, Sarah 150
IVERS John 150, Michael 150
JACKSON Angie 151, Cecil 151, George 151, Mabel 151, Mr. 75, Sarah 219
JACQUES Delos 151

JAHN Anna 151, Anthony 151, Arthur 151, Elizabeth 151, Paulina 151, Rosa 151
JAMES Frank 151, George 151, James 151
JAQUAY A. Cortez 151-152, Earl 151-152, Kenneth 151-152, Mortimer 151-152, Otto 151-152
JEFFERDS Claribel 152, F. 152, Melville 152, Samuel 152, Willard 152
JEFFORDS Emma 332-333, Liberty 152
JEMISON Mary 344
JENKEL Frank 152, Henry 152
JENKINS Mr. 347
JENKS Latisa 152, Lovett 152, Mr. 312, Orson 152
JENNINGS Mary 258, Mildred 76
JEWELL Angie 152, Joseph 294, M. A. 52, Moses 152
JEWETT Mr. 85
JIMERSON Eli 241, 276, Robert 153
JOB Sarah 105
JOBE Anna 355, Clarence 355
JOCKLEY Mr. 188
JOHN Elizabeth M. 140
JOHNS Edris 153, Edward 153, Harold 153, John 153, Thomas 153, Wesley 153
JOHNSON Almira 266, Almon Lee 154, Bela 154, Calvin 154, Celia 154, Corydon 154, Deborah 153, Elida 153, Elisha 129, 233, Ellen 153-154, Elton 153, Florence 154, Frances 154, Francis 246-247, Giles 14, 154, 309, Harriet 233, Hattie 153, Hema 129, Henry 154, Jacob 266, James 170, John 153, Juliatte 247, Kate 153-154, Lillian 259, Lucinda 153, Marcus 243, Maria 55-59, 266, Milton 154, Mr. 26-27, 249, Olga 154, Parkman 246-247, Ralph 55-56, 153-154, Raymond 154, Richard 153-154, Seraph 246-247, Thomas 153, Warren 246-247
JOLLS Angie 155, Ara 155, Earl 155, Elbert 155, Elizabeth 155, Hilda 155, John 155, Merle 155, Warren 155, Willard 155
JONAK John 317
JONES Anne 155, 157, Benjamin 156, C. M. 156-157, Catharine 155-157, Catherine 155, 157, Cathrine 155, 157, Charity 156, 157, Charles 156, 192, Daniel 156-157, David 155-157, Diana 18, Elizabeth 155, 157, Ellen 156, Emma 157, Evan 156, Frederick 156-157, Hattie 156, Homer 156, Hugh 155-157, Isaac 156-157, James 153, 156, John 155-157, Lloyd 156, Lydia 156-157, Lyman 156-157, Mary 155, 157, Morris 155-157, Mr. 330-331, Olive 156, Oliver 156-157, Ora 157, Permelia 156-157, Richard 155-157, Sarah 192, Silas 156, Sophia 156-157, Thomas 155-157, Verna 156, William 155-157
JORDAN Clare 157, Ruth 157
JOSLIN Frank 329
JOSLYN Adelaide 157, Edith 157, Martin 157
JOY Catherine 157, Mary 157
JUDD Harrison 202, Louise 3
KAFER Jacob 159
KAMMERER John 233
KAMMIRE Carl A. 52
KANE Casey 159, Daniel 159, Edward 159, Eliza 159, Ella 159, Eve Eliza 159, James 159, John 159, Margaret 159, Mr. 107, Otis 159, Peter 159, Thomas 159
KARCZWESKI Pauline 159, Stanley 159
KARL Bessie 159, Claude 159-160, James 159, John 159-160, Joseph 159-160, Lena 29, Mary 159, Michael 159, Ruth 159-160, Winnifred 159-160
KASPRICK Martin 292

KAST Charles 114
KAUTZ Ada 160, Oscar 160, Paul 160, William 160
KEARSTEAD See Kierstead
KEATING Minnie 160, Patrick 160, Winifred 86
KEELER Bertha 304
KEEN Luella 160
KEENAN Michael 160, Patrick 160
KEHOE Jennie 82, Margaret 86-87
KEIM Julia 160
KEISER George 240
KELLER Arthur 160, Eugene 160, Eva 347, George 347, Helen 160
KELLEY Bernard 161, Elmer 160, Ezekiel 160, George 236, Joseph 160-161, Mary 160-161, Mr. 216-217, Sarah 160-161, Thomas 160-161, Vesta 160
KELLOGG Albert 310, Edwin 310, Mr. 51, 59, Sylvia 310
KELLY Eddy 161, James 338, John 86, 161, Mary 161, 247-248, Mr. 349, Nelson 161, Warren 161
KELSEY Darwin 161, James 190, Jane 190, Kathalo 161, Maria 161, Mr. 316, Samuel 161, Stephen 161, Truman 161, Wealtha 161
KENFIELD Felton 343
KENNAN Adeline 162, Lucius 162
KENNEDY Catherine 162, Cornelius 162, Elizabeth 162, Francis 162, Henry 162, Margaret 162, Mary 162, Mr. 106-107, Nora 162, William 162
KENNER Levi C. 79
KENNICOTT See also Kinnicutt, Anna 163, Ella 162, Leander 162-163
KENT Bessie 163, Emma 163, Ezra 26, James 163, Justus 163, Kenneth 163, Mary 163, Mr. 63, William 63
KENYON Also see Kinyon, Aletha 52, Charles 52, Kittie 52, Mary 52
KEPPEL John 163, Lizzie 163
KERPKA Albert 168

KERR Lucinda 105
KESLER Catharine 163, Frank 163, Leopold 163, Loesa 163, Magdalina 163
KESSLER Andrew 163, Charles 163, Daniel 163, Frank 164, George 163, Lena 163
KESTER Charles 164
KEYES Herbert 164, Orson 164, Rosanna 164, Truman 30, Vernie 164
KIDDER Carry Adell 4
KIERNAN M. W. 164
KIERSTEAD William R. 164
KILBURN Delaney 141, Manley 141
KIMBALL Caroline 228-229, Eli 228-229, Emeline 228-229, Ezra 228-229, Sally 228-229
KIMBLE Byron 164, Charles 164, Cynthia 164
KING Adelia 164-165, Anson 164-165, Charles 164, Edwin 30, Elizabeth 164, Fred 164-165, Harriet 164-165, Mary 164, Nora 165, Reuben 164, Sophia 164-165, Verna 164, William 164
KINGMAN Aurora 217
Aurora 218
KINGSLEY Abi 165
Augusta 165
Nelson 165
Orril 165
Sarah 165
KINNE Mary J. 55
Mary J. 56
KINNEY Caleb Williston 177
KINNICUTT Adalissa 202, John 162-163, 202, 324, Leander 202, Lucius 202, Mary 202, Sophronia 162-163, 202
KINYON Betsey 165, Daniel 165, Lovisa 165, Lydia 165
KIRBY Sally 120
KLINK Mary 165, Wm. C. 165
KLOCK George 165, John 165, Manning 165

KLUTSENBAKER Mr. 126-127
KNAPP Anthony 166, Carrie 166, Emily 166
KNICKERBOCKER Harmon 218
KNIGHT A. D. 166, Adelia 81, Bertha 166, Daniel 166, Ellen 166, George 107, Jane 166, Mr. 153, Oliver A. 81, Parma Dulcenia 107
KNOLL Anastina 166, Anna 166, Bessie 166, Edith 166, Hattie 166, Henry 166, William 166
KNOW Mary 167
KNOWLTON William 146-147
KNOX Adella 166, Andrew 166, Ann 166, Frederick 166, George 166, James 166, John 166, Mary 166
KOBER Anna 167, John 167
KOBINSKI Peter 322, May 322
KOHN Adam 167, Catherine 167, John 167, Latham 167, Simon 167
KONKLEWSKI Baldwin 167, Frank 167, Sopha 167, Thomas 167
KOOP Mr. 2
KOTTS Frederick A. 167
KRAMPF Joseph 167, Mary 167
KRAUS John 167, Margaret 167
KRAWCZYNKSI Anton 168, Bronislaw 167-168, John 167, Ladislaus 167-168, Maria 168, Mary 167-168
KREBS Adolpha 168, Caroline 168, William 168
KREHL Frederick 168
KRENCER Bertha 168, Joseph 168, Rose 168
KREPKA Mary 168
KREUZER SEE KRENCER
KRIEGER Addie B. 168
KRITTER Alfred 169
KROTT Anna E. 123
KRUSE Amelia 169, Dena 169, Henry 169, John 169, Mary 169
KRUSOS Spero 310
KUEHL Albert J. 169, Anna 169, Conrad 169, Gustavus 169, Helen 169, Margaret 169

KUJAWA Alezandria 169, Frank 169, Joseph 169, Josephine 169, Mary 169, Stephania 169
KURTZHALTS Annie 313
KWAITOWSKI Leonard 169, Frank 169, Joseph 169
KYLER Bessie 170, Ezra 169-170, Lloyd 169-170, Mark 169-170, Tessie 169-170
KYSER George 170, Horace 170, Susan 170
LABUHN Mr. 317
LACY Carlos 171, Carrie 171, Francis 171, Lewis 171, Permelia 171, Wallace 171
LAFEVER Helen 171, Lewis 171
LAFFERTY Joseph E. 115
LAIDLAW Gilbert 66-67, 171, Rena 66-67
LAING J. D. 54
LAKE Eveline 171, Ezra 171, George 171, Lampson 171
LAMB Mr. 167
LAMMIE Daniel 206-207, Ella 172
LAMPER Acta 172, Nancy 172
LAMPHERE Mary Ann 172, Silas 172
LANCKTON Jerusha 177
LANG Agnes 160, Nicolas 330
LANGHAM Albert 172, Ella 172, William 172
LANGHANS Ruth 172, William 172
LANGMADE Aceneth 313, Bertha 172, Capitola 172, Emily 172, Grace 172, Lydia 172, Miranda 313, Nathan 313, Nettie 172, Stephen 172, 313, Whitman 313, William 172
LANGWORTHY Fred O. 95
LAPOINT Charles 312
LARABEE Amos 129-130, Celina 129, Fayette 129-130, Lorinda 129, Nathan 129-130
LARKIN Caroline 172, Thomas 172
LARSON Jennie 240, John 240, Mr. 345

LATHAM Lucy 342
LATHOM Lucy 326
LATTIN Alice 173, Benton 173, Berton 173, Grace 173
LAUGHENTHALL John 159
LAUGHLIN Catherine 173, Diamus 173, E. Lucille 173, Francis 173, James 173, Katherine 173, Margaret 173, Mary 173, Mr. 266, Patrick 173
LAULER Catherine 173, Eveline 173, Joseph 173
LAW Doris 174, Eliphalet 236, Eveline 173, Ezra 173- 174, Mr. 45, Reuben 173-174, Sylvia 174, Vernia 173-174
LAWLER Eugene 101, Katie 271-272
LAWRENCE Harriet 174, Herbert 260, Orrin 106, Polly 174, Reuben 174, Richard 174
LAWSON Mr. 256
LAWTON Alfred 174, Alice 222, Cynthia 174, Emma 174, James 174, Maude 222, Merton 222, Orrinda 174, Peleg 174, Wilson 174
LAY Alice 174, Edward 174, Florence 174, Ruth 174
LAYTON Edith 278
LE BLANC Bessie 175, Blanch 174-175, Charles 174-175, Ella 175, Robert 174-175
LE ROY George 175, Simeon 175, Willard 175
LEACH Albert 175, Bettie 175, John 175, Kathryn 175, Ralph 175
LEARN John 263, John 291, Lydia 175, Mr. 203, Orlando 175
LECKEY Robert 175
LECOUR Mr. 182
LEE Anna 175, Edward 175, Elva 175, James 175-176, 215, Nellie 13, William 175
LEIGHTON Adeline 19, Henry 19
LELAND Asa 176, Harrison 176
LELOUR Mr. 182

LENHART Mary 209
LENT Helen 176
LEON Ann 176, Carrie 176, Daniel 176, John 176, Timothy 176
LEONARD Dora 176-177, Eleanor 176-177, Flora 176-177, I. R. 147, John 176, Leon 176-177, Louise 176, Melvin 176-177, Milton 176, Mr. 173, Satie 176-177, Stella 176-177
LETTIS Mary E. 107
LEVINING Edward E. 201
LEWIS Alfred 177, Amanda 177, Cary 177, Charles 177, Daniel 177, Edward 177, Elizabeth 177, Floyd 177, Forest 177, Jane 177, Jerome 177, Joe 261, Laureat 177, Miles 177, Mr. 179, 249, Myrtle 177, Nathan 177, Paul 177, Sally 177, Stanley 177, Stillman 177, William 34, 117, 177
LEXER Frank 275, Myra 275
LIECHTE Barbara 168, Freda 168, John 168
LILLY Zillah 322
LINCOLN Charles 178, 219, F. E. 178, Lottie 244, Lucius 177-178, Mary 177-178, Pratt 177-178, William 178
LIND Charles 178, Josephine 178
LINDERMAN Mina 314
LINGENFELDER Cornelia 28
LINGENFELTER Joseph 310, Mr. 126
LINK Anna 178, Barbara 178, Jacob 178
LINTON Charles 178, Edward 178, Fred 178, Joseph 178
LION Elizabeth 202
LIPPART Betsey 242, Betsey 243, Minnie 178
LITCHFIELD Edward 178, Ensign 178, Eugene 178, Molly 178, Royal 256, William 178
LITTLE Frances 179, Frederick 179, Jane 179, Mary 179, Miriam 28, Mr.

70, 107, 133-134, Noah 133, Richard 107, 178-179, 205, William 179
LIVERIDGE Edward 222
LIVERMORE Mr. 153, 333
LLOYD Cora Belle 179, Leola 179, Lysle 179, William 179
LOADER Addie O. 179
LOBDELL Lucretia 235-236, Peter 236
LOCKE Mr. 301, Philander 31
LOCKIE Andrew 339, James 339, Julia Ann 339
LOCKWOOD Jacob 179, Jessie 179, Laurence 25, Mary L. 118
LOFTUS John 179
LONDON Flora 81
LONG Andrew 179, Carl 179, Charles 179, Emerson 179, Frances 179, Harold 179, Mary 179
LONGHANS John 140
LONGLEY Mr. 200
LOOKER John 323
LOOMIS Anna 19
LOONEY Alice 179, Mary 179, William 179
LOOP Lennie 180, Mr. 33, Walter 180
LORD Charles 180, Derrick 180, Ellen 180, Ethelyn 180, Mary 180
LOSEE Augusta 293, Azael 303-304, John 180, Owen 293
LOUIS Sophia 92
LOVETT Mr. 109
LOVEWELL Lucinda 107
LOWDEN Charles 180, James 180
LOWE Collen 243, George 180, James 180, Marian 146
LOWELL Lucius 117, Verna 117
LUBBERTS Mary 180
LUCAS Frank 180, Jennette 180, Pantha 180, Theodore 180
LUCE Caroline 180-181, Charles 181, Clara 181, Franklin 181, Fred 181, George 181, Grace 181, Hiram 181, Irwin 181, James 181, John 180-181, Lucas 223, Lucius 181, Mark 332, Milford 180, Mina 181, Orvis 181, Phebe 181
LUDDINGTON Alice 181-182, Alonzo 181-182, Ernest 181-182, Frank 181-182, Harvey 181-182, Maude 181-182, Ruth 181-182
LUDWIG Mr. 211
LUNTZ Isidor 182, Molly 182, Ory 182
LUTHER Hattie 182, Jessie 182, Mary A. 182
LUTTMAN Annie 182, Christopher 182, Martha 182, Theodore 182
LUTZ Roger H. 182
LYCETT Beulah 182, Gertrude 182, Kenneth 182, Michael 182
LYMAN Mr. 54
LYNCH Mr. 221, Robert 182
LYNDE John A. 15
LYNE Mr. 51
LYON James 72-73
LYONS Lillian 182, Marguerette 183, Maria 183, Martha 52, Thomas 183
MABEE Abram 346
MACAPES Major 4, 317
MACARTY Susan 185, Thomas 185
MACCOLL William W. 185
MACDONALD Mr. 340
MACK Ella 185, May 185, William 185
MACKEY Byron 263, Conrad 185, Hannah 185, William 263
MACKMER Albert 185, Beulah 185, Elizabeth 185, Frederick 185, Rachel 185, Ralph 185
MADARA Josiah 138
MAGNER Bertha 200, Thomas J. 200
MAHANY Catharine 185, Cornelius 185, Joseph 185, Margaret 185
MAHER Clara 339
MAHONEY Mr. 341
MALLERY Fred 185
MALLORY Anna 186, Burt 186, Cecil 186, Finice 186, George 186, Hazel 186, Ira 186, Izola 186, Lloyd

186, Malvina 186, Mr. 68, 191
MALONE Andrew 186-187, Celia 186, Emma 187, James 187, Mamie 186, Mary 187, Minnie 187
MALONEY Catharine 187-188, Charles 187, Edward 187-188, Frances 188, James 187-188, John 187-188, Margaret 187-188, Mary 187-188, Patrick 187-188, Virgil 187, William 187-188
MANCHESTER Roy G. 188
MANLEY Annie 188, Elizabeth 188, John 188, Laura 188
MANN Mabel 104, Matilda 10-11, Silas 20
MANNING Mr. 139
MANTENFALL Bertha 188, Louisa 188, Mary 188, Peter 188
MARBLE Betsey 72-73
MARKHAM Frank 188, Lucretia 188, Marsha 188, Mary Ann 90, Mr. 215-216, Sophronia 49, Wm. 188
MARONEY Bridget 188, Frank 188, John 189, W. H. 189
MARRON Mary 157
MARSH Adams 18, Adelbert 189, Anna 189, Arba 189, Artemisia 189, Duane 189-190, Emily 189, Emma 347, George 351, Harry 189, Harvey 189, Hattie 189, Leon 189, Marshall 189-190, Mary 189-190, Mr. 181, Nelson 189, Orris 189-190, Reuben 347, Sidney 234-235, Virginia 347, Walter 189, Wellman 189
MARSHALL Ada 190, Edward 190
MARTH Elizabeth 57
MARTIN Adaline 190, Elta 50, Jesse 190, William 325
MARTINA John 190, Peter 190
MARTINDALE Kirby 190, Roy 190
MARVIN Hester 190, James B. 190
MASON Carrie 49, Edgar 190, L. 190, Mina 190, Mr. 49
MASONER Katharine 190, Margaret 137

MASTERSON Florence I. 11
MATESON Myron 190-191
MATHER Edna 191, Emor 191, George 191
MATHIAS Allison 339
MATTESON George 309
MATTFELDT A. H. 191
MATTHEWON Clinton 58
MATTHEWS Alida 191, Anne 191, Jane 191, John 191, Margery 191, Maria 191
MATTHEWSON Ava 191, Clinton 58, 191, Dacie 191, Dora 191, Hale 191, Henry 191, Marvin 191, Mr. 76
MATTOON Bernice 192, Elida 192, Ida 192, James 192, Jennie 192, Jessie 192, Mary 192, William 192
MAUER Catherine 62
MAULBETSCH Catherine 192, Christine 192, George 192
MAXSON Barton 253, George 192
MAXWELL Edna 192, Elizabeth 192, Henry 192, Joseph 192
MAYBEE Alvira 192-193, Clyde 193, Frankie 192-193, Jeremiah 192-193, Myrtie 192-193
MAYER Christine 193, Elizabeth 193, Gretchen 193, Rudolph 193
McARTHUR Frank 193, Mary 193, Plin 193, Sarah 193, Thomas 193, Ward 193, William 283
McAULIFFE Estella 310, Mr. 335
McCABE Anna 104-105
McCADDEN Mr. 191
McCAFFERY Charles 193
McCALL Alexander 71
McCANN Irene 134
McCAPES Mr. 243
McCARTHY Timothy 212
McCARTY Daniel 193, John 193, Marie 193, Ruth 193
McCLELLAN Agnes 198, Arthur 194, Joseph 193-194, Kate 193-194, Thomas 198, William 194, Wm J. 193-194

McCLELLAND David 194
McCLORY Christopher 194, Emily 194, John 194
McCLOSKEY Bartholomew F. 64
McCLURE Addie 285, 288-290, Caroline 194, Della 300, Eunice 194, Frederick 194, Henry 68, 194, Ina 300, James 194, Maria 68, Nelson 300, Samuel 194
McCOLLISTER Mary 194
McCOVEY Cassie 293
McCOY Bethuel 79, 191, John 266
McCREADY John 204
McDEGRAUS Mary 322
McDERMOTT Michael 162
McDIVITT Ada 190, Alice 190, Daniel 190, Lucille 190
McDONALD Archie 194, Hugh 194, Mabel 194, Mary 194, Milton 195, Susie 194-195, Thomas 194-195, W. W. 194-195
McELFRESH Mr. 80
McELROY Jennie 195
McFADDEN Emma 195, Leo 195
McGARVEY James 195
McGAVERN Clair 195, Clifford 195
McGEORGE William 9
McGILL Arthur 195, Celestine 195
McGINNIS Ellen 195, John 195
McGUIRE Belle 195, Bertha 195, Flora 195-196, James 195-196, Jane B. 196, Sarah 195, Thomas 196
McINTOCH Mr. 341-342
McINTOSH Edgar 196, Silvertus 226
McINTYRE Anna 196, Arthur 196, Frank 196, Martin 196, Mr. 27
McIRNEY Bridget 196
McKAY Amelia 196, Bernice 196, Daniel 196-197, Francis 196, John 196, Lulu 196, Napoleon 196-197, Richard 196, 220, Roscoe 196, Sally 196- 197, Silas 196, Thomas 196
McKERN Mr. 325
McKERNAN Anna 197, Charles 197, Ellen 197, Francis 197, James 197, Mary 197, Michael 197-198, Thomas 197
McKIBBIN Edward 198, Margaret 198
McKINLEY Agnes 198, Elizabeth 198, Hazel 198, Henry 198, John 198, Lizzie 198, May 198
McKOON Rosith 141
McLANE MR. 351
McLARNEY Mr. 5
McLAUGHLIN James 46, 198, Mary 46, 198
McLOREY Elnora 176
McMAHON Edward 305, Helen 198, James 216-217, John 198, M. Louisa 198, Mary 198, Mr. 305
McMASTER Adalaide 199, David 199, Emily 199, Ira 199, Jane 199, Susan 199, Wallace 199
McMILLAN Lydia 336
McMILLEN Alden 215-216, Charles 215-216, Charlotte 199, Christiana 215-216, Eliza 108, John 199, Martha 199, Mary 215-216, Polly 199, William 215-216
McMULLEN See Page 109
McMURRAY James 157
McNALL Clara 260-261
McNINCH Lee 326, Nellie 326, Sarah 326
McPHERSON Frances 199, 339, Jessie 339, Ray 339, Roy 199, Wallace 199, 339
McQUAID Martin 199, Mr. 331, Rose 199
McSTAY Jennie 106
McVEY Arch 199, Christina 199, Elizabeth 199, James 199, Margaret 199, Susan 199, William 199
MEACHAM Harlan 200, Henry 200, Jeremiah 200, Le Roy 200, Martha 311, Mary 300, Milo 311, Moses 200, Orator Warren 30, Rhoda 200
MEAD Mr. 196, 263
MEADE Henry G. 200
MEDLEY Bessie 263

MEECH Melvin 312, Minerva 312
MEIER Joseph 272
MEIGHS Hattie 328
MELE Carl 200
MELOY Mr. 185
MELROSE Clifton 39, Ebenezer 200, James 200, Mary Belle 39
MERCER Betsey 139, James 139
MERIDAN Jacob 200, Teresa 200
MERKT Charles 200, Edith 200, Eugene 200
MEROW Estella D. 200
MERRICK Ethel 200
MERRILL Almira 332, Charles 28-29, Frank 201, Hattie 201, Henry 201, Mr. 14, Willie 200-201
MERSCH James 65
MERSE William 323
METCALF Armena 12, Charles 201, 331, Ella 201, Harry 201, Leroy 201, Mr. 51, Raymond 201
METTS Mr. 137
MEYER C. 201, Dorothea 201, Leona 192-193
MICHLER Gottlieb 1
MIDDLETON Amanda 117
MIGHELLS Elizabeth 201, Ellen 201, Elliott 201, Florentine 201, George 201, Marian 201, Sophronia 201
MILES Arthur 201, John 201
MILK Anna 202, Benjamin 202, David 202, George 202, Giles 202, Hiram 202, John 202, Martin 202, Mary 162-163
MILKS Alexander 2, 202, Archie 202, Benjamin, 162-163, Etta 282, Giles 162-163, Hiram 162-163, 202, Jennie 202, John 162-163, Jonathan 202, Lucy 220, Luther 202, Manley 126, Martha 202, Martin 162-163, Mina 202, Mr. 80, 282, Rose 202, Ruth 202
MILLER Abram 203-204, Albert 202-204, Amy 203, Annice 328, Ansel 202-203, Anson 203, Asa 203, Cadelia 202-203, Charles 202-204, 341, Christiana 138, Clara 202-204, Clare 24-25, David 202-203, Edna 203, Elizabeth 202-203, Ellen 202-204, Elma 203-204, Elnora 94, Emeline 203-204, Frances Anna 203, Frank 94, 203, George 202, Harriet 203-204, Henry 245, Hubert 128, 202, Hurbert 204, James 203, Joseph 202-204, Laurentine 328, Leon 204, Lottie 256-257, Louisa 245, Mariah 202, Marion 280-281, Mary 203, Max 280-281, Mr. 69, 210, 225, 287, Nancy 204, Nellie 202-203, Peter 12, 203-204, Rose 203-204, Sarah 203-204, Silas 202, Thomas 202-203, Thurman 203, Walter 203, William 203-204
MILLHOLLEN Emily 11, 310
MILLS Dexter 332, Ione 204, Jesse 204, Merrill 63, 204, William 204, 349-350
MINER Charles 204, Frank 204, Henry 204, Jesse 204, Julius 204, Lillian 204, Nettie 77-78, 204, Thomas 204
MITCHELL Carrie 204, Charles 204, John 204-205, Margaret 204, Mary 42, 277, 297, Thomas 270, William 218
MIX Mr. 345
MIXER Sally 71-73
MOBERG Ada 205, Edgar 205, Lena 205
MOENCH Caroline 15
MOHR Andrew 205, Clarence 205, Edward 205, Julia 205, Lucretia 205, Margaret 355, Mary 205, Walter 205
MONG Anna 205, Cornelia 205, Willson 205
MONTELEONE Anthony 323
MONTENFFEL See Mantenfall
MONTGOMERY Nellie 205
MONTON William 122
MOODY Brad 177
MOON Leroy 206, Mary 205-206,

Orville 205-206, Thomas 205-206
MOORE Anna 132, Blanche 292-293, Charles 206, Edgar 157, 206, Edward 197-198, Harlow 206, Jacob 108, Joanna 197, Josephine 206, Oliver 206, Romanzo 206, Wesley 141
MOOT Minnie 206
MORAN Donald 206, Sarah 206, Sarto 206
MORGAN Almira 206-207, Anna 208, Arthur 207, Atcelia 206, Christiana 206, Christina 207, Congdon 207, Cornelia 206-207, E. Atcelia 207, Ernest 207, Harriet 206-207, 347, Henry 206-207, Hiram 206-207, James 206-207, Mary 207, Mercy 207, Mr. 71, 238, Newell 207, Permelia 206-207, Philip 207, William 207
MORIARTY Ellen 207-208, Francis 207-208, Johanna 207-208, John 207-208, Michael 207-208, William 207-208
MORRILL Franklin 208, Herbert 208, Lucy 208, Mary 208
MORRIS Arminta 208, Austin 338, Calphernia 94, Catharine 242-243, Charles 208, Daniel 208, David 208, Hannah 208, James 208, 311, John 208, Julia 208, Louisa 208, Phebe 12, Sidney 230, Thomas 208, William 208
MORRISON Charles 209, Elizabeth 200, Emma 208, Francis 263, James 209, Lottie 209, Mary 209, Maud 209, Thomas 209, William 208
MORTON Agnes 209, Anna 209, Ara 209, Daniel 209, DeForrest 209, Frank 209, George 209, H. Edith 209, Hugh 209, James 209, Mr. 134, Nelson 209, Robert 209, Sarah 282-283, Wm. 298-299
MOSCRISS Lillie 94
MOSHER Betsey 209, Minerva 209, Thomas 209, William 210
MOSZAK Peter 210
MOULD Mary 85
MOYER Alice 210, Estella 210, Eunice 210, John 210
MUDGE Charles 210, Edwin 210, Geraldine 210, Helen 210, Seldon 210, Winifred 210
MULCAY Dora 210, James 137, 261, John 210, Nora 210
MULLER See Miller
MULLIN James 210-211, John 211, May 211, Ralph 293-294, Theresa 211
MURPHY Anna 211, 301-302, Blanche 211, Daniel 211, Emilie Coast 54, Frank 211, James 211, John 211, 249, Maggie 211, Marcella 211, Margaret 49, Mary 211, Matthew 101, Mr. 144, 326, Rose 211, Sarah 211
MURRAY Anna 211-212, Bertha 211-212, Clifford 212, Ella 211-212, George 178, Hayward 211-212, John 211-212, Lena 211-212, Margaret 211-212, Margarite 211-212, Mary 212, Michael 212, Novella 211-212, Sara 211-212
MYER Joseph 272
MYERS Aaron 212, Adelaide 212, Albert 212, Arthur 212, Edith 66, Joseph 251, Louisa 212, Mary 212, Olive 212, Stephen 212
MYLES Alice 212, Frank 212, James 212, Mary 212, Rose 212
MYRICK Clarence 213, John 212-213, Mary 213
NAPIER Edward 215, James 186-187
NASH Adaline 215, Adelbert 215-216, 283, Adell 215-216, Amos 215-216, Charles 216, 283, Corydon 215-216, Dewit 215-216, Dewitt 215-216, Emmet 215-216, Eugene 143, 188, 215-216, Oramon 255-256, Perry 215, 283, Sally 215-216, Victoria 215-216

NEAR Maranda 215-216
NEFF Andrew 57-58, 286
NEILSON Stanley 149
NELSON A. E. 217, Alexander 216, Beth 217, Eliza 218, Emily 217, Flora 217, Frank 217-218, Frederick 216-217, Hattie 296, John 216-217, Lana 216-217, Marion 217, Morris 216-217, Nellie 217, Orrel 217, Robert 217, Samuel 216-217, Staley 217, Walter 217, Wilber 217, William 216-217
NENNO Amos 218, Charles 218, Edward 218, Fred 218, Gertrude 218, Lewis 218, M. W. 218, Michael 218
NEUGART Bart 274, Berthold 218, Frank 218, John 218, Mina 218
NEUMAN Bessie 286
NEWCOMB David 218, Etta 218, Freddie 218, George 218, Hulda 20, John 218, Mary 218, Thomas 20
NEWELL Frank 304, Sidney 338-339
NEWKIRK Jane 153
NEWMAN Adelia 219, Anna 218-219, Eunice 219, Ira 218-219, Mansel 219, Mary 218-219
NEWTON George 121, Lyman 219, Martha 219, Milton 219, Myron 219, Nellie 328
NICHOLS Charles 219-220, Grace 219-220, Hosea 220, John 219-220, Marietta 219-220, Mr. 167, 174, Nellie 219-220, Nelson 219, Orlando 219-220, Richmond 219-220, Robert 219, Sarah 219-220
NICKLESS Heman 121, 172
NICKS Mr. 155-157
NIES Amelia 220, Carl 220, Charles 86, 220, 291-292, Christian 220, Fred 220, Irving 220, Paulina 220, Pauline 220
NILES Annabelle 220, Charles 220-221, Ethel 220, Gaylord 221, Harriet 220, Howard 220, John 220, Lovina 220, Mr. 246, Sarah 220, Stephen 220, William 220
NIX Charles 221, Eda 221, Malvina 221
NOLDES Betsey 90
NOLTON Caroline 190, Martin 190
NOONAN Clarence 221, Frank 221, Harry 221, James 221, Patrick 221
NORDINE Clara 94
NORTH Anna 221, Edwin 221, Jennie 182, 221, Mr. 289
NORTHRUP Aaron 221, Elizabeth 222, Eva 221-222, Jessie 221-222, May 221-222, Moses 221-222, Mr. 271, 272
NORTON Bessie 121, Elizabeth 222, James 222, Mary 88, Nellie 222, Nelson 88
NORWOOD Agnes 222, Emma 222, Fred 222
NOTTINGHAM Bessie 261, Claude 222, Electa 222, Elnora 222, Harry 222, Jacob 222, Mabel 222, Ned 222, Solomon 222, Starl 222, Wellington 261
NOURSE Amy 350, Edward 223, Emma 223, John 223, Louise 223, Orrin 223
NOYES Betsey 97, Frederick 97
NUDA Mr. 138
NUTTING Edwin 223, Eva 223, Ida 223, Lucien 223, 349, Matilda 223, Melissa 223
NYE Edward 108, Samuel 223
OAKES Alice 225, Jasper 225, Jesse 225, Mr. 286-287, Nellie 225, Nichols 225
OAKLEAF Edward 328, James 328, Jennie 328, Marion 328
OAKLEY Ada Blanche 225, Amanda 225
OAKS Caroline 225, Ellie 225, George 225, Ida 225, Millie 225, Mr. 324, 336, Sarah 206-207
O'BRIEN Ambrose 225, Anthony 226, Bridget 225, Charles 35, 225, Daisy 225, Dennis 225, Ida 225,

James 225-226, Jennie 225, John 225-226, Michael 226, Mr. 180 Patrick 226, Rev. 104, Sarah 226, Simeon 226, Stephen 226, Zilla 226
OCHERICH Johanna 138
ODELL Mr. 78
O'DELL Albert 226, Amelia 226, Daniel 226, Emma 226, Mary 226, Orrin 226
O'DONNELL Anna Belle 292-293, Benjamin 292-293, Cornelius 226, Elizabeth 226, 292-293, Stephen 226, Susie 343, William 226
O'HERN Ellen 47-48, Mary 47-48
OHMER Mildred 130
O'KEEFE Patrick 83-84, 127
O'LAUGHLIN Peter 33
OLCUTT Emma 249, Henry 326
OLDEN William 194
OLDENBURG Mr. 129
OLDER Mr. 45, William 194
OLDHAM Harvey 226
OLDS F. C. 227, Frances 227, Fred C. 119, Harriett 227, John 227, Laura 227
O'LEARY Mary 227
OLTHOF Henry 123, Mary 122
O'MARA Bryan 227, Catherine 227, Ellen 227, John 227, Julia 227, Mary 227, Michael 227
O'MEARA Francis 228, Harry 228, Norman 228, Patrick 228
ONDRA Mr. 206
OOSTERHOUDT Arthur 228, Emeline 228, Ida 228, Louisa 132, 228, Mary 228, Mr. 132, Samuel 228, 290, William 228
O'ROURKE Edward 228
ORSBURN Mr. 142
OSBORN Lillian 237
OSGOOD Catherine 32
OSTERSTUCK Adeline 228-229, Angeline 228-229, Charles 228-229, Emery 228-229, Eveline 229, George 228-229, John 228-229, Mary 228-229, Warner 228-229, William 228-229
OSTHAUS Carl 229-230, Ette 229-230, Johanna 229-230, Walter 229
OSTRANDER Andrew 230, James 230, John 230, Lany 230, Margaret 315, Mary 230, Mr. 190, Nellie 230
OSTRUM Bertha 143, Helen 143, Thomas 143
O'TOOLE Mr. 198
OVENSHIRE Jenny 326
OVIATT Lucetta 230, Miles 230
OWEN Carrie 332-333, Emma 230-231, Flora 230-231, Jessie 230-231, Josephine 230-231, Lemuel 230-231, Mabel 230-231
OWENS Esther 231, Evan 95, Margarett 95, Martha 231, Nina 231
OYER Betsey 231, David 217-218, George 231, Hannah 140, John 231, 275, Levi 231, Loretta 38, Margaret 217, Mr. 230, Peter 174, 217-218
PADLO Frank 237, Joseph 233, 237, Louis 237, Philomena 237, Vincent 237
PAGE James 233, Jane 233, Joseph 233, Tracy 233, Wilson 233
PAINTER Eva 121
PAISLEY Mr. 102, 120
PALM Andrew 233, Anna 233, Charles 233, Florence 154, James 233, Mabel 154, Raymond 154
PALMER Edmond 236, Mr. 28-29
PARBS John 233, Mary 233
PARISH See Parrish, David 233, Jane 251, Mary 233, Shubel 251, Smith 64, 233
PARKER Adell 140, Albert 234-235, Alice 234-235, Amy 234-235, 248, Asa 234-235, Beulah 235, Chauncey 234-235, Cora 234-235, Corwin 17, David 234-235, DeForest 314, Edwin 234, Ellicott 234-235, Emma 234-235, Ernest 233, 235, Eunice 235, Eva 234-235, Ezra 234, Flora 234-235, George 344-245, Heman

235, Ida 140, James 234-235, John 233, 235, 339, Lola 343, Mary 234-235, Mira 234-235, Mr. 1, 102, Myron 293, 295, Permelia 17, 234, S. Arvilla 234, Sabina E. 10, T. J. 140, Urson 234, Ward 233, 235, Washington 235, Wiley 233, 235, William 235, Willie 234
PARMETER Benjamin 235, Gratia 235, Lydia 235, Mary 235, Osborn 235
PARRISH See Parish, Clark 236, Cynthia 236, John 235-236, Leonard 235-236, Marvin 235-236, Orisy 235-236, Shubil 235-236
PARSELL Corilla 331-332, John 331-332, Rebecca 331-332, Warren 331-332, Worden 331-332
PARSONS Amos 97, Howard 236
PASSMORE Samuel 36
PATCH Abram 236, Alson 236, Judith 236, Olive 236
PATON Belle 236, H. Isabel 236, H. Janet 236, Mary 236, Mildred 236, Nettie 236, William 236, Wilma 236
PATTERSON Annie 237, Eugene 89, Genevieve 237, Grant 237, James 237, Maggie 237, Nathaniel 237, Sophia 237, Violet 237
PATTESON Annie 237
PATTON Earl 83
PATTYSON Darius 237, James 237, Mary 237
PAULY Eva 355
PAYNE Mr. 241
PEABODY Charles 237, Clyde 237, Minnie 237, Mr. 4, Raymond 237, Wilma 237
PEARCE Benjamin 237, Marjorie 237, Mary 237, Rounsville 237
PEASE Arthur 237-238, Chauncey 237-238, Cora 237-238, Elsie 237-238, Frank 237-238, Martha 237-238, Samuel 237-238
PEASLEE Daniel 93, Elizabeth 93, Joseph 77, 92, 203, Snytha 93

PECK Cyrus 238
PECKHAM Edwin 238
PEET Abram 238, David 238, Evan 81, 238, Flora 338, John 238, Thomas 238, William 238
PELTON Tober 238
PENDLEBURY Mr. 110
PENDLETON Perry 240
PENHOLLOW Doris 301
PEPPERDINE Chloe 238
PERAINO Mr. 225
PERCIVAL Frederick 239, James 238, Nettie 238-239
PERIN Edward 239
PERKINS Carrie 239, Daniel 234-235, Francis 239, George 239, Harry 239, Herbert 92, John 89, 177-178, 242, Mabel 239, Riley 239
PERNO Mr. 225
PERRIGO Flora 239
PERRIN Eliza 239, Hosea 239, Mary 239
PERRY Ann 209, Hubert 246, Josiah 350, Satira 126
PERSONS Charles 239, Mary 239, Samuel 239, Wilber 239
PETER Aloysius 239, Catherine 239
PETERS Arthur 239, Clara 240, Emma 220, Frank 240, Mr. 93
PETERSON Carl 240, George 133, 240, John 240
PETTINGELL Mary 240
PETTIS Lydia 50
PETTIT Elta 62, Henry 240
PETTY Marcia 240, Margaret 348, Rufus 240, 257
PETTYS Carrie 240, Celia 240, Irma 240, Levi 240, Merritt 240
PFLEUGER Catherine 122, 282
PHELPS Charles 37, 241, Charlotte 240-241, Cyrus 240-241, James 133, Lucy 240, McKinley 241, William 37
PHILLIPS Daniel 241, Ann 260-261, Charles 327, Clara 241, Delos 350, Henry 322, Jared 241, John 241,

Jonah 350, Mary 222, 241, Milo 241, Minnie 241, Mr. 31, 43, 83, 319, Ross 126, Sarah 241, Sophronia 144, Susan 241, Sylvenus 241, William 241
PHINNEY Andrew 249, Emeline 249, Eugene 249, John 249
PIATT Ruth 5
PICKETT Ruth 352
PICKUP Emeline 332, Frank 332
PIERCE Aldra 241-242, Alice 152, 276, Caleb 242, Clarissa 242, Count Polasky 241-242, Dolly 242, Emeline 312, Ezekiel 161, Fernando 242, James 242, John 241-242, Joseph Frank 242, L. B. 241, Lanie 257, Leander 276, Marcia 242, Mary 241-242, Mr. 123, Nehemiah 242, O. W. 86, Patience 241-242, Phebe 313, Richard 242, Sarah 242, William 59-60, 140
PIERSON Mr. 30
PIFER Charles 243, Edward 242-243, Mary 242-243, Peter 242-243, Sophia 242-243
PINGREY Melzer 18-19
PITCHER Alice 243, Iona 243, Laura C. 243, Spencer 34
PITTMAN Ellen 24
PIXLEY Orrin 243
PLACHER James 243, Mary 145, 243
PLANK Mr. 265
PLUMMER Ina 243-244, James 243-244, Lawrence 243-244, Susie 243
PLUTZ Augusta 334
POLAND James 215-216
POLLARD Mr. 315
POOLE John 307
POOR Franklin 303, Maria 303
POPPLE Josephine 244, Maud 244, William 244, Willie 244
PORTER Anna 244, Edward 244, Henry 244, Isaac 244, John 244, Mary 244, Samantha 244
POTTER Catharine 244, Gideon 244 Mr. 172

POWELL L. F. 244, Luther 347
POWERS Edward 244, Kathryn 244, William 244
PRATT Albert 246, Alpha 245, Altna 245-246, Amos 245, Benjamin 245-246, Claribel 114, Clotilda 245-246, Darius 267, Delos 141, Ella 246, Emily 245, Fannie 246, George 245-246, J. Huldah 245-246, Jenett 267, John 245-246, Judson 245, Julia 245, M. Calvin 245, Mary 245, Milton 245, Noah 245-246, Phoebe 245, Roxana 267, Sally 141, 245
PREBYNSKE Anthony 292, Katherine 292, Michaelino 292
PRENTICE Alice 246, Edith 246, Mary 246, Simeon 246
PRENTISS Solomon 238
PRESACK Elizabeth 246, Frances 246, Irene 246, Joseph 246, Lizzie 246
PRESCOTT Jennings 246, John 76, 246, Lillian 76, 246, Minnie 165, Mr. 206, Norton 76, 246, Urban 76, 246
PRESTON Bridget 86, 160, Emily 247, Hiram 246-247, James 86, 160, Juliaetta 246, Orrin 246-247, Rossell 246-247, Samuel 246-247, Warren 246-247
PREY Florence 247
PRICE Alfred 276, Elbert 247-248, Elfie 247-248, Elizabeth 247-248, Emma 276, George 247, Hale 248, Lewis 247, Lucinda 276, Mattiah 276, Merta 247-248, Mr. 143, Samuel 247, Speda 247-248
PRIESS Hans 248, Henry 248
PRIEST Mary 221
PRINCE Halsey 165, Mr. 165
PRINGLE Mr. 91
PRITCHARD Frank 316, Mr. 127, 137
PROCTOR W. H. 353
PROSSER Andrew 248, Caroline 248, Daniel 153-154, Emily 153-157,

Michael 248
PUDDY Dorcas 103
PUGH Mr. 262
PUPPLE Mary 131, William 131
PURDY Carrie 261
PUTNAM Caroline 248, Eliza 248, Henry 248
PUTNEY Edwin 248, Sarah 248
QUACKENBUSH David 249, Ella 249, Frank 249, Harlan 48, Jane 249, Spencer 249
QUIGLEY Agnes 249, Clara 249, Daniel 249, Eleanor 249, James 249, Jane 249, John 249, Mary 249
QUINN Catherine 249, Frank 249, Mary 249, Michael 250, Thomas 249
RACHFORD James 251, John 251, Mary 251, Patrick 251
RACKOWSKY Katherine 251
RADLEY J. Wilson 20
RAINEY Mr. 26-27
RAMSAY Florence 251, George 251, Kate 251, Mary 251, Silas 251, Sylvester 251, William 251
RAMSEY Franklin 332, George 251, Mary 251, Silas 251, Sylvester 251, William 251
RANDALL Charles 252, Clinton 251-252, 264, Cora 251-252, Daisy 251, Edna 252, Edward 252, Elisha 331-332, Elma 252, George 251-252, Harvey 252, Helen 251-252, Ida 252, Jacob 252, Lottie 251-252, Lucy 331-332, Ruth 252-253, 264
RANSOM Addison 253, Alonzo 253, Betsey 253, Leslie 291, Orrin 253, Smith 253
RATHBURN Clarissa 253
RAUB O. J. 253
RAUBER Albert 253
RAY Daniel 253
RAZEY Ada 253, Almadorus 13, Charles 253, Chloe 253, Emma 13, Frances 253, Horace 253, Lorenzo 253, Mary 253, Sarah 13

READ E. W. 140, Elgene 326, Maud 156
REASZ Albertine 253-254, Catherine 253-254, Edith 253-254, Frances 253-254, Frank 253-254, Isabel 253-254, Willard 253-254
RECK Iva 254, Caroline 306-307, Charlotte 108, Cora 221, 254, Elvira Cora 221, 254, Emery 254, Isaac 139, Maud 278, Mr. 166, Newton 108, Pearl 254, Phebe 139
REEDY Rose 159, T. F. 159, Thomas 254
REESE Eleanor 254, Esther 254, Joshua 254, Mr. 95, Sarah 254, Thomas 254
REEVES Clinton 254, Edna 254, George 248, Lizzie 248, Mr. 147
REIHM Jacob 254
REILLEY Fred 255, George 254-255, Lillie 254
REILLY Fred 254
REITZ Catharine 255, Frederick 255, Henry 255, John 255, Leona 255, Mary 255, Molly 255, Raymond 255, Theodore 255
REMINGTON Heman 255-256, Marcella 255-256, Mr. 323, Oramon 255-256, Robert 255-256, Ruth 255-256, Seth 255, Stephen 255
RENWICK James 256, Jane 256, Robert 256
RETTER John 256
REUSCH Bertha 256, John 256, Margaret 256, Michael 256, Regina 256
REUTER John J. 25
REVETT Clara 256, Geneva 256, George 256, Mary 256
REYNOLDS Arthur 257, Bertha 257, Callie 258, Carrie 177, Catharine 271-272, Charles 256-257, Dennis 257-258, Edward 256-257, Elizabeth 256-257, Elmer 257, Emma 257, Erma 257, Frances 257, Henry 258, Ida 256-257, Jacob 257,

James 256-257, John 256-257, 271-272, Levi 242-243, Lovinia 257, Margaret 256, Mary 256-257, 271-272, Millard 257, Minnie 282, Mr. 311, Pamelia 258, Permelia 257, Richard 256, Robert 256-257, Roberta 256-257, Semantha 256-257, Walter 257, William 177, 271-272
RHOADES Mr. 12, 129
RHOADHOUSE Nelly 258, Vernon 258
RHODES Addie 258, Clara 220, George 258, Marcus 258, Merrill 258
RIAN Mabel 258, Nelson 258
RIBBLE Mr. 34
RICE Abel 139, Alice 136, Caroline 258, Charles 258, Clark 139, 258, Elmer 258, Emily 258, Lorette 258, Mariet 258, Mr. 284, Polly 139, Sally 258, Sarah 341, Sylvia 139 William 258
RICH Bessie 259, Lewis 259, Lillian 259, Lynn 258, Mr. 139, 264-265, Philip 7, Raymond 259, Victor 258-259, Wallace 142, Walter 258
RICHARDS Helen 259, Jennie 259, John 259
RICHARDSON Beulah 259, Emily 190, George 259, Harry 307, Henry 259, Jennie 259, Leander 259, Morris 259
RICHEY Beulah 260, Cecil 259-260, Evelyn 259-260, Hugh 259-260, Lela 259-260, Lola 259-260, Pearl 259-260, Robert 259-260
RICHMOND Augusta 3
RICKARD Andrew 140-141
RICKARDS Eliza 206, Nelson 206
RICKARS Andrew C 100
RIDDLE James 70, Joseph M. 70
RIDOUT Elma 260, Eva 260, Maria 1, 260, Mr. 1, Nathan 260, Nellie 260, Wesley 260
RIGGS Coral 260-261, Eliza Ann 260-261, Franklin 260-261, H. L. 260-261, L. S. 260-261, Lewis 260-261, Miles 260
RILEY James 261, Mary 261
RINK Gifford 261, John 261, Mina 261, Nellie 261
RITCHIE Ella 261, John 261
RITTER Eva 261, John 261, Joseph 261, Mary 261
RITZAUR Christopher 85
ROACH David 225, William 225
ROBBINS Albert 262, Charles 236, Egbert 262, Ellen 261-262, Esther 261-262, Frank 262, Fred 262, Horace 236, John 236, Mary 261-262, Peleg 262, Richard 261-262
ROBERTS Everel 262, Harriet 262-263, Katie 262-263, Mary 254, 262-263, Owen 262-263, Robert 262-263, Sarah 237-238, Willie 262-263
ROBERTSON Whetten 263
ROBESON Idella 223, John 223
ROBINSON Catherine 263, Elizabeth 263, Eunice 263, Horace 263, Jane 18, 263, Mary 263, Mr. 159, William 263, 286-287, 290-291
ROBLEE Mr. 303
ROBSON G. L. 311
ROCKWELL Mr. 317
ROCKWOOD C. H. 310
RODGERS Augustus 263, Maria 263, Mr. 296
ROFF Albert 263, Della 263, Florence 26, Lysander 263
ROGERS Ada 263-264, Isaac 263, Jos. 130, Lafayette 29, 263-264, Leo 264, Mr. 108, Oma 29, 263, Roquel 1, 277, T.H.B. 346
ROHAN Catherine 264, Ellen 264, Johanna 264, John 264, Mary 264, Nancy 264, William 264
ROHRICK Frederick 140, John 140
ROJEK Joseph 264
ROLFE Mr. 129
RONDOLL Clinton 264, Ruth 264
ROOD Anna 264-265, Edith 265, Evelyn 264-265, Herbert 264-265

ROOT Emma 265, Nancy 265
ROPPS George 265
ROSE Mr. 145
ROSEN Louise 265
ROSENBERRY James 265, Richard 265, Sarah 265, Thomas 265
ROSS Amelia Ann 71-73, Ann 71-73, Asa 265, Clara 265, Edwin 71-73, Ella 265, Florence 265, Floyd 265, Joseph 71-73, Walter 265, Wilber 71-73, Zenos 71-73
ROTSCHKY Frederica 265, Gottfried 265-266, Margaret 266, Mary 265-266, Sophia 266, Theresa 266
ROUNDS Lane 221, Mr. 270
ROUPE J. S. 296
ROWAN Mr. 42
ROWLAND Charles 306, John 266
ROYAN Anna 266, Charles 266, Josephine 266, Hiram 266, Horace 266
RUBLEE Allison 171, Frank 171, Jane 171, Leroy 171
RUCKH William 290
RUF Louis 266
RUGG Charles 266, J. Wilson 266, Mr. 277
RULISON Fannie 266, John 266, Mr. 171
RUMRILL Betsey 228-229, Lewis 229
RUNGE Marie 58
RUNYON C. A. 266, Lydia 266
RUPLE Mary 266
RUSH Calvin 267, Jacob 267, Mary 267, Poltus 267, Sabelia 267
RUSSELL Mr. 263-264
RUST John 165, Norman 50, Quarteus 327-328
RYAN Catherine 267, Francis 267, James 355, Mary 267, Michael 267, Patrick 267, Roger 335, William 267
SAAR Mr. 321
SACKET Frederick 269, Garry 269, John 269, Jonathon 269, W. Gilmore 269
SACKINGER Elizabeth 9
SACKRIDER Daniel 269, Sophia 334
SAFFORD John H. 129-130
SAGE Mr. 115
SALISBURY Ann 269-270, Barnard 269, Cyrus 269-270, Foster 269, Jane 269-270, Jenette 269-270, Lavancha 269, Lorentus 269, Martin 13, Maryon 269, Mrs. 190
SANDERS Asa 43, Cora 325, David 253, J. C. 325, Jay 325, Mr. 35, 240
SANDERSON John Sewall 142
SANDSTONE Charles 270, Hannah 270, Henry 270
SANDY Edith 301
SARTWELL Mrs. 195
SAUNDERS Hezekiah 270, Julia 270, Nelson 270
SAVAGE Elizabeth 270, Frank 270, Marguerite 270, Nellie 270, Patrick 270
SAWERS Jane 49
SAXTON Adelle 171, Albert 270-272, Baker 270-272, Ebenezer 270-272, Emma 271-272, Faithy 171, Florence 271-272, Fred 271, Frederick 270-272, Genevieve 271, Hannah 270-272, Henry 171-172, 270-272, Horace 171, Leonard 271, Lucy 270-272, Mariette 271-272, Melvin 171, Perry 171, Seymour 171, Walter 270-271, William 271
SAYLES Mr. 42, 297
SCANLON Leo 198
SCHAAK Joseph H. 233
SCHAEDER Mr. 16
SCHAFFER Carl 288
SCHAICH Mr. 120
SCHEIER Laura 272, Theresa 272
SCHLITTLER Elizabeth 272, Frederick 272, George 272, William 272
SCHLOSSER Frances 272, John 272, Joseph 272, Theodore 272
SCHMALZ Emma 272-273, Gottlieb

272-273, Jennie 272-273, John 272-273, Mary 272-273, Michael 272
SCHNELL Arthur 273, Delia 273, Edwin 273, Erwin 273, F. H. 273, Irene 273, Norbert 273, Violetta 273
SCHNEPEL Charles 273, Edward 273, George 273, John 273, Mary 273
SCHOLL Burdette 273, Catherine 273-274, Gilbert 273, Mamie 273
SCHOONHOVER Mr. 138
SCHOONOVER Nellie 274
SCHOTT Walter W. 274
SCHRADER Mr. 154
SCHULER John 274, Nicholas 274, Philip 274
SCHULTS George 274
SCHULTZ Carl 186-187, Charles 200, Christopher 186-187, John 186-187, Mr. 274
SCHULZ Henry 186-187
SCHUSTER Emma 274, John 274
SCHUTT Clifton 274, Ethel 274, Fred 274, Henry 106, John 106, 274, L. D. V. 274, Mary 274
SCHUTTS Clyton 222
SCHWALB Anthony 274
SCHWENK William 338
SCOBEY Anna 274, Hannah 274, Ruth 274
SCOFIELD A. Burdette 110, Willis 274
SCOTLAND Helen 346
SCOTT Amanda 225, 325, Bert 122, Charles 275, Elbert 122, Elwin 275, Frankie 122, Hollis 137, Justus 120, Mary Jane 4, Mr. 175, 239, Nettie 275, O. P. 275, Thomas 52
SCUDDER Ada 136, Alvin 275, Amanda 275, Delevan 136, Ezekiel 136, Hezekiah 136, Samuel 275
SEARL Eliza 55, 266, Florence 275, Frank 275, James 119, Justin 266, Matthew 55, Theodore 275
SEARLE Mary 275, Roberta 275, Theodore 275, William 275
SEARLES Dennis 275, Dorothy 276, Eliza 275-276, George 275-276, Harmon 275-276, John 275-276
SEARS Albina 276, Charlie 276, Clarence 276, Delevan 276, Eliza 276, Lucy 276, Resolved 276
SEEKENS Lara 171
SEEKER Runette 276
SEEKINS Manley 276, Martin 276, Monroe 276
SEELEY Silas S. 104
SEELMAN Mille B. 140
SEELY Mr. 104, Silas 188
SEIBERT Grace 281
SELLINGER Mr. 90
SENEAR Jesse 276, Oscar 187
SENECA Lucinda 152, 241
SENTER James 118
SERA Mr. 100
SESSIONS Albert 276-277, Edna 277, Henry 277, Israel 277, John 276-277, Martha 277, Mr. 237, Sophia 277
SETOFF Louis 277
SEXTON Elisha 351
SEYLLER Alphonse 277, Julius 277, Louise 277
SEYMOUR George 325, Henry 277, Mina 277, S. H. 85, Silas 61-62
SHACK Mr. 245-246
SHAFFNER Eugene 277
SHAFNER Mr. 108
SHAKELY Miles 40
SHANNON Aggie 277, Bessie 277, Eliza 277, Ella 277, Emily 277, James 277, Samuel 277, Truman 277
SHARP Margaret 195, Mary 277
SHARPE John W. 31
SHATTUCK Cladius 278, Lewis 278, Mary 278
SHAW Adell 278, Cortland 278, Emma 278, Hamlin 278, Herbert 278, Irene 278, James 3-4, Leo 278 Mr. 71, Nellie 278, William 278

SHAY Johanna 264
SHEA Patrick 315
SHEAN John 278
SHEAR Emma 278, Libbie 278
SHEARS Emma 9, Mr. 9, Sarah 9
SHEDD John 278
SHEEHAN Lawrence 278, Michael 278
SHEHEN John 279
SHELDON Leslie 279, Ruby 279
SHELEHAN Mary 315
SHEPARD Chandler 279, Leverett 279, Lucinda 296, Luther 279, Sarah 279, Thomas 296
SHERLOCK Amarette 279, Jay 279, John 279, Judd 279, Judson 279, Sylvester 279
SHERMAN Bennie 279, Dora 279, Edward 279, James 208, Latusia 279, Selana 279, Theodora 66, Theodorus 279
SHERRY Anna 279, James 279, Margaret 279, Peter 279, Will 279
SHERWIN Susan 189, Sylvester 189
SHICKS William 227
SHIELDS Caroline 280, Christina 280, George 280, Henry 280, John 280
SHIMERSKI Julia 152
SHINGLER John 280
SHIPMAN Edith 110, Hosea 110, Lizzie 280
SHIPPERD H. H. 5
SHIPPY Alfred 280, Charlotte 280, Isaac 280, Kate 280, Mr. 13, Rosell 280, Sarah 280, Seville 280
SHIRLINE Henry 280
SHOEMAKER Millie 280
SHOFF Brady 281, Clair 280-281, Elizabeth 280, Lucille 280-281
SHORTS Ella F. 99
SHRADER Mary 130
SHROEDER Clara 281, Deana 281, Grace 281, Julia 281, Leo 281, Louisa 281, Mary 281, Samuel 281
SHULTES Emma 281, Henry 281

SHULTS See Schults, Ida 281
SHULTZ Minnie 218, William 218
SHULZ Mary A. 42
SHUM John 327
SHWAKERT Mr. 163
SIBLEY Eben 237-238, Judson 237, Sherman 237-238
SIBLING Mr. 88
SIGGINS Helen 10, Isaac 10, Mary 10, Pauline 10, Walter 10
SIGMAN Albert 281-282, Alice 281-282, Andrew 281, John 281-282, Laura Maria 281-282
SIKES Caleb 316, Hawley 316, Hiram 316, James 316, Julia Ann 316, Lura 316, Salina 316, Shadiak 316, Stephen 316
SILL Clare 282, Clyde 282, Mamie 187, Ona 282
SILVERHEELS George 282, Lawrence 282, Lillie 282
SIMMONS Adam 282, Etta 283, Frederick 283, Lola 282, Loretta 282-283, Richard 283, Seth 282-283
SIMON Simon J. 75
SIMONS Charles 283, Chas. 176, Dora 283, Harry 283, Helen Elizabeth 283
SIMPSON Harriet 19, Joseph 19, Mr. 64
SIRLINE Charles 283
SISSON Ada 283-284, Clara 283-284, Elmer 283-284, Helen 284, Henry 283, Malvina 283, Mamie 283-284
SKEELS Alsina 284, Burt 284, Daniel 284, Luther 284
SKINNER Anna 284, Archie 284, Ethel 284, Nathan 234-235, Roxanna 234-235
SLATER Alida 284, Georgia 284, John 284, Levi 65, 284
SLATTERY Andrew 284, John 85, 284, Maria 164, Matthew 284, Michael 284
SLAWSON Celia 285, Minnie 284-285, Mr. 294-295, Newton 284-285,

Rose 284-285, Silus 284-285, William 284-285
SLOCOM Elizabeth 285
SLOCOMB Cyrus 38
SLOCUM Abner 285, Albert 285, Almanzo 285, Ansel 285, Etta 285, Georgia 285, Gilbert 285, Harley 285, Henry 285, Jersey 285, Mary 285, Ruth 285, Sarah 285, Sylvia 285, Willard 285
SLOVER Adeline 285, Anna 285, James 285, John 285
SMALLWOOD William R. 9
SMITH Adam 290, Addie 288, 290, Adeline 290, Alpha 286-287, 290-291, Alva 65, Amanda 237-238, Andrew 286, 288-289, Anna 240, Anson 287-288, Athalene 288-289, Augustine 287, 290, Bessie 286-288, Betsey 286-287, 289-291, Buel 334, Caroline 287, 289-290, Celia 288, Charles 86, 190, Charlotte 287, 290, Chester 286-287, 289, 291, Clyde 289, 290, Cora 57-58, Cornelius 177, Daisy 287, 289, 291, David 286, Desdemona 286-287, 290-291, Earl 286-290, Edwin 182, 221, 289, Elijah 286, Elizabeth 286, 290-291, Ella 286, 289-290, Ellen 171, 274, Elon 247, Elva 286, 290, Emery 286, 289, 291, Emma 233, 290-291, Ettie 290, Flora 288-289, Frances 53, 286, 288, Fred 287, Frederick 289-290, Fredrick 140, George 287-288, Goldie 287-288, Grace 286-287, Harlan 287, Harry 71, Harvey 337, Helen 286, 288-289, Henrietta 286, 288-289, Henry 189, 287, 289-290, Hiram 287-289, Ichabod 32, Ida 286-289, Isaac 287-289, J. J. 288, James 287, 289, Jane 286, 288-289, Jasper 204, Jefferson 287-289, Jennie 285, 290, Jessie 288, John 290, Julia 288-289, Leena 286-287, 291, Lewis 287, 289-290, Lloyd 285, 288, 290, Louisa 287, 289-290, Lucy 286-288, 290, 313, M. Athalene 286, Marguerite 286, 288, Marvin 290, Mary 249, 286-287, 290-291, Mason 68, Matilda 287, 289, May 286-287, 290, Minerva 312, Minnie 286, 289, Monroe 287, Mr. 1, 114, 139, 162, 189, 211, 303, 346, Nathaniel 286, Nellie 287, Ophelia 287, Ora 290, Otis 290, Percy 285, 288, Ralph 286-287, 290, Ray 286, Rolla 290, Rosetta 189, Royal 288-289, Russell 288, S. W. 287, 290, Sarahett 286-287, 290-291, Silvester 286-287, 290, Stephen 190, Willard 190, William 30, 32, 287-288, Willis 286, Wilma 286-289, Z. W. 286, 289-290
SNIDER Joseph 291
SNOW Chauncey 328, Jane 152, 241, 276
SNYDER A. W. 291, Augustus 291, Carl 291, Clyne 291, Elva 291, Emeline 15, Esther 291, Eugene 291, Hellen 291, Homer 291, Lynn 291, Merl 291, Mr. 89, Norman 15, Phalismen 263, Robert 291
SOBKOWIAK Anna 291-292, John 292, Stanislaws 291-292, Victoria 291-292, Wladislaw 291-292, Zelka 291-292
SOLAREK Clara 292, Edward 292, Harry 292
SOMERS Mr. 6
SOMMER Edward 292, Hattie 292
SOULE Chester 293, Lucy 293
SOUTHWICK Abiah 292, Frank 292, Phebe 164, Waity 341
SOWL Elbert 292-293, John 292
SPARK David 293
SPAULDING Alice 293, Eleanor 203, Eliza 293, Ellen 203, H. P. 293, Harry 293, L. H. 293, Preston 293, Roby 129-130, Ryland 293, William 293
SPEARS Amy 293, Ezra 293, Sarah

SPENCER Anna 293-294, Azarah 294, Burton 293, Clara 293, Collins 145, Della 293, Doris 294, Earl 293, Floyd 293, Isabel 293, Jacob 294, James 276, 293-294, John 294, Maggie 294, Marion 294, Mr. 54, 345, Rachel 249, Rose 64, Stephen 293
SPIESMAN Anna 294, Harry 294, Mary 294, Matthew 294, Theresa 294
SPINDLER Mr. 343
SPINK Mr. 315
SPOOR Abram 294
SPRAGUE Amy 295, Arthur 295, Christopher 295, Delos 295, Dulcenia 295, Henry 294-295, Lois 294-295, Lorenzo 294, Mr. 81, William 295, William Jay 293
SPRAKER Clarence 295, George 295, Harold 295, Susan 295, William 295
SPREATOR Catharine 295
SPRING Alfred 295, Catherine 295, Ellen 295, George 295, Levi 295, Samuel 295
SPRINGER Gertrude 280
SQUIRES Edward C. 79
ST. JOHN Selleck 199
ST. LOUIS Louie 131, 321
STACHOWIAK Eva 218
STACY Carrie 296, Charles 296, Jennie 296, William 295
STADLER Leonard 296
STADY Fred 296, John 353
STAFFORD Austin 171, Bertha 171, Grant 171, McClelland 171, Minerva 171, Orsell 171
STANICK Frances 292
STANLEY Addison 296, Ellen 296, Isaac 296, 303-304, Joseph 18-19, 296, 303-304, Juliatte 296, Luther 296
STANNARD Henry C. 130
STAPLES Goodwin 287-289
STAPLETON Mary 296

STARD David 72
STARKS Alyertta 89, Ava 25, Chester 89, Dora 191, Eliza 296, Eugene 296, Fred 89, G. W. 25, J. W. 89, Malissa 89, Warren 25, Wesley 89
STARKWEATHER William 296
STARR Maria 296, Thomas Irwin 150
STEBBINS Bertha 293, Emerette 123, Francis 296, Lyman 296, Mary 293, Silvanus 296, William 89
STEEL Ella 296, Myrtle 296
STEELE David 288, Jacob 296, Mary 260-261
STEFFENHAGEN Frank 297
STEIGER Amelia 297, Erik 297
STEIN Flora 42, Frank 297
STELLEY Mr. 15
STEPHEN Anne 297, William 297
STEVEN Edna 9
STEVENS Carol 297, David 297, Fred 298, Horace 297, Inez 297, Lawrence 297, Levi 251, Lottie 297-298, Madge 297-298, Mary 297-298, Mr. 3, Nancy 297-298, Ruth 297, William 297-298
STEVENSON Angeline 298-299, Cora 298-299, David 298-299, Ella 298-299, Frank 298-299, Harriet 30-33, James 298-299, Joseph 298-299, William 298-299
STEWART Allen 299-300, Anson 299, Catherine 175, 300, Elihu 156-257, Elisha 276, Eliza 276, Eva 299-300, Fenton 300, Frances 299-300, Ira 299-300, Joseph 299-300, Leo 300, Wesley 299
STICKNEY Catharine 123
STIER John 300
STILES May 108, Margaret 328,
STILLMAN Frederick 300, Marie 300, Thomas 300
STILLWELL Henry 300, Horace 300, Lewis 300
STIMPSON Lorena 228-229, Lovina 228-229
STIMSON Charles 218-219, Hiram

218-219, J. Edward 300
STOCKING Truman 125
STODDARD Theodore 104
STOECKEL Carl 230, Phoebe 230
STOLL Elizabeth 301
STONE A. O. 42, A. W. 42, Anna 301, Anne 42, Anson 301, Bradley 301, Burney 301, Dewitt 246, E. L. 42, Esther 301, Eunice 301, Frances 301, Gertie A. 42, Imogene 66, 69, John 301, Johnstone 301, Lena 301, Minnie 42, Olive 301, R. L. 42, Ralph 301, Ross 301, S. D. 137, Sidney 301, Wilber 301
STONEMAN G A. 166
STOTHARD Alexander 302, Annie 301-302, Euphemia 301-302, James 301-302, Mary 301-302, Sarah 301-302, William 301-302
STOUT Etta 32, Herbert 32, Minnie 32
STOWELL Ailen 302, Calvin 302, 352, Fannie 302, Fredrick 302, George 86, Grace 302, Louis 302, Sarah 302
STRAHUBER George 94
STRAIGHT Allen 303, Amelia 285, Charles 303, Emily 303, Jennie 303, Mabel 303, Mr. 188
STRAIN Marshall 82
STRICKLAND Clara 293, Dan 303, Emeline 215-216, John 293, 303, Laura 303, Marietta 66, Walter 303
STROHUBER Anna 266, George 266
STRONG Abigail 303-304, Bertha 303, Clement 303-304, David 303-304, Emeline 303, Mary 303-304, Romeo 303, Wallace 303
STROPE Betsey 304, Eveline 304, Franklin 304, Frederick 304, Levi 304
STRUBLE Adeline 304, Bessie 304, Paul 304, Robert 304, William 304
STUART Barbara 304, Cora 304, Glenn 304, Maud 304, William 304
STUDLEY Mr. 44

SULLIVAN Dennis 304, Jerry 305, Josie 304, Mary 101, Michael 305
SUMNER Etta 305, George 305
SUNDERLIN E J 266
SUTHERLAND Carrie 305, Edward 67, 305, Elizabeth 68, Ettie 305, Hewitt 305, Inez 305, Isabella 67, 305, Mary E. 68, Mary Elizabeth 67, Mary 305, Ralph 67, Vera 305, William 305
SUTTER George 306
SWAIN Gertrude 306, Helen 306, John 306
SWARTHOUT Alexander 311, Ann 311, Jane 311, John 311, Marcy 311, Oakley 311, Phebe 311
SWARTS Lena 62
SWARTZ Elenora 306, Elmer 306, Francis 306, Frankie 306, Hattie 306, Henry 180, Ida 306, Katherine 306, Mary 306, Peter 306, William 306
SWEET Ada 306, Alice 306, Edgar 306, Grace 176, Lizzie 306, Mary 306, W. C. 176, William 306
SWEETEN John 94, Marshall 94, Martha 94, Wallace 94
SWEITZER George 307
SWETLAND Amelia 141, Ella 97, Mr. 234
SWIDERSKI Stanley 128
SWIFT Alfred 67-68, Alfred 305, George 307, Harlan 171, Lucy 307, Simon 307, Volorous 67-68, 305
SYLVESTER Mr. 205
TAFEL Mary 249, Mr. 278
TAGGART Sarah 154
TAITE Mr. 117
TALBOT Asher 309, Bessie 309, Roxanna 309, Stephen 309, William 309
TANNER Charles 298-299, George 298-299
TAPP Carrie 309, Harold 309, Margaret 309, Parma Belle 309, Theodore 309, William 309

TARBOX Alice 309-310, F. Grace 309-310, Irving 309-310, Luther 309
TATAR Stephen 310
TATSIS Gust 310
TAYLOR Asahel 310, Benjamin 310, Charles 102, 310, Emma 11, Emory 310, Frank 350-351, Ira 310, James 310, Mary 310, Mr. 211, Ruth 310, Sam 310
TAYLORSON Margaret 237, Mary 237, William 237
TEITZ Elizabeth 314, Ernest 314, Mary 314
TELLER Weltha A. 172
TENY Charles 258
TERHUNE Edwin 310, Genevieve 310
TERRY Arabella 310, Augusta 132, Ransom 147, Rebecca 322, William 310
THAYER Amariah 311, Charles 311, Daniel 311, George 311, Jacob 311, Lemuel 311, Martha 311, Monroe 311, Rosina 311, William 311
THEIMER Catharine 311, Christian 311, Ellen 311, Pauline 311
THOMAS Benjamin 147, Charles 269, Edgar 311, Elizabeth 269, Frank 242, Janet 269, Justus 140-141, Mary 312, Morris 312, Mr. 203, Shepard 269
THOMPSETT Vera M. 156
THOMPSON Archibald 312, Emma 101, Frank 312, Fred 312, Jennie 312, John 312, Lewis 312, Mary 312, Mr. 109, 240, Rachel 312, Seth 327, Welcome 312
THORNE Anna 313, Faith 313, Rhea 313, Sanford 313
THORTON Alonzo 299-300, Anna 313, Eleanor 313, Ernest 313, George 313, Hiram 299-300, Lucina 313, Marion 313, Richard 313, Samuel 313, Sarah 313, Thomas 313, William A., Rev. 129
THRALL Donald 314, Mary 314, Stephen 313-314, Virginia 314
THRASHER Louis J. 48
THURBER Ada R. 1
TICKNOR Frank 314, Olive 314, William 314
TIETZ Emma 314, Viola 314
TIMMERMAN Anna Matilda 315, Caroline 314, Cary 314, George 314, Hazel 314, John 314, Muriel 314, Robert 314, Ruby 314
TINGUE Joanna 315, Mary 315, Peter 315, Will 315
TINKCORN James 315, John 315
TITUS Ira 315, Mr. 221-222, Nellie 315, Sarah 315, Starr 315, Stephen 315
TOBIN Bridget 315, Carthage 315, Leo 315, Loretta 315, Louise 315
TOLLETT Mr. 89
TOMPKINS Harry 316, Martha 316, Norman 316, Orrin 351, Rempson 315
TOPLIFF Betsey 18
TORRANCE Garwood 68-69, Joel 68-69, Mitchell 68-69, Persis 68-69, Sarah 68-69
TORREY Laura 316, Naoma 316, Seymour 316
TORRY Edward 52
TOTHILL Edward 316, Fannie 233, Fanny 316
TOUCY Charles 256
TOUSEY Alva 316, Lillis 316, Marcia 316, Rue 316, Ruth 316
TOWERS Rebecca 316
TOWNLEY Agnes 209, Frank 209
TOWNS Emma 317, Jessie 317, Oscar 316-317
TOWNSEND John 234-235
TRACY Daniel 23
TRAVIS Mr. 200
TRAY Thomas 211
TREADAWAY Mr. 41
TREPUS Mr. 325
TRIPP Lucy 66

TROMMER Clara 317, Henry 317, William 317
TROWBRIDGE Marion 317
TRUBY Ernest 35, Fred 31
TRUE Mr. 270
TRUMBULL H. J. 278
TUCKER Albert 317, Ellen 131, Lottie 258, Sarah 317
TULLIE Mr. 80
TUOTO Mr. 225
TURNER Bery 317, James 317, Maurice 317, William 317, Zella 317
TUTTLE Mr. 346
TWOMLEY Lyman 110, 317, Minnie 110, Urania 110, 317
TYLER Albert 318, Jennie 318
TYMA Maciej 318
ULMER Jacob 103
ULMSCHNIEDER Charles 319, Emma 319, Ida 319, Louise 319, Mary 319, Matthias 319, Rose 319
UTLEY Electa 319, Rodney 319
UTRICH George 319, John 319, Joseph 319, Louisa 319
VADERFOOT Father 12-13
VALANCE John 17
VALENCE William 17
VALENTINE Harry 321, Mr. 78
VALKENBURG William 100
VALKENBURY William 100
VALLANCE Alexander 321, James 321, Margaret 321, Robert 321
VALLELLY Archibald 226, Elizabeth 226, Mary 226
VALLELY James 315, Mary 315
VALLEY George 321, Harry 321, Joseph 321, Mary 321, Paul 321
VAN BENSON M. 133, Martin 223
VAN DEUSEN Eugene 99, Carrie 321, Ida 321, Nellie 321, Wm. 321
VAN ETTEN Ernest 321, Horton 321, Mariam 321
VAN MARTER Frances 322
VAN RENSSELAER Abram 322, Ann 343, Clarissa 322, Minerva 322, Phillip 322, Sophia 322,343
VAN SCHOONOVER R. B. 180
VAN SYCKLE George 322, 343
VANDYKE Nelson 265
VANGILDER Abram 322, George 322, Milton 322, William 322
VARNUM Addison 323, Ann 322-323, Michael 322-323
VAUGHN Carl 117, David 113, Eda 117, Harrison 93, 113, Helen 205, Mr. 109
VEDDER Alice 323, Betsey 323, Comodore 323, John 231, 323, Mary 323, Rachel 323
VENA Anthony 323, Carmella 323
VENABLES Huldah 267
VENBURG Ellen 323, Florence 323, Mary 323, Paul 323, Peter 323
VERGITH Mr. 129
VERY Cora 323, Elijah 323, Martha 323
VIBBARD Lincoln 76, 246, Shep 116, 196
VICKERY Clotilda 323, Eva 323, John 323
VINCENT Lydia 7, 324, Oscar 323
VINING David 324, Hannah 324
VINTON Caroline 324, Charles 324, Lathrop 324
VOLK John 315
VOLLMER Annie 324
VOSBURGH Annette 132, John 132
VREELAND Anna 324, E. B. 336, Edward 305, 336, Laura 336
WADE Lena 325, Mr. 275
WAGNER Claudia 292-293
WAIT Catherine 88, John 88, Mary 66
WAITE George 325, Hudson 282, Ida 325, Mr. 26, 140, Nellie 325
WAKEFIELD Avaline 325, Mary 325
WAKELEE Anna 325, John 325
WAKELY Cornelia 325-326, Dolly 325-326, Henry 325-326, Lela 325-326, Martha 325-326, Walter 325
WALDO Milton 28
WALDRON Charles 85, Emma 326,

Olive 326, Otis 326, Robert 326, Roy 342
WALKER Janice 326, Jennie 78, L. Jane 326, Preston 326
WALLACE Emma 117, Georgia 326, Robert 345
WALLER Jeannette 326
WALRAD Alice 326, James 326, Jane 326
WALRATH John 291, Walter 107, 137
WALSH Daniel 326-327, Ella 126, James 326-327, Jane 326, John 326, Margaret 326, Mary 326, Timothy 326
WALTON Mr. 270
WARD Anna 327, Charles 327, James 327, Minnie 327
WARING George 327, Henry 327, James 327, John 327
WARNER Alonzo 327, Alpheus 310, 327, Amie 310, Carrie 327, Charlotte 327, Ellen 327, Emma 327, Lizzie 327, Louisa 327, Mr. 109, 193, Perry 327, Riley 327, Wm. 327
WARREN Eliza 111, Jerome 327, John 237, Mary 327, Mr. 237
WARTERS Frank 178, Joseph 82, Lena 81
WARTZ Joseph 280
WASHBURN Amelia 327, Charles 210, Clarence 328, Daniel 327-328, Eglantine 210, Emily 49, Emma 50, Howland 327-328, Martha 327-328, Melvin 327-328
WASNICK Stanley 225
WASSON L. 310, Mr. 351, Wallace 328
WATENPAUGH Eunice 55-56, John 55-56
WATERS Bert 328, Fred 328, Henry 328, Lee 328, Roy 328
WATKINS Fred 182
WATSON Edward Wallace 328, Jacob 328, Joseph 199, Lewis 312, Lovina 328
WATTS Aria 328
WAY Mr. 127
WEAST Amos 164-165, George 110-111, Sally 328
WEATHERLY Heber 346, Mr. 114
WEAVER Charles 328, Katherine 328, Mr. 141
WEBER Elizabeth 329, Henry 329, Lawrence 53
WEBSTER Annis 329, Caroline 153, Edward 329, Eveline 329, Hugh 153, Julia 329, Levi 329, Lucy 329, Mr. 68, Samuel 255, Warren 329
WEDLOCK Mr. 52
WEED Henry 42, 261, 327
WEEDEN Joseph 296
WEEKS J. Grant 329
WEEMS Florence 322
WEIBLE Mr. 132
WEIR John 234-235, Sarah 234-235
WEIRCHOCK Mary 119
WEISER Anna 329-330, Clara 329-330, Emma 329-330, Herman 329-330, Joseph 329-330, Theresa 329-330
WEISS Elizabeth 330, Jacob 330, John 330, Magdaline 330
WELCH Bridget 330-331, Ellen 330-331, Gertrude 330-331, James 330-331, John 330-331, Lizzie 330-331 Margaret 330-331, Maria 77, Mary 330-331, Mary Ellen 331, Nellie 330-331, Patrick 330-331, Raymond 330, Rose 330 1
WELDON Emma 331, Frank 331, George 331, Herbert 331, Howard 331
WELLER Godfried 331, John 331, William 62
WELLNHOFER John 331, Leonard 331, Mary 331, Peter 331, Theresa 331
WELLS Alice 332, Almira 332, Beatrice 326, Bernice 332, Champion 332, Clarinda 331-332,

Ellen 332, Franklin 331-332, George 140, Gershon 332, Hannah 332, John 332, Luther 332, Rebecca 332, Sarah 312, Sophronia 331-332, William 331-332
WELSH Sarah 138
WENTWORTH Alexander 166
WENTZ Charles 332-333, Erwin 333, George 332-333, Jacob 332-333, John 332-333, Lewis 332-333, Ramel 332, Sarah 333
WERICH John 333
WESCOTT Anthony 333, Clarence 333, Clark 333, Edwin 333, Flora 333, George 333, Grace 333, Joseph 333, Sally 333
WEST Ernest 334, Fred 334, J. L. 353, James 123, 334, Jennie 334, Lany 230, Lela 334, Minard 334, Sheldon 334, Walberga 334, Walter 104, Willard 334
WESTBROOK Elroy 210
WESTFALL Albert 334, Allen 334, Herman 334, Lewis 334, Martin 334, Sophia 334
WESTIN Andrew 229, Mr. 229
WETHERLY Eugene 334, George 334, Henry 334
WEXLEY Alexander 256-257, Alta 256-257
WHALEN John 335
WHALEY Charles 335, Eugene 335, Guy 335
WHEAT Mr. 277
WHEATON Carroll 335, John 335, L. S. 335, Mark 335, Mary 335, Neva 335, Rose 335, Roy 335, Samuel 335
WHEDON Charles 335, Fred 335
WHEELER Benjamin 335, Catherine 335, Elitha 335-336, George 335, John 95, 335, Lewis 280, Lyman 336, Mr. 48, Nettie , Ruel 335, Sarah 351, Semantha 335-336, Warren 335-336, William 30, 45
WHELAN Fenton 336, Hattie 336
WHIPPLE Belinda 336, Benjamin 355, Burdette 336, Clarissa 336, David 161, 303, Emeline 336, Fred 336, James 336, Martha 336, Morgan 336, Samuel 336, Theron 336, W. W. , Dr. 336
WHITCOMB Eugene 87, Franklin 336-337, Mr. 297, 351, Newell 336-337, Oren 336-337, William 336
WHITE Albert 290, Almer 337-338, Amelia 177, Arvilla 338, Calvin 337, Charles 337-338, Earl 337, Edmund 337-338, Ellinora 337, George 337, Hannah 337, Harriet 337, Henry 87, 337, James 84, Joel 337-338, Luke 337, Manly 338, Margaret 337-338, Mary 337-338, Mr. 108, 235, Phineas 235, Richard 337, Robert 337-338, Sarah 337, Thomas 32, Truman 337-338, Wesley 337, Wilbur 337-338, William 18, 337-338
WHITEHEAD Mr. 114
WHITFORD Agnes 338, Alice 338, Charles 338, Elias 338, Ella 338, Inez 338, Mr. 70, Rufus 338
WHITING Amana 2, George 30-33, James 350
WHITLOCK Mary 338, Almond 339, Benazah 339, Emily 338-339, Eugene 339, Hattie 339, John 339, Katie 338-339, Mary 339, Moselia 338-339, Spencer 339, Theodore 338-339
WHITMAN F. J. 339, George 339
WHITMER Alice 339, Christina 339, Milford 339
WHITNEY Charles 339, Lambert 118, Mr. 81, 208, Sarah 209, 339
WHITTIER Ann 340, Charles 340, Frank 340, J. F. 340, Mary 340
WHITTON Augustus 340, Charlotte 340, Clara 340, Ethel 340, Eva 340 Gertrude 340, James 340, Thomas 340, William 340
WHOLEBEN Maggie 340, Martin

340, Phillip 340, Sophia 340, William 340
WICHERT Charles 340-341, Charles 341, William 340-341
WICKER Harry 341, Susie 341
WICKHAM Lucius 341
WICKWIRE Dorothy 341, Eliza 341, Ruth 341, Wallace 341
WIDRIG Fred 131, 341
WIEDMAN William G. 125, Wm G. 203
WIEGAND Mr. 121
WIERCHOCK Mary 120
WIES Ernest 107-108
WIGGIE Mr. 327
WILBER Albert 341-342, Charles 341, Florence 342, Helen 341-342, Mark 341, Nellie 341-342, Pearl 341-342, Robert 341-342, Ruth 341, Vivian 341
WILBERT Mark 342
WILCOX Dorlesca 342, Elizabeth 45, Ella 342, Frank 342, Hiram 342, Hosea 45, John 176, Mr. 246, Sarah 45, Timothy 301, William 311
WILDRICK Fanny 342, Helen 342, Mr. 123, Sophronia 342
WILETOWICZ Michael 167
WILEY Grace 342, Lynn 342, Martha 342
WILHELM Arthur 326, George 326, 342, Loise 326, Walter 326
WILKINS Charles 350
WILKINSON Arthur 342, Edith 342, Henry 342, Millard 32
WILLARD Clare 343, Doris 343, Dorothy 343, Erastus 167, 279, 343, F. Estelle 343, Franklin 282, Harriet 342, Herbert 343, Luarancy 152, Owel 152, Robert 343, Virginia 343
WILLCOX Ellihu 18, Hosea 18, James 18, Jonathan 18
WILLIAM Eliza 165, Mr. 137, 225
WILLIAMS A. Laura 345, Allen 243-244, 343, Almon 344-345, Carrie 344, Delos 344, Eleanor 343, Emma 343, Eugene 344, Frank 344, Fred 344, Friend 343, George 343-345, Henrietta 322, 344, Herman 344, Ida 344, James 343, Jane 344-345, John 206-207, 238, 254, 343-345, Joshua 345, Lauren 343, Lena 343-344, Levi 344, Lloyd 344, Louise 345, M. D. 344, Margaret 344-345, Marian 343, Martha 343-344, Mary 206-207, 238, May 343, Mr. 33, 328, Myron 343, Nathan 243, 343, Oliver 344-345, Ralph 343, Robert 206-207, 238, Sarah 344, Simeon 344-345, Simon 243-244, Sophia 344, Thomas 344-345, Wayland 344, William 343, Wm. 344
WILLIS Albert 345, Carrie 345, Chauncey 345-346, Daniel 345, Hezeriah 345, Josie 345, Leroy 345, Loretta 345, Polly 345-346, Sarah 345
WILLOVER Mr. 171
WILLSON Urbern 346
WILSON Agnes 341, Alva 85, Buel 346, Claude 346, Elzora 346, George 346-347, Henry 347, J. H. 347, James 191, Jessie 346, Louisa 346, Lucina 346, Luria 346, Luther 346, Lynn 346, Mary 346-347, Maud 346, Norman 346, Oscar 319, Pearl 346, Ray 346, Reid 347, Sarah 346-347, Sarah Hayden 346
WILTER Mr. 287, 289-290
WILTSE Maude C. 42
WIMPLE Charles 347, Hattie 347, Henry 347, Willie 347
WINCHELL Caroline 347, Ellen 347, Henry 347, Jacob 347, James 347, Lydia 347, Miranda 347
WIND Anna 348
WING Clifford 348, Mae 348, Pauline 348
WINSHIP Adaline 89, Charles 89, 288-289, 348, Esther 348, Evaline 89, Isaac 89, 265, 336, 348, Joseph

348, Nathan 348, Truman 348
WINTERS George 241, Margaret 167
WISER Anna 348, Catherine 348, Elmer 348, Henry 348
WITHEREL Robert E. 53
WITHERELL Aileen 349, Doris 348, Ethel 348-349, Musetta 348, Robert 348-349
WITTER Elbridge 338, Gertrude 349, Jay 349, Leroy 349, Mr. 88, Myrtle 349, Rufus 349
WOLF Anna 349, Frank 349, Virginia 349
WOLFE Edward 349
WOOD Ann Eliza 106, Bessie 349-350, Daniel 350, Elbert 349, Ellsworth 349, Emery 189, 350, Ethel 350, Gabriel 349, Genevieve 349-350, George 349-350, Gilbert 350, Hazel 349, James Frank 350, John 106, 201, Mary 350, Mattie 349-350, Melissa 349, Mildred 349, Mr. 76, 125, 155, 223, Nathan 327, Nellie 217, 349-350, Permelia 189, Sarah 332, Staley 217, Thomas 350, Wm. 349-350
WOODARD Ara 350, Ephraim 350, Jenette 350, William 350
WOODBURY Helen 251, Henry 252-253, 364, Mahaley 251-252
WOODIN Eri 350-251, Georgia 350-251, Harriet 350-251, Homer 350-251, Mary 350-251, Tharecia 350, William 350-251
WOODMANSEE George 351
WOODRUFF Amelia 351, Angelette 351, Austin 351, Charles 351, Frank 351, Franklin 351, Henry 351, Kate 351, Louisa 351, Maryette 351
WOODS WIlliam 351
WOODSWORTH Horace 89, Mr. 351
WOODWORTH Betsey 146, Charles 26, Delia 26, Juliette 26, Olive 26, Victor 26, Zebbie 26
WOOLHEISER Ina 300
WORDEN Frank 352, George 352, Irving 33, 91, 233, J. E. 25, Justus 126-127, Minnie 352, Ruby 352
WORTHINGTON Henry 352, Randolph 352, Squire 352, Sylvester 352
WOYAN John 352
WRIGHT Alpheus 299-300, Arthur 28, Charles 204, Cordelia 352, Eleakim 28, Eliza 336-337, Florence 28, Frederick 351, George 242, Harvey 352, Howard 352, Leander 346, Luna 352, Lyman 336-337, Mary 242, 352, Mr. 164, 170, Rachel 336-337, Rollin 20, Samuel 237-238, Sanford 336-337, Sarah 242, Seth 336-337, Silas 242, Susanah 336-337, W. 36
WUERSETT Michael 62
WULFF Emma 352, Gustave 352
WURTZ Joseph 280
WYMAN Abbey 88
YAGER David 353, Frank 353, Glenn 353, John 353
YARNELL Mr. 91
YAW Charles 353, Eliza 314, Emily 353
YEAGER Mr. 90
YEOMANS Vine 236
YESLEY 257
YEWDELL Mr. 272
YORCH John 86
YORK Abigail 353, Catherine 353, Mary 353
YOUNG C. Verne 353, Catherine 353, Harold 135, Helen 297, Horace 123, James 353, Lafayette 135, Louise 297, Mr. 200, Muriel 353, Olive 104
YOUNGS Lizzie 353
ZAPH Anna 355, John 355
ZAUMETZER Mr. 20
ZELUFF Catharine 355
ZIEDEL Isabel 103
ZIEGLER Effie 263, Florence 263, Frank 263

ZIMBAR Frances 355, Mary 355, Matthew 355
ZIMBAUER Anna 159
ZIMMERMAN Benedict 239
ZINGG Ella 355
ZINN Albert 355, Estella 355
ZOGHIBE Seid 343

www.ingramcontent.com/pod-product-compliance
Lightning Source LLC
Chambersburg PA
CBHW050832230426
43667CB00012B/1966